BARCLAY FOX'S JOURNAL

Barclay Fox

BARCLAY FOX'S JOURNAL

EDITED BY R. L. BRETT

ROWMAN AND LITTLEFIELD
TOTOWA, NEW JERSEY

First published in the United States 1979
by Rowman and Littlefield, Totowa, N.J.

ISBN 0 8476 6187 3

Printed in Great Britain by
Ebenezer Baylis & Son Ltd
Worcester

Contents

CONTENTS

Illustrations

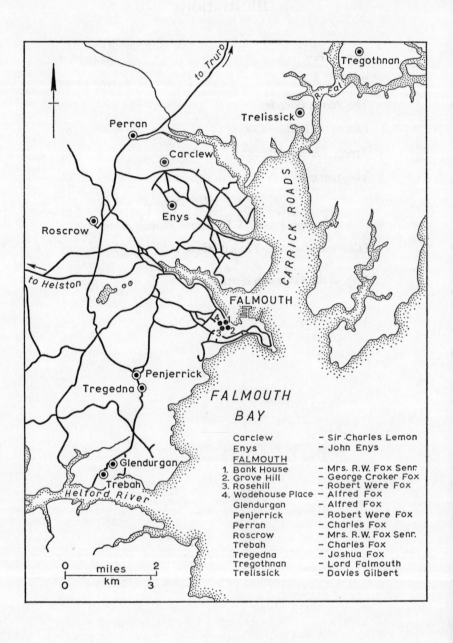

Carclew — Sir Charles Lemon
Enys — John Enys
FALMOUTH
1. Bank House — Mrs. R.W. Fox Senr.
2. Grove Hill — George Croker Fox
3. Rosehill — Robert Were Fox
4. Wodehouse Place — Alfred Fox
Glendurgan — Alfred Fox
Penjerrick — Robert Were Fox
Perran — Charles Fox
Roscrow — Mrs. R.W. Fox Senr.
Trebah — Charles Fox
Tregedna — Joshua Fox
Tregothnan — Lord Falmouth
Trelissick — Davies Gilbert

Preface

The Journal from which the following selections have been made consists of ten volumes. It runs from January 1832, when Barclay Fox was fourteen, to October 1854, but the bulk of the Journal is from 1832 to his marriage in October 1844, after which he ceased to keep a daily record. There is a gap from September to November 1835, about which one can only conjecture, but it is likely that a notebook which he used on his travels abroad during this brief period has been lost. The Journal has never before been published in any form, unlike the Journal of Barclay Fox's sister, Caroline, selections of which were published in 1882 and again in 1972.[1] Caroline Fox's Journal is a very different piece of work from her brother's. Though it was never intended for publication it was written for reading aloud to the family circle and has literary style. Barclay Fox's Journal, in contrast, is the record of a busy and active life; it was sometimes written in hotel rooms or on board ship, and often in the brief intervals of a day crowded with business engagements. Most of Caroline's Journal was destroyed by an over-scrupulous family and almost all that concerned her personally was omitted from the published selections. Though it remains a lively, sensitive and at times entertaining narrative, we are left in almost complete ignorance of the daily and domestic details of her life. Her brother's Journal, while it may lack the elegance of his sister's writing, provides these details in abundance and adds to them a wealth of information concerning the business interests of the Fox family. Barclay Fox also travelled a good deal both at home and abroad, and his Journal is not restricted to Cornwall. While there is some overlap between the two Journals, they remain very different productions, in contents, style, and the interests of their authors.

I have not attempted a facsimile version of the original. The major omissions in the text will be clear from the dating of the entries, but I have not indicated shorter omissions since this would become unnecessarily tedious to the reader. I have also silently expanded some abbreviations, corrected spelling mistakes, and added punctuation where necessary to present a rendering of the text that is readable while remaining accurate.

Acknowledging kindness is always a happy task. First I should like to

1. The first version was entitled *Memories of Old Friends: being extracts from the Journals and Letters of Caroline Fox* and was edited by Horace Pym; it was reprinted, in two volumes, the following year. The 1972 edition by Wendy Monk is a selection from the original one. Wilson Harris's *Caroline Fox*, published in 1944, gives a delightful account of Caroline Fox and her family, and has furnished me with much useful information.

thank Mrs Waldo Trench Fox of Penjerrick, near Falmouth, who has the bulk of the Journal in her possession, and Mr R. T. Fox, who owns two of the volumes, for their ready agreement to its publication and for allowing me to borrow it. Mrs Trench Fox has shown me many kindnesses on my visits to Cornwall and I am indebted to her and her daughter, Mrs R. Morin, for their help. From the beginning my wife was an interested partner in this venture and has sustained me with encouragement and constructive criticism. Professor Peter Mathias of All Souls College, Oxford, read the completed typescript and made many valuable comments from which I was able to profit; I am most grateful for his advice and counsel. I am also indebted to my friends, Dr Philip Larkin, who read the typescript and suggested improvements, and Professor A. G. Dickens, whose interest was helpful and generous.

The published text is only a fraction of the original manuscript which had to be turned into a typed version and I owe a debt of gratitude to the following for their skill and care in undertaking this work: Miss B. Coates, whose efficiency was matched only by her enthusiasm, Mrs J. Naylor, Mrs M. Barker, Mrs P. Wren and Mrs G. Cowper. I have been fortunate in the help provided by several libraries, especially the staff of the Brynmor Jones Library, the University of Hull; the late Roger Hale, Librarian of the Cornwall County Library, Truro; Miss R. Beckett, Librarian of the Falmouth Branch of the County Library; and Miss Lesley Webster of the Friends Library, London. I am glad to record my thanks to them and also to the Geography Department of the University of Hull for preparing the map of the Falmouth district which accompanies the text. The portrait of Barclay Fox is taken from what appears to be an ink and wash picture, a photograph copy of which is owned by Mr Robin Hodgkin of Bareppa, Falmouth. I am grateful to him for his kind permission to reproduce it here.

The publication of this book has been assisted by grants from the following: the British Academy, the Chairman and Directors of Barclays Bank Ltd, and the Joseph Rowntree Charitable Trust. I am most grateful to these bodies for their generosity and support.

Finally I wish to express my indebtedness to Mr Simon Kingston of Bell and Hyman Limited, not only for supervising the book's production, but for his patience, interest, and encouragement.

R. L. BRETT

Introduction

Robert Barclay Fox was born in September 1817 at Falmouth in Cornwall. The contemporary records that remain all speak of him as a popular and attractive character, but the Journal itself provides the best evidence of his personality. Its varied contents and its vivid and spontaneous style reveal a young man, full of energy and with an interest in all that goes on around him, and though serious when the occasion demands it, never pompous or sanctimonious. He is quick to sympathise with human weaknesses, but equally quick to laugh at cant and humbug when he meets them. He takes a fresh and intelligent look at men and their affairs, but is sensitive to the beauty of the countryside and has a genuine concern for animal life. His pages provide a graphic account, enlivened by youthful good spirits, of what life in Cornwall was like in the 1830s and 1840s, but he was aware of the larger issues of the day, political, spiritual, and intellectual, and personally acquainted with some of its leading thinkers. One could hardly have a more observant, thoughtful, and yet entertaining recorder of his times.

The Foxes were a wealthy Quaker family who had been settled in Cornwall since the seventeenth century. Carlyle, in *The Life of John Sterling*, described them at this time as

> . . . the well-known Quaker family of the Foxes, principal people in that place [Falmouth], persons of cultivated opulent habits, and joining to the fine purities and pieties of their Sect a reverence for human intelligence in all kinds. . . . The family had grave elders, bright cheery younger branches, men and women; truly amiable all, after their sort.

Barclay's father, Robert Were Fox, was a scientist of some distinction, a Fellow of the Royal Society whose entry in the *Dictionary of National Biography* lists his important scientific achievements. Like other eminent Quakers of the time, his commercial ventures combined with his scientific gifts to produce technological inventions that served industry and society. His business interests in mining and shipping led to inventions and discoveries in mining engineering, geology and navigation. As a young man he collaborated with another Quaker who lived in Cornwall, Joel Lean, in developing Watt's steam engine and increasing its power by the use of high-pressure steam. His knowledge of geology was also of considerable help to the Cornish mining industry. But he will be chiefly remembered in the history of science for his invention of navigating instruments and especially the new dipping-needle compass which was used by Sir James Clark Ross and

Captain Nares in their Polar expeditions. Ross told the inventor that without his compass he would not have discovered the South Magnetic Pole.

In 1814 Barclay Fox's father married Maria Barclay of Bury Hill, near Dorking. Her sister, Lucy, four years previously had married Robert Were Fox's cousin, George Croker Fox. This double union between the two families brought Barclay Fox into the circle of the Quaker establishment of the period. The Barclays were the founders of the banking and brewing firms, one of which still bears their name, and were connected by marriage with the Gurneys, Buxtons and Hoares, who formed the influential circle of Quakers centred on Earlham near Norwich. Barclay Fox's maternal grandmother was a Gurney, and Elizabeth Gurney, later Elizabeth Fry, the famous philanthropist and prison reformer, was his mother's cousin.

At this time marriage outside the Society of Friends led to 'disownment' and there came into existence a close-knit group of wealthy Quaker families who, since their membership of the Society virtually led to their exclusion from the professions, exercised their talents in commerce and industry. The number of great commercial and industrial enterprises owned and managed by Quakers at the end of the eighteenth and the beginning of the nineteenth centuries was out of all proportion to the size of their membership. The cocoa and chocolate firms of Fry, Cadbury, and Rowntree are household names, as are the bankers Barclay and Lloyd. But one can add to these firms like Allen and Hanbury, Reckitt and Colman, Huntley and Palmer, and individuals like Abraham Darby, who started the famous ironfoundry business at Coalbrookdale, Edward Pease, who constructed the first railway line that ran from Stockton to Darlington, and a host of others. A variety of reasons has been given for the large part played by Quakers in the Industrial Revolution in England. They could not enter the universities of Oxford and Cambridge until subscription to the thirty-nine articles ended in the 1850s and so were denied access to the professions which depended on higher education. But this was so for all Nonconformists. Their many moral virtues of integrity, honesty, thrift, and a capacity for hard work, combined with a high intelligence, must have played a large part. But supporting these was a theology which believed in works as a manifestation of faith, and which regarded the material and the spiritual as two aspects of one reality. It was a theology which saw the truth expressed especially in the parable of the talents and the story of the Good Samaritan. It led both to independence and to help for one's neighbour.

This was the larger Quaker circle which formed such an important part of Barclay Fox's world, but within this there was the smaller and more intimate circle of his own relatives at Falmouth. At the centre of this were his parents and two sisters who together formed a very affectionate, warmhearted, and gifted family. The eldest of the three children was Anna Maria, born in 1816, and the youngest Caroline, born in 1819. Caroline has become the best known of the three because of the publication of her own Journal. Readers of this all testify to her remarkable qualities. It shows a sensitive spirituality combined with a shrewd observation of her fellow men that expresses itself with wit and irony; the kind of journal Jane Austen might have kept if she had belonged to the Society of Friends. Anna Maria, though her memory has hardly survived her own lifetime, was nevertheless a person of great talents. At the age of seventeen she originated the plans for setting up the Falmouth Polytechnic which became, with the grant of a royal warrant in 1835, the Royal Cornwall Polytechnic Society. This institution figures frequently in the pages of Barclay's Journal and has made a major contribution to the life of Falmouth ever since.

Around this family group was a large circle of relations who lived in the neighbourhood of Falmouth and were prominent in its affairs. Scarcely a day went by without some visiting between members of this circle and frequently they would join together for breakfast or tea without any formal invitation. Family ties were strengthened by business interests and interlocking enterprises that contributed to the Fox fortunes. They ran the shipping business of G. C. Fox & Co., a company still in existence, had a large interest in the famous Perran Foundry, in the tin mines, in pilchard fishing, and, with their relations the Prices, in the Abbey Iron Works at Neath in South Wales. These enterprises were all flourishing at the time when Barclay Fox began his Journal and the decline in Cornwall's economy was still some years away. With increasing affluence his father and uncles were buying up land outside Falmouth and building country retreats for their leisure hours and eventual retirement. Barclay's father acquired Penjerrick, while his uncles Alfred and Charles bought the neighbouring estates of Glendurgan and Trebah, which are still famous for their gardens today.

Barclay's uncles and aunts were a varied lot. George Croker Fox was not properly speaking an uncle at all, for he was a cousin of Barclay's father, but he was senior in the family hierarchy and looked up to with respect, tempered by the realisation that 'Uncle G.C.' could be at times a pompous bore. He had literary aspirations and some classical scholarship and his translations of Aeschylus and Sophocles had been published in London. He and his wife Lucy were saddened by having no children of their own. Both Uncle G.C. and Aunt Lucy flirted for a time with the idea of leaving the Society of Friends and becoming members of the established Church. They thought better of it, but a generation later this path was to be trodden by many of their fellow Quakers for a variety of worthy and less worthy motives.

Uncle Alfred had married Sarah Lloyd, one of the Birmingham banking family, and had six sons and six daughters. Although they lived next door to Barclay his cousins were too young to be his companions. His connection was more often with Uncle Alfred himself, whose particular interest in the family business concerns was the pilchard fishing. Uncle Alfred sometimes appears in the Journal standing at Barclay's bedside at dawn with the intelligence that pilchards had been sighted off Mevagissey and with a request for his nephew's assistance.

Barclay's favourite uncle and aunt were the Charles Foxes. Uncle Charles was manager of the Perran Foundry. His wife, Sarah Hustler, came from the North of England and knew Wordsworth and the other Lake poets. She was ardent and sympathetic, a ready confidante of her nephews and nieces.

Uncle Joshua had caused a scandal by marrying outside the Society of Friends a lady who had lived in Paris and was rumoured to be a dancer. But all this was behind him by the time of the Journal and we meet him in its pages as a widower and the father of three high-spirited girls, living at Tregedna, just outside Falmouth and next door to Penjerrick. Uncle Joshua had a romantic, even a sentimental strain in his make-up and unlike his brothers was totally unsuited to business affairs. He was more interested in natural history than finance and his love of animals and birds was legendary. Both Barclay and Caroline record in their Journals how the birds he tamed would settle on his head and take crumbs from his mouth.

If Uncle Joshua's past had been a cause of alarm and censure, the real black sheep of the family was Uncle Lewis whose deathbed repentance is recounted by Barclay. Of his father's sisters, Charlotte married her cousin, Samuel Fox of Tottenham; Elizabeth, who married William Gibbins, died a few years after the Journal opens; and Mariana married Francis Tuckett of Frenchay, near Bristol.

All the Foxes were Quakers and had been ever since the seventeenth century when Francis Fox and his family joined the Society of Friends soon after its establishment in Cornwall. There were branches of the family at Plymouth and at Wellington in Somerset, and these were also Quakers, but there is no evidence that any of them were related to George Fox, the founder of the Society. At the time when Barclay Fox was writing his Journal, the Society was undergoing some changes. The main change was a theological one, but like all such changes it was to have an effect upon the practical affairs of the Society. Hitherto the Society had placed great emphasis upon the guidance of the Holy Spirit operating in the minds of believers, and gave this far greater importance than the study of the Scriptures. But the Evangelical movement which was working in the Anglican and Methodist churches of the day had its influence also upon the Quakers, leading some of them to revalue the Bible and to embrace a doctrine of personal salvation in terms of an Evangelical interpretation of the Atonement. It was to lead some Quakers out of the Society of Friends, but for those who remained it meant a reassessment of old beliefs and practices. The theological issues were being debated by Barclay Fox's contemporaries and the friendships which existed between his family and leading Evangelicals like Wilberforce and Thomas Fowell Buxton made him particularly aware of them. But he grew up in the traditional practices of the Friends. He and the rest of his family wore the traditional Quaker dress and used the old form of 'thou' and 'thee' in addressing each other. They would not go to a theatre even if the play were by Shakespeare or some other dramatist whose work they would read with pleasure and approval. The strict Quakers would not have pictures or even looking-glasses in their homes, regarding both as forms of vanity, but the Foxes were not like this; they played games, enjoyed music and though some of them (along with Christians of other denominations) were led by the temperance campaigns of the times to adopt teetotalism, they took drink in moderation. Many of their friends belonged to other denominations, not only distinguished churchmen such as F. D. Maurice, Charles Kingsley and Dean Stanley, but local clergy of all denominations. Caroline Fox in starting her Journal for 1846, wrote, 'I have assumed a name today for my religious principles – Quaker-Catholicism – having direct spiritual teaching for its distinctive dogma, yet recognising the high worth of all other forms of Faith; a system in the sense of inclusion, not exclusion; an appreciation of the universal, and various teachings of the Spirit, through the faculties given us, or independent of them'.

One of the characteristics of Quaker religion has always been its philanthropy; its relief of suffering and its practical concern for all in need, a concern not limited to co-religionists or even to Christians. The Foxes were foremost in any project that helped the citizens of Falmouth, giving generously not only of their money but their time and energies. The great concern (to use the Quaker terminology) of the Society of Friends at this time was still the abolition of slavery. Although as a result of the campaign which had been waged by Wilberforce and his followers, slavery had been abolished in British territories, it still existed in the southern states of the U.S.A., and the slave traffic was still carried on in parts of Africa. Even in the British West Indies slavery had been succeeded by a system of labour which exploited the black population. The anti-slavery campaign was one of the topics which regularly exercised the minds of those who attended the Yearly Meeting in London when the concerns of the Society of Friends were discussed. Barclay Fox's family attended the London Meeting at least every other year and played a part in the larger affairs of the Society. The other great 'concern' which comes into the later pages of his Journal is the Irish famine. The Quakers played an honourable part in the relief work in Ireland and Barclay Fox himself was active in it.

The interests and friendships of the Foxes were not limited to the Society of Friends. Barclay's father was acquainted with many leading scientists of the time and the family regularly accompanied him to the meetings of the British Association. A near neighbour and great favourite of the family was Davies Gilbert, who was President of the Royal Society from 1827 to 1830. Gilbert was a man of parts; as well as being a geologist of considerable reputation, he was Member of Parliament, first for Helston and then for Bodmin, and a patron of Humphry Davy and Brunel. He lived at Trelissick, a beautiful estate overlooking the River Fal, midway between Falmouth and Truro, and now the property of the National Trust. The scientific interests of the Foxes brought them into touch not only with the eminent but with the very humble members of their community, for they were eager to bring advances in scientific knowledge to improving the working conditions in the Cornish mines. Through the Falmouth Polytechnic they offered prizes for the invention of what were called 'man-engines', that is winding-gear for lowering and raising miners in and out of the pits. Barclay describes the testing of such engines and how they made obsolete the exhausting and dangerous use of ladders for ascending and descending the shafts.

Among the Foxes' Cornish friends were Sir Charles Lemon of Carclew, the Member of Parliament for Truro, John Enys of Enys, and the Molesworths, a family of versatile talents which included Sir William, the Member of Parliament for East Cornwall, who had been expelled from Cambridge for challenging his tutor to a duel, but subsequently became a minister of the Crown and the editor of Hobbes's *Works*.

There were two not entirely unrelated matters that exercised the minds of the leading people in the district at this time. The first of these was the future of Falmouth as a packet port. Falmouth was one of the ports which received and despatched the country's mail; it was responsible for the mail to and from America, the West Indies, Spain, Portugal and the whole of the Mediterranean, and the mail packet boats were protected by a naval vessel stationed at Falmouth under Admiralty orders. These ships carried passengers as well as mail and there was a considerable traffic in and out of Falmouth which was the most westerly port of importance in the kingdom. During the Napoleonic wars ships' masters had made for Falmouth as the nearest landfall and its sheltered estuary provided safety both against the enemy and the storms of the South-Western approaches. With the end of the war and with the coming of steamships there was the risk that all this would change and that Falmouth would be superseded by Plymouth or even Southampton. It would soon be much easier to take a steamship into either of these and then complete the journey to London by fast coach or by the projected railway. The only way to circumvent this threat to the fortunes of Falmouth was to build a Cornish railway that would link the town through Exeter to London either by a north or south line. The other great question for the people of Falmouth was the choice between these two routes, but while the debate went on the Government were already threatening to take the packets away from Falmouth. Barclay Fox gives us an account of the running fight he and his fellow Cornishmen put up to safeguard their interests, but more important than this to the modern reader is the light his Journal throws on the changes in travel in this age of railway expansion. At the beginning of his Journal the journey to London was generally by ship to Plymouth, where the passenger transferred to another ship to Portsmouth for the last stage of the journey by mail coach. By the end of his Journal the traveller could go by coach to Exeter and there catch a train to London. It is not only travel within the United Kingdom that we learn about from the Journal, for Barclay made an extended tour of Italy as a young man.

Barclay's Journal would always have been more than the chronicling of provincial life in the first half of the nineteenth century, for Cornwall was rather different from the rest of the country and, moreover, his family knew a wide circle of interesting and distinguished persons outside the county. But a strange quirk of fortune brought Barclay the friendship of three of the most intellectually gifted men of their generation, two of whom at least played a major part in shaping the life of Victorian England. These were John Sterling, John Stuart Mill, and Thomas Carlyle. It is not only for the glimpses his Journal gives us of these three remarkable men, interesting as these are, that we read his pages with curiosity, but for the way in which they influenced a serious-minded young man from a wealthy family, engaged in commerce and industry, struggling to relate his beliefs to the demands of the times.

Ill health and an early death robbed John Sterling of any outstanding achievement, but he was one of the most gifted men of his day. He had been a Cambridge Apostle, a disciple of Coleridge and in attendance on the poet in his declining years at Highgate; he was a brother-in-law of F. D. Maurice and with him had edited the *Athenaeum*, and was the founder of the Sterling Club, a debating society which numbered among its members J. S. Mill, Carlyle, Tennyson, and Monkton Milnes. He was generally regarded as one of the most brilliant talkers of his generation. Julius Hare, who had been his tutor at Cambridge, wrote in his Life of Sterling, '. . . his conversational powers were certainly among the most brilliant I have witnessed. In carrying on an argument I have known no one comparable to him.' Barclay Fox was tremendously impressed by Sterling. In April 1841, he wrote, 'His eloquence was like a clear cascade. His knowledge seems almost universal. You name a writer or an event and he can tell you all the details. His mind is European, his liberality unbounded. His insight of character is like an infallible instinct, his imagination rich to overflowing. To know him is a privilege the highest might be proud of; to know what he knows is an affluence few might bear.' Sterling was an immense influence upon Barclay and the tone and spirit of the Journal change perceptibly after his arrival at Falmouth. He opened up wider horizons than Barclay had been used to and gave him what he had lacked by not going to a university. Barclay's father was intelligent and cultivated, but his interests were scientific and practical. Sterling's interests were artistic and literary and his mind wide-ranging and speculative. In one respect, especially, Sterling stood as the symbolic intellectual figure of his generation. This was in the field of religion.

Sterling had visited Germany in 1833 and had been introduced early to the unsettling effects of the so-called higher criticism of the Bible. He had taken Orders, but had then resigned while Hare's curate at Hurstmonceaux. Hare in his memoir of Sterling maintained that the resignation was only because of ill health and this may be true, but we know from the letters of F. D. Maurice, which have now been published, that Sterling's friends were concerned about his religious doubts and questioned whether Carlyle's friendship was a help to him. Carlyle, who was proclaiming his own secularised version of Christianity, believed that Julius Hare's life of Sterling glossed over these issues and had attributed to Sterling a faith he did not possess. So passionately did he feel this that he wrote his own biography and gave Sterling a posthumous fame more extensive than anything he had enjoyed in his brief lifetime. Whether Carlyle's account of Sterling is more accurate than Hare's is difficult to tell; his portrait of Coleridge in this book is so much a caricature, even if a brilliant one, that one must doubt his objectivity. Before Carlyle embarked on his book there was some talk of J. S. Mill's undertaking a Life and though nothing came of this, it is an indication of the regard Sterling's friends felt for him and of his place in the religious controversies of the time.

Hare had consulted the Foxes when writing his memoir and there is no doubt that their sympathies lay with his version of John Sterling's life and beliefs. On 25th January 1847, Caroline Fox commented in her Journal, 'Julius Hare has, I believe, done his part admirably well'. Carlyle's *Life of John Sterling* was published in 1851 and it is significant that after its appearance there is no record in either Caroline's or Barclay's Journal of their calling on Carlyle, though both of them had always looked forward to their visits to Cheyne Row when in London.

John Sterling first came to Falmouth in February 1840 with the intention of taking the mail packet to Madeira. Although he was only thirty-three years old, his health was precarious. Ten years earlier he had gone with his newly married wife to the West Indies in search of a cure which he did not find, and most years since then had been driven to winter abroad by a weak chest. Another invalid to arrive in Falmouth at the same time was Sterling's friend, Dr John Calvert. The two men had first met in Madeira in 1837 and Calvert, like Sterling, was once again fleeing the rigours of an English winter. But their plans were frustrated; a gale in the Channel delayed the packet so long that they both decided to remain at Falmouth for the winter.

Yet a third invalid to arrive in Falmouth at this time, hoping to embark for Madeira, was Henry Mill, the brother of J. S. Mill, who was accompanied by his mother and his sister Clara. Henry Mill was in the last stages of consumption and he died the following month while still at Falmouth. Sterling, who was a friend of John Mill, naturally looked for lodgings not only for himself but for this sad trio who arrived with him. He was helped in this by Barclay Fox, who was working in the family shipping office, and so began Barclay's close friendship with Sterling and Calvert. John Stuart Mill came to Falmouth to be at the deathbed of his brother and his gratitude for the kindness the Foxes had shown his family developed into a friendship, less close than that between Barclay and Sterling, but nevertheless sincere and cordial.

Both these men were ten years older than Barclay and this of course modified his relationship with them. He regarded them not only as friends but as mentors, and looked to them as an undergraduate might look to his tutor for advice, inspiration, and educational guidance. Both of them encouraged him to read more widely and Sterling especially played the part of tutor. He gave constructive criticism of Barclay's poems and public speaking, encouraged his ambition to visit Italy, and above all strengthened his determination not to give all his time and energies to business. Through them he met the Carlyles and became a welcome visitor at Chelsea. Carlyle was much older than Sterling and Mill; he was forty-five in 1840 when Barclay attended his public lectures on Heroes and Hero-Worship and met him afterwards. By this time Carlyle had become a popular writer and lecturer. Barclay regarded him, as a growing number of his contemporaries did, as a prophet. Brought up in a home that encouraged scientific and rational enquiry and soon aware of the great religious issues of the time, he was not satisfied as so many of his fellow Quakers were with the Evangelical piety of the Clapham sect. Puseyism, the other alternative for so many young and serious men of his generation was equally unattractive to him. The doctrine of inner illumination to which the Quakers attached great importance and their belief that no special sacraments are needed as channels of God's grace, but that all life is sacramental, made it very easy for him to welcome Carlyle's 'natural supernaturalism' whose 'one Bible', as he put it in *Sartor Resartus*, was what was 'felt in my own heart'. The entries in the Journal that concern Carlyle all speak of him as a liberating and inspiring influence.

After his first stay in Falmouth which lasted three months, Sterling brought his wife and children and settled as a resident there in April 1841, until his wife died in May 1843. He then went to the Isle of Wight, but remained in close touch with the Foxes and visited Falmouth in the July. The guarded entries in Barclay's Journal reveal that early in 1844 he proposed marriage to Barclay's sister Caroline. They make it clear that Caroline was in love with Sterling and that his proposal presented her with a heart-rending decision. When he proposed marriage Sterling was in a wretched state of health and had only nine months to live, but it is unlikely that this would have deterred her. Barclay's Journal gives a clear indication of parental pressure and there would have been the knowledge that marriage entailed expulsion from the Society of Friends. In an article entitled 'Cousin Caroline', published in the *Friends' Quarterly Examiner* in 1945, a grand-daughter of 'Uncle Alfred' (Mrs L. V. Holdsworth who was the daughter of Thomas Hodgkin and Lucy Anna Fox) relates how her mother said of Sterling and Caroline, 'Yes, he and she did love each other; but he was not sound in his beliefs so they could not marry'. There must have been a strong conflict between her own deep feelings on the one side, and on the other, a stern sense of duty towards her family and her religious convictions. We know that Caroline passed through a most painful ordeal and became ill under the strain. The first editor of her Journal tells us that 'In the years 1844 and 1845 came a time of great sorrow, and a considerable blank occurs in the Journals of these and some of the succeeding years; what she wrote at this time containing, save so far as is extracted, nothing but a sacred record of great personal suffering and inward struggle'. Not only was there the struggle over giving Sterling an answer to his proposal of marriage, but the rapid decline in his health which culminated in his death in September 1844, would have filled her loving and sympathetic nature with a longing to be near him.

Tradition has also held that Barclay's other sister, Anna Maria, was in love with John Calvert. It would be no surprise if this were true. Dr Calvert emerges from Barclay's Journal, as he does from Caroline's, as a most engaging person. Carlyle in his *Life of Sterling* describes him as a man who '. . . loved art, a great collector of drawings; he had endless help and ingenuity; and was, in short, a very human, lovable, good and nimble man'. He and Sterling were old friends, bound closer together by sharing the same malady. They had wintered in Madeira and had visited Rome together. During Sterling's first visit to Falmouth they shared lodgings and then Calvert moved to lodgings of his own where he was joined by his sister. As a medical man Calvert knew well that he could not expect to live very long and in fact he died in Falmouth less than two years after his arrival. His increasing frailty prevented Calvert accepting all the invitations he received, but his purchase of a pony prolonged his mobility until in the end he was confined to his lodgings. But Calvert was never bitter and always displayed a fine sense of humour. Caroline records a conversation he had with his sister in November 1841, only a few weeks before his death. 'Dr. Boase paid him a long visit. His sister asked what he had recommended. "An apple," answered the Doctor. "Dear me! that does not seem a matter of great importance." "Oh yes," said her brother, "an apple drove Adam and Eve out of Paradise, and perhaps this apple may drive me in." ' Anna Maria was especially devoted to Calvert and since he had great sympathy with the Quakers and might easily have become a member of the Society of Friends, no obstacle would have been put in the way of a match between them. But his ill-health and early death made this impossible. When Calvert died in January 1842, John Sterling wrote a moving epitaph for his friend. It says something of the narrowness of religious sentiment at the time that the last two lines of this, though they won the praise of Wordsworth, were censured for their suspected heterodoxy:

> Reason thy lamp and Faith thy star while here;
> Now both one brightness in the light of God.

Wordsworth would have had a certain interest in this epitaph for John Calvert was the son of his old school fellow and friend, William Calvert, and a nephew of Raisley Calvert whose bequest of £900 had enabled him to devote himself to poetry. Calvert was not the only link between the Foxes and the Lake poets. We have already mentioned that 'Aunt Charles' knew Wordsworth, but 'Aunt Alfred' was a Lloyd of Birmingham and related to Charles Lloyd, the poet, who had lodged with Coleridge and later became a neighbour and friend of the Wordsworths at Grasmere. With such connections and so great an admiration for Wordsworth it was a great occasion for Barclay while attending the Yearly Meeting in London in 1842, to meet the poet, who by this time had become the Grand Old Man of literature and, as the Journal reveals, rather enjoyed the part.

Coleridge died in 1834, two years after the Journal opens, and Barclay never met him, but the Fox family were interested to hear the accounts Sterling gave of his last years at Highgate. An even closer link was the poet's son, Derwent Coleridge, who was headmaster of the grammar school at Helston only a few miles from Falmouth. Until he went to London in 1841 to become the first principal of St Mark's College, Chelsea, he was a frequent visitor at the Foxes and figures in the Journal as an attractive and witty person with some of his father's conversational abilities. There had been talk of S. T. Coleridge's joining his son at Helston, but when it came to the point he could not bring himself to leave the Gillmans and Highgate. If he had managed to settle in Cornwall he would have found a warm welcome at the Foxes, for they greatly admired his writings; not only his poetry but his later prose works, especially his *Aids to Reflection*.

These selections from the Journal end with Barclay's marriage to Jane Backhouse. He had first proposed to Richenda Fowell Buxton, the daughter of Sir Thomas Fowell Buxton. Lady Fowell Buxton had been one of the

Gurneys of Earlham and was therefore related to the Foxes, but on marriage she had left the Society of Friends and joined the Church of England. Sir Thomas was a leading Evangelical and had taken over the leadership of the anti-slavery movement on Wilberforce's death. With these credentials one would have thought Richenda an impeccable choice as a wife, for she was also intelligent, beautiful, and devout, but Barclay's family had some doubts about the match, for it would have meant marrying outside the Society of Friends. To their credit they were ready to accept Richenda as a daughter-in-law and to give Barclay their blessing, however painful the outcome might be. Fortunately for his family, if not Barclay, Richenda did not feel disposed to accept him. She, too, had her religious scruples and would not become a Quaker, nor did she encourage Barclay to think she would accept him if he left the Society of Friends.

Jane Backhouse belonged to a Darlington family of Quakers and her mother was yet another of the Gurneys. Barclay's courtship was a delicate matter since his great friend W. E. Forster (later to become the famous Liberal statesman, but who moves in and out of the Journal as a young man with an abundance of high spirits) had already been rejected as a suitor by Jane. Barclay had given William Forster every encouragement and had been his confidant in this unsuccessful suit, and the situation now brought about a reversal of roles that one expects in the theatre but not in real life. William Forster is one of the most attractive characters in the Journal and his generous nature is demonstrated in the support he gave Barclay in these two court-ships and more especially in the later one when his own feelings were so deeply involved. Barclay was successful where his friend had failed. W. E. Forster was later to marry a sister of Matthew Arnold; a marriage that brought him great happiness. It meant that he had to leave the Society of Friends but fortunately it did nothing to disturb his friendship with Barclay Fox.

The Society of Friends at the time of Barclay Fox's Journal

There are many references throughout the Journal to the various 'Meetings' of the Society of Friends. The Meetings for Worship which were normally held on Sunday, or, as the Quakers called it, 'First Day', were the gatherings which corresponded to the services of other churches. In addition to these were the 'Meetings for Discipline': the Yearly, Quarterly, and Monthly meetings which were responsible for the conduct of Quaker business and the life of the Society as a whole. These were divided at each level into a Men's Meeting and a Women's Meeting, but ministers of either sex were allowed to speak at both if they felt they had a 'concern' which warranted this. The Yearly (or London) Meeting took place at the Headquarters of the Society,

Devonshire House, Bishopsgate. All members of the Society were entitled to attend this, but a minimum attendance was guaranteed by those who were nominated as representatives from the Quarterly Meetings, which acted as a means of communication between the Yearly and the Monthly Meetings. The Quarterly Meetings covered a region, often the size of a county, or sometimes (dependent upon the distribution of Quakers within its boundaries) several counties. Their membership, too, was guaranteed by representatives from the Monthly Meetings, which covered a number of local congregations. At the bottom of this pyramidal structure were the Preparative Meetings made up of one or several local congregations.

The Yearly Meeting was the Parliament of the Quakers; questions of policy were debated there and the direction of the Society over the next year, or several years, was determined by its discussions. It issued Queries to the Quarterly Meetings to ascertain the condition and needs of the Society as a whole, together with Epistles and Advices to make known those issues which 'concerned' the leadership of the Society. The Monthly Meetings provided the information required and in addition decided such questions as whether to accept certain applicants for membership or to expel (or disown) members. They registered births and deaths, arranged the details of Quaker marriages, and collected subscriptions.

Parallel to this structure were the Select Meetings, or the Meetings of Ministers and Elders, whose purpose was to strengthen and organise the affairs of the ministry. It was these Meetings which granted 'certificates' to permit ministers to travel at home or abroad on the business of the Society. The ministers had no direct pastoral concern as had ministers in other churches; their special function was to preach. Men and women equally could be chosen as ministers but all ministers were unpaid, non-professionals who followed their own lay callings. Any adult was free to speak at Meetings, but when it was felt to be appropriate the Monthly Meeting gave him the status of minister. Similarly, the elders were unpaid, lay men and women, often those who had no vocation to preach, but whose experience and counsel were recognised by this status. Their duty was to support the ministry, giving it advice and encouragement when needed.

An office of great importance was that of Clerk. At all the various Meetings the Clerk acted as both chairman and secretary. At the smaller local Meetings the same person might act as Clerk for many years, but the Clerk of Yearly Meeting was usually chosen for a year at a time. Votes were never taken; decisions were arrived at by 'taking the sense of the meeting'. When this had been reached it was the task of the Clerk to formulate and record it.

Since the Yearly Meeting could not deal with the many issues that arose throughout the year, a standing committee was needed. The name given to this was the Meeting for Sufferings, a title that descended from the days of

Quaker persecution, when members might be imprisoned and their needs demanded discussion and action. It met at monthly intervals and, although it acted under the control of the Yearly Meeting, its authority and powers were considerable. It scrutinised the debates and legislative measures brought before Parliament and took action to see that Quaker interests were protected and Quaker opinion was expressed. It collected funds for special purposes, supervised the activities of Quaker ministers travelling abroad, and kept in touch with Quaker membership in other countries. If the Yearly Meeting was the Parliament of the Society, then the Meeting for Sufferings may be called its Government.

The Society of Friends required its members to adopt 'plainness of speech, behaviour and apparel', but at the time when Barclay Fox was writing some Quakers were beginning to interpret this injunction more liberally than had been customary. Hence arose the distinction, referred to in several places in the Journal, between 'plain' Quakers and 'gay' ones. 'Plain' Quakers were strict in their religious observances and retained the traditional dress and the old form of speech with its use of 'thou' and 'thee'. 'Gay' Quakers were beginning to modify these customs and some women members were prepared to wear discreet colours instead of plain grey, though ministers and other officers of the Society were still expected to conform to tradition. A 'gay' Quaker would sometimes change to being a 'plain' one as a result of a deepened religious conviction or a new sense of vocation. This happened with Elizabeth Fry when a girl, but another person mentioned in the Journal, this time one of the younger generation, W. E. Forster, is recorded as deciding to abandon wearing the old-style Quaker coat. Barclay Fox himself clearly approved such a change and welcomed a more liberal spirit.

FAMILY TREES

THE FOX FAMILY

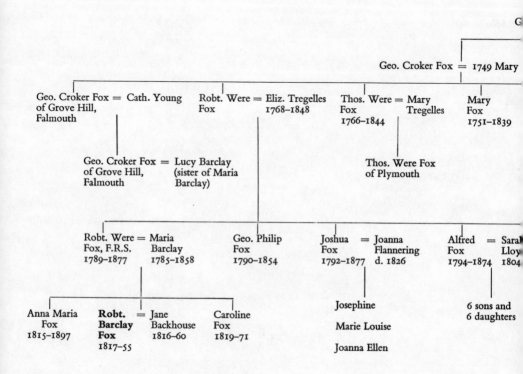

G

Geo. Croker Fox = 1749 Mary

Geo. Croker Fox = Cath. Young
of Grove Hill,
Falmouth

Robt. Were = Eliz. Tregelles
Fox   1768–1848

Thos. Were = Mary
Fox   Tregelles
1766–1844

Mary
Fox
1751–1839

Geo. Croker Fox = Lucy Barclay
of Grove Hill,   (sister of Maria
Falmouth   Barclay)

Thos. Were Fox
of Plymouth

Robt. Were = Maria
Fox, F.R.S. Barclay
1789–1877   1785–1858

Geo. Philip
Fox
1790–1854

Joshua = Joanna
Fox   Flannering
1792–1877 d. 1826

Alfred = Sara
Fox   Lloy
1794–1874 1804

Anna Maria
Fox
1815–1897

**Robt.
Barclay
Fox**
1817–55

= Jane
Backhouse
1816–60

Caroline
Fox
1819–71

Josephine

Marie Louise

Joanna Ellen

6 sons and
6 daughters

26 Anna Debell

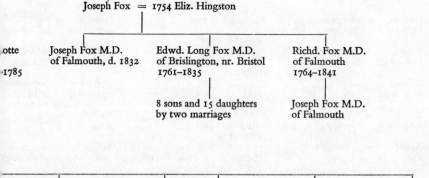

Joseph Fox = 1754 Eliz. Hingston

..otte

..1785

Joseph Fox M.D. of Falmouth, d. 1832	Edwd. Long Fox M.D. of Brislington, nr. Bristol 1761–1835	Richd. Fox M.D. of Falmouth 1764–1841
	8 sons and 15 daughters by two marriages	Joseph Fox M.D. of Falmouth

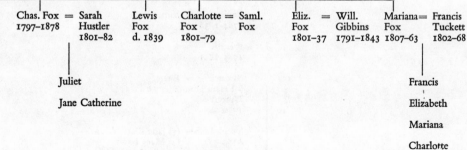

..ry

..809

| Chas. Fox 1797–1878 | = | Sarah Hustler 1801–82 | Lewis Fox d. 1839 | Charlotte Fox 1801–79 | = | Saml. Fox | Eliz. Fox 1801–37 | = | Will. Gibbins 1791–1843 | Mariana Fox 1807–63 | = | Francis Tuckett 1802–68 |

Juliet

Jane Catherine

Francis

Elizabeth

Mariana

Charlotte

THE GURNEY FAMILY

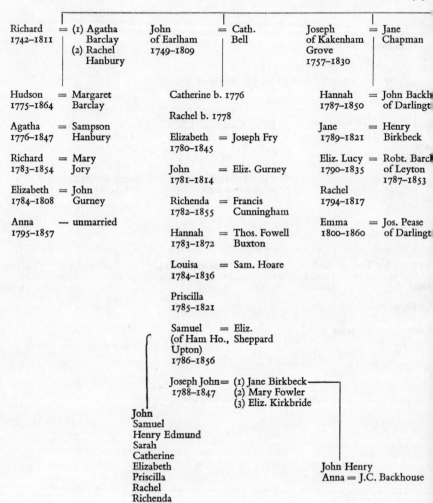

John
of No
1715–

| Richard 1742–1811 | = (1) Agatha Barclay (2) Rachel Hanbury | John of Earlham 1749–1809 | = Cath. Bell | Joseph of Kakenham Grove 1757–1830 | = Jane Chapman |

Hudson 1775–1864 = Margaret Barclay

Agatha 1776–1847 = Sampson Hanbury

Richard 1783–1854 = Mary Jory

Elizabeth 1784–1808 = John Gurney

Anna 1795–1857 — unmarried

Catherine b. 1776

Rachel b. 1778

Elizabeth 1780–1845 = Joseph Fry

John 1781–1814 = Eliz. Gurney

Richenda 1782–1855 = Francis Cunningham

Hannah 1783–1872 = Thos. Fowell Buxton

Louisa 1784–1836 = Sam. Hoare

Priscilla 1785–1821

Samuel (of Ham Ho., Upton) 1786–1856 = Eliz. Sheppard

Joseph John 1788–1847 = (1) Jane Birkbeck (2) Mary Fowler (3) Eliz. Kirkbride

Hannah 1787–1850 = John Backh of Darlingt

Jane 1789–1821 = Henry Birkbeck

Eliz. Lucy 1790–1835 = Robt. Barcl of Leyton 1787–1853

Rachel 1794–1817

Emma 1800–1860 = Jos. Pease of Darlingt

John
Samuel
Henry Edmund
Sarah
Catherine
Elizabeth
Priscilla
Rachel
Richenda

John Henry
Anna = J.C. Backhouse

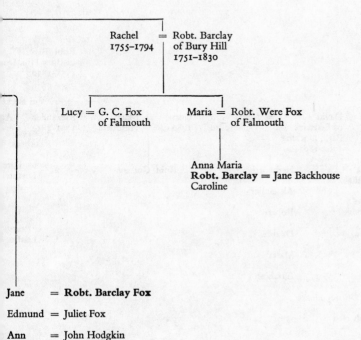

Rachel = Robt. Barclay
1755–1794 | of Bury Hill
1751–1830

Lucy = G. C. Fox
of Falmouth

Maria = Robt. Were Fox
of Falmouth

Anna Maria
Robt. Barclay = Jane Backhouse
Caroline

Jane = **Robt. Barclay Fox**

Edmund = Juliet Fox

Ann = John Hodgkin

THE BARCLAY FAMILY (of Bury Hill)

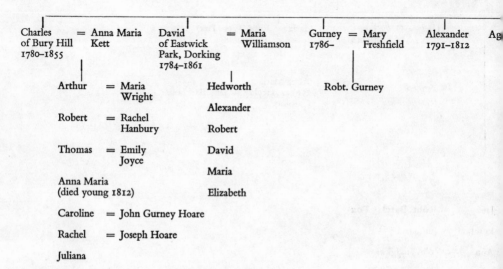

Robt. Barclay
of Bury Hill, Do▮
1751–1830

Charles = Anna Maria	David = Maria	Gurney = Mary	Alexander	Ag
of Bury Hill Kett	of Eastwick Williamson	1786– Freshfield	1791–1812	
1780–1855	Park, Dorking			
	1784–1861			

Arthur = Maria   Hedworth   Robt. Gurney
         Wright

Robert = Rachel   Alexander
         Hanbury   Robert

Thomas = Emily   David
         Joyce
            Maria

Anna Maria
(died young 1812)   Elizabeth

Caroline = John Gurney Hoare

Rachel = Joseph Hoare

Juliana

ιel Gurney

garet Hodgson (no issue)

| house 1 | Anna = Jacob Reynolds | Lucy = G. C. Fox of Falmouth | Maria = R. W. Fox of Falmouth | Martha = J. Bromhead |

1832

BARCLAY FOX was fourteen when he began his Journal; his sister Caroline was twelve and his sister Anna Maria fifteen. It will be noticed that at the start of his Journal he follows the old Quaker practice of referring to the day of the week and to the month simply by numbers. This practice was founded upon a dislike of names derived from heathen deities. The first year's entries are devoted to an account of their schooling by their young tutor, John Richards, and of Barclay's schoolboy interests and hobbies, together with family concerns. The year includes a visit to London to attend the Yearly Meeting of the Society of Friends, where he meets many of the foremost Quakers of the day. While there he also attends an anti-slavery meeting at Exeter Hall.

FIRST MONTH

1. 1st day. Breakfasted at Grove Hill. A cold day, got a cough, stayed home from the afternoon Meeting. Papa gave me this book.
7. Mamma has had a letter from John Wall to say that Cavendish[1] will come the week after next – how delightful. Rather wet weather. I bought a centre-bit today for 14s.
9. Commenced schooling today by myself in the new schoolroom and made an address to it in 6 Latin verses. I knocked out a pane of glass with my whipping top. A very wet day. I have begun to go to bed at 9 instead of 10.
10. 2 Aunts came to breakfast, we all read our poems to them. After breakfast I went with Papa to Perran to try the intensity of the magnet[2] with William Henwood, first in the valley and then on the top of the hill. We found the needle varied $\frac{1}{2}$ a degree. In the evening we 3[3] went to the Bank and read our poems again to Grandmamma and Aunts. Rather wet day.
12. I commenced my studies with J. Richards[4] today. In the morning he

1. Cavendish Wall, who was to come to Falmouth to be tutored with Barclay.
2. Barclay's father experimented with magnetism and invented an improved dipping-needle which resulted in a greater accuracy of the navigational compass at sea. Perran, on the Restronguet Creek, was where the Foxes had established their famous foundry, which was managed by Uncle Charles Fox. Uncle Lewis also lived at Perran.
3. i.e. Barclay and his sisters, Anna Maria and Caroline.
4. The young tutor (he was only eighteen) who was to supervise the education of Barclay, his sisters, and Cavendish Wall. A schoolroom was fitted up at their home, Rosehill, for this purpose.

examined me in the Greek Testament, in the afternoon in Virgil and Geography and gave me some Latin verses to do in the evening. Took tea at Grove Hill where I met Fanny Gould who was rather agreeable. Passed a very pleasant day tho' it was raining so that it nearly washed Aunt Lucy away. I think I shall go on very pleasantly with J.R.

17. Recommenced French with Alfeston.[1] A cold frosty day. J. Richards has begun to teach Carry mathematics. Learnt 37 lines of Virgil this evening.

20. Wind changed to the South tho' no rain yet. Passed a pleasant day. Dear Uncle Francis arrived at Falmouth today on a love visit to my aunt M.[2]

26. Put on a long coat today. Show'd myself in it to Papa, but he did not like it so I've left it off again. Construed 52 lines of Virgil & 3 pages of Justin today. Fine day. Carry was turned out of the schoolroom today for laughing. Put up a little cup to hold the monkeys' nuts. The one that had the sore tail is much better. Cut my finger with a chissel rather badly.

29. 1st day. Introduced Uncle G.C. to my monkeys. He was much pleased with them. F. Tuckett dined here. Took a walk with Uncle G.C. after Meeting, did 15 verses in the Greek testament for John Richards. Delightful day.

SECOND MONTH

1. John and Cavendish Wall came today. Cavendish is a very nice good tempered fine fellow. I like him very much. He has a great cut across his right eye caused by the kick of a cart horse. I settled him in to some Greek this evening. He says he is very stupid. John Richards came to tea.

14. Fine but cold day. Had a narrow escape together with J. Richards & Cavendish, from the tide coming up & enclosing us on a rock. At last we managed to climb up the cliff and arrived at the top without loss of life. Bought 2 bladders & some quicksilver for footballs.

18. Bought another bladder & I have burst it. Lost my gold watch-chain and after a vain search had it cried.[3] Mamma gave me a gold seal to make up for the loss. Read our themes on domestic life. Called on Aunt Mary in the evening.

20. I had my chain brought back. J. Richards has an inflammation on the chest & came to School an hour too late. Had a leather case made for the foot-ball. Bought another bladder.

1. A teacher of French who, with a drawing-master named Prout (followed by Jordan), supplemented John Richards's tuition.
2. Aunt Mariana, who was to marry Francis Tuckett of Frenchay, near Bristol.
3. i.e., by the town-crier.

3RD MONTH

1. Rode to Perran with Papa to meet Uncle & Aunt Charles who came home yesterday. A rat bit one of the monkeys in his paw.

4. 1st day. Very wet. Lucretia Crouch spoke in the morning. The afternoon Meeting was silent. Saw a rat in the house with the monkeys and have been devising schemes for destroying them. The monkey's paw is well. Tip[1] continues very ill. Mamma & Carry have slight colds.

9. A whole holiday. Most beautiful weather in the morning. Cavendish & I had a game of cricket in the afternoon. We rode to Perran to tea when we visited the foundry & came home in the evening. Tip seems much better. Caught a little fish & brought it home alive.

23. Drawing day. Prout took a sketch of Pendennis.[2] In the evening J. Richards & Cavendish Wall came to tea, after which Papa gave a sort of lecture on mineralogy to which J. Wall was expected but did not come. Rather rainy. Caught a curious crab with very large claws & brought him alive with 2 rather large fish as companions for the eel which seems to be thriving.

27. J. Richards, Cavendish & I went on board the *Alchymist* with Uncle Lewis. Explored the cavern at Pennance with Cavendish in the afternoon. John Wall went back to Bridgenorth this morning to his sister's marriage. Fine day.

4TH MONTH

4. The marriage-day of Cavendish's sister – a holiday of course. In the morning rowed with Cavendish to the *Aurora* frigate. In the afternoon some of the Classical School[3] boys came to a game of cricket & tea, after which Papa showed us some experiments on galvanism &c. Very fine day.

16. The Reform Bill passed today at its 2nd reading with a majority of 9, on account of which the town was decorated with Flags & Laurel. The weather was fine between the showers.

18. Poor Tip died today suddenly. Rainy day. Carr, the temperance man, dined here with Uncles Alfred, George, & Francis elect. Attended Carr's temperance lecture in the evening which was very interesting. Mamma, Aunts & many others became members.

1. The family dog.
2. Pendennis Castle stands at the mouth of the Fal estuary and with St Mawes Castle, across the strait, protects the entrance to Falmouth harbour.
3. The Classical and Mathematical School had been founded in Falmouth in 1825.

19. Began Logarithms in Trigonometry. Cavendish was poorly this morning but has taken some Doctor Pritchard & is, I hope, rather better now.

20. Cavendish is rather better than he was yesterday but has kept his bed all day. I finished a box for Cos. Thomas. Good Friday & therefore a holiday.

23. An awful account came this morning in a letter to Cavendish of his sister & her husband being struck by lightning & deeply wounded, though the doctors think not dangerously. Cavendish was well enough today to come to school & to take a ride with me in the evening.

25. The cholera reached Falmouth today. One old woman has been seized. Uncle G.C. in a great fright.

26. Measured the distance of the Manacles[1] from Gillan Vaise & found it 8½ miles. Rode to Perran to tea in the afternoon with Cavendish. The cholera has not spread yet. Fine day but blowing.

5TH MONTH

11. Fine day but cold. Cavendish has had a better account of his brother & sister. A.M. dined at the Castle.[2]

13. Uncle & Aunt Charles & Uncle Lewis dined here. Rode with the latter to Perran after the afternoon Meeting & slept there. Had accounts from London that Duke of Wellington is appointed Prime Minister. Fine but cold day.

14. A reform meeting held at Falmouth today. The King & Queen were insulted at London. I dined at Grove Hill & Cavendish took tea there. Fine in the morning, but very wet night. There seems to be some doubt about our going to London. It would be a disappointment to stay at home in some respects, yet there are so many things which we should risk if we went just now that they nearly counter-balance it.

15. Breaking up day. Plenty of packing up & confusion. A temperance meeting was held this evening which I attended.

16. Papa, Mamma, A.M., C. & Kitty[3] set off for London this morning in the carriage. I rode to Penjerrick after Meeting to take leave of Uncle Joshua. Dined & lodged at Grove Hill. Cavendish drank tea there.

17. Took breakfast with Cavendish at Grove Hill at ¼ past 6. We got on board the *Sir F. Drake* a little before 7. Changed her for the *Brunswick* off

1. The dangerous rocks between Falmouth and the Lizard.
2. Pendennis Castle. The Lieut-Governor of the castle was Lieut-Colonel Fenwick, a friend of the Foxes.
3. The Foxes' maid.

Plymouth, the wind right against us. Passed a fine shoal of porpoises, nearly ran a boat down. I was a little sick. Fine day but wet night.

18. Got up at $\frac{1}{2}$ past 5. Landed at Portsmouth about 9 a.m. Set off for London by coach. Ran over a sheep in our way & killed it. Arrived at London about 7. Took a hackney coach for Austin Friars where I was most kindly welcomed by Cos. R. Reynolds.[1] Met his father in the evening, drank tea & lodged there.

19. Walked about town with Cos. R. Reynolds. Papa arrived here at 2. Accompanied him to our lodgings. Met Mamma, A.M. & C., then dined with them. The lodgings seem very comfortable. Had a row on the Thames in the evening.

21. Took a walk about town & visited St. Paul's. Made some purchases. Cavendish called here. Took a walk with him & went with him to see the Riding School, thinking it was a public place, but a man on horse-back came up & turned us out.

22. This evening Uncle D. Barclay & Cos. R. Reynolds called. They told us the brewery[2] had been on fire & they calculated £50,000 damage done.

30. Attended Gracechurch Street Meeting after which I went with Mamma, H. Tuckett, A.M., & C. to see the ruins of the brewery. I met Uncle & Arthur Barclay there. From the brewery we went to Austin Friars to dine, where we met a number of the Chapmans, Cos. R. Barclay, Betsy Fry,[3] &c. Attended the Meeting at Devonshire House[4] in the morning. It was long & rather dull. Called on Grandmamma in the evening. Wet day.

6TH MONTH

4. The morning was extremely warm. It came on to rain in the forenoon & continued all day. We breakfasted at A. Dale's & came to London afterwards to attend an anti-slavery meeting. F. Buxton[5] spoke. At $\frac{1}{2}$ past 3 we went to

1. Anna, the sister of Barclay's mother, was married to Jacob Reynolds.
2. Barclay, Perkins and Co., at Southwark, which had been taken over from Dr Johnson's friend, Henry Thrale, in 1781. Several Quakers were brewers at this time, but drew the line at distilling spirits. See P. Mathias, *The Brewing Industry in England, 1700–1830.*
3. Elizabeth Fry, the famous Quaker and prison reformer.
4. The headquarters of the Friends in Bishopsgate. Friends had occupied it from 1666. In 1924 the headquarters moved to Friends House in Euston Road.
5. Sir Thomas Fowell Buxton had married Hannah Gurney and was therefore related to the Foxes. He was an evangelical churchman and M.P., who carried on the leadership of the anti-slavery movement when Wilberforce resigned it for reasons of health. In 1833 a Bill was passed which ended slavery in all the British colonies, but the campaign continued to get it abolished in all countries.

Grosvenor Place,[1] Papa & Mamma to dinner & we children to Juliana's tea. We stay there till 6th day.

5. Took a walk about Hyde Park with the 4 girls & Juliana's governess, after that went with Papa & another gentleman to Perkins's exhibition which was opened today, where we saw 3 little steam boats working in long troughs, a number of models, fossils, pictures, &c., & lastly a cannon fired by steam. But the most interesting of all we saw was large sparks produced from a magnet by quickly removing a piece of soft iron that was on it, & above all, we each obtained a shock from it, which it is not known that anybody had before.

8. Took a walk with Papa & saw a number of sights viz, 1st the King's horses, carriages & State coach, which last is very magnificent, 2ndly to Westminster Hall & Court of King's Bench where the court was then sitting, 3rdly the House of Lords, & lastly a part of Westminster Abbey, not having time to see the whole. From the Abbey Papa went off to Tottenham whilst we went to Grosvenor Place just in time for luncheon, directly after which we drove off in the carriage to Upton[2] where we were heartily welcomed. We dined there & had a game of Question & Answer & 12 Nouns[3] in the evening. Took a ride in the afternoon with Samuel & Betsy Gurney & A.M. & C. I rode 'a remarkably quiet horse' as it only kicked 5 times & ran away once.

11. Left Upton soon after breakfast & came to Austin Friars. From thence we went to Sonde Place calling on R. Barclay in our way. We took luncheon there at about 1 & arrived at Sonde Place at 7 where we were warmly welcomed by Grandmamma[4] & Cos. Louisa.

14. Fine day. Went to Bury Hill[5] in the morning. It is being much improved. Took a ride in the afternoon on a mare Uncle David lent me.

24. Took a ride with Caroline & Sam Gurney up Boxhill. Took an early dinner at Betchworth from whence I went to Dorking with Sam Gurney to see the 'wonderful large pig', 13 hand high & 12 ft. long. Had some archery with Caroline, Juliana & Sam Gurney. The two latter drank tea at Sonde Place, where we all went into the hayfield. Made a large nest & had strawberries & cakes there.

26. Went to London by the 7 o'clock coach. I was there by 10. Found Papa

1. The London house of Charles Barclay, brother of Barclay Fox's mother.
2. Samuel and Elizabeth Gurney lived at Ham House, Upton, near Stratford in Essex. The estate today is West Ham Park.
3. A game played by the Fox family in which a dozen nouns were contributed in any order by those playing. The winner was the writer of the best passage which incorporated all twelve in the order in which they had been listed.
4. His maternal grandmother, Mrs Robert Barclay, who lived at Sonde (or Sondes) Place, near Dorking.
5. Bury Hill, Dorking, the country house of Uncle Charles Barclay.

at Austin Friars. Went with him to the Surrey Zoological gardens & saw the beasts fed. We saw also the bones of the great mastodon, the enormous crystal vase & the model of a Cornish copper mine.

27. Set off for Bristol in the Company's day coach at 6, arrived there half past 8. Found Francis Fox with his gig. He drove me to the *Gloster Hotel* to see Grandmamma & Aunts & from thence to Combe.[1] Was kindly received and slept there.

28. Grandmamma & Aunts came to Combe to breakfast. Francis Tuckett called there. With him I went in to Bristol & saw the ruins of Queen's Square[2] &c. Grandmamma & Aunts called for us at the warehouse. We went with them to Frenchay to see Francis Tuckett's old mother & new house. Went on to Cross in the evening, Francis Tuckett accompanying us.

30. Breakfasted at Exeter & went on to Plymouth. Arrived there between 8 & 9 well scorched by the sun which has been roasting us all the way from Cross.

7TH MONTH

5. After an early breakfast went on to Perran. Found Thomas[3] waiting for me there & we drove on to Grove Hill. Went in the afternoon to see the monkeys &c. at home. Walked with Uncle G. in the evening to Penjerrick and saw our colt.

6. Breakfasted at Aunt Alfred's & rode with Uncle G.C. to Tregothnan,[4] dined there. It is a beautiful place. Came home to tea. Weather cold and showery.

9. Began schooling again today with John Richards. He has just taught me the Hebrew letters. We had a delightful bathe under Pennance.

8TH MONTH

16. Measured the distance between Pendennis & Pennance points with the azimuth compass. Found it to be nearly 2 miles. Bathed at Gillan Vaise.

---

1. Combe was across the Clifton Downs and where his mother's sister, Aunt Agatha, lived. She was married to the Bristol shipbuilder, George Hilhouse.
2. Queen's Square and the Bishop's Palace had been burnt down in the Bristol Riots the previous year.
3. One of the servants.
4. The family home of the Earl of Falmouth.

Took a row with Cavendish in the afternoon & had some archery in the evening. Aunt Lucy dined here. Catch of pilchards by our seine at Curnock of 150 hogsheads. Began the 5th Book of Euclid to day.

9TH MONTH

5. Half holiday. Sailed with Cavendish & the Wodehouses to Tregothnan. Dined there amongst the trees. Saw the house, grounds, church, &c. Were becalmed in our way back & did not get home till between 9 & 10. Very fine weather.

6. Drove to Perran with Cavendish to dine at Grandmamma's cottage. Took a row after dinner. Saw some casting.[1] Got home between 8 & 9 in pelting rain. My 15th birthday.

10. Fine weather. I had some archery in the forenoon. Went to see various curiosities in the afternoon. Took a long walk in the evening. Aunt Lucy drank tea here. We found this afternoon that one of the monkeys had broken or put out of joint its arm. Thomas & I mean to set it tomorrow if we can.

11. After breakfast caught the monkey & held an examination over its arm, found it broken between the elbow & shoulder. Between 12 & 1 went with him to J. Field, but his mistress being poorly in bed he thought the screams would frighten her. So I went down to cousin Joseph's,[2] but he was not at home. John Richards & Cavendish dined with me, Papa & Mamma being gone to the Quarterly Meeting at St. Austell. Directly after dinner, John Richards & I went down with Jack to Cos. Joseph's, found him in & we commenced the operation. With a great pair of leather gloves I held him on my lap holding his head fast that he should not bite. John Richards held his arm out straight, while the doctor bound in the splints which he managed very well. Poor Jack's screams were most pitiful. However, it was soon done & I took him home & put him in a box with a bed of hay for him & I hope he will do well. Drank tea at Grove Hill.

12. The monkey had no appetite for his breakfast but he ate some grapes & does not seem to be in pain. Cavendish dined with me. After dinner I took a row with him. Drank tea at Grove Hill. Papa &c. came home in the evening. Removed the monkey to my bedroom.

14. Monkey going on nicely. Half holiday. Went with Papa & J. Richards to Meudon beach on a geologizing, conchologizing & botanizing & natural historising excursion. Cavendish poorly & not able to come to school.

16. 1st day. Rather poorly. Took some rhubarb in the morning & a walk in

1. At the Perran foundry.
2. Dr Joseph Fox.

the evening with Papa & Aunt Alfred. The monkey not quite so well in the evening, he seems in pain & I fear his arm is swollen.

17. I was showing the lame monkey this morning to his comrade when he leapt out of the box & ran to him in the stable & climbed up into their bedchamber, bandages & all. Now he is gone there I shall let him stay.

24. Took a row & a bathe with John Richards & Cavendish. Drove down to the Plymouth coach & brought home Amelia Opie[1] to dinner at 5. She means to stay here for some time. Very fine.

28. Damp foggy day. Took our first lesson with Jordan, our new drawing master. Papa dined at Carclew.[2] After dinner Cavendish & I rowed to St. Mawes. We went about the town & castle & then came home. We were ½ an hour going & ½ hour coming back.

10TH MONTH

3. Windy & rather cold. Called at Grove Hill & Uncle Alfred's where A. Opie dined. Her nephew & a Mrs. Austin called on her today. The Walls, Uncle G.C. & Aunt L. drank tea here when A. Opie took very good likenesses of Uncle G.C. & Henry & Cavendish Wall. The former goes tomorrow.

20. Almost frosty. Read my theme on Genius got a 9 for it. A. Opie contributed. Cavendish drank tea with us. Began wearing a tail in preparation for the ordeal I must go through tomorrow at Meeting.[3]

21. 1st day. Got through coat very well. Mamma began to visit the poor. Called on Aunt Mary. Walked with Papa & Amelia Opie. Fine day.

11TH MONTH

1. Wet drizzly afternoon. Blowing very hard in the morning, which has most probably detained the steamer as she was expected yesterday afternoon, on account of which Cavendish's mother is not arrived yet.

2. This morning J. & E. Wall arrived in the *Drake* steamer, having been 2 days & 2 nights in their voyage from Plymouth. Took a walk with Cavendish in the afternoon. Very wet drizzly weather.

1. Amelia Opie, the widow of John Opie, the painter; she became a Quaker in 1825 and played a prominent part in the anti-slavery campaign.
2. The home of Sir Chas. Lemon, M.P. for Truro.
3. To be admitted to full membership of the Society of Friends. He was required to wear a tailed coat without revers, the traditional Quaker dress.

4. 1st day. Have got a cough & stomachache. Took 3 of Morrison's pills in the evening. A.M. has also a cough and Carry's is believed to be whooping cough.

7. Cough much worse. Was confined to the house all day. John Richards now gives me lessons in the dining room.

13. In the evening took an ipecacuanha pill & had my back rubbed with rum & turpentine.

20. Cough very bad in the night & being in Mamma's dressing room for change of air it frightened her & Papa out of bed. Had no schooling today.

23. Cough much the same. Had a drawing lesson with Jordan. Game of battledore and shuttle cock with Cavendish & kept up to 260. Weather rather wet. Find these whooping fits most miserable. Caroline is getting better & A.M.'s is nothing more than a common cough.

25. 1st day. Last night most wretched. Very bad all day, 3 tremendous fits in the evening. Mamma has a sympathetic cough.

26. On account of his brother's having the scarlet fever J. Richards has been dismissed the service pro tempore. My cough very bad tho' I think not worse than yesterday. Took some salts of Tartar & oil of almonds in the evening.

28. Much the same. Aunts called here. A day of thanksgiving for not being visited by the cholera. Wet & cold weather.

12TH MONTH

5. Quarterly Meeting at Truro. Got a sore throat to which internally I applied a gargle & externally a flannel. Finished a picture of John Baptist's head.

9. We go to Penzance on 6th day. Took a long walk in the garden which I enjoyed extremely.

12. Uncle & Aunt Charles dined here & gave us 5 of Au du Bon's birds.[1] Aunt A. spent the evening here.

14. At $\frac{1}{2}$ past 9 set out for Penzance for change of air with our carriage & the Grove Hill horses & Lucy.[2] Arrived at our lodgings about $\frac{1}{2}$ past 2. We found the rooms small but pretty comfortable. Papa & Kitty arrived in the evening, having come in the gig & been upset in the way – nobody hurt. Violent storm in the night.

1. i.e. five plates from Audubon's *Birds of America*. John James Audubon (1780–1851) was a famous ornithologist and his book was a lavishly illustrated publication which has since become a collector's piece.
2. The adopted daughter of Uncle G.C. and Aunt Lucy.

15. Called on the Walls who lodge 3 doors from us. Afterwards took a walk with Cavendish about the town, quay, beach &c.

18. Cavendish came in to have a chat & game of marbles with me. Little Lucy poorly. Caroline has a sore throat & relapse of the whooping cough, my cough is now almost well. Wet nearly all day & much hail.

25. Christmas day.[1] Walked to Trengwainton (Sir R. Price's) with Cavendish & A. Note. Pretty fine.

28. Took leave of Penzance at ½ past 10. I drove the gig & Kitty to Helston where Papa took my place. We got home a little before 4.

30. 1st day. Went to Meeting for the first time since my whooping cough. Found one of the monkeys was fled to its last home. Alas poor Jack.

1. The Quakers made very little of Christmas, carrying on the Puritan dislike of the Feast as a Popish 'mass'.

1833

THE YEAR opens sadly with the death from scarlet fever of his young cousin, Jane Catherine, the daughter of Uncle and Aunt Charles. In July Barclay goes on a walking tour to Land's End with his cousin, Sam Gurney, and his tutor, John Richards. There is fear of cholera which had struck Newlyn the previous year. Cavendish Wall receives bad news about his brother John, who had gone to Malta in search of health. Cavendish himself becomes depressed and ill because of this news. But in spite of illness and death there were things that brought pleasure: fishing trips, excursions and picnics, and the visit of his Gurney cousins. The year also saw the establishment of the Falmouth Polytechnic Society in which his sister Anna Maria played a leading part.

1ST MONTH

5. Jane Catherine taken ill with the scarlet fever.

9. The account of Jane Catherine early this morning alarmingly worse. After Meeting a little better, but the evening's intelligence was very discouraging. The symptons are very bad – great difficulty of swallowing, the mouth quite black & the doctor says if she survives the night there will be some hope. Today we read our journals of 1832 for which Papa gave us each a sovereign.

10. The account early this morning from Perran was still worse. It was from Uncle Charles who appears to have given up all hope. At dinner time the intelligence reached us which we could not but expect of her happy release from all her sufferings on earth; Uncle & Aunt Charles are calm & as well as can be expected, though Aunt Charles has a slight sore throat and complains of exhaustion.

14. John Richards came. Read Virgil with him. Jane Catherine was buried at Feoc at 11. Anna Maria was the only one of our party that attended the funeral. Cavendish came at 6 this evening. Tolerably fine.

15. We heard to day that Juliet[1] has taken the scarlet fever. Dr. Fox was sent for directly, he says the symptoms are more favourable than those of Jane Catherine. Cavendish began schooling to day.

19. Juliet has been very weak & a little wandering but Dr. Fox thinks upon the whole she is as well as can be expected. Cavendish & Tom Fox[2] dined

1. Juliet was the other daughter of Uncle and Aunt Charles.
2. One of his cousins from Plymouth.

here. I don't admire the latter much. Henry Wall arrived very unexpectedly from Penzance this evening to settle Cavendish in a new lodging. He drank tea with us.

22. H. Wall left this morning. Cavendish poorly with head and stomach-ache so as to be incapacitated from attending school. I administered some Dr. Pritchard which has done him good. Bought a leaping pole.

25. Juliet going on even better than could be expected.

2ND MONTH

1. Jordan came from 10 to 12 this morning. Introduced Cavendish to Aunt Mary. E. Wall arrived today from Penzance. In the evening received a very handsome writing case from Aunts for which I returned a note of thanks.

13. Tremendous storm in the evening which besides doing much damage in the neighbourhood managed to get between the roof of our house & the lead which it blew against one of the chymneys & knocked it down besides making a hole in the roof.

14. All hands very busy this morning in refixing the lead whose obstreperous-ness together with the strength of the wind nearly gave Little John (Bryant) a leap from the top of the house. Tonight the storm was even more violent than the preceding.

20. Monthly Meeting at which the 3 couples, to wit E. Fox & Man, M. Fox & ditto, & A. Carkeet & ditto, passed the meeting[1] which they did in an orderly manner though none except F. Tuckett spoke loud enough. Company to dinner.

3RD MONTH

21. It being again a half holiday Cavendish & I descended Uncle Joshua's mine where I made a most unfortunate speech by pointing out a copper lode to Cavendish which proved to be the black produced by the smoke of a candle. Came home & had my hair cut.

28. A very large party of the wedding guests to dinner & one of the bride-grooms (William Gibbins), the other being so much indisposed that there are

1. His Aunt Elizabeth was to marry Wm. Gibbins, his Aunt Mariana to marry Francis Tuckett, and Anne Carkeet to marry W. Bryant. All three couples had to seek permission to marry from the Society of Friends.

some fears of his not being able to attend meeting tomorrow in case of which Cos. J. T. Price[1] proposes an adjournment to his bed-room.

29. Holiday of course as

> This is my ladies' wedding day.
> And we are come for to be merry.

A delightful morning & we all as smart as we could possibly & consistently make ourselves! Arranged the procession in the upstairs room. In half an hour both pairs were joined in the holy bonds of matrimony. Some very good and appropriate sermons were given on the occasion. After the marriage we adjourned to the Bank for some cake & wine after our great exertions, after which many of the party took a walk round our garden & returned to a ½ past 2 o'clock dinner which proved to be at 4. There were 45 at it & it was a dinner indeed. After dinner we returned to the drawing room where we mustered 60 strong. Passed a very pleasant evening. Talked to all the agreeable young women, had a short meeting in the evening & having taken an affectionate leave of the brides (who went to Perran direct) we all departed to our respective homes.

4TH MONTH

13. Being invited last week I accompanied Cos. F. Fox to Perran to dinner where we walked round the grounds, looked at Audubon's birds, played with the monkey & did many other like interesting circumstances. Uncle Charles told us of an odd speech of his gardener. On asking him his opinion of the character of a poor woman then in a dying state, he said, 'She was a sturdy sort of a body, had never been before her betters (magistrates) & agen one thing was knacked agen another he thought she'd go safe'.

23. Walked to Penjerrick directly after dinner with Cavendish who bought Uncle Joshua's boat. Grandmamma & Aunts &c. drank tea here. Settled the prizes and subscriptions for the forthcoming Polytechnic society[2] with Uncle Gibbins.

25. Received a handsome desk from Anne Dale who dined here with Cos. Richard. The Daubuzes drove through W. Carkeet's window & did considerable damage this afternoon.

1. Joseph Tregelles Price, iron-master of Neath Abbey in S. Wales. The Price family had been partners with the Foxes of the Perran foundry before moving to Neath.

2. The Falmouth Polytechnic Society was set up in 1833 largely at the suggestion of Barclay's sister, Anna Maria, but all three children played an active part in its affairs. It prospered so quickly that in 1835 it became the Royal Cornwall Polytechnic Society under a royal warrant granted by William IV.

26. Cavendish's boat brought home to day. She will have to undergo much repair before she is fit for use. I had my hair cut. A wet evening.
30. The repairing of Cavendish's boat finished. Took her up on the beach under the bank & cleaned her out. Leapt with Cavendish in the afternoon 6 ft.[1] Fine day.

5TH MONTH

24. Extremely warm. Bathed with Cavendish at Gillan Vaise. Drove him out in Aunt Lucy's pony chaise to Penjerrick where all our party & the Grove Hillites dined (at their cottage). After dinner walked about the place, inspected the plantations, colts, orchard, &c. We called on Uncle J. & came home about ½ past 7. Carry's 14th birthday – her present to me was a silver toothpick.[2]
27. Took a row & a bathe. Was introduced to the Marquis of Palmella[3] who called.
31. Bathed with Cavendish & J. Barnicoat at Gillan Vaise. Whilst bathing we saw a steamer coming in which we found to be the *Hermes* & having got John Richards's leave we rowed out to it with the full expectation of bringing back J. Wall perfectly recovered, but on enquiring for him the doctor of the steamer told us he remained at Malta, it being out of the question for him to attempt returning as he was not able even to move in bed. He said there was not the least possible hope for him, which was confirmed by another doctor on board. It was a tremendous blank to Cavendish – he scarcely spoke all the way home. He came to consult Mamma about whom he should write to & he sent a letter to Henry & another to T. Boddington.[4] In the afternoon he walked with me to Ashfield & was in better spirits.

6TH MONTH

6. Most dismally wet, ½ holiday. I dined at Grove Hill with the French

1. This was a game played with a jumping-stick.
2. It was the family custom on birthdays for the presents to be given by as well as to the person whose birthday it was.
3. A Portuguese nobleman. In 1828 the Queen of Portugal had called at Grove Hill. In 1826 her father Pedro IV had renounced the crown in her favour but her uncle Miguel had seized the throne in 1828 and declared himself King. In 1832 Pedro with help he received from England raised an army and landed at Oporto. In 1833 Chas. Napier destroyed Miguel's fleet off Cape St Vincent and so Queen Maria was enabled to return to the throne.
4. His brother and his brother-in-law.

Ambassador & his suite, with Captain Coatsworth & a gentleman from the *Mauritius*. The Count is a fat chattering old fellow. His admiration for Uncle G.'s paintings would not stop his sitting still.

15. 1st day. Uncle & Aunt C. & Uncle Lewis dined here. The former gave me a razor every part of which is made out of London Bridge. Uncle Lewis has brought me a set of crayons. Drank tea at Grove Hill & walked with Uncle G.C. to Penjerrick. Caught in 3 heavy showers & was thoroughly wet through.

16. Saw Cavendish off by the Penzance coach. He had given a porter orders about taking his great trunk but he had forgotten it & though sent off as soon as we reached the coach did not arrive in time for it. However, Pearce[1] promised to send it by the Exeter Mail. Bought a chain for our boat. Attended the Classical School examination which I did not think much of.

17. Went out fishing in the harbour. Uncle Joshua's children & governess came to dinner. Papa gave them some cuttings & Caroline a pair of doves with which they were much delighted. Waited for the *Cornubia* some time in the evening on the Quay as there was a possibility of the Gurneys[2] coming in her.

18. *Cornubia* arrived but not Gurneys. Wet drizzly morning. Dined at Aunt A.'s at a $\frac{1}{4}$ to 1 intending to have fished at Durgan but the wind & rain continuing we set to making a wheelbarrow for Alfred, but at 4 it cleared off so beautifully that we determined to go. We were becalmed about 5 miles from Durgan & did not get back to Falmouth till $\frac{1}{2}$ past 11 with my spoils in a bag. All were gone to bed but Thomas at last came down & opened the back door.

24. A day full of matter. At 6 ran down to the Bar with a note to the Treweekes to ask some of them to accompany us to Kynance, but they were prevented by indisposition, so at 7 we started in 3 carriages. We arrived at Gweek at about 10 & had a most splendid breakfast, went on through Trellowarren to Cadgwith, where we met the rest of the party, viz. George Banks, Sir James Gardiner, his son & W. Aldham, Jnr. making in all a party of 15. We went to the Devil's Cauldron which was much admired by all & some of us took sketches of it. From the Cauldron we proceeded to Kynance Cove which the party liked better than anything they had seen in Cornwall. We took half our dinner on the sands & thence proceeded to the Lizard. On our way the spring of one of the carriages broke & G. Banks was pitched but sustained no damage. We dined at the lighthouse, ascended it, admired its reflectors & view & set off for home. I was stowed in with Isabella & Dame Banks who half stewed me before we got home by having only 1 window down about 3 inches & all the rest up. We got home at 12 much delighted with our day.

1. The inn-keeper.
2. His cousins from Ham House, Upton.

26. The *Firefly* steamer arrived this morning from Malta. I rowed off to her as soon as possible for any news of J. Wall but could obtain none, they not having been permitted to leave quarantine. I turned about to go home but found such a tremendous gale to encounter that there seemed no possibility of returning. After rowing about ¼ of a mile all my strength was spent, the wind was perceptibly rising & I felt in rather an awkward predicament. At last I saw a boat sailing from one of the packets. I hailed her & she took me in tow & landed me safe & sound. About ½ past 12 we set off for Tregothnan with a most splendid wind which took us up in an hour, everybody enjoying it but Dame Banks who was sick, frightened & fidgety & moreover had a tumble by sitting on a loose winch. After taking some bread & cheese we wandered over Tregothnan house & grounds for about an hour & then returned to King Harry passage where we found the carriages waiting & went on with them to Perran. We spent a very pleasant afternoon there walking about the garden, & looking at Uncle C.'s insects & returned about 12.

28. Rescreage's mare came to be tried but Papa did not like her. Ordered a fustian suit for our intended pedestrian tour. The Gurneys came at ½ past 4, much delighted with Cornwall. They walked about the garden, to the beach &c. In the evening we were much surprised by the entrance of Henry Wall, who came to hear the first news from the steamer & go to Malta if necessary. The Gurneys are delightful girls.

7TH MONTH

Journal of a Tour through Cornwall.

2. Preparations being at last ended, weather favourable & all things propitious, Sam Gurney & self set off for Truro at 9 a.m. on foot, having sent on our knapsacks in the van. Walked as far as Perran, amusing ourselves on the way with the various speculations of the passers-by. Our dress was such as to bespeak us very suspicious characters – a large fustian coat & trousers surmounted by an oilskin cap, stick in hand & knapsack at our back made us look uncommonly wicked. At Perran we entered the van & being the sole occupants were not long arriving at Truro. On entering the inn the waiter stared at us & enquired if we wanted to go into the tap, but on speaking in an authoritative tone to let him know we were somebody, he showed us into a parlour & dinner soon made its appearance. After dinner we strolled about the town & vicinity & frightened W. Tweedy junr. by accosting him in the street. At about ½ past 8 we were joined by J. Richards. After tea we went to Garland's smelting house. The people there all very surly.

3. Rained heavily till 8 o'clock when we set off for Mitchell. In our way

visited St. Erme's church, a curious building in the form of a cross. Took some luncheon at Mitchell. After resting an hour there we walked on to Lower St. Columb where we dined on a rasher of bacon & some bread. An original old man was there with whom we were much amused. He told John Richards he was a drunken farmer. John Richards asked him if his health didn't suffer by it? No, he was as healthy as any man in the parish. If his affairs weren't the worse for it? No, he always struck a better bargain drunk than sober. If his conscience did not prick him for it? Not in the least. If the Parson didn't scold him for it? Parson – law, bless your heart the parson ha' got drunk with me scores of times. Thus beaten on every point John Richards was obliged to sound a retreat. Not being able to obtain beds at Lr. St. Columb we walked on to Mawgan. Arrived at Mawgan about 8 & were much struck with the neatness of the village & the beauty of the situation. We had a most comfortable little inn & agreeable landlady. On entering the inn a crowd collected round the door for play bills, thinking us a set of strolling players.

4. At a ¼ to 7 attended mass at Lanherne nunnery,[1] an old edifice built by the Earl of Arundel. What I heard & saw has by no means determined me to turn Roman Catholic. After breakfast we visited the nunnery again in hopes of being introduced to the Prioress but were disappointed. We were received by the Portress, a little lively old woman dressed in the Carmelite costume. We bought some of the little fripperies made by the nuns & sold for their benefit & having done this we departed. From Mawgan we turned our steps towards High Cove cliff about 3 miles to the N.E. Weather very wretched, all got wet through before we got half-way. Having dried ourselves in a cottage & the rain almost ceased we proceeded to the cliffs which are extremely magnificent from 2 to 300 ft. in height & composed of a black slate. Whilst amusing ourselves by rolling stones down the cliff we startled an eagle from her nest, which soared up above our heads in a most superb manner. She was soon joined by her mate & they followed us till clear off from their nest. We walked along the cliffs to Bedruthan, the scenery being much the same all the way. We then turned back along the coast & arrived at Lr. St. Columb Porth, after 7 hours rough walking, as hungry as wolves. After devouring a huge lump of bread & a bottle of porter we proceeded to Newquay, a village about 2 miles further. We got some slices of bacon there, half an inch thick & salter than anybody could eat if only half-starved, with some cheese. From Newquay we turned our faces Perranzabuloeward. About 7 or 8 miles distant we crossed Gannel Creek, which is close by Newquay, in a boat. As we went on, the road became worse & worse, being nothing more than a succession of mounds of loose sand 20 & 30 ft. high covered

1. The house was given in 1794 to English Carmelite nuns from Antwerp, who were refugees from the French Revolution.

with a prickly rush which stung our ankles at every step, & perforated with rabbit holes into which we were constantly slipping. On our way we visited the top of a church steeple which was buried by a sand drift about 30 years ago. At about ½ past 9 we arrived at Perran, having walked 20 miles at the very least & were glad enough to turn in.

5. A most lovely morning. We breakfasted at W. Carne's at 8 o'clock. He kindly showed us about the mine & gave us a guide to Cligger Head about a mile & a half distant. Our guide was a very intelligent old man of 63 called Uncle Jacka. He pointed out the places amongst the rocks where the *Hanover* packet & a sloop were lost. We descended Cligger Head, a strikingly magnificent cliff composed of alternate layers of porphyry slate & red sandstone, the dip of the strata seemed to have undergone some singular convulsion. We climbed the cliff with some difficulty & continued our route to St. Anne's. Near St. Anne's there are 2 curious wells & some tradition connected with them, also a hole in the rock which communicates with the sea. The story goes that a certain giant Boulster, an inhabitant of these cliffs, fell desperately in love with St. Agnes, who wearied with his importunities, at length consented to accept him on condition that he would allow her to bleed him into the aforesaid hole till she filled it. The giant not aware of the secret channel, accepted the proposal & consequently bled to death. At St. Anne's we took some bread & cheese with Capt. Verran, a very intelligent man. We chatted with him for an hour & then ascended St. Anne's beacon from whence the view is remarkably fine & extensive. We could see Pendennis from it & equally far in the opposite direction. From St. Anne's we proceeded in a boat for a mile, keeping as near the shore as possible to observe the cliffs which are all slate. There are some very fine caverns along the coast one of which we entered. Having landed we walked towards Portreath. On our way we stopped at Wheal Towan mine about 3 miles from the sea & looked at the engines &c. which are in excellent order. At ½ past 10 we arrived at Portreath Hotel, found the door locked & the inmates gone to bed. After some thundering knocks a female form in nocturnal habiliments made her appearance at the window. After duly inspecting us & making sundry enquiries concerning us she sent unto us one of her hand-maidens, who on opening the door stared at us for a few seconds & then slammed it in our faces, bolted it & set off. We thought this rather strange conduct & stood in the porch ruminating where we should spend our night when the damsel again appeared & admitted us. We got some bread & butter & milk – tea being unattainable as the fire was almost out. As soon as our beds were ready we turned in. Sam & I in one wretched little buggy bed hardly big enough for one, and to escape being eaten alive I was glad enough to reenter the fustians & therein pass the night.

6. After breakfast we proceeded to Gwithian, a distance of 5 miles. On our

way we saw 2 enormous whales at a great distance, spouting up the water & wallowing in the foam like porpoises. Came over the sands to Hayle about 3 miles & a half to dinner. The sand was very loose & the weather very dismal so that between the both we had no great enjoyment in the walk. The weather continuing very wet, we departed from Hayle in a van in which we had 14 companions. We arrived at Marazion about 7 & there found a box of clean things for Sunday wear which were particularly acceptable.

7. Attended Marazion Meeting in the morning & walked from thence to Penzance having received an invitation from E. Crouch with whom we dined. From a hill near Newlyn we watched a shoal of mackerel in the water. We then saw a seine go out after them & shoot;[1] it was a very interesting sight.

8. Ascended the tower of the new church at Penzance from which there is a very fine view. Surveyed the Geological rooms & other Penzance lions till one, when we turned our faces towards Lelant where we arrived late in the afternoon.

9. Sam having a head-ache we sent him back to Penzance this morning by the van. John Richards & I continued our route along the coast towards St. Just. At Zennor, a village between St. Ives & St. Just, the people took us for scissor grinders. We explored Gurnard's Head a remarkably bold promontory. On the western side is the junction of the granite & killas.[2] We climbed down the cliff & on ascending it further on, John Richards was in imminent danger, the grass being very short & slippery so as to admit of no hold. However by dint of taking off our shoes & sticking our nails into the cliff we at last reached the top. Arrived at Morvah about 4 very ready for dinner. They supplied us with fried eggs & bacon, the former much the nature of oil, the latter of Lot's wife. Having inspected Levant & Botallak mines in our way we reached St. Just about ½ past 9. Took up our abode at the *Star Inn* & found our hostess very civil.

10. Very dismal foggy morning. Inspected the remains of an ancient amphitheatre at St. Just. It looks nothing more than a round field with a mound around it. Proceeded to Cape Cornwall which is extremely magnificent. We stopped there nearly an hour waiting for the fog to clear away but being disappointed we proceeded to the Land's End where we had the pleasure of meeting Sam who had come in a car from Penzance. We found him near the point waging war with the gulls. Having bestowed our admiration on the rocks, the cavern & Capt. Arbuthnot's horse's foot marks,[3] we returned

1. i.e. throw out the net or seine.
2. The Cornish term for the high ground rising above the slate.
3. In *Household Words* for 1852, General Sir Robt. Arbuthnot gives a true version of a story which had been exaggerated. In June 1804, while a captain of dragoons and stationed at Falmouth, he had visited Land's End with two companions. He led his horse on foot to the edge of the cliff and when a few yards away remounted to return.

to the little inn to dinner. The weather continuing wretched we went in the car to Tolpeden-Penwith, which having duly admired as well as all the neighbouring cliffs, we proceeded on foot to the Logan rock. In our way had a grand hawk hunt & very nearly succeeded in the capture. We reached Logan Rock about 7 & ascended to the top. Rocked it as we all firmly believe, descended the cliff there & having been much delighted therewith proceeded in the car to Penzance.

11. Having waited till 10 o'clock for a letter we proceeded to St. Michael's Mount, went over the castle, sat in the chair, descended into the dungeon. walked round the Mount, bathed & departed. Took some luncheon at Marazion & proceeded towards Helston. Between Marazion & Breage is an old castle called Pengersick.[1] It is now turned into a barn, the upper part we strongly suspected was kept for illicit purposes as the cottager who kept the key refused positively to let us go there. It is also near the sea & except the cottages that surround it there is no house within a great distance of it. Leaving Penjersick we went through Breage to Wheal Vor[2] where having looked at the Engines, Stamps, Buddling apparatus[3] &c. we proceeded to Helston where we slept.

12. Having sent on our knapsacks by the van Sam & I set off for Falmouth at 10 & arrived at home about 2.

13. Rode with Sam to Poldice mine intending to go underground but were disappointed, the men being all up to receive their pay. Rode back to Perran to meet the girls who were gone with Uncle & Aunt C. to the North Coast. They arrived about 8. Slept at Perran.

15. Set off for Tregothnan at 1. Had a charming excursion, dined on the grass, went over Trelissick[4] & returned about 8.

24. Sam departed at 7 & I saw him off. At 1 o'clock I went with the girls to the gypsies whom we sketched. Took a beautiful little gypsy girl over the garden, gave her a handsome nosegay, put an elegant wreath on her head, took her to Grove Hill & introduced her to Lucy & then returned her to her clan laden with flowers, cake, pence, books & a doll. We drank tea at the Tregelleses.

1. A sixteenth-century fortified house which has now been restored. The origins of this house remain a mystery but it was thought locally that it had been built by a murderer.
2. One of the most important tin mines which at this time was producing about a quarter of all the tin in Cornwall. In 1832 a beam engine with an 80-inch cylinder, the biggest of its time, had been installed.
3. A trough for separating ores in running water.
4. On the River Fal, halfway between Falmouth and Truro, the home of Davies Gilbert, President of the Royal Society, 1827–30. It now belongs to the National Trust.

The horse then became unruly and plunged towards the precipice. While still four feet away Arbuthnot managed to free himself and leap from the horse which went over the cliff to her death below.

27. The party returned from Truro where they have much enjoyed themselves. Gave our boat a regular wash. The Gurneys & A.M. are gone to Grove Hill where they stay some days. Called on them in the evening & at 9 went down to the *Regulator*[1] where I had the infinite satisfaction of meeting Cavendish. He is well & brings us a good report of his mother. Gave me 12 Indian arrows.

8TH MONTH

14. Went to Brougham to have a tooth out but he advises me to go to Truro and have it stopped, which I intend doing. Dined at Grove Hill but came home directly after tea to a magnetic lecture by Papa which was very interesting. Saw a young crocodile in town.

16. The Gurneys went at 7 this morning. Had an affectionate kiss at parting. We sketched with Jordan. Cavendish dined early with me & we rode to Truro to consult N. Stephens about my refractory tooth. I had him stopped together with 4 of his brethren, which was no delightful operation.

19. A.M. fearing she should be mistaken for a boy, has at length begun caps.[2]

23. Received a note from Aunt C. inviting Cavendish & me to accompany them to Coverack to fish. Having obtained leave we set off for Trebah, dined there at 1 & immediately after proceeded in Uncle A.'s boat to Coverack. Had a fine breeze all the way. Nearly got upon a rock by catching our keel in the floats of a crab pot & the wind dying away at the same moment. There had been a catch of pilchards the night before about 2 miles off, so having landed Uncle & Aunt C., we proceeded to the seine & got 300 for bait. Landed amongst the rocks & walked back to Coverack. After tea we took another boat to Uncle A.'s which was anchored at the fishing ground. Pascoe had set 2 boulters (100 fathom lines with a large hook at every fathom). Having got into Uncle A.'s boat we commenced fishing & were very successful.

24. There being no spare bed in the inn besides what Uncle & Aunt C. occupied, we laid our great coats down on the parlour floor & went to sleep. Rose at 6 & bathed. Breakfasted at 8 & two horses being brought to meet us we rode in tie to Helford taking our way through St. Keverne. Crossed the passage & got to Trebah about 1, lunched & rode home in time to read our themes.

27. The Horticultural Meeting takes place tomorrow at the Classical School,

1. The stage-coach.
2. i.e. begun to wear a cap.

consequently today was employed in decorating it & getting the plants in, in which we all assisted. The room was hung round with flags. There was an arch of ever-greens at the entrance gate, one over each of the side gates & a treble arch of ever-greens & flowers over the door. The stands for the flowers were hung with garlands from post to post. We contributed a large circle of dahlias & laurel alternatively, with a magnolia in the centre, which was hung up nearly opposite the door. There was also a pyramid of dahlias & a crown & star of evergreens. The stands were placed all round the room. Upon the whole it looked uncommon well.

28. Attended a Jewish marriage[1] at 1. It was very interesting. Four Jews held four poles which supported a blue canopy under which the priest stood in his sackcloth & pontifical cap. When the music struck up, the bride entered supported by her mother & aunt, who led her round & round several times under the canopy while all the Jews sung Hebrew. Having finished her revolutions they placed her by the side of the bridegroom who rammed on a ring to her fat little finger, repeating at the same time some words after the priest. After this the priest read something in Hebrew which sounded like a marriage contract. They then sung some more Hebrew & for a finale the priest put a wine-glass on the ground which the bridegroom stamped upon, & congratulations succeeded. Having taken some cake & wine we proceeded to the Horticultural meeting. There was a tremendous cram so that Sir Charles Lemon was obliged to hold forth outside. After dinner Cavendish & I went to look out for the steamer which soon arrived. We rowed out to her & found Col. & Cos. H. MacInnes & their 2 children on board. I got into their boat & took them to Grove Hill. They were both well & very hearty. Grandmamma, Aunt C. & Uncle A. who returned yesterday, drank tea with us. Spent the rest of the evening at Grove Hill.

9TH MONTH

6. I'm 16 to day on which interesting occasion Mamma gave me Butler's *Analogy*,[2] Carry a pair of braces, A.M. the pious *Minstrell*.[3] All the party but Cavendish & I are gone to Perran to meet the grandees.

8. 1st day. Had the pleasure of meeting Cos. Josiah Fox, brother of the late John Fox. He has come with his 2 sons from the banks of the Ohio to take possession of his brother's property. He is a very singular clever & interesting person. He constructed the American Navy & wears a pig-tail.

1. A Jewish synagogue had been built in Falmouth in 1766.
2. Bishop Butler's *Analogy of Religion*, 1736.
3. Probably James Beattie's poem *The Minstrel*, 1771-4.

9. In the afternoon I rowed with Cavendish to Little Falmouth to look at the *Stansmore*, which has been much injured in passing over a coral reef. While at the rock whom should we meet but friend Josiah & his 2 sons inspecting the dock yard with Dick Symons, who made us all drink tea with him.

10. All but Carry & I gone to the Quarterly Meeting at St. Austell. Cavendish & I drank tea at Grove Hill where I attained at least one new idea, viz., when writing, as one does not like to be troubled with continually snuffing the candle, place the candlestick at such an inclination that the wick shall project beyond the flame which will consequently gradually fall off in ashes & the flame will be steady.

19. Having changed the half-holiday from tomorrow to today I adjourned at 12 to the Bank to dinner. Having finished, Uncles Alfred & Francis Tuckett & A. Burgess & self set off in our gig & on the pony for Glendurgan on a fishing excursion, being well supplied with bodily comforts both external & internal. Uncle G.P. followed us & Uncle C. joined us on the beach & off we set in 2 boats & came to an anchor about a mile beyond the Manacles. We lit a fire & having taken tea we commenced operations; the evening was delightful. The bright fire with the men lying smoking round it & the clear moon shining on the rigging made the scene very picturesque. Having got to an end of our bait we found we had 2 doz. very fine hake, 9 or 10 congers, a cod, dog-fish, bream &c. We then managed to tuck in a hearty supper & set off for home with the tide against us. We had to row all the way. Got home about 3 in the morning. Found a famous fire when we got home where we put our things to dry & having taken a 2nd tea we all turned in, 2 in a bed, half undressed, all agreeing that we had passed a delightful afternoon & night.

22. Uncle G.C. in great alarm about the cholera which is reported to be at Falmouth.

23. The cholera is in the town it was ascertained today at a meeting of the board of health. Papa & I spent a solitary evening at home.

24. The Tregelleses, including our new cousin Jennifer, & Dr. Fox & Cos. Anna drank tea here. Papa introduced his electro-magnet which excited much astonishment. We teased Cos. Jennifer to tell us some Irish stories which she did uncommonly well. Cavendish & I took a row in Uncle Joshua's boat. Saw on the beach some cholera bedding & clothes being burned.

10TH MONTH

1. Thomas whilst taking out the breakfast things was seized with faintness

& sickness which so terribly frightened him that his groans were heard at the next house. Having put his feet in warm water & taken some medicine under Col. MacInnes's directions, been put to bed, &c., he gradually recovered. He told Col. MacInnes that he could compare the motion of his bowels to nothing but a pump, which destroyed the Doctor's gravity.

2. Thomas much better but Grace was seized in something the same way.

4. Took a gentle ride with Cavendish who felt better after it. Dined at the Bank. Walked to the castle with Uncle G.P. We heard Aunts' Scotch journal in the evening.

5. Took a ride with Cavendish. He felt refreshed, but it tired him. He longs so for change of air that he is to go to Penzance the day after tomorrow, where I probably join him at the end of the week.

6. 1st day. Cavendish low and poorly. Packed up his things for him in readiness to go tomorrow, but he sent a note in the evening to say he was not equal to it, consequently his place was transferred from tomorrow to the next day.

7. Cavendish still poorly & nervous. Walked here & sat in the sun in the arbour. Mamma gave him a dose of Pritchard, which we heard in the evening Dr. Vigurs extremely disapproved of. Cavendish says he shall not be able to go tomorrow. Grandmamma & Aunt C. & Uncle G.P. came to tea, the latter spouted *Alexander's Feast*[1] & parts of Milton in the evening.

8. Cavendish low in the morning but got much brighter in the course of the day. Had some fish with a relish. Dr. Vigurs admitted that Mamma's medicine had done him no harm. Cholera still on the decline.

18. The papers state the arrival of Capt. Ross[2] in England, having long ago been given up for lost. He has been absent four years in the Arctic Ocean and has lost only three of his crew. Rode with C. to Glendurgan where I assisted Uncle A. in cutting down his trees & drinking his tea. We returned to Falmouth together.

19. Read our themes on Glass which were approved of. The subject given for our next is a circumstance which happened very lately, viz. the loss of the *City of Waterford* on the coast of Portugal. She had much of Donna Maria's[3] property on board and amongst the rest her sceptre, which was nearly the only thing saved. A box from the Gurneys today brought besides many presents for the girls, a beautiful silver & gold pencil case for me from Sam. They give a long detailed account of the robbery of their house which

1. A poem by Dryden.
2. Captain, afterwards Sir James, Ross determined in 1831 the position of the North Magnetic Pole. In 1839 he was to set off for the Antarctic, and it was on this voyage that he sent a message to Barclay's father to tell him that the Fox dipping needle compass had led to the siting of the South Magnetic Pole.
3. The Queen of Portugal, who had returned to reclaim the throne which had been seized by her uncle Miguel.

happened a few days ago. The only thing they have lost of any value is a French clock which stood on the chymney piece. Papa is much disturbed by a cold in the head.

22. Rather a worse account of Cavendish. It really seems an anxious thing for this attack to hang about him so long, but I think it may be partly attributed to his nervousness. Grandmamma, Uncle G.P. and Aunt Charles stay with us till the end of the week. A most singular whirlwind took place today. It seemed to come from Helston. It upset much of the furniture in Selly's Hotel & swept over to Flushing, capsizing two boats and whirling two men out of another.

26. Most boisterous day. A number of people collected on Gillan Vaise & Swanpool beach to secure any parts of the wreck of the *William & Mary* which struck a few days ago on the Manacles. Cavendish returned in the evening. Went directly to see him but found him nervous and very little better.

27. 1st day. Vigurs has been to see Cavendish & pronounces his complaint to be a worm. He is accordingly to be dosed with turpentine tomorrow.

28. Heard of the death of Mathew Stevens in the night, most probably of apoplexy. Cavendish under the effects of his most horrible dose.

29. Cavendish feels much more comfortable. John Richards not being able to attend this morning, having taken some calomel, I went to Cavendish & got him out & walked with him. Aunt A. spent the afternoon with us.

30. Fine sunny day. Walked up & down the terrace with Cavendish who dined with us. Called with Carry on Emily Wright. She is going with her husband to Woolwich in the *Hermes* & wishes Cavendish to accompany them as he has had a strong invitation from Henry to come to Oxford for a change of air.

31. Cavendish has determined to accept the Wrights' proposal & go with them tomorrow. I expect a thorough change of air will be of great service to him. Capt. Wright gave me a chameleon. I have already seen it change colour at least a dozen times. A box from Madeira arrived in the evening with a splendid bunch of feather flowers for Mamma made by the nuns, as well as some clay figures.

11TH MONTH

12. The Tregelleses read Chemistry with us which they mean to continue regularly. There was a letter from the Government yesterday stating that if a clean bill of health was not returned, the packets would be removed to Plymouth. Accordingly a clean bill was issued this morning, very soon after which three new cases [of cholera] were reported.

15. Directly after Jordan's lesson I rode to Perran to meet Mildred Hustler, a first cousin of Aunt C. and about my own age. He is going to stay at Perran a year to be instructed in all the mysteries of merchandise in Uncle C.'s counting house. He seems very sociable and open hearted. I like him very well. Had a letter from Cavendish with a much better account of himself.

16. The *Firefly* steamer arrived two days ago having made the Mediterranean voyage as far as Greece and back in 27 days, the shortest passage ever known. I returned from Perran this morning to breakfast.

12TH MONTH

1. 1st day. Very wet. Aunt Mary much worse, she is thought to be in great danger. We called on her today. Uncle C. & Mildred Hustler dined here. Aunt C. not at Meeting, having an attack of erysipelas. Spent an hour with Aunt Alfred in the afternoon.

4. A committee to settle the affairs of the Polytechnic Society was held at our house, but on account of the boisterous weather not many attended; it was agreed to adjourn the next committee till 2nd day.

6. Directly after drawing rode to Perran to lodge. Consulted Capt. Tregaskes about the model of a mine I am making for the exhibition. He told me many of the technical terms in mining &c.

14. Dined at Grove Hill with A.M., came home directly after & went on with the mine. Have been doing a map of the world this week instead of a Theme. Broken up today for a fortnight. Had a better account of Cavendish today.

23. Day of days. The committee of Judges assembled at the Schoolroom at 10, the members at 12. W. Carkeet & I were door keepers where we took £5. 6. in shillings. The Exhibition went off admirably beyond our most sanguine expectations, the attendance was large & many articles extremely interesting, particularly the steam engines, Papa's electro-magnet, A.M.'s box of minerals, T. Hastings' painting, the mine &c. &c. A great quantity of prizes were given, the largest part of which were to the poor. A.M. had 5 prizes, I 3, & C. 1; mine were a very complete dressing case for the mine, a book of monkeys for Passamonde[1] & a mother of pearl paper knife for a map of the world. Sir Charles Lemon, J. Enys, G. Borlase, D. Coleridge,[2] & R. Taylor dine here.

1. Pasamond, or Passement, is gimp, made of silk or other material, for decorative trimming.
2. Derwent Coleridge, the son of the poet, was headmaster of the grammar school at Helston.

29. 1st day. After meeting accompanied Uncle & Aunt C. to Perran in the carriage. Called on Uncle Lewis in the evening who has been poorly. The Methodists at Falmouth are much interested about the Ascension of Elizabeth Elliot, who while at prayer in the class meeting, was plainly seen to ascend within a foot of the ceiling, which being accomplished she con-descended to resume her former station, much to the astonishment of all beholders.

31. Wet morning but fine afternoon as yesterday. It was a thanksgiving day at Falmouth today for the departure of the cholera.

1834

CAVENDISH WALL returns after Christmas still unwell and depressed. In May there is another family visit to London for the Yearly Meeting, followed by visits to Upton, the home of the Samuel Gurneys, and Bury Hill, Dorking, the home of the Barclays. From London Barclay accompanies his father on a visit to the Rhineland and Holland. The record of this has had to be omitted for reasons of space.

1ST MONTH

2. S. Wood commenced at Falmouth a course of lectures on Architecture &c., which we attend. The subject of today's was the progress of civilisation as shown in the advancement of the art of building. John Richards and I settled into schooling today. Cavendish is expected in a week.

14. General committee of the Polytechnic members which now amount to nearly a hundred. Uncle C. put a proposal to the meeting offering a premium for some contrivances to assist the ascent of miners from the mine. The first prize to be 10£, the 2nd 5£, & the 3rd 3£. This is the first fine day we have had for many weeks.

18. H. Fenwick & her 3 brothers, & Tom, Charles, & Arthur Fox drank tea here. The evening was employed in practical charades. T. Fenwick much brushed up by his military life. Cavendish arrived this evening by the *Regulator* but I was not allowed to go and welcome him on account of my cold. Thomas went as proxy & did not bring a very encouraging report of him.

19. 1st day. Went to see Cavendish before he had left his bed. Found him looking much better than I had been led to expect, the only thing that appears to be amiss with him is weakness and occasional great depression. Whilst at Cheltenham he was in continual fear of death, but is now better & glad to settle into his studies again. He brings a good account of his mother. He dined with us.

27. Grandmamma gave me the gold handle of a cane which belonged to my great grandfather. We drank tea at the Bank. Uncle G.P. lost a gold seal. Uncle A. advised him to have it cried[1] & concluded by telling Uncle G.P. that if he would give him 6d. he would engage to procure it for him.

1. i.e. by the town-crier.

Uncle G.P. agreed & Uncle A. produced the seal which Aunt A. had found the day before. But my worthy uncle fought shy of the agreement.

30. The wind shifted to its old quarter and we are again favoured with drizzling warm weather. A fine 74 is now anchored in the bay. Our new schooner the *Trefusis*[1] made her first debut at Falmouth.

2ND MONTH

3. Saw a kingfisher just outside the garden in the evening. Walked with Cavendish to the *Trefusis* which they were paying[2] by the blaze of tar barrels. The picture was a complete Rembrandt.

5. Went with Cavendish over the *Trefusis*, our new vessel, She is a tolerably sharp stylish schooner, & wind & weather permitting, sails for Italy tomorrow.

9. 1st day. Paid a very entertaining call on Aunt Mary who gave me a gold coin of the reign of James 1st. A.M. read Aunt Mary a letter from Frenchay which gives us reason to expect an additional cousin in the course of a week.

13. S. & M. Sutton & Cavendish dined here. The Tregelleses came directly after to attend our chemical experiments. J. Richards was of course head man & on the whole we managed very well, though without Papa's help it would have been a most meagre affair. However we succeeded in making oxygen, hydrogen, chlorine, nitrous gas & carbonic acid gas &c., with which we tried many & interesting & brilliant experiments. We attempted making nitrous oxide but somehow or other failed. The party separated a little before 12.

21. A.M.'s 18th birthday, on which important era various donations were given and received. Today the poor chameleon breathed his last.

3RD MONTH

4. Took a walk with Cavendish. Find him still melancholy & expecting soon to die. He is nevertheless determined to be a surgeon. We paid a visit to Vigurs's surgery together & afterwards a professional one to a man whose leg was broken by a cart running over it.

5. Whilst walking near the Quay today a boat was swamped off Trefusis. There were 4 men & a boy on board, 3 of whom were sitting on the windward side, but on a sudden violent puff they let go the sheet & the boat

1. G. C. Fox & Co. were shipowners as well as shipping agents.
2. i.e. painting with tar those parts which required protection from water.

over-balanced by the weight of the men on the other side, heeled over & was of course instantly filled; one man jumped overboard intending to swim. However another boat put off to them as soon as possible & afterwards 2 others & brought them in under Capt. King's. We watched their landing, they were all looking desperately pale & frightened as well they might be.

7. Being a half holiday I rode to Truro & had 3 teeth stopped. Cavendish rode part of the way with me, but fearing he should get tired prudently went back. Returned to Perran to tea & to lodge. Employed the evening in skinning birds with Mildred.

8. Got up between 6 & 7 to return but found Trade had broken out of the field in the night. I rode Mildred's mare in, which ran away with me. Took a walk with Cavendish. Read our Themes on the modes of preserving health. Cavendish's displayed some knowledge of his subject. Carry's was a very good cut at Cavendish's numerous precautions.

10. Drank tea at the Crouches. Cavendish who has been much employed lately in studying medical books, has found that aberration of mind often attends dyspeptic nervous affections & has at last come to the conclusion that he is at times rather cracky himself, in which I perfectly agreed.

13. Walked pretty much with Cavendish who is decidedly much better since his arrival. Called at Vigurs's surgery which is Cavendish's centre of attraction.

20. According to engagement with Uncle C., Cavendish & I rode to Trebah soon after 7 to breakfast. Uncle C. & Mildred arrived a little after. After breakfast we proceeded with Uncle C.'s gig & Uncle Tom Pencluna, rather a rough passage for the horses. At Helford we divided parties, sending on our feeble young friend Cavendish with our venerable Uncle Tom in the gig to prepare dinner for us at Coverack. Mildred, Uncle C., & I walked across the country to Porthalla & from thence to Porthoustock, Uncle C. distributing tracts for their Sunday School at each village. From Porthoustock we kept along the coast to Coverack, when within about a mile of that place Uncle Charles strode into a quagmire which enveloped about $\frac{1}{2}$ his length. However with much scrambling he emerged & Mildred & I, as soon as our risible faculties would allow us, set to scraping off the mud with our sticks. Having reached Coverack we most thoroughly enjoyed our dinner and then proceeded to Cadgwith, sending Cavendish & Uncle Tom as before to get our tea. We kept along the coast & saw some most splendid cliffs & arrived at Cadgwith about $\frac{1}{2}$ past 7, having walked 19 miles. We got 2 comfortable little beds between the 4.

21. Directly after breakfast we proceeded to Kynance, visiting the Devil's Cauldron on our way. We did not see Kynance to advantage, the tide being too high. However, we scrambled about a good deal, till gig &c. made their appearance with the prog, which we quickly despatched & proceeded to

Mullion. The cliffs uncommonly splendid & covered with gulls & cormorants. Shot a pretty little bird near Mullion whose name none of us could tell. Having arrived at Mullion we turned Uncle Tom adrift & proceeded in the gig to Gweek where we were met by Thomas & our gig, so taking leave of Uncle C. we drove home & arrived soon after 7.

22. Had my hair cut & all but clapped my hands on a gentleman's eyes in the town mistaking him for Cavendish. Aunt Lucy is very poorly with the influenza.

25. The *Melville* that arrived today can bring no intelligence of the *Thais* (Capt. Church) which has been due 7 weeks. She had not arrived at Halifax when the *Melville* left. Took the colt an airing round the lanes. He is very much admired by all the knowing ones. Aunt Lucy not better. Mamma there most of the day.

4TH MONTH

16. Some Friends dined here today & as our religious society have founded a boy's school at Ashfield, the engaged master not being able to attend for another quarter, his highness J. Richards is appointed to the exalted post of vice-mastership of the school, which he is to attend after leaving us. I wish him prosperity & joy.

29. Drove A.M. to Falmouth soon after 7, as till we break up we go to school an hour earlier in the morning & come out an hour sooner in the afternoon to allow J. Richards to attend his Ashfield duties which he commenced yesterday & thinks the boys pretty promising. Uncle C. was seized today with an attack of influenza. Received a very handsome self-interpreting Testament as a wedding present from Anne Dale.

5TH MONTH

1. Was awoke soon after 5 by infantine hornery ushering in the summer. Grandmamma & Aunts took leave. They set off for Town tomorrow morning. Took a row with Cavendish.

10. Very busy packing up &c. for the journey. All except self go on 13th day; I set off on 15th by the Irish steamer.

12. Bustle, Bustle, Bustle, morning noon & night. Went over to see about the carriage which is shamefully after time. Companies after companies coming to take leave.

1.Rosehill, Falmouth

2.The Perran Foundry today

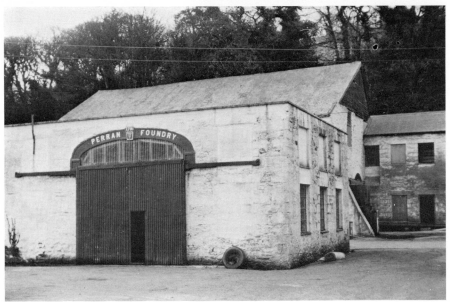

3.Falmouth, 1825. *William Daniel*

4.Truro, 1830. *Thomas Allom*

13. The party set off about 8. The gig accompanied them to Truro & of course brought home a list of omissions to come with the boy who goes by the steamer to frank[1] the rest of the rubbish. Between 10 & 11 went with Uncle G. to Tregithey. Had pouring rain all the way to Helford but a fine afternoon. Came back to Penjerrick to dinner where Aunt & little Lucy met us.

15. Fine. Removed the books from the schoolroom & got everything ready for setting off tonight which is the proper, though on account of contrary winds, not the expected time of the steamer's arrival. Slept at home with Cavendish & had our luggage taken to the Counting House beforehand but all in vain. No steamer yet.

19. Breakfasted at 6, set off in the *Drake* with Cavendish at 7. One pleasant passenger on board from Gibraltar. Changed to the *Brunswick* off Plymouth. Found her overstocked with passengers so as to oblige me & some others to sleep on the floor. One nice intelligent little fellow on board from Sierra Leone. He had 2 Dumboo monkeys which gave us much amusement. Cavendish rather sick.

20. Arrived at Portsmouth soon after 8. The coach started an hour & half after our arrival. Found 2 great boxes of family luggage rather bothering companions. After an unadventurous but hot & dusty ride we arrived at London Church-town at $\frac{1}{2}$ past 6. From the inn I went to Austin Friars, Cavendish having left me at Piccadilly for his uncle's. Took the luggage & Mamma to our lodgings in Barton Crescent in the evening.

21. The Yearly Meeting commenced today at 10. It was principally occupied in reading Epistles. Shopped a little with Mamma & the girls & returned late. Papa attended a grand Geological meeting in the evening.

25. 1st day. After an early breakfast went to Westminster Meeting & had some good sermons. After an early dinner adjourned to Aunt Gurney's & met the Backhouses[2] there, very nice girls. Drank tea there & accompanied them to Meeting.

31. Father & mother having departed to the select meeting we, their pups, sallied forth at 9, sight-seeing. We first adjourned to the National Gallery of Arts & Inventions. Many very interesting things there, amongst others a canvas tube for a man to slip through from any height in case of fire. A man descended by it to the Square for our edification. From this place we adjourned to the Fleas[3] taking a pastry cook's & sundry other shops in the way. Messrs. Flea & Co. gave great satisfaction dancing, driving, riding,

1. i.e. to transport free of charge.
2. The Backhouses were a Quaker family from Darlington. Jonathan Backhouse had interests in railways and banking. Hannah Backhouse was a minister of the Society of Friends.
3. An exhibition of performing fleas.

duelling &c. From the fleas we went to a very good oxy-hydrogen microscopic exhibition. After staying there an hour we walked to the new Bazaar
which was extremely splendid. We made numerous purchases. We got home
to dinner at 3 middlingly fagged. After dinner walked off to the Stratford
coach & drove to Upton where we spent a very pleasant & sociable evening.
I took a walk of about 2 miles to Joseph Fry's[1] new house & wife.

6TH MONTH

3. Jane & Ann Backhouse joined us at breakfast. They are particularly nice
girls, the former is quite beautiful. After breakfast Papa & Mamma went to
the Examination of the Borough Road School & we chits to the Distribution
of the Prizes at the Art Society. It was exceedingly interesting especially when
the young ladies & children received their medals, which were given by the
Duke of Sutherland. The girls & I took a shopping excursion in the afternoon & bought some amazingly cheap books.

4. Directly after breakfast went to Grosvenor Place to join the party in an
excursion to Harrow to hear the boys' speeches. Some of them spoke well
& others the contrary. We dined at Kennedy's the head master's & then
returned. Arthur drove me in his phaeton. We spent the evening in enrobing
him in his Turkish costume, beard, moustache &c., in preparation for a
masquerade he attends tomorrow. Our party went to Upton today at 3.

7. After breakfast all the juniors except the 2 youngest set out in the phaeton
& on horseback for Greenwich. We called in our way on Grandmamma
Sheppard & her happy idiot daughter, Anna, who screamed with delight on
seeing us. We went 2 miles down the Thames in wherries & arrived at Greenwich at 1. We first went into the dining room and talked with the Pensioners, who seem a very entertaining original set. Their livery is a blue
surtout with gilt buttons, knee breeches, & a 3-cornered hat. We visited their
sleeping apartments & the picture gallery: a painting of Lord Nelson's death
struck me as the best. We next went to the chapel, the ceiling of which was
very magnificent. We saw Nelson's hat & coat and then engaged in our
labours of love, distributing tracts among the Pensioners' wives, sons, &
others, who mobbed us so for tracts that the ladies soon communicated their
inclination to move on. We accordingly walked to the Park & lunched
under a tree in great style.

9. We got to Austin Friars in time for luncheon after which the rest of the
party went on to Eastwick[2] & I to Hampstead by the coach to see the Hoares.

1. A son of Elizabeth Fry.
2. Eastwick Hall near Great Bookham, Surrey, had been bought by his uncle, David
Barclay, in 1833.

I got there just at dinner time & though I had never seen any before but Gurney, who was not then arrived, they were all very easy & sociable.

10. Breakfasted at ½ past 7. Set off for Town at 8 & from Charing Cross at 9 for Eastwick. Met the Backhouses in my way. Arrived at Leatherhead a little before 12 & walked to Eastwick, distance a mile & ½. Uncle & Aunt David very cordial. Took a ride with the party through the forest &c. to see the estate, which is uncommonly fine. It is very beautifully wooded & the land appears very fertile. The house is square & very large, the drawing room is 75 ft. long & contains 4 large red marble pillars.

30. Papa thinks of taking me on excursion up the Rhine. Uncle Barclay thinks it a capital plan & gave me £5 to spend in Holland. Took leave of Grandmamma.

7TH MONTH

1. After much hesitation on Papa's part on account of Grandmamma's indisposition, we at length set off by the 9 o'clock coach for Town after taking an affectionate leave of Mamma & the girls. We reached the Elephant & Castle at 12 from whence Papa went to the West End on various commissions while I proceeded into the City with the luggage. I called at Austin Friars for letters. Went from thence to the Steam Navigation office where I obtained a paper giving all the necessary particulars. The steamer to Antwerp starts at 10 tomorrow morning. I then called on Cos. Sam Gurney in Lombard Street & delivered sundry packages for Upton from the girls. None of their party can accompany us as we wished. Then went to Watkins & Hill's where I met Papa who sent me to the Foreign Office to get a passport from Lord Palmerston, the Secretary of State. I called there but by stupidly misunderstanding Papa's orders could not obtain it without the payment of £2.7.6. I afterwards found that at the Dutch consul's or ambassador's I could have got one for nothing. However, as it is always best to look on the bright side of things, we are by this people of much greater importance. It secures more attention & will probably save so much trouble. Lord Palmerston did not say much. He looks oldish[1] & is very deaf. I went to Prince's Street to get the passport visaed by the Dutch ambassador but he was not at home. Took some dinner at a Pastry Cook's & met Papa at the *White Hart*. I wrote to Aunt Mariana & then went to the Dutch consul's to get the passport visaed by him but he was not at home. Wrote to J. Richards to tell him my plans. We slept at the *White Hart*.

1. Palmerston was 49 and lived until 1865, dying in office after being Prime Minister for a total of more than nine years.

13. 1st day. We landed at the Custom House about $\frac{1}{2}$ past 3 & after a hasty dinner set off for Upton. The party were quite astonished to see us. We went to a Meeting & spent a very pleasant evening there. Some of the Buxtons were staying there.

14. Set off directly after breakfast for Town & had much trouble at the Custom House on account of $\frac{1}{2}$ a bottle of Eau de Cologne & some tobacco. The Eau de Cologne I got free but the custom was so enormously high for the tobacco that I let them seize it. Slept at the *White Hart*.

15. Started at 9 by the Portsmouth coach from the *Spread Eagle*. We passed the new Western Steam Carriage which had met with some accident. Arrived at Portsmouth at $\frac{1}{2}$ past 5 & went on board the *Brunswick* immediately. We had a fine voyage & the berths were comfortable.

16. Got up in time to have a view of Torbay which looked exceedingly beautiful in the morning light. We exchanged steamers off the breakwater. On board the *Drake* I met Derwent Coleridge & family, a son of Davies Gilbert on a visit to Enys, & a most disagreeable insinuating old infidel with whom D. Chapman & I had a long discussion on the doctrines of the Fall, Atonement &c. We landed at $\frac{1}{2}$ past 7. I went directly to Grove Hill, but finding the natives were staying at Penjerrick I went to Cavendish who received me as might be expected. He accompanied me to our house where I was warmly welcomed by the servants & from thence to Uncle Alfred's where I slept. A letter today from John Richards stating his intention of being home by 2nd day.

24. Wrote to parents. Rode with Thomas to a farmer's in the country, of the name of Box (who is to be tried for smuggling the day after tomorrow), to see a horse for sale, but both horse & master being out, we proceeded to Penjerrick & looked at the colt, fields, plantations, Aunt Mary's cottage &c.

25. Painted the boat for an hour & then set off to Glendurgan on another fishing excursion carrying with me a bundle of clothes, 2 doz pilchards & a lot of fishing tackle. Having got everything on board we were joined by Uncles Gibbins, Tuckett, Alfred & Lewis, & Mildred & off we started in high glee, but Uncle Gibbins's enjoyment was soon concluded, being seized by violent sickness, which not at all abating when we came to an anchor, we sent him home in the little boat. We only caught 18 hake & then commenced our homeward voyage.

26. On arriving at Glendurgan at 3 this morning we found Uncle Gibbins so ill as not to be able to stand. We physicked him with brandy & tea & he then laid down for 3 hours. On awakening we found our troubles were not yet over, for Watkins, Uncle Alfred's man, having slung up the hammock in the kitchen very high, the rope broke & he was tumbled out on the stone floor & hurt his hip severely, though we hope the accident is only temporary. After breakfast Uncle Gibbins felt much better & we all proceeded

home through driving rain. Uncle & Aunt G. returned to Grove Hill yesterday so that I now am regularly settled there.

8TH MONTH

1. Whole holiday, being a day of National Thanksgiving for the Abolition of the Slave Trade which took place at 5 this morning. Uncles Lewis & Francis & myself with 2 fishermen employed the time about 7 miles off St. Anthony's in catching bream. We were extremely successful. After catching above a 100 fish we returned & got home a little before 11. The distance from Falmouth was 10 miles, 6 of which were against wind & tide. I rowed all the way. Cos. A. Fox's baby died today.
2. After concluding the painting & having launched the boat I ran home & found the dear people had arrived before me. They were all well & in good spirits & condition, delighted with their tour & glad to get home & much satisfied with home alterations. Employed the evening in paying with them visits of greeting.
9. Uncle J. came in the evening with whom the Friends held a meeting.[1] Cavendish came in to borrow some money, walked in amongst them most unceremoniously & was walking up to shake hands with Uncle Joshua, who sent him off marvelling greatly.
10. 1st Day. J. Barclay & his son spent the day & lodged here. Lovell Squire[2] dined.

9TH MONTH

1. According to appointment Papa & I proceeded to Trevince to breakfast, which having been accomplished & surveyed the garden, John Michael Williams escorted us to Wheal Jewel, & about ½ past 11 with Captain Dee, John Michael, galvanic batteries &c., descended in Michael's shaft, furnished with miners' dresses, hats, candles & all other 'appliances & means to boot'. We stopped at the 70 fathom level to arrange the apparatus, but finding the

1. Uncle Joshua had been disowned by the Quakers for marrying outside the Society, but as he was now a widower, there may have been discussions about his re-admission. Cavendish must have intruded into what was a very private meeting.
2. Lovell Squire had just moved to Falmouth. He was a Quaker and was to marry Henrietta Crouch, one of the Falmouth Quakers. He was a meteorologist and later became Supt. of the Meteorological Observatory at Falmouth, but at first started a school in the town.

galvanometers were left 'at grass', we were obliged to send a miner for them
& meanwhile descended to the 80 fathom level, where we blasted 2 rocks with
sand & surveyed a very fine & promising lode which is yielding the adventurers nearly £3000 per month. We returned to the 70 fathom & meeting
the galvanometers there, settled down to experiment on the galvanism in the
veins, the results of which were very satisfactory. We afterwards visited other
rich parts of the mine. A tin lode has been lately discovered & is very promising. After a stay of 7 hours in the lower regions we returned to upper air by
an ascent of 109 fathoms, having undoubtedly far outstripped the similar
exploits of Orpheus, Ulysses & Aeneas.

2. Have not felt a moment's fatigue from yesterday's labours. Uncle G. had
intended setting off for France this afternoon but deferred it till tomorrow,
partly on account of Grandmamma's very precarious state & partly from
want of resolution.

3. Morning wet & blustery. After a row with Cavendish went to Grove Hill
to take leave of Uncle G. Found he could not decide on leaving till he had
heard Dr. Fox's opinion of Grandmamma's case, as should it be such as to
induce Uncle C. to return, the object of his tour would be defeated. I went
to the Bank but found the Dr. was then with Grandmamma. When he came
down I found he took a darker view of her case than I had any idea of. He
advises Aunts not to urge Uncle C.'s return but at the same time believes that
the symptoms in Grandmamma's case are preparatory to a general breaking
up of the system. Uncle G. waits till tomorrow to see what Aunts write
Uncle C. respecting his return.

4. Uncle G. after much hesitation set off this evening for Bath, from whence
he will proceed to the continent or remain there as he feels inclined. That he
will pursue the latter course I have not the least doubt. I drank tea with him
& saw him off.

6. 17 years ago the illustrious author of this work made his entree into the
sublunary world. On which signal anniversary various donations were given
& received by the diverse members of the family.

12. The Ashfield boys with their master & J. Charlton came soon after 4.
We played sundry games of cricket & quoits. All the Stephenses except the
father came to tea, after which Papa gave a lecture on magnetism at which the
Tregelleses & their girls joined, so that we mustered pretty strong by supper
time. They all went away a little before 10.

20. Waited in the harbour for the steamer an hour. On her arrival we went
on board & found Cavendish's brother & sister Boddington on board, whom
we rowed with their luggage to their lodgings. They seem nice, sociable
people. Falmouth lamps commence being lit this evening.

10TH MONTH

3. Dined directly after drawing & took a row with Cavendish to the Turkish brig, boarded & inspected her & her crew, a queer group of Turks and Greeks. Came home & bathed.

4. G. Thompson drank tea here. He goes to Cambridge next week. In the evening he & I dressed up like Turks with turbans, sword, beard & moustache, &c., &c. We first came to our house & having alarmed the servants, applied to Papa for passports. He referred us to Uncle Alfred, where we went, & on his refusal threatened to stab him. We then went to the Tregelleses, who unfortunately were out, but the servants & children being in, we asked them in broken English if the Turkish Consul lived there. They all assured us with the greatest anxiety that he did not & were extremely earnest in explaining where he did. This we pretended not to believe & the whole household being collected, I stalked in, laying my hand on the hilt of my sword, at which two screaming rushed upstairs, and one into the parlour & slammed the door. I pushed it open, but finding only a little girl there screaming her lungs out, I marched out & the door was immediately barred & bolted behind. In about an hour a message came to our house from the Tregelleses to know if G.T. & I were or were not the perpetrators of all the alarm. I went over to know the meaning of the message & heard as exaggerated accounts of ourselves as possible. The servants would not be persuaded it was us but said that either was twice as big as me, that we swore dreadfully, that I drew my sword & the other a knife from his bosom (probably the pipe that G.T. was smoking), that we had black legs & that our feet looked very suspicious of being cloven. After all this I think we could not have wished better success.

16. Sir J. Franklin,[1] the celebrated northern voyager, dined here. He is a stout man with a splendid forehead and piercing eye, but very blue about the beard. He gave us some very interesting accounts of his own adventures & sufferings. He is expecting his wife every day on her return from a little excursion through Russia, Scythia &c. She has travelled through Egypt twice, ascended the great Pyramid, & has spent much time in Italy, Greece, &c. Sir John was delighted with Papa's instrument. He left us at half past ten.

12TH MONTH

17. Squaring accounts at the schoolroom, this being the last week before the

1. Sir John Franklin (1786–1847), the Arctic explorer and discoverer of the North-West passage.

holidays. Went with Aunt C. and the girls to a small show of wild beasts. Cavendish much the same. He has had a letter from his mother hinting the possibility of his not returning to Falmouth after the holidays.

21. 1st Day. A Portuguese man-of-war brig arrived for the purpose of conveying the Duke of Leuchtenberg, King of Portugal,[1] to his young queen. A royal salute was given & returned.

---

1. Augustus, Duke of Leuchtenberg, married the young Queen Maria in 1835, but died a few months later.

1835

In August Barclay finally leaves the schoolroom behind him. His friend Cavendish Wall goes off to be apprenticed to a surgeon in the Midlands, as a preparation for 'walking' one of the London hospitals. Before settling into the Counting House at the family's shipping firm, Barclay embarks with his father and Uncle Charles for a visit to Dublin, where a meeting of the British Association is to be held. The Association was still in its infancy for its first meeting had been at York in 1831, but already Barclay's father is an accepted figure among the scientists of the day and at Dublin he reads a paper on his research into magnetism. W. E. Forster enters the Journal for the first time. Although they never live near each other, he and Barclay are to become close friends and confidants. The Polytechnic Society receives royal patronage and becomes the Royal Cornwall Polytechnic Society. There is a gap in the Journal for the months of September, October, and November. From later references it is likely that during this period Barclay accompanied his family to France and the notebook in which he recorded the details of this visit was probably lost.

1ST MONTH

1. The weather has completely turned with the year. The wind is to the North & the air is cold & dry. Uncle C. & I called on Sir C. Lemon who is much fagged by his electioneering exertions. Mamma called with Aunt Lucy & brought a letter from Cavendish containing the sad news of his intentions of going to Cardin, a Worcester surgeon, in a month, and so here is *finis* to our pursuits together at Falmouth. I have the satisfaction of knowing that from the time of his coming to his departure, we have never had an approximation to a quarrel, but I hope & believe our friendship is not to end here & I look forward to days when we shall again enjoy each other's society as of yore. But alas for the rest of my time with J. Richards. How changed will be the schoolroom!

9. Alfeston recommenced his labours. I now take my French lesson with the girls. J. Richards came & we set to work to form a new 'synopsis studiorum'. The girls are to join us for one hour each day. Their schoolroom occupations with me are to be Italian, Somerville,[1] Mathematics & Arithmetic. Went to

1. Mary Somerville (1780–1872), whose *The Connection of the Physical Sciences*, 1834, is probably referred to here. Somerville College, Oxford, was named after her.

Perran in the gig with Parents who returned after receiving an improved account of Uncle L. I lodged at the House according to arrangement to meet the Coleridges, who are extremely interesting people. Derwent Coleridge has most wonderful conversational powers & appears to be master of every subject. His wife is brilliant & handsome. Papa has discovered & clearly proved that electricity does not act by currents as was supposed, but by pulsations.

20. The Duke of Leuchtenberg, present King of Portugal, arrived at Pearce's to-day at ½ past 7. I went down there & had the pleasure of seeing his highness, first going from his chamber to his drawing room & afterwards from thence to his dining room. He is a tall, slight & handsome young man with light hair & moustaches.

21. Frost all last night. The girls & I went to Pearce's at ½ past 7 to see the Prince embark, which he did at ½ past 8. He went on board the *Monarch* steamer to breakfast, after which he departed with another steamer and 2 frigates in attendance. Monthly Meeting whereat Catherine Lidgey & her swain Edward Bastion passed the meeting, which they performed satisfactorily. Jordan & J. Richards drank tea here & experimented with Papa till past 11.

2ND MONTH

19. Pouring wet the greatest part of the day. Paid a visit to the gypsies & gave one of them, a very handsome girl of the name of Boswell, a sketch of her niece, Saphira, done when the Gurneys were here, & which all the party declared to be very like her. Had a most interesting dinner visit from Davies Gilbert, the sweetest old man I ever saw in my life, & J. Enys & J. Hull, the collector, who seems an agreeable person.

3RD MONTH

2. Went to the gypsies early this morning & according to promise, gave Ed. Boswell's wife (who is expecting to be shortly confined) sundry old carpet ends & an ancient piece of drugget, as the covering of her tent was very scanty. They were highly delighted & insisted on my breakfasting with them, which of course I did. We had bread & cream & cold beef & capital tea. They are very hospitable, civil & industrious. Their conversation was really superior & the wit at times quite sparkling. We are all high friends. If Mrs.

Boswell's child be a boy it is to be christened Barclay in honour of your humble servant. Walked to Penjerrick in the evening.

11. Satisfactory Polytechnic meeting, D. Gilbert in the chair. He is to request his most gracious Majesty graciously to deign & condescend to become Patron of the Cornwall Polytechnic Society in the place of our late, much beloved, lamented Lord Dunstanville.

31. A gypsy, Elias Barclay Boswell, was born today at 6 a.m., just steering clear of Fools' day for the honour of the name.

4TH MONTH

5. 1st day. Called on Aunt Mary. Walked to Penryn & engaged Tremaine, the colt rider, to come & commence breaking in Bayard tomorrow. The Ashfield boys dined here.

6. Tremaine came at 8. He led the colt a long walk & found him on the whole tractable, though not so much so at shoeing. They are obliged to leave the hind shoes till tomorrow. Spent a pleasant evening at Cos. A. Fox's.

7. Uncles & Aunts Gibbins & Tuckett dined here. After dinner we went en masse to look at a farm for sale belonging to Stephens, as Uncle Gibbins wants some land wherewith to try the allotment system.

8. Tremaine backed the colt today who bore it moderately. He looks uncommon well under good grooming. Took the boat to Berryman's to have a locker put in her, after which I shall paint her.

5TH MONTH

4. Rode with J. Richards to Carclew to ask Sir Charles to sign the address of the Polytechnic Society to his most gracious Majesty, requesting him to become our patron. Sir Charles much approved the address. We called at Enys but the squire was not in. The Tucketts, Gibbins, Grandmamma & so forth, spent the evening here. Archery & bowls in the afternoon.

22. Had a good deal of riding in the course of the day principally on account of trying the black mare. Whilst Carry was riding it the saddle slipped off & she, of course, accompanied it. When I had put it right & resettled her on it, I was about to mount the colt when he gave a little jump forward & slid me out of the stirrup which was remarkably slippery. He then stepped on my foot & threw me down, in which state of prostration he took the liberty of standing on my leg for some time. However, I crawled into the ditch &

after a short pause & rubbing & making wry faces, I recovered, remounted & rode to Penjerrick with the rest. I felt very stiff in the evening & on going to bed put on a poultice which much relieved the stiffness.

6TH MONTH

13. Went to meet the coach at 7, in which I had at length the gratification of meeting Bessy & Priscilla Gurney with their governess. The coach drove up to our house, the girls in wonderful spirits & excitement, delighted with everything & very well. They are by this time most probably dreaming away with all their might.

15. The Gurneys *almost* the most charming girls I ever saw. Took them with their governess to Perran for breakfast. They were delighted with everything. Walked to Pendennis in the evening. Sad accident at Penrose. A man named Moyle, being employed by Uncle G. in making a road from the beach & blasting a rock, retired for shelter into a cavern, the roof of which by the concussion fell upon him & crushed him to death. He has left a widow & 2 children.

17. A large party dined here, W. Forster Junr.[1] amongst the number. In the afternoon R. Tweedy & I took the ladies a row to the *Astraea*,[2] they & we taking the oars by turns. In the evening went to see a large hydro-oxygen microscope, the *animalcula* very good & well shown.

18. Took a ride with Bessy and Carry in the morning & a walk to Pennance with the party in the evening, where we romantically reclined on the grass while Bessie repeated the *Lady of the Lake*.

19. Rode to Trebah with Jordan at ½ past 11, Bessie driving all the girls in the gig. We met Uncle and Aunt C. and W. Forster at their cottage & went up the river to a woody valley called Tremaine where we landed & sketched. We dined on the grass & after a very pleasant & merry walk, especially to us boys in handing the ladies over the hedges, we returned to the cottage to tea & went home directly after the Gurneys. They thoroughly enjoy Cornwall & I like them better than ever.

20. Rarest fun at Grove Hill where we all dined together with W. Forster. Immediately after dinner he & I according to agreement went home & dressed like Turks, he being my wife (6 ft. high). We met Bessie & Carry in their room at Grove Hill, the former being in a thorough Swiss costume &

1. W. E. Forster, the son of William Forster, a minister in the Society of Friends, was to achieve eminence in later life as a minister in Gladstone's government. At this date he was sixteen and soon to be apprenticed in the woollen trade.
2. The *Astraea* was the supply ship for the packets based on Falmouth.

the latter an antiquated hag of the last century, also in a very appropriate dress. We four went in together and all acted their parts to admiration. My wife flirted with Uncle G., whilst I carried off Prissy by force as a substitute. W.F. & I went out on Eastman's Hill & got mobbed famously. We returned & danced on the lawn.

24. Dismissed the preceptor. Hurrah & so I'm now a finished man – how very funny! I believe I'm soon to buckle to at the Counting House & most likely have J. Richards up a few hours each week till we've finished Differential Calculus. The Infant School children took tea on the lawn. W. Forster & I played at blindman's buff & ran races with them. Uncle G. & Aunt L. drank tea here & in the evening we had a most admirable practical charade. *Courtship* was the word, so the last scene in particular gave rise to rare fun, W.F. & I courting Bessy one after the other, the former in the character of a sentimental beau & self as a rough Jacktar. W.F. slept here. Wrote to Cavendish.

29. Bayard is laid up & blistered for a splinter in the leg. Dined at 1 & started for Quarterly Meeting. I drove Prissy & Carry to St. Austell. Bessie drove Uncle Gibbins's gig containing the parents. We stopped an hour & $\frac{1}{2}$ at Truro & visited the Museum & Mary Tregelles, whilst Carry had her teeth titivated. We made a superb supper at St. Austell & by accident or design got adjoining rooms separated only by a thin door, so that the girls were carrying on a long gossip in bed till an audible 'hem' from myself chained the clappers & annihilated much information.

30. After breakfast walked to Carglaze with the girls, notwithstanding a dense fog almost amounting to a skew. However, after leaving the mine the weather cleared up & we were able to visit Lanescote mine under the convoyance of J. Carkeet. The engine was most beautiful & is of the greatest power of all in the country. The girls were determined to go below & descended till their heads were under ground. The jigging machine was capital. We dined at Lostwithiel on lamb chops & nominal cheese (really a conglomeration of maggots) & arrived at Liskeard about 5. After tea the parents went to Select Meeting whilst the offspring scoured the town & called on the worthies. We heard of the birth of a daughter to Francis Tuckett of Frenchay, leather factor, & Mariana, his wife. Mother & child doing well.

7TH MONTH

1. Uncle & Aunt C. with A.M. & W. Forster arrived to breakfast. Satisfactory Quarterly Meeting, at which nine sermons were delivered & two Yearly Meeting Epistles were read. We children all dined together at the

Elliotts, much to Aunt C.'s horror. Nevertheless our conduct there was most exemplary(?). We left Liskeard at 4 & reached Lostwithiel just as heavy rain commenced. But on its clearing a little some of us managed to get to Restormel[1] which looked to great advantage. On leaving it we had a very severe thunder storm with much rain, which continued till we reached St. Austell. We were as wet as fish & shifted as soon as we arrived.

2. W. Forster & I awoke the ladies at half-past 5 by dressing like ghosts & in that semblance twitching their noses in order to take a walk to Carglaze; they were, however, forbidden by their rulers so we went ourselves. I never saw it look to so great advantage. The view also of Fowey harbour from thence was very beautiful. We breakfasted at the Browns'. In our way home Aunt C. favoured us (W.F. & me in particular) with so many lectures for trivial offences that I employed my ride from St. Austell in composing a ridiculous satire on the subject, which I humbly dedicated to her. Took a walk with the girls on our return.

13. J. Richards came at half-past 9 to continue Differential Calculus (he will probably come every morning till we have finished) and at 12 o'clock I made my grand entry to the Counting House & was duly installed in a little cage-looking sort of a pew opposite E. Seccombe. My first essay was copying a Consular letter to America, then some bills & then checking a Russian bill of exchange which was unconscionably hard.

8TH MONTH

3. Settling my affairs in preparation for going to Dublin tomorrow. Spent a very pleasant afternoon at Tregedna & had some good singing from some Budock girls.

4. Very busy day packing up, &c. Turned the last lock on the schoolroom door, which gave rise to a little sentimentality. Dined at Uncle A.'s. Uncle C., who goes with us, lodges here. The steamer is after her time.

5. The Gurneys left us by this morning's coach. A very warm parting. We have very much enjoyed their visit & to my best belief so have they. Many people have settled one of them for me – but it's no go – not mind enough. They are nice girls, but can't converse – & so on. At 8 the steamer made its appearance, so after breakfast Papa, Uncle C., & I bade adieu to home. We had 400 passengers on board, amongst others Sir J. & Lady Franklin, Lady Whitmore, & many gentlemen bound to the Scientific meeting. The wind sprung up as soon as we weighed & before we reached the Lizard we had a

1. Restormel Castle, a ruined Norman castle, which crowns a hill overlooking the River Fowey.

regularly fresh breeze. We overhauled another steamer off Mounts Bay. She raced us for some time, but driving to leeward the Captain got a little alarmed & in altering her course one of the engines broke, & he fired signal guns & hoisted a flag of distress. We sent a boat on board but the Captain did not require assistance; however he thought fit to put back to Falmouth. The swell round the Land's End made us speedily settle our accounts. The ladies whose cabin was right aft & the steerage passengers, who were very crowded & dirty, were in most dismal pickle & to use the words of the poet, 'So fled the night, so dawned the day'.

6. Towards noon we came in sight of Ireland & consequently were in smoother water. We anchored off Kingstown, the tide not permitting us to proceed to Dublin tonight.

7. Weighed anchor at half-past 7 & reached this elegant metropolis in an hour. We found comfortable-looking lodgings prepared for us & after making arrangements about members' tickets, &c., we hired one of their strange unsightly & unsociable cars to go & view the lions. We went first to the Botanical Gardens, which are of 30 acres extent, beautifully laid out & which contain many splendid trees & plants, both rare & beautiful. Went from thence to the Zoological Gardens which are also good. A great number of the Irish fashionables were there. An elephant loose & exhibited by a boy of 8 or 9. The Irish ladies are good figures & some of them are very hand-some. In the evening went to Kingstown on the railway.[1] Delightful motion. 30 miles per hour & no roughness. My first Steam Carriage excursion. Kingstown contains very good houses but wears, as I fancy, a dreary appearance. Returned also by steam.

8. 'Oh! I have passed a miserable night', I may well say, as a greater man said before me. The Irish Flea Association were so occupied in holding a section on human Physiology upon my devoted body that it was out of the question to think of sleeping while transactions of such interest were going forward. Early in the morning I assassinated 4 of the committee together with their President, Mr. Bug. After breakfast Papa attended the Committee, but Uncle C. & I, not being of the Elect, were excluded. However, to employ the day we thought we might as well excurse a little into the country so at 12 we entered a barouche & drove to Enniskerry, a distance of fourteen miles. We put up at Enniskerry & proceeded in a car to Lord Powerscourt's, a distance of two miles. It is a very deep & steep ravine, beautifully wooded, with large masses of granite rock appearing through the leaves, a remarkably clear stream flows at the bottom over a very rocky channel which causes every here & there a tiny white cascade, & in the distance the sugar loaf, a hill 2000 ft. in height, makes a grand finish to the scene. We got back to Enniskerry to dinner about half-past 4 & reached home at 8. Papa returned a

1. This was one of the earliest steam railways in the British Isles.

little before midnight, having been at a regular flare-up dinner at the Provost's.
10. Commencement of scientific Labours and Dissipations. Uncle C. & I
went to Trinity Examination Hall at 10 to get our tickets, which we did with
much difficulty. They gave us at the same time a small map of Dublin which
is very convenient. Uncle C. & I took our seats at the Geological &
Geographical Section. The lecturer was a man called Griffith.[1] He began with
a geological account of Ireland, illustrating it by an excellent map of his own
making. A fine young man called Price rose & asked 2 or 3 questions about
the scarps & gravel pits & gave some account of the geology of the North of
Ireland. The turn of the meeting followed, viz. Professor Sedgwick,[2] a fine,
commanding-looking man with a wide brow & raven hair. He expressed
his warm thanks to Griffith for his clear explanations of several important
points, spoke of geology in general & Irish geology particularly, & after
saying some very pretty & clever things to the Irish, he sat down. He has
wonderful fluency & abounds in imagination & wit. F. Tuckett dined with
us. Papa had attended the section on Physics & did then & there read a paper
on the subject of the non-magnetic effect of melted iron. After dinner
Uncle C., F.T., & I took a stroll as far as St. Patrick's Church to see the statue
of Dean Swift. At 8 we rigged out & went to the General meeting at the
Rotunda, the Vice-Roy's court. The room was splendid; a great crowd of
ladies in spic & span evening dresses, & multitudes of marvellous men. On a
platform raised about 6 ft. above the rest of the meeting were Lord Mulgrave, the Vice-Roy, with two Aides de Camp. He was magnificently
dressed in blue with light blue sash & silver epaullettes. He was handsome &
young but looked too effeminate to please me. About him were Wheatstone,[3]
Lardner,[4] Sir J. Franklin, Sir J. Ross, Sir T. Brisbane, R. W. Fox, &c., &c.,
& last & *least* (in stature *only*) T. Moore[5] himself. I saw Lady Morgan amongst
the fair assemblage below. I had a very good view of Moore as he perambulated the room in search of pretty girls. Broke up a little before 12.
11. Attended meeting at 10. Shirked the meeting for discipline & went to the
Geological section; the lecturer was giving a discourse on organic remains.
I did not stay long but went to the Physical section (which was exceedingly
interesting). Snow Harris[6] was engaged in describing some electric dis-

1. Sir Richard Griffith (1784–1878), Professor of Geology and mining engineer to Royal
Dublin Society; created Baronet, 1858.
2. Adam Sedgwick (1785–1873), Professor of Geology at Cambridge; prebendary of
Norwich, 1834.
3. Sir Charles Wheatstone (1802–75), Professor of Experimental Physics, King's College,
London.
4. Dionysius Lardner (1793–1859), Professor of Astronomy, University College, London.
5. Thomas Moore (1779–1852), the Irish poet and biographer of Byron.
6. Sir William Snow Harris (1791–1867), knighted in 1847 for his improved lightning
conductor; lived at Plymouth and was a friend of the Foxes.

coveries of his with some interesting experiments. A young man called Russell[1] read a very good paper on canal conveyance. He told us that in opposition to the generally received notion that resistance of the water increased as the velocity of the floating body, he had discovered that after reaching the velocity of eight miles an hour this law changed & the resistance decreased as the velocity increased. I made a rush for the Dejeuner at the Zoological gardens. Uncle C. & I got in with great difficulty on account of their not having sent us our admission tickets. We got seats, however, at the fag end of the fag table & consequently did not fare sumptuously. The public were admitted at 4 & the gardens were soon crowded with upwards of 4000 pieces of gaiety. The elephant & camel & Lord Mulgrave paraded the ground & excited much attention. Went to the Rotunda at 8 where Lardner gave a lecture on Steam which was very dull. It was however compensated for by the delicious refreshments given at the close.

12. At 11 we attended the Physical section. It was commenced by Harris with a paper on measuring Electricity. Papa was then introduced with his instrument which he explained, but the committee were puzzled & bothered him with questions instead of letting him get on. I fear there were few who were up to it, but those who did understand seemed very much interested by it. The Quaker was succeeded by a Catholic Priest called Macauley, who exhibited a model of his of a plan for making magnetism a moving power & which he looks forward to superseding steam. The model was very ingenious & worked well but his paper was very long & dry. We dined at home. I wrote to the sisters. I couldn't go to the Rotunda in the evening on account of an ugly cold which I caught, together with those other vermin the first night of my sojourn.

13. I discovered this morning that I am one of the first Practical Experimental Philosophers of the day. Necessity is the mother of invention. My experiment was this. I bought yesterday evening a phial of Spirits of Turpentine. On going to bed I soaked two pieces of paper with the aforesaid & placed one at the head & the other at the foot of the bed, under the clothes. I rubbed my hands with the same & turned in. That night I was free from flea persecutions. There's an invention, simple, practical & of universal interest. I went to the subsection of Physics which was devoted solely to mechanics. Russell was lecturing, when I entered, on the most advantageous forms for ships. An elderly man of the name of Hawkins then came forward to describe a plan of his which he intends in a measure to supersede railways: it consists of a system of ropes & pulleys. A horse is to move a rope at a certain rate which will convey the carriage at ten times that rate. To turn corners the carriage is to strike against a side rail & be reflected at the

1. John Scott Russell (1808–82), naval architect who later developed wave-line system of ship construction; constructed the *Great Eastern* steamship.

required angle. I don't much admire the plan. J. Taylor then gave a very interesting account of the duty performed by Cornish Steam engines & spoke of the very great superiority of South Welsh coals over Newcastle. That ought to bring in customers to our colliery[1] anyhow.

30. 1st day. Received a letter from Falmouth informing us of John Richards's conversion to Irvingism.[2] They say he has made a public confession of his faith. I have no doubts he is sincere, but what news it is! Much was said about the proposed continental tour. Papa & Uncle C. sat in council upon it & the bill will, I fear, be thrown out. It will have a 2nd reading at Malvern where we proceed shortly. Took leave of the various Friends. Uncle C. started for Liverpool Steamer in the afternoon.

31. Very busy packing up, settling accounts, &c. About 6 we got under weigh in a great hurry, proceeded per railway to Kingstown & embarked in the Holyhead Steamer.

12TH MONTH

18. Delicious weather. Rode to Penjerrick with the girls. Colt & other affairs doing well. Dr. Simon, the electro-magnetic man, favoured us with his company at dinner, after which I took the opportunity of shaving him to display the excellencies of my new importation.[3] The scene was not bad. My poor parents laughed themselves to tears. We attended the doctor's second lecture, amusing & that's all. B. & H. Newton to the astonishment of everybody made their appearance at Falmouth this evening.

22. Took a pleasant ride on Bayard & on returning found Sir C. Lemon, his nieces, & J. Enys at luncheon. We accompanied them to a fourth lecture of the doctor's, rather better than the preceding one. The Newtons' object in visiting Falmouth is to warn all men of the errors of Irvingism.

28. Resumed or rather recommenced the duties of my calling at the Counting House. Of course they are as yet only a shadow, an indistinct, prospective image of a mercantile life & a long time must elapse before I shall be able to comprehend & enjoy the scheming, the speculations & intricate manoeuvrings to which man is forced to resort in this money-loving age. I am convinced that a life of action is the happiest. My hours are from half-past 9 to 2, and

1. The coal mine near Neath in South Wales in which, along with the Abbey Iron Works, the Foxes had an interest.
2. Edward Irving (1792–1834), a friend of Carlyle and a popular Presbyterian preacher in London, who was expelled by the presbytery of his church for heretical views. His followers founded the 'Catholic Apostolic Church' in 1832.
3. A razor he had presumably brought back from Paris.

after dinner from 5 to 7, so that I shall have time enough in the evenings for keeping up, & perhaps adding to a little, the scrapings of knowledge acquired during the last 11 years. We had a famous family dinner at the Bank. I do like the large Christmas assemblings of kith & kin.

1836

Barclay continues working in the shipping office of the family firm. His routine is enlivened by the arrival of a ship-wrecked crew who had resorted to cannibalism to survive and by a mutiny among soldiers embarked for Spain. In May he visits London for the Yearly Meeting of the Society of Friends and this is followed by social gatherings and visits to places of interest with his young cousins. From London he travels to Dorset to stay with W. E. Forster and from there they both walk to Bristol. He goes to Bristol again later in the year for a meeting of the British Association and some of the scientists make their way to Cornwall to attend the opening of the new premises of the Royal Cornwall Polytechnic Society at Falmouth. In the autumn Cavendish Wall returns for a visit to Cornwall. Falmouth sees many interesting visitors, but none more colourful than the Begum of Oudh who arrives at the end of the year.

1ST MONTH

1. Cornish weather still, mild & moist, not by any means like a New Year's day. Called on Uncle Geo. who presented me with a handsomely bound copy of his first-born, Translations of *Prometheus* & *Electra*. Those Newtons have been making sundry grand disturbances in the family. The Irvingites increase instead of being annihilated by their opposition.

6. A brig called the *Agenoria* arrived from St. John's bringing 11 men, the crew of a timber vessel, whom they had picked up in the most forlorn condition. They were capsized on the night of the 3rd in a tremendous storm. Having cut the lanyards with much difficulty the vessel righted & the crew, with the exception of 3 who were drowned, congregated on the quarter-deck. All their provisions were washed overboard & they continued till the 18th enduring the extremity of starvation and misery. On that day they came to the decision of drawing lots for who should die for his comrades & a young man of 19 was the victim. After prayers he took the knife & cut his arm across & across, but no blood appearing they cut his throat & drank the blood & devoured a considerable part of the body before it was cold. On the 20th another man being on the point of death, they cut his throat to save the blood & on the 24th another for the same reason. Having finished their horrible meal on that day a sail was discovered by the crew with tears of joy. This was the *Agenoria* which took them on board. They are now settled in the two Poor-Houses & where they are all likely to recover.

9. Attended a sale of damaged hemp & sacking &c at Boyer's Cellars. They sold high. After dinner visited Captain Gorman, master of the unfortunate vessel I mentioned on the 6th. I had from him the whole horrid particulars of their sufferings & took notes at the time with a view to drawing up an account in order to make their case known & excite interest. I met at the same time Captain Gillard, master of the *Agenoria*, who confirmed all the statement of Capt. G. as far as he was competent. I saw the penknife belonging to Capt. G. with which the 3 men were butchered. I saw sticking to the blade – horrible, horrible! – a piece of human flesh, a relic of their cannibal meal!

30. Inspected all Uncle L.'s improvements & plannings in his new garden which I admire much. Went to Enys with Papa & Uncle C. to meet De La Beche,[1] the great geologist employed in making a complete geological map of Cornwall. He was interesting & agreeable. His daughter was with him. Went back to Perran to dinner & drove Mamma & the girls home.

3RD MONTH

12. The *Westminster*, a fine American ship, & a large East Indiaman came in today on account of contrary winds.

14. Went on board the *Westminster* with Cap. Moore. She is a superb ship. The fitting-up of the cabin beats everything of the sort I ever saw. It is very long & panelled with highly polished satinwood & cherry & bird's-eye maple, & large mirrors. In an inner cabin sat a tempting party of ladies working &c. round the table. Lady Nesbit & her beautiful niece & Mrs. This That & the other with whom I chatted for some time. We went with them outside the Castle head as we had agreed to take the pilot on shore. We parted high friends.

21. Last night 30 soldiers deserted from a company going to join the Queen's army in Spain per *Royal Tar* steamer. They seized an old collier belonging to Downing which was lying alongside to supply coals. They cut her cable & drifted into the middle of the harbour where they anchored for the night. A boat was immediately employed to cruise round her to prevent provisions being taken off or any of the mutineers going on shore, which was their object. This morning Capt. Symons[2] & some other gentlemen went on board the collier & towed her alongside the steamer. To this the men made no resistance & even helped to ship the coals, but swore never-

1. Sir Henry Thomas De la Beche (1796–1855), began at his own expense a geological map of England; appointed by government in 1832 to conduct geological survey; knighted in 1848; became a friend of the Foxes.
2. The captain of the *Royal Tar*.

theless not to go on board the steamer. They complained much of the treatment of their officer & the wretched prospects of the expedition. There were 3 desperate ringleaders, most perfect looking villains. The doctor went on board & reasoned with them & Capt. Symons did the same. One only was persuaded to return. I then went on shore with Capt. Symons & accompanied him & the officer & E. Seccombe to Pender's & Downing's; to the former to obtain a warrant for the ringleaders & to the latter to induce him to prosecute, which he readily agreed to. After dinner at the Bank, Uncle Francis & I returned on board the steamer. The men persisted in their refusal & their numbers seemed rather increased. The coals were shipped; persuasion, entreaty, threatening &c. were used in vain by the officer. The ringleaders answered only with a short denial or a scowl of defiance. We remarked one fine, falcon-looking soldier amongst the faithful ones. There was a certain dignity & air of command about him which his private's dress could not hide. He watched the mutineers silently & laughed at the absurdity of not being able to quell the row, which he would stake his head to do in a few minutes. He confessed to us that he was not what he seemed to be, that he went by the name of Brown, that he was in very good circumstances but that family disagreements had forced him to take this step. Capt. Symons shortly came on board & addressed the mutineers, telling them that the warrant was ready, the constables were coming, & as sure as they were taken on shore they would be transported. But the rascals at this information declared it was what they most desired. The constable now came on board, a single, old stick of a fellow, with a warrant for all the deserters, a sort of job the old fellow didn't seem to like. However, the names of the ringleaders were inserted & they were personally arrested, but the men flocked round him & declared all were equally guilty & one should not go without the rest. Meanwhile a chain was slipped round the foremast of the schooner, the steam was got up & away went the hostile parties perforce hand & glove. The deserters looked uncommonly silly at this unexpected step. We stopped again off Castle head & most of us went on board the schooner. Persuasion was used to the utmost & gentle forcing & 3 or 4 more were brought back. Capt. Symons, however, now declared to the officer he could not afford time for any more trifling so that he must either give them up or force them on board at once. The latter course was decided on & a rush was made. The resistance was as strong as 24 hours' fasting would allow. They fixed themselves behind the tiller in a compact body, drew their knives & swore they would stab the first man that touched them. Symons led the attack for the officer was employed too busily in loading his pistols. The conflict was short but desperate. The *Royal Tar*'s men were determined to gain their point. Brown was in the thick of it & seized the chief ringleader. In ten minutes all were brought on board. One man, however, jumped overboard & not being able to swim was after much struggling picked up by Benson's boat & brought on board. The men were marched off to the quarter-deck & a sergeant with a musket stationed over them. Meanwhile we observed another of the deserters swimming towards Curtis's boat. The officer was taking aim at him with his pistol but I prevented him & the man was taken on board. The business being then over we left the steamer, towed the collier back to her anchorage & got on shore a little before 8.

27. 1st day. Took a walk with Uncle A. who spent the evening here. The wind increased from 6 in the afternoon & by 10 was blowing a most awful tempest from the southward. All very anxious about the Indiaman in the bay. Heard 4 or 5 guns but could see nothing.

28. Got up early & had the satisfaction of seeing the Indiaman riding safely at her moorings. The storm was but little abated but blew from the N.E. so that she was sheltered. A brig, yesterday at anchor near her, had disappeared. I learned that the brig, *Traveller*, with a cargo of coffee from St. Domingo & which had applied to us, had gone ashore on Trefusis Point & was knocked to pieces. Her starboard topsides & deck as far as 2 planks was visible above the surf. The Bar beach as far as Castle head was literally strewn with wreck & the water's edge in many places white with coffee. Edward & I walked round there & stopped many who were walking off with planks &c. Set a great many fellows to work to haul the timber up under the cliffs from whence it was carried away by waggons. Three of the clerks were off by the wreck saving what they could. The chronometer, 6 bags of cotton & 3 or 4 of coffee have been brought ashore. Have been wet through 3 times in my rambles along the Bar. The captain it seems was on shore, the vessel drifted & the men lost their presence of mind.

29. Saving as much of the cargo as possible. Between 4 & 5 tons of coffee were landed, washed & stored.

30. Landed 3 trawler-loads of spars, sails, cables &c, and some coffee from the *Traveller*. Some poor French fishermen complained of the boys' pelting them with stones & in attempting to catch them one fellow fell overboard. We went out & caught one of the gang & horsewhipped him. Wind got round to the S.W.

31. Superintended the landing, washing, storing, & noting 2 boat loads of coffee with some of the vessel's stores. Three trawler-loads landed in the evening. The brig was towed alongside the pier by night. Her stern & a great part of her larboard side are carried away. Visited nearly all the Jews in town with a French captain to sell some doubloons. More arrivals & a world of business to get through in the evening. I introduced Percy Fenwick to the shop & set him to copy letters on rough sheets. At present he is more in the way than of any use, being a slow coach & clumsy fisted. He is to come at present only in the evenings.

4TH MONTH

4. The Counting House crammed with passengers for the 3 steamers which start today for Gibraltar & thereaway, some very interesting people. Went on board the *Glasgow* steamer to see H. Baring & his wife who are taking a voyage for the health of the former – pleasant people. Three young men named Bibby, Constable & Ellis dined here, the two latter going via Suez to India. The former is son of the first merchant of Liverpool, very gentlemanly & 'smart'. Constable is the son of Sir W. Scott's partner & therefore could tell us much about the poet – on all hands agreeable. They left soon after dinner.

5. Little Alfred poorly, complaining of much pain when he coughs. Misericordia[1] sale. Horribly cheated by the ladies who refused to give change. Mary Coleridge & the Powles lunched here. Miss Powles brought a little deeply-smitten lover of hers named Vyvyan. Commercial duties increasing.

6. Misericordia auction at which Uncle Gibbins & I officiated as auctioneer's boys. £67 profit was cleared in all. Brilliant assemblage & some fun. Little Alfred in an anxious state; leeches applied by Dr. Fox's orders, who considers his complaint to be a tendency to inflammation of the lungs.

11. The wreck of the *Traveller* & all thereto belonging was sold today. The hull brought £65 & the total amount £335.

13. Rode to Perran with A.M. to breakfast. She remains there till tomorrow. Aunt A. arrived this evening bringing her niece, Rachel Stacey, with her to sojourn for a season. She is well but she brings a melancholy account of an accident which happened to her brother J. Lloyd's eldest child which fell out of a coach & was run over & killed. A smuggler with 104 tubs taken by the *Dove*.

23. Busied about the farm at Penjerrick in which Papa & I are become partners.

25. The De la Beches & J. Enys came at ½ past 10. The gentlemen philosophized for some hours & then set off on a geological tour. I drove the ladies in the gig to Penjerrick where I capsized it, but fortunately not the females, they having got out to walk across the hill. We cut the harness & lugged the horse out with a rope & put the gig on its proper footing. Took Bessie De la Beche over Tregedna House & gardens & the two Penjerricks which she was polite enough to specify as Faeryland. Went from thence to Glendurgan. Took a cruise up Helford river, walked up Trebah valley, ate our third luncheon under the big oak & got home just in time for a 6 o'clock dinner. Bessie is a very nice girl.

---

1. The Misericordia Charitable Society had been founded at Falmouth in 1810.

5TH MONTH

11. Drove Mamma to Enys before dinner & visited the new house which they expect to enter in 3 weeks. Took leave of the Clarks (Uncle A.'s party where I found E. Powles & her two little sisters arrived to proceed under our escort tomorrow).

12. Set off per *Regulator* at 6, Papa with the three ladies inside & self on the box by coachey. At Penryn we were joined by young Vyvyan *en cavalier*, E. Powles's most melting swain. He rode by our side to Truro & there took his final & sentimental leave; by the aid of a salts bottle which he procured for the lady he contrived to muster up some veritable tears for which he was rewarded by a white rose from the whiter hand of the beloved. We journeyed on to Exeter with nothing particular except 3 extra passengers & palpable eclipses of dust which much inconvenienced the outsiders. Not able to procure places per *Telegraph* as intended we proceed tomorrow morning to Bath.

13. We reached Bath at half-past 5. After dinner, being fortunate enough to get the whole inside of the Bath mail, we proceeded to Town through the night, which was passed more comfortably than could have been expected considering that two children were of the party. E. Powles & I kept up a chatter pretty late. She is agreeable & clever & is not accusable of hiding her talent in the earth.

14. We reached Town at 6. Dropped our traps *en passant* at St. Paul's Coffee House & Papa at Gracechurch Street. I escorted the ladies in a hackney shay to their house on Stamford Hill & surprised their Papa in the act of sitting down to a solitary meal. Took a cab and called on Sir C. Lemon, then at Grosvenor Place where we found the party just starting off for the Horticultural Exhibition at Chiswick. We accordingly joined them at the most brilliant floral show. The azaleas & cacti were superb; the ladies not so much so as I had expected, though there were 3 or 4 stars. There were a thousand carriage loads of fashion & aristocracy. The gardens very beautiful & two splendid bands performing all the time. Returned with the party as far as Belgrave Square, where we called, & after a stroll as far as Charing Cross returned to dinner. The family all well & the house very handsome. A pleasant sociable time. Music in the evening.

15. The Backhouses were at Meeting. Hannah Backhouse gave the most impressive forcible sermon on giving up the whole heart unreservedly, I ever heard. Her husband, son & daughters dined at Ham House. Jane as lovely as ever. The Buxtons also there. Richenda[1] is a striking creature. H. Braithwaite & her starry daughter called in the evening.

17. Removed to Uncle C.'s after breakfast with bag & baggage. While Papa

1. The daughter of Sir Thos. Fowell Buxton.

dissipated at the W. End, I went out shopping with Uncle & Aunt C. Called on Bohn, the bookseller, & Ridley, the miniature man, where Uncle C. was drawn but not quartered.

18. Yearly Meeting began with various sermons. Attended a teetotal meeting afterwards & heard Hocken, the Birmingham blacksmith, who spoke in a most animated & naturally eloquent strain, but was too severe on Barclay, Perkins & Co. to convert their relation or even to induce him to stay.

21. Had the pleasure of walking with Sarah Grubb & Caroline Braithwaite to Lombard Street; the latter is certainly a most graceful being. At the end of the evening Meeting Isaac Crewdson rose & said that he had been much pained by the little growth of truth experienced in the Society & queried whether there were not some important point not enough attended to, seeing the attention that was paid to dress & address &c., & hoped the Meeting would encourage social evenings for reading the Scriptures, meditation & prayer.

24. Dined at the Backhouses. Had a chat with Jane afterwards – refined but staid. In the afternoon Meeting the subject of Friends serving as magistrates was brought forward. Some discussion took place on Church rates & then the whole account of John Williams, the Irish Friend imprisoned for tithes was recounted.

31. Met Wm. Forster according to appointment at our lodgings at ½ past one, & having snapped up a dinner we cabbed to the Buxtons (54 Devonshire Street) where a fine show of ladies was already assembled & we almost immediately walked to the Colosseum to see the feats of five Bedouin Arabs. Having satisfied our curiosity we proceeded *en masse* to the Zoological Gardens, increasing snowball fashion in our course, so that we assembled in the garden above 40 girls & boys & a few old ones. We had a glorious time of it. The Hoares of Hampstead joined us. Caroline Braithwaite was considered the star, though some admired Richenda Buxton as much. We rode to Devonshire Street in complete Gurney style. In the Gurneys' coach were 8 girls inside & 6 men & boys out, Wm. Forster & I sitting on the top & alarming the insiders through the windows. Thus figured we rode through Regent's Park. We were joined by sundry more at tea, after which we attempted a practical charade.

6TH MONTH

1. Reached Holborn at 11 & rummaged its high & low vicinity in search of old books. Dined at Devonshire Street at 3 & left directly after. Had a warm parting from Anna & Richenda who though different characters are both

charming creatures. Reached our lodgings just in time to accompany Papa to Upton. We took Caroline Braithwaite & most of the girls a row on the canal till 10. She was dressed in Sam's cap & a boa & looked most captivating. She sung nightingalely. If Sam isn't touched I'll never pretend to connoisseurship in these matters. For my part I have found my heart effectually guarded by *bewilderment*. I have wandered about this last week in a labyrinth of sweets & that's a very different thing to a man-trap!

3. Bade adieu to our dirty lodgings, dirty landlady, dirty household at 9 & stowed away my luggage & self in the Bridport coach, having engaged to spend a few days with W. Forster. Papa went to Dorking & we are to meet at Frenchay the week after next. We made a glorious supper at Dorchester & reached Bridport at 2 in the morning. Glad enough to turn into a snug bed.

4. 1st day. Walked to Bradpole[1] to breakfast. It is a sweet little spot most luxuriantly covered with vines & roses & the Forsters were kindness itself. Spent the day in going to Meeting & walking & talking on various interesting matters with William.

9. At half-past 7 took leave of the most hospitable friends I ever saw & in company with William coached off to Street. Whilst lounging about for 2 hours till the other coach came we bought *Tom Thumb, Blue Beard* & other edifying works to read on the journey. Two females having joined us on the hind seat we very politely offered *Tom Thumb* to one of them to amuse herself with whereat she turned up her scornful nose, ejaculating, 'Nursery tales indeed!' Reached Street at 3 & were warmly welcomed by J. & Ellen Clark. Both were very pressing to make us sleep at their house, but they prevailed not. J. Clark accompanied us to Tor Hill where is one of the most extensive views in the kingdom & where the last abbot of Glastonbury was hanged by Henry VIII. Glastonbury Abbey then claimed our attention & admiration. We tramped on 7 miles further to a village called Wookey but were turned off & proceeded to another village called Easton, but the woman of the *Pig & Whistle* not really liking our looks sent us on another mile to Westbury where we with much difficulty persuaded mine host to rig up a berth for us. He was in a state of muddle & good humour so we got some bread & cheese & beer. Our bed was, of course, many degrees below mediocre. Nevertheless we managed well.

10. At 7 joined our landlord in his family breakfast & made off for Wookey Hole. We cut a mile 'cross country' through much rain & slush to Farmer Duckett's house where we were speedily provided with candles & a boy. The entrance to the cave is kept locked. We entered & proceeding through a low passage & down some rough steps we suddenly found ourselves in a high spacious apartment called the Witch's Kitchen. Going through another low opening we came to another chamber of equal size in which was a

1. The home of W. E. Forster's parents which they were soon to leave for Norwich.

stalagmite figure of a lion, lapdog &c. A black-looking stream runs through it & flows out in a cascade. Having seen sundry other crannies & passages & being much delighted with all, we returned to the realms of day & pushed on to Cheddar. After a lunch & a nap we walked through the cliffs which are well worth seeing. Reached Banwell at ½ past 5. Made a glorious supper & our coats being wet through, the landlady kindly clad William in the great coat of her departed lord & me in her own black silk cloak which made me look much like a young priest.

11. Walked to Churchill on the Bristol road where a coach gave us a lift of 6 miles from which point we branched off across the country to a village called Butcombe in search of a curious ancient sepulchre. We called on the parson for information. He told us the land had been bought & the place destroyed. We returned to the Bristol road, boarded the *Exquisite* & in an hour were busily cleaning ourselves in Francis Fry's hospitable dwelling.

12. 1st day. William & I took a fly & flew to Frenchay. Found the family in good spirits. Met Papa who arrived this morning. All the Bank party there.

15. At half-past 10 took leave of the Frenchay circle, Uncle F. escorted us to Bristol & saw us on board the *Exquisite* (Exeter coach) & took his leave. Reached Exeter at 9. Had great difficulty in securing a single place per *Regulator*.

18. Resumed Counting House labours & greeted my office-mates. Called at Grove Hill.

29. A cutter's man whilst working in Symons's loft was accidentally shot by a boy named Sampson who was playing with the other's pistol & not knowing it was loaded took aim & shot him through the head. The man dropped immediately. The boy was taken almost as lifeless as his comrade to Chard's. Took my first bathe – truly delicious.

30. Attended the inquest held over the body of Johns, the first I had seen. The body was that of a young man of one-&-twenty. No expression of pain in the countenance but the wound was ghastly. Verdict, accidental death.

7TH MONTH

2. A man was seized with a violent fit outside our house. He was lifted on the bank & we performed various Samaritan offices without avail. Sent for Brougham who bled him copiously, but at 6 o'clock he being still quite senseless, ½ a dozen of us bore him to the Poor House, stripped him, put him to bed & bathed his feet in warm water. We then proceeded to ransack his pockets. His worldly possessions seemed to consist of ¼d. – the contents of his purse. His letters, however, were interesting. It appeared from them

that his name is Ormond, that he was about to sail from Plymouth to St. Sebastian on board the *Televera*, a 74, to join the Queen's troops, that the ship gave him the slip, by which means his outfit, on which he had expended £34, was transported to St. Sebastian & his unfortunate self left on Plymouth quay. From thence he came to Falmouth in order to start by the *Royal Tar* steamer. For the last three days, having spent his all, he wandered about in utter destitution. He went on board the *Royal Tar* without Capt. Symons's knowledge, who discovering him when 3 miles off shore & having no authority to take him, put about & sent him ashore.

3. 1st day. Paid two visits to Ormond who has recovered his senses, but remains in bed. He is very gentlemanly & well-spoken. Told me much about himself. Sent him broth, &c. Uncle & Aunt C. dined here.

4. Found Ormond better. Lodged at Perran on my way to Liskeard Quarterly. Most languid weather.

5. Set off from Perran as outrider to Uncle & Aunt C. in their gig. The weather broiling hot, almost unsupportable, notwithstanding I stripped to the utmost confines of decency. Got a glorious bathe at Lostwithiel in a river. A fair at Probus. Reached Liskeard about 10.

18. At 3 the Methody Sunday School paraded round the garden, amounting to about 600 with upwards of 100 teachers. The children did ample justice to huge baskets of gooseberries, mazards[1] & gingerbreads, whilst their more delicate mouthed preceptors contented themselves with 7 bottles of wine to the dregs. They went away pleased, or ought to.

26. Whilst at the Counting House Dr. Fox appeared in pretty considerable affliction because his grand-child Edward had just been bitten by Blanco whom he feared was mad. I conveyed my medical cousin to our house to inspect the beast. He was chained & looked forlorn, refused water but lapped some milk, after which he tore the mat, rubbed his nose in the earth & performed other odd antics which much alarmed the physician. We collected evidence against the culprit who had snapped at a great number yesterday & today & Dr. F. thought it advisable to proceed at once as if it were a case of hydrophobia. So having mustered Brougham & Appleton & Rachel Tregelles we visited the child. Dr. F. left the house, Appleton & I held down the patient while Dr. Brougham excised each tooth mark so as to make a clean wound of it, & then cauterised each with nitric acid. It was soon over. Whilst it lasted there was a sufficiency of kicking & squealing but a lollypop at the end seemed to set all right. I took Brougham to look at Blanco. He thought the symptoms suspicious of incipient madness. In the afternoon there was an alarm that Blanco had broken loose & was scampering off nobody knew where. A general hunt was established & he was taken in the garden in about 10 minutes, but in that time we found that he had bitten Harriet Tink

1. Cherries.

in the hand very badly. Brougham attended her & treated her the same as the other. It made us all extremely anxious.

27. Called at the Tinks' in my way home & found the invalid pretty well but suffering from the operation. The dog shows no symptoms of madness, but we have been holding council of life & death over him. I think his really serious illness will save the headsman.

29. Dog dying; went in to him but he couldn't rise. Pope's pilot boat was wrecked last night near Crab Quay by missing stays & driving on the rocks. Had a glorious pull with Charles & Percy against a strong wind.

30. Alas poor Blanco!, he has yielded to the inexorable tyrant – he was found dead as mutton in the stable. A thumping stick was firmly grasped in his forepaws apparently to defend himself against any unhallowed power that might claim him after death. We subjected him to a critical post mortem examination in Brougham's workshop; the two apprentices, Dr. Fox & Surgeon Williamson & self were in attendance. To my great triumph & to the greater discomfiture of the faculty no symptons of madness were discovered. The bite in his head had penetrated the skull & in the natural course of things caused his nervous irritability & speedy death. I called on the Tinks & set Harriet's mind at rest about hydrophobia.

8TH MONTH

2. Rowed the girls to Flushing. Ormond & the second Todd went off this morning to Spain per *Glasgow*. I saw Aggy Burn's *mamma* amputated by Brougham &c. Horrible! Horrible![1]

5. Another chasse-maree with salt arrived this morning. Uncle A. being at Glendurgan, rode there to inform him & to know his pleasure. It appeared to be rabbit-hunting in which I joined & did more than all my comrades except the dogs. We concluded with three corpses. We dined at Trebah & whilst there found Dash kicking on the ground having been grievously bit by an adder. We immediately bled, sweet-oiled & physicked him. Some currants arrived today from Plymouth much damaged. Unfortunately the cash is already remitted. A Lieut. Burney who is going to accompany Sir J. Franklin to Van Dieman's land spent about 14 hours here today learning the instrument.

20. Accompanied my sire & Uncle Hilhouse to Bristol. Met there Uncles C., G.C., F., &c. &c. We went en masse to the Committee room & got tickets

---

1. This sentence is written with the letters of each word reversed, a device he occasionally used for items he would not wish to read aloud in the family circle.

for the Association[1] & meandered amongst the Dons. Saw Whewell,[2] Dalton,[3] Wheatstone, De la Beche, the Commercial Rooms, Institution, & other lions animate & inanimate.

26. Bundled up between 5 & 6 to embark on a philosophical excursion to Portishead.[4] We mustered 110 sages on board the *Killarney* steamer. We landed on the argillaceous deposit of Portishead with much difficulty but made a glorious dinner in a large marquee on the green. Our lecturer, however, from excitement, exhaustion & habitual abstemiousness went a little beyond his high-water mark & unfortunately swamped himself. His friends got him on board with difficulty & had greater difficulty in preventing him from speaking & making a fool of himself. We landed at Ham Green, the beautiful residence of R. Bright, Esq. His sons were waiting on the shore & escorted us to their house. We found the old gentleman lying on a sofa, having broken his thigh, but he received us with the utmost politeness & hospitality. They showed us into another room most sumptuously supplied with fruit & pastry & we readjourned to the other for tea & talk.

27. Up again at half-past 5 & had a gallop across the Downs to Clifton with Uncle Hilhouse to see the laying of the foundation of the bridge[5] which is to be, the undertaking of Brunel. We joined the processions & marched away after our noble Marquis in a coach & six, with drums & trumpets & dozens of flags. The stone was laid on the opposite side to Clifton. The Marquis made a little appropriate speech which was followed by a flourish of trumpets, cheers on cheers from both sides, royal salutes, the ascent of 3 balloons & other diversions. We wound back in indifferent order, scrambled into boats & after being carried away by the current & giving ourselves up for lost, we poked each other out on the mud & scampered to the *Gloster Hotel* to breakfast. Joined the girls at the Miss Hilhouses & accompanied them & Aunt A. & Co. to the zoological gardens which are young but very promising. The evening meeting was well attended but too much wasted in parting speeches, thanks & compliments. At the end of the meeting a motion was handed to T. Moore[6] & forward glided the little Bacchus to the table & having bowed to the audience as none but himself can bow, addressed them in such a lively sparkling strain, so elegant, so witty, & so beautiful, that the building rung & rattled with continual acclamations.

1. The British Association which was meeting in Bristol.
2. William Whewell (1794–1866), Master of Trinity College, Cambridge; natural scientist and philosopher.
3. John Dalton (1766–1844), chemist and meteorologist.
4. At the mouth of the Bristol Avon.
5. The Clifton Suspension Bridge, the foundation stone of which was laid by Lord Northampton, President of the British Association.
6. The Irish poet.

9TH MONTH

4. 1st day. Walked to Penjerrick to beg Uncle J.'s attendance as Polytechnic judge & other matters. The gentleman, however, was taking it so easy on the drawing room sofa that all my endeavours to awake him were fruitless.

5. The New Polytechnic edifice makes something like a show today. The Room is well filled. Paintings very good. Some ingenious inventions for measuring the supply of water to boilers, a galvano-motive engine by Jordan, three mine-descent models, steam-engines, &c. &c. But the two things that delighted me most were an engagement between Richard & Saladin in chalk & Christ's Sermon on the Mount in pen & ink, both original & both first-rate. We had a dinner party of about 20; the principal ones were Buckland,[1] Johnston,[2] Powell,[3] De la Beche & daughter, & Davies Gilbert. Wheatstone expected but did not arrive.

6. Bade adieu at 6 this morning to 19 sunny years. Heavy rain, with but occasional interruption, was the order of the day. A large phalanx of sages marched with us to the grand Hall at 11. Professor Wheatstone just arrived. Buckland passed many just encomiums on Mr. Fox, spoke of the value of the Institution, his gratification, &c. Sir Chas. Lemon read a letter containing Victoria's & her mother's ready & warm assent to become patronesses of the Society. The gentry repaired to the Ordinary at Pearce's where Uncle G. invited them to Grove Hill & they came to the number of 80. We had a glorious soirée of it, flirting or philosophising as fancy led us. Wheatstone is a little prince in his way & the Gilberts are quite loveable girls. Davies Gilbert is altogether superb & so is Georgina Treweeke. Escorted her with sire & sister, & their friends the Pascoes, to the Quay as they wanted to go to Flushing. Boatmen all in bed so we routed out old Clements & adjourned to the Counting House, while he got up & braced up his leg. The clerks opened their eyes at the new consignment.

7. Polytechnic was the general rendezvous. It is to be open two days more. The makers themselves had to explain their own inventions. The sages marvelled greatly at Cornwall's natural genius. Phillips of Hayle, a very clever fellow, had 4 apparati to speechify on: an improvement on the method of dialling a measure for the supply of water to a boiler, a plan for lowering miners, &c. Papa – a model of Wheal Jewel, his new balance which weighs 1/20,000 of a grain, a new mode of correcting the magnetic needle by turning the axis 180°. Jordan – his galvano-motive machine which consists

1. William Buckland (1784–1856), Professor of Mineralogy, Oxford, 1813; Dean of Westminster, 1845–56.
2. Alexander Keith Johnston (1804–71), geographer; published first English atlas of physical geography, 1848.
3. Baden Powell (1796–1860), Savilian Professor of Geometry, Oxford.

5. The man engine for raising and lowering the miners at Dolcoath
copper mine

6.Dolcoath copper mine, Camborne, 1831. *Thomas Allom*

7.Falmouth Harbour, 1831. *Thomas Allom*

of a wheel rotating within a frame & magnets being placed at equal intervals in both with a plan of alternately reversing the poles.

9. The morning proving auspicious to our hearts' content we started for Kynance soon after 7. Dr. Buckland with Uncle A. in his phaeton & Wheatstone, Johnston, Fox & self in a coach and four. Kynance had its usual & due share of admiration & geological research. The bellows did its best to give satisfaction & on the arrival of Dr. B., who had made a circuit of the coast, we proceeded to satisfy our creaturely appetites. Dr. Winterbottom & C. Bullock had joined our party per car from Helston & we settled down in much jollity & good fellowship. We had a squab & chicken-pie most philosophically heated by quicklime on the spot. After dinner I was clever enough to get into the water waistcoat-pocket-high. Had to strip, empty my boots, & wring my shirt, to the high amusement of the sages. On our road saw a jack o'lantern for the first time, a bright blueish light – it vanished almost immediately. Chatted with Wheatstone unceasingly while the others reposed. He is a man of the most versatile genius, almost as literary as scientific. We talked of Coleridge, Moore, Shelley, Milman,[1] ghosts, music & such-like. After supper he played several tunes on another instrument of his called the Symphonia, its compass is greater than the concertina.

18. 1st day. After dinner the heads of the House conferred long & weightily on the subject of attending Sarah Squire's public meeting at Breage. Having decided on so doing, we entered Tregurtha's vehicle & set off at half-past 3. Reached Meeting half-past 6, $\frac{1}{2}$ an hour behind time. Our tardiness was occasioned partly by an asthmatic affection of the horse & partly by a contretemps which happened to his master at Falmouth Turnpike. The change somehow lost its way & wandered down his leg instead of abiding in his pocket, which necessitated John to step into the 'Pike & unrig, to the great amusement of the ladies. S. Squire spoke & prayed nearly the whole of meeting time, accompanied with groans & pious ejaculations from her audience. Her burden seemed principally to be unholy conversation. We reached home at 10.

20. Sarah Squire paid us a religious visit at 11. After much counsel &c. to us in family assembled, she had a private interview with me in the dining room in order to go more into particulars. No doubt if I could keep her precepts I should be much better than I am. She informed me inferentially that there was room for improvement. Methought I could have told her that & much more if I thought it necessary.

21. Monthly Meeting. Mammy laid before the meeting a concern to visit the meetings of Monmouthshire, Worcestershire & Wales & the General Meeting next month. Lucretia Crouch wished to accompany her. Unity was

1. Henry Hart Milman (1791–1868), Professor of Poetry, Oxford, 1821–31; Rector of St Margaret's, Westminster, 1835; Dean of St Paul's, 1849.

expressed. Ann Tweedy sent by her husband a concern in the same direction, so the Welsh Friends will have enough of it.

26. Parents started per *Regulator* at 6, the one on her religious excursion through S. Wales, the other to escort her as far as Ilfracombe. The girls gigged off to Trebah at half-past 7; we all stay there during Father's absence. Walked to Penjerrick & took my dinner with me. Rode to Trebah to tea with a villainous headache but a dose of sal volatile having nigh vanquished it, the evening passed in interesting reading & bright & profitable talk. Had a snug little berth where I coiled up & slept like a dormouse. Mucky, smudgy, slushy weather all day.

10TH MONTH

3. Captain Fitzroy of the *Beagle*[1] dined here. He is just returned from a 5 years' voyage of discovery about the Southern regions. My father showed him his dipping needle &c. with which he was highly pleased.

4. Capt. F. breakfasted here & reports that he was not able to sleep from the philosophical excitement of last evening. He and father were engaged in comparing observations with their respective instruments in the field all the morning. Walked to Penjerrick.

11TH MONTH

5. Whilst sitting over my books in the evening, Cavendish was announced & in he marched. We greeted as he & I were wont to greet & sitting down amongst the women, we talked as may be imagined. He looks much the same as ever, a little taller, very sedate & tired by his journey. He is going to winter here for his health. Not being able to persuade him to lodge here, I accompanied him to Pearce's.

6. 1st day. Showery. Uncle L. dined here & Cavendish, of course. Much chat together over old times. Had to tend the shop in the evening about some letters, our two active Partners being in the West. Cavendish lodged here.

14. On coming home after breakfast this morning I found a young swell of the name of Ellis (the radical candidate for the Division) in the drawing room, entirely at his ease, having borrowed a pocket handkerchief & begged

1. **Charles Darwin** was one of the expedition on this voyage of H.M.S. *Beagle* and published his account of it in 1840, but he did not meet the Fox family on disembarking at Falmouth.

for a breakfast. Thought him a great chatterbox & a great fool. He attempted a political argument but found his head not strong enough for the head of the house. He babbled Italian & German & thought to astonish the natives.

21. Walked to Boyer's with Uncle A. Found the Anti-dry-Rot Tank finished & the women begun to pack & press the fish. On our way back found that the Liverpool steamer had just arrived with refugee Portuguese. Called on them at Pearce's & found them to consist of the Duke of Palmella & two sons, Count Villa Real & son, Baron Randulfe, Master of Finance &c., who had bolted during the late disturbance & thought themselves lucky in getting off with a sound skin.

22. Henry Wall arrived last night, the ghost of himself. He is about to embark for Madeira. Cavendish removed today to Wilson's lodgings in the New Street, very comfortable. A.M. & I dined at Grove Hill to meet the Duke & his family. The old gentleman was very agreeable & much obliged for the attention shown him. His elder son, the Marquis de Fayal, quite a nice fellow, is engaged to a young girl, the daughter of Count Sampejo. They leave for London tomorrow by the Devonport coach.

28. From 8 to 9 a.m. it blew the most tremendous hurricane ever remembered in this place. While standing at the Counting House window I saw two whole chymnies blown bodily down within 5 minutes. 22 in the town suffered the same fate. The slates were about the streets so as to make it perilous to walk through them. 20 panes of glass in 2 adjacent houses were shattered thereby. We watched a sloop belonging to Willoughby drift from the harbour to the rocks under St. Mawes castle where she was wrecked. The wind was N.W. Every house I believe suffered more or less. Uncle A. had a chymney & the yard wall blown down & Uncle G.C. 3 large trees &c. The schooner *Violet*, Capt. Perryman, having been lying here under our care above a week, drove against the chain of a West Indiaman by which she would soon have been cut in two had not the crew cut away the rigging & the masts, the foremast close to the deck & the mainmast about 10 ft. above. Philip & the Capt. & I went off to her & succeeded by the close of the day in getting her yards &c. on board, mooring both masts astern & with the assistance of a crew from the *Astraea* warping her off to a snug berth & anchoring her there. The Capt. did nothing himself except occasionally swearing at the men for not doing right. The mate put all the fault on Capt. Turner of the West Indiaman who, he said, could have slacked out more chain. He, on his part, declared when I went on board that he had it all out. I went below & got some sustenance; 2 gentlemen passengers, the captain's wife & a bride of 17 were there. Returned to the schooner & found the Capt. very sulky. Found our good people at home in a state of intense anxiety & nervous irritability on account of the lost youth.

12TH MONTH

1. A fine day at last, a thing we had almost despaired of. The Begum of Oudh, wife of Moolree Mohammed Ishmael Khan arrived here today with her suite per Cork steamer.

2. The girls &c. went to Pearce's to pay our respects to her brown Excellency Marriam Khan. Her Hindoo servant directed us to Capt. Clavel's where we found her. She is an oddity if human being ever deserved to be called so. Her person dark olive, broad nosed, black jaguar-like eyes, body & limbs so supple as to assume any form at pleasure, dress inexplicable except that it seemed a most uncouth jumble of fine & gaudy materials. Her language was English words mispronounced & ingeniously misplaced. She stretched out a brown leg & pulled up her trowsers to show the material. It was altogether great fun.

3. At ½ past one I accompanied the girls to Marriam Begum. She was squatting cross-legged, half in & half on her bed which was spread on the floor; bundles of clothes & messes were scattered about within her arm's length. Her Hindoo girl attended on her & a little idiot protegée huddled up in a heap against the wall. She was stockingless & wore two rings on one great toe. She made many shrewd & original remarks on our government, religion &c. With a little coaxing she exhibited her chest of jewellery, which is of the most massive and superb order I ever saw, also her magnificant India and Cashmere dresses some of which she put on for our edification. She flattered me much by observing a striking likeness to her son, gave me a pressing invitation to Oudh, promising me 1000 rupees a month to enter into the Rajah's service. She gave me one, I presume as bounty money.

28. The Ambassador from Oudh, husband of our friend Marriam Begum, paid us a long visit with his secretary; he embarks tomorrow per *Atlanta* steamer for Bombay. He is a very odd fellow with tiger-like eyes & came to the office with a remarkably odd story that he had £50 wrapt up in a handkerchief in his coat pocket & that in pulling out his duplicate handkerchief for use he supposes he forked out the former therewith, money & all, so that he is here penniless. We advanced him enough for his expenses, much to his satisfaction. When I called on him at Pearce's he had a wife & child sitting by the fire whom he immediately ordered out of the room. He visited *the* Instrument with which he was highly delighted, being head astronomer to His Majesty of Oudh.

1837

THIS YEAR sees the death of the King and the beginning of Queen Victoria's long reign. The proclamation of Victoria's accession to the throne is accompanied at Falmouth by the inevitable procession and band. More important for Barclay is his accession to the estate at Penjerrick. Later on the estate is to be developed as a second home for the Fox family, with the two original cottages converted into a house set in beautiful gardens, but Barclay begins by farming and appoints as manager Thomas Evans, who begins a long and happy association with him. August and September are taken up with a family excursion to the North of England and Scotland. They travel by carriage and railway (the carriage accompanying them on the train) through Bristol, Cheltenham, Birmingham, Sheffield, Leeds and York, to Darlington, where they stay with their friends the Backhouses, and where Barclay's mother conducts a ministry to the local Friends. They return through the Lakes, where Barclay meets Southey and Hartley Coleridge, and Liverpool, where they attend a meeting of the British Association. Barclay and his sisters are now approaching maturity. Anna Maria, the eldest of the three, celebrates her twenty-first birthday, and Barclay himself is drawn more and more into the business affairs of the family.

1ST MONTH

2. Wind fell back to the N.W. & the thermometer rose many degrees. Nevertheless I skated for several hours so as to make the most of the time left. Lieut. Chumleigh of Pendennis, a Miss Todd in each hand, a skate on each foot, & a quizzing glass knowingly stuck before one eye, floundered bodily in about knee deep, to the high delight of the by-standers. Chumleigh ended the exhibition by making a spring at the shore, a second break followed & the hero lay, with his stomach in the water, his heels in the air & his face prostrate at Miss T.'s feet. 'It was a glorious sight to see.'

2ND MONTH

1. The girls' inventive faculties have been hard at work & the result is an admirable newspaper entitled *The Falmouth Foolscap*, containing Politics,

Advertisements, Puffs & Varieties extraordinary with all the other component parts of a popular paper & the valuable addition of illustrations. Cavendish has fixed on going to Plymouth for a change.

2. Dismal, muggy weather & not able to do anything with comfort out of doors. Called on General Soublette, a Venezuelan just arrived from Town. He sails tomorrow per *Express*. He returned the call, a fine gentlemanly man. Old H. Tippett & Dicky Symonds of Little Falmouth were carried off last night by the influenza. Bad account from Plymouth of Aunt Abbott. 20,000 there laid up with it.

21. A.M. attains her womanhood today, but the celebration is deferred till next week.

27. Cavendish dined with us today. Beat up old & new clothes shops for costumes for our intended exhibition of tableaux vivants on the celebration of A.M.'s birthday.

3RD MONTH

2. The day of days! The most important era in our house since Caroline's birth, the celebration of A.M.'s arrival at womanhood; the first of her generation. All Grandmamma's branches & ramifications, except Uncle G.P. & some of the minuter ones, honoured our house with their presence. The Grove Hill party, Cavendish, Eliz. Crouch & Bessie de la Beche were afterwards added to our party. The company flocked in at 2 & settled down to dinner after which poured in a brilliant display of presents from all quarters. Mine consisted of little more than love and good wishes dressed up in a little rhyme for decency, but it was followed up by something of a more exciting & far more substantial character, called £1,000 lent to the Neath Coal Co. & paying 4½% interest. This was something like doing the genteel thing & never did a recipient deserve it better. Took a walk with Uncle C. & came back to tea & immediately after set to work at the evening revels. A frame was set up at the end of Mother's dressing room, plenty of drapery was procured & a lamp was suspended in front. Uncle G.C. first appeared in the character, dress & attitude of Titian's Charles V. The effect was wonderful. A better deception cannot be conceived. After a minute and a half's survey, the door was closed & Uncle Joshua then made his appearance as a Greek chief with admirable dress, turban, pistols, sword, beard &c. I never saw such a splendid man in my life as the light flashed from his black eye, looking sternly out of the picture. The two girls made beautiful Spaniards. Uncle A. was Garrick, between Tragedy & Comedy, who were Bessie & Eliz. Crouch. Cavendish & I were misers, & so on. Everything answered to admiration;

only one sad cloud was cast over the evening by Aunt E.'s breaking a small vessel in a fit of coughing whilst talking with Bessie. No serious consequence is apprehended from the incident itself, but it is a melancholy confirmation of her long suspected disease of the lungs. It happened near the end of the day, but it could not but shed a damp over the rest of the time. The finishing stroke of our revels was a most elegant, luxurious & tasteful supper & the party separated a little before 11.

11. Attended an intensely interesting trial at the Town Hall of Capt. Edwards & his mate, of the schooner *Ada*, for the murder of one of the crew by atrocious ill-treatment on their voyage from St. Michael's. The evidence was a passenger & two seamen who were examined separately by Cornish. The same questions were put to each & their accounts agreed precisely. The barbarity of the prisoners, especially the mate, which came out in evidence, was beyond conception & excited the generous indignation of the crowded audience, showing itself in groans of execration & other demonstrations more deep & fulsome than I ever heard. The sole offence of the deceased was drinking a little coffee from another man's kettle. For this he was first beaten by the captain & mate, then hung up to the gaff by his heels, thrown overboard & having a little recovered his senses, towed in the water for ¼ of an hour, & when brought up senseless & almost lifeless, beaten by the mate with a mop till the head flew off & then with a stick on the mouth & eyes. The miserable victim died that evening & was thrown overboard the next morning. The Capt. is a young respectable looking man, the mate is in all appearance a villain – in reality a fiend. They were committed to the Admiralty on a charge of manslaughter.

19. 1st day. Walked two miles before breakfast & to Pennance Point before dinner & to Penjerrick before tea. On my return from the latter my father made me the following proposition, which of course I jumped at like gold, viz. Penjerrick estate (which is now let to Uncle G.C. at £20) together with the cottage & four fields adjacent, the croft & all the orchards at the same rent, with the proviso for him to take one or two of the fields at any time should he want to plant &c. & half the produce of the orchards. To come into hand at Michaelmas. This is an object which would suit me best of any I could name. The loveliness and interest attached to the spot from old associations, invest it with a charm to my mind far beyond any pecuniary advantages I can hope to reap from it.

20. Found myself on Penjerrick farm at half past 7 this morning & visited every field & returned to breakfast. Had a most glorious sail out of the harbour on board the *Havre*, the magnificent French brig. It was blowing fresh & I came home in the pilot boat, gunnel under. Aunt E. better.

21. Rode round the country & visited all the principal farmers in search of grass for the colts &c. None to be had for love nor money owing to the late

very severe weather. The frost last night was as sharp as any part of the winter. Visited amongst others Farmer Martin of Polvoose, an odd old original, a shooting comrade of my grandfather & intimate acquaintance of my great grandfather, whom he described as a fine hale old man with a wig like a bishop's. He lived & died at Penjerrick.

22. The *Transit* at length made her appearance. Uncle Charles & I went on board directly to settle some preliminaries about shipping Aunt E. There being no other lady, she will have the whole ladies' cabin to herself & there being only 8 gentlemen, each will have a separate room. From taking longer than was anticipated in shipping the coals, the steamer was not able to haul alongside the pier to take Aunt E. on board. However, the business was very easily managed. At 5 we deposited her in the sedan in our large lighter. She & her husband & Uncle C., Edward & Ann Taw were the voyagers. On coming alongside the tackle was made fast to the lashings of the sedan, which was immediately hoisted on board & Aunt E., with scarcely ten seconds exposure to the air, descended to her cabin & settled in. We took leave & went on shore. Grandmamma & Aunt C. started for Frenchay directly after. The former, just before leaving, made me a present of a cow, or a calf which it is to have, I am not quite clear which.

24. Good Friday. Snow 3 inches deep. It snowed most of the morning but the weather cleared up after dinner. Cavendish dined with us, after which he & I trudged out to Penjerrick. Sent a man into the plantation to cut furze for the cattle.

4TH MONTH

2. 1st day. The *Iberia* arrived from Lisbon with a letter to Mother from Aunt E. It brought a capital account of the invalid & much better than could have been at all anticipated. They wrote from Lisbon but looked forward to a trip to Cadiz last 5th day.

8. Was engaged to Grove Hill to dinner, but at 4 o'clock was met by the intelligence that Glendurgan was on fire. Rode there directly with Uncle A. We found the tragedy concluded & the four smoking walls with a smokeless chymney at either end all that remained of its former magnificence. The crowd of villagers there assembled were eager in their condolences with his Honour [Uncle A.], who showed himself the hero throughout & caused, I imagine, admiration & wonder. He was the merriest of the party, looked on the bright side of it & gave all the operatives some porter, which was the finest trait of all. We found nearly all the furniture saved & stowed away in the loft over the stable. Nobody knows how it happened. The thatch

caught first & it is conjectured that it was occasioned by a spark. It was not insured.

5TH MONTH

1. Ushered in by the usual horrors of kettles, horns & other unearthly clangours. All Lovell Squire's boys were announced directly after dinner. Conducted them to the higher field & passed the time till tea with rounders, leapfrog, leaping poles, troco[1] &c. After tea practical charades were performed in pretty good style. An unimproved account from Lisbon.

11. Tried the colt & am very well pleased with him. He is one that will much improve by good keeping, which I mean to give with full relaxation for a year. He is to be a denizen of Penjerrick & to pay for board & lodging by occasional assistance in the cart & plough. Called at Wm. Coope's new house[2] where I had the pleasure of being introduced to Wightwick,[3] the architect & wit. He is beautifully ugly & carries the confidence of genius in every tone & action. Wm. Coope showed us his stables & appurtenances, with three superb coach horses. He is an agreeable, unassuming, gentlemanly man.

26. The *Transit* steamer was seen at a distance of 25 miles about half-past 7 this morning. As she came nearer we could make out a flag on the larboard paddlebox, the signal that our expected party were on board. About ½ past 9 she came in & Uncle Francis Tuckett & I immediately went off to her. We jumped on board long before the old Doctor came off to clear her & had the pleasure of seeing Uncles C. & W.G. looking all the better for their excursion. We did not see Aunt E. of course, but the account Uncle C. gave of her was discouraging. He spoke of her having lost both flesh & strength since she left England, yet he was quite satisfied of the rightness of the step. Dr. Fox visited her as soon as he came on board & found her more emaciated than he expected. Uncles G.C. & W. brought Aunt E. on shore in about an hour, for the sedan was in attendance on the quay. She was immediately carried to the Bank & Aunt C. settled her on the sofa upstairs. We staid below & had a long chat with the two travelled uncles. I rode to Penjerrick after an early dinner to inform Uncle J. of the arrival. Began to burn the skim which I was much pleased to see.

1. Lawn billiards, in which balls are directed into rings by wooden cues.
2. William Coope had just been appointed Rector of Falmouth.
3. George Wightwick of Plymouth, a friend of Charles Mathews, the actor; renowned for his lectures on Shakespeare; he was to design the new building for the Royal Cornwall Polytechnic at Falmouth.

28. 1st day. Walked to Penjerrick before dinner & found that the rain of yesterday had completely stopped the burning operations & will, I suppose, throw me back some days. Aunt E. not so well this morning. A smuggler in one of the Cawsand boats brought in today by two of the Mullion preventive men with 112 kegs.

29. Took a cruise to St. Anthony where I had some chat with Armstrong. I found he had spent many years on the Mediterranean where he was a great yachter & knew Byron intimately. He promised me an autograph. He was present with him when Shelley was dragged up; he was so disfigured as to be quite unrecognisable. His little schooner bore evident marks of having been run down.

6TH MONTH

5. Went to the Bank & found Aunt E. had revived a little & was then taking some beef tea. Dined there after which I walked to Penjerrick according to engagement to measure my field. On my return Thomas met me with the intelligence of Aunt E.'s death between 5 & 6.

9. Much rain. A convict ship put in here on her way to Botany, with 250 convicts on board, amongst others Edwards & his mate of the *Ada*, who were tried at this place.

20. Before tea whilst discussing Neath Abbey business in the long walk, Cos. J. T. Price started a proposal to take me to Wales to instal me into all the mysteries of Colliery & Iron manufactory which he undertook to do in six months. The subject was much discussed. My father & Uncle A. liked it. The conclusion seemed to be that nothing could be fixed at present. There would be several decided advantages in the plan & with one or two important stipulations I should feel quite willing to go.

21. Rode to Penjerrick & farmed for about half an hour before breakfast. The field is sown today. Emma Sutton and Miss Warren called to take a botanical excursion with A.M. They drank tea here after which I trudged home with them. In the evening arrived the intelligence of the King's death which happened early on 2nd day morning. We are now under the dominion of Queen Victoria, making the third European nation at present under petticoat government. Meanwhile peace to the dead. Without being a man of energy or ambition, he has made his reign glorious throughout futurity by the enactment of the Reform bill, the Emancipation of the slaves, & the general extension of popular privileges.

23. Broiling weather. Bought some mangel wurzel seed & walked to Penrose with it in the evening as Nichols will sow the remainder of my field the beginning of next week.

27. Proclamation of her Majesty Queen Victoria, for which purpose a procession about a quarter of a mile long formed in the Moor at 12 o'clock, consisting of Constables, Clergy, Army & Navy, the Herald on a grey horse, between twenty & thirty nice little girls in white with crepe hats & chaplets, preceded by young cavalry pages of nine or ten years old & flanked by foot ones, a very pretty group. Then came the Mayor & Alderman & other dignitaries in the full pride & glory of office. Then a long train of the very respectable inhabitants, then shoemakers, schools & other riff-raff. A company of Royal Marines closed the procession. There was an abundance of banners and three bands of music. The proclamation was made at about six places in the town; in no very good style for the poor herald seldom failed to confound kings and queens & the genders of pronouns in a most lamentable manner. By far the best part of the pageant was Jack's notion of a march, setting all rules thereof at utter defiance & snatching a swill of beer or a kiss occasionally *en passant*. They seemed the only ones who looked at the thing in its proper view. Indeed the rest might have been taken for a funeral except for the flags & music. The whole affair went off very well, no blunders of much consequence & no lives lost in the general rejoicing. That there was no blood shed is more than I would answer for, as the streets in the evening presented no scene remarkable for sobriety or order, what with dancing through the town in a long train, music in the middle, fireworks going off in all directions & all loyal men as drunk as pipers. All the confusion due to the day seemed to be religiously observed without. Within, in Pearce's, the loyal nobility, gentility & respectability of the place were comforting their insides & fumigating their brains at 15/– a head in honour of her Majesty.

7TH MONTH

29. Whilst cramming some luncheon down my hatchway the Coleridges made their appearance. After a bright little chat they departed to pay sundry calls, with a promise of returning to dinner. Meanwhile I rode as far as Perry's & settled for the keep of my colt. Installed Thomas as steward at Penjerrick with a fee of 10% on the profits during my absence. The Coleridges came punctually & a most brilliant dinner we had. I was engaged to Grove Hill to meet the Gordons, but this was a chance not to be lost. The subject was a strong political argumentation between the philosopher & the poet, which rose from a difference of sentiment between them in regard to the exercising of any influence over a voter. My father alleged that it was not just & Derwent Coleridge that it was both lawful & desirable. By degrees these points of discussion multiplied so that all were resolvable into a battle between

the stationary & progressive principles in society. Derwent Coleridge is a high Tory; his language was poetry, his ideas were vivid & quick as summer lightning, but the stuff his arguments were made of did not, I thought, stand the test of sober & dispassionate reflection. Of course, neither yielded an ell.

8TH MONTH

1. At 10 as punctually as could be expected we started on our travels in our carriage with Grandmother's horses & our gig behind. We had sorry weather & worse to cheer our spirits. On our arrival at Redruth we were informed that the Hayle steamer was lost, but the truth turned out that she had only been delayed by the tremendous weather on 7th night and had landed her passengers at Ilfracombe. Reached Hayle at 3. We got the carriage on board with the greatest ease & bade adieu to our three attendants, Thomas, Pearce & Glasson, and steamed off. A good deal of rolling & shivering & smelling & other disorders liable to the race of steamers, but Capt. Vivian was very civil & the kind steward also.

2. Got up between 5 & 6 after what's called a very light night. In fact the minimum of sleep permitted me barely amounted to forgetfulness, owing to the heat, the heavy swell, the whistling wind & rattling rain. Spent the day on the cabin sofa with Charles Lamb & Isaak Walton & came to in King's Roads about 2 o'clock. We loaded at Lamplighters Hall[1] in the steamer's boat whence I escorted the ladies to Combe & my father proceeded to Bristol in order to visit Frenchay & start early tomorrow for Swansea. The Hilhouses gave us a liberal welcome. They gave us a prime dinner, & phrenology, chess & chat occupied the evening.

3. Another wet day. Rode to Clifton with Uncle Hilhouse to see the carriage & give directions. Found a note there from my father to say he had left last evening for Cardiff per *Lady Charlotte* steamer. A precious night he must have had of it. Saw the New York steamer, 1,250 ton. It seems very doubtful whether she can carry fuel enough to provide for all contingencies.

4. Took leave of Combe at 11 with pleasurable remembrances of our visit. The lord & lady were remarkably well. Aunt Agatha & the two girls accompanied us to Frenchay where we met Grandmother & Aunt C. Spent a snug, sociable time agreeably varied with a fair specimen of dinner. We took leave & journied on very pleasantly over good roads to Cheltenham, which we reached at 9, & took up our abode at *The Plough*.

5. Visited the Montpelier Spa before breakfast & saw a smack of Cheltenham fashionables. None worth looking at. We left this town of palaces at 1 o'clock

1. At Shirehampton on the River Avon between Bristol and Avonmouth.

highly pleased with mine inn which is a little world of itself. Stopped an hour and a half at Worcester to give me an opportunity of seeing Cavendish. He was looking very well but lame from a fall with his pony about a fortnight since. He hobbled up to the inn to see Mother whence I went to the Cathedral to look for the girls. The postboy took us to Kidderminster which made the distance to Birmingham six miles more, in consequence of which we did not reach Jos. Gibbins's till half past ten, cold & hungry. He was very hospitable & gave us a noble supper after which we were glad enough to turn in.

6. Attended Meeting at 10. I walked to the farm with Sampson Lloyd, Aunt A.'s handsome brother. Sampson is sentimental & Wordsworthian but on some subjects very sensible. Paid a few visits to Friends of this diocese with mother, amongst others the Cadburys, a prim party consisting of Pa & Ma, four sons & four daughters.

7. Today was devoted to seeing the wonders of Birmingham. After an early breakfast at the Sturges, next door, we set off, being joined by the girls & Aunt A., to the various manufactories. We first visited Armfield's button manufactory. The work is all done by machinery; the workman has only to place the button under its influence & poke it off as fast as possible. From there we went to Thomason's omni-manufactory, as it seemed to me. Plating, medalling, buttoning, lapidarying, cutlering, &c. I stamped a railway medal, which is effected by a die, forced down by a huge screw, loaded so that the pressure shall be about 24 tons. We next surveyed the fabrication of papier maché. It is made as hard as & more tough than wood. Some of the painting upon it is really beautiful. We 'flied'[1] it from thence to T. Gibbins's house & demolished the cold collection he had prepared. We were escorted by him over his own province, justly styled the Battery works. It is the manufacture of brazen vessels & ewers, brass candlesticks & wire & copper pipes. Jos. Gibbins joined us here & we went *en masse* to the superb Town Hall. It has been finished only two or three years & ruined the two contractors. Had the pleasure of meeting Christopher Wordsworth, Master of Harrow & nephew of the poet, a man apparently of strong sense & erudition but too bigotted a Tory for these enlightened days.

8. Set off to the Railway station after an early breakfast. The buildings & appurtenances at the station are gigantic & really handsome. Being joined there by the girls we took leave of our overwhelmingly kind friends & proceeded to Matlock. The road from Derby to Matlock is rich in the extreme, abrupt limestone hills on one side, splendidly wooded, & rich meadows with cattle feeding, on the other. Matlock itself is pitched in the most romantic point of all. Whilst daylight lasted we climbed to the heights above the inn, called the Dungeon Tors. We made a most voracious tea,

1. i.e. took a fly, a fast, hired carriage.

having had no meat since our early breakfast at Birmingham & after somewhat satisfying the cravings of nature with a huge dish of mutton chops, the girls & I returned to the hill behind the hotel & ascended to the summit. Our inn, the *New Bath*, is very comfortable & moderate, the people civil & obliging.

9. Chatsworth, one of the Duke of Devonshire's private palaces, is about eleven miles from Matlock. With the exception of one or two royal ones it certainly is the most superb residence I ever saw; too much so, for comfort, I think. We were conducted from suite to suite, from saloon to saloon, of the utmost magnificence. Dined at Bakewell, drizzly rain, tremendous hills, vile ponds & other discomforts by the way made a snug tea & a speedy turn-in at Castleton truly acceptable.

10. Strolled to the Peak before breakfast. It is only about 300 yards from the inn. We reached Sheffield about 9, another dirty, smoky, ragamuffin manufacturing town. Our inn, the *Tontine*, not over good.

11. Took a survey of the town before breakfast. Immediately after it we all visited Rogers's show-rooms & manufactory of plating & cutlery. The form exactly the same as what we saw at Thomason's in Birmingham. All their steel is made from Swedish iron, put in a huge furnace alternately with layers of charcoal where it remains for seven days. It is then melted in large crucibles from whence it is cast in moderate sized bars & afterwards worked through various stages of smithing, grinding & polishing to all manner of edged instruments. Rogers employs 500 workmen. We spent between £5 & £6 in his irresistible show-room. We were glad to get clear of Sheffield; it is a vile dirty place as all manufacturing towns are. I hate the whole of them. On our road we passed Lord Fitzwilliams's Wentworth Castle & sundry fire-spouting chymnies, changed horses at Wakefield & reached Leeds between 8 & 9. This amongst all others of its species is the vilest of the vile. At a mile distant from the town we came under a vast dingy canopy formed by the impure exhalation of a hundred furnaces. It sits on the town like an everlasting incubus, shutting out the light of heaven & the breath of summer. I pity the poor denizens. London is a joke to it. Our inn was consistent with its locality; one doesn't look for a clean floor in a colliery or a decent hotel in Leeds.

12. Made various fruitless enquiries for Jos. Pease & others of Mother's friends; but no satisfactory information could we obtain. The inhabitants are as dull as lead & the smoke 'has entered into their souls'. After breakfast we visited the huge woollen mart, containing upwards of a thousand sellers' stalls. Piles of broad cloth everywhere met our view, guarded by a regiment of wool dealers armed with little brooms to defend their goods from flies and furnace dust. The whole spot was pervaded with a close clothy smell, but the heavy countenances of the dealers seemed well adapted to their scene

of action. We left this dingy town directly afterwards & in about three miles travelling got beyond the influence of its murky atmosphere. We reached York, a distance of twenty-five miles, about one. Were pleasantly impressed by first appearances. Took our station at the *Black Swan* & having dressed and cleaned ourselves we proceeded to the Minster. This did indeed soar far above our highest anticipations. We entered & were led through nave, aisle, transept, chancel, vestry, & chapter by a chattering sacristan whose lengthy chapter of details much took off from the solemnity of the great whole. We were shown the place where Martin hid himself behind a tomb. He burnt down the whole of the chancel.[1] The wonders of that pile would take more time than I can spare, but I shall never forget them. We went from there to the Museum. The Geological & Antiquity departments interested us most. After dinner the girls & I went to the castle where an execution took place this very day, the first there has been for two years. The view from Clifford's Tower is very extensive. The burial mound of Severus, the minster, the city, & the meandering Ouse with a large steamer on its bosom made a striking sort of view. We went over part of the prison. Saw the spot where the unfortunate Thos. Williams was hanged today, the gallows had only just been removed, but the sight of the most intense & horrible interest is the collection of murderous instruments & relics. I never saw any collection which called up such a train of fearful & thrilling thoughts. After lounging away another hour amongst old book & engraving shops, we returned to tea. My father & I called on Saml. Tuke[2] in the evening. We are all highly pleased with York, its contrast to Leeds is very striking.

13. 1st day. Met Lydia Barclay at Meeting this morning. She & my mother gave us long & interesting sermons. Sundry of the convalescent patients from the Retreat were present. We walked to Saml. Tuke's home to dinner; two sisters, two daughters, & two sons from his circle. None very taking except himself, whom I have long looked at with a sort of veneration for his Christian dignity & his mild & impartial sway over the Yearly Meeting. After dinner our party, except Mammy, went to the Retreat & joined the assembled patients in a little meeting room in the establishment whilst Thos. Allis, the governor, read two or three chapters & psalms & then held about half-an-hour's meeting. A most sad sight at best. We afterwards went over the asylum with Thos. Allis. It seems as thoroughly comfortable as such a place can be.

14. Left York for Darlington about 8. Diverged some distance from the direct route to visit Fountains Abbey which is about three miles from Ripon.

---

1. This happened in 1829.
2. Samuel Tuke (1784–1857), tea and coffee merchant in York; grandson of William Tuke, the founder of the Retreat, the first institution of its kind for the humane treatment of the mentally ill; social reformer and friend of Wilberforce.

It is certainly finer than Tintern which I consider saying a good deal. The tone of ancient solemnity was much disturbed by party after party of chattering, graceless, unfeeling, sight-hunters. Light thoughts & words have no business in such a place. Arrived at the hospitable mansion of Polam Hall[1] about 8 o'clock. We were heartily welcomed.

15. Got up at the unconscionable hour of half past five to attend a Monthly at Catherstone, 20 miles off, a beautiful drive, passing by Barnard Castle, the luxuriant Tees & romantic Deepdale.

17. Today we spent at home, i.e. Polam Hall. Meeting day. Called on sundry Peases & Backhouses & Robsons. I believe there are no other Friends' names in Darlington.

20. Mother gallivanted twenty miles off to hold a meeting at Osmotherly at 6 o'clock this morning. Being a Sunday it was a home day with us. In the morning meeting we had a sermon from Hannah Backhouse on the indwelling Spirit of Christ, another from John Pease whose ministry I like much.

23. Our time at Darlington has been one of unalloyed pleasure. The prevalent tone of mind throughout the circle is of no common order. Its most promising characteristics, I think, are refinement & cultivation, active religion, philanthropy & self-esteem. Jonathan Backhouse I love for his own sake, I admire for his benevolence, I pity for his indecision. His wife I like because she likes me & has done everything to make us comfortable. I look up to her powers of mind with almost awe. The only thing I could wish otherwise with her is a clearer comprehension of the word *wife*. I think poor hubby sometimes gets hardly his due. Jane is a statue-like being, cold & beautiful, with delicacy of soul and just appreciation of the good & beautiful. She has a high & a proud heart at some times amounting to scornfulness. She evidently knows her standing and receives attentions as homage due to her. With all this & amazing firmness into the bargain, she would make a prize of no common value to any that would undertake her, but she being thoroughbred, it must be a master's hand to train her to the bit. Ann is goodness itself, without any external attractions but a look of eternal good nature. She has a mind nearly as well stored as her sister's with a finer perception of goodness & a sincere love of truth. We bade adieu to Polam and Mother at half past one & reached Durham before 5. Visited the cathedral, museum, & University.

1. The home of Jonathan and Hannah Backhouse at Darlington where they stayed while Barclay's mother conducted her ministry in the neighbourhood.

9TH MONTH

8. Got up at 6 & had a row with Mother on the exquisite Derwentwater. There could not have been a lovelier morning & scarcely a lovelier scene. After breakfast we ascended Skiddaw, I on foot & the rest on steeds of a nondescript variety. Our mother managed the ascent most valorously. The mountain air seemed to restore her forgotten youth. Having spent about an hour on the top of the mountain we turned our faces southward & descended, I ran on before in order to call on Southey, who lives just at the foot. I had no introduction nor indeed plausible pretence for the call, but summoning my stock of impudence which has often stood me in good stead, I knocked at the door. The Poet was dressing for dinner during which operation I had the good fortune to be left in his library. There hung a small alto-relievo of himself in wax over the oak chymney piece & another I suppose of his son. The tone of books on his shelves well bespoke his peculiar tastes: various rare editions of classical works, old Spanish historians & poets, Moorish antiquities & Catholic legends in the same tongue, German & Italian works, Massinger & others of the old English Dramatists, & a small book entitled The Poets' Pilgrimage which on opening I found to be a MS. poem of his describing his visit to Rome, dedicated to his daughter Katherine. After employing about twenty minutes in this supervising manner, I heard a quick step coming down stairs, the door opened & in he walked. His manner was at first nervous & hurried. He bowed stiffly, with a what's-your-business? sort of look which almost threw me aback. However, I introduced myself as a particular friend of his nephew,[1] Derwent Coleridge, & had merely called to offer my services in taking him any parcel or letter he might wish to send. Having declined this as he had sent a parcel a week or two before, the conversation seemed to come to an end. However, the idea came to my aid of asking his advice as to our route through the Lakes. This opened him a little. He spoke fluently & was gradually betrayed into something like a glowing description of Lake scenery. He is a tall, gentlemanly, studious-looking man with a bush of white hair, a large hooked nose & a prominent restless nervous eye. His complexion & manner also bespeak nervous irritability, but I have since heard that he is remarkable for evenness of mind. This may be his nature, but I should rather think it a conquest. Returned to the hotel, made a glorious dinner & after a little shopping, ordered the carriage, reached Grasmere at half past nine. Thinking it too late to call I sent off Aunt C.'s letter to Hartley Coleridge & we proceeded to despatch tea. In the evening between 10 & 11 as I was coolly mending a pen, A.M. suddenly nudged me & pointed to the door. On looking up I saw an odd little fellow about 5 feet 4 or 5, standing on the threshhold going through a series of low bows like a very

1. Southey and S. T. Coleridge had married sisters.

polite Mandarin. There could be no mistake. I jumped up & shouted 'Hartley Coleridge'. He rebowed all round and sat down. He required as much drawing out as a twelve-jointed spy-glass. His manner reminded me of Uncle G.P. but his voice was like no-one but himself, such a strangely small, shrill pipe. Having talked over the usual introductory topics interspersed with long & frequent pauses, he took his hat & bowed adieu. I walked home with him by way of seeing a little more of the genius.

9. Before breakfast walked to Dale End, Aunt C.'s cottage, with Mother & the girls. It is a most sweet place as the dullest spot on that exquisite lake cannot fail to be. After breakfast my sire & I posted off to Coleridge's. We met him on his way to the hotel. He showed us Wordsworth's cottage[1] behind his own at the foot of the mountain & which De Quincey inhabited afterwards. The girls joined us & we walked with Hartley Coleridge over the mountain to Rydall, the elders going round in the carriage. The Poet is not yet returned but we found his lady at home, rather prim in manners, but of a benevolent & well-intentioned aspect. Rydall Mount is considered by many the loveliest spot on the Lakes. In the drawing-room is a likeness of the poet taken at Rome this year & considered the best. There is a beautiful bust of him in a niche over the stairs. On one side of the door hangs a painting of the 'old grey thorn', and on the other Bolton Abbey with 'the white doe of Rylstone' in the foreground. Dora Wordsworth is with her father. They say she is an exquisite creature. Mrs. Wordsworth escorted us over the grounds. The mountain views from various points are highly striking. There is a brass plate inlaid in an old projecting stone at the foot of the garden on which is graven a stanza of Wordsworth's referring to his rescue of it from the builder's hands.[2] The parents having joined us with the carriage, Hartley Coleridge conducted us to Rydall Falls which are in the grounds of Lady Fleming close by. Hartley Coleridge accompanied us to Ambleside in the carriage three miles further. On arriving he went off to pay some calls & we posted down to the lake. We were cruizing on Windermere nearly an hour. Hartley Coleridge joined us at dinner during which he was very brilliant. He talked on various subjects in a most original strain: his abhorrence of oaths, his views on the independence of intellect & morality, with much gossip about the Balls & Braggs of Hawkshead. He would prefer mere beauty of person in a woman to mere intellect; the one he designated a negative possession, the other unswayed by moral sentiments the true character of a fiend. He certainly is a strange compound of genius & oddity. We reached Hawkshead about 8, a dull little place, but a pretty landlady.

10. 1st day. Skewy morning. Attended Hawkshead meeting at 10. A queer little place & an attenuated body, only eight members, including non-attenders.

1. Dove Cottage, where the Wordsworths had lived on first coming to Grasmere.
2. The lines beginning 'In these fair vales hath many a Tree' were published in 1835.

11. We set off in a flood of rain which lasted all the way to Kendal, a most agreeable accompaniment to a succession of rough steep hills, up & down like furrows. Reached Kendal at one & drove at once to G. Crewdson's. We took Ellen on board & drove on to Sizergh Hall,[1] three miles on. It is an old Tudor castle turreted & moated, belonging to the Strickland family. W. Crewdson & his lady received us at the door, the latter not much altered. They led us through a lofty suite of rooms to the drawing-room, which is a princely apartment. Left Sizergh at half past six & reached Lancaster soon after nine.

12. After breakfast we called on the Dockery's. D. Dockery escorted us round the castle, the scene of Geo. Fox's frequent imprisonments. Pushed on briskly, dined at Boskbridge & reached Liverpool about six, distance fifty-four miles. Landed the parents' luggage at J. Crossfield's & then transported the girls & theirs to R. Fry. I went back to the town, settled the carriage at the *Adelphi*, ran to the Crossfields' & dressed in time to attend the British Association soirée at the Town Hall at eight. Here I was soon joined by Uncle A. who arrived yesterday. Paraded with him round & round on an observational. The evening dresses & other settings-off of the fair failed to supply the place of real beauty of which there was a modicum. The strong point seemed to be backs & shoulders. Great cram of about 2,000 persons. Ran home a little before eleven.

16. All the sections were over yesterday except the Geological. Instead of giving it my countenance I got a ticket & joined the expedition to the salt mines. We went by the Grand Junction Railway. They gave us a push at starting which sent us through the tunnel a mile and a half long. The steam carriage waited for us at the other end & took us in tow. We reached Hurtford, the nearest station to Northwich in an hour & two minutes, a distance of 31 miles. We were politely received at the Works by Messrs. Perth & Worthington & ushered down in a bucket, four at a time. A hundred and ten yards descent brought us to one of the most magnificent scenes, a vast level, ceiled chamber half a mile in length, supported by long ranges of columns all of pure & glittering salt, & lit up by 2,000 tapers fastened to the walls & pillars. We wandered through it in wonder & rapture. After an hour and a half's wonderment we were conducted to a long table in the centre of the mine amply garnished with meats & wines. There were sundry speeches after dinner. We returned to the mouth of the shaft & all that could, before ascending, sung God Save the Queen & then a stanza from a hymn. I thought it rather out of time and place.

22. Mother's passport[2] arrived from Falmouth, permitted her to go forward

1. Sizergh Castle is now the property of the National Trust. George and William Crewdson had both married members of the Fox family.
2. i.e. the certificate from the Society of Friends to authorise her ministry.

& stablish the saints which are at Darlington. This decided our plans. We children snapped up a hearty dinner, took leave of our parents & our most liberal & kind entertainers, & embarked the carriage on the Birmingham railway at half past two. Our parents fixed to start for Leeds this evening. We reached Birmingham at half-past seven. Found a gentleman & a pair of horses waiting for us. Beds had been secured at the *George Hotel* & we drove there at once. Birmingham is crammed full of musical artists & amateurs. The festival was over this morning. A fancy ball at the Town Hall was the business of the evening. After tea I strolled thitherward but did not see more than ½ dozen in costume & that nothing particular. The crowd was immense. The price of beds during this week has been one & two guineas per night. We were lucky enough to get them at 5/–.

23. Reached Frenchay at half past seven. Made a noble tea & had a snug cozy chat till bed-time. Uncle Francis is a good hearty fellow.

25. Took leave of Frenchay at 9 o'clock. Uncle Francis & I proceeded to Bristol in his gig & I sent out post horses for the girls & the carriage. We reached Combe at half past three & were warmly received.

27. Bristol Quarterly Meeting. Rode in after breakfast & met my father, who brings a good account of his lady from Leeds. Returned with him to the *White Lion* where the evening was spent in a thorough talk over Neath affairs.

28. Took leave of Combe a little after six. They have been most heartily & unaffectedly hospitable. Drove to the *White Lion,* were with the Prices half an hour & then pushed homewards as fast as we could persuade the postboys. My father & I paid Sidcott[1] a visit in our way. There are nine Cornish boys there, three of them Foxes. Visited the school & ran over the establishment to see the arrangements which are good, cleanly & comfortable; the demarcation between boys & girls strictly observed.

29. Set off at half past six. Breakfasted at Launceston at half past eleven. A pleasant Cornish feeling. The 'Cornish boys' don't lose by comparison with their manufacturing brethren. We were blessed with thorough summer weather & travelled very well. Indian Queens to Truro, thirteen miles, in 80 minutes, i.e. a mile per six minutes. Found Pearce waiting for us at the latter place with Grandmother's horses which whirled us home by 8 o'clock. All the 'helps' greeted us with most pleasant looks & everything was looking just as it should be. Spent the evening in unpacking & settling in. I come today into possession of Penjerrick. Though somewhat abused it is a hopeful material to work on.

---

1. Sidcot is a Friends' school at Winscombe in Somerset.

10TH MONTH

2. Thoroughly resettled into the Counting House duties. Walked to Penjerrick after dinner. Surveyed the state of things there as left by my predecessor & went into a settlement of accounts. Neither process at all satisfactory. Held a council of war in the evening with Thomas as to future arrangements.

3. Had a regular flustration with Matthey[1] in the turnip field. I accused him of unreasonableness in his charges, upon which he worked himself into a state bordering on insanity. I have made up my mind to get rid of him if possible. Weather still in the dismals. Met W. E. Forster per *Regulator*. We have both been manoeuvring to meet for some time past & he has at length managed it. Spent a royal good evening together.

5. Walked with William to Penjerrick to see Matthey. Asked his terms for working for me steadily in order to have a fair excuse for ejectment.

7. Took a ride with William. Galloping ahead of him my steed kicked a splash of mud in his face which was so fairly distributed between eyes & spectacles as to blind him. In this state he rushed on an unfortunate pedestrian, which I was made aware of by a yell of terror, and on looking round I saw the man in a state of dismay, brandishing a huge knobstick over his head to keep off the animal. William did not see him till encountered. He was at last able to 'haul his wind' without any personal injury.

9. Walked to Penjerrick with William at half past six. William in raptures. He walked on to Trebah & I returned to make some enquiries about a man called Bishop, as I have determined on parting with Matthey. William received a letter from his father with a message from his employer which renders it necessary to set off tomorrow. So all our bright plans are quashed. William & I having many topics left to discuss, felt constricted to pass the night by the kitchen fire with chat, books, letters & other documents, besides a sufficiency of bread & cheese & porter. Made a tour of the town at 4 in the morning & altogether made the most of our night.

13. Before breakfast I walked to Penjerrick & gave Matthey to understand that he must look out for another place. He never has suited me. I can't abide him. Never had such a cunning fellow to deal with; he tried every tack & urged every tie which bound him to the place, finally offering to work as low as the lowest offer I had received. However, my mind was made up. I offered him several sacrifices on my part to get out before the end of next month. A man called Evans came up in the evening to offer himself as Matthey's successor. I hear a good character of him & mean to give him a fair trial.

16. Geological meeting at Penzance. Started on horseback a little past six.

1. The tenant and farm manager at Penjerrick.

Whilst the pony baited at Helston I called on the Coleridges. Found them at breakfast at which I joined them & then accompanied Derwent Coleridge through his new schoolroom & other private accommodations. He showed me his books & bust of his father. Talked about the mystery of *Christabel*. He considers it to be founded on the Roman Catholic notion of expiation for others' sins; that Geraldine is a divinely appointed penance imposed on Christabel for the redemption of her lover who had committed some crime.

17. Rode to Penjerrick & had a second specimen of Matthey in the tantrums. He intimated he would give me all the trouble in his power in getting out. However, if he will run his head against a wall he shall see which is the harder.

11TH MONTH

3. Rode to Penjerrick & had a settlement with Matthey up to the present time. No house unfortunately is ready to receive him. The brig *Anna* came in much damaged. She sprung a leak two days ago & they had to fling part of her cargo overboard.

14. Spent an hour with Aunt C. & Eliz. Crouch at Trebah. The former was suffering from a wretched headache occasioned by a letter from Uncle L. today, enclosing a notice of resignation to be presented at the Monthly Meeting tomorrow. It is what I expected & wished for. It certainly seems ridiculous in any man who is his own master to keep up an appearance of what he decidedly & declaredly is not.

12TH MONTH

7. Walked to Penjerrick where my ears were blessed with the joyous tidings that Matthey had arranged with Hill to enter his house at Christmas. From henceforth my affairs are all smooth sailing.

20. An odd consignment has come to us per *Express* packet in the shape of a 60 gallon rum puncheon containing in spirits the mortal remains of Mrs. Hodges, the late wife of the Vice-Consul at Jacmel. The inconsolable partner consigns her to us in a most thoroughly mercantile letter to be forwarded to order.

21. Found that Matthey has arranged to quit me tomorrow. Had a longish interview with Thos. Evans, my new tenant, in the evening. Drew up certain articles of agreement which we both signed in due form.

25. Trudged out to the farm & employed a couple of hours with Evans in

superambulating every field, inspecting the erections, stock, implements &c., arranging for the present & fixing for the future & so on. Returned to the cottage & partook with the lady & gentleman of the place of a dinner of roast beef & plum pudding I sent out in the morning. They were much gratified & seem highly pleased with their present lot.

29. Walked to Penjerrick. Found Evans ploughing the lower corner field which I shall prepare for potatoes. Took his place at the plough's tail but my furrows proved, like myself, not too regular. Dined at Tregedna & then walked with Evans to Tregarn where there is to be a sale next week.

1838

THE YEAR opens with terrible storms in January and February. Barclay is busy with the ship repairs that follow the gales, but manages to find time for his farming at Penjerrick. The rest of his family leave in March for a visit to France and Switzerland and in May he rejoins them in London where they all attend the Yearly Meeting of the Society of Friends. From London he goes to Norwich to spend a holiday with his friend W. E. Forster and then returns to London in time for the Queen's Coronation in June. He is lucky in obtaining a ticket for the stand outside Westminster Abbey where he has an excellent view of the Queen's procession. In September Barclay celebrates his twenty-first birthday. The Royal Cornwall Polytechnic begins to take seriously the invention of machinery for raising and lowering miners in and out of the mines. Barclay's father and uncles offer prizes for the most successful 'man-engines' invented. The year ends as it began with storms and with damaged vessels seeking shelter at Falmouth.

1ST MONTH

16. The Revd. Mr. Hodges called at the office. He has come from London to escort his sister-in-law who has been lying in the Custom's warehouse, encasked & enspirited, back to her native town. Snow in the day. Frost at night.

24. Most tremendous gale from S.E. from 12 till 4. Many vessels drove. One smack slipt anchor in order to run up to little Falmouth, but not daring to carry sufficient sail was driven to leeward & struck at the back of Hobbs's. She knocked in part of the wall, carried away her bowsprit & was at last got off, but the men not being able to work her to windward, having left all the head sails on shore, ran her in on Green Bank beach where they secured her & scrambled on shore as they could.

26. Miserable weather. Cold out of doors & colds in. Mother's cough troublesome. Percy arrived last night. He had a tremendous ride from Exeter, horses tumbling down, coach walking into the ditch & scraping acquaintance with the hedge & similar manoeuvres.

2ND MONTH

2. Walked to Enys to breakfast to see the result of a ploughing match which

took place there two days ago. Only six ploughs appeared on the field five of which were Scotch. The Cornish one broke down before half finishing its work. There were two samples of ploughing which might show with any in England.

15. A most terrible night was followed by an equally tempestuous day. Wind S.E. Took a run before breakfast, but found it no joke to make head against the storm. The snow driving in your face like a simoom & stinging like hail, & lying on the ground in vast drifts to the depth of one & two feet. Found at the office that a packet had driven ashore at Trefusis Pt. & in the intervals, when the snow became a little less thick, we could make her out lying on the rocks on her beam ends, with top-gallant masts & all the yards set. We could also see that the *Asia*, a Dutch East Indiaman of 1,100 tons, had driven awfully near the point. On coming home to breakfast I found that the lead had departed from the top of our house to cover a shed in Capt. Daniel's yard. I hardly passed a house which had not suffered more or less damage. After breakfast the weather was clearer though as boisterous as ever. I could make out the packet clearly. She proved to be the *Ranger*, Lieut. Turner, in a most awful plight. Trudged up to Boyer's Cellars to look at the devastation along shore: a sloop belonging to F. Symons, knocking to pieces at Market Strand, having carried away a corner of the *King's Arms*; another at Green Bank, hammering away at the pier in which she had bored a great cavity, was going to destruction as fast as possible; another was run ashore at Boyer's. We blocked up the doorway with bales of wool. The old brig was rolling it out at two anchors, but the Dutch galliot at Symons's yard was blown clean over, her bulwarks, cross-trees, & a little bit of deck were just visible above the waves. It required one's whole strength to make headway against the wind across Green Bank Terrace. I was wetted to the skin in spite of a host of envelopes. Changed & returned to the charge. Capt. Plumridge, Smith & Jennings went over to Trefusis to render assistance. We could make out a vast body of men employed in landing & saving the stores. In the afternoon two schooners slipped & ran ashore between Penryn & Boyer's, one the *Ditton* with oranges consigned to us, the other the *Hope* from Limerick with bones. The bark *Harvest-Home* ran ashore at Restronguet. The gale continues. We can form as yet no idea of the whole of the extent of the injuries, but shall know more tomorrow. It has been a most exciting day.

16. The gale died a natural death in the afternoon. I walked with the surveyors to the examination of the two schooners. No London mail yesterday or today. We hear that the stoppage is on this side of Exeter. The *Drake* towed out the Indiaman into deep water. The *Ramona* arrived at twilight, having ridden out the gale in Scilly where two Dutch ships are ashore.

17. The mail that should have arrived on the 15th came in after dark this

evening. Ran out into the country & found Evans making the most of a large catch of seaweed on Maenporth beach. Two trees growing from the hedge by the well were blown down. No other damage. Some lame ducks put into port.

22. Rode in to Falmouth & attended a meeting for the consideration of what steps to take towards deepening the harbour. The Mayor was in the chair & the representatives of Lord Wodehouse & Lady Basset on either side. Lieut. Green presented a paper of his to the secretary & after a long farrago of crude matter utterly irrelevant to the subject, he mentioned his having at the meeting the model of a mud-boat adapted for the purpose. C. Carne requested Lieut. Green to exhibit his model. This his Highness flatly refused & flew into a most tremendous rage with every individual in the room for not showing more respect to his valuable communication. His voice became a shout & he swore that they were not worthy & should not benefit by his invention. Parson Coope after endeavouring to pacify Green, got into scalding water about an account of the last meeting which appeared in the *Express* paper. Coope, who I have no doubt was the writer, scolded the Mayor for lecturing the editor. Bond proceeded to read the subscriptions. Lord Wodehouse's subscription is £100, the paltry, contemptible, close-fisted curmudgeon. I should consider this virtually puts a stop to the whole proceedings.

26. I witnessed a scene at the Methodist meeting at Perran Well which I never could have conceived possible had I not seen it with my own eyes. It was a revival of the first order. The meeting was held for prayer & singing, but the congregation having been in an awakened state for a week or more, rendered the voice of the prayer-leader totally inaudible. About thirty were under impression or revived, or taken down, as it is called. They were all young boys & girls. Such confusion, such contortions, such savage uproar as would have disgraced an assembly of savage idolators. Every pitch of the voice, every attitude that the human body could be thrown into, with demoniacal howlings. Their cries were 'Glory, Glory', 'Bless the Lord', 'Praise God', &c., &c., uttered in a style of religious frenzy, or rather an outrageous mockery of religion, which utterly disgusted me.

27. Called at Boyer's Cellars. Quay work knocked down. T. Olive has never known the tide so high; the water was 9 inches in his parlour. Magnificent Swedish brig in the pier with her rudder gone. All hands very busy. Dined at the Bank & rode to Penjerrick. Saw Uncle Joshua's new shaft, or rather pit, in which he has just discovered by far the richest tin of all he has raised. Found the farm in a wholesome state and two lambs added to my stock, one 2 days & the other 2 hours old.

28. Beautiful morning. Uncle C. dined with us at our house & we trotted back through wind & rain to tend on eighty of Aunt C.'s school whom she

was feeding & rewarding with all manner of natty prizes, after which Uncle C. electrified & shocked their small systems & amazed them with magic lantern & other phenomena. Drank tea with Uncle L. & attended with him a regular Methodist meeting. Impressive, rousing & exciting sermon preached by a Mr. Wood. Prayer & singing alternately, both extremely interesting, occupied the rest of the time. Towards the conclusion there was a perfect hurricane of revival.

3RD MONTH

7. The plans for France & Switzerland seem pretty well settled. Our party, save myself, with the Perran party will form five carriage-loads & start from Southampton, probably tomorrow week.

9. Superb weather. We have a regular picture gallery arranged in the state-room at the Counting House, being part of the cargo of the French brig. They are mostly poor things & far too French for eyes polite. There are two or three of a really high order. A female portrait called a Leonardo da Vinci is beautiful. Rode out to the farm. Got in my oats, grass seed, &c., in good order. Another lamb born. Rode on to Treverva with Evans & bought some hay & potatoes.

15. Delicious weather. Attended a sale & bought a mast & some cordage. It is fixed for me to escort the ladies of our party to St. Austell the day after tomorrow so as to break the neck of the journey. Launched my craft & moored her in her old berth.

17. Started on our travels about 1 o'clock, i.e. Mammy, the girls, Eliza & Jane. My father is to meet us at Bodmin the day after tomorrow. Reached St. Austell without adventure or mishap.

19. My father arrived at 6. Having missed the coach, he came by the Plymouth one as far as Lostwithiel & thence across country in a postchaise. We all of us started at 9, they to Switzerland & I homewards (via Lostwithiel per returned chaise).

20. Removed my kit to the Bank where they provided me with a bed, a table, & a chair. Had a satisfactory visit to the farm.

23. By way of a change I lodged at Penjerrick, carrying with me my dinner & night shirt & mould candle. Worked hard all the afternoon. Chalked out forty-six trees for the slaughter & cut down several. Made a choice of the best saplings in the orchard of various sorts to supply their places. Worked as long as daylight lasted. Spent a truly enjoyable evening in solitary sway with books & paper beside a glorious wood fire in the inner parlour & turned into bed with a keen relish.

25. 1st day. Superlative weather. Dined at Uncle A.'s. Uncle L. spent the afternoon here. Walked & talked with him. Was told of young Sammy Pellew's inveterate & undying hate towards unfortunate me. I met him on the terrace three weeks ago bearing down under full sail with a blustering, bullying swagger, as though determined to carry the world before him. As we passed I looked at him rather hard, an as-good-as-you sort of look. Just as he shot by I heard him ejaculate 'Dear me!', as I thought, but now hear it was an imprecation of a similar sound. I turned short round to know what he meant. He bowed with both hand & head, exclaiming, 'No reference to you, sir', & raced on. However, I had second-hand his description of this transaction; the utter contempt with which I always survey him & on this occasion my haughty expression was such that he could not avoid cursing me aloud as he passed, that his hate towards me is inexpressible & much more.

4TH MONTH

13. Most luxurious weather. Good Friday. Everybody else went to church, I receded to Penjerrick. Dined at Uncle J.'s. Sam Rundell, with Ann Tweedy of course, held a publick meeting at Mawnan. Coope Senior had a frightful accident this afternoon. Returning from church in his phaeton with the two little girls, the horse set off by Hall's. He lost control entirely & the horse carried it all his own way till he at last ran his head against the Penders' wall, close by Grove Hill gate, & capsized the carriage. The two little girls were shot out like peas & fell on the horse's side & ran off unhurt, but the old man was pitched out against the wall, broke his collar bone & cut his head & knee very badly. He was taken senseless into Broad's & finally carried home in a sedan by four men. I called there in the evening. He was lying in the next room & his groans were audible with every breath. The family were anxious but not much alarmed. Vigurs said that he was not apprehensive of the slightest danger & did not admit the idea of any internal injury.

18. Today we had hail, sleet & snow. Received a capital account from the voyagers written from Clermont, Mammy in high spirits & sitting out of doors. A comfortable fire, well-aired bed, books, candle, & independence. It was a hermit's luxury.

24. Bleak rainy day. Coope Senr. was buried at 10 this morning. In spite of the weather the attendance was large, three chaises & four with more vehicles of lesser magnitude. It was a melancholy sight. The Rector, we hear, means to reduce his establishment. People say that they lose an annuity of £1,400 by the old man's death.

25. Took an instructive & edifying walk with Eliz. Crouch. Wm. Coope

is evidently a loser by his father's death in the way of property to a considerable amount. He gives up his horses & carriages, & people say all his menservants except one gardener. If this be true he is much to be felt for, being overhoused & over-establishmented by another's improvidence, but I think things are not as bad as they appear.

28. Busy painting & white-washing my house; it improves it vastly. Glorious weather but fresh wind. Took a row with Uncle G.P. in his new craft in the evening. An elopement took place yesterday of Miss Hobbs, the seedsman's daughter, with Stoner, the guard of a coach. They were pursued by her sire but without success.

MAY

3. Elizabeth Crouch taken violently ill. Weather in the dismals. Returned to Penjerrick late in the evening & was much concerned to find that Betsey Evans[1] had been siezed with an attack resembling paralysis, though only temporarily. The seizure passed off in about five minutes, but has left great debility & occasional fainting fits.

16. Found a letter from my parents desiring me to be in Town tomorrow morning & procure lodgings for them as they look forward to arriving there on the following or the day after. Elizth. Crouch dined with us. She goes with me tomorrow. I shall escort her as far as Bristol from whence she proceeds to Manchester. Intensely busy all day. Sent out eight ducklings to Penjerrick. Paid six farewell visits & happily completed packing & arranging by half-past eleven. Took a loving leave at the Bank. Slept at home. Visitors & parcels flocking in till bed-time.

17. Up at half-past four & breakfasted with Elizth. Crouch. Set off in high glee & journied in solitary happiness till the stage after Truro when we were joined by a woman with two young children, the younger only three months. The consequences as Sam Weller says, are 'hobvious'. This was a great nuisance. She produced a bottle of 'lickor' from her pocket & earnestly pressed us to partake of it. She said it was for the child's use, who was bad in its nasty little bowels & moreover very sick. The pleasure of this part of our ride may be conceived. She left us at Camelford. We reached Exeter a little before 8 & found comfortable rooms prepared for us. Elizth. having a little headache I deposited her on a sofa & read her to sleep.

18. Off at half-past seven per *Exquisite*. We reached Bristol soon after 4, where having shipped Elizth. in a fly to her friend J. Sturge's & taken my place by a 6 o'clock coach, the *Monarch*, to London, I hurried on to Dr. Fox's

1. Thomas Evans's wife.

in Berkeley Square, where I had the delight of finding Uncle G.C. & Aunt Lucy, the latter looking better than I had expected. She is improving much under Dr. Fox's care, to whom both attribute her existence at this moment. Uncle G.C. walked with me to the inn & chatted whilst I devoured a mutton chop. I couldn't get an inside place for love or money, so made interest with the guard for a great coat.

19. Soon after midnight about three miles beyond Marlborough, the guard having to descend to drag the wheel, set his foot on a young woman's head, who was perched on the bottom step of the coach. She was pretty & respectably dressed & said she was going to London (a 75 mile walk). The guard was inexorable & displaced her. Both her appearance & circumstances bespoke her a runaway. We reached the *Belle Sauvage*, Ludgate Hill, at 8 o'clock. Having devoured an astonishing breakfast at St. Paul's Coffee House, I posted off to Barton Crescent in a hunt for lodgings.

20. 1st day. Took an early breakfast & went into Town. Lost no time in finding my way to the Customs House & had not waited ten minutes when the Rotterdam steamer arrived. I jumped into a wherry, pushed off & in two minutes had the delight of hailing all our party in renewed health & high spirits. We bundled into a hackney coach & cab & drove to our lodgings where a fire was lit & breakfast laid. We sat down together very happy, talked, made meeting, & had, as Friends say, a very united time.

21. After breakfast came the Customs House business. Eliza & I posted thither with the keys & got everything overhauled, repacked & on the whole satisfactorily settled in an hour. I obtained a pair of horses, drove to Barton Crescent & disgorged the contents of the vehicle & finally stowed it away in a neighbouring coach-house.

23. Commencement of the great Sanhedrin.[1] The whole day was occupied by Answers to Queries & four testimonials. The principal temptation in our Society appears by the Answers to be frequenting taverns & drunkenness! After the evening meeting the girls & I pattered through the black mud to the Backhouses' lodgings in Finsbury Square. Jane looked well & handsome but unfortunately laid up with a broken arm occasioned by a fall from a pony. Hannah Backhouse was poorly upstairs. Jane, Eliza, Ann, the girls & I spent a cozey uninterrupted couple of hours.

24. Still answering Queries. I walked with Fred Tuckett to the India Docks to see the launch of the new steamer *British Queen*, 1836 tons, larger by 500 tons than any other on the ocean. It was a superb sight. Her début from the dock was as if a mountain removed into the midst of the sea.

25. Immediately after Meeting the girls & I posted off to the grand anti-slavery one at Exeter Hall. Having a platform ticket we secured a good place. About two or three thousand people present, Lord Brougham in the chair.

1. The Yearly Meeting of the Society of Friends.

26. The morning meeting was taken up by two very interesting questions. Joseph Eaton, Bristol Branch, teetotal-temperance-travelling Secretary, brought forward his views very strongly. The other question was that of appointing a Committee to visit & assist Westmoreland Quarterly meeting, many of whose members have been baptised & otherwise deviated from the practices of Friends. Meeting lasted till nearly 4. Ran home to dinner, then back to Bishopsgate & met W. E. Forster just arrived from Norwich by appointment.

6TH MONTH

1. We had a fine show of young cousinhood at breakfast, viz. Jonathan & Edward Backhouse's juveniles with their gentle cousin Eliza, & W. E. Forster. We proceeded by McAdamised roads, on account of Jane's broken limb, to Deville's lamp shop (367 Strand). We found the little old gentleman in his phrenological gallery containing 3,200 casts. We settled down in turn & were manipulated; the operation took about a quarter of an hour each. His characters of Eliza & Ann Backhouse with whom he commenced, appeared to us awfully correct. When our turn came, however, we thought we detected several discrepancies & a sort of family resemblance with those who had undergone the ordeal before us, as though he were pronouncing our characters under the influence of that impression. Mine according to Caroline's notes was as follows. 'Great kindness shown to young persons & those wanting protection. Strong in friendships but made with fear. Anger strong when offended, but rarely shewn. Firm in views & opinions. Sensitive to approbation but conscious of his own powers. Very high sense of honour & justice. The desire of property, but not sought parsimoniously. Respect for Religion but not led away by wild notions. For intellectual occupation, the development extremely good. Language, Classics, Literature, Science & the Physiology of things well understood & readily applied to highly useful purposes. Advice rather *given* than *taken*. Advice received if it convinces the *reason*.' The leading trait seemed to be that I am confident in my own powers, probably overmuch, & if I ever come forward in public life it will be from this confidence. Caroline's character he gave well, I think, laying much stress on her sensitiveness, but described her as diffident with strangers, which is glaringly false. A.M. he made an upright character with superior talents, but neither her moral nor intellectual influences did he place as high as they deserve.

2. I accompanied the girls to an appointment with Davies Gilbert. Found the old gentleman waiting for us. He put on his hat & accompanied us to the Royal Society's rooms at Somerset House. In the first room we entered was

Newton's reflecting telescope made by his own hands, the manuscript copy of the *Principia* most neatly & legibly written, the entrance book in which are all the members' autographs from its commencement. The lecture-room contains paintings of all their eminent men; the likeness of Davies Gilbert is very good. Met William Forster at Jonathan Backhouse's & carried him off to scour the city. Amongst other places we called on Baron du Potet, the animal magnetiser, and arranged to attend his experiments on 2nd day, also a penny panorama of the Fire of London, Death on the Pale Horse, & mass in the church of St. Jean, which proved, especially the first, very good & well worth the money.

3. Dined at Edward Harris's who is a thorough nice fellow. We had a good dinner & a good company to partake of it. He has three daughters, Isabella the youngest a pretty, lively, arch girl. Sounded her slightly & found her fair metal.

4. The girls & I proceeded after breakfast to lionize in the West End. Met Aunt C. & W. Forster at the Pantheon from whence we formed one party to the dwelling of the Baron du Potet, Physician extraordinary. He was operating on five patients when we entered. Some were put into a sound sleep, others became drowsy & spasmodic, starting as if under the influence of electric shocks. The action was produced by the Baron's drawing his hand in a peculiar manner from the eyebrows & chest of the patient. Generally speaking, in a few minutes the patient dropped into a sleep or something deeper, & as the manipulation continued, became violently convulsed, the hands clenched, the muscles rigid, &c. A child of eight years was brought & placed in a state of sympathetic magnetism with a young lady. Both fell asleep & were convulsed. Presently the child began to talk in a most strange, fearless, flippant way, her character seemed changed. She left her chair & said she would go to the Baron, which she did, though her eyes were closed fast. The Baron then set her in front of her co-patient who was immediately contracted & bent forward in the shape of a horse-shoe. Her muscles were so stiff that we could take her up in this extraordinary attitude & she retained it. The awakening took some time in one or two cases. I questioned some of the patients & was convinced that they had neither power nor purpose to play a hoax.

5. Accompanied the girls to St. Paul's hotel where they amalgamated with Uncle C. & Co. to pay a breakfast visit to Lady Geo. Murray. I amused myself with a little sight-seeing. First the Water Colour Exhibition. I then went to Moxon's, Chas. Lamb's publisher, & had a chat about that wondrous man. I bought *Elia* for W. Forster & wrote some lines at the beginning. Visited also Glagliardi's & Madame Tussaud's waxworks exhibitions, both of which are remarkably good. The subjects of the latter are the principal characters of the age & seem to be accurate likenesses. I nearly spoke to a

figure of old Cobbett which was sitting on one of the settees. We reassembled at St. Paul's & went back to Upton. Found that all our possessions were removed to Ham House where we accordingly dined & took up our abode.
13. Started about 7 in the gig to Leyton to meet the *Telegraph*. My companions were one drunken sailor who was rather troublesome & three great geese who pretended to be politicians & talked nonsense, so I read most of the way. We bowled along at 10 or 11 knots. Reached Norwich about 7 & found faithful W.E.F. in waiting.
14. Monthly Meeting. Anna Forster[1] paid us a visit in discipline. The way of carrying on business was rather singular. Some poor Friend, who had received 8/– per week from the Monthly Meeting, died & after the expenses of her funeral a balance of £4 remained, which Robert Blake insisted the Monthly Meeting ought to resume as their own property. This may be Quaker law but it seemed to me very unlike common law. Immediately after Meeting William & I hastily devoured some sustenance & set off in a gig for Northrepps Hall.[2] Reached Northrepps about 7. We proceeded to the coast. The country, bare & sandy, reminded me of Perranzabuloe.
15. About 9 we set off in a barouche in a coasting excursion. Proceeded & bundled out again at Mundesley to look at vegetable deposits & encroachment of the sea. Pushed on again till we reached Happisburgh where we ordered dinner & ran down to the coast. Bathed & explored & then returned to our inn. The landlord & landlady suffering from the dissipation of yesterday's fair delayed our dinner beyond the bounds of human patience so at last we obtained some fried pork & two or three dozens of eggs with which we managed to satisfy the cravings of nature. We then turned & got back to Northrepps to tea. Spent the evening in chess & conversation. William & I settled in soon after 2.
23. Started per *Phenomenon* at half-past six. William accompanied me to the coach office & took leave. He's a fine fellow. The coach cram full & refused about 20 applications for seats on the road. Reached Stratford at half-past nine whence a porter conveyed my traps to Ham House.
25. S. Gurney drove me to Town. A little tug steamer took me down to Westminster Bridge, landed there & walked to the Abbey to look at the preparations for the approaching ceremony. Booths were erected in every direction & by great good luck I secured a seat in one adjoining the Abbey-entrance for £1–1s. I joined Robert Barclay at half-past four, who drove me down to his house (The Grove) at Tooting, a comfortable place. Rachel adopts a sensible plan whilst alone, that of sending the servants out of the room during dinner. Spent a pleasant chatty evening varied with conjuring tricks, puzzles & chess.

1. The mother of W. E. Forster, whose parents now lived in Norwich.
2. The home of Sir Thomas Fowell Buxton who was a brother of Anna Forster.

26. Quarterly Meeting at Devonshire House. Met our party there who were well & in good spirits. We ordered post-horses & I escorted my Mother & sisters to Ham House. As they could not give me a bed I accompanied the former to John Fry's. The Master & Missus were out riding but I found from the servant that there was only one spare bed. I left my Mother & bolted. I made application at the only respectable inn at Stratford but was refused. I accordingly put up with accommodation at a public house over the way called the *King's Head*.

27. My bed was not of the finest or cleanest which enabled me to rise at half-past six. The bill amounted to 2/6. This included the comforts of tea, a bedroom, a sitting-room with 5 windows, 4 candles, slippers, &c. Breakfasted at Ham House. Catherine & Chenda Buxton came in afterwards. We took a pair of post horses & Bessie & Priscilla accompanied us to King's College to meet Professor Wheatstone by appointment. He exhibited the various wonders of his laboratory. We parted from the Gurneys & we three proceeded to the W. End. Walked through Hyde Park & looked at the enormous preparations in the way of fair & fireworks for tomorrow's festivities. London was never known so full. Progression on foot is no easy task, but in a coach in some parts of the city next to impossible. At the W. End the array of aristocratical equipages forms two continuous processions, one up & the other down, leaving hardly sufficient interval for pedestrians to cross.

28. We all posted off about 6 to see the raree-show. Dropped the girls at the Athenaeum & proceeded to my seat in the 'Abbey Box'. A squadron of life guards soon arrived & formed in front of the crowd so as to keep a clear space in front of the Abbey. From the time of my arrival at 7 to that of the procession at 11 there was one perpetual stream of the English nobility, principally peers & peeresses who all drove up to the door in their ermined scarlet robes with their coronets on their laps. At length the gun fired which told of the procession having started from St. James's & in about half-an-hour it appeared, a most unutterably imposing array. From where I sat I could see them all dismount but had the best view as they passed in order in front. The Duchess of Kent is a very striking woman. Her coach was stopped just in the right place for about a minute during which we cheered her lustily & she bowed on all sides. Some of the peeresses were magnificent creatures. The maids of honour preceded her Majesty in twelve of the royal coaches. They were all in white like so many sylphs & from the back of their heads flowed a zephyr-like gauze veil which reached to the ankle. But all the enthusiasm shown before was as nothing to that on the appearance of the grand actress herself. Her Majesty was dressed in white satin with her hair simply arrayed & looked every inch a queen, only one could have wished there were a few more inches of her. Whilst the ceremony proceeded we made a rush for victuals & succeeded though at a most exorbitant rate. Between

3 & 4 the coaches again drove to the door, the foreign ministers first appeared, then the ambassadors extraordinary. At length the royal coach drove up & our 'virgin queen' ascended the steps with regal dignity & self-possession. We greeted her with one tremendous & continuous cheer. As soon as the pageant had passed I bolted & cutting across St. James's Park to the Athenaeum fell in with the procession again. I pushed through the crowd & gained a nearer & better view of her Majesty than before. Joined my father & the girls at the Athenaeum & we proceeded to Buckingham Palace, but we got separated in the crowd & I found that not being able to thrid it they had returned home. I met a pleasant party at Grosvenor Place, Gurney Hoare & his wife, Robert & his, Arthur & his, with all the young Bromheads. After tea five of the gentlemen including myself took a ramble through Hyde Park where a remarkable fair is held, full of all description of entertainments & festivities, which is to last for three days. From thence Gurney Hoare & I made a thorough tour of Pall-Mall, Bond St., St. James & the adjacent streets to see the illuminations. The Ordnance, Crockford's, the National Gallery, the Duke of Sutherland's house, some of the Hotels & most of the Club houses were most brilliantly, gorgeously & tastefully be-lamped. But the fireworks in St. James's Park which began about 11 sent every other show all to nothing. It ended soon after 12 & I trudged my way back to mine inn. The Strand was in one blaze of light from the illuminations & transparencies. Reached home & turned in about half-past one, highly delighted with the retrospect of this never-to-be forgotten day.

29. My Mother arrived in the carriage soon after 9 but we were not fairly under weigh till nearly 11. My father remained behind having business to do. We dined at Reading & slept at Hungerford. Had some thunder & lashing rain in the afternoon.

7TH MONTH

3. Started a little before 8. We took the Tavistock & Callington road & notwithstanding hills right perpendicular we had good cause to be satisfied. At Morton we stopped to mend the dray & I had a sentimental opportunity with a pretty girl in the churchyard & a daft old crone she had led out to sun herself amongst the tombs. From Morton to Tavistock we had the agreeable variety of twenty miles of Dartmoor. From Callington to Liskeard it was superb.

4. We dined at the Allens, started at 4 (my father having joined us from Plymouth) & reached home at 11. The servants gave us a substantial welcome & we found our way into bed.

5. Went to the shop & gossipped with the clerks concerning all transactions commercial & amatory. Saddled our new black pony & rode to Penjerrick. I never saw a place looking more luxuriant, the oats fine, potatoes immense, carrots grand, but weedy as a man's heart, vetches very fair, hay quite ready to cut, sheep fat, horses in excellent order. The Evanses were really glad to see me, but Betsey still feeble.

11. Today had been fixed for a hay party to make merry at Penjerrick but it was otherwise ordained. The morning was ushered in with a drizzly skew which waxed into rain & though the afternoon was kinder it was too late to make the attempt. Called at Grove Hill & much admired a Murillo which Uncle G.C. picked up at a sale for 30/–.

21. The Tregelleses & a very agreeable Hanoverian of the name of Dagenhert dined here. He is a commissioner of some Colombian mines & a man of much science & general information. He told us that in the Hartz mines they have adopted a plan of ascending & descending similar to one laid before the Polytechnic Society; that of two vertical rods furnished with stages at certain distances, one of which is continually moving the length of a stroke which is the distance between two stages.

8TH MONTH

7. Joined the Harbour Committee at the Bar to see Lieut. Green's wind-sail dredging apparatus applied to the mud in the harbour. As I sagely foretold it proved but an airy scheme & ended in flatulence. The unhappy apparatus not only could produce no mud for our edification or propel the model one inch, but could not even carry itself round for a minute together when thrown completely out of gear so as to have no encumbrance or friction.

9. The Treweekes joined us in the evening. Georgina, the eldest, is one of the finest girls I ever saw, marvellous black eyes, all features in good keeping, beautiful symmetry & complexion. She stutters, which is a great drawback. They staid till 11 & seemed to enjoy themselves.

26. 1st day. My father went to Redruth on Meeting business. Uncle & Aunt C. dined with us. The latter engaged us to come & comfort her widow-hood at Trebah during the absence of her lord & ours when engaged at Scilly in the work of the ministry.

27. Engaged a Pilot boat to take Cos. Edwin & the rest of the mission to Scilly. My father being the leader of the party & this being his last day at home, he had a conference with me as to present arrangements & future prospects. As I become of age next week I am to have a third of his share in the business, commencing from the end of last 6th month which will prob-

ably be worth to me £120 per annum, with £1,000 now in the hands of Neath Abbey Co. & paying 4%. For this first year of my majority I am not to be considered a partner till my mind is made up as to how far I have capacity enough to undertake a share in the management & liking enough to stick to it.

9TH MONTH

3. Paid the queerest call on an elderly gentleman & his wife of the name of Durtnall. He is a doctor learned in tongues & well skilled in the interpretation thereof to the tune of 20 or 30 languages, a huge waddling mass of flesh surmounted by a very shiny bald head & the most everlasting talker I ever heard.
6. Twenty-one! I have emerged from the grub state! I am the same fellow as yesterday & yet there is a change, a sort of promotion in society of which I seem to have a vague sensation akin to that of a half-fledged mid just dubbed lieutenant. I had no celebration, no festivity, no fuss, three things I detest, but the lasting memorials I highly prize, viz. Loudon's Encyclopaedia of Agriculture, the family contribution, & Adam Clarke's Bible in 6 huge volumes, Uncle G.C.'s. It was a wet mawky day which prevented our taking tea at Penjerrick, the only spree we had projected. A rare letter from W.E.F.
13. This being the day appointed as celebration of the momentous event which occurred 21 years ago, I ordered in the cart from Penjerrick for Caroline & myself & the prog, & the rest of our party bestriding the beasts we congregated at the Farm to the amount of 16. We all stowed away in Evans's parlour, pretty close work, & attacked the cake built for the occasion, the syllabub, peaches &c. with much satisfaction.

10TH MONTH

2. Polytechnic opened today. There were 26 new inventions which shows that our Cornish barbarians are not much behind the progressive spirit of the age. My father explained his galvanic manufacture of veins & spoke well. We had a 'cold collection' set at the Bank where resorted all that would. At 7 o'clock Snow Harris gave a lecture on Magnetism which was well attended. We persuaded the Treweekes to lodge with us. Georgina is a glorious-eyed creature with a warm heart, comparative simplicity & an absence of affectation considering the admiration to which she must be liable.

3. This day in my estimation very much outstripped the one before in interest. The prizes were given at 12 & the competitors had to ascend the rostrum & explain the principles of their improvements. My father entered at length into the importance of the adoption of some plan for raising & lowering miners on the score both of humanity & economy. He explained the one in use in Germany & called on his fellow countrymen not to let themselves be outstripped by foreigners. He then informed the meeting that Uncle C. had that morning offered £100 to any mine that should first put into practice most effectively this desirable object, to this he added £50 & my Uncle G.C. £100. This noble act was received with shouts as it deserved. At 7 o'clock Wightwick gave the most brilliant lecture I ever heard; his subject was the Romance of Architecture.

9. Very busy with 4 pair of hands digging potatoes at Penjerrick. They turn out about 19 bushels, a tolerable produce for 28/-. Joined the Frys at Trebah. Uncle C.'s ground sean was shot by way of amusement & a very fair catch was made. The Frys charmed with Uncle & Aunt C. like everybody else. We returned about 9, pitch dark.

11. Despatched the Frys per *Drake* between 7 & 8, bearing with them our old chariot & took leave of my progenitors & invalid sister[1] at 11, they being bound on a valetudinarian expedition to Perranzabuloe where I look forward to joining them next week. Brownie the colt at last broken in, was seized with a most alarming attack of inflammation in the bowels. Bled and dosed him. Quartered at Grove Hill by day & return to Bank at night.

13. Attended a sale of damaged oats at Boyer's Cellars & bought a few hogsheads cheap. Poor Brownie in agonies of pain. Questioned whether it were not better to shoot him. Rode to Trebah to tea & lodge. Caught cold somehow. Hope not scarlet fever.

14. Walked before, & rode in to Synagogue[2] immediately after breakfast. Found the colt considerably better; the medicine had at length acted, & an external stimulant applied to the chest & stomach succeeded in producing perspiration which much relieved him. Called on Appleton who was with Cavendish in Town about a week since. Gives a very good account of the same. Dismal weather throughout the day.

15. The weather such as to prevent my driving Anna Maria to Perranporth, I started after breakfast solo except the companionship of Uncle G.C.'s black mare which carried me well. I entered the family mansion just in time to assist at the last rites over the fragments of a roast rabbit. All the inhabitants appeared to have undergone a thorough renovation in health & vigour. C. is all the better for her fever & my father took me a walk after dinner & astonished me as much by his rejuvenated physical powers as the sublimity

1. This was Caroline.
2. i.e. the Meeting House.

of the scenes of rock & billow to which he conducted me. Slept at the Inn.
16. Spent the morning in galloping across the sands with my sire exploring
some very striking caverns & then taking a run 'cross-country' to Wheal
Prudence, a little mine just beyond Cligger Head at the top of a cliff 360 feet
high. I descended to the bottom. The views on that spot are of the sort the
grandest I ever saw. So much of the terrible that it requires strong nerves to
look down on the mad surges which lash their sides & roar like wild beasts
as they are driven back in foam. Set off on a homeward voyage immediately
after dinner. A dismal drizzle was 'our portion' nearly the whole way.
Arrived at length, however, & once more assembled in full family at home.
Our happiness was clouded by the sudden death of poor Brownie.
17. Two Bible Society Secretaries quartered at our house to attend the
meeting appointed for tonight. The morning occupied in despatching 2
packet loads of passengers, amongst whom we had the pleasure of taking
leave of our old friends the Mexicans, & by the West India Packet we embarked a second batch of Abolitionists, to see that Blackey gets two half-
pence for his penny.[1] The Bible meeting which occupied the evening was
very well attended & proved I think above par. Andrew Brandram's[2] speech
I liked much, being matter of fact, to the point & free from twaddle. The
rest were much like other Bible meeting sermons. Aunt C. received such an
alarming account of her brother J. Hustler that she has determined on starting
for Bradford tomorrow morning.
23. Trudged to Penjerrick. Called at Tregedna. Marie Louise & J. Ellen left
the room & returned the most uncouth-looking black rascally chymney
sweepers I ever saw – old hats, coats, breeches & boots, with their faces &
hands blacked to the hue of ink. Such a pair as I wouldn't meet in a dark
lane for something. They sat on the sofa & conversed in Cornish. A knock
was heard at the door, which they immediately attended to & frightened a
poor Milliner's man & boy almost into fits.
26. I staid at Trebah & had an interesting & improving time with Uncle C.
Spent the afternoon in a long ramble on the other side of the river & the
evening in the study of magic & legerdemain. An interesting letter from
Aunt C. containing a better account of her brother.

1. These would have been Quakers who were visiting the W. Indies to see that the
emancipation of slaves was carried through with justice. Slavery in the colonies had been
abolished in 1834, but for a time the former slaves were still apprenticed labourers to
their owners. This arrangement produced injustices until complete emancipation took
place in 1838.
2. Andrew Brandram was secretary of the Bible Society.

11TH MONTH

1. Weather still far from settled. Exercised well nevertheless, calling at the Collier's about a horse, & Dr. Durtnall to make enquiries. Found him as usual all fullness & fluency. He is resolved to lecture on Michael Angelo for the benefit of the Polytechnic gallery.

2. Rode to Trebah to breakfast, after which rode with Uncle C. to Gunwallow & Mullion on the Mount's Bay. Stormy weather & the waves grand. Lunched at Mullion. On returning to Helford found the river too rough to transport the horses & had to leave them behind. Borrowed a small boat and pushed off when a blustering fellow came down & demanded a passage. Uncle C. too civil to him & took him across. Turned out to be Lieut. Lawry of the *Delight*. Heavy rain as we reached Trebah for a good fire & good dinner. Turkey & champagne. Spent a rational social evening.

6. Drove my father to Truro to attend a meeting of the Institution.[1] We had rain all the way & back again & were scantily repaid for the effort. Sir C. Lemon's speech was interesting tho' rather in matter than manner for he stammered sadly. He brought forward his scheme of founding a school for miners to educate young men in the scientific & mathematical principles on which mining operations depend. He agrees to support it entirely the 2 first years of its existence & endow it on his death, provided the County will do their share. The Truro Institution gives a room for the lectures. A paper of Uncle C. on a new variety of shark caught by a Durgan fisherman was read. We came home to a 6 o'clock dinner hungry as hunters.

7. An almost hopeless account from Bradford. Uncle C. much affected. Had the pleasure of a visit from no less a man than O'Brien,[2] founder of that Sect, a shrewd old fellow enough for that line of life, with all the verbiage & scriptural idiom common to his followers, but apparently unrefined & but little educated. His appearance & manner speak the sectarian & zealot. He had just returned from America & was very full of the exposure of Free Masonry which has lately taken place there. Bought one of his books containing the Ritual & all the Mysteries of that Body.

8. Attended an abstinence meeting held by a man called Cassell, a Liverpool carpenter. His address was liable to the same objection as almost all the others of his clan, enlarging on the evils & horrors of drunkenness, in which all agreed, instead of the benefits or expediency of their peculiar system, the point in question. He nevertheless appeared to be gifted with a peculiar native eloquence, much humour, & a forcible earnestness of style & manner.

1. The Royal Institution of Cornwall, founded 1818.
2. William O'Bryan had been born in 1778 at Luxulyan, Cornwall. He changed his name from Bryant. He was the founder of the Bryanites or Bible Christians and had emigrated to America in 1831.

14. Tried a horse & found it wanting. The *Splendid* arrived with our cargo of hemp. Had a biggish dinner party. Dr Durtnall talked one unceasing torrent. He never can be profound with such a length of the 'little member'. His wife is intensely silly & without sense enough to see that she is so, interrupting others' conversation with the most absurd & frivolous remarks.

20. At 8 o'clock in the morning Uncle A. appeared in my room announcing the arrival of an E. Indiaman, put in with 7 feet of water in the hold. It is the *Larkins*, Capt. Ingram, between 7 & 800 tons register. 2 nights since the Scilly pilot ran her on the Nundeep rock & knocked a great hole in her bottom. Yesterday the Captain landed at Penzance to procure a steamer to tow his ship up the channel. Failing in this he proceeded to Falmouth & applied to us for the same purpose. Whilst discussing the subject with Uncle A., about ½ past 9 the ship entered the Roads, the Coverack pilot who took charge of her in Mount's Bay having sent on shore to Cadgwith for men at about 5 o'clock & procured from thence 30 able hands belonging to our sean, with R. Rundell at their head. They boarded just as the crew had lowered the long boat & fixed on abandoning the ship. The Surveyors having given their report as to the necessity of discharging, White and I went on board, engaged 2 smacks in our way from 30 to 40 tons each, loaded them & brought them to the cellars. A temporary clerk, P. Buckett, engaged. Moved the ship up on the mud with the evening's tide. Sent a fresh gang of men off to the pumps & got the water under about a foot. Her cargo consists of saltpetre, jute, indigo, sugar, silk, rice, turmerick &c. worth from 50 to 60,000 £s. It is a fine thing for the place. We employ every man that can wheel a barrow & have not much idle time ourselves.

21. Hard at work all day loading and discharging. We put the indigo, silks, &c. in the bonded warehouse & the goods of inferior value in Boyer's Cellars.

22. Boarded Capt. Plumridge before he was dressed & then the *Astraea* & 4 or 5 packets to get sailors to strike the ship's topmasts. Engaged about 20 hands & went on board to give notice & get a snack of breakfast. The water pumped up continuing to taste very strong of saltpetre, I took off a large boat with 7 great rumpuncheons & a hawse & filled them with the water coming out of the scuppers. We were discharging lighters till nearly 10 when stopped by the rain.

23. Engaged in commercial, agricultural, & chemical engagements. Began the day by discharging goods, principally sugar & linseed. Then got a puncheon down into the Bank kitchen with some labour & filled their boiler over the furnace with the nitrous water. No crystallization or sediment, however, by the end of the day. Undertook the landing of a cow & 3 China pigs from the Indiaman. Much difficulty in getting the former on shore. Carried the 2 little pigs whilst Edey drove their mother with a great root of seaweed to a temporary residence. Landed 6 lighter loads today. Got

on shore another cargo of the pump water, but on tasting found it to contain no nitre. The evening's report accounted for this; the fresh gang of men have reduced the water to 18 inches, which is below the bottom of the saltpetre.

24. Today ushered in by a storm from the Eastward. Loaded 3 lighters notwithstanding & discharged at Boyer's. Whilst engaged in settling with the porters in the evening, Sampson entered the office aghast and announced that Firefly's leg was broken. I went with him to the Bank stable horror-struck & held an examination. Went in search of Vigurs. He pronounced it a dislocation of the little pastern with the coffin bone. Anthony maintained it was a fracture. The former is clearly right, the shortness of the bone making breakage all but impossible. It was the consequence of shameful carelessness, the Bank groom having taken up the iron disc which covers the drain, to be repaired, & leaving the hole open & covered by the litter. Sampson while hanging up a martingale, put the mare in the stall & on taking her out, her hind leg slipt in, she plunged & fell on her side. Sampson drew out her leg & found the pastern projecting over the hoof. We bound up her leg in flannel saturated with a cooling mixture which we moistened every half hour. Dined at Grove Hill. Ran to the stable immediately after & rigged up an old sack with a rope at each corner which we passed under her belly & made fast to 4 staples fixed on each side of the stall. This was a great relief to her. Sampson sat up with her all night.

25. Sunday. A cold dark day, wind strong from the E. Ran down the first thing in the morning to visit the invalid. She is doing better than I expected. There is little or no swelling nor apparent inflammation. She eats with an appetite & occasionally rests some weight on the frail member. The slings are a great help to her in changing her position. Called on young Powell, son of the consignee of part of the *Larkins'* cargo. He escorted here the Captain's wife. Uncle Charles dined & 3 of Squire's boys did tea here.

27. A thorough hurricane from SSE all night & greatest part of the day, but it fell dead calm by night. Many vessels coming in damaged. We hardly know yet to what extent. Two vessels were wrecked a little the other side of St. Anthony's point this morning, a chasse-maree, with wheat for Plymouth, 3 men drowned, & a schooner from London, also with wheat, run on the beach. P. Buckett went over there. Found the remaining 4 Frenchmen at old Miss Martin's. Nobody there could understand them & the poor fellows were glad enough to find somebody who could give explanations & recom-mendations in their own language. Wind changed to SW.

28. 19 individuals showed themselves at Meeting; the storm was terrific. The harbour sometimes appeared all in a smoke so as to eclipse the vessels. Glass never remembered so low, about 27°.30. Neap tides. Nevertheless the water was running thro' Cos. Hester's shop, up to T. Olive's House, sweeping

all over Gillan Vaise & Swanpool. Magnificent waves dashing bodily over the cliffs. Never saw such beauties here.

29. Still very heavy gale from SW. More damaged vessels coming in. Held survey on a brig from San Domingo & ordered her to discharge. Uncle C. & Juliet came to lodge &c. Busy as an ant. Hardly time to write this.

12TH MONTH

3. The *Iberia* arrived, having put back with loss of rudder. All people, nations & languages appear to be flocking here, Americans, Swede, Dutchman, Bremener &c. arrived today in addition. Went on board the Indiaman alongside Flushing quay. We are discharging the damaged goods left in her hold, the *Ruby*'s coffee, & the *Swift*'s silver at the same time, so our hands are tolerably full.

5. Business with a vengeance. I was not able to leave the desk except 10 minutes for dinner from 10 till 7. We had 8 extra hands at work. The Dublin Steamer came in during the morning & had to wait while we shipped the money & made out Bills of Lading. This latter department fell to my share & was no joke, tho' I had 4 volunteers assisting. Our share of the prey was 800,000 Dollars for which 72 Bills to make out. However, we vanquished the enemy by tea-time, discharging 3 or 4 vessels at the same time.

6. Called on Captain Smith of the Norwegian man-of-war *Ornen*. I was received in state. Ladder manned, &c. Tight time of it when I came on shore, making out about 30 accounts & writing the specie owners. At it till 20 minutes to 12.

7. Turned up at 6 & went on board the Indiaman to see if she could be moved that tide. Failed however. Captain Ingram in a rage. Ran out to Penjerrick. Borrowed a launch & anchor & called on Clackworthy at ½ past 11 at night to get another to warp the *Larkins* into the Roads.

8. According to last night's arrangement I turned out at ½ past 5. Went on board the *Astraea* at 6. Found, as I feared, that no second launch had been engaged. Managed to borrow one, however, from the frigate & a kedge anchor from the coffee brig in the pier. Wrote an order for it on the back of a letter & got the captain to sign it in bed. Sent the anchor on board the *Larkins*. Meanwhile 3 sails were set & 3 launches had her in tow. It was a beautiful morning & a fair wind & we got her out prosperously. Called on Captain Ingram to inform him of the same. He appeared as yesterday *in nocturnalibus*. Call from the Norway Captain. Plenty of fag at shop. Dinner party at 5. Captain Ingram & wife, Captain Wathen, & Dr. O'Gorman, British Consul general at Mexico, & brother, & W. Fenwick. A pleasant party – no drag. It went off well & everybody was pleased.

11. Very interesting day. A Captain Ellerby has arrived on the part of the Underwriters to settle with the parties who claim salvage on the *Larkins*. The hearing of the case occupied the day till ½ past 4. Rundell & his men were first heard. After a statement of services rendered they asked £1500. Ellerby made a tender of £300 for the 23 men & £40 for Rundell. This they positively refused & stated £1100 as their lowest. Lieut. Brewer, Revenue Officer, accompanied by his Commander, Captain Morgan, was next heard. His claim was for boarding the ship from Cadgwith & tendering his services which were declined, it seems, by the mate. In about an hour he desired his men to join Rundell's at the pumps & remained on board till she reached Falmouth. He made no claim but waited for the offer. This was the same to his men as had been offered Rundell's with £11 odd per man & £20 for himself. This was at once refused but no specific claim made. He was then dismissed. The Pilot (James) being introduced he considered himself the ultimate cause of the vessel's safety, in having staid by the ship & sent for the men. He demanded £500. £100 was offered together with his Pilotage £8. Refused. Came down to £400 as his lowest. Ellerby writes the Underwriters tonight a statement of the several claims, & requests an answer per return. The men engage not to enter into legal proceedings in the meantime on his pledging that it shall not be to their prejudice. A heavy cold confined me after dinner.

15. A letter being received from the Underwriters who refuse to make any advance on their offer to the claimants on *Larkins*, the pilot first & afterward Rundell's party consented to accept it rather than throw it into the Admiralty court. R. Rundell throughout has acted exceedingly well. Lieut. Brewer had before consented to let his claim be decided in the same proportion as that of Rundell's crew, so now all is settled & much better for the Underwriters than I at all expected.

17. Dined at Grove Hill. Met the Ingrams, Captain Ellerby, Durtnalls & my amiable friend Sammy Pellew. The evening went off sociably enough. The Doctor had his full swing & his sea-faring auditors went away duly impressed with his gigantic intellect. His wife as ridiculous as ever. The lord of the manor[1] very gracious & gentlemanly.

18. Finished those stupendous accounts of the old ship by tea time. The Captain examined every item with the eye of a ferret, blustering at the Commission &c. & behaved in a far from gentlemanly manner. However, it was at last satisfactorily closed & we had the pleasure of seeing his back & wishing him a fair wind. I had a small private breeze with him in the morning being told that he had cavilled at my insufficient charge of 4/- for a week's keep of his beasts. I told him a bit of my mind. Returned the paltry sum he grumbled at & insisted on his retracting what he had said as to shabby conduct, which he did with a bad grace & pocketed his bawbees.

1. i.e. Uncle G.C.

23. Mild & moist. Called at Grove Hill. Duchess of Palmella arrived bound to Lisbon.

24. Dismal stormy weather. Called on the Duchess & escorted her, her daughter's suite, & luggage on board the Tagus Steamer in a launch we borrowed of Capt. Plumridge for the purpose. It was a thorough gale of wind. We shipped several seas & some of the ladies were not a little frightened. The Duchess is a dignified & ladylike woman. Bought a black mare of a man called Trerise for 15 guineas. Took another very pretty one belonging to Captain Sampson of Chacewater on a week's trial.

25. It was a merry way of spending Xmas Day with a vengeance that of attending Monthly at Truro. We persuaded our mother with some difficulty to stay at home. Rode Captain Sampson's mare. I liked her much, she was amiable, gentle & lively. Full Meeting. Wind changed to NE. Frost.

26. Wind backed to the SW & brought with it a searching driving rain which lasted the whole day. Returned to Truro, it being Quarterly. W. Hoskins & S. Rundell gave us good sermons. Ann Tweedy visited our Meeting & gave us a close discourse on restraints & small departures in appearance & ended with a controversy with the little lads' cloth caps.[1] My father resigned his Commission as Clerk. A. Jenkins promoted to the office. Rode home directly after Meeting & got a drenching as I anticipated.

27. Our ordeal came at length; I thought till yesterday we had escaped, but the Committee's report of not having finished their family visitations destroyed the sweet delusion. On returning from my morning's avocations I found them assembled in full conclave, consisting of Messrs. Allen, Budge & Veale, Eliza Allen & Mary Jenkins. We 'dropped into silence' without any loss of time & after being in a 'gathered' state for a $\frac{1}{4}$ of an hour were interrupted by a violent ring & a loud 'Is Mr. Fox at home?', which we recognized as the voice of Sir C. Lemon. I went out to our most unseasonable visitor who popped in as it were on purpose to give the Committee an idea of worldly associations. I explained that my father was particularly engaged & bowed him out of the house. On returning the lecturing commenced, but the handling was so lenient that it hardly deserved the name. E. Allen's strain was that of affectionate interest & desires for our best welfare which was taken I hope with thankfulness. I couldn't see on what grounds they made a regular meeting of it, for though some of them were regular ministers, they were not appointed in that capacity, but as individuals to enquire into the state of the society & administer counsel when needed. They dined with us but left soon after.

1. There was a good deal of discussion at this time in the Society of Friends about the preservation of the traditional dress and speech of the Quakers. As late as the Yearly Meeting of 1849 there was a discussion concerning the insistence laid by the Society on the mode of dress and speech as a qualification for office, however minor, in the Society.

28. A family of the name of Lyne particularly introduced by the Sabines arrived today from Dublin.[1] The party consists of a young clergyman, wife, sister & 3 young children. I accompanied them to Flushing & had a grand hunt to obtain lodgings, it being their object to pass the winter there on account of the gentleman's having burst a blood vessel. We found no house suitable except the Molesworths' who are from home. We accordingly at length fixed on the Tregelles's for a week during which time arrangements are to be entered into with the Molesworths for their house during the winter. They are, I think, something of an acquisition. He is a man of intelligence but a great invalid. His wife is pretty & vapid, but his sister is a girl of excellent sense, judgment & energy & is evidently the managing partner, careful without fidgets, & planning without bustle. My father & the girls rode to Carclew for a morning call but Sampson only returned. He brought a note to inform us that an Egyptian Bey & Dr. Bowring[2] had arrived for a day or two & they had decided on lodging there; then followed particular directions for various articles of female attire which pass under the comprehensive name of 'things'. Mammy & I spent a pretty sociable evening.

29. Called on the Lynes. They are comfortable. Brig put in damaged & must discharge. Our truants did not arrive till after 10. They came in a state of high excitement of delight with all they had seen & heard. Dr. Bowring was the charmer & Edhem Bey the curiosity of the party.

1. The Lynes were to become close friends of the Foxes. Major (later Sir Edward) Sabine was a distinguished explorer who had accompanied Ross and Parry on their expeditions to the Arctic, 1818–20. He and his wife were friends of the Foxes.
2. Dr (later Sir John) Bowring became editor of the *Westminster Review* in 1825. He was a disciple of Jeremy Bentham and became Liberal M.P. for Kilmarnock in 1835. He was an advocate of Free Trade before Bright and Cobden. Having lost his seat for Kilmarnock in 1837 he visited Egypt and brought back with him Edhem Bey, the Egyptian Minister of Instruction. A fuller account of Bowring's visit is given in Caroline Fox's *Journal*.

1839

BARCLAY FOX continues to be busy with the affairs of the family shipping firm. He spends a good deal of his spare time at Penjerrick, where he sets up bachelor quarters, cultivates the estate, and engages in small-scale farming. There is a constant stream of visitors: friends and relatives; those seeking health in Cornwall or embarking at Falmouth for a warmer climate abroad; foreign dignitaries, ships' captains, men of science, business associates. In the autumn the house at Penjerrick is enlarged to provide a second home for Barclay's parents and sisters, as well as himself. In October of this year we meet the first reference in the Journal to the construction of railways in Cornwall. In 1834 the Bodmin and Wadebridge railway had been opened and plans were afoot for a line from Hayle to Tresavean, with branches to Redruth and the Roskear and Crofty mines. These projects were connected with the transport of ores from the mines, but the leading citizens of Falmouth were concerned with the protection of Falmouth as a packet port for overseas mail. With the advent of steamships they realised that the packets might easily move further up the English Channel to Plymouth, Southampton or Portsmouth. With the possibility of quicker land transport by railway, they calculated that they might meet this challenge; their hopes were not in fact realised, but the Journal records the efforts made to preserve the fortunes of Falmouth and to expand those of the rest of Cornwall. At the end of the year there is the excitement of an impending by-election for Falmouth and Penryn.

1ST MONTH

1. Resolved even whilst putting this pen to this paper to be less prolix from this time forward except on particular occasions. Penjerrick. New Year's dinner with tenantry, goose & plum pudding. Balanced farm account.
4. Drove to Truro & ordered a Britzska[1] of Carvosso for £71 all complete, estimate having been sent before. Called at Carclew. Dined at Bank.
8. Called on Monsignor di Silvera, Dom Pedro's[2] Minister of Finance, a snuffy old chap & deaf. Report in town that I aided & abetted an abduction, the little girl whom I escorted on board the *Tagus* with the Duchess of Palmella proving to be the stolen bride of the Marquis of Fayal.

1. A light four-wheeled carriage.
2. See p. 47n. above.

10. Rode to Perran to breakfast. Found the inmates very so-so with bad colds, Aunt C. especially, but she was not looking amiss, & was cheerful. The Manchester & Birmingham train broke down with her which obliged her to stop 1½ hours on a bank under a tree in middle of the night. Brings bright account of her brother. Mammy's night much disturbed by cramp. In a low spot all day. Had to act the part of arbiter & pacifier in a grand squall between Thomas & Sampson.

11. Sampson gave warning,[1] or rather expressed an intention of so doing, which I hearing, kept him to his word. Great lamentation amongst the maids who thoroughly spoilt him. Dined at my cottage. Season of slush. Mother better.

19. Called on Suttons & Lynes who are settled at Flushing with addition of a mother & aunt. My father wrote C. Tottie, Swedish & Norwegian Consul, to appoint me Vice Consul instead of himself. Wind strong from N.

23. Received from C. Tottie (Consul General) my appointment of Swedish & Norwegian Vice-Consul at Falmouth; the grace of the act was however destroyed by his charge of £10.10 as Secretary's fee.
Note:– This I declined paying – & never did.

24. Called at Little-in-Sight before breakfast to enquire after T. Evans's brother who was all but killed the day before yesterday, being knocked down in the street by a horse at full speed which had broken to pieces the gig to which it was fastened & set off with the shafts bang thro' the town. He was today if anything better but still insensible. The back of the skull they fear is fractured. The Doctor gave his long talked-of lecture on Michael Angelo & came off much better than I expected. We had a sizeable dinner party who came some to attend the lecture & some the Polytechnic annual meeting held this morning. C. Taylor dressed up in my mother's things in preparation for the fancy ball tomorrow. It had a remarkable effect.

31. Winter at last. Woke in a world dazzlingly white. Snow ankle deep. Snow storms at intervals thro' the day. Mail not in till 2. Attended meeting of Budock Landowners to settle on Surveyor & Tithe apportioners for the Parish. Fixed on an Irishman, W. Smith, for the former, who tenders to do it & map it at 8d. per acre, & on W. Rowe, Corfield, & Edwards for the latter business for £100. An Apparition 6 ft. & a half high entered the dining room in the evening. A letter of introduction it brought to my father explained it to be a runaway American slave called Moses Roper who is lecturing thro' the country on the system of Yankee Slavery.

---

1. i.e. gave notice.

2ND MONTH

1. A sharp frost last night, succeeding yesterday's snow, made a noble slide of the roads. Called on Roper. He is son to General Roper & has written an account of his escape, which he sells at the end of his lectures: he is a sensible shrewd fellow, but very sparing of his words. Splendid day so ran out to Penjerrick. Dined with Uncle J. In the evening the wind changed, rapid thaw.

2. Mild & slushy. Finished *Oliver Twist*. Wonderful & admirable work. The workhouse, the parish apprentice, the whole system of villainy practised by the thieves & their employers, are laid open with a consummate knowledge & a graphic power which Dickens alone of the present day possesses.

4. Wet weather all day. Called at the Lynes & our gigantic friend Moses, who dined with us & afterwards lectured at Baptist meeting on American slavery. His accounts were diabolical. The iron chains, anklets, &c. & other similar mementos as ornamental as useful, were exhibited from the pulpit. If his statements are true on the whole, allowing for personal prejudice, the 'free & enlightened' planters are the most inhuman & detestable tyrants on the face of the earth.

6. The great & long expected day arrived. Proceeded to Grove Hill at 6 where soon assembled a party of 20 to 30. The Dr. was the star. At half-past 7 all adjourned to the Dining Room which was handsomely prepared for Dr. Durtnall's recapitulation of his lecture on Michael Angelo. It was a lecture with a vengeance, the body thereof being all a digression. He ceased by $\frac{1}{2}$ past 11, after his audience had dropped off by ones & twos, having 3 auditors to hear the finale. (The fact was – between you & me – the Dr. was drunk!) He flew at length into a consummate rage with his audience for want of taste & broke up in a huff.

7. Sale of *Leander*'s sulphur. Sold well. Called at Grove Hill. Aunt Lucy bowed down with mortification. Called at the Dr.'s who was in good spirits & said he should have gone on till 5 had he not been stopped. Rode to Penjerrick. Bank party came to stay a few days.

18. Called on the Duke of Palmella & daughter, Sampejo family, & the 3 principals of Gribble, Hughes & Co., gentlemen on their way to Canton to establish a House. The Steamer not in till after 9 p.m. instead of starting at 10 a.m., the effect of taking coals at Plymouth. The *Alert* put back with loss of topmasts. M. le Baron landed & re-embarked on the *Reindeer*. Uncle A. returned from Wales. Attended Polytechnic Committee.

24. 1st day. Called on Aunt Mary who I think very ill.

25. Spent 2 hours in Aunt Mary's bedroom till 10 in evening. Uncles J., A. & G.P. were also there, doing the little that could be done to soothe and comfort her. Her appearance was much altered, deathly, hands clammy,

voice feeble & broken, pulse 107, continual feeling of oppression & choking. By opening both door & window a strong current of air was produced, yet she still cried out for more air. Her 2 servants supported her up in bed. We were alternately employed in fanning & administering tea, brandy & water, narcotic medicine &c. It was evident that Nature's conflict could not last long.

26. This morning brought the news that I anticipated. My Aunt Mary's long pilgrimage is over, the flesh has sunk beneath its burden of years & the spirit is gone home, a blessed change no doubt. She died this morning about ½ past 3 being in her 89th year. The poor & fatherless will long lament her loss.

28. Splendid fire on Eresey Terrace. Ran up there but too late to do anything; the house being thatched was very soon burnt down. It was late in evening. Scene very Rembrandtish & picturesque.

3RD MONTH

6. The mortal part of poor Aunt Mary was consigned to the grave today. A large concourse attended. The Meeting solemn & interesting. The coffin was brought into the Meeting-House. The generation above us dined at Uncle Thomas's. The younger branches assembled there in the evening.

7. The Reading of the Will by the executors took place today. Each of the children of the Plymouth branch have £250. Uncles A., G.P., & J. £1,000 each. Rest £100. Poor old Jimmy Drew, father of Susan, toppled over the quay-head this afternoon & was drowned. Intense cold. Thermometer last night 23°.

8. Morning clear & cold. Accompanied Aunt C. to Perran to breakfast. Walked thence to Truro to inspect progress of carriage &c. Called on Capt. Pengelley, to try his horse. It being out he agreed to bring it to Falmouth next week. Met Tom to my astonishment who speered me out at the Coach-makers. Having his pony, we took turns thereupon to Perran, where we ballasted & proceeded in same style to Penjerrick. Spent pleasant evening & trudged home together.

18. Ran out to Penjerrick. On return found Don M. Moreno (Buenos Ayrean Minister to London) at office, just landed from *Seagull*, highly indignant at the unsubservient disposition of the Custom House officers in not allowing his baggage to pass unsearched in virtue of his office. On return-ing through the Moor[1] heard 2 of the 'Chartists' (deputies from 'the grand

1. The town square at Falmouth.

Convention'[1] in the North) holding forth to the populace on the oppression of the poor, tyranny of government, slavery of governed, & they bitterly complained of the unnecessary tax of a war establishment after 23 years' peace, the injustice of every Englishman not being entitled to vote, the iniquity of new poor law &c. Called on all to come forward & sign their petition.[2] 'We *demand* universal suffrage &c.' Said Christ was crucified between 2 thieves & so were the English people between the Whigs and Tories. Both speakers were eloquent, one especially so, very specious & plausible, adducing from the mass of statutes just those which bore out his position & produced an effect. Both were inflammatory, not to say seditious, shrewd designing scamps, *ignes fatui* misguiding honest men with a blaze of enthusiasm. Can't do much harm here, I think. People too well off to kick up a row. The hearty cheers seemed to indicate that a flame was lit, but I know enough of Falmouth zeal to feel pretty sure of its going out unless well fanned.

21. Attended a Polytechnic Committee in which Jordan introduced & described his new photogenic inventions. One application of the sensitive paper to self-register barometric observations, the other to diary the sun's light, the aspect of the day &c., very simple & pretty.

27. Saw my father off by the *Regulator* at ½ past 6 for Bodmin. At Fish Strand saw a horse in a cart belonging to a woman of Illogan. I tried him in saddle & harness & bought him before breakfast for £20. Some doubts expressed afterwards of his soundness, on which account the woman is to call again at end of week, & if we don't like him, take him back with 10/- for loss of time. Filled up voting paper for guardians[3] for Budock.

28. Attended vestry at Budock to count votes for guardians. Some demur made by parish officers to the presence of us non-commissioned ones.[4] We however staid & saw the numbers made up, which were Fox 123, Symons 113, Falck 185, Hamilton 174. So the laird of Grove Hill is held less worthy of the office than the Penryn 'Kiddlywinker'[5] by 51 votes.

30. Tackled the 'Chouster' & called on her to fulfil her agreement & take back horse. Got a swarm of fishwomen with their male appendages about my ears & that was all I received in the way of satisfaction. Highly annoying.

---

1. The Chartist Movement drew up the 'People's Charter' in 1838. This demanded, amongst other things, universal suffrage for all adult males. A body called the National Convention was elected by the Chartists in 1839.
2. A petition in favour of the Charter, signed by a million and a quarter people, was presented to Parliament in June 1839.
3. The Poor Law Act was administered by Boards of Guardians elected by householders in groups of parishes known as unions.
4. i.e. those who were not householders.
5. Ale-house keeper.

My father vexed at the business. Consulted Tilly[1] who gives little encouragement & advised us to make the best of it. Floods of rain.

4TH MONTH

3. Old Moll Rowe, father of the porters, but a drunken old scamp, fell over the quay & was drowned in the night.

5. Attended a Polytechnic Committee. Model of a mine ascent machine sent from Fowey Consols.[2] Proves to be precisely Lean's[3] plan which gained first premium.

9. Joys of a Monthly. Sundry pepper & salt sermons in the discipline meeting. Called at the Lancastrian School,[4] which is going to the dogs as fast as neglect on the part of the late master and refractoriness on that of the boys can send it.

13. I have been disturbing the dust of generations in hunting thro' old ledgers half a century back to trace out Aunt Mary's account in order to make a final settlement. Walking with my father before dinner he made the following proposition: to exchange the £1000 given me on my majority for 1/64th in the Neath Abbey Works & 1/64th in the Colliery, the money not being clearly transferable from its present place. To this I gladly acceded.

14. Joseph Robinson, traveller of the Colebrook Dale Iron Co. to tea. They turn out 1400 tons per month besides small castings. They now have an order for 800 tons of rolled plates for the Gt. Western Co., who are building another steamer,[5] larger than the former & all of iron, which seems to be a material likely to come into general use for ship building.

17. A day of general excitement to the Falmouth fair, being the *Misericordia* Sale. Misericordia, the name, appears to allude to the perilous situation our hearts are placed in on these occasions, as the fair sellers whilst puffing off the charms of their delicate merchandize are not quite forgetful of their own & often do as much business through the attraction of the one as the other.

1. Tobias Tilly, solicitor of Falmouth.
2. Fowey Consolidated Mines at Tywardreath, where experiments were made with a 'man machine', or winding gear, for lifting men out of the mine.
3. Joel Lean (1779–1856), mining engineer and friend of the Foxes.
4. Joseph Lancaster (1778–1838), an educationist, introduced a primary school system in which the older children taught the younger. He set up his first school in the Borough Road, London, and adopted the monitorial system there. No fees were charged but parents contributed what they could afford. Lancaster was a Quaker but was disowned by the Society of Friends because he could not settle his debts. The Lancastrian school in Falmouth was founded in 1812.
5. The *Great Britain*, designed by Brunel and built 1838–44.

There were but few stars of considerable magnitude, but the articles for sale were above average & altho' there seemed to be no attendance except from the immediate neighbourhood, the result surpassed any former year, wanting but a few shillings of £100. Hercules being ill & unable to sleep all night I visited him before dressing & thought it best to send for Cos. Joe who pronounced it scarlet fever. We accordingly lit a fire in the schoolroom put a bed therein & having made it comfortable removed him there & sent for his mother who has a bed in the adjoining room.

18. Hercules better. Dr. Joseph retracts his opinion as to the nature of his complaint, pronouncing it now a violent cold & at his mother's request he was removed to Perran. The auction of the 'lave'[1] of yesterday's sale brought £26.17.8. Things went low. Called on the members of the Committee of the Lancastrian School & assembled them on the spot at 11 o'clock. Received a report of general behaviour, ranged the black sheep, 10 in number, against the wall, went into their offences, lectured all & condemned 7 to expulsion this day week, unless a very decided amendment be manifested between this & then.

21. 1st day. Uncle Thomas accosted Uncle Charles today in a most wrathful & ungentlemanly manner on the subject of Aunt Mary's accounts, accusing him of cruelty for not having given them him before, but that he had some spirit left & he would resort to other methods to obtain what he required. Nothing could be more uncalled for. Arranged an excursion to Caerhays Castle[2] tomorrow by water.

22. Started at 9 in the Clarks' trawler, our party consisting of our family & guests (barring Mammy), Uncles C., G.P., & A., the latter bringing his 2 boys & Hannah. Had glorious weather all day, a little too calm. Dined on board & landed at 1. Caerhays is a remarkable old place just this side the Deadman.[3] A fine long rambling Gothic castle with turrets & towers in abundance, curiously situated very near the sea, the late seat of Squire Trevanion, whose style of living was that of a nobleman; he is now an outlaw & all his goods & chattels, House, Stock, & Estate are brought to the hammer by Sheriff's order: a melancholy moral on extravagance & dissipation. The Sale was proceeding in the stable yard. The only things worthy of admiration were the house itself, the horse 'Marvel', the St. Bernard's dog, a splendid & gentle creature, & some of the bedsteads, the furniture generally inferior & the library decidedly 2nd rate. Left at 4 & had a pleasant cruize home, which, however, took us 5 hours, the wind being nearly ahead. Drank tea on board & came to our moorings as the clock struck 9.

1. A dialect word meaning 'the remainder'.
2. St Michael Caerhays, a castle rebuilt to the designs of John Nash, by the owner, John Trevanion.
3. Dodman Point.

25. Attended the Committee meeting at the Lancastrian School & expelled 2 reprobates, who have passed thro' their week of grace without amendment. Called on Tilly & requested him to apply for a summons for M. A. Roberts, mother of one of our boys, who hearing of her son's being kept in for some offence made a forcible entrée into the schoolroom & knocked down our worthy little master.

5TH MONTH

1. The 1st of May was duly introduced with all the horrors of tin horns & kettles & little boys, a consequence was that the oratorical powers of our school committee were exercised on only a dozen or two little urchins who hadn't pluck enough to take leave for a holiday. Called on the parents of 2 of the refractories who made the same remark that I have often heard, 'That we cannot expect to keep up proper discipline in a school, much less reform a rebellious one without some system of punishment therein'. Miss Drummond sent out her cards to all her young compeers to come and celebrate her nativity. We had a maypole & snap dragon & various species of romps, highly amusing & instructive.

2. Rode to Perran to breakfast & there remained *till tomorrow*, completing Aunt Mary's accounts from data obtainable there. Whilst thus engaged, in walked Uncle Lewis who reappeared the day before yesterday after a 7 months' absence. He looked paler than before his departure, but equally, if not more bulky. He has been laid up with illness in London for 8 weeks. (More than reason to fear that he has plunged deep in the waters of dissipation & has reaped & is reaping its bitter, bitter, fruit.) Walked with Uncle C. through Carclew woods. I never saw them looking lovelier. Aunt Lucy & her Lucy came out to dinner.

15. A most dreary day indeed. We have plunged, as it were, into the heart of winter. The lilacks in full bloom are weighed down with the weight of snow & the lawn is a sheet of spotless white! Such a day as late as this never remembered here. Went with Uncle J. on board the *James Tuscan* from Manilla on a monkey hunt. Uncle J. bought a monkey & I a pair of handsomely worked nautilus shells. Lashing snow storm on our way back.

19. 1st day. The Hustlers arrived yesterday & were at Meeting today, but returned to dinner. William is a fine ingenious fellow as far I can judge. The girls are small. Called on the Osbornes, a family from Cadiz.

23. Started at ¼ past 8 for Truro to bring home the carriage & see a horse. The former much improved. Latter a miserable rip. Called at Stephens's &

had tooth filled. A ticketting[1] going on at Pearce's. I called & took a seat at the Williamses tables. It seemed a quick, simple, & fair mode of sale. Stopped at Perran to dine & lodge. Called on Uncle L. who was in bed. He has been ill ever since his return & looked dismal. I talked on indifferent subjects for half an hour & went to the other house where Uncle & Aunt C., Dr. & Mrs. Durtnall, the Borlases & Mr. Wilson, together with the Hustler party formed a pretty good-sized party. The Dr. as voluble as ever, – Arabic roots & Hebrew criticisms. P. Hustler rather struck by his learning. Borlase, who is a blunt clever fellow, didn't admire him. After visitors were gone we sat up till tomorrow telling queer stories.

29. Oak day[2] with all its fooleries. We received an answer to our application to the Commissioners of Treasury to have all things bonded at Falmouth. This was granted with the exception of silks. Drove to Enys to a 2 o'clock dinner. Met the juveniles from Perran there & rambled over grounds.

30. Scorching hot. Lord James Perry's yacht in harbour. *Such* a beauty! Drank tea with the Lynes. Such tories! I believe all women are so by nature – if they turn out otherwise it is the effect of education, example, or reflection.

6TH MONTH

1. Cornelius Lyne & wife returned from Madeira. He looks like a corpse. Helped them to get their luggage thro' the paws of the customs. Hard rain all night.

4. Accompanied the Lynes to Mylor to hunt for lodgings for their invalid, who appears to be sinking rapidly. We were unsuccessful.

12. Called on A. Tsiolkowsky of the Russian Royal School of Engineers, an agreeable & intelligent fellow, as they all are. He dined here, as did the Trebah party & a Miss Bamfield. The swanlike Helen Molesworth looked in in the afternoon & was beguiled to staying till evening. Had the pleasure of escorting her home. She is a thorough *woman*.

14. A Danish ship the *Christian* was towed in totally dismasted. She applied to us of course. Luxurious cruise before breakfast. After an early snack I rode to Penjerrick, taking Perran in my way to see Uncle L. who says he is better & yesterday out of the Doctor's hands. He looks dismal. Found my carrot field as weedy as a man's heart. Men & women at work upon it but make small progress. Evening close as an oven.

1. A procedure used in sales in mining districts by which ore is sold to the highest bidders who make their bids by ticket.
2. Oak Apple Day, the anniversary of the Restoration in 1660 and to commemorate the occasion when Charles II hid in an oak after the Battle of Worcester.

15. Capt. Sill of the American ship & the Durtnalls dined here. All went off well. Capt. Sill is an intelligent man, but a high tory. He says there is a large party of them in America. Dr. Durtnall was entertaining & gave us plenty of spoutation in the evening. At a pathetic part his lady rubbed her eyes & said it was 'too much for her'. Wrote to the owners of the Dane at Altona, the Capt. preferring not to commence repairs till we hear from them.

20. A circumstance of no everyday occurrence happened today. A merchant of the name of Budd of the firm Budd & Lee, which failed 16 years ago, being about 160 pounds in our debt, called this morning & gave a check for £80 & stated that he hoped to be able to wipe off remainder next year. The man is an Irishman, which is the more extraordinary! Much rain with thunder & lightning.

21. Started at 10 on a cruise up the river with Capt. Sill in his boat. We landed under Craigmurrion about a couple of miles beyond Tregothnan, found our way to the old house & enquired for old Penhallow Peters whose stock Capt. Sill wished to see. We found none but his sons were there, the old gentleman having removed 4 years since to a farm called 'Kergerral', the former residence of his bride. His son Joseph showed no great pleasure in speaking of the match; however, he politely directed us to his estate & to his bull-house, which lay in another farm, Penhallow, but not far out of our road. We accordingly went there & saw 5 magnificent bulls weighing from 12 to 14 cwt. One was led out to show us, & he *was* a picture! The man who conducted us to his master's informed us that the old gent 4 years since, being then 73, married a buxom widow or old maid, I know not which, of 40 odd, called Martin. This proved very galling to the children who thought the match below him & the old man was obliged to live at his wife's house as there was a complete break in the family. He, however, holds all the land & farms it himself, from 1000 to 1500 acres, the sons doing nothing. On reaching the house we found the Squire was out, nevertheless we introduced ourselves to his amiable partner. She proved a specimen which I should be very sorry to have missed, without exception the most complete mass of vulgarity I ever encountered, ugly, huge & tawdry with a most unprepossessing squint & a voice like the boatswain of a man-of-war. What could have induced the old spooney to marry her I can't conceive. She entertained us (I may well say) till the arrival of her lord, or more properly, her slave, for she is as completely installed in the *pantaloons* as any wife I ever saw. Poor old man, I pitied him. He had, it seems, been to Falmouth on purpose to find Capt. Sill (Tilly having informed him of his wants in the ram & hog line). He gave us a hearty welcome & a hospitable dinner, the lady occasionally ordering her husband to keep his seat & not to leave the room, & varying the conversation by an account of O. Cromwell's visit to that identical house, & regaling himself from that identical cupboard, & 'that

was truth & sterling truth'. She made throughout a most lamentable effort to appear genteel & particularly recommended her plan of pickling *her* hams with treacle & saltpetre. The old man having left the room with farmer Tyacke of Merther to bargain about an ox, I drew her out on family matters, as she evinced no particular delicacy on the subject. Sill & I occasionally writhed in the agony of suppressed laughter (particularly when she told us that the cause of Joe's lameness was the 'rheumatics or siatick in *these parts*', patting the place she alluded to). However, the sweetest scenes must have an end and we bade adieu to the fair dame of Kergerral, her husband disposing us in his double bodied phaeton with a sister-in-law & niece Jane, and convoying us ahead on a pony. The ladies were packed in for the sake of an airing & were as easy as needs be. Ere we reached Trelistian, the site of the rams, we were as thick as pickpockets. Having admired the old patriarch & bought one of his progeny, 11 months old for £10.10, the Squire returned & sent the gig & women on with us to Filley-way,[1] where our boat awaited us. Such roads as we went over effectually destroyed all *distance* on our parts, 3 or 4 times being all but capsized, & jolted into each other's laps, which we all thought high fun, old lady & all; & going down such a desperate hill at such a desperate rate that we had to hold firmly by each other to keep our bodies up. We parted on the beach high friends as needs be, without knowing each others' names. Had a tough pull of it home, the wind being strong & right ahead. Sill & I laughed ourselves fairly out during the homeward voyage. On returning found the family not come back from Penjerrick, so ordered tea & a fire & made myself comfortable after the labours of the day.

24. A day of grand havoc at Penjerrick. The new owners, Uncle G.C. & my father, made a day of it, slashing the big trees right & left. We had 7 men with hatchets, ropes, & saws, & by evening the lawn looked like a battle field – heaped with prostrate corpses of trees. The ladies joined us with prog & we dined & tead on the walk in front of the house.

27. The Mayor & Aldermen paraded Town, marking the bounds thereof, and naughty boys followed the procession with mud & turfs & marked the backs thereof. There was a beautiful sweepstakes race in the afternoon. Mayne's *Blue-Eyed Maid* showed them all her heels. Whether the *Jackdaw* or *Watersprite* came next is a disputed point. There was some splendid sailing & good manoeuvring. Heavy showers.

28. Saw C. Lyne off in a pilot boat for Penzance with his wife & brother James. He looked miserably fallen away & is most certainly gone there but to die. Escorted his sister to the Omnibus. All overflowing with gratitude for the small attentions we have shown them. Breakfasted with Capt. Sill, an entertaining companion. Another day at Penjerrick. Did much execution. Place wondrously improved. The ladies joined us with prog & all hands

1. Probably Philleigh.

enjoyed the rustication. The owls can't understand the meaning of it for the life of them.

29. A.M. held her first juvenile horticultural exhibition on the lawn; it was a pretty sight – there were 59 girls from various schools in Falmouth, Budock, Penryn, & Constantine, with flowers in pots, nosegays & wild flowers of their own rearing or own collecting, as well as 53 spectators, the female aristocracy of the neighbourhood, & 6 old widows from the Retreat[1] with their little batch of pots on a table before them, & sundry other hangers on, gardeners' families, &c., altogether a party of 130. After a too munificent distribution of prizes, consisting of rakes, watering pots, spades, trowels &c., the juvenile competitors were regaled on buns & rice & treacle & the elderly ladies on tea. After which races, &c., were the order of the day. The small detachment from the workhouse were a pattern for orderly behaviour. All went off highly pleased, having been first addressed by my father & then by the 3 gardeners in succession.

7TH MONTH

1. Started en pleine famille at 8 a.m., to attend the adjourned Monthly Meeting at Truro where the concerns of W. Hoskins & E. O. Tregelles were both taken under long & weighty deliberation. After a snack at Cos. M. Tregelles's we continued our journey Eastward. We left our horses at St. Austell & posted to Lostwithiel where we visited Restormel as a matter of course.

2. According to previous arrangement with Uncle C., we were up at 5 & joined him in the mail which brought us to Liskeard at 7. After a good breakfast we took a gig & started for Gunnes Lake. A precious 15 miles we had of it. I never drove up nor down such steep hills as we passed over today, but we had a good horse & a beautiful country on all sides & splendid weather. We reached our destination at half past 11, ordered dinner & trudged to the 'Clitters', Uncle C.'s larch estate, where we spent all the morning in marking trees for amputation. I stripped & swam across the Tamar & landed in Devonshire with some difficulty, the current on the opposite side being so strong as to carry me away. After a good dinner at the little inn we drove 3 miles to Cothele Castle[2] belonging to Lord Mt.

1. The Widows' Retreat at Mount Sion, Falmouth, which had been started in 1810 by Lord Wodehouse and Samuel Tregelles.
2. Cotehele House is one of the best remaining early Tudor manor houses in England. It belonged to the Edgecumbe family until 1947 when it was acquired by the National Trust.

Edgecumbe. It is well worth seeing, a good honest genuine antique with all the old furtniture, tapestry &c., in statu quo it was in 500 years since. The fine old entrance hall is hung round with firelocks, carabines, petards, swords, long pistols, hunting horns, old English bows, armour &c. Very interesting. Queen Anne was born & brought up here. The rooms are tapestried & have doors concealed behind. The massive furniture of oak & ebony, richly carved, puts to shame the flimsy work of modern days. We reached Liskeard at half past 8 & did justice to a hybrid between tea & supper.

3. Quarterly Meeting. It was to me in Friendly parlance a far from satisfactory opportunity. The first meeting was largely attended. The matter was weighty, the manner simple & beautiful & it breathed the spirit of pure religion throughout. W. Hoskins then laid his concern[1] before the Quarterly Meeting & here I was indeed annoyed, not to say disgusted. It was taken up by the *women*, discussed by the *women* & finally thrown out by the *women*!, the men taking scarcely any part in the whole proceedings! O tempora! O mores! We have lost the breeches public that's certain, – and then the poor honest good old man! How I felt for him. Had it been the judgment of grey haired men, there would at least have been no *indignity* in it, but to be voted unfit for a service which he believed was his duty to perform, by a pack of old women, with Ann Tweedy & C. Abbot at their head, the former of whom ought to be ashamed to open her mouth in a meeting for discipline, after altering the day of one to suit her convenience & then never appearing nor sending an explanation, the other a bigot to the backbone; to say nothing of Catherine Lidgey, who is evidently insane. Oh it was sad, sad! After sitting 5 hours, we went to Cos. J. Allen's to dinner. Having got half through we had to decamp, the carriage being ready. We came by the new road to Bodmin, the most picturesque woody & beautiful stage in the country, perhaps in any country. Slept at St. Austell.

4. Got home to a late dinner. Broiling day. We couldn't have got on at all had we not had an extra horse clapped on in front of ours. I stopped at Truro & called on J. Prideaux[2] who is come to give a course of Chemical Lectures at the mining school in that town. I have half a mind to attend. I reached home in a melting state. At the office I saw & took leave of Capt. Sill who sails tomorrow.

5. Received a very interesting letter from R. Pearce, informing us of the death of Cornelius Lyne. He ruptured a vessel the day before & died yesterday about 2 o'clock. He speaks in the highest terms of the family who bear their affliction as becometh Christians. Drove my father to Penjerrick after breakfast where Uncle G. joined us & we made much progress amongst the

1. To visit the Quakers in Ireland.
2. John Prideaux was Professor of Chemistry at the Cornish Mining School, Truro, 1839–41. His mother was a member of the Fox family of Plymouth.

trees in the higher 'Tub field', opening new vistas before unknown, until the womenfolk arrived with dinner.

12. Drove my father to Redruth to join in a consultation for a companion for Edwin. My father was devoted to the service, much contre gré,[1] but was obliged to submit. Penjerrick after dinner. Carried second field of hay.

15. After much preparation, leave-taking & last words, we bade adieu to our beloved head, together with E. O. Tregelles and his sister Lydia on the deck of the steamer, with every prospect of moderate weather & a fair passage. Invited the elite of the Lancastrian boys to a tea-party on the lawn tomorrow.

16. Took a cruise solo to St. Mawes. Favoured with the company of our Plymouthian relatives to a half past 2 o'clock dinner, & the 18 best Lancastrian boys to their long-talked-of tea visit at 4. After some highly improving and exciting pastimes, such as Moppedhidey, Buckeyhow, & Hunt the fox,[2] we sat down to eat & drink; the plebeian occupying one table, & the upper-class boys, consisting of Cos. Joe Fox's, W. Hoskins, Adeline & her 2 brothers, Hustler & son, 'Master' Pollard, & our honourable selves, the other, side by side on the lawn. After which we ran races & went into the mysteries of the magic lantern & the little lads departed in good time, highly pleased with their 'treat'. Not so the aristocratic part of our guests, with respect to time at least. In spite of obvious hints they lingered on till past 10, till we grew sick of boys.

19. Storm all night and this morning. Dined at Fenwicks to meet J. Lyne. Chess, – the usual substitute of conversation at that house. Ran out to Meudon & Tregedna, to ask Uncle G.P. & Tregedna girls to join in taking German lessons of Professor Schweitzer, who will come here from Plymouth if he has sufficient encouragement. The latter acceded. Wind & rain have much injured the wheat crops.

22. According to engagement we were joined by all the Trebah party at 10 & off we started for Tregothnan. Had a fine fair wind up. Surveyed house, church, &c. Dined gypsy fashion & returned. Landed at King Harry passage. Walked through Trelissick & then & there down it came sure enough, a regularly pepperer. The poor girls waded thro' the wet grass like Niobes. Rain continuing heavy, a large detachment of our party landed at Mylor and walked across to Flushing. Home, tea, a good fire, & dry clothes, were luxuries fully appreciated. Talking of clothes, whilst about it I thought that standing as I did in my father's shoes I might as well sit in his breeches, but to fill up vacancies, found it necessary to stow 3 or 4 nightshirts behind, in which

1. i.e. reluctantly. E. O. Tregelles and his sister Lydia were to embark on a visit to Friends in Ireland.
2. All were versions of Hide-and-Seek. In Mop-and-Hide-away, or Moppy Heedy, the seeker has to race the hider back to base.

costume I made a very respectable appearance. Uncle A. started on a packet deputation to Town.[1]

24. Being appointed with P. Hoskin to canvass a district of the Town for contributions for the 12 widows and 40 orphans of the crew of the *Melville*, we went our rounds. A very poor district was allotted to us, nevertheless, including our family's subscriptions we collected £21.

27. After breakfast in solitary bliss I ran down to shop as usual. Called on Professor Schweitzer, M.A., late German Professor in the Royal College, Belfast. He professes to teach *Deutsch* in 6 lessons sufficiently well to enable his pupils to continue it by themselves. His manners & appearance savour of the quack, but his testimonials are very good. I had already engaged for him the 3 Tregedna lasses as well as myself. Ran out to Penjerrick. Everything growing with wonderful vigour. After tea the Professor appeared & we set to till past 10, reading, parsing, analysing &c. His system is certainly good. Called afterwards at Grove Hill to return to Dr. Durtnall a letter he lent me from Bohn,[2] expressing the approbation of several learned men of Uncle G.C.'s new work, 'The Death of Demosthenes & Translations from Aeschylus'.

30. Received letter from my father giving a good account of himself & E. O. Tregelles but holding out no prospect of return yet. Rain again all day. Most calamitous weather. The corn in certain situations much battered down. Two thirds of the hay that has been cut in the county (or nearly so) still out, & most of it decayed. Rode to Penjerrick to attend sale of our timber. The net profits about £47. Being wet through below, I accoutred myself in Mary Anne's stockings & John Toy's shoes & thus managed in comfort to consume my dinner which I had carried out in the crown of my hat.

8TH MONTH

2. Picked up another small guest this morning who came 'consigned to order' & bound to Coleridge's. Took compassion upon him & fed & lodged him. Thomas went to Plymouth for the ladies by steamer. Visited Uncle L.

1. At the time when the Journal begins there were 39 mail packets (6 of them steam-ships) working out of Falmouth, all of them under Admiralty orders. In 1834 the P & O Steam Packet Co. and the Royal West India Steam Co. jointly petitioned the Government to give them this traffic and to allow them to operate from Southampton. Falmouth resisted this proposal, but in 1841 the Royal West India Steam Co. were permitted to carry the West Indian and Mexican mails (still using Falmouth however) and the Cunard line the North American mails from Liverpool. By 1850 Falmouth had ceased to be a packet port.
2. The publishers. G. C. Fox's work was published by John Bohn, London, in 1839.

whom I found in bed recovering from a bad 'attack'. He looked more like himself & was cordial. Rode from thence to Penjerrick.

3. Between 6 & 7 per *Drake* arrived the female segment of our circle as well as Uncle Alfred & Thomas, the former on his return from the deputation on the Packet business. I fear they have effected nothing but a sensation, the Government having gone too far to retreat. Our people well & happy.

6. A well-managed, well-attended & well-appointed Regatta. The day fine, breeze fresh. Of the 5 head prizes for sailing boats, it was satisfactory to observe that 4 Falmouth & 1 Truro boat walked off with the whole. All the 2nd prizes were won by Plymouthians. The scene was beautiful, the company enjoyed themselves, & accidents none. Capt. Plumridge entertained 300 guests aboard the *Astraea* & the day closed with fireworks, &c.

13. Grand teetotal festival. The ranks of the saints paraded the streets in procession with ribbons & evergreens, music playing, & banners waving. Amongst the devices was a dismal drunken scene, the wife dropping the child headlong from her lap, & the husband, too far gone to lift the last glass of spirits to his mouth, is kindly aided by the Arch Enemy, who is guiding his wrist. At 2 as many as chose went yachting in the harbour in 3 sand barges decked with laurel. All this is very distasteful, tho' I am not prepared to say it may not be useful. Susan & Robt. Sutton dined with us & then accompanied us in the cart & britschka to Penjerrick, which looked lovely. Whilst engaged in tea before the old house, we were visited by a sybil bearing a paper flag, written over in a large hand that she was sent from above to advocate the cause of the establishment, i.e. Wesley's clergy, to rouse men from the apathy of their sins to warn them of the 4 sore judgments about to come on the earth. She informed us that she wrote it under the immediate inspiration of the spirit, that she was called on to live a life of faith & had done so for 39 years, preaching to men in the streets & calling on them to repent, that teetotalism was a system sent down from heaven to prepare for the coming of the Son, – with much more in as wild a strain. A sample of a religious enthusiast. Her insanity appeared to be only on the subject of her call & inspiration.

17. Penjerrick in the morning. Busy about railings to enclose the farm yard. It will be a great improvement. On arrival of the *Drake* took off a boat to bring on shore our guests, R. Barclay of Leyton, with Gurney & his four sisters, a formidable show of female hobbledehoys. Convoyed them to our house & entertained them to the best of our ability.

20. Tourised the Barclays to Kynance Gove, Cadgwith, &c., calling on Sir Richard Vyvyan[1] en route, who is a 70th cousin of theirs. I never talked to him before; he is every inch a gentleman, perhaps a wee bit too aristocratic, but it keeps well with the place. We saw his library, chapel, pictures, &c.

1. Sir Richard Vyvyan of Trelowarren, M.P. for Helston.

At Cadgwith we took boat & entered the O.G.'s cauldron[1] and a magnificent cavern beyond. At Kynance we baked pie with lime & dressed chops with burning brandy. I tumbled into a cavern amongst the rocks & had to swim for it. We reached Helston about 8, on our way to Monthly at Penzance. Spent an Elysian hour at Coleridge's, who preached a crusade against Infant Schools & made the old dame schools appear glorious in comparison thro' the magic of his eloquence & music of his voice.

21. Attended Monthly at Penzance. Dined at Joel Lean's with 3 of the Barclays. A queer little old man was there called Richards, who at cheese time stood up in his place & shook hands all round by means of stretching across the table about 7 feet, & departed. J.L. was amusing. He showed & explained his patent (now expired) to produce motion by compressed air acting on 2 sets of vanes in a cylinder, &c. Very ingenious. Wet evening.

24. Breakfasted at 8 & news being received of a catch of pilchards at Porthoustie, we voyaged thither at 9 in Uncle A.'s boat. Arrived just in time for the second tuck.[2] It was a beautiful sight. 25 hogsheads were taken into the boats in our presence. On our return we met the ladies just arrived. We walked to the beach & had 2 hauls of the groundsean. It was a fairish catch & as we felt very peckish we accordingly set to at the knife & fork business. Gurney was rather low in his spirits because the ladies instead of bringing our smart clothes, which we had packed up & placed under their charge, brought only their own bathing things & some of my dirty linen &c. We were therefore obliged to appear in the bathing smocks. After dinner, all hands went to Tregedna. Uncle Joshua charmed the ladies, & his daughters sang their best. On returning home we had the delight of meeting my father who has suddenly leapt among us from Wales, 4 days before expected. He looks, & is, well & in good spirits. We sat up chatting pleasantly till a late hour.

28. News of large catches of pilchards at Mevagissey. Coward sent up there.

29. Accompanied the Barclays with our carriage as far as St. Austell, thence to Carglaze & took leave after dinner. They for Ilfracombe, our people for Falmouth & I for Mevagissey. The Barclays are a family that grow upon you. The father is a loving father, but a dreadful fidget. Gurney has high principle, good sense & application to his favourite pursuits, but too much squeamishness for a man. His sister Jane is one of strong, practical, good sense, energy & penetration. Elizabeth, the 2nd, a being composed of quiet sentiment, want of animation, but good features. Anne, 3rd, a beautiful temper & disposition, but has odd eyes. Emma, the youngest, is the flower of the flock & consequently the pet. Her father's preference is too marked &

1. The Devil's Frying Pan, into which at high tide the sea roars through a natural arched entrance. O.G. is probably 'Old George', the Devil.
2. To 'tuck' is to empty a seine by a 'tuck seine' inside the main one.

bad for her. When my gig & lame steed reached the noted town of Mevagissey & J. Morris's equally well known inn, I proceeded at once to S. Coward's room, whom I found fast asleep. Pulled him by the nose & made him tell me the news. There appear to be from 4 to 5000 hogshead, enclosed & cellared. I waded my way to our cellar & found W. Roberts at the head of 50 or 60 women bulking the fish. The town was given up to confusion. Everybody beside himself & no such thing known for 20 years – such a catch taken so early. Scoured the town with Coward who congratulates every acquaintance he happens to meet. I was extensively introduced to old friends by name tho' not by person. At 8 there came in a load of fish from the *Bee*, concerted with our Mevagissey one, & about 9 came our turn to discharge. Such a scene I never saw. We were obliged to keep watch with lanterns all the way from the quay to the cellar to keep off the pilferers. I had the jetty, & had to threaten one man with Bodmin[1] & use other more forcible arguments. The temptation was too strong to resist. The place was covered with men, women, children, & baskets all come to buy, beg or steal, as way might open. However, with close exertion we got off with comparatively small plunder, and kept the women hard at it till 11 in the cellar. W. Roberts is a famous fellow for it. He has not been in bed for a week. Drank tea at 12. Fish disappeared in the evening. It is said they struck the rock & went off at a tangent. The knowing ones assert that the shoal is gone for good. Bed at half past 12.

30. Up soon after 5. 8 to 10 boat loads of pilchards at the pier, but no seans shot in the night nor any appearance of fish in the bay. Consequently I thought it best to send express to St. Mawes to prevent the 3000 bushels of salt being sent as ordered yesterday by Coward. I spent the morning in looking after the cellar & boats. In consequence of a letter from Falmouth, advising catches to the westward & very small supply of salt, we raised the price to 2/9! Before dinner I went round to nearly all the cellars in the place & made up the total amount to be about 2874 hogsheads & as near as we can guess about 1200 now in the seans. I left at 7 in a gig. This 'town of stinks & wenches', as Coleridge says of Köln, – such muck, such hurry, such holla-ing, in cellar & out, such universal pilfering whenever there is opportunity. Such are the sweet characteristics of Mevagissey in fishing season.

9TH MONTH

4. Dr. Francis Fox of Brislington[2] & his wife to dinner & lodge, having been

1. The county gaol.
2. Dr Fox, one of the Bristol Foxes, who had established at Brislington, near Bristol, a hospital for the mentally ill.

touring down west. A youth called French also to dinner, a sharp little prig of a Londoner.

5. I had arranged to take the Dr. & his lady to Consols & the carriage drove to the door, when an alarm being given of a schooner being stranded under the Rector's House, we changed tactics & proceeded thither. This proved to be the *Spy* loaded with wheat from Odessa. On receiving her orders she tried to beat down against a strong S. Wester & in going about missed stays & was driven ashore. P. Buckett with the gig's crew was in attendance & carried out a kedge to windward, on which she rode while weighing anchor & setting 3 head sails. As soon as the time cleared her of the rocks, she paid round & got off with little or no damage.

6. Dr. Fox & lady left us per coach at half past 5. Agreeable domestic people, *he* very intelligent, *she*, what is called 'sweet'. Tried our new & very elegant 4-wheeled gig, which Thomas brought home yesterday from Truro. Afternoon indoors having a cold.

10. Breakfasted at Penjerrick. I sent over for Ching & gave orders about whitewashing the rooms & repairing the roof, back at half past 10 & off for St. Austell with three generations of female Friends, my father being too unwell to act as escort. We reached our destination about 5. Whilst the select meeting was sitting, I attended a lecture given at the National School on Peace by David Moses. Found it all very true & very trite. Came away without a new idea on the subject.

12. Gregory, Lecturer on Education, called offering his services to organise the school.[1] Called with him on the Committee & obtained their sanction.

18. Rode to Penjerrick in the evening to make arrangements for settling there tomorrow. I have got the place into comparative comfort with the aid of mason & carpenter. I found that by Hercules' carelessness in leaving open the stable door, the sow & progeny had got in & devoured all the duck's eggs on which she has been sitting almost a month. Very mortifying. One of the other ducks fell a victim to its taste for experimental philosophy by tumbling into the tar pot, to the great detriment of his personal appearance. We have had to shave him in consequence.

19. All hands removed to Penjerrick. I joined them at tea after attending Webbe's sale & buying sundry furniture for the place. Beautiful moony night. A real unfeigned pleasure to be at last settled in at Penjerrick as a home. Fires in each room, doors & windows put in repair, & upper storey whitewashed. All snug. The large room above allotted to me. Lay awake long, drinking the beautiful moonlight which streamed down the lawn in a flood.

20. Up at 6 & saw the men set to work trenching the little left hand garden. By evening a mighty change was produced in the effect & much more in contemplation. I went to Flushing & brought home purchases. Attended

1. The Lancastrian School of which Barclay Fox was a governor.

Polytechnic Committee. Rode in cart to Penjerrick after dinner; evening at Tregedna & then home to sleep in order to start early tomorrow for Mevagissey, the fishermen there having advertised a sale of 1075 hogsheads of pilchards & Uncle A. having departed this evening. I go in order to inform him of any additional orders & to help him in advising the London Houses of price.
21. Lovely morning. I started soon after 8 & crossed to St. Just. I had a beautiful ride to Mevagissey & reached there at half past 11. I found Uncle A. at one of the Curers & set to work & prepared a whole lot of letters for our London friends, leaving a space for price. After dinner the curers assembled in one room, the merchants in another. After a little haggling about conditions, the former sent the latter individually their price, which was 70/-. The latter then sent in their terms. Ours was 40/-. They lowered to 60/-, but there being no present prospect of a nearer advance, I took horse & started for King Harry passage. It was a dark & intricate road & I went about a mile out of the way – 15 miles to King Harry. Holla'd for the ferry, which came in about ¼ of an hour. I took nearly as much time to get the horse in for he was very refractory. I had to hoodwink him, but succeeded at last & got across. I tried to get a feed at the public house, but in vain, so pushed on for Perran 5 miles further & reached it at half past 9, I hungry & the horse tired. Attended to latter & then broke in on the maid servant who soon prepared a luxurious tea & comfortable bed.
28. Penjerrick. Fresh changes & improvements have opened a beautiful vista of the meadows below. With their fringe of fine trees they are a vast additional beauty. The Enyses, Dr. Daubeny,[1] &c. dined here. A pleasant evening. Lots to do at shop. Have bought 2500 hogsheads of pilchards. Too much at present high price.
29. 1st day. I received a letter from W. Forster saying that J. C. Backhouse had started for Falmouth in hopes of having my company in a tour thro' Spain & Portugal. I ran down to the inn & found my gentleman in bed. Came home and mooted the subject at the breakfast table, but it met with so much opposition from the throne that I quietly withdrew the bill. I sent J. C. Backhouse an orthodox coat[2] to appear in at the Meeting. He dined with us, a nice unassuming fellow, & accompanied us to Penjerrick in the evening, but it was a dismal walk, dark & wet. Called on H. Livermore, an extraordinary creature who is bound on a pilgrimage to Jerusalem. She told me that she was called by the Spirit in 1833 to go forth & minister, as plainly as she heard me speak.

1. Chas. Daubeny (1795–1867), Professor of Botany at Oxford, who wrote a paper for the Journal of the Royal Institution of Cornwall on the gardens at Grove Hill and Penjerrick.
2. The Quakers' traditional dress; the coat referred to would be a plain, drab tailed-coat without revers.

30. Town after breakfast, returned to dinner & walked J. C. Backhouse with the girls over Tregedna, Penjerrick West, Crill, &c., then with Aunt C. halfway to Trebah & made a noble tea on the strength of it. Uncle Joshua called in the evening to see John Jose,[1] who seems to be sinking fast. Humble, calm & comfortable in his hopes. Took leave of him thinking he might not survive the night.

10TH MONTH

2. Up at half past 4 & breakfasted in order to reach Kynance whilst the tide would admit of our entrance, but having to go round by Gweek & losing our way once or twice we (i.e. J.C.B. & self) did not succeed & could not get into the cove. A sweet ride we had across the moor to Cadgwith, sticking occasionally in mud to the horses' hocks, & they poor things utterly exhausted by their ante-breakfast excursion. We breakfasted at Cadgwith & inspected the fish & then turned our horses' heads Helford-wards. A most deplorable ride we had. We were soon wet through, for the rain fell in torrents. The horses were jaded, the roads abominable, yet nevertheless we were sorry to lose them, which we did from time to time. We reached Trebah at last, arranged ourselves in borrowed plumes & did justice to a good dinner provided exactly to suit our case. We attempted to ride home but were obliged to leave Niger at Penjerrick. Took J.C.B. to Counting House & procurred passport, cash &c. Rode 33 miles today & walked 3 or 4.
3. Saw J.C.B. off per *Drake* at 7 this morning for Jersey, whence he means to cross to France & tourise out his furlough.
4. A busy morning. Equinoctial gales, N.E., heavy showers & so on. My father & the girls attended the Geological at Penzance. I dined at Bank with Mammy & ran out to Penjerrick. Took some grapes & rudiments of gruel for Uncle John. With the former he was highly pleased. He was rather revived & much freer from pain. I spent the evening at Tregedna. The night was pitch dark & I rode home occasionally feeling my way with a stick. Employed at the Polytechnic Hall arranging & hanging paintings in conjunction with G. P. Nash & Armstrong. The former rather bulky for ladder work. Saw Sam Patch, the famous American diver, who jumped from the top of the lower mast of a schooner, about 50 feet head foremost into the pier, hung himself by the legs, then by the neck, & performed sundry other dainty devices.
7. In harness with Armstrong & G.P. Nash at the Polytechnic Hall arranging, hanging pictures & cataloguizing. By evening we were able to send

1. The steward at Uncle Joshua's estate at Tregedna.

down the catalogues to the printer, much to his dismay, having to work at it all night. Very good display on the whole, but having been confined to the higher regions of art (all the paintings being hung in the gallery) I am not able to give an opinion as to the scientific objects which were ranged in classes on tables below. Met Wightwick amongst the judges. Then Snow Harris rolled in, having sent his wife & 3 children to our house, Buckland, Sir Charles Lemon & various others. A party of 18 to dinner, Davies Gilbert, who stays with us over the Polytechnic, The Harrises, the Warres, Lieut. Sulivan,[1] J. Enys, &c.

8. The grand day, Miss Poly's 7th birthday. Everything went off well. The chair was taken by our venerable Vice-Patron at 1. Abstracts of the essays for various modes of amelioration of miners were read & much speechification followed. A great assemblage of the Dons, – Baronets, Members of Parliament, & all that sort of thing, too many to mention. Held a mongrel between lunch & dinner at 3 to which all were bidden. Buckland gave at 7 an illustrative lecture on De la Beche's Geological Map of Cornwall. The best of his, I think, that I ever heard. He considers that we live on a superficial crust surrounding a red hot fluid mass, which is now disgorging fiery flop thro' 170 volcanoes, that the lodes are caused by up-heaving of this upper crust, which breaks, & extraneous matter is squeezed up through the cracks. Finished about 9. Our house being full, I stowed away 8 of our party at Grove Hill for the night.

10. Last day of the Exhibition. A man from Perran explained 2 useful inventions of Capt. Tregaskes's; one for discharging vessels with dispatch, the other for deepening shallow rivers. Both are in operation at Devoran & by the aid of the latter they have already deepened the river in front of our right, say 150 fms. & 18 inches. Phillips explained his new levelling instrument & J. Prideaux lectured on a new method of his of boring rocks by first softening them by chemical means. Snow Harris was in the chair. Dined at Carclew at 7; Father, A.M., Harrises & self. Handsome dinner & delightful party. The celebrated Miss Brune,[2] charming person, keen, clever, naive, handsome & very distinguée, Sir A. Buller[3] & 3 daughters, & 2 sweet Miss Tremaynes, sociable easy unaffected creatures who played & sung duets like nightingales.

20. Sunday. Rain, as yesterday promised. Wm. Hoskins after a very good sermon was seized with the spasms to which he is so liable & was supported out of Meeting by his son. Hearing a very poor account of Jn. Boyne,[4]

1. Later Vice-Admiral Sir Bartholomew Sulivan. He was a lieutenant in H.M.S. *Beagle* on her voyage round the world, 1831–36.
2. Miss Mary Jenny Prideaux-Brune, daughter of the Rev. Chas. Prideaux-Brune of Padstow.
3. M.P. for Liskeard.
4. A master at Lovell Squire's school.

I called on him. He was sitting before the fire in his bedroom & looking as hollow & haggard an object as I have often seen. Yesterday he thought himself dying. He felt better today, but complained much of his forlorn & lonely condition. Thinks there never was a man so separated from his friends & all society. Has vowed against all Doctor's stuff henceforth & for ever. Longs for air & change. He takes rather a more hopeful view of his spiritual prospects than he did. I don't think his lungs are diseased, for his voice is strong & his cough gives him no pain, but I think the malady is rather in his stomach (with which he has been playing such strange & absurd freaks) & also in the nerves, which act reciprocally one on the other. He is very hypochondriacal & fanciful. I have no doubt that change of scene, air without exertion, & cheerful society would be the surest restoratives. There is much of interest in him in spite of his oddness. He has fixed on leaving Lovell Squire's, if ever well enough. Called at the Bank to see the Tucketts who arrived yesterday.

22. On coming in I found Hercules very bad, feverish cold, toothache, &c. Sent him to bed & dosed him to produce perspiration. Called on J. Boyne who has been out in the Bath chair, but rather overdid himself by walking. He is a deplorable object. Called at the school where things are going on well. Attended a vestry at half past 6 to consider the state of Swanpool road[1] & what means should be pursued to readapt it to land carriages instead of water carriages as at present: it was resolved that our Way Wardens being summoned before the magistrates do appear & do all they can to throw the blame on Lord Wodehouse in order to make him undertake the clearing of the tunnel.

23. Hercules the same. Jn. Boyne rather weaker & talks much of approaching dissolution. He has removed to Godolphin's Lodgings. Committee of Polytechnic at 1. An interesting Dr. Steinkopf dined and lodged with us as did Uncle & Aunt C. A Bible meeting at half past 6, which was tolerably attended considering the weather. I was much pleased with Steinkopf's fervor & simplicity. His bad English even is pleasing to my ear. He gave us a sermonet after reading.

24. Paid an interesting visit on Jn. Boyne today. He expressed in his peculiar manner, but beautiful language, his full hopes & clear prospect of a blessed immortality, & then apologized for his imbecility, saying that it might be expected 'a man of his literary acquirements would express himself more lucidly'. He requested me to accept his Bloomfield's Greek Testament as a present, & take any other of his books that might suit me at half price. This I agreed to do. It is quite a scholar's death-bed.

1. Swanpool is a lake adjacent to the sea on the outskirts of Falmouth. In 1826 a tunnel was cut through the rock to allow surplus water to drain into the sea, and a road was made on the bar between the sea and the pool.

26. J. Boyne last night was highly delirious. It took three men to hold him even in his attenuated state. He fancied himself a glorified spirit & insisted on stripping himself of his 'filthy rags' & lay down on the floor naked attempting to fly. It appears that an injudiciously large quantity of morphia was administered to him thro' want of definite instructions. When I called he wanted much to get out. I managed to dissuade him with difficulty. He seemed oppressed with a vague recollection of last night, & said he was under a strange hallucination. On Cos. Joseph's entering the room he took him to task in style for making 'such a blunder', as he called it, referring to the morphia. The day before yesterday, Aunt A. asked him whether he had any brothers or sisters. After endeavouring to evade it, he cried out, 'O tribulation of body! Misery of Spirit! I was not born in wedlock!' This was news to me. I understand it was a distressing scene.

27. J. Boyne sinking fast. I called but did not see him. After an early breakfast drove my father to Redruth to meet some applicant for membership.[1] Waiting for the conclusion of the committee, I stood outside with Mary, the antique warden of the Meeting house. We watched the people coming from church & she gave me much valuable information as to the names, birth, parentage & circumstances of the passers-by, — was a son to Bill Mitchel, the carpenter, & — was a maiden up to Miss Jenkins's, a quiet maiden, — & — & — whom I called ladies in my ignorance, were nothing but shopwomen. Low people showed up so smart now-a-days that you wouldn't know a *stinking ould maiden* down to Bal[2] from a lady born, and many such like moral reflections did we pass on the degeneracy of the age. By dint of hard driving we got home in time for the afternoon meeting. I spent the evening at Lovell Squire's &, by J. Boyne's request, selected from his library some books that would suit me, which he wishes me to take at ½ price.

28. Poor J. Boyne died today about 2 o'clock, the only present were Lucretia Crouch & Thomas. It is a happy release for him, poor fellow. His sufferings must have been dreadful for the last 6 months, the morbid state of the stomach acting on the nerves & these again on the stomach, & with all this incubus on his spirits, to be subjected to the drudgery of perpetual annoyances of a school, with the continual contact with a set of noisy & uncongenial companions to which an usher is doomed, & the sense of loneliness, & friendlessness, & base birth. No wonder it has brought him to an untimely grave. The girls & I dined at Enys, my father being confined with a bad cold. We met Sir Geo. Staunton,[3] the celebrated Chinese traveller, & the Phillpotts.

1. i.e. of the Society of Friends.
2. A reference to 'bal maidens', i.e. women who worked in the mines, breaking up the lumps of copper ore.
3. Sir George Staunton (1781–1859), a noted Sinologist who published an authoritative book on the laws of China.

The former is a very peculiar man about 50 with a remarkable petitesse & nervousness of manner. His conversation was not interesting nor was there anything striking in his appearance, but a man that has been twice to Peking & can talk Chinese must be a lion for all that. Returned about 11, & having taken a place by the *Quicksilver* mail, sat by the drawing room fire till 29. ½ past 1 when I started for Bodmin to attend the County Railroad meeting. I had the coach to myself till a stop beyond Truro, when 2 women gave me their company. Very cold night. Reached Bodmin at ½ past 5 & turned in till 8. Met a large party at breakfast, principally Falmouthians, joined afterwards by Freshfield, Lord Falmouth & son, & other dons, & business commenced about ½ past 10, i.e. a preparatory meeting to draw up resolutions to lay before the large meeting. There were Sir Chas. Lemon, Sir H. Vivian, Sir R. Rolfe, P. Hoblyn, High Sheriff, Carteret Ellis, Hon. G. Fortescue, J. Tremayne & many other of the County Gentlemen. The Resolutions set forth the importance of the undertaking in various lights & to various interests & to the nation at large of continuing Falmouth as a Packet Station, which would be done of course if the Railroad were established. Finally a committee of 13 active men were appointed to prosecute every enquiry short of an actual survey & gain every information on the subject & to lay the result before another County meeting. Subscriptions were made to enable them to do this thoroughly. Lord Falmouth was in the chair & spoke well on all points but one, which was that he could not see the necessity of raising a subscription for the committee, but thought if they absolutely wanted money they might have power granted them to raise one afterwards. Sir H. Vivian said properly enough that the committee would not stir one step without it. Professional men would charge for every scrap of information they gave. Adjourned at 12 to the Town Hall where a very large & respectable concourse was assembled. Above 500 at least. The High Sheriff was in the chair. Lord Falmouth moved the first 5 resolutions! & dwelt ably, but perhaps too much for a County meeting, on the superiority of Falmouth as a Packet Station, something acknowledged unequivocally by the Government of 1807, 1810 & 1822. At one of these periods the packets were absolutely moved to Plymouth on account of disorders amongst the crews, but they were obliged to restore them in the following year. He spoke in general terms on the advantages which would be felt by our trading, agricultural, commercial & social interests, & finally squatted with vast applause. Sir Chas. Lemon seconded him & shewed by rather a wild mode of calculation, more like a baronet than a merchant, that the House of Messrs. Foxes of Falmouth in the matter alone of Expresses to London would save £1500 a year, & naturally concluded that the members of that House would give the capital *that* represented, viz. £30,000, or a considerable part of it. This, of course, was said in a joke, but might as well have been omitted. However, his speech in other respects was good & sensible. Pendarves moved the next resolution, which was seconded by Freshfield in a very able speech, shewing the advantages this undertaking presented over others of a similar nature in being the undertaking of a County instead of a Company. A large item in Railway expenses was owing to the opposition of land owners, whereas in the present instance they would support it. All this would give confidence in the undertaking to the Capitalists of the Kingdom. Lord Boscawen was delivered of a short speech with tolerable success considering he has no palate to signify. Paynter of Boskenna seconded a resolution moved by Sir H. Vivian in a most able & admirable address, on the vital necessity of a railway to Cornwall, that while other counties were traversed by them she remained without, that she did not remain stationary while others outstripped her, but retrograded. It could not be questioned that no port in the kingdom was equal to Falmouth as a packet station, but if a Railroad were carried to Plymouth & not to Falmouth, that would doubtless supersede the latter. But he doubted not that a Railway would be carried thro' Cornwall; there was not a man, woman or child in the County but would feel the benefit of it. As to the objection of Cornwall being no thoroughfare, he contended that it was the outlet to the S & the W & was backed by all England. Falmouth would become the port of London, as ship owners would ever be glad to avoid the dangerous channel navigation, &c. The estimated cost was £14,000 per mile. This was extraordinarily low – the Great Western[1] cost between £30 & £40,000. He called on Cornishmen & Devonians, one & all to support this measure. Every man that possessed £25 would find it worth his while to give £5 towards the undertaking. He sat down amidst great cheering. Tremayne returned thanks to the Chairman & he in his nervousness thanked the gentlemen for the polite manner in which they had drunk his health. I joined the passengers per *Regulator* at their dinner, & arrived at Falmouth by that coach a little before 8. I met a pleasant intelligent fellow on board, a Lieut. Bacon of the Horse Artillery, author of 'First Impressions of India'. I got inside a stage beyond St. Austell & met Cos. E. O. Tregelles & Lydia on their return from Ireland & Wales, the former looking all the better for his trip.

11TH MONTH

7. Rode down to Penzance to attend the Wheal Rose[2] account meeting.

1. The Great Western line from Paddington to Bristol was being built at this date and was completed in 1841.
2. A mine near Penzance.

Paid the Coleridges a call in my way, who gave me some luncheon. Derwent Coleridge & I somehow got into a long politico-theological controversy. It commenced in his complaining of the clergy not being represented in the House of Commons. From this we got to the connection of Church & State. He said that holding as they did as a most certain & undeniable fact that their church was the true visible church of Christ, in case of a separation taking place they could not but look upon the State as heavily guilty as disconnecting itself from Christ's Church. I said that tenet had been held by every dominant sect in succession, Roman Catholic, Presbyterian, Independent, & Church of England, each one considering itself the true Church of Christ. 'But,' he said, 'we maintain it on the grounds of our outward, visible & actual succession.' Consequently, I said, you derive it from those who have denounced you as heretics. This, however, he thought did not alter the case in the least. Reached Penzance at 4. Meeting at 5. The purser & many of the Adventurers[1] being teetotallers we had a tea instead of dinner at the hotel. Afterwards business, the result of which lengthened the faces of some of the guests, viz. a call of £5 per share.

8. I had a dismal ride home sure enough. Rain the whole way. However, having a good steed under me I did not feel very miserable. Reached home at 2 & joined the party at Penjerrick at tea. Sad account in the papers of an incursion of about 8000 Chartists into the Town of Newport,[2] headed by John Frost, an ex-magistrate, their object being it seems to be revenged on the magistrates, free from gaol a man called Vincent, one of their kidney, & it is said burn & pillage the town. They wounded the mayor & the sergeant who was quartered with about 40 regulars in one of the hotels. At the first fire, however, they started & Frost has since been taken & lodged in limbo, so there, probably, the matter ends.

12. Attended a very interesting meeting held by the Hon. Capt. Elliot to advocate the cause of the Sailors' Home & the Destitute Sailors' Institution, twin societies & the most admirable in their working & most judicious in their management of any Benevolent Societies in the Kingdom. Elliot spoke feelingly & beautifully. Capt. Plumridge, who was in the chair, cried like a child as did several others.

14. The cartmen who are carrying clay for me from Pennance complaining that the horses & the cart wheels sink into the gravel which has been loosened by the inundation of Swanpool, I sent 2 men to clear out the tunnel, a point

1. The Adventurers were those who took shares in a company. This was before public companies with shares quoted on the market had come into existence.
2. In June 1839 the 'People's Charter' which demanded political reform had been presented to Parliament, but the House had not considered it. As a result there were outbreaks of violence in several places. In this outbreak at Newport ten people were killed. Vincent was one of the Chartist leaders.

now in dispute between the parish & Lord Wodehouse. This Herculean task they effected in about an hour & the water poured forth in a torrent. Spent evening at Tregedna. A little small talk, singing & music.

17. The family came in at 10 after bidding adieu to Penjerrick for the year. The weather is become too slushy for any comfort in the country without 7-league boots. W. Indiaman, Capt. Turner, put in with loss of bowsprit &c., having been run foul of in the night.

18. 2 more lame ducks today. Large bark with loss of rudder & Russian bark, dismasted, towed in by 2 pilot boats, both to our shop. Called on Uncle Lewis. He is restless & weary in consequence of a sleepless night, but sociable & agreeable. Bullmore thinks the colon is oppressed by an accumulation of undigested matter.

21. Plumridge has declined standing for Falmouth. Queen Victoria has announced her intention of marrying Albert in April next. I hope she is not going to make an April fool of herself. News from America that all the Banks, except of Boston & New York, have stopped specie payment. Duke of Wellington has had an alarming seizure. I read & wrote in solitude till $\frac{1}{2}$ past 1, when having burnt out all my candles except one end, I went to bed.

23. Uncle Joshua having given me last night rather a worse account of Uncle L., I rode to Perran to dinner. I found him much worse than I expected & Grandmother is very anxious. His pulse intermitted this morning for first time. He looks cadaverous & has hardly strength to hold up his head. Speaks in a whisper & that with difficulty. It is a melancholy wreck. I staid about 4 hours doing what little could be done in raising him, changing his position &c., which he is too weak to do without help. Bullmore came about 5 & suggested calling in a doctor, confessing he saw a great change for the worse. In riding home I accordingly called on Dr. Wise & requested him to be there tomorrow morning.

27. Rode to Perran after meeting & saw Uncle L., whose appearance & manner speak a great improvement since the 23rd. He sleeps well. This is to be attributed to the anodines, but the effects are nevertheless very perceptible upon him. He takes a very little jelly & beef tea & a few tea spoonfuls of wine, which is all the nourishment he can bear. Found him grateful & affectionate.

29. The weather clearing a little I walked to Penjerrick in the afternoon. John Jose is somewhat better. Farming operations are thrown back by the wet of the 3 last days. At 7 I attended a meeting of the Liberal Electors of Falmouth & Penryn to fix on a suitable representative to succeed Rolfe,[1] who

1. Sir R. M. Rolfe had been elected M.P. for Penryn and Falmouth in 1835. He vacated his seat on being made a Baron (i.e. a judge) of the Exchequer Court, a court which wars later abolished.

is made Baron of the Exchequer. S. Blight Esq., Mayor in the chair. Reid of Penryn mentioned Capt. Sir Thos. Usher as a man every way suited to represent Falmouth. After this had been discussed some time, Drown came forward & in a very passable speech told the meeting that he had the honour of an intimate acquaintance with the most distinguished man in Europe & he had expressed his willingness to stand. He ended by stating that his friend's name was Dr. Bowring. Incidentally during the discussion of the comparative merits of these two individuals, Pender received as sound a lashing as any man could desire, for his underhand conduct in canvassing for some nameless individual after the unanimous selection of Capt. Plumridge at a former meeting at which he was present. Cornish gave it him first, then Harvey & then Tobias, who added to the effect by quoting not only the unfortunate gentleman's words, but his most unhappy & most characteristic manner. Tilly considered that Bowring, eminent as he was, was unsuitable on 2 or 3 accounts, the principal of which he could not name at a meeting like the present (he referred to his being a Unitarian) & at length almost unanimously, the mayor was called on to send an invitation to Sir T. Usher to present himself & declare his political sentiments & to stand for the burgh if approved of. There was a good deal of fun & some really good speaking.

30. I walked to Perran after an early dinner. It was evident Uncle L. had lost ground, but we avoided questioning him as he shows great disinclination to talk. Bullmore came down before tea & said that he felt it his duty to state that he saw a very considerable change for the worse during the last 24 hours. To Aunt C. alone he expressed his full belief in the great work of the Saviour & its efficacy & regretted with deep humility that hitherto his mind had been in that enfeebled state as to prevent his feeling the deep contrition which his past transgressions required.

12TH MONTH

1. Uncle L. slept soundly, the effects of the composing draught. He was asleep when I came in to Falmouth.

3. A note from Aunt C. before breakfast brought us all on the spot by 11 o'clock. A great change took place last evening. We sat round his bed without speaking, Aunt C. occasionally wetting his lips with water & Wm. & Mary at the head of the bed attending to the pillows &c. My mother prayed for him very sweetly. Bullmore & Wise called, one after the other, & so satisfied were they that the change was very near, that each left a particular request that he might be informed by tonight's post at what hour he breathed his last.

6. A little after 10 a note from Aunt C. reached us stating that the close of poor Uncle L.'s sufferings took place at 9 this morning. We drove to Perran at once & found the family party assembled in the chamber. The face of the dead was the finest I ever saw, a dignified repose, an expression of gravity & gentleness unlike anything human. We looked, & felt no doubt of his blessedness. We read a chapter of Ephesians II in the room, which my mother followed with a very sweet address. We dispersed in the garden till dinner time. In the evening Uncle Joshua, Caroline & I, succeeded in taking tolerably correct profiles by the shadow.[1] The Tucketts here. Returned after tea.

11. A most dismal, drenching and deplorable day. We assembled at the Bank at 10. The family sat round the coffin in the drawing room, a large concourse of friends & acquaintances assembled in the dining room. By dint of almost physical force we persuaded all the female part of the procession to avail themselves of a postchaise & car & proceed at once to the Meeting House. Aunt C. & the Tregedna girls were the only ladies who walked. The weather was utterly unfit for any. The coffin was carried by the servants. A very short time was spent in the yard & we went into the Meeting House before they commenced filling in. After a long & solemn silence we had addresses from Sarah Rundell, Ann Tweedy, J. Budge & Ed. O. Tregelles. A large party assembled at the Bank to dinner. All the relations in town or nearly so, & several others.

13. At 7 attended a meeting of the Falmouth Electors at Pearce's, to hear Dr. Bowring's declaration of his political creed, previous to his offering himself as candidate for our 'Siamese'[2] borough. He appeared half an hour after his time & was duly introduced by G. Drown, who was moved to the chair. He then stood up, giving me a good sight of his very expressive face; a high & noble forehead, a keen penetrating eye, deep set & brilliant even thro' his spectacles, a nose bespeaking power & taste, a finely chiselled nostril dilating with the interest of his subject & a very peculiar & uncommon mouth, the lips somewhat prominent, but firmly set with an expression of high & fixed purpose not easily to be shaken. His speech was worthy of his appearance, philosophical, terse, energetic & powerful. He began by referring to his Cornish origin, his public career & the principles which had ever influenced him. He spoke of the measure for National Education as the most important which could come before a Legislature.[3] He upheld a system which should embrace all denominations, without respect to the sectarian bigotry of any frivolous creature who would confine all that was good within the narrow

1. i.e. silhouettes of Uncle Lewis.
2. The twin boroughs of Falmouth and Penryn were united in 1832, returning two M.P.s.
3. The Education Act which provided universal state education was held up by sectarian differences until 1871.

limits of his own polemical opinions. He enlarged on the principles of free trade. England contains a vast fund of industry, activity & intelligence. Why then at the same time is there so much misery? If legislation prevents the import of the surplus food of another country to this, & another legislation the importation of the surplus manufactures of this country to that, here are 2 checks on the fruitfulness of man's labour. This is absurd, impolitic & contrary to reason & humanity. He adverted to some other great political topics & then came to the Cornish Railway question, which he warmly approved of, & should he have the honour of representing us in parliament, pledged himself to support to the utmost of his abilities. In his travels thro' many lands he had always found railways the Representatives of Civilisation. Finally he begged to re-explain that should any other liberal candidate appear on the field whom the electors might think a fitter man to represent them in parliament, he would that instant joyfully withdraw. Immense applause. Then followed his political catechism from various electors as to his opinions, first on church rates, then tithes, floggings, ballot, duration of parliament &c., all of which he answered readily & satisfactorily. He is a decided advocate for the ballot,[1] seeing how well it has worked in Spain, France & America; abolition of church rates, on the principle that power gives no right to oppress the conscience of the weaker; the same of flogging in the army & navy & so on; thro'all declaring himself a supporter of the present ministry but by no means their tool; & a determined advocate for the rights of the people, his motto being 'the greatest good to the greatest number'. The resolution moved by Harvey & carried without dissent was that Dr. Bowring be considered by this meeting a suitable person to represent the borough in parliament. The Tories of whom many were present behaved remarkably well.

14. Heard from Tilly of 2 other candidates likely to appear on the field, Hutchins, nephew of Sir J. Guest, a liberal, recommended by Rolfe and Sir H. Vivian, and Cable, a Tory barrister, of whom nobody appears to know anything. It is very important that there should not be 2 Reform candidates, the party can't afford anything like a split. Dr. Bowring dined with us at 5 and a most pleasant, easy and interesting visit we had. He is evidently discouraged by his interview today with the Penryn constituency, but talked little on these topics, dwelling principally on his travelling experiences in Egypt and the Holy Land. He had an interesting interview with the present Pope, Clement 16, and was allowed to kiss the ring on his finger.

15. Wet incessant. My father confined with a cold. Called on Dr. Bowring, who was out, & on Lovell Squire & lady with whom I had a pleasant chat. We heard in the evening that Dr. Bowring has relinquished & leaves tomorrow, not choosing to oppose Hutchins.

1. i.e. the recording of votes in secret, a practice not yet adopted at elections.

20. Broke up school. Assembled committee and gave prizes according to the boys' marks. I was glad to see that they almost universally preferred books. Despite wet morning I trudged to Penjerrick after early dinner. John Jose was as weak as water, notwithstanding, he says he takes a brave bit of stew for dinner and a pure piece of bread and makes a breakfast of fish and potatoes. I overhauled the Penjerrick accounts with Tom Evans. The alterations in the grounds and stables have cost nearly £60. I spent the evening at Tregedna taking likenesses or silhouettes, by tracing the shadow on a sheet of paper. Those of Uncle Joshua, Joanna Ellen and self were very good. A novel catastrophe for the family was discovered today. Thomas, shutting the pantry door, in awful tone imparted to me the pleasing intelligence that he and Hercules (tell it not in Gath) had picked up the — itch![1] Both were sent off with all their traps to Symons's to try the effect of his sulphur baths.

25. Christmas was ushered in like other days by heavy rain. I was wakened a little after 5 by sweet music. Got up & walked thro' the town. Fine moonlight. Band playing solemn music in the street. Others singing. Christmas dinner with T. Evans. Roast beef and plum pudding. We wound up farm accounts by way of dessert. They turn out pretty satisfactory. Tea at Tregedna.

1. Scabies.

1840

THE YEAR starts with the election of a new M.P. to represent Penryn and Falmouth, and with the usual visits from those using Falmouth as a port. In February there occurs the first mention of John Sterling who was to play such an important part in the lives of the Foxes. Sterling arrives in Falmouth with Mrs Mill (the mother of John Stuart), her daughter, Clara, and invalid son, Henry. Sterling's residence at Falmouth introduces the Foxes to some of the leading intellectual figures of the day and brings an interest in philosophy, literature, and the arts to a family whose senior members are concerned more with science. It leads Barclay to read Carlyle's *Chartism* which had appeared in 1839, and to consider more deeply the political questions raised by the Chartist riots of the previous year. The leaders of the Newport riots had been sentenced to transportation and the convict ship taking them to Australia is forced by storms into Falmouth harbour. In March Barclay sets out for the Abbey Iron Works at Neath. From Wales he travels to London, using the new railway line from Reading. While in London he attends two of Carlyle's lectures on Hero-worship and pays visits to the Carlyles and the Mills. He then accompanies his family to Ipswich and Woodbridge where his mother is engaged on a preaching mission.

JANUARY

5. After dinner we had a visit from a Turkish prince, Nadir Bey, returning a call from me 3 months ago. He is a remarkably acute & well informed man with good manners and fluent & interesting conversation. He is between 30 & 40, dressed in European costume, but retaining beard & mustachios. We were highly pleased with him. He says he learnt English in 5 months; he never could learn to spell but as soon as he knew the letters, he attacked Shakespeare & Milton. He had no fault to find with England except the weather and the cab drivers. A lady in Town accusing the Turks of worshipping the sun, he replied, so would you Madam, if you ever saw it. He so detests steamers that on one of his voyages, being sick past endurance, he attempted suicide with a pistol, but was prevented by the Captain. Took leave of him at the Meeting House door where he shook my hand warmly and said, 'I am going to pray for you and I hope you won't forget me. We don't worship in the same house but I hope we serve the same God.'
6. Called on my worthy friend the Bey before his leaving by the steamer.

He lost last evening, he says, a pocket book containing notes to the amount of £300, with letters and a picture which he values more. Had it immediately cried and posted, offering a reward of £100. Whilst attending a meeting of the Adventurers in Carrick dues and *Bray*[1] held at the Counting House, an old lady came down to inform us that she saw 2 little girls pick up a pocket book yesterday and run into their house. Edward and I, as we were starting on this scent, met 2 constables who put us on another, having seen him with companions last night who were notorious thieves. We went to their roost and the constable searched the house while we stood guard outside, but all in vain. We proceeded to the other house and saw the 2 little girls whom Mrs. Williams had specified and saw the book they picked up, which belonged to the under-boots at Selly's. Returned fruitless. My father doubts the existence of the book.

10. The Penny Postage Act came into operation today.[2] It will be a vast boon to the merchants and may be to the poor if they will avail themselves of it.

20. Frost & 4 other ringleaders in the Newport Riots condemned to be hung & quartered.

23. The girls breakfasted at Perran to meet Moultrie[3] & D. Coleridge. They came home glowing with the reflected intellectual brilliancy of the morning. The Phillpotts[4] happening to call at our house at the right time & being bound as well as myself to Perran to dinner, gave me a place in their carriage. E. Phillpotts was in a low spot about Marie[5] whom she took under her wing during Aunt Lucy's absence, & she turns out a bad 'un. Moultrie is a large coarse-featured man and tho' marked with an expression of candour and honesty, shows no impress (to my perception at least) of that elegance of mind and refinement of feeling which his poetry denotes. He is remarkably silent in company, apparently more from constitutional indolence than any poverty of ideas, for they were good when they did come. Coleridge was the mouth of the party and shone as much or more than usual. He descanted eloquently and sensibly on the good and evil of Puseyism. He strongly objects to the idea of there having ever been a golden age of the church. The apostolic writings show a very low state of morality and religion amongst the early converts. All the party left early. Slept at Perran.

24. Went into Falmouth on the Truro bus & met a very intelligent fellow therein. We had much chat on politics and public affairs. I found his name to

1. The Carrick dues were for anchorage in Carrick Roads at Falmouth. The *Bray* was a ship in which the Foxes had shares.
2. Before this Act, introduced by Rowland Hill, which started a national penny postage, the charge for mail was by distance covered.
3. John Moultrie, friend of Derwent Coleridge, was himself a poet of some reputation in the Victorian period.
4. Rev. T. Phillpotts was Vicar of Gwennap.
5. One of the maids at Grove Hill.

be Latimer, a reporter of the *West Briton*. Torrent of rain all the morning. Got out at Guildhall to see the polling. Found things all right. No chance for the Tories, notwithstanding the unceasing exertions of a party of young cadets, passengers of the *Sophia* Indiaman now lying windbound in the harbour, who in a barouche & 4, decked in red ribbands, were traversing the town & bringing Tory voters to the poll, old Jimmy Thomas amongst others. The bribery oath was administered to all at Falmouth; a wicked measure, a sort of compulsion to perjury. I doubt if it prevented the vote of a single individual. The poll closed at 4. Liberals 222 ahead! So much for Falmouth Toryism unbacked by cash. The result was announced & greeted by reiterated shouts. Speeches followed from Cornish, Broad, Coppock (Reform club man), Harvey, Bond, Rickerby &c.; exultation & triumph, stigma on the folly of their foes, & imprecations loud & deep on one (whose sacred calling at least should have prevented him) who it appears has withdrawn his custom from Edey for refusing to break his promise to Hutchins. In the evening the new member addressed his new constituents at Pearce's & was followed by many of his supporters, but the scene below stairs distracted my attention from the proceedings aloft. The cadets were in high wrath, vowing vengeance on Sammy Richards who had chucked a glass of water in one of their faces, but having returned to the dinner table they couldn't get at him. Meanwhile 2 porters, one dressed in a military & the other in a naval uniform, both 3 sheets to the wind, came in and addressed the assembled multitudes, as a burlesque on what was doing above stairs. The cadets finished the day by getting the band into the house & followed the meeting by a ball with Pearce's maids, & that by making Rickerby[1] as drunk as an owl, tattooing him & other great indignities, & finally wheeling him through the streets in a wheelbarrow & capsizing him in the gutter.

31. Uncle A. started for town to be present at the coming trial of Crane against Fox. The former's object is not at present to take the bone out of the latter's throat, as in the fable, but the bread out of his mouth, to the tune of £20,000 or so, – at least by his computation. A Swedish ship *Minerva* in ballast put in much damaged. I sent surveyors & master tradesmen on board to estimate the cost of repairs, &c., to send to Hamburg where she is insured. They report £4 to £500.

FEBRUARY

3. Ours is a varied scene. I paid devoirs to a Hungarian prince in the morning

1. Wm. Rickerby, editor of the *Falmouth Packet*.

& was concerned in the evening in smuggling a Greek outlaw out of the clutches of the bailiffs. We were informed yesterday that a writ was issued against Capt. Inglissi of the *Popidone* on account of Col. Hunters' infamous demand. Today it came sure enough. I sent off to warn Capt. Inglissi, who came on shore to consult. We advised him to return on board, or submit to the officer, who happened to enter the outer office while he was in the inner one. Meanwhile the scene within was dramatic. Capt. Inglissi wept & raved & swore he would rather kill himself than go to prison. Accordingly when shades of evening fell, P. Buckett's heart being touched by his hapless condition, he was enveloped in Capt. Andrew's old cloak & smuggled up to P. Buckett's house where he remains in concealment till Gilliat's answer instructs him what to be after.

5. The wind becoming somewhat more fair, I persuaded the Greek Captain to write a letter to Gilliat, authorising him to draw on him or his consignees for whatever was just in Col. Hunter's bill & then get ready for starting in the night if possible. This he readily did. We engaged a pilot & sent orders to the mate to weigh one anchor & have all in readiness for starting at 2 in the morning. Called on Capt. Inglissi & took leave. He seemed very comfortable & up to the fun.

6. 3 lame ducks swam into the port: an American with loss of sails, &c.; a Dutch galliot much damaged, with a cargo of sugar which she must discharge to the benefit of our neighbours; and another Dutchman damaged, with a cargo of cotton, of which she must discharge part. Capt. Inglissi was not able to start last night, the wind having backened to the Westward.

8. I had a call from a very superior intelligence in the person of a consumptive clergyman called Sterling,[1] who came on behalf of a Mrs. Mill[2] to enquire about her forfeited passage money; she with her daughter & son having arrived just too late for the packet, the latter being ordered there for his health, a blessing he is never likely to see by all accounts. I called on the family with Sterling. Saw the 2 ladies, who are ladylike. Looked for lodgings for them in the afternoon. Sterling is a person with whom you cannot converse 5 minutes without being struck by his vigorous intellect & fluency of expression. He was well acquainted with Coleridge & was his bedside companion during his last days.

10. Rode in to breakfast. This being the nuptial day of our gracious Queen, our loyalty was shown by dining all the poor of the town in their own houses. A liberal subscription was raised in the town & upwards of 2000 had a good dinner on this day, many of whom hardly knew the meaning of the word. The town was of course decked with flags & favours & such frippery & a band paraded the town. Took Dunstan's lodgings for the Mills. Escorted

1. See Introduction, pp. 17–20.
2. The mother of John Stuart Mill.

Sterling over Grove Hill to look at the paintings, he being a connoisseur.
11. At the Counting House all day. Evening at the Fenwicks next door, where I had the felicity of meeting Johns,[1] our new little curate, whom Derwent Coleridge describes as a 'harmless man', which I should think was just. Johns says Sterling is or was Editor of the *Athenaeum*.[2]
13. I rode to Perran with John Sterling according to agreement. A glorious day & a most interesting ride. His conversation is as good as any man's. He refuted, I thought well, the foundation & ground work of Puseyism, particularly as regards the authority of the fathers, whom he shows to be in many points speculative dreamers and self contradictory. Thinks the evangelical party as far surpass them in vital religion as they do them in theology. Arrived at Perran just in time to see the casting of the great bob,[3] – 14 tons. A most superb sight; the impetuous lava stream, the eager anxiety of the men regulating the speed & direction of the dazzling flood, and the blood-vessel-bursting excitement of Richard Cloke[4] was altogether a scene quite cyclopean. Derwent Coleridge, the Warres, Sterling, C. & I adjourned to the house to a handsome 'cold collection', then visited Uncle Lewis's garden & library, with the latter of which Sterling was highly delighted. Our ride home was very interesting. We discussed Providential interferences & supernatural visitations in both of which he is a sceptic.
15. Very busy day. Read some of Sterling's poems[5] which his friend Dr. Calvert[6] lent me & an original & vigorous work on Chartism by Carlyle.[7]
16. Called on the Mills who are comfortable in their present abode on the Terrace. Letter from Uncle A. about the result of our trial. The decision appears undecisive. The judge stated that there was no case to go before a jury & therefore awarded a pro forma verdict of damages, with permission to the defendants to bring an action for costs when the case will be discussed by the judges.
18. A luminous call from John Sterling who made some good remarks on Calvinism & on the mathematical accuracy of the scheme which he concluded made it so popular, & the completeness of all their deductions from wrong premises.
20. Hard sleet and bitingly cold. Rode to Penrose to visit poor Nicholls in his affliction, his wife having died in her confinement 2 days ago, leaving

1. The Rev. C. A. Johns of Helston. Ironically, in view of Derwent Coleridge's remark, he succeeded Coleridge as Headmaster of the Grammar School at Helston.
2. Sterling had edited the *Athenaeum* for a short time with F. D. Maurice, who later became his brother-in-law.
3. The beam of a steam engine. This beam was the largest yet cast at the Perran foundry.
4. The foreman at Perran.
5. Sterling had had a volume of *Poems* published in 1839.
6. See Introduction, pp. 20–1.
7. Carlyle's *Chartism* had d appearein 1839.

7 young children! He was striving to bear the blow like a man & took his affliction in the face, at the same time his sorrow was deep, fervent, & expressed with all the devotedness of a lover & the simplicity of a genuine unsophisticated man. I sat with him 3 quarters of an hour and he went through the whole lamentable story, by which it appears clearly that she was lost through the utter inefficiency of the old nurse, which aggravates the affliction much. Nicholls talks of leaving Penrose as soon as his master returns, not feeling equal to manage so large a place & attend to the requirings of seven children as well.

23. Biting, blustering, glorious weather. Walked to Pennance with my father & 2 females who were almost blown to pieces. The waves were tumbling & galloping & thundering over the black rocks in their maddest & magnificentest style.

26. Called at the Mills & the Mamma being out, Clara Mill invited me upstairs to see her brother. It was an opportunity I should be sorry to have missed. He was sitting in an easy chair muffled up in a long dressing gown. His face was beautiful & full of expression, refined & highly intellectual. His brow was like marble, but the hectic flush on his cheek & the glassy brightness of his large blue eyes spoke consumption unmistakably. On my entering he stretched out his hand which felt like death & said in a low, musical voice, 'I was anxious to see you to thank you for your great kindness to me which I shall never forget'. I begged him not to speak more than was necessary & then talked to his sister in order to save him the effort. He, however, made a few remarks on the flowers we sent him, &c., which evidenced a most refined & sensitive mind. I did not stay more than 5 minutes & left deeply interested by him.

27. A ship put in last night with maintop & mizentop-mast carried away. On enquiry before breakfast I found her to be the convict ship *Mandarin*, having on board Caspar Abraham & the others implicated in the gold dust[1] robbery & also the illustriously infamous Frost[2] & his companions. I talked with the captain who does not know much about the prisoners. They are very strict to admit no one on board more than is necessary. Walked to Penjerrick & dined on fried eggs. On return called on the Town Council, Capt. Plumridge & others, for signatures to a request to our Town & County members to be in their places the 5th of next month to support a motion for the abolition of capital punishment.[3]

28. Determined to see Frost if possible. Accordingly I went off with P.

1. Gold had been found and mined in Cornwall at this time.
2. The Chartist leader who had been arrested at the Newport rising in the previous year.
3. In practice at this time the death sentence was imposed generally for murder alone, but there were still over 100 crimes punishable by death. The Quakers were in the van of those who pressed for the abolition or reduction of capital punishment.

Buckett who had to settle the account with the captain & told him to introduce me to the doctor who has charge of the prisoners. I gave him a newspaper & tried to make myself agreeable. I found that Dr. McKechnie had
been visiting Frost in the capacity of doctor & had no intention of going
again, so that if I wished a sight of the lion I must assume a character which
should be a sufficient excuse. Accordingly I took that of missionary & tract
distributor, which however ill it became me, effected my purpose. Dr.
McKechnie introduced me as a friend come to enquire if any tracts or
religious books would be acceptable. Frost came forward and answered with
the most consummate contempt for all children's & old women's books. He
'would be obliged for a Pilgrim's Progress or some solid reading however'.
He had made religion his study for 13 years. In answer to my question
whether he did not consider the government had acted as leniently with him
as it could, he answered with great emphasis, 'Not a bit of it. They have
commuted my sentence to a much harder one. I should vastly prefer hanging
to this slow lingering torture to which they have condemned me.' Jones &
Williams who were in the same cell asserted the same. Altho' there appeared
to me to be a deal of swagger & affectation in this I was glad to hear them
profess it. It showed that transportation was held by this class of men to be
something more than a mere removal from one country to another. Frost's
is a face one cannot easily forget, wan & haggard & indented with deep
furrows, a small piercing grey eye & a beetling brow surmounted by a shock
of grey hair. Much character without decided talents in his face. All the bold
badness, without any of the sublimity of a Revolutionist. Jones & Williams
are inferior animals. The former affected a light carelessness & unconcern
which ill became his circumstances, the other appeared to be nothing more
than the brute man. We returned through a double row of convicts chained
by the leg & emerged through the massive grating guarded by a sentry with
sword drawn. On returning on shore I collected some tracts for the doctor
to distribute & a Pilgrim's Progress for Frost, which I begged him to
acknowledge, which he did in a short note.

29. A hard working day, but crowned with a halo! – viz an evening with
Sterling & Calvert at their lodgings, the former conversationalizing in his
highest strain, the latter equally engrossed in the disembowelment of sea-
birds. Sterling entered into some metaphysical analyses on various abstract
subjects. He then got on a dissertation of Genius & Talent which he holds are
utterly distinct.[1] The effect of the former appears supernatural, the latter is
that of a piece of mechanism, the effect of which may be wonderful but the
mode of its production is traceable & may be imitated. Lamb's talents were
perhaps of no very high order, yet his scintillations of genius are not to be
mistaken. Tho' compared with Coleridge he was a silver penny besides a

1. This distinction was very much a part of S. T. Coleridge's literary theory.

doubloon, yet were they coin of the same mint. He talked of Goethe whose own early life supplied him with the first half of *Werther*.

MARCH

1. 1st day. Bitterly cold. Young Mill worse.

2. Rode to Penjerrick. Making a beautiful entrance to that place. Sent off 2 letters tolerably well signed, one to our Country & the other to our Town members requesting them to give their support to Ewart's[1] motion on the subject of capital punishment.

7. Took a stroll with Sterling who chatted very pleasantly on Carlyle, H. Taylor,[2] Landor, Heine, Southey, &c. The last is sinking into a morbid lethargy as if he were worn out.

8. 1st day. Most superb weather even as yesterday. Ewart's motion for the abolition of capital punishment *in toto* lost by a majority of 70. The fault of attempting too much.

10. Stole away from the Temple of Mammon in the middle of the day to saunter through the sunny lanes & enjoy the brilliance of Sterling's conversation & Georgina Treweeke's countenance, Hender Molesworth's goodness, & Harriet Mill's[3] quiet companionship. These with sisters, 2 Welsh ponies, & self, formed an unusually agreeable company. Visited Tregedna & sat an hour with the Prince Regent.[4] We surveyed the improvements in our Penjerrick garden; my second visitation, having laid out a new entrance drive before breakfast.

22. Had the long anticipated pleasure of meeting John Mill, the exquisite writer in the *London & Westminster*.[5] His voice, face & manner betoken delicacy of feeling, mildness, clearness & correctness of view, with that entire absence of assumption & affectation which distinguishes the really great from the really little.

23. Till 5 o'clock this was not materially unlike other days of the year, but from 5 to half past 10, one of a thousand. Mill dined with us & Sterling joined us on the departure of the ladies. What a time it was! What clear exposition

1. Wm. Ewart (1798–1869) in 1837 introduced successfully a Bill to abolish capital punishment for certain petty crimes. In 1840 he pressed unsuccessfully for total abolition of the capital penalty.
2. Sir Henry Taylor (1800–86), wrote a number of verse dramas, especially *Philip van Artevelde*, 1834.
3. Either Mrs Mill or (see below) another of her daughters, also named Harriet.
4. i.e. Uncle Joshua.
5. John Stuart Mill became editor of the *London & Westminster Review* in 1836, but resigned in 1840. His important philosophical works had not at this time been published.

of eternal principles, high thoughts, & sound feeling. Sterling had most to say, but what Mill said was ever exactly to the point & ever original. The first theme was flowers. Culture will improve, but not change the character of a species. Then somehow we tumbled on geology. Sterling & pater held a long & spirited argument on seeking to reconcile the Mosaic account of the creation with certain physical facts. Sterling insists strongly on the importance of not twisting the palpable meaning of scripture to accord with what is known to be matter of fact. He would prefer saying so, once there is a discordance which we cannot understand. Lyell's[1] system was reviewed & flung overboard. As the evening advanced we dived deeper into the mysteries of human nature. Sterling propounded high moral maxims which Mill clarified & glorified in his own felicitous manner. Both insisted much on not striving to be or appear to be a different character to our own.

24. Busy preparing for departure. I walked to Penjerrick to meet the girls and Harriet Mill with whom we had a pleasant walk discussing the beautiful character of her younger brother. I spent the evening with Sterling who gave me a letter of introduction to Carlyle.

25. Walked with Mill and Sterling after dinner. Mill sketched simply and beautifully the opposite habit of mind of himself & Carlyle; he being a generalizer, Carlyle an individualizer. His own turn was abstraction, Carlyle's realization; the former is characteristic of the moral philosopher, the latter of the poet. He had once or twice actually realized scenes of which he read and from that experience could easily understand the fancied inspiration of poets. For historic events to come home to him with the reality of actual presence would be more than his nerves could bear. When he first saw the great Truth 12 years since, that the *earnestness* of a writer is the only thing about him worth attempting to imitate, and the inevitable inconsistency of a copied style makes it more than vain, it seemed to him like a Revelation. There is a sincerity of depth of assent in his emphatic *Yes* which is very peculiar. He is the most candid, genuine and clear-reasoning man I ever met with.

26. Took leave of the Tregedna party and met the girls with Clara Mill and their usual attendants Mill and Sterling at the cottage. We had a deeply interesting walk home. We divided lions, C. and I taking Mill, the others Sterling; Mill all the way uttering the wisest things with the greatest modesty. His counsel was weighty and encouraging, his truths high and irresistible, his language the eloquence of sincerity and earnestness. 'Be ever striving at some point beyond you and above you, but not beyond the sphere of your natural tendencies. Never try to deceive others with the appearance

---

1. Sir Chas. Lyell (1797–1875) was a pupil of the Foxes' friend William Buckland. He published *The Principles of Geology*, 1830–33, and *The Elements of Geology*, 1838. His work changed men's notions about the age of the earth and the nature of Creation.

of being what you are not, but above all never try to deceive yourself. For the aim of your strivings, consult the inward guide which will infallibly point out your own peculiar legitimate end and province. Much will be gained in the pursuit indirectly which was never contemplated. Never relax nor give way to self indulgence or desultory habits, and your reward will be ample according to your self denial. There is work to be done by every man and some work or other *can* be done by every man. Carlyle's favourite motto: 'A man never knows what he can do till he tries. Don't let your power of discernment outstrip your powers of execution. Keep the latter up to the former.' With much more in the same strain too good to be forgotten. We parted warmly and the pressure of his hand more than his words spoke his sincerity. He pressed me to visit him at the India House, which I shan't be slow to do when in London.

27. Started per *Regulator* at half past 6. Snow nearly all the way to St. Austell. Unadventurous journey to Exeter where we were glad to avail ourselves of the many comforts of the New London Inn.

28. To Bristol by the *Estafette*. I had a remarkably agreeable companion in the person of a nameless fellow countrywoman, evidently of some birth and breeding, altho' her appearance at first sight indicated neither. She was from Padstow and a great friend of Miss Brune's. After lavation at the Red Lion we 'flied' (not flew) to Combe, where we were cordially greeted by Aunt Agatha and her two fair steps. Mary is a noble looking girl, with all the bloom and freshness of nature, unsullied apparently by boarding school education. Uncle G. very kind in his way. He talked us into a state of semi-consciousness or luminous crisis, agreeable after the fatigues of the day. He is more liberal in his views, and takes a hopeful view of public affairs, which indicates an improved state of the liver.

29. 1st day. Took leave of our host at ½ past 7 and drove 'cross country' to Frenchay to breakfast. Made much of by Aunt Mariana. Their house is wonderfully improved. Uncle Francis has changed some nondescript back premises into a most elegant and tasteful little drawing room, furnished in the choicest manner and communicating with the dining room through the prettiest little greenhouse I ever saw. As the Friends here find their spiritual hunger satisfied by a morning meeting only, Uncle Francis and I enjoyed ourselves in the sun in the beautiful grounds of the Duchess of Beaufort, and his garden, where I saw a plan of growing pears worth remembering. The pear is grafted on a quince stock and when it has attained the height you wish, the top is cut off and all the lateral branches tied down to impede the flow of sap. The strength of the tree then produces flower instead of new wood. The produce is very great, and no room is lost in the garden.

30. Took leave of my kind host at 7 and started behind his little pony for Bristol. Took inside berths per Welsh mail and proceeded to our final

destination. A beautiful passage across the Severn.[1] In the coach was a gentleman who gave me much information about Mrs. Fry,[2] her interview with the Queen and her present mission. He informed me that she was 'a ladylike woman, though a Quakeress'! Got out at the Abbey[3] with books and baggage. At the door appeared Cos. J. T. Price, N. Tregelles and C. Waring. The former led us at once to business in the office, to consult about accepting an offer for the *Beresford*.[4] This settled, we proceeded to 'The Cottage' and greeted Aunt Price and daughters and a good tea with beef and oysters. They gave me a hot berth with a vengeance, right over the kitchen. I was soon perfectly kiln dried.

31. Rain appeared. Paid C. Waring a call, then to Glyn Clydach. It is a remarkably pretty, genteel-looking place which belongs to the Coal Co. I was formally introduced to business and spent the morning in going through the upper and lower works. The din of hammers and furnaces and the swarthy creatures toiling at the formation of mysterious unintelligible instruments made the scene very cyclopean. The hot air furnace was interesting; a third 'tweer', i.e. bellows snout, was applied yesterday. The tweers are guarded by water passing round them just where they enter the furnace. The air is heated to 600° in a furnace, before driven in to supply the main one. The main works are devoted to the manufacture of boilers. After dinner J. T. Price drove us to Briton Ferry, our new purchase from Lord Jersey, a very attractive spot with an elegant and comfortable house overlooking the mouth of Neath River, where we are forming a shipping place by cheating the tide of the low water mud and making a channel with bargeloads of slag to enable vessels to get alongside at all tides. J. T. Price and we then strode down to our present shipping places higher up the river. Upwards of 6000 tons of good coal thereon; stone coal,[5] very fine. It is un-come-off-able on rubbing it with your finger.

APRIL

1. Proceeded to business after breakfast. Visited the furnace mouth 40 feet above where it is tapped for casting. It carries at present 40 charges per 24 hours, each charge consisting of 5 cwt Welsh ore, 1½ Cornish, 3 cwt of coal, besides culm and limestone. The result, since the 3rd tweer has been applied,

1. The route from Bristol to S. Wales involved a crossing by ferry which operated where the Severn Bridge now stands.
2. Elizabeth Fry.
3. The Abbey Iron Works at Neath.
4. A ship owned by the Company.
5. i.e. anthracite.

is not yet known. Its average turn-out has been 60 tons per week. Whether it will now pay its way or not seems to hinge on the quality of the iron. After dinner we visited the forge. One hammer weighs 2½ tons and gives the iron a pretty smart jab.

2. Christiana, after my twice declining, set at me again this morning, pressing me to make the 'Cottage' my home during my stay. The first thing therefore on reaching the Abbey was to hunt for lodgings. I found the best in the village unoccupied, 2 comfortable rooms at 5/- per week. The husband was out but the old lady will give me an answer the day after tomorrow. After meeting, drove to Briton Ferry and went at once to our embankments which are a capital idea. By their means 50 vessels will be able to lie alongside our wharfs and the coals will be run out of the mouth of the colliery on a tramroad direct to the shipping place. Rigged as colliers we took a lamp and explored the colliery. They have driven a level into the hill about 230 yards; the size of the vein in the end is 2 feet 3″. Men drive and arch up with stones, say 6 feet high, at 12/- per yard. In the last 'stall', that is, a driving upwards from the main level, the air is consumed in a short time and the workman is obliged to leave it. We are driving into the old workings in order to gain ventilation.

3. After breakfast we 3 (i.e. the Co.) started in J. T. Price's vehicle up the vale of Neath to inspect operations. After 8 miles of first-rate Welsh scenery, we arrived at Pwllfaron, our anthracite colliery, where we rigged as colliers, squatted in a tram and were drawn by horse into the bowels of the mountain. We have driven in here about 1300 yards; the vein is 4 feet thick, all hard glittering stone coal. The mode of working is to drive the heading 6 feet high and proportionate width, to admit of a horse the whole way. On each side the main artery small passages are driven at about 20 feet apart, called 'stalls', merely the height of the vein of coal, but a considerable width. The coal is slid down to the main passage where it is taken by the trams. We are at present only working the 4 ft. vein, from which we get 3 boat-loads per day or 60 to 70 tons. Having bread-and-cheesed, as Wilberforce would say, we emerged to the light of day, which after all is pleasanter than the carboniferous scenery within. We harnessed the animal and proceeded to our iron mines. The first thing one sees is an inclined plane something like ¼ of a mile long, with a wheel at the top by means of which the loaded trams going down draw up the empty one. We have 4 levels, i.e. workings, with an arched mouth in the side of the hill, for they are all what we should call adits, except one making our fifth, which is open like a quarry, in which 6 veins are visible. Having given notice a month since of a reduction of wages, the men trooped about us in swarms. We put off any final decision till the expiration of the month when the furnace will have been proved. Got home at ½ past 10 and Aunt Price scolded her big boy for being so late.

5. 1st day. My father passed a feverish night which made him doubtful whether he should be able to cross tomorrow. However about half-past 5, the afternoon being fine, we started per mail for Swansea, having fought our way through the vehement opposition of the 'Cottage' people to this plan. Spent a pleasant evening with my father till bedtime.

6. I saw my father off at 6 a.m. per *Bristol* steamer for Ilfracombe, and am left on my own foundation in this principality for 6 weeks to study our various interests therein. J. T. Price joined me at Capt. Moyse's (our agent here) and took me to our Graigola coal bank to see operations, then to Graigola Company House, where with Parsons we overhauled the accounts. I dined at Capt. Moyse's with 3 strapping daughters and accompanied him across the water to our 2 shipping places at Port Tennant. We visited en route another shipping place of ours by some old Copper Works, called Quaker's Bank. I spent the evening with Charles Waring tracing out map of our holdings from the Lords of the Abbey.

7. After breakfast I went with Cos. J. T. Price and Charles to the main colliery and had a thorough inspection of plans and sections, to examine as far as possible the actual position of the end of our workings in relation to those of the old works, now deserted 50 years and filled with a column of 40 fathoms of water. From the vagueness of the information on this point we decided on not driving further in the direction of the old workings. After dinner I rode with him to Briton Ferry and went underground.

8. In the morning I laid in a stock of groceries by the sly and after dinner surreptitiously conveyed my goods and chattels out of the cottage. I was discovered with my portmanteau by Christiana whilst gliding through the front door. She seized thereupon, but after a sharp tussle I secured my property and sent it down to my lodgings at Peter Godfrey's. I spent the afternoon at Graegola with Cos. J. T. Price to see the first launch of trams down a new inclined plane 310 yards long. A fine improvement and made for £50. I took tea at Godfrey's house, comfortable rooms, civil landlady and, what is most important in a lodging house, *clean*. I received brilliant letters from the girls, but reporting the death of Henry Mill, calmly and quietly as the dissolving of a snowflake.

10. Rode up Neath Valley with Cos. J.T.P. to look into Pwllfaron & meet the miners at Abernant. We went into the open work called the Patch, the best of the levels, where the ore lies very regular, wide & of good quality. The men being assembled about 80 in number, Cos. J.T.P. speechified, saying that owing to the improvement in the furnace we found it unnecessary to require a reduction in their wages. They were pleased & asked for a quart apiece to drink our health. J.T.P. told them he didn't like that, because he understood that people put poison in the beer, called alcohol or the devil: he therefore drank nothing but water himself, & of that he had no objection

to their drinking as much as they liked. He left £1 amongst them as a compromise. Ate fried eggs & ham at our overman's house and rode home.

12. A Sunday which was no sun-day. Wet, close and dismal. Tea at the Cottage to receive last directions from Cos. J.T.P.

13. Saw him and his sister Junia off per coach at 7. He will accompany her thro' her ministerial labours which will probably detain him 4 weeks. This is a bore, as I lose in great measure the purpose of my visit. The furnace is doing badly owing to the Abernant coal of which we shall use no more.

14. Up at ½ past 5 & in the works before the bell ceased. The furnace is still bad. That Abernant coal is ruination. I watched the poor wretches trying to tap the furnace in vain till ½ past 10, when I went home, pitying them from my soul. They did not succeed till 2 in the morning. The severity of the work consisted in 3 men standing at the very mouth of the furnace. (I could not stand within 20 feet without being scorched.) One of these held down the tapping iron to guide it, the other 2 drove it in with alternate blows, till the sweat literally ran from them in streams. They rushed from the place when they could no longer bear it & others took their places. The tapping iron broke off in the furnace which much increased the labour.

16. Last night they couldn't get a cast at all from that perverse furnace. After Meeting rode to Briton Ferry with Charles to see into things. On return found Cos. Nathaniel in high excitement on board his new tug, whose paddles were floundering & she springing forward against the big chain which curbed her like an impatient steed pawing to be off. The chain was at length cast off & she plied amidst shouts of triumph down Neath river & back again, loaded with Abbey boys and 2 or 3 directors. I found in the evening that I had left my purse containing a guinea & the key of my writing case in a shop at Neath.

17. Good Friday. Rode to Neath before breakfast to enquire after my lost property, but heard no tidings & never shall. Received a letter from home enclosing one of Sterling's to Mammy, and another to self from J. Mill, 2 sheets and a half long, – such a beauty. He has given us a complete series of the London and Westminster.[1]

22. In the afternoon Charles & I experimentalised on the small coal from Briton Ferry which we mixed with river clay in different proportions & concreted it with lime water. Then we cut them into square cakes & placed them on a flue. There seems no reason why this should not make good fuel & so turn to account thousands of tons which are now lost.

23. Meeting in morning. The furnace is slowly recovering. Proved our small coal cakes in a kitchen fire & they seem to burn remarkably well. Received

1. In return for their kindness to his dead brother Henry, J. S. Mill sent the Foxes a complete run of the *Westminster Review* with marginal notes in his own hand and in some instances identifications of anonymous articles.

the key of my desk from home which enabled me to get at certain locked up letters which have not seen the light for a week & send home a pretty considerably fat parcel.

25. Called on J. Wickens, agent of the Abbey Lords, who is just arrived on his annual visit, to feel his pulse on the subject of our turning a meadow at the bottom of Glyn Clydach into a pond, by building a substantial dam across the valley, as a reservoir for the works. This is a point of vital importance to us. He listened attentively & evidently liked the scheme, but requested us to send him our proposition in writing, that he might consider it properly & answer in a day or two. Our object is to get from him a black on white engagement that such an operation shall not prejudice our interests if we wish to renew our lease, as the present terminates in 12 years. This point requires delicate handling.

28. Breakfasted with J. Wickens (the Lords' agent) at Redwood's and then accompanied him & Cos. Nathaniel to the field we propose turning into a pond. He made no objections & I drew out a memo of agreement between him & the Co. & sent him for his signature, which he accordingly affixed, promising therein to give us a lease of the ground for 21 years if we desire it. Cos. Nathaniel says it is the best day's work done at the Abbey for years.

MAY

1. No ushering of the day with horns, kettles and garlands. The Welsh look on the first footstep of Summer in moody silence. In office all day.

3. 1st day. Wrote home & heard thence. Fixed to be up at 3 tomorrow in order to be off per *Bristol* from Swansea for Ilfracombe at 5.

4. I was awakened by vehement ringing at 4 from C. Waring and Ed. Boon, who had brought the beasts to the door and were come to see after me, being an hour after time. I turned out and drove down like mad. Reached Swansea just in time. An awful passage. A fresh easterly gale was meeting a strong tide from Westward and a pretty bobbery they kicked up in the middle of the channel. All laid low except one passenger and self. I landed and made a royal breakfast at the *Britannia*. Scoured the Town, reading rooms, heights, rocks, beach, clambered up the cliff and returned to dinner. Reshipped at ½ past 4 and had a fine smooth passage back. Called on Capt. Moyse and reached home about 9. Kind letters from home.

6. After breakfast I rode with Charles to Pont-Neath-Vaughan 12 miles up the valley, calling en route on Jevons, the Mills' friend. Cos. J.T.P.'s clay works are at Pont-Neath-Vaughan, situated in a most romantic ravine above a rocky stream. We followed its windings for 2 or 3 miles in perfect rapture.

It is decidedly the loveliest spot I have yet seen in Wales. The lady's fall is here in winter; now it is nothing but a little spout of water as it were from an ebullient tea-kettle. But the wild and richly clad crags which surround it were looking in great perfection from the various hues of the young foliage which covered them. Rode back just ahead of the rain, after dining on mountain river trout and what looked exceedingly like horse lice in the porter. Home in time to write a few letters to Falmouth.

7. Dined at the Abbey and then accompanied Cos. Nathaniel in his gig to W. Parsons' rolling mill to gain hints for ours. The machinery is simple enough, a water wheel turns the pair of rolls by means of toothed pinions, and a fly wheel communicates with each to accumulate force. The refinery iron is run in hot to the puddling furnace, in which it is stirred up into balls of clidgy semi-fluid iron, which are put under the big hammer, & 2 or 3 blows flatten them enough to go through the rolls, which makes them sheets about ⅜ inches thick which are then snipped square with a big shears & sent off as boiler plates. We then drove to Swansea and separated to go about our respective business. I was pleased to hear from Capt. Moyse that our coal at Port Tennant is beginning to move a little more briskly. Got home at 8.

8. Went with old Charley Jordan to Merthyr per coach to look at the construction of a pond amongst the hills. The road was beautiful & bad, & both in the superlative. The men of Merthyr are the crudest looking material in human shape I have yet seen. The pond is in a wild spot in all conscience. Whilst examining the construction and sketching the sluices we got a regular soaking, for which on returning to the inn I had to rig out in the landlord's garments. After dinner I had just time to run over a portion of Crawshay's ironworks at Cyfarddfa, in front of which is his barrack-looking castle, whence he can watch operations from his drawing room windows. He keeps 7 furnaces going in a row, worked by 2 blowing engines, each furnace making 85 tons weekly. To see the big hammer chewing up the blob of red iron like a schoolboy over a taffyball & that blob then run thro' the rolls, groove after groove, till it came out almost as fast as I am writing it, a long bar as thick as my finger, was something like. He has 2 complete ranges of rolling mills. The water after passing over the wheel is pumped up thro' 2 6-feet pumps and repeats its duty. He employs about these works between 2 and 3000 men. Home by ten past 7.

9. Taking leave and finishing maps. Cos. J.T.P. returned in evening.

11. Went down to works at 6 and explained to Maister what I had done in his absence as locum tenens. He's too much afraid of laying out money. Talked to him about Briton Ferry & the necessity of having an experienced efficient person stationed on the spot to superintend affairs. Looked over furnace account which proved disastrous as I expected. Last month the best week showed a loss of £20 & the worst week a loss of £85. J.T.P. blew on

my experimental compressed fuel, saying it would not be saleable on account of its colour. After breakfast he went to Swansea. I accordingly spent the day in packing up & taking leave.

12. Parted with my landlady with good feeling on each side (a rare occurrence) & mounted the Bristol Mail at 7. Reached Cardiff at 11 & took a cup of cocoa at E. Waring's. I sat an hour or more with his wife and daughter, who complain of the dullness & want of society. Visited Cardiff castle & saw the horrid den where Robert of Normandy was confined by his brother for 13 years. The old castle is a well placed venerable ruin. Facing it is the modern one, the residence of Lord James Stuart, but the property of the Marquis of Bute. An omnibus conveyed me to the steamer which lay in the basin at the end of the Marquis's docks. They appear an amazing work, but the water appears to me very inconveniently high for loading vessels. It is said that these docks cost him £300,000! Reached Clifton soon after five. After a wash at the hotel my first point of attraction was Sterling's,[1] whose house I found at last with wonderful difficulty. He lives in 19 Lower Crescent. I found him not looking well, just returned from Town, very cordial & interesting. He introduced me to his wife & children & to his sister-in-law, Mrs. Maurice, the wife of the High Church Maurice,[2] well known amongst the controversial-theology-reading-world. He gave me a note to Carlyle's wife, an *alto relievo* likeness of himself, and moreover a substantial tea which proved very acceptable. I took leave and drove to Joseph Raikes for orders from Granny, Ma having written me that she would reach Bristol today and proceed under my escortship. Drove to Baldwin Street & found him, but no note, nor did he know that she was expected at Frenchay. However, he sent a clerk with me & we ferreted about at the coach offices for tidings, but in vain. I waited for the *Nonpareil* till after 10, but with no arrival, and with some misgivings I took my place per *Emerald* for tomorrow morning.

13. A wet morning, so changed my berth for an inside. Dull companions, but country beautiful. Got on the Railway at Reading & travelled by that mode the last 38 miles[3]. The carriage was the most superb of any railway carriage I ever saw, a regular drawing room with large plate glass windows, & 2 tables surrounded by velvet sofas. The motion is, however, the worst I know on any rails. Reached Town about half past 6 & took up my quarters at St. Paul's Coffee House.

1. Sterling was living at this time at Clifton (now a part of Bristol), but later moved with his wife and family to Falmouth.
2. The Rev. F. D. Maurice and John Sterling had married sisters. In his early career Maurice commanded the support of the Tractarians, but he was not really a High Churchman. His theology, like that of Coleridge (of whom he was a disciple), was based on Christian Platonism.
3. Brunel's Great Western line from Paddington to Bristol was open only as far as Reading at this date.

14. Called on W. Forster at Sandersons but he was out. Buss'd down to Barton Crescent and spent all the morning lodging-hunting; no easy job. I found one beauty, the only difficulty was that the two principal rooms were already engaged. Called a second time & found the landlady in. I pointed out what desirable lodgers we should be and put her up to get t'other ones off, which she'll try, & will write me. Returned to City and called on John Mill at the India House, most cordial affectionate & in short J. Millish. Recalled on William & found him. I walked with him & Cos. Francis to York Hotel where the Tucketts are quartered. Found from them that a rod in pickle awaited me from Granny, who with Aunt C. was expected that afternoon per railway. Accordingly I rattled down there with William in a cab & after waiting an hour received & safely deposited them in the coach, I bundling inside as a No. 5, & entered into full explanations which proved quite satisfactory. I packed them all up neatly in a hackney coach with luggage & dispatched them to Tottenham. William & I got on board a coach & bundled down to his lodgings in Hampstead, where we found ourselves ready for tea, it being past 9. From tea-time till 2 we had a glorious chat, embracing past, present, & future. After discussing common acquaintance, letters & metaphysics, we got on *the* subject, which is in a state of awful muddlement, & the poor youth is much put to it to disentangle honourably to himself & considerately to another. I gave him what counsel I could.

15. Streaming day. Lodgings are ours. After a round of calls, seeing plenty of relatives & hearing all about everybody, I entered a bus & visited my landlady with whom I completed all final arrangements & fixed to begin on 2nd day. Livery stable. Thence to Fraser's to get tickets for Carlyle's lectures on Hero Worship. Dined at Vasey's & proceeded to the Lecture room. Waited at the door & waylaid Clara Mill. We secured a good place & were much interested till Carlyle's arrival in examining the fine study of heads & faces around us. Leigh Hunt was there, Milman, I heard whispered behind me, & I soon discovered the Calmuck countenance of Whewell vis-à-vis. The female show was remarkably fine, mostly striking from intellectual expression and high breeding; but there was one girl in a white veil in a distant corner of surpassing loveliness. I pointed her out to Clara who was much struck. Jane Backhouse's style, but far superior. At length the hero of our worship arrived, as much like his picture in Sterling's library as Rome is to the cork model; a black-haired, beetle-browed, wooden-faced, earnest genuine *Man*, the champion of Truth, the deadly foe of quackery, the defender of all sincere believers, be their belief what it may. He began with some nervous hesitation, but as he warmed with his subject he became eloquent, impressive, earnest, irresistible, sublime. This was his 4th lecture, the subject, 'The Hero as Priest'. He chose as illustrations of his present subject

Luther & Knox. He gave us a sketch of the former's life in a few, spirited words & scouted the idea of his being instigated to his resolute opposition of popery by private pique. He was prompted by a love of truth to search for the Real; he consulted his bible & his conscience. He was deputed to Rome: he looked at the professions, the ceremonies, the observancies of Roman Catholicism & saw that they were miserable unrealities. His conscience told him that he must openly teach the people that the decretals of a Pope could in nowise save them, being but ink & paper. He pointed out the man's sincerity of belief & its fruits, & spoke as in bitterness of spirit of the hollow forms, the miserable half-beliefs & the spasmodic efforts of some to believe that they believe, now prevalent in the world. He then started an original idea on the subject of idolatry, which in its proper application is not of necessity sinful. Idolatry means symbolism. These symbols were mostly applied to false gods & hence the denunciations against idolatry, but nevertheless we are all idolators. Even the Puritans when they waged war with all images & symbols of the invisible, looked at the bible as a sacred symbol. He then entered on Knox & the false ideas entertained of him. His was not a low, plebeian, insult to Royalty, but he felt he had a work to perform & a truth to declare, & woe to him if he did it not. When Clara & I trudged out it began to sputter & when we reached Oxford Street the clouds were rent in twain with a peal of thunder & down came the rain in streams. I put her into a shop and finding she had no conscientious scruples to cabs, got one, stowed in & drove to Kensington Gardens, thro' which we walked to their house, the rain having abated. After a social time with the mother & sister I took leave & trudged 2 miles to St. George's Hospital. I found that Cavendish[1] had left about 10 minutes before. I ferreted out his lodgings a mile & a half off, but he had just left there & I had to retrace. I was quite ready for tea when I reached St. Paul's.

16. I met my father at the *Spread Eagle* on his arrival from Bury Hill. He looks well & professes to have regained his usual health and strength. He has taken my quarters at St. Paul's. We strolled down to the Lowther Arcade, looking en route into a shop to see some beautiful specimens of the Electrotype. The Adelaide gallery surpasses what I ever saw before; an oxyhydrogen microscope showing all manner of awful animalculae yards long, the decomposition of water by electricity, the process of glass-blowing and spinning, beautiful specimens of polarisation, a steam-gun, a mode of welding lead without solder & what was most interesting of all, the electric eel. Started per Dorking coach at 4 & reached Bury Hill to dinner at ½ past 7. Hugged Parent & girls & paid my respects to Uncle Barclay & family. A pleasant social dinner & companiable evening.

18. We took leave of Bury Hill at 7. I have never left the place so favourably

1. Cavendish Wall was now a medical student in London.

impressed with Uncle Barclay. His calm, feeling, but manly way of looking misfortune[1] in the face & counting the alleviations is a credit to his head & heart. We reached Town about 10, dropped Mammy at the Meeting House & took the girls to our lodgings which look promising. Having deposited the vehicle at a livery stable, we 3 posted down to the West End. I deposited them at the Royal Academy & proceeded to Belgrave Square. Called at No. 8. Uncle David was out & Aunt David not dressed (12 o'clock). However, she appeared in about 10 minutes in the magnificent drawing room & after 10 minutes indifferent chat I continued my route to Carlyle's, 5 Cheyne Row, Chelsea. Neither he nor his rib was at home. Left Sterling's note of introduction with another, enquiring what day would suit him for me to call again. Joined the girls at the National Gallery where met Uncle and Aunt Charles. Dined at Uncle Charles's lodgings & then started en masse on a Queen-hunt. We waited nearly an hour at Hyde Park corner, in vain. We saw, however, the old Duke of Wellington on horseback, his open honest face unmistakeably stamped with his own straightforward, upright, manly simplicity. Home to tea at 8. Met Cavendish at the door, looking unchanged except rather pale, probably from confinement & hard fag. Took him in & gave him some tea. His apprenticeship will be out this month, when he will have to walk the hospital, 2 years in Town, & then go to Edinburgh and fag for an M.D-ship. He & my father & self went out about 10 for a spree to Mme. Tussaud's wax figure exhibition. Found it closed of course. Rain.

19. Mill's to dinner. Only the family party to meet us, which was satisfactory. All were brimful of kindness & cordiality. John twice remarked that he couldn't persuade himself it was real. Clara is the 2nd best in the family, but he is pure intelligence, such a combination of giant intellect with feminine modesty, is rare indeed. He walked with us thro' Hyde Park to Knightsbridge, whence we took a fly. All the way he discoursed on high themes; Will, Self-subsistence, Christian Church, Sectarianism. He foresees much further splitting up of sects & finally a reduction of the creed of the universal Christian church to a few general articles in which all can unite & nominal distinctions be thenceforth abolished, tho' each individual be still allowed full freedom of opinion. This is the great consummation to be desired.

20. Opening of the great Sanhedrin.[2] Fell in with numerous acquaintance in the yard. Several prefatory addresses and ere the business commenced we had a visit from Priscilla Green & Sarah Grubb. From the latter we had one of her marvellous sybilline sermons. She pointed out the fulfilment of her many prophecies in regard to the Society & denounced those who attempted to remodel it. She made some well-deserved, honest, uncompromising

1. The death of his wife.
2. The Yearly Meeting of the Society of Friends.

home-thrusts about money-loving, money-getting spirit. A sermon which would have pleased Carlyle.

21. Dined at the Backhouses'. A sizeable party; Jane was looking very splendid. Cut the latter half of the afternoon meeting & posted down to the Athenaeum to find Snow Harris. He showed me over the Institution & then we started for the Royal Society's Room at Somerset House to meet Prince Albert. We saw some singular characters whilst waiting in the ante-room: a Persian in full costume, Buckland, Wheatstone, Faraday, Roget, Marquis of Northampton, the President, &c. We strangers entered as our names were called and were entertained by the dull proceedings of this dull society till a servant announced the Prince. The little Marquis ran out & ushered him in. He was attended by 2 lords, Aberdeen & another. He walked up the room with dignity, bowing as he went. He is a well-built, handsome young man, with more intelligence in his face than the pictures indicate. Having reached the table the President took his fin & palavered in a very courtierlike style, but in too low a voice to be heard, whilst the Prince bobbed very graciously ever 3½ seconds. Having thus duly installed him & finished our transactions we refreshed with coffee & separated.

22. Attended our parish church, the Westminster Meeting House. Met Cos. Elizabeth Fry & Bessie Gurney there. At ½ past 2 Caroline & I cabbed off to Edward Street to attend Carlyle's last lecture, the subject, the Hero as King. He considers the Parliamentary war the most interesting thing in English History. It was first the war of belief against unbelief, taxes against Freedom of Conscience. He drew a masterly sketch of Cromwell, who is one of his heroes. In his cool way he said, Perhaps I am the first man that ever dared to assert that Cromwell was an honest man. Cromwell's rise to the supreme power if fairly examined will be found to have been produced by the necessity of the times & not by his own ambition. Cromwell had a great Truth within him which was his armour & confidence, but his acts were the result of circumstances. He died in 1658 & one century after, arose another like unto him, but a lesser, Napoleon Bonaparte. The age in which he lived, the 18th century, may be called the century of quacks. The tremendous French Revolution was a Truth clad in thunder & horror, but still a Truth. It was the assertion that the world is more than a machine & the people who form it have a spirituality within them. In Bonaparte there was a great truth but not without a mixture of falsehood. We found the afternoon meeting engaged in considering the state of the Society as shewn by the answers to the queries. A great deal was said on attending other places of worship. Joseph Eton endeavoured to persuade the meeting to issue a recommendation to the Society against the use of all intoxicating drinks. This the weightier parts of the body declined.

23. Reached Carlyle's at 6. He had not returned from a ride, but his wife & I

had a pleasant chat. She told me of the tremendous effort these lectures had been to him & how he suffered from them. 2 Scotch gentlemen wandered in; one, a Mr. Dunlop, a great abstinence advocate, the other nobody as far as I could discern. After a short time the hero entered and greeted me very warmly. He took his chair & scintillated in broad Scotch to the delight of his hearers. There is no effort & no affectation in his style of discourse. Familiar, earnest, emphatic & ever ready to appreciate a good thing, which he greets with a most boisterous shout of laughter. He is a delightful companion, without any affectation of greatness; his conversation is such as no one could listen to for 10 minutes & not be convinced he was an extraordinary man, – a great living Truth. Mill calls him a Hebrew Prophet. He talked T-totalism with Dunlop with much interest. Then we got on Methodism, Revivals, Superstition &c. He calls the Conference[1] the hundred Popes of England's Jesuitry. He told us of a sick child in Scotland that had been induced to say it was a changeling & then tortured, roasted & killed by its parents & relations, which he says is about the most affecting thing he ever heard. After the others were gone & he and I were alone, he became much more interesting. He talked of Sterling & wondered how he ever could have taken orders with his latitudinarian views. We discussed Royalty & Loyalty & the absurdity of the 'Divine right'. He gave me a deeply interesting sketch of his own life. His sense of the unrealities of the world commenced at 15. He ascribes his emancipation to Goethe & some of the Germans. After talking of belief for some time, I asked him how the belief once fixed, we were to gain a certain knowledge of what is our own particular work on the earth. He said, 'Goethe's counsel on that point I have found the best. Ever do the good that lies nearest thee.' He does not like the idea of taking up one particular aim or object & striving after the fulfilment of it. He considers that vanity is closely allied with such a scheme & that great men have never entertained it. He adduced St. Simon[2] as an instance of the ill effects of it. However, this was not an illustration of what I meant. I left between 10 & 11, but omnibuses being scarce at that time, I did not reach home till midnight.

24. 1st day. Joined the girls at Ham House after breakfast. Found the old English hospitality of the place undiminished. Met Fowell Buxton & Edward & Kitty & their lovely brace of boys at dinner. Kitty very sweet & as good wives love to be.

25. I dined with Cos. Francis at the old Jewry and then called on Mill at the India House Museum. I had a choice chat with him for $\frac{3}{4}$ of an hour. He says that the French are incapable of the combination of humour & earnestness, consequently their laugh is confined to absurdities & is of the characer of a sneer. They could not both admire & be amused by Cervantes. They could

1. Presumably the Methodist Conference.
2. Saint-Simon (1760–1825), the founder of French Socialism.

not love & laugh at Pickwick. This was given rise to by speaking of Carlyle's characteristic laugh. After meeting proceeded homeward, which we reached at length after sundry farcical adventures, composed of wrong omnibus, drunken companion, taking a coach, getting out again, re-entering & leaving an umbrella somewhere on the road. Letter from Uncle George from Florence.

28. Nothing very exciting at the morning meeting. I dined in an awful hurry with Aunt Chas. at whose lodgings I had the pleasure of meeting Dr. Calvert, who accompanied us to the India House Museum, where all the Mill party & Professor Nichol[1] & wife were waiting for us. After seeing the gorgeous spoils of the East, barbarian weapons, & illuminated Persian MSS., we wandered through the chambers of stuffed natural history, more occupied in each other's converse than the circumjacent stuff.

29. J. Mill & his 3 sisters to breakfast. One thing John Mill said 'reached my witness', – 'nine tenths of society have a deportment & manner purely conventional, the other tenth have also the conventional for society & reserve the natural for their intimate friends'. He accompanied us to Bishopsgate. Soon after the meeting assembled. It is a strange thing to watch the discussion of a question in this strange synod. There are differences of opinion, but the question is ever decided without a division & without votes. Feelings are expressed & the Clerk adroitly gathers the predominant feeling of the meeting & all settle down in perfect satisfaction with the decision. How such a proceeding would astonish an M.P.!

30. Joined A.M. at 11 & went to Kensington per bus where we took a flying dinner with the Mills & proceeded according to previous appointment to Hampton Court with Clara, Harriet & George. Within we passed through suite after suite of galleries of paintings, some very striking; a large Vandyke the best I ever saw, several Titians, one full length of Ignatius Loyola, a fine Rembrandt, & the Woman taken in Adultery by Ricci, a superb work of art in every respect. We returned satiated with magnificence. A vast number of apartments in the palace are occupied by the poor nobility.

JUNE

1. Grand Exeter Hall Anti-Slave Trade Meeting. Prince Albert in the chair at 11 o'clock. Met the Mills at 9 & secured a good place close to the platform; about 4000 present. Albert was received with vociferous cheers. He bowed with grace & dignity & took the chair with much modesty, he spoke the

1. John Pringle Nichol (1804–59), Regius Professor of Astronomy at Glasgow University and a friend of J. S. Mill.

opening speech distinctly & well, tho' too low to be generally heard, glancing pretty frequently at his notes. Thomas Fowell Buxton then moved the first resolution in a manly dignified & forcible address, representing the increased horror of the present system which exports & destroys 500,000 victims annually, & gave a general idea of the object of the Society,[1] namely to commercialize, civilize, & Christianize Africa, making treaties with Kings, settling & cultivating & trafficking. He was followed by Wilberforce[2] (the 'Venerable' so called – age about 30). His speech was decidedly eloquent, worthy almost of his Pa. Sir Robt. Peel made a fine speech, assuring his Royal Highness that he need not consider the situation he was in at present unworthy of his station. O'Connell[3] came in & was loudly cheered. 2 or 3 bishops spoke & several Earls, but amongst the number the name of the City King, Samuel Gurney Esq. must not be forgotten. His speech was like himself, straightforward, manly & to the point, & without a shadow of pretension. He confined himself to the commercial part of the business (which had not been touched before) & handled it like a man who understood his subject. Prince Albert left when the meeting was half over & Earl Ripon took the chair. The end of the meeting, which lasted 4 hours, was interrupted by incessant cries for O'Connell, but the Platform Government was inexorable. Ripon wound up with a short speech & as the last word left his mouth the organ struck up, which overpowered any row that would have been, but made the O'Connellites leave the meeting almost foaming. The proceeding was injudicious. They should have let him speak when the business was over.

2. Breakfasted at the Backhouses to arrange a party to Norwood. Took Jane back & we, except Mammy, were about to start in a hackney coach, when in walked the queen B (i.e. Hannah Backhouse) herself, saying she had walked out of the monthly meeting, ex Gallery & all, to go too! Norwood, the model industrial school contains 1100 of the offscouring of the Middlesex parish workhouses & the faces of the children indicate what a very raw material it is. However, the system works admirably. The literary part of the education & handicraft trades go on at the same time, tailors, tinkers, shoe-makers, carpenters, sailors &c., under different masters in separate rooms. Beautiful order & cleanliness throughout. We saw the Lilliput sailors go through the whole gunnery exercise, man the top gallant yard &c. A proof of the working of the system is this: they are restricted from keeping a child after 16 years of age & such is the demand for Norwood children that they have but 10 out of 1100 above 14.

1. The African Civilisation Society.

2. Samuel Wilberforce (1805–73) at this time was Archdeacon of Surrey. He later became Bishop of Oxford. He was a son of Wm. Wilberforce.

3. Daniel O'Connell (1775–1847), the Irish orator, who had helped to bring in the Catholic Relief Bill of 1829. From about 1840 he began to agitate for Home Rule for Ireland.

3. Spent the morning in the City & did a deal of business. I joined our people at Hampstead where we paid a remarkably pleasant little dinner visit to Gurney & Caroline[1] & then drove 'cross country' to the Mills', where we met Carlyle & wife. I spent most of the evening in listening to the first & chatting with the second. His opinion of O'Connell is that could he see one inch further into things than he does he would renounce his present occupation for ever. He spoke in strong reprobation of the want of sympathy with the working classes & takes a gloomy view of their present state. He talked of Geo. Fox,[2] whom he greatly admires. On coming out at ½ past 10, we found the post boy as drunk as a lord, at first hardly able to speak. It was too late to get either another pair of horses or a hackney coach, so we at length proceeded with him, making him walk the horses a considerable way & then relaxing into an easy jog trot. We reached home 10 minutes past 12.

4. We settled our worldly affairs to the mutual satisfaction of ourselves & our landlady & drove down to Upton to a 6 o'clock dinner, in which hospitable quarters we settled ourselves for a few days.

6. I went into Town with Samuel Gurney & paid 14 or 15 calls on old or new commercial friends of ours, to brush up old connections & to confirm new ones. I met generally with a friendly reception, tho' some were rather short, as if they knew their own business best, when I set forth the advantages of Falmouth as a place for orders for vessels. They mostly prefer Cowes on account of its nearness to London. Drank tea at Upton Lane, 'the Frys'. Cos. E. Fry produced the letters she had received from various crowned heads or rather, as A.M. remarked, 'from crowned hands'.

7. Sunday. The lane to the Meeting House presented a full fair sight before & after meeting hours. The original drab has become unpopular & 'black spirits and white, dove coloured, & grey', speckled the road in very picturesque groups.[3] Dined at the Listers.[4] Mary is a clever girl. I had a close confab with Caroline Braithwaite in the evening on change of costume & on Baptist Noel[5] & such like holy men. She evidently worships him & fancied she had in me an incipient convert. Dined with Cos. Francis at the Old Jewry & accompanied him & Wm. Forster to an anti-slavery conversazione at the Society's room. I smuggled myself in as an anticipatory delegate whose credentials were not yet arrived. I met a most extraordinary collection of animals, many of them Yankees deputed for the express purpose of attending

1. Gurney and Caroline Hoare. Caroline was the daughter of Uncle Barclay of Bury Hill.
2. The founder of the Society of Friends; no direct relation of the Foxes of Falmouth.
3. The Quakers were beginning to discard their traditional dress at this time.
4. Joseph Jackson Lister (1786-1869), developed the modern microscope; father of Lord Lister, the great surgeon; a Quaker connected with the Gurneys.
5. Baptist Wriothesley Noel (1798-1873), a Baptist clergyman and popular preacher.

the Grand Convention. Lucretia Mott[1] the celebrated Hicksite preacher & her husband, dressed after the straitest fashion of quakerism, & a Miss Neal, a she-delegate of 18! The only gentleman amongst them was a Dr. Burney, an intelligent, clear-sighted man. After a sufficient time spent in tea & twaddle, the Revd. Mr. Knibb, a Baptist preacher from Jamaica, was stuck up to be asked questions as to the working of emancipation in that island. He is a great bull-dog-looking fellow & made out that it had answered in every respect. He said too much & impressed me as not entirely void of humbug. After he departed we discussed American slavery & Yankee prejudices very fully. Burney explained how Congress could not compel the states to adopt any measures for the extinction of slavery, Congress being in fact only a delegated power from the states & they individually being the supreme Government. L. Mott gave tongue in fine style. She has a happy knack of telling a story & gave us a minute account of her companion being tarred & feathered, her own efforts to be his substitute or share his fate; the burning of the Town Hall at Philadelphia & many other particulars, showing no disposition to stop when once set agoing. It being nearly 10, William & I started & got to Hampstead at some time of night where we enjoyed supper & chat till morning.

11. Went to Hampstead with William to lodge, after calling at the House of Commons to see Dr. Lushington.[2] Today the news has been confirmed & widely spread of a deed which will make yesterday a black spot in our calendar. Our young & unoffending Queen was yesterday shot at by a lad whilst riding up Constitution Hill. He fired 2 pistols at her when within 8 yards. Happily neither took effect.

12. Came in early with William & found at the old Jewry my appointment as delegate to the grand anti-slavery convention, whither we accordingly repaired. It was held in Freemasons' tavern. Between 4 & 500 delegates present. Old Thos. Clarkson[3] came in after the meeting was assembled & took the chair. We all rose as he entered. He spoke very feelingly of his unity & interest in the operations of the society & invoked the blessing of Heaven on its undertakings. Jos. Sturge[4] stood by his side & undertook all the business

1. Lucretia Mott (1793–1880), a famous American preacher of the Society of Friends. The 'Hicksite' separation in America (1827–8) occurred because of an uneasiness felt by some Quakers at the teaching of Elias Hicks, who emphasised the Inner Light and minimised the person of Jesus Christ.

2. Stephen Lushington, M.P. (1782–1873), a supporter of the anti-slavery movement. In 1840 he brought in a Bill to abolish capital punishment, but it was defeated.

3. Thos. Clarkson (1761–1846) was not himself a Quaker, but he had worked closely with the Quakers in the anti-slavery movement and spent his fortune and his energies in this cause.

4. Joseph Sturge (1793–1859), railway pioneer and one of the first newspaper proprietors in the modern manner. His *Morning Star* propagated Free Trade, Cobden's Anti-Corn Law League, and peace. He was a leading Quaker.

part of the meeting. After a time a large form rose near the table, took off his hat & displayed to the enthusiastic audience the full sunny face & black curly locks of Dan O'Connell. He treated us with a thorough specimen of characteristic eloquence, delicious to listen to, urging the Society to make some decided stride in advance, to do something; to have met & effected nothing would be vastly worse than not having met at all. He offered whatever talents he possessed in the cause and expressed his intention of addressing the Irish slaveholders in America by a letter circular. When Clarkson left the room, Brother Phillips, a delegate from Massachusetts, brought forward in a very clever manner the indignity offered to his co-delegates by the council by not admitting their credentials nor allowing them a seat in the convention. He referred to Lucretia Mott & Co., the Amazonian phalanx who sat round 2 sides of the hall, but outside a bar which divided them from the Council. This led to a hot & furious argumentation which waxed hotter & more boisterous for 3 hours & a half, on the rights of women & whether it was fit that they should or should not sit as delegates in this convention.

13. Went in to town. Took leave of Mill & proceeded to Carlyle's for the same purpose. Found the philosopher in a glorious state of disgust & declamation at what he calls the 'laissez-faire principle', adducing the late attempt on the Queen as a proof of the misery & discontent of the lower classes. An extraordinary specimen of female Yankee coarseness, vulgarity & shrewdness was there when I arrived. When she cleared out, Sterling's father came in, the *Jupiter tonans* of *The Times*,[1] a sort of whirlwind of a man. He thanked me very warmly for our attentions to his son. He & Mrs. Carlyle packed off in his carriage & the cynic taking his pipe invited me into his back garden where we walked up and down for half an hour, he philosophising on Irving's character, woman's place & sphere, the injury done by controversialists & the absence of faith in the world, in very sublime style. He parted with me very warmly, pressing me to come again.

14. 1st day. Met the travellers, who returned yesterday – Sarah,[2] burnt bright brick colour, Chenda,[3] beautiful as ever. I walked with her to Meeting & listened to her clever descriptions of their journey, incidents, &c. Dined at Ham House, a party of about 30.

15. After a few calls I went to the Convention. Heard a glorious speech from O'Connell, which though a golden maze of digression & metaphor was practically directed against the slavery of the Southern States. He recommended that addresses be sent to the heads of the various religious sects in America, urging on them the incompatibility of slave-holding & Christianity.

1. Sterling's father, Capt. Edward Sterling, was one of the chief leader-writers of *The Times*.
2. Sarah Gurney.
3. Richenda Buxton (daughter of Sir Thos. Fowell Buxton).

Many came to him on his taking his seat to ask for autographs & to shake hands with the giant. A Professor Staunton spoke next & gave some striking facts showing that no efforts in Africa would put down slavery in America whilst some of the Northern States were in fact the Congos & Guinea coasts of the Southern States. He referred to Texas, which O'Connell described as supported on the 2 bloody pedestals of slavery of the African & destruction of the Indian.

17. Drove to town after breakfast in our carriage, having taken leave of part of our kind hosts, & 3 of the ladies accompanied us to the National Gallery. After transacting some business in the city I joined them there, but only in time to miss them, they being in the act of adjourning to a pastry cook's. However, they left Sarah Gurney & Chenda Buxton behind, which attraction, united to the National Gallery, had somewhat more charms for me than the cook's. We did not stay long, the ladies having a prison-discipline meeting to attend. At half past 4 we got under way for Ipswich.

20. After breakfast paid a call on Chas. May, the first man in this section of the body in regard to talent. He is now in business with the Ransomes, agricultural implement makers.[1] He showed me over the foundry. Their patent plough share is highly ingenious, all cast in a mould, the bottom of which is iron, the effect of which is to harden the lower surface considerably & the upper one consequently wears away the fastest thus always sharpening itself.

21. 1st day. Called on certain good friends & in the afternoon drove to Woodbridge 14 miles off to attend a meeting of Mammy's, & more especially to see Bernard Barton.[2] He joined us at tea at John Alexander's & he & I became soon exceedingly sociable. I questioned him about Chas. Lamb, on which subject he became very communicative, quoting long passages from his letters which were too racy for Talfourd[3] to publish. I was altogether much better pleased with him than I expected. It is said he never utters a good thing except in quotation. Took leave of our parents at Woodbridge who proceed on their ministerial duties & join us at Norwich.

22. Took leave of our hospitable entertainers at 10. Having glorious weather,

---

1. Chas. May (1801–60) had started business as a retail chemist in Finsbury, but in 1836 he took over the engineering department of Ransome and Sons. Ransomes had begun in Norwich, but moved to Ipswich in 1789, where they took out a patent for chill-cast ploughs and built up a great business in the manufacture of agricultural implements. May patented an invention for fastening railway lines to sleepers and subsequently became a F.R.S.

2. Bernard Barton (1784–1849), a minor poet who became a friend and correspondent of Chas. Lamb. He had worked as a clerk in Alexander's bank in Woodbridge but was supported by an annuity raised by the Gurneys so that he could devote himself to literature.

3. Lamb's correspondence was first published by Sir Thos. Talfourd in 1834.

good roads & good posters we rattled on happily enough & reached Earlham[1] at 4.

25. Quarterly at Norwich. Streaming wet. Dined at Aunt J. Gurney's with a Quarterly Meeting squadron. Took leave of the family & returned to Earlham to pack up for packing off tomorrow morning. The Earlham gardener was discharged last night by the Doctor's advice, he showing strong symptoms of insanity. In the excitement of the moment he went to the surgeon & attempted to stab him with his pruning knife. In the hurry of business he made the attempt on the wrong man. Spent a remarkably pleasant sociable evening with the Earlhamites.

26. Left Earlham a little before 7 & went to Town per *Telegraph*, a capital coach. Left luggage at *White Hart* & ran down to Upton. Sam Gurney not well & feels disappointed at the narrow-mindedness shewn by the Convention in refusing to hear F. Buxton on the subject of his Society.[2] Slept there.

27. Returned to Town after breakfast. Completed sundry bits of business & called on the Buxtons in Brick Lane. Started per railway to Southampton which I reached at 9.

28. Started at 9 by the *Vivid* coach to Exeter, outside. Mild evening. Reached Exeter at (29th) ½ past 9 in the morning, which allowed time to cleanse & replenish before arrival of the Devonport Mail, which brought me at Falmouth by ½ past 1 in the morning. Hot day. Glorious for travelling, but too much of it for the hay, which in this county of Devonshire is thinner than I ever saw.

30. Effected an entrance to our house at that unconscionable hour by rattling out Thomas from his first slumber with gravel & terrific howls. Gave me a warm welcome as far as words went, but had neither food, drink, fire nor bed to offer. However I managed to scrape together something resembling a supper & by stealing a sheet from Kitty & blankets elsewhere rigged up a tolerable ex tempore bed, which I was glad enough to turn into. Garden looks well, but lawn brown & horses thin. Great scarcity of hay owing to 3 months drought. Ran out to Penjerrick after dinner. Honest Thomas Evans was most loyally warm & conducted me over the farm. Hay crop wretched. One crop of potatoes failed entirely, field ploughed up & resown. Rest of the crops looking well. John Jose still clings to life, but his grasp is apparently all but unfastened. He is a mere skin-covered skeleton & cannot move a limb from weakness.

1. The home of Joseph John Gurney at Norwich.
2. Sir Thos. Fowell Buxton's scheme for an expedition up the Niger to settle the land and develop it on modern lines included armed vessels, and this caused most Quakers to withdraw their support.

JULY

2. Wet day, but highly acceptable to the country. Settling in satisfactorily to my accustomed sphere. Reading De Tocqueville's *Démocratie de l'Amérique*, recommended by Sterling, & Brown's *Philosophy of the Human Mind*.

4. Had John Lyne to dinner with me; he is on his way to France to winter for his health. Good account of the family. He is a singular fish. By his own account he is doing great execution amongst the Cornish & other belles. An American brig called for orders. Made the passage from N. York in 17 days!, consequently before any advice of her sailing could have arrived.

8. A man called Read yesterday whilst discharging wheat from a lighter fell down the hatchway & with a sack of wheat on his neck. He did not speak after it for 4 hours. I called today after Meeting. Found him better but he had not been bled, refusing to submit to it. I insisted on having it done before I left the house. After taking ½ a pint he fainted. Brougham thinks favourably of his case. He was in our employ. Received a letter from the girls & a note from my father. In the evening sent for Swan, the depredator of certain peasticks during our absence, & sat in judgment on him. The poor fellow had nothing to say for himself & the wife could only whimper & beg for mercy. I sentenced him to pay damages & costs, 10/–, and let him off with a long sermon on thievery.

AUGUST

1. New volume & new month, & new style of an old journalist. Reader henceforth I write for myself not for thee. Paid attention in the morning to a burly corn merchant introduced by D. Alexander, in the evening to a recent importation of the Irish, the Miss Robinsons. By their account the new sect in Ireland appear to be nothing more than ultra-Quakers. Their neophytic clothing arises from the principle that all dyes are superfluous & therefore vanity.

4. I took the Bells, my father, sisters and H. Molesworth to the lighthouse in my boat. We joined a pleasant tea-kettle party on the rocks under Meudon in the afternoon, the Tregednites, Miss Griffins, Kirkness &c. Shrimped, fished, boated, sung & carted home afterwards. A grand teetotal festival in Falmouth. There was an enormous procession, 2 barouches & 4 banners & bands with cruizing on the harbour & a Tea in the evening. It was partly I imagine a clap-trap, partly a fan for the flame of Abstinence & partly a show of strength. Human nature does love notoriety whether for good or evil report. Also, as Carlyle says, Man must have symbols. The bulk are by no means philosophic enough to rally round an abstract idea.

5. A Committee meeting at the Lancastrian School, attended by the new Baptist Minister, Mr. Watts, who takes a warm interest in it. He is convinced, as I have long been, that there is not *moral force* enough in a lad like our present master to exact the respect due from his scholars, who are a refractory perverse, unmanageable mass of material. No mistake seems to me greater than to choose a schoolmaster for his cheapness.[1]

7. We all dined at Carclew taking J. Richards with us. No other guests but J. Enys & four Dykes.[2] Philly Dyke expressed her conviction of the fallacy of two moral maxims duly instilled in copybooks as to the undesirableness of money & beauty. She considered both highly desirable, & without either a woman has no chance. I thanked her for her candour in expressing what others of her sex only thought. There is however some melancholy truth in her reflection that without those adventitious advantages, so far from anything like personal merit, an unfortunate female is obliged to remain a natural conservative however contrary to her inclination; & such is the harshness of the world that instead of sympathy she reaps derision or something like it, thereby. It seems to me that jokes on old maids are exactly as unjustifiable as on cripples or idiots.

8. Dr. Bowring called on us in the morning & was agreeable. He talked of the French regulation of Railways. The Government guarantees to adventurers 4% for their money & then has the supervisorship of the business. For want of such law in America, in one state the Railway cannot be used for letters on account of the charge, & the Government has to send them by its own coach. Bowring thinks that some law should exist to prevent the inconvenience of such a monopoly in this country.

11. The melancholy rumour is confirmed that we are to be despoiled of our packet establishment & Dartmouth is to reap the benefit of the change.

13. Much pleased today with a trait of genuine simple goodness of heart. Walking to Penjerrick I overtook a little fellow about 4 years old trudging to school with his little bundle in one hand & in the other an apple of which he had just had the first nibble. This he held out to me as I pass'd him. 'Is that for me?' 'Yes.' 'Why? Don't you like it?' 'Yes.' 'Then why give it to me?' 'Because you are a stranger', – a noble principle to act upon & yet he never studied moral philosophy. Returned the little chap his apple with a penny & told him always to be kind to strangers & he would never repent it.

15. Animated picture on our lawn today, 140 little girls seated in companies. Some with flowers in pots, & some with nosegays, for exhibition & prizes, & about 70 onlookers, besides a row of old widows from the Retreat. It was the 2nd annual exhibition of A.M.'s Juvenile Horticultural Society. Sir C.

1. The Lancastrian monitorial system was a cheap form of school organisation since it employed the older scholars to teach the younger and dispensed with teaching staff.
2. Sir Chas. Lemon's nieces.

Lemon & his Rectorship adjudged the prizes, & Sir Charles made an appropriate speech. These things which bring the 'classes' (as they are called, as if these were different orders of men) into juxtaposition must have a healthy effect on each. The great want in the present day seems to be a sufficient 'sympathy' between these said 'classes'. Not that there is any want of provision for the poor in the way of Union houses, Alms houses, & an infinite variety of 'Charities' ostentatiously so called, but there is a want of familiar intercourse, & reciprocal acquaintance, & interest, which would be found much more than bald official charity to bind & solder & interweave the different interests of our social system together. It is this which would produce Union & Ties of affection which neither Chartism nor any other antagonist-'ism' could dissolve.

17. Polytechnic Committee. Councillor Hall, that Genius of Blunder, gave notice of a proposition for our next meeting, to throw open the Hall for all purposes except Religious, Political, or Dancing, raising again the ghost of a controversy which had with much difficulty been 'laid'.

18. Count Von Beust, Director General of Mines in the Prussian dominions, called at the office to ask for introductions to the Mines &c. He is a man of remarkable energy, intelligence & rapid perception. We took leave of our father at 1, who started for Wales in his way to Bristol in search of his wife, & proceeded ourselves to Penzance Monthly Meeting, taking L. Squire in the carriage to fill up. Called on the Coleridges & put up at Marazion.

19. In the 2nd Meeting A. C. Stephens was reported as 'inclinable to marry in a manner contrary'.[1] Started homeward after a hasty snack at J. Lean's, reading on the road Carlyle's extraordinary phantasmagoric adumbration entitled 'Das Mahrchen'.[2] I should imagine, a composition the most German ever launched from English brains. Tea at the Coleridges'. Derwent Coleridge was unfortunately out. Mrs. Coleridge agreeable, also a Mr. & Mrs. Drury.[3] Mary Coleridge's fixed idea is the absolute duty of a veneration for church & state & all thereto appertaining. Drury is more liberal.

25. Ethel Crouch to breakfast which gave us an opportunity for open chat on experiences & opinions. She is, as I supposed, decidedly one of the Evangelical church party, sincere & conscientious in her belief to the best of my discernment. Her home treatment is a great mistake, cold looks & want of tolerance cannot but be injurious to a mind so sensitive as hers. I trust that exclusive dogmatism & magnification of distinguishing traits are not Quaker characteristics, but they certainly are sectarian ones & opposed to the comprehensive brotherhood of the true catholic spirit.

1. i.e. wished to marry outside the Society.
2. Carlyle's *German Romance*, 1827, a collection of folk-stories translated from the German *Märchen* or *Mährchen*.
3. Rev. Henry Drury (1812-63), archdeacon of Wilts.

SEPTEMBER

1. Met Charlotte & Fanny Gwatkin at Falmouth with their uncle Sam Trist. Walked & chatted with them over old reminiscences. Fanny's intended is somewhere in the East, in the situation of many vessels now in port, i.e. 'waiting for orders'. Having attained that, he must clothe himself with a curacy at least, before he presents himself for matrimony. On returning to dinner found the place invaded by the Dykes who had three hours to put away while their Uncle attended the Board. Having no time to spare to do the agreeable, I asked them to join me at dinner, which consisted of a noble dish of stew at one hand & a plain pudding at the other. Tea at Tregedna. Evening stroll with Uncle J. & the girls.

2. Packed off 20 to 30 fish circulars. We have full 2500 hogsheads in the cellar. Began *Sartor Resartus*, having finished that extraordinary epico-dramatic poem called *The French Revolution*.[1] It seems to me the work of the greatest 'force' of the present day.

4. Betty Jose told me today about her poor old sposo. 'You ceant think how he 'es gone together! Why, his belly 'es sunk, into the back of 'un & tes nothing but a girt pit, big enough for a cat to lie in!' What a forcible not to say poetic description of an abdomen!

5. The Lords of the Admiralty arrived at Falmouth on their annual inspecting tour. The inhabitants take the opportunity to present their refutation of certain statements in the Commissioners' report respecting the comparative merits of this & Dartmouth.[2] Closeted some time with Uncle J. & Tilly, going pretty fully into the merits of the question between him & the directors as a rehearsal previous to an interview with one of them this evening.[3] His case appears as clear as the sun, but the fight will be between single-handed honesty & many-headed knavery.

8. All except self started for St. Austell to attend Quarterly Meeting. Busy morning. Dined with Lord Yarborough on board his yacht, the *Kestrel*, at $\frac{1}{2}$ past 6 with a small naval party. A fine old fellow that Lord Y., old school, no nonsense, combination of Jack Tar & John Bull. No ceremony, but a dinner worthy of an earl. Talked of old ships & old admirals & what he did & saw among the Greek isles during the Navarino months. Started in my 7 ft. punt at $\frac{1}{2}$ past 9 which made them stare.

11. My father spoke to me about a ridiculous rumour of my attachment to Georgina Treweeke which being not only without foundation but also

---

1. Carlyle's *Sartor Resartus* had been published in *Fraser's Magazine* in 1831–4 and in volume form in 1838. His *French Revolution* had appeared in 1837.
2. i.e. as ports for the mail packet service.
3. Uncle Joshua had involved himself in legal proceedings over the sale of mining shares.

without the *appearance* of a foundation, receives only my utter contempt. 'No lie can live.' Let them talk.

12. Pit of stomach to edge of desk; point of quill to face of paper. Such has been the work of today. Surely I may write myself – a man of *letters*. What a fuss old Paul would have made had he been a clerk of ours, bragging as he used to when he had written 'a *second* epistle with his own hand'. That however was before the times of clarified goosequills & superfine Bath post.

14. Attended the examination of the School of Mines at Truro. There were but 8 boys. The questions were of the highest class of mathematics & mechanical science, introducing adfected quadratics, differential calculus &c. The boys quitted themselves nobly. Sir C. Lemon's speech at the close was much to the purpose, offering, if the county would now take up the work he began & carry it on, to present a site for a building, £500 towards the erection & £10,000 at his death, increasing it if necessary to £20,000. Unfortunately in his plan of education he lugged in the subject of religion & declared his intention of its being a Church of England establishment, at the same time using no coercion to other sects. It would have been better omitted.

15. Started soon after 6 with C. Pearson for Portloe in the *Stormy Petrel*, fine wind but somewhat puffy, had to luff & strike sail once or twice. Sent Tom back to St. Mawes with the boat to wait us there, while we examined fish & made much of the curers. They have done badly in the fishery this year, however I got the promise of nearly all caught & proceeded to St. Mawes & did likewise. The Gurneys, i.e. Sam & Ellen & her sister M. A. Reynolds, arrived in the evening to stay over the Polytechnic.

16. A wild day & no mistake. Monthly at Redruth attracted all the weight of the family. C. & I remained at home to do the hospitable to the Gurneys. In a walk to the beach unhappily broke in on the sacred privacy of a loving pair seated in a cavern intertwined like vine-stalks. Recognised 2 old acquaintances, Miss Kirkness and J. Tresidder. Two iron steamers in the harbour bound on a secret expedition & secretly belong to the East India Co.

20. S. I pity Sam, not that he seems unhappy, but his lot would surely make *me* so. Ellen has good sense, but for a life companion – how flat! & moreover if not cold, at least tepid, & a wee bit too authoritative. She has the effect of a taste & feeling naturally good, but injured by education & soured by disappointment. I think the want of progeny has something to do with it. Her sister is Reynolds all over. She has not gone through the world with her eyes shut.

29. The Polytechnic Exhibition commenced today. The Exhibition was decidedly a good one though not so multifarious as sometimes. Sir C. Lemon took the chair. At 4 our garden looked like an adjournment of the 'Quality'; Rashleighs, Tremaynes, Carlyons, Sir C. & his Dykes, Sir W. Molesworth, Treweekes, Scilly Smith alias Lord of the Isles, Taylors, Molesworths &c.

Sir W. Molesworth[1] is a young-looking, slight, sanguine complexioned man, with a genius-like eye & peculiarly unforgettable mouth. Walked round the garden with him & chatted amongst other things about John Mill, whom he considers one of the first men in England, but inferior to his father. 'Ah', he said, 'he has become somewhat sentimental. He was brought up a Benthamite & is now Coleridge-bitten, & in trying to reconcile the 2 philosophies I think he has made a jumble.' Harriet Tremayne is a remarkably bright intelligent creature. It is a real pleasure to talk with such. Attended Snow Harris's lecture on gravitation in the evening, mostly elementary but some of his illustrations new & clever.

OCTOBER

15. Gave a great boy-entertainment at Penjerrick. L. Squire's horde & a few others, making upwards of 40 in all; dined them without the superfluity of table or plate, making them squat on the lawn & eat pasties, after which we got 2 carts under weigh & put about a dozen in each & occasionally a boy on each horse & so with the sound of a great tumult, but happily with no personal injury (except to the cart) we reached Bream Bay. Here was fine fun in store for them, a large pool in the rocks black with a shoal of lances, beautiful little fish, measuring from 1 to 3 inches. All hands set to & by means of handkerchiefs & other contrivances caught between 18 & 20 lbs weight. C. Pearson & I bathed. After tea the mass of Boyhood moved off highly delighted with its afternoon's work.

16. Trudged in before breakfast with a load of fish for potting & pickling. Morning occupied in painting the tent at Penjerrick. My mother joined us at dinner. Soon after I started for the Phillpotts to a late dinner where I met young Seymour Tremenheere, Mr. Flamank & the Enys party. The Phillpotts' youngest child, a girl of 2, has actually got a nose & is as much like her father as she can stare; eyes &c. almost equally formed. Tremenheere is a sensible fellow. He is one of the Govt. Commissioners on the National Education Grant[2] & consequently is examining & supervising all schools in

1. Sir Wm. Molesworth (1810–55), M.P. for E. Cornwall and then for Leeds, was a man of parts. He had been expelled from Cambridge after challenging his tutor to a duel. An infidel and philosophical radical, he was a disciple of Grote and James Mill. He was the editor of the *Works of Hobbes*, which appeared in sixteen volumes 1839–45. His family came from Pencarrow, near Bodmin.
2. The Government had made a grant available to schools, subject to an inspection and report on the schools' efficiency. Hugh Seymour Tremenheere, whose family came from Penzance, was appointed an Inspector of Schools in January 1840.

this part that have received aid or ask his company. One he visited today in Gwennap he thinks the best he has seen. The mining districts generally he finds do not shine in their schools. T. Phillpotts is a remarkable pleasant gentlemanly fellow without much of the cleric about him. Slept at Falmouth.

21. Mankind as with one accord dedicated this day to meetings. My sire had to start at 6 for Bodmin to attend the great Railroad County meeting & the great County harbour meeting to memorialise the Govt. in opposition to the foolish Commissioners. Then there was our regular meeting for worship at which were some good-intent common-place sermons, then a second meeting at which our dear mother expressed her concern to hold public meetings at some of the villages in the neighbourhood & was set at liberty. Then the monthly meeting where we received Richard Richards's reply to his disownment, & a very simple & touching report of the Committee who had visited Nathan the dentist on his approaching marriage with a Gentile[1] & who reported him incorrigible. Aunt C. & Juliet stayed with us over night. Gossiped with the former till 1.

28. A.M. & I during a ride to Falmouth chalked out a design for a book club for the benefit of the population of Penjerrick & Budock. Accordingly we made a dash at it after meeting & bought 2 guineas worth of suitable books, useful & entertaining, mostly people's editions of standard books, which with considerable additions from our own collection, will form a very respectable nucleus to increase upon. A meeting of the literary population called for Friday morning. I hope the parson won't be at us for this heretical attempt to diffuse *light* which he may consider an infringement of his patent.

30. At half-past 12 we held our village committee, all under the rose, as if we were doing some clever, naughty thing. Myself in the chair. 7 admirable regulations were read & adopted for the government of the Society. They were perfect, of course, I having prepared them all last night, but I managed so that all present might think he or she had a hand in the making. Then we produced the books & passed out our subscriptions in advance & were all so clever & witty on the subject and felt so well satisfied both with ourselves & our society that we parted in much harmony & brotherhood.

NOVEMBER

1. W. Hoskins was today laid in his narrow cell. Pouring weather. I was not able to attend the funeral, thinking it more important to attend to the dying than the dead. I made arrangements for the daughter of Lady Jane Taylor, who should have arrived today from London on her way to Malta, being

1. i.e. to someone not a member of the Society of Friends.

far gone in a consumption according to Margaret Gurney's account of her. 2. Busy day of it. We removed Miss Taylor from the *Montrose* to the *Oriental* in Capt. Plumridge's barge which we borrowed for the purpose. We had to carry her in & out of the boat, an interesting dying girl. Major Taylor & his daughter were exceedingly obliged for the attention shown them. The seal of death is evidently set on the latter & it seems a cruel thing to me to send one so helpless & forlorn & far gone, away to a foreign shore to die. The *Oriental*'s saloon is gorgeous. Returned to Penjerrick in the evening. Held a 2nd book club meeting to receive additional subscriptions &c. We have now 27 members.

7. Paid old John Jose my last visit. He drew his breath with difficulty, spoke inarticulately & his fluttering pulse was almost imperceptible. It was evident he was dying, but his spirit had not departed when the family left Penjerrick after an early dinner. In the evening we had a grand rat-hunt; master, servants & all, waging war to the poker with a giant fellow who had ensconced himself in a hole in the bathing room, where he was at length done to death by severe & repeated blows, but was clever enough to conceal his corpse & baulk us of the triumph of a pyre bequeathing us only his fragrance & the memory of his daring deeds.

8. News was brought that the patriarch of Penjerrick died today. A 43 years sojourn has closely associated him with that spot & gained the respect & esteem of all who knew him. He was a worthy upright & honourable old man. A very clever letter from Anna Gurney & a still more so from Chenda Buxton. She is a noble, high-souled creature with her father's moral greatness & her mother's earnestness of purpose. She is fitted by nature for a high sphere.

12. Rode to Constantine with my father to attend a Bible meeting held by C. Dudley & Lieut. Wilson, who were conveyed there by Uncle & Aunt C. from Trebah. When C.D. had done, he said, 'Perhaps Mr. Barclay Fox will now oblige us with a few words.' I screamed out from the body of the meeting that I had nothing to say & there were others present vastly better able to speechify than myself. However it was no-go, I had to scramble up on the platform, long-lashed whip, spatter-dashes & all, to give tongue to the best of my ability. After stating what had been done, I spoke a little of what remained to do. I instanced France, Sweden & then the world at large. A man earning 10/- & giving 1d. per week expends but 1/120th part of his wages on this cause, yet supposing him to live 23 years, by that small effort he puts 100 copies of the text in circulation, which supposing a book to last 100 years, is tantamount to circulating 10,000 copies through the world for one year. Then urged them to join the Association, conspire to work their collectors to the bone by the burden of copper, & when they could stand it no longer they should club together & give them a donkey. 'I've nothing

more to say', I stammered out, took a run and a jump off the platform & vanished. 26/- collected at the door. Dark stormy night. Rode to Trebah. Rain, wind & I all the way struggling for the mastery. The tide was all over the road by Pender's mine & the colt refused to venture. I had to splash into it on foot & lead her after me. A glorious tea & fire made ample amends. We sat up till near midnight telling ghost stories by turns.

16. Begged all this end of the Town in company with his Worship Sam Blight on behalf of the Railway survey. Though by dint of importunity we raised a fair collection, this work by no means raises human nature in one's opinion. There were however some lights in the picture & on adding up our pelf we mustered (including large donations from 2 parties previously given) as much as £258. £400 was fixed as Falmouth's quota, which I think will be obtained.

17. Accompanied Sr. Pedro Aronaza to Perran & thence to the United Mines to examine the engines & machinery. He is concerned in large iron works & collieries near Malago and is wanting engines. The new engine at the United Mines which was made at Perran is a beautiful sight. 85 inches. They expect it will do 85 million when everything is complete.[1] Being somewhat wolfish after inspecting the engines we waylaid the maid coming downstairs with a basin of broth, which we proceeded to incorporate. Our plan was to go on to Consols, but the Don declared he 'nevare saw such bad vedare in his life' and pleaded hard to return to Falmouth. He seems to know more about bull fights than iron works. There are colleges, he tells me, to educate bull fighters, with professors & books; some supported by the Government. Storm of wind & rain all the afternoon.

19. All day employed on turning the Polytechnic Hall into Arcadia. All was in preparation for tomorrow's flower bazaar, conceived and put in practice by my sister for the honest purpose of discharging a Polytechnic debt. Met our new Secretary, R. Hunt[2] of whom my first impressions are of a useful agreeable & highly intelligent fellow. He came from Plymouth in order to assist on the present occasion.

20. The doors were opened at 12. The contributions of flowers were bountiful, nor did my vegetables make a despicable show. The outside of the building was planted with fir trees. The entrance steps & passage were turned into a covered way of laurels, through which you gazed through a fir avenue, whilst a wreathed mirror at the other end, betwixt stands of flowers, doubled

---

1. The measurement of 85 inches was the size of the cylinder and the figure of 85,000,000 was the 'duty' of this pumping engine, i.e. how many pounds weight could be raised one foot by the consumption of one bushel of coal.

2. Robt. Hunt (1807–87), scientific writer, was firstly secretary of the Royal Cornwall Polytechnic Society and later president. Appointed professor of experimental physics at School of Mines and was elected F.R.S. in 1854.

the imaginary extent. Unfortunately the attendance was insignificant, the townspeople keeping aloof, & not above £28 were taken. Hunt to dinner. He has much simplified the mode of preparing the Daguerreotype[1] & has made some curious experiments on the properties of the chemical & calorific rays in reference to vegetation. He sowed a row of cress in a box on which he admitted light through a succession of vials imitating in colour the solar spectrum. The portion under the shade of the blue bottle shot up quickly & flourished vigorously; under the green it slowly appeared but grew; under the yellow some plants appeared but never became green; under the red none of the seeds germinated. He then reversed the position of the bottles & the effects were also reversed.

23. News of the birth of a princess[2] announced with sound of cannon. Mother and child doing well. A bit of high life at Carclew where my father & I dined. Met the Grotes[3] there & Sir W. Molesworth, the Bassets, Taylors &c. A handsome, well dressed party, & a handsome, well dressed dinner. Sir William & I had a chat before dinner on J. Mill, Benthamism, Coleridgism &c., I spoke of them as leaders of 2 opposite schools representing 2 great antagonist principles, the progressive & conservative. He professes to have no sympathy with the mere utilitarian according to the rules of the *Deontology*,[4] which he asserts to be a piece of Bowring's quackery, but nevertheless thinks utility in its broad sense the only principle on which any system could be based. On that hypothesis, I asked, what is the meaning of the words 'ought' & 'ought not'? There he admitted the question hinged, because no principle of utility could include those if they really existed. 'Then what does utility imply more than self-interest as the sole motive of action?' He defined his credo as 'the greatest possible happiness obtainable for yourself & your fellows'. Lounging over a settee while the Queen's late production was commented on as a blessing interposed between us & Cumberland tyranny,[5] 'I think', he said, 'he would do for us very well. *Then* would be the palmy days of Radicalism.' 'The next thing we shall have to do', said Grote, 'will be, I suppose, to vote the young lady £6000 a year to provide her with cradles & baby linen.' 'Ah,' said Molesworth, 'enough to keep 40 families in comfort.' Grote seems a man of good sound sense without pretension to

1. Robert Hunt published the first English treatise on photography in 1841.
2. Queen Victoria's first child, Victoria Adelaide Mary Louisa, was born on 21st November 1840.
3. Geo. Grote (1794–1871), a friend of the Mills and Bentham, one of the founders of London University, and a philosophical radical. His wife, Harriet, was a woman of strong intellect and character.
4. The title of a book by Bentham concerned with ethics.
5. The Duke of Cumberland and King of Hanover (1771–1851) had been opposed to the Reform Bill of 1832 and when he became King of Hanover in 1837 had made himself absolute monarch.

much beyond, a man of a fine presence & parliamentary air. But his wife! I had her to myself all the evening after dinner & found her gifted beyond the lot of woman – perhaps beyond the sphere of woman. We were looking over some architectural lithographs, which led to some clever remarks on Cathedral building, ancient & modern, Ecclesiastical power, & Roman Catholicism. The beautiful Mrs. Basset sailed across the room in glistening satin & joined us, interposing her swan-like neck, but Grote kindly took a chair & engrossed her, leaving his wife to me. We then got on various topics, Carlyle amongst the rest, whose disciple she is not, though she admitted his universality & ability of tracing the good in everything, however distasteful, as very admirable. She designated his *French Revolution* a series of strong chalk drawings, illustrative of the time, or perhaps a phantasmagoric exhibition, & himself a sort of literary showman. She thinks his barbarous eloquence unsuited to the polish of the 19th century; it reminds her of Job. He should have lived in the patriarchal times. Reached home about 11.

26. I heard an extraordinary romance of real life from 2 of the actors therein. The *Nirene*, a French brig bound from Dunkerque to Marseilles with a cargo of oil, was struck by a sea on the 13th, which completely capsized her, carrying away 3 of the seamen as well as both masts. The mate, my informant, was with the captain in the cabin. After she was turned over they managed, by breaking down a bulk head, to crawl out of the water into the hold on the top of the casks, where there was just sufficient room for them under the keelson. 3 men who were forward at the time managed with vast difficulty to join them in this dismal den, for 60 hours without food or light, floating they knew not whither, and gnawing the hoops of the oil casks for nourishment. A pilot boat it seems had them in tow for 2 days without their knowing anything of it. On the night of the 15th, however, they cast them off, thinking it was coming on to blow. Early in the morning of the 16th they felt the vessel ground. She was on a reef of rocks: the water found entrance & lifted the casks, leaving the men scarcely room for their mouths above the water & against the vessel's hold. One man was wedged down by the casks & drowned. The mate was dragged above the water by the captain by his hair. As the tide fell, they were able to descend & endeavoured to break open a passage where the topside was shattered. This they could not do, but to their amazement at length saw a hand appear under the bulwarks. The captain exclaimed 'C'est le bon Dieu' & grasped it with such a death grip that the pilot who owned it was so frightened by this unexpected evidence of life, human or demoniac, that he has since taken to his bed. However a hole was soon cut, through which they were dragged, & in a flood of tears fell on their knees amidst the surf & thanked Heaven for their resurrection. Pearce sent these men to us as Consul. We shall forward them to Plymouth, no French vessel being in port.

DECEMBER

1. Had a visit from 3 young Egyptians now recalled by the Pasha after 4 years' education in this country. They were shrewd intelligent fellows. One of their comrades has married an Englishwoman & lives at Camborne.

7. Rode to Penjerrick with my father. The new pond has reached the hobbledehoy stage & is really a great set-off to the place. I accepted my father's offer of a salary (£89) on condition that it shall not interfere with retaining my daily exercise & evening pursuits.

14. A brig laden with culm got on the rocks under Pendennis last night. We sent 5 men to assist her, who threw 30 to 40 tons overboard. It blew hard from N.E. & she got some unpleasant bumps on the rocks. On the evening's tide she was got off by the aid of Captains Plumridge & Innes & about 60 of the packets' crews, but is very leaky. Self busy all day with Capt. Stang of the Norway Brig, *Madswiel*, doing necessary at Custom House & landing his cargo which consists of bark, rice, pepper &c. Hard frost. No time for sentiment.

15. T. Evans laid low from the effects of a fall across a granite trough which bruised his chest. The intercostal muscles are injured & thence the lungs affected. Ran out to see him; leeches have been serviceable. Busy landing & stowing *Madswiel*'s cargo. C. Clift laid low & extra work at the office. Hard frost. This weather makes the difference between rich & poor not only *seen* but *felt*. What a blessing it is in truth never to be obliged to forego a bushel of coals for want of means!

16. I should say that England was verging towards a mesocracy, or the dominion of the middle classes, which corresponds with what is democracy in America. De Tocqueville considers that all the world is hastening towards democracy, & says truly that every great event in history, the invention of gunpowder, of printing, the post, the Reformation & the various Revolutions, have all been a germ of increase of power to the people. He rather overlooks, I think, plutocracy or the influence of wealth, which will probably outlive most other -ocracies. Frost hard enough to slide on. Found T. Evans better & downstairs. Hard fag at the office till 11.

18. A heavy fall of snow last night which continued through the greatest part of today. Cutting weather. Uncle A. at Mevagissey about the purchase of fish & I had to send an express to him in consequence of a fresh order. The man came back in 40 minutes saying the horse could not travel from the balling[1] of the snow. Sent him off on foot via St. Mawes. Had an interview with Capt. Sutor of the *Hannah*, an uncivilised-looking barbarian, one of whose men stabbed him on the 24th Oct., so that his bowels protruded from the wound. I took the man in custody & went with him & the Captain before

1. The forming of balls of snow on the horse's hooves.

the Mayor. Cornish being out of town the case is remanded till tomorrow. Joined my father at Penjerrick, snow ankle-deep.

19. Close work at the office till a late hour. Much time taken up by Capt. Sutor, who persisted in proceeding against the man in a manner that we warned him would take the matter out of the magistrate's hands, which was verified by the court. Capt. Sutor was bound over to prosecute him at the Central Criminal Court for stabbing with attempt to kill. Attended to the crew of a Russian ship picked up at sea by a Norwegian captain who has left them under our care. Manufactured ice creams with great success.

21. Distributed a few orders for meat, bread, & coals, that some of my poor neighbours may enjoy a dinner on Christmas day. Mail not in till 4.

24. Met my father at Penjerrick, where the pond-scenery lit by a bright sun looked surpassingly lovely. Where the old muddy lane was, is now a beautiful glade (the hedges being thrown down) sloping to the pond, from whence 3 or 4 elms, a towering poplar, and a noble ash start up in the foreground in fine bold drawings, beyond the pond which mirrors back the tall trees bending over it.

25. The day when the Word was made flesh & dwelt among us. How little we appreciate the full significance of this anniversary. Kept it in my usual way, – a roastbeef dinner with T. Evans & family & settlement of farm accounts afterwards: all looked well pleased, happy & contented, which, to my mind, in a clean comfortable English cottage, is as fair a sight as a man can look upon. Had to attend to business annoyances in the evening, in which we were obliged to have legal advice, the bankers in London attempting to shuffle out of their responsibility to us for the purchase of a pilchard cargo.

26. Long & interesting letter from J. Mill, in which he remarks on the Atonement & Divine Justice; not thoroughly sound, but next door to it, & a vast stride from his old Benthamism. He evidently cannot bring his reasoning faculty to admit that Divine Justice could require or accept the sacrifice of the Guiltless for the transgressions of the guilty. He speaks of Molesworth as a man complete within his own limited sphere, of Mrs. Grote as the caricature of her husband's opinions, of Guizot as immeasurably the first statesman in Europe.

28. Had a monstrous boy party, 12 to dinner with additions at tea. Walked them out to Penjerrick & left them there to demolish trees & work off their surplus energies. Despatched Ed. Seccombe to London for mail about this troublesome business of Gandolfi's.

29. An hour or two after, Hannah[1] on the spur of the moment gave birth to a boy, the miniature likeness of his dad. The mother going on tolerably, but excited & given to chatter. As the Firm had no doubt a hand in expediting this business, C. proposes that it be called 'G. C. & R. W. Fox & Co'.

1. Hannah Seccombe, the wife of the Foxes' clerk.

30. Filling Ed. Seccombe's place at the office allows but little time for reading & little power for thinking. By diurnally poring over the cash-book, my thoughts insensibly grow cashiferous till it seems strange to apply them to anything beyond arithmetic, which confirms me in my belief that our bent of mind is much more the result of external circumstances than we like to admit. Achieved a mighty triumph over self in rising with the dawn for the last 3 mornings, finding the day far too short for its work.

31. The knell of the old year is about to strike. It has been one of no common interest; the three great facts, or salient points of it to me, are my acquaintance with Sterling, Mill, & Carlyle. They are the three seasons of my mind's year.

1841

BARCLAY CONTINUES to be busy with the affairs of the family and spends much of his spare time laying out the grounds at Penjerrick. In February Dr Calvert returns to Falmouth, somewhat worse in health, but an intellectually stimulating companion. In April he is followed by Sterling, who buys a house in Falmouth and decides to settle there. This is very much to Barclay's taste, for Sterling becomes increasingly his mentor and it is on his advice that Barclay decides to devote part of his time to study rather than business. Sterling also encourages him to plan a visit to Italy. The Royal Cornwall Polytechnic Society flourishes and Robert Hunt, its Secretary, gives Barclay instruction in chemistry. There are courses of lectures during the year on education and phrenology, and in July Barclay attends the meetings of the British Association at Plymouth. Several of the distinguished scientists there make their way to Falmouth after the meetings and grace the proceedings of the Polytechnic Society.

JANUARY

1. A fresh year has opened, with its work. Was introduced to E. Seccombe's first born now four days old. No reason was *visible* for placing it higher than that which it most resembled, raw beef, with one exception, viz. that it was *dressed*. It is difficult to look on such little animals & honestly believe that there are souls inside of them. Spent a remarkably pleasant New Year's day at Penjerrick where the servants also spent their holiday.

5. Heard from Pellew a curious story for this enlightened 19th century. In consequence of various troubles & losses, a horse & bullock, & 7 pigs feeding & not fattening, &c., on the 2nd he trudged to Redruth to consult Tammie Blee, a wise-woman or witch-detector. He had to wait in a lower room from morning till dusk before his turn came, so many were the applicants for the results of her supernatural wisdom. On being admitted, she said, 'I know what you are come about', then told him his initials, his wife's & his son's, that he was a parish officer, that he had a horse & bullock ill, which she described minutely & correctly, that he had lost a pig & that several more were doing badly, & that he had been for some time disabled from work by something in the right arm. The accuracy of all her statements made his hair stand & the sweat issue freely. She further explained to him that it was all the work of an 'ill wisher', & that there was a certain minute

218

in every day when evil wishes took effect. She could guard him from their power, which she did by a written paper, which he was to hang round his neck &c. For his cattle she gave him powders, which he was to rub into their bodies after pulling out a few hairs, repeating during the operation, 'May the power of God keep me from evil'. This he has done & finds them already improving. He as much believes in the power of the old lady as in the truth of any part of the Gospels. She must be worth knowing.

7. The hard frost of last night tempted C. Pearson & me to walk to Perran to try the ice at Carnal & we were well repaid by some hours fine skating. What a glorious wind-like exercise it is! I had several thumping falls as was natural for a bungler. Full moon, cloudless sky, white earth, the very ideal of a winter's evening.

9. News reached us of the loss of a steamer at the beginning of this week on the rocks of Scilly. Out of 61 persons on board, only 3 females & 1 sailor were saved. It seems that in a snow-storm they mistook the Scilly light for the Longships & so ran on the rocks. It is the saddest loss that has happened on our shore for many years.

13. I have been reading Niebuhr's colossal fragment of Roman History.[1] It is full of profound learning & evidences the most extraordinary research. A letter from A. Gurney says that the thermometer at Keswick indicated 16° *below zero*!

22. Busied with my father at Penjerrick about the rockery. At 6 I attended a preliminary meeting of the E. Kirrier Farmers' Club at Selly's. Tilly in chair. About a dozen present. Formed rules & plans for future proceedings. Appointed officers & a committee to which I was pressed to belong, but declined. Lady Basset is our Patroness, & has presented us a good commencement of a library. At each meeting a member is to introduce an agricultural subject which is to be discussed, & amongst so many long heads & practical farmers no doubt much light may be gained. About 50 names are down as members. I like the plan much.

24. S. Cold northerly. Low nervous letter from J. T. Price, who hints about leaving business & settling his worldly affairs &c. He evidently writes under the yoke of influenza, the depressing effects of which I know.

27. Penjerrick again. The news circulated through the town yesterday made people look glum, the transfer of the packets to Dartmouth, of which the Mayor has received official intelligence. I prophesy they won't stay there 12 months.

28. Called on Dr. Calvert who yesterday dropped in on us as it were from the skies. He will probably remain here through the winter. He appears to be on the whole worse than this time last year, the formation of water being

1. Barthold Niebuhr (1776–1831), distinguished German historian, whose *Roman History* was translated by Julius Hare and Connop Thirlwall, 1828–32.

perceptible in the swelling of his legs; his complexion, however, looks less bilious. I had a remarkably pleasant little chat with him over old associates and interests. He has as kindly a heart inside of him as any man breathing. Sterling, he tells me, is writing a tragedy.[1] He contrasted the energetic impulsiveness of his character with the unruffled simplicity of Mill's. He spoke of H. N. Coleridge's late publication of his Uncle S.T.C.'s *Confessions of an enquiring Spirit*[2] in which he discriminates between inspiration & dictation, overturning the notion of literal inspiration *in toto*. I am rather surprised that H.N.C. with his High Church doctrine should edit such a work. Calvert has taken lodgings on the Terrace.

31. With Calvert in the evening. Carlyle said to Dr. C., 'Calvert, I wish Satan nothing worse than to have to eat through all eternity with my stomach; no brimstone would then be needed.'

FEBRUARY

2. Town meeting on the Packet question at the Guildhall. Jeffries, the linen draper, was the wit & butt of the meeting. He recommended a deputation of the most amiable females in the town to our gracious Queen to avert the dreaded calamity, & happily compared the recommendations of Dartmouth, viz. the dangerous rocks at the entrance making it inaccessible in many winds, to Sancho Panza's description of the charms of Dulcinea, who was blind of one eye whilst the other ran brimstone & vermilion. A petition for a Committee of Inquiry having been previously prepared, was read & passed. One of the Resolutions was placed in my hands, viz. to call on the other boroughs in the county to co-operate with us in the work. Happily no speech was necessary. Family party at dinner at Uncle A.'s. Hard frost.

4. Spite of deep snow & furious Easterly wind, my father & I trudged to Penjerrick & accomplished some very effective grouping & building with the large rocks carried yesterday. The snow enabled us to slide them into their allotted sites with great ease. Attended agricultural meeting at Selly's. The subject of discussion was grain-dressing. No very definite conclusion arrived at. Heard of W. Forster's having actually offered himself to Jane Backhouse.

5. An interesting call on Dr. Calvert, whom this bleak winter weather confines to his bed. Talking of books he said, 'What I want is a man who will

1. *Strafford: A Tragedy* was published in 1843.
2. Coleridge's *Confessions of an Inquiring Spirit* was published posthumously in 1840 by Henry Nelson Coleridge, the poet's nephew, and his wife, Sara, the poet's daughter. In this work Coleridge argued persuasively against the literal interpretation of the Scriptures, or what he called 'bibliolatry'.

state things simply as they are & not view the world whether moral or physical through the focus of his own theory'. 'Mill,' I said, 'does the least so of any man I know.' He quite agreed. It is religious writers principally that fall into this most mischievous error. In their unwisdom, they think to derogate from God's glory unless they make out that good & evil actions are rewarded & punished in this life; as false a doctrine as ever was propounded, that is, as far as *visible* reward or punishment extends. Ran out to Penjerrick but heavy rain & sleet prevented our working.

6. One of the finest specimens of a stormy sea I ever beheld at 5 o'clock today was dashing out its brains on Swanpool beach & making a sheet of foam all the way into the Pool, carrying the Bar & everything before it. Called on Dr. Lloyd[1] who stays with his sister some weeks. Whilst standing round the fireplace after breakfast, the chymney caught fire & saluted us with a lava stream of burning soot from the crater above. Turned the carpet up & let the beast burn itself out. Wrote to Sterling.

8. Letter from W. Forster from Polam, telling me what I knew before.[2] I think she'll have him. He's the man for her as far as decision of character is required, but the curb rein will require delicate handling. The cold is still upon me. I have little faith in remedies. I believe it must have its course & its appointed time & then die of itself. Ran out in the middle of the day to see the roads which I could easily have skated over.

9. Another holiday through this very convenient cold. A famous opportunity for getting on with my reading. A call from T. Warre, who kindly volunteered to give me a German lesson, but found the part I was reading harder than he counted on.

10. Whole holiday again. It's as good as Christmas used to be 10 years ago. By vegetable diet & water I avoid all feverishness. I feel not the least annoyance from this cold & laugh at the numerous messages of sympathy.

11. The 55th chapter (No. 36) of Master Humphrey's Clock[3] is exquisite, equalling in simple pathos Shakespeare's 'King John'. That man (Dickens I mean) is a poet. Still in house. Sundry callers. Hard rain out, but Elysium within.

12. Spring. Walked to Budock & Penjerrick. Fell in on returning with Jane Tresidder, an old crone famous for her cures & charms (not personal). Had much conversation with her & insinuated myself into her confidence, so much so as to learn many of her most valuable receipts & most solemn charms. She is an enthusiast in her art & blest with as much faith as any of

---

1. The brother of 'Aunt Alfred'.
2. W. E. Forster had proposed marriage to Jane Backhouse.
3. The framework in which Dickens set *The Old Curiosity Shop* and *Barnaby Rudge*. It started to appear in 1840 in parts, but Dickens abandoned this framework and wrote the two separate novels instead.

her patients. She attributes the beneficial effects of charms as much to the faith in the operator as in the patient, as in animal magnetism the intense action of the will of the operator is stated by its supporters to be the efficient cause. She described trying Hezekiah's remedy of boiled figs on a boy with a gathering in his neck & with signal success.

13. Hard rain. Indoors all day. Dr. Calvert called & took his part in a glance at men & manners. Dr. Lloyd to tea. He spent the evening in giving A.M. a practical lesson in bird skinning, which he did *con amore* and evidently thought it unprofessional to submit to the vulgar prejudice of washing one's hands after such operations. A letter from W.E.F. saying he *is not quite killed* & that's all. I think he counts on ultimate success. I read a beautiful article of Mill's in the L. & W.[1] called 'Signs of the Times'.

MARCH

5. Called on Dr. Calvert to consult him as to the disposal of a poor family, the husband having bolted in debt & the wife, mother-in-law & little girl, left with nothing to live on whatever. Calvert says they want to get by some means to Ilminster, where they know a charitable lady, on whom, as far as he can learn, 'they have about as much claim as we have on God Almighty, i.e. that they have received numerous favours from her already & therefore think themselves entitled to more'. Read a queer book today called *Artificial Memory* by Von Feinaigle,[2] which at first smelt strong of humbug, but on trying it with a little attention found the effects extraordinary. Having peopled a room with imaginary symbols, you thereon hang the idea to be remembered in some visible form. By this plan I found that once reading over I could perfectly well remember the succession of the Kings of England & the exact date of each reign, & this backwards as well as forwards. Walked to Penjerrick in a flood of rain.

6. Dr. Calvert called. We talked of the malaria, which is now supposed to be caused by sulphuretted hydrogen generated by the decomposition of vegetable matter (especially the cruciform plants, which contain much sulphur) in salt water. It seems to exist in bands of country in Africa. Acting on the above theory the African expedition go provided with chlorine to absorb the noxious exhalations.

19. The Prussian barque *Juno*, laden with salt, put in last night with loss of sails & rather leaky. About 8 o'clock they found $2\frac{1}{2}$ feet water in the hold, & after pumping some time, found the water gained on them, upon which

1. *The London and Westminster Review.*
2. Gregor von Feinaigle (1765?–1819), author of *The New Art of Memory*, 1812.

they hallo'ed they were sinking & got the boats out & proceeded to save their chests & bedding, having made up their minds to abandon her at anchor in the harbour! The mate of the *Merina* with a boat's crew came on board on hearing the shouting about 11 o'clock; finding the crew panic-struck & unfit for anything, they immediately unshackled & slipped the chain, set mizen & foretopsail & ran her up on the mud on this side of Mylor. Today we sent off surveyors who order the cargo to be discharged.

22. Received to dinner Aunt C. & Juliet, together with an antique piece of furniture called Juliet Smith. Not being versed in antiquarian subjects, it excited in me no other interest than as a curiosity of the old school. Getting in my carrots which are mostly in a state of germination having been in a pile of sand for nearly 3 weeks, which gives them a vast advantage over their enemies, the weeds.

23. Commenced a course of lessons in the chemical analysis of earths & metals with R. Hunt. My fellow-pupil is T. Warre. We assembled in Hunt's laboratory at 5 & concluded at ½ past 8, all more or less edified. Carrot seed all in. Bought a new cow.

24. Made some glorious purchases at Col. Williams's sale, pre-eminent amongst which was a portfolio of Morland's[1] lithographs, 36 in number, genius in every stroke, – & all for 13/6d. Called on widow Vincent, whose husband died last week (in consequence of a blow on the head received whilst working about the rockery). One simple remark of hers conveyed more of the feeling of widowhood than the most high-wrought expressions could have done. He used to work, she said, on that hill in front of the window, so that I could often look up & see him while I went on with my sewing, & so from habit I catch myself looking up there now, & when I don't see him in his old place, it do come across me that I shall never see him again. I said some of the common-places of comfort, to which she listened, but only answered with a sigh. Here was no wound to be healed with words. I respected her feeling & changed the subject.

26. Gave notice at Penryn of a public meeting to be held there in the evening by Junia Price, who is now at Perran with her brother. In the course of my peregrinations called on an old woman & sympathised with her various afflictions physical & moral. She was a Methody now & had shaken hands with John Wesley, but had taken to the Quakers in her youth because she went, as child's maid, to a Quaker's family, one Mr. Price. She was not a little interested that it was one of those children she had the charge of 50 years ago that appointed this very meeting. I went to the other end of the court to notify farther, when a woman came out & taking me for a Home Missionary, begged me to visit a sick old woman upstairs. So we ascended & found a wretched old crone of 92, groaning & complaining of torments of pain, to

1. George Morland (1763–1804), the painter of country scenes and animals.

whom I preached a sermon on patience, which edified us all except the object of it. Walked to Penjerrick after my morning's work & got through some farming satisfactorily.

29. A letter from Sterling from Torquay whence it is not unlikely he will proceed to Falmouth. He speaks of Carlyle's last work, *Hero Worship*, as, on the whole, the most valuable of all his writings. The Prices proceeded on their mission Westward. From Cos. Junia's opinions (as expressed yesterday) respecting birthright membership I entirely & deliberately dissent. If there must be sect at all, which in the low state of religion, is perhaps at present a necessary evil, I would have the children of Friends instructed in the true principles of Quakerism more than is now the practice, but at the age of discretion they should *not* be considered members of the body without a deliberate voluntary avowal of their conviction.

31. *Fox* v. *Glover* comes on tomorrow at Bodmin, with a special Jury. Erle is counsel for Fox (for non-payment of Glover's acceptance of a bill for £319). The defendant's plea, fraudulent misrepresentation. Tilly intimating by a note that the defendant was likely to defend his case contrary to our expectations, I took a place by the night-mail for Bodmin in order to see the fun.

APRIL

1. At ½ past 12 last night I coiled myself up in a corner of the mail, which I had to myself, & reached Bodmin at ½ past 4. Laid on a sofa till 7. I joined Tilly at breakfast in the Lawyers' room with 2 or 3 others of the fraternity; they were funny fellows with their own professional jokes & so on. Uncle J. slept at St. Austell & did not reach the Court till his cause was being concluded, which process occupied about 5 minutes in all. Erle rose, as soon as the jury were sworn, simply stated the complaint, that the burden of proof rested with the defendant, the defendant had not thought proper to defend his case & therefore a verdict for the plaintiff was the only course. This was given by the judge immediately, with the interest, the jury not having a word to say. Another case was then brought on; nothing interesting except the examination of Oliver's barmaid, who having been brought up to the bar, was a match for her questioners the bar-men. Accompanied Uncle J. home in his gig. Bankhart, Secretary of the Company in London & the machinator & prime-mover of all the roguery, was present, looking as sour as vinegar. The costs will be nearly £400. We dined at St. Austell & had a pleasant drive home despite the rain, Uncle J. in the heroics of course. Friendship, Integrity, his Autobiography, Christianity & Intolerance, were a few of the topics. The gratification it gave him would alone repay me for the trip, no others of the family being there.

2. Our Grandparent & Aunt C. gave us their company at Penjerrick. We regaled on stew & spent the afternoon in planting wild flowers. Spring is calling them forth in myriads, spangling the old borders & long-walk-hedge with a prodigality of beauty.

6. Rode to Portreath to meet the partners of the Company there in a consultation on having a new basin wherein a dozen colliers may lie & discharge.[1] Had a fight with W. Reynolds about what Lady Basset should give to induce us. We ask £2,000 & 2^d per ton off the quay, dues on coals which are now 8^d per ton, ore 6^d. We could not exactly come to terms, but he will probably give in.

10. On returning to tea found Sterling! – sitting by the fire & haranguing as in olden times. He looked pale & worn, but animated, cheerful & energetic as ever. H. Molesworth was of the party and he could not only listen, but understand & appreciate. Occasionally when Puseyism, Church History, or German Literature, was touched on, his eloquence was like a clear cascade. His knowledge seems almost universal. You name a writer or an event & he can tell you all the details. His mind is European, his liberality unbounded. His insight of character is like an infallible instinct, his imagination rich to overflowing. To know him is a privilege the highest might be proud of; to know what he knows were an affluence which few could safely bear.

11. Sterling left us at 7 for Penzance to be with Calvert till his father's arrival at Torquay recalls him. He wishes me to go to Italy & to give part of business-hours to study. Junia Price held a public meeting with the sailors at their room in the evening.

12. Ran down to Plumridge's quay to look at the naval hero of the age, Commodore Napier,[2] who arrived yesterday in the *Oriental* from Alexandria. He is the sort of man that I conceived from his exploits & style of diplomacy, a thorough *tar*, with a jolly face, a sparkling eye, & a stout sturdy hull, worthy of containing the heart of oak within. His voice & manners show the energetic mind, the prompt decision & daring which have marked his actions. He was in quarantine, so could not land. I offered our services to send off anything he might want from shore. I want nothing but Pratique,[3] said he. Send me that & I'll thank you. The Leans arrived & stay with us over the approaching Quarterly Meeting. Talked of steam engines all the evening.

15. The Prices left. Narrowly escaped breaking my back by tumbling out of

1. Portreath Haven, near Hayle, was the harbour on the west coast which served the mines of the Redruth district. A 'railway', or tramroad, brought the ores to the harbour and fetched the coal from South Wales back to the mines. The harbour was on land owned by the Bassets of Tehidy.
2. Chas. (later Admiral Sir Chas.) Napier (1786–1860), who was given command of the land forces at Beirut and won a notable victory there. Became M.P. in 1841.
3. Licence for a ship to make contact with a port after quarantine (or on showing a clean bill of health).

a cart on my way to Penjerrick. Reading Carlyle's *Hero Worship*, his lectures now published; a wondrous deep-sighted & eloquent work.

16. A letter from Glover's solicitors yesterday to Tilly, informing him that their client is insolvent. The scoundrel, – to accuse a man of fraud & thus oblige him to prosecute & then avoid the consequences by such a subterfuge! It is no doubt just as likely to be false as true.

19. Uncle A. started for Birmingham. I take his place at the desk. Sterling appeared in our system from Penzance in the evening. I met him at the coach & conveyed him to our house to lodge, where Aunt C. being also located our evening was not altogether a flat one. His mission is after J. Carlyon's house, next door, to be sold tomorrow. Kept it up with Aunt C. in her room till 1 in the morning.

20. Inspected the house with Sterling & attended the sale: he bid £1050 – it sold for £2000! Tables of finery with young gentlemen on one side & young ladies on the other, & flirtations across them, a variety of small fascinations practised as usual for the benefit of the poor. The 2 belles, G. Treweeke & M. Gardiner. Sterling dined with us in quiet. He was more of the lamp than the meteor today. Sterling made enquiries about 2 or 3 other houses & one of the new ones on the Bank will probably prove his future residence. It is a grand idea. He left us in the afternoon accompanying Aunt C. to Perran.

23. Rode to Penjerrick & thence took a run across the country to Trenarth, the old family estate of the Nicholases, which is for sale on the 26th. It is a wild & thorough Cornish valley with great capabilities, with a mansion & other houses about 200 acres. It extends down to Helford River & might be made beautiful. Much pleased with a man called Peters, whom I found quarrying & carrying stones to build himself a house on the side of a piece of croft, which he had taken on lease & was going to bring into cultivation. I found he was the owner of 5 little meadows of the richest pasturage in the valley, which I admired in passing by. He took them 5 years ago when they were moor & growing nothing but reeds & sedge. He skimmed, burnt & drained it, & his corn in 5 weeks lay prostrate with its luxuriance. He cut it green & gave his cattle, & before harvest had to cut it down a second time. How he is well rewarded for his trouble. He was a miner, he said, & worked at Wheal Vyvyan and when he belonged to the night corps, he worked on his meadows all day & when to the day corps, he worked through the night if there was any moon. If we all laboured in our vocations like this man!

24. After a little farming & final orders, walked home by ½ past 7. In the evening Wm. Forster appeared by the *Regulator*, on a flying visit to talk to me of love, in the interval between visiting one & another woolstapler, as he is beating up commissions in the West. He does not look much pulled down by his exercise. We deferred our talk till tomorrow but I discerned on alluding to the subject, that he had not given it up.

25. William & I employed the day principally in walking & talking & that not altogether unprofitably. We sat up till near 1 going over the late affair between him & Jane *ab initio*, chapter & verse, correspondence & all. She evidently had a very hard try with her feelings before she refused him. Her proceeding throughout was that of a thorough Quaker. She did not wish to have her attention distracted by explanations or protestations, but placed the disposal of herself in the hands of a Higher Counsellor than her own heart, having sincerely sought, as she expressed it, 'right direction' in the affair. She was led thereby, as she believed, to decide in the negative after two visits. He has determined to try again, undecided only as to what interval he should allow to elapse. As far as I can judge, nothing that Jane said would encourage any such renewal. My father started per mail for Plymouth at ¼ past 12 in order to see the Niger expedition, on his way to Wales where the Neath partners meet to consult about a rolling mill.

26. Started William at 7 per Penzance coach from whence by means of taking a gig & driving across the country he was able to join me at Penjerrick at 4 where dinner waited him. After showing him the place & farm, we went in to Tregedna where Uncle J. & he got on well. The girls warbled & we devoured bread & cream. The latter part of the evening, i.e. till ½ past 1, we spent in Penjerrick parlour & on the terrace comparing notes as to many things. He is decidedly deepened in his views; he won't admit that his present disappointment has been useful to him but I am sure it has. While sitting at my desk Sterling suddenly flashed in upon me. In ½ an hour we had seen Oliver & inspected his house, the one next to the Bank, & in ½ an hour more the bargain was concluded (750£) and Sterling has actually planted himself at Falmouth! A brilliant morning's work. He walked home with me to luncheon. Somehow or other my mother & he fell into a discussion on Friends' dress, by which both parties were confirmed in their previous views.

27. William & I trudged in to Falmouth to breakfast. After attending to the day's work, I joined him at Perran & we proceeded together to Truro for the sake of last words. After he had attended to his wool business & I to a hollow tooth, we sat in quiet, conversing, canvassing opinions and living over old times to our mutual edification. He retired to the sofa till the arrival of the Devonport mail & I turned in, not having sentiment enough to sit up & see him off.

28. I think Wm. will have Jane in the end. The fact is he is determined to win her, he is convinced she loves him & will give way in the end. Breakfasted at Perran. Bathed for the first time. Horrid cold.

30. Freshfield's motion for a Committee of enquiry on the question of Dartmouth as a packet station was carried by a majority of 4, & against the ministers. An interesting lecture from Hunt. The effects of the spectrum on paper sensitive to light are curious. We could *see* the invisible ray beyond the

red by looking thro' a blue glass – it appeared of a deep crimson. Warre & I both took a little of the nitrous oxide or laughing gas. He was more affected than I, tho' neither of us much, owing to the smallness of the quantity. The sensation was pleasurable but dizzy; a larger dose would probably have removed this.

MAY

2. S. A great public baptism in the sea at the Bar took place today of 9 or 10 converted sinners in the presence of thousands. The operators are, I believe, a sect without a name but that of Christians. I do not know the peculiarity of their views, but their appearance is somewhat of the primitive Methodist species. I heard 2 of their preachers holding forth near Capt. Plumridge's, with great energy & zeal, dealing largely in damnation, & arousing the dead in trespasses by strong chiaro-scuro painting of Heaven & Hell & the like, a style of discourse suited perhaps to their audience but certainly not to calm reason. They spoke however as if their hearts were in the cause, & their desire was to save souls. After all, I believe we lay far too much stress on views and doctrines. Faith & sincerity of heart are the things needful. A man who holds a false creed may be a more acceptable worshipper than another who holds a true one.

5. Sterling came yesterday & took tea with us. He proposes making a frieze round his parlour of the plaster of Paris Elgin marbles, a pretty idea. He looks pallid and pulled down. I have taken lodgings for him for a week & he is busied all day about his new purchase. A meeting of the incipient Falmouth & Southampton Steam Co. at our office today in which we fixed that Cos. E. O. Tregelles should go and inspect the *Beresford* & report. The Chancellor of the Exchequer's proposal to build up our inadequate revenue is to lower the duty on sugar to 36/– per ton from £3.3/–, & to lower Baltic timber from 55/– to 50/– per load, & raise our colonial timber 5/–. The rest he proposes making up by a property tax. The sugar suggestion will no doubt raise the opposition of the Slavery Abolitionists[1] and I trust will be quashed.

6. Farmers' club in the evening. Subject of discussion, turnip culture. Introduced by a farmer called Earle & followed up by Rowe, Northcote, Tilly, Selly &c. The general conclusion seemed to be that during the first week in June was the best time to sow, that there was no remedy for the fly but by forcing the plant beyond their attacks, that to effect this the dressing (bone dust) should be shallow. Earle states that in Middlesex they use their turnips for feeding pigs after saving the seed from them.

1. The close connection of the West Indian sugar trade with slavery caused many Quakers at this time to forego the use of sugar.

7. Evening with Sterling. Lit up with flashes from the spheres. Discussed Capital Punishment. He does not go my length & contends that if the State has no right to take away life, it has no right to take away freedom. Also upheld the monstrous error that capital differs from secondary punishments not in kind but only in degree, as if an exile from the body and an exile from Gt. Britain were merely modifications of the same species of banishment. He is however in favour of abolishing Capital Punishment for all offences except murder & rape.

8. My father returned from Neath via Plymouth at 2 this morning, bright & well. Gives a somewhat more encouraging report of Neath concerns. Eccleston & Sterling to tea. The former is a self-satisfied puppy and if he be a sample of the Society,[1] the Ethiopian will hardly change his skin through their scrubbing. However I have got up a lecture for him for the 10th & hope he won't disgrace me. Received a rich letter from Mill. Finished my essay on Capital Punishment.

9. S. Wet again. At Sterling's after dinner & met there an intelligent, free spoken, good-natured friend of his called Lawrence,[2] a magistrate and collector of the Revenue in India. He spoke of Lord Clive as equal to the Duke of Wellington.

10. Eccleston with me after breakfast. I took him to the Rector's, who talked reasonably on the objects of the Society, then to the Town Hall, where the Rector having taken the chair, Eccleston spouted for 2 hours to the assembled multitudes (some 30 or 40). His speech came up to its pretensions, which is something. He gave us geographical information as to the course of the Niger & Chadda which was new. Their junction is the point proposed for the settlement. The collection at the door exceeded £2. Sterling's friend Lawrence was there. His object at Falmouth is 'Love, all love', in the shape of a very pretty, simple girl, a Miss Gresley, who is staying with the Dawsons. How to get an interview puzzled him. As he does not know the Dawsons I offered to take him there & introduce him to the Lieut., for which he was profoundly obliged. After being there a few minutes the young lady entered the room looking the picture of sweetness & innocence. They were soon in close chat & I took my leave.

11. Attended Redruth Manor Court in the capacity of 'lord'. W. Williams was with me an hour, but sounded a retreat when dinner was announced as his doctor had forbid large pasties & hot rooms. I was consequently obliged, much against the grain, to preside & take the head of the table, which was surrounded by between 30 & 40 tenants, shopkeepers, mine-captains &c.

1. The African Civilisation Society.
2. This was John (later Lord) Lawrence (1811–79), who became one of the most famous figures in the history of British India. He was later the hero of the Indian Mutiny and became governor-general of India.

It is no joke to carve a tough rump of beef for a party of that size. Kept up conversation by dint of topics political & agricultural. After dinner when the lords were toasted in due course, I had to get on my legs & speechify. After acknowledging the compliment, I told them it was not our practice[1] to give toasts, on which ground they would excuse my proposing their healths & believe my wishes for their health & welfare equally sincere.

14. The lover Lawrence on the verge of despair because his lady love did not appear at the Horticultural meeting yesterday. The Dawsons & she came to see the garden. Sterling met them according to a private plot between us, in order to sound the lady herself & to convince her cousin, Mrs. Dawson, that his friend was not an adventurer & was in fact 'worth looking after'. Miss Gresley I found very artless, intelligent, lively & good looking & in all respects worthy of being fallen in love with.

15. Boarded the Braganza Steamer immediately on her arrival, to pay attention to the Countess of Durham with her brother & children, on their return from Cadiz. It was by Uncle D. Barclay's special request who, I fancy, looks to making some use of her at the next election for Sunderland. Walked with Sterling & Lawrence. Both approve of the government measures for increasing the revenue, tho' I see the commencement of a split in the Anti-Slavery Society in consequence, the London Committee having declared themselves opposed to the Sugar Bill. Uncle A. has returned from Wales in high spirits about Briton Ferry coalset, which he counts on yielding £10,000 per annum by means of a vein only discovered during the last visit of the partners.

17. Sterling poorly, – blistered & cupped. Sat with him in his bedroom.

19. Monthly meeting at Redruth. Aunt Lucy's resignation was read & admitted with but little remark. It was brief & well written, stating her attachment to the Church of England and the inconsistency she felt it to remain a nominal Quaker. I hear that Uncle G. states his entire coincidence in her views.

20. Collected the Town with the Mayor for the sums subscribed for the Railway Survey. People look strikingly unamiable when asked for their money. Sterling so much better as to drive out to Penjerrick. Calvert arrived at Falmouth for a permanence, I hope. Lawrence dined & then rode to Penjerrick with me. It was a small plot in which however we were foiled, for the Dawsons had engaged to come with the lady & at the 11th hour disappointed us, at which he raved not a little. He is an amusing, companionable fellow.

22. We mustered strong at the Warres to drink tea & see fireworks which were tolerably commendable. Lawrence was there & the Dawsons with Miss Gresley. She showed him all due civility, but what I should consider

1. i.e. the practice of Quakers.

poor encouragement for a lover. I believe he took it in the same light. Saw Dr. Calvert on his pony. He considers himself improving fast, but shows much feebleness & languor; so does Sterling, he has been spitting blood. Poor fellow, he is too good to last long.

24. A message from Uncle J. that he wished to see me led me to Tregedna after breakfast. I found him writhing in an agony of pain, his face of an ashen hue & the cold sweat starting from every pore. He could hardly speak to me, but his eyes were rolling wildly & he could not bear to remain in one position for 2 successive moments. I never saw a fellow creature in so great apparent suffering. The attack had only come on 3 hours before & was increasing in violence. As it had all the appearance of inflammation, & finding he had only sent for Brougham, I started off for Penryn at a smart gallop, found Dr. Wise at home & despatched him at once to Tregedna. To my surprise on riding thro' Falmouth I met Brougham in the street going leisurely to attend a patient. I therefore packed him off without loss of time & went to business. I ran out in the middle of the day & found to my delight that 13 gr. of calomile & a mustard plaister had entirely removed the pain. The Drs. were at dinner, & Uncle J. quietly in bed, luxuriating in the departure of pain. Having seen all this very satisfactory sight, trudged back to Falmouth to attend a meeting of the *Beresford* Shareholders at our office. I trudged out again at 9.

26. Hearing that some of the Buonaparte family were in the harbour on board the *Iberia*, I made a push to see them. Lawrence accompanied me. I got a newspaper, went off & enquired of the captain, for M. Adolphe Maillard, some American Secretary of Legation, who belonged to the suite. I introduced myself to him as the Consul's son & offered our services & the paper. As he had one or two, I gave it to an old gentleman the other side of the table, who thanked me. After talking to Maillard for 10 minutes, I said I supposed the prince was in his cabin (as I had heard that he was so infirm that Hull & Cornish who went off to see him were only allowed to stay with him 2 minutes). Maillard said, 'Oh, this is the prince', pointing to the old gent, to whom he then introduced me. He was very polite & chatty & we talked for about 10 minutes on various subjects. This was Joseph Buona-parte,[1] ex-King of Spain, now Count de Servilios. He had the square Napoleon face & bright blue eyes, but was evidently feeling the infirmities of age. I then asked Maillard for the prince of Canino, Charles Buonaparte, son of Lucien[2] & nephew of Joseph B. The prince jumped up & bowed

1. Joseph Buonaparte (1768–1844), eldest brother of Napoleon, ex-king of Naples and ex-king of Spain. After Napoleon's defeat he went to America and became an American citizen. He returned to Europe in 1832 and died in Florence.
2. Lucien Buonaparte (1775–1840), Prince of Canino, brother of Napoleon. His son Charles, who inherited the title of Canino, was uninterested in politics but established a reputation as a naturalist and ornithologist.

& said, 'I am he.' He was a stout, uninteresting but very civil fellow. After a little chat I took my leave, the ex-King pulled off his glove & shook hands, as did the prince. Joseph talked French, but Charles very fair English. On going on deck I found Lawrence walking up & down. I persuaded him to make a push & go below, which he did & was introduced to the party while I spent the time in admiring young Buonaparte, Charles's son, a very handsome boy & the image of Napoleon. We were well satisfied with the success of our visit.

30. Sterling arrived with wife & children from Hayle. Glorious afternoon. C. & I walked out together & discussed the importance of a mate not being a pleasant companion only, but a yoke-fellow. It is bad for a man to have a wife who does not understand him, but still worse, one who much over-appreciates him. Love & obedience is milk & honey to the object of it but worship is pure alcohol.

31. Meeting of the *Beresford* shareholders to take steps to give actual birth to the concern. There is a melancholy absence of pluck in the Town for a project of this sort.

JUNE

2. Canvassed several Falmouthians in the morning with E. O. Tregelles about the *Beresford*. Read the *Election*,[1] a very clever poem lent me by Calvert.

3. Tea at the Dawsons with all the Tregedna party. There is a peculiar freshness about Miss Gresley which is highly pleasing. We attended the first of Smith's lectures *en masse*. His subject was Physical Geography. A full audience. Lecture was not very anything. Seas & tides & rivers & springs, mountains, caverns & mines, were his theme & were well illustrated on a screen by a magic lantern behind. He is a specimen of a man of the pump-spout faculty, never at a loss for word, never original or imaginative. His stale jokes, which were at his fingers' ends, carried with them the musty smell of having been always packed up with his magic lantern. The boys & especially Tom Evans, were however highly pleased. Rattled back in Uncle J.'s waggon with my horses at mail coach speed.

4. Paid an ecclesiastical visit to the churches, accompanying T. Phillpotts, in his inspecting tour as Rural Dean's assistant. We took a boat at Durgan & went across to St. Anthony's church, a sweet retired little spot which we passed across & landed under Mawnan Glebe. We scrambled up & devoured sandwiches on a sunny grassy spot, enjoying them & each other in pleasant chat. We then broke in on Kinsman, after peeping through his church win-

1. A poem, in seven books, by Sterling, published in 1841.

dows to see that he kept his temple in a reputable state. We found the Incumbent at dinner & sat down to assist him. After a few clerical jokes we started for Penjerrick & arrived in time to catch the cart, in which we crammed 7 of us & set off for the Magors, where we tea'd & collected like a snowball into a very formidable mass, to do honour to Smith's second lecture. In the midst of a good deal of twaddle he gave some ideas which were new to me. The gulf stream is part of a great whirlpool 8000 miles in circumference, commencing at Guinea & going round by Mexico & Newfoundland at the rate of ½ a mile per hour. The Trade winds are a whirlwind following the same course, both the results of the earth's form & motion. He properly called the sea 'the highway' & not 'the barrier' of nations. His polar illustrations were good.

6. S. Sterling speaks in the highest terms of Emerson's Essays,[1] which have all the originality & earnestness of Carlyle, with more philosophy, & without his savageness. Called on Calvert who continues very languid. Slept at Falmouth on account of the Census, which returns the numbers that sleep in every house tonight.

7. Attended a Harbour Committee, at which Capt. Plumridge's evidence before the Committee of the House was read. It was energetic, manly, full, & straightforward. The united evidence in favour of Falmouth must be irresistible. Smith's lecture on mountains, lakes, & cataracts. His lectures show (if nothing else) how much ease & brass may be obtained by practice in addressing the public. Hunt followed him with a few remarks on photography & took a photographic picture with the oxyhydrogen light.

8. Smith's last lecture on volcanoes, earthquakes & boiling springs, & more especially his own fame, & the great importance of his educational lectures which he means to favour us with this week & next. Generous man. He must have cleared £50 at least by Falmouth. I believe it is essential to a public lecturer that he be, to some extent, a humbug, in fact to all who have to do with the public, for it is an animal of the Gull species that lives on humbug more or less disguised. I interfered in a domestic quarrel, the audible signs of which stopped me in the street. I went in & found a drunken father had been beating a daughter in her own house, for harbouring a lodger who bred strife in the family. I endeavoured to calm the tempest & persuaded the lodger to pack off her traps & start, which she agreed to do.

12. Falmouth sick with a political fever. Knots of politicians in all street corners & the candidate, Capt. Vivian, frisking from house to house with his tail of lawyers, playing the agreeable & omni-assentient to every elector. What a charm must lie in those two magic labials M. P. to induce men to

1. Ralph Waldo Emerson (1803–82), American philosopher and poet, visited England in 1833 and met Wordsworth, Coleridge and Carlyle. The first volume of his Essays appeared in 1841.

resign peace, comfort & some odd thousands, for the sake of them & the humorous idea that they are governing the nation, instead of the nation governing them.

19. A letter from Freshfield brought the glad intelligence that the Committee of Enquiry had returned a report favourable to Falmouth & decisive against Dartmouth. Electioneering going on strong, another Tory candidate, Mr. Sartoris, in the field. The idea of such a man, without the shadow of any connection with Falmouth & being profoundly ignorant of our local interests, representing us in Parliament seems preposterous.

21. Rode with Dr. Calvert to Perran to look into the accounts & make a choice of a pig. On our return, Dr. Calvert conversed in an interesting manner on the mission of mankind & the purpose of existence. On this subject he professes himself diametrically opposed to Sterling. That men should be sent into the world to teach their brethren, he considers a fallacy as old as St. James, who complained of the many masters or teachers. He contends that we are all sent to be learners & through a process of progressive refining, to be fitted & prepared for glorification. When I look at John Sterling, he said, as a man pressing on to learn & to use & to become an infinitely improved John Sterling, I look at him with vast respect. But when I look at him as a man having attained Truth & Perfection, & consequently a Teacher of Mankind, I laugh to think what a complete dwarf he is. People are a deal too fond of giving advice when they know little or nothing of the peculiar circumstances of the individual, which in fact is as necessary to know as for a doctor to know the disease of his patient. I fully concur in the general bearing of the doctor's sentiments. But, on the other hand, I see something of the one-sidedness of a confirmed invalid, who feeling his own inability for active usefulness, will not appreciate the gift of the active Few.

24. The wits of the less thinking part of the Falmouth electors are wondrously set off by the Whig band & procession which bear, amongst other veracious symbols, a very big loaf, & a little one, on long poles; the former the prospective Whig loaf, the latter the present Tory one. The Canon has published a very stupid, narrow, short-sighted address to his tenantry to vote for Lord Boscawen, with his reasons for so doing, & which, the *West Briton* wittily remarks, proves that all canonical writings are not inspired. Called on Dr. Calvert in the afternoon. Found him in a languid dropsical state. He says he keeps himself alive with rectified spirits of wine & gin, eating nothing that can oppress the stomach. This, he is certain, cannot last. It is only like living in oxygen. Spoke highly of Howell, the cleverest of the London Practitioners, & who still undertakes to prescribe for him. 'The science of medicine as well as that of morals will no doubt be much further advanced 50 years hence than they are now, but I feel happy in having been able to obtain the benefit of the highest experience in both, as far as they have been

attained in the age which God Almighty has placed me. For the rest, what I suffer is partly my fault & partly a design for my good & it is my place to bear it patiently as long as it lasts. As to enduring another winter of it, I have no idea of that.'

27. S. Called with Sterling & his lady on Calvert, who appears to be losing ground by inches. He is patient, interesting & cheerful. He rallied Sterling on his renewal of allegiance to Mother Church, since he had attended the morning service. Sterling loudly protested against the platitude & inanity to which he had to listen. Marsh preached &, according to Sterling, preached twaddle such as 'that God is good we cannot doubt, for the Scripture tells us so'. Sterling says he only goes to church vicariously for his children.

30. Gave a glorious hay-party in the cross close, whereat I was honoured by the company of Sterling with wife & children, the dwellers of Trebah & Tregedna, the 2 boys from Glendurgan, & W. Lean of Birmingham & C. Pearson. Most of the party never entered the house the whole time, but as we pitched a tent & built a nest & had the solace of a syllabub, strawberries & cream, &c., there was not any grumbling. The children were wild with pleasure & the parent birds grew young in watching them; all of which is very delightful & as it should be.

JULY

1. The cause of Truth has triumphed at Falmouth. For the first time in our annals we have returned two Whigs! – Vivian 84 & Plumridge 50 – above either of the Tories. The whole constituency is 1,500.

2. Visited Batty's caravan with the Tregednites &c. The group of lion & lioness, with 2 panthers in the same den, was superb, and the terms which existed between them & their keeper were wonderful. A magnificent tigress in the next cage & a lioness in the one adjoining broke their partition a week since & had a most desperate & bloody encounter. We separated & met again at Trebah in the evening together with John & Capt. Sterling, his brother, who is much his inferior in appearance, but sensible & matter of fact.

10. Breakfasted with Tilly at Tremow & spent the morning in surveying his various farming operations. I was convinced of the great advantages of the horse hoe & ordered one accordingly. The rotation he most approves is this, – cut your grass, feed down the ley, plough or comb it & leave through the winter, then oats without dressing, then turnips with bone dust & dung in preparation for the wheat which succeeds it, then grass seed & let it out. Tilly is a good tempered, energetic, intelligent, shrewd-headed fellow, who thinks boldly for himself & is somewhat latitudinarian. There is a want of

delicacy of mind, and also of liberality, tho' none is louder in the profession of it. Attended a Polytechnic Committee.

11. Called on Calvert who is now reduced to bed. His weakness is excessive, but he suffers little or no pain. He told Peters he should not survive the present attack, poor fellow. He will be a loss indeed.

12. Rode to Penjerrick before breakfast & held a survey on Swanpool Beach with J. Falck, to fix on the how, where & wherewithall for making a new road across it, which if done at all, must be done by individuals, as both parishes disclaim the ownership of it.

13. Attended in the evening Rumball's first lecture on Phrenology which interested me much. His phrenology maxims are these: Size is power, other things being equal, & Form indicates quality. Dr. Gale's attention was led to the subject 70 years ago by observing that boys who remembered words had protruding eyes. Cornish attempted to controvert some of his views after the lecture, but his own cranium being at the time somewhat vapoury, he was not in a state to theorise on those of others.

15. St. Swithin wept! and mankind sorrowed for his woe. At a library meeting Sterling brought forward his proposal of a book club attached to the library & cemented into brotherhood by an extra pound per head for ordering new works, the great deficiency of the library. It met with proper support. Attended Rumball's second lecture, – & such a lecture! After attending Smith it is like quitting Russell's van for the *Quicksilver* coach. His character is energy, his reasoning lucid & convincing, his style eloquent. I delight in him. In the pauses you might have heard a pin drop. He began with alimentativeness as the first tendency developed by the child. The consideration of its nature, connected with facts, led him to the discovery of gustativeness as a distinct organ by which food is discriminated. The first implies a mere love of aliment without reference to kind. The first leads if indulged to gluttony, the second to drunkenness & epicurism. People broad in the cheekbones have the former; a hollowness in that part of the cheek indicates the latter. It also indicates a dyspeptic habit which he asserted to be a *low state of nervous power*: not a derangement or weakness of the coats of the stomach. The remedy therefore obviously is *Brace the nervous system*, by exercise, bathing, friction, &c. He then came to destructiveness, an animal instinct given us as carnivorous animals & for highly useful purposes in conjunction with the moral faculties. He then came to combativeness, which means a desire to *oppose*. He gave some remarkable examples & illustrations. Acquisitiveness, – a love of acquiring, – as money now represents everything tangible, it usually takes that direction. Magpies have it large. A lady of large property was transported the other day for stealing a pair of stockings. Her acquisitiveness was morbid, producing monomania. She ought to have been sent to an asylum. All these faculties are means to ends; when their

indulgence becomes the end, not the means, this is a perversion which is always evil, & in excess may amount to insanity. This may apply to misers. As acquisitiveness is the desire *to gain*, so secretiveness is the desire to keep; the cat, the squirrel, the fox, the magpie, all have it. He then came to Fear, improperly called caution & shewed the difference between them. Sam Scott, the diver, had none whatever. Cornish objected after the lecture closed, but only indulged in assertion & quoted Blumenbach,[1] who admitting that there was both Novelty & Truth in the Science, added, 'but then unfortunately whatever it has of true is not new & what is new is not true'.

16. After inspecting the performance of my new horse-hoe at Penjerrick, I joined a large & joyous party at Glendurgan. The day was a realised idea of summertime & 3 boatloads of us, on the mirror-surface of Helford river, basking in the sunshine & watching the drawing of the trammels felt it altogether a luxury of existence seldom equalled. Being pressed for time for the lecture, I doffed my jacket, girded my loins & ran home from Glendurgan in 55 minutes. When I arrived, Rumball had reached love of approbation & self esteem, which qualities, though generally allowed, he denies to the brute creation, wrongfully as I think. He then came to Firmness, of which he gave a just & subtle analysis. It is utterly distinct & independent of physical courage, but must enter into the feeling called *moral* courage. Cranmer manifested it by holding in the flame the hand which signed his recantation. Likewise, a Dr. Beale, curate of a parish near Tavistock, who tried to make him think he belonged to the navy, but whose head showed an entire absence of combativeness & destructiveness. Rumball told him plainly he had no courage, saying he was as fit to be a post captain as himself was to be a bishop, & ably distinguished the form & content of his courage, which would not preserve his wits if a single footpad sprung on him from a hedge, but would enable him to face 10 if he had time to reflect & was convinced it was his bounden duty. Women have it larger than men; combativeness less.

18. S. This was a memorable day at Grove Hill, being the first time that the lord & lady wended their different paths to separate worship. I found Uncle G. very low under it in the evening. He thinks it cannot continue so, but he must needs follow her. From the Chapmans' report of Coope's sermons, both in the morning & evening, it will never suit a mind like his, & Aunt L. was much distressed by this first sample of what lies weekly before her.

19. Evening at Sterling's where we met the Stangers, Dr. Calvert's relations. The beloved physician is wonderfully recovered from his late attack. Sterling exhibited some superb engravings of Raphael's frescoes in the Vatican, with one complete set of heads taken out of the picture of Poetry

1. Johann F. Blumenbach (1752–1840) was one of the most distinguished German physiologists and anatomists of the time.

over one of the windows. Ran over to Rumball's lecture to hear the end &
to make an appointment with him to repeat it the day after tomorrow for
the benefit of those who were prevented from attending.

21. Monthly Meeting at Redruth. Stayed at home having much to do at
the shop. At ½ past 7 we posted off to Rumball's last lecture. It was on the
moral faculties, & of course more than usually interesting. Something led
him to refer to the present constitution of the House of Commons, which
as well as other Legislative Assemblies, presents this absurdity. The man who
goes there with his mind open to conviction & not pinned to a party, is set
down as a waverer & worth nothing. Yet weeks are spent in bursts of
eloquence & the most acute reasoning to prove this assertion or that, when it
can be estimated at the very outset, to 2 or 3, how many will vote this side
or that.

28. Started with Uncle C., the Balls, & A.M. & C. in the former's carriage
for Plymouth. Slept at Liskeard.

29. Breakfast at the Allens's between 6 & 7. Reached Plymouth soon after 10.
Procured a ticket of life-membership,[1] & after visiting the Abbots and
recognising sundry old friends, deposited the girls at the Geology section &
went my rounds. First, to the Chemical section, where Hunt was concluding
his lecture on photogenic drawings. The president & other table-men were
about ½ a dozen, & the audience about twice that number. At the Statistics
section H. Woolcombe was droning out the remarkable circumstances &
characters connected with that remarkable city, Plymouth. Met Wightwick
there whose patience was tired as soon as mine, & we decamped to the
Mechanical Section. An animated discussion was going on about steam &
locomotives. In reference to atmospheric resistance on railways, Scott Russell
showed that the experiments with a wedge front to the train proved nothing,
as from a blunt wedge no sensible acceleration could be expected. In perfectly straight railroads there is always a very perceptible oscillating motion,
& this causes a preference to a slightly curved road, where the oscillatory
motion is counteracted by the curvilinear one. Rendel,[2] a first rate practical
engineer & pupil of Telford, told us that a railroad which enabled the train
to average 20 miles per hour, proves in the end the most satisfactory to all
parties. At the physical section I heard nothing, but saw some fine specimens
of the female race. At the Geology where Wightwick & I finally came to an
anchor, Dr. Buckland was talking about earthquakes & about keeping a
saucer of treacle in our bedrooms to show the intensity & direction of them,
& counselled us always in case of an earthquake at night to jump out of bed
& take refuge in the window or doorway. An elderly man called Walker

1. i.e. of the British Association which was meeting in Plymouth.
2. James Rendel (1799–1856), a surveyor under Thomas Telford, the road and bridge
builder. He built the Birkenhead docks.

read a paper to prove that the breakwater & all other limestone edifices under water were in process of being eaten up by small varmint called sanicava. He attributes the depth of water at Dartmouth & other limestone harbours to this circumstance. Buckland learnedly suggested something about snails which he discovered at the bottom of some extensive limestone borings near Boulogne. This led to a learned disquisition on snails, as to how they bored & where they bored, & why they bored, & whether they really bored, or no. Thought I, if they don't, I know who does. It reminded me not a little of Pickwick's scientific discussion of tittle-bats.

30. At the Zoological Section Dr. Hodgkin[1] read a paper on man & his varieties. The picture of a tribe of N. American Indians in process of extirpation suggested the image of the gladiators in the Roman amphitheatre. He deplored the indifference of his countrymen as to the extinction of a race of men whilst the loss of the Dodo created an intense interest. He proposed as a valuable object a human zoological garden, but suggested as another means of attaining the same object to support his Aborigines Protection Society. At the Chemical Section Daubeny was holding forth on manures, which interested me much. He contends that they are not stimulants merely but nutritives; in many cases isomorphous constituents of manure can be substituted one for the other, magnesia for lime, &c. At the Mechanical Section, Scott Russell was holding forth on his experiments on the best *forms* of ships. He did not enter into particulars, but laid a voluminous report on the table & stated that the resistance to a floating body is considerably more in shallow than deep water. Joined a large party at Elford Leigh, Cos. W. Fox's new purchase, a very large house about a mile from his lodge, with a forest & park, looking very imposing, but sadly gone to seed, the effects of heavy mortgages & non-residence of its former proprietor.

31. Rode in with Tom between 6 & 7 in the morning to join an excursion to the Eddystone in the *Carron* steamer. From 50 to 100 of us mustered on board. Conybeare, Lloyd, Daubeny, Walker & Lord Ebrington were the principal lions. The wind being fresh & your philosopher being more of a land than a water animal, there were sundry revelations of what before lay concealed in the depths of human nature, with sundry white & lengthened visages. Dr. Daubeny, with whom I was having a profound discussion on the action of manures, made a sudden rush in the midst of conversation to the ship's side. On the whole, however, it went off pleasantly enough. From Benjn. Docking I learned a good deal about Lord Byron's page who accompanied him in his wanderings. His name is Rushton & he is a very respectable schoolmaster near Nottingham. He wanted to know if I knew anything of a Mr. Sterling whose poetry he had been highly delighted with & some of

1. Thomas Hodgkin (1798–1866), the physician after whom 'Hodgkin's disease' was named. He founded the Aborigines Protection Society in 1838.

which he had copied. We saw the Eddystone[1] to advantage, though it blew too fresh to land. Smeaton, the engineer, took the idea of its peculiar form from the stem of the oak, which he has copied.

AUGUST

2. Breakfasted at the Sleemans'. Met a worthy little priest called Alford there. At the Statistical Section a letter from M. A. Gilbert was read on the advantages of spade husbandry, by the adoption of which she had eased her parish of 90 paupers, whether with gain or loss to herself was not stated. Sir C. Lemon then read a paper of his (to which I had the honour of contributing) on the agricultural statistics of Cornwall. It appears that in 1794 $\frac{1}{3}$rd of the county was cultivated, $\frac{1}{3}$ was croft broken up once in 25 years, & $\frac{1}{3}$ entirely uncultivated. At that time carts were hardly known in the county & it did not more than feed its own inhabitants. In 1839 the population having more than doubled, being 345,000, the produce in corn fell short of the wants of the inhabitants by 35,000 qrs. or their equivalent. He made out that we pay one twelfth of our annual exports for food. Accompanied the girls & Dr. Donnelly to his house from whence, after a handsome luncheon, proceeded to the Dockyard to see the *Hindostan* launched. Heavy rain all day prevented many, nevertheless multitudes were present. It was the grandest sight of the sort I ever saw. She was christened by the lady of General Ellis with a bottle of port. With a blow of the mallet on a chisel she then cut the rope which confined 2 pigs of ballast, which falling perpendicularly were meant to have struck off the dogshores on both sides. It required however 5 minutes coaxing to induce her to make the plunge & enter her new home.
4. No sections held this morning, but a grand evening finale at the Town Hall, Devonport. The meeting was occupied by blarney, served up hot & laid on thick, sure enough. Robinson & Buckland lowered themselves in my esteem. The next meeting is appointed to be held in Manchester in June '42. Grants are made to various committees & individuals for various specified objects to the amount of £3350, of which £100 or £200 was granted for pursuing investigations in some highly interesting species of fossil mammalia, and the munificent sum of £7.11/- for investigations in the races of men. We left before the proceedings were half concluded. I have taken a ticket for life membership. We have engaged a batch of philosophers to proceed to Falmouth & attend the Polytechnic. Took leave of a large round of acquaintances.

1. Smeaton's lighthouse was built 1757-9, but as the rock on which it was built became undermined it was taken down and replaced by another in 1879-82. The removed upper part of Smeaton's tower was re-erected on Plymouth Hoe.

5. Returned home. Dismal weather. Parents received us with cordiality. Observed much of the corn, especially barley, beaten down by the rain.

7. A hard working day at the Polytechnic Room arranging hanging, &c. Professor Lloyd[1] & his wife arrived & quartered at our house. They are a delightful pair, married about a year. He reminds me a little of J. Mill. She is a sweet girlish thing, very pretty & perfectly simple.

9. Hard work at the room most of the day. Held a meeting of *Beresford* owners in the morning in which we advertised her to make various trips tomorrow & the 2 following days. Walked over to Budock to attend our Library meeting in the evening. It was well supported & 11 new books of a superior stamp were proposed (principally by the villagers), which I am ordered to procure. A party of 18 assembled at dinner. I sat by Hicks of Bodmin, who kept me in a state of intermitting hysteria by his fun & wit & stories of an eccentric political economist in his asylum.[2] Our house being brimful of guests, I had to lodge at Grove Hill.

10. 1st day of the Exhibition. Professors in abundance. Representatives of science great & small. Lions & lions' whelps, all served to swell the ever-rolling sea of life which flowed through the entrance door. The body of the Hall exhibited a larger collection of the respectability, talent, intelligence, & wealth of the country than one ever sees together but on these occasions. The 'notables' were ranged for exhibition on the platform. Owen's[3] lecture in the evening was a beautifully clear & simple description of the succession of organized life which inhabited the succession of worlds antecedent to the present. I met him at Grove Hill afterwards in company with other philosophers & was delighted with him. Ritter,[4] the German Geographer was there, a magnificent old man, and Conybeare, the ungainly, & Sterling & Daubeny & other celebrities of great & small repute.

11. Today's proceedings were all pretty much the same, with the addition of a Regatta, with a change of dinner guests & a change in the evening lecture. When Conybeare concluded, Sterling was called on to follow Geology with a dissertation on its application to the Arts. He came unprepared. 5 beautiful casts were on the table before him for prizes. These he took as his text & preached thereon such a lovely sermon on *Art*, & *Style*, & *feeling* for the Beautiful, that it seemed as though our eyes were opened to behold the

1. Rev. Humphrey Lloyd (1800–81), D.D., F.R.S.; in 1838 became Director of the Observatory in Dublin; wrote on optics and magnetism; later became Provost of Trinity College, Dublin.
2. Samuel Hicks was steward of the Cornwall Asylum at Bodmin.
3. Sir Richard Owen (1804–92), F.R.S., was the first Hunterian professor of comparative anatomy and physiology. He was one of the foremost scientists of the day, but was to attack Darwin's theory of evolution in the 1850s.
4. Karl Ritter (1779–1859), professor of Geography at Berlin, began a new epoch in the subject, as the founder of general comparative geography.

inscrutable mystery of Beauty. He pointed out the difference between the Greek & Roman mind & the corresponding difference between Greek & Roman sculpture. He sketched the leading characteristics of the 5 wondrous men whose busts were before him, Dante, Homer, Pericles, Augustus & M. Angelo, in such a manner as none but himself could do; & as he warmed with his subject, his poetry, his eloquence, his deep earnest enthusiasm, rivetted his astonished audience beyond the power of words.

12. Today was devoted to a Regatta at Falmouth & a philosophic excursion to Kynance Cove, the latter under the direction of my father. In the evening Hunt read an essay at the Hall on the Influence of Poetry & Painting on Education. Poor Hunt! – Sterling was in the chair. He concluded the meeting by giving us an idea of what poetry *is* & what it requires. It is no light art to be taken up & flung aside at pleasure. Of this the other man had small notion. But Sterling with his flashing eye, his earnest, energetic delivery, with his pale face & feeble frame was a sight both fearful & beautiful. I thought of the pelican that is said to feed her offspring with her own blood.

13. The *Beresford* steamer arrived last night & we today held a meeting of the shareholders on board. She is a very superior looking vessel & will act as the best advertisement of herself. We fixed an excursion for her to Penzance on the 16th. The Lloyds left us for Carclew. The Listers came to stay with us.

14. Took our guests to Penjerrick at 1 & after duly exhibiting all the lions, returned to a large dinner party, amongst whom were Prof. Lloyd's brother & 2 sisters, just arrived from Dublin to spend a fortnight here; evidently superior people. Settled them to a game of Lavater[1] in the evening.

11. Commenced acting on a resolution to rise daily at 6 on pain of forfeit, to eat sparingly & to read regularly, at least as far as circumstances permit. If the permanence of the will in its present braced up state could be insured! But habit will do much in this way.

19. Having planned a pedestrian excursion to Tintagel with C. Waring we started in the evening for Perran, where we occupied the time with sundry jeux d'esprit & Lavater, in honour of the Harrises who depart tomorrow.

20. Set off on our travels at 7, our party consisting of Professor Lloyd's brother Bartholomew, I. & W. Hustler, C. Waring & self. Quitting our barouche at St. Columb Porth we braced on our knapsacks & proceeded under those magnificent & many coloured cliffs to Pencathan, the estate of a Squire Peters from whence we chartered a cart to Padstow. W. & I spent a part of the evening in calling on the justly celebrated she-squire, Mary

---

1. Johann Kaspar Lavater (1741–1801) was a Swiss theologian and physiognomist who claimed that personality could be read in the features. It is likely that this was a game devised by the Foxes which tested this claim on a series of portraits. Caroline Fox's Journal relates how they falsified Lavater's claim by adding cut-out hats, coats, cigars, etc. to the illustrations in his books.

Prideaux-Brune of Place House. The old butler was particularly shy of ushering us into his lady's presence seeing it was a dark dismal evening and we bore a peculiarly scampish appearance. We were however cordially received & entertained by that high-spirited lady.

21. C.'s heel not permitting him to walk, we despatched him to Wadebridge in a gig to carry our traps, engage beds & meet us at Tintagel. We others crossed Padstow river & landed on muddy sand half-knee deep. We trudged through some wild country & amongst some really fine cliff scenery to Port Isaac, passing through Portquin, a queer little fishing town at a creek-head. At Port Isaac after dining on some fish & cheese, we chartered a fishing boat which landed us under Tintagel Castle. We had a deal of swell on our way & no easy matter was it to land & get the boat off safely through the surf. But the 2 men were very fine fellows & fought a hard battle with the breakers which they at last overcame. Tintagel is indeed a wonderful place, independently of its historic or rather romantic interest. It must have been a magnificent stronghold at the time when Uther Pendragon sought shelter there in the likeness of its owner.[1] We trudged on to Boscastle, where C. Waring & a fly waited for us. After satiating our love of the sublime & beautiful we were glad to turn our attention to the needful & substantial in the shape of a hearty supper at Wadebridge.

22. S. A dismal day. Lloyd left us after morning service. He is an uninteresting, common-place sort of fellow. We attended a meeting of 5 members besides ourselves in the morning, & church in the evening, there being no second service in our chapel.

23. We went by Railway to Bodmin to breakfast. We took an hour & a half to go 8 miles, the train before us getting 3 times off the rail. Called on Hicks who engaged us to stop to dinner to meet Wightwick & to occupy the morning by a survey of the asylum. We spent about 5 hours in doing so, which contained more of interest to me than all the rest of our tour together. I was introduced to many of the patients and saw madness in many of its phases & many degrees. The more one sees of it the greater mystery does it appear. A madhouse is the most impressive sermon possible on that text, 'I am fearfully & wonderfully made'. Hicks took us first to see a man styled Measter, who was boiling food for the pigs, apparently a hard working farmer. His mad point is a concern for the County rates. He considers himself the manager of the establishment & his intense concern at having to keep so many fellows in idleness is highly ludicrous. He abuses Hicks like a pickpocket & tells him 'He will not put up with it, no longer. Take & send 'em off one to a time to Tor point & ship 'em aboard the *Royal Sovereign*. Send

1. According to Geoffrey of Monmouth, Arthur's father, Uther, fell in love with Igerna, the wife of the Duke of Cornwall, and was changed by Merlin into the likeness of the duke, so that he could seduce her. Arthur was the child of this union.

'em to Americkey & swop 'em for balk, or put 'em to cultivate Dartymoor. They shall not stay here', &c. Whilst listening to his extraordinary protest we saw poor Flamank wandering about the garden & throwing stones into a pond. Hicks called him & he came directly, recognized me & W. Hustler & greeted us warmly. He then informed us that Quaker & Quack doctor were words from the same root, but followed it up by asserting that the spirit of Quakerism & the Holy Spirit of God were one & the same. He then spoke of some nameless one who had deeply wronged him. I was lost in admiration at his deep pathos, & the occasional grandeur of his ideas; his wit was perfectly meteoric, so wild, so strange, so brilliant. We had wandered some way from the rest when we were called to speak to a religious enthusiast, a Bryanite, I believe, who was washing potatoes under the pump. He told us with an air of the strongest conviction of various extraordinary visitations to him, mostly in the form of clouds, some of which spoke to him. 'Do you know what clouds are?' asked Flamank. The latter was in a state of boisterous, uproarious merriment & turned all that the poor fanatic uttered into the wildest possible fun. In spite of it all, the other admitted that Flamank's sermon yesterday on the Pharisee & Publican had affected him so that he was on the point of falling on his knees when the congregation went out. Flamank only laughed louder & said it showed his spiritual pride. Then clambering up on the pump, he indulged in such a flood of puns & extraordinary witticisms, incessant, quick-flashing & extravagant, as kept us in one continual shout of laughter. Being left off on poetry he gave us several other specimens of his uncommon genius. So he went on, quoting Greek & Latin at a most surprising rate. The aptness & beauty of his quotations & the poetic fervour with which he utters them or descants on characters that interest him, make it a high treat to be in his company. He went with us into the drawing room where his attentions to a young lady, whom he called his Queen, were the very quixotism of devotion. She was pretty & played her part well. Leaving them in the parlour, Hicks took me hastily over the asylum which seems well conducted, orderly, clean & ventilated. He introduced me to a singular character, called Sukey Provis, apparently a very plain Friend. She professes to be convinced, & made many enquiries of me respecting the state of the Society. Amongst the women was one poor, wild-eyed maniac, whose reason fled when her heart was broken: her lover had been false to her. I should think a madhouse contains more *character* within it than any other building. We all dined at the Asylum & met a large party there, but alas Wightwick was not of them. We had a somewhat brilliant evening. Hicks's conjuring & fiddling & the ladies' vocal harmony, together with coffee & conversation, made us part very good friends.

24. Breakfasted with Hicks & posted back to Falmouth.

30. General meeting this morning of the *Beresford* owners, self in the chair

for the first time. Found no great difficulty in gathering the 'sense' of the meeting, that being comprised in a small compass. There is hardly a public meeting held but may be entirely led by the nose by 3 men who are masters of the subject & have laid their plans beforehand. All the details are now settled & the *Beresford*, Capt. Goodfellow, is to commence running on the 7th prox.

SEPTEMBER

1. Juvenile Horticultural Exhibition on the lawn. About 150 children present & plenty of 'quality' as spectators. A pretty animated sight. Prizes were given to most, & something to all, & they departed in high good humour. Tea at Sterling's.

4. The Owens came to breakfast & stay over tomorrow with us. He is a glorious creature & his wife a microscopic curiosity. We spent the day till dinner time in collecting all manner of sea prodigies, zoophytes, anomia, cypridae, &c., a rich banquet for the microscope, which kept us peeping & ejaculating 'How beautiful' till nearly 5. A lesson of this sort immensifies one's ideas of creation beyond anything I know. Amongst other treasures we found a cypria, all alive & with her mantle on, which the professor declared was alone worth coming from London to see.

5. Walked with the Owens under Pendennis Cliffs, where a vast sermon was preached to us, visibly & audibly on the adaptation of things, Owen being the priest & the shells which covered the beach the sermon of Nature. We scrambled up the cliff at the peril of our limbs & wended back our laborious way. After dinner Owen & I had a phrenology dispute. He calls it stuff & nonsense, because there are no corresponding convolutions of the brain to organs, indicating different qualities. He thinks animal magnetism is all humbug. It is the nature of science to deny what is incomprehensible according to physiological laws already established. Owen spoke beautifully on the superstitions, ignorance & opposition geologists have to contend with. Galileo had to endure the same, & even Newton. And yet when all these several so-called contradictions to Scripture had been clearly established, Religion & Revelation had not been overthrown. In the evening we persuaded these choice people to stay over tomorrow.

7. Started per *Lord Beresford* for Mevagissey with Uncle A. which we reached in 2 hours, though blowing fresh with an ebb tide. Met old T. Stark on the quay & perambulated the fish cellars. In our peregrinations we visited the new mansion of Mrs. & Miss Cock. A more striking incongruity one seldom sees than between this house & its inhabitants. No expense seems to be spared in

order to strike due reverence into the soul of Mevagissey for the possessors of so much magnificence & taste. The mother is about as homely in manners & appearance as might become any other decent fisherman's wife; the young lady has picked up a few boarding school elegancies, which fit her as well as a coronet would a coal-heaver, & has devoted her life with incomprehensible assiduity to the working of chair-backs & bottoms to adorn her drawing room. They are considered a sort of raree-show at Mevagissey & are certainly very handsome. From thence Uncle A. and I ascended into a very different atmosphere, moral & physical, the drawing room at Heligan[1] where we found the ladies & Lady Dunstanville at their morning occupation. The house is furnished in a style of lordly hospitality. The mistress though a perfect lady is more simple than a quarterly meeting Friend, gentle, affable & modest. The daughters are noble creatures. Harriet is high souled, warm-hearted & indued with intellectual perception & penetration of character beyond almost any girl I know. She is above all conventionality & despises sham most sincerely. Whatever is earnest finds sympathy with her. Her appearance is in keeping with her high character. Her sister Mary would be called a charming creature anywhere, but till Harriet is married, she must be content to remain a star of second magnitude. Our party did not arrive till 3. They brought the Owens with them, who were persuaded to stay over the night with our triad,[2] our parents proceeding to St. Austell. After seeing the gardens, which are laid out in good English taste, with grass walks & beautiful vistas, C. & I rode out with Mary on horseback & the rest in the carriage. We 3 soon left them & dived into the deep shade of Heligan Woods, amongst which are some of the finest oaks in the county. After a ride of 8 or 9 miles we returned to dinner at 7. Old Tremayne appeared at the same time, warmly greeting in one breath, & warmly protesting in the next against 2 uncon-scionable lawyers who had tired out his patience & appetite. He is a fine slouchy old figure of a man, in a coat that might have belonged to his grandfather. We spent a peculiarly pleasant evening. I sat between Mrs. Owen & Harriet T. & had some good conversation with the latter. Owen was not very communicative, but all he says is worth listening to. Lady D. is fluent & agreeable. We had a little singing of a very high order from the 2 girls & separated about ½ past 11. Tremayne is a much more liberal Tory than I supposed.

8. All the family joined us at a ¼ past 8 breakfast & then shipped us in their carriage to St. Austell, to attend the quarterly meeting. We had dinner at the Veals where there was more ceremony far than at Heligan. A Quarterly Meeting dinner party are more given to Spanishizing than any people I

1. Heligan House at St Ewe, near Mevagissey, was the home of the Tremayne family. Lady Dunstanville was Sir Chas. Lemon's sister.
2. i.e. Barclay and his two sisters.

know. Reached home at 9 & took leave of the Lloyds, who go tomorrow, highly pleased with their stay here.

14. Breakfasted at Penjerrick. where my father emigrated in the evening to try hermit life & change of air for a feverish attack which has prostrated him for the last 2 days. Took the girls up St. Mawes Creek in the *Petrel*. It blew fresh & she did her work in style. Attended a dispensary general meeting & became a subscriber & governor.

17. Went to Mevagissey per *Lord Beresford* to attend the sale of pilchards. Before dinner, called at Heligan. I found Harriet the only Tremayne at home & had a pleasant $\frac{1}{2}$ hour's chat with her. My asking whether her friend Trelawny[1] was likely to contest the E. Division again with Lord Eliot, brought forth a beautifully womanly eulogium on his excellencies, the purport of which was, that he is far too good for the House of Commons, but may do well enough for something nearer home. There was an ingenuousness & warmth of expression which delighted me.

18. Very busy day discharging 3 cargoes of wheat & selling one of codfish. Spent the evening at Sterling's. The Tregedna party was there. A little music & singing from the girls & then Sterling read us an essay on Dante which he had written this morning; an extraordinary production for so limited a time.

19. S. Wet & cold. Had a discussion in the evening on the question of Recognition in a future state. The arguments seem rather to preponderate in favour of it, supported as it is by the strong convictions & full assurance often expressed by good people immediately before death. Saw Aunt A. probably for the last time for some weeks, the time of her trial being come. In the garden I asked the 2 boys how they liked the prospect of a new brother or sister & to my astonishment found they had not the slightest idea of the 'coming event'; and Theodore with a calculating earnestness enquired whether it was going to be a boy or girl, & whether Mamma had *told* me there was going to be a baby.

20. Women are decidedly more sensitive both of praise & blame than we are, i.e. they are more dependent on the opinion of others than men. The dearest treasure of a woman is her reputation; that of a man his honour. This was exemplified by a circumstance today. 2 days since a young man named King was arrested for £2,300 when going on board the packet. Anna Chapman, in describing the affair to me as she came full primed & loaded with the story from Uncle A.'s lips, heightened the pictorial effect of the scene by speaking of him falling on his knees and shedding tears in his entreaties to Uncle A. to become bail for him. This proved to be untrue although *her* statement was not groundless. This morning however Uncle A. in a playful way slipped a book into her hand, marked at some child's story

1. Sir John Trelawny, who unsuccessfully contested East Cornwall in 1841. He became M.P. for Tavistock in 1843, having married Harriet Tremayne the previous year.

on the effects of exaggeration. This act the girl has taken so deeply to heart that she cannot get over it, saying that a lie is imputed to her & her word never was suspected before & all that commonplace twaddle. In her absence Uncle A. came in & I was highly amused & pleased by the manner in which Katey fought her sister's battle. She is a very fine ingenuous character. Her sister with a desire to perform her allotted part in this world, is unfortunately, soft, silly & superficial.

21. Martin, the servant at the Bank, died suddenly of inflammation. My mother was with her. She was one of the most civil, obliging & good tempered persons that could be & many an act of good-natured kindness has she done me. I trust she is happy. Equinoctial gale accompanied by lashing rain.

22. Sterling, Patey, Hunt, my father, Uncle C., & self met on the subject of establishing weekly lectures in connection with the Polytechnic Society. We obtained promises enough to make a trial of the plan for 3 months, which we accordingly mean to do. Went to a Polish quack & had 2 corns eradicated, much to my satisfaction. Dinner at Grove Hill.

24. The *Blanche* with our cargo of wheat from Spain arrived today, just in time to enter the lower duty. Sailed down to Maenporth after dinner. There was plenty of sea, but went through it like a witch. C. & I spent the evening at Tregedna & were kept weather-bound for the night there & at Penjerrick. Spent a highly profitable hour with Sterling this morning criticising some of my productions. He pronounced a favourable judgment thereon & discovers a marked improvement, but still complains of verboseness & ambiguity. He lays great stress on expressing the thought in the fewest & most definite words you can select. Jos. John Fox[1] to dinner, an intelligent youth, who by close application has mastered chemistry, anatomy, & botany enough to distinguish himself in each & gain honours at the London University.[2]

30. An edifying walk with Sterling. He confirms my conviction of the duty 'also to see Rome'.

OCTOBER

1. Last day of the 2/8d. duty on wheat. It rises tomorrow to 10/8d., consequently the corn merchants are in a great fuss. We paid duty on about a dozen cargoes. I rode to Penjerrick with Katey Chapman. There is a spring-freshness & warmth about her which is very pleasant.

9. Only 15 hours of business, including meals. Left the office at $\frac{1}{2}$ past 12.

1. The son of Dr Joseph Fox of Falmouth.
2. University College, the original 'London University', opened in 1828.

Despatched about ½ a hundred letters & then some bread & cheese, which we found more congenial. Calvert very poorly. The *Alert* came in this morning, with plenty of dollars, but alas without her Commander, our old friend Dawson, who died of the yellow fever on his way to Havana.

12. All minor facts in this day are lost in the blaze of the one great fact, not of the day only, but of the month, perhaps the year – to me; Sterling's lecture on the 'Worth of Knowledge', delivered at the Polytechnic Hall, as the inaugural discourse of the series which is to succeed. It was eloquent, profound, impassioned, true! An address like the sound of a trumpet to rouse his hearers from the dull lethargy of the conventional & the common-place. The soul of the man was in his subject & his winding up, which re-capitulated the great truths he wished to enforce, seemed like a message from some higher intelligence, so weighty it was, so solemn, so deep, & so full. The audience were as dumb as stones, not a breath, not a rustle of silk, was heard, & once when an impulse to clap manifested itself, it became imme-diately subdued by Sterling's quiet rebuke of 'My friends, I desire not your applause but your attention'. My father was in the Chair. He expressed in appropriate words the universal feeling of the meeting at the close of the lecture.

13. Sterling, I grieve to say, is quite overdone by the exertions of yesterday. I spent some time with him & he entered into explanation of some parts of his lecture which seemed obscure.

16. Sterling much better. The shadow of an approaching cold kept me prisoner in the evening, which enabled me to get on with my reading. Called to see a poor man, Thos. Thomas, who has been injured in our employ by inhaling the dust of the wheat whilst trimming it in a vessel's hold. He has been insensible & delirious nearly ever since & the doctor has very little hope of his recovery. The death of a labouring man is a public loss, that of a gentleman only a private one. The one spends all he possesses (his labour) for the benefit of the community; the pittance given him in exchange for it enables him to keep himself & family alive in order to continue to work. An example to us whose powers of doing good are greater but the result less.

23. Woke with half my countenance closely resembling that of Henry VIII, the combined effect of cold & a decayed tooth. Chapmans to dinner. Chess with Katey. In the afternoon I read Ellen Chapman's account of the last illness & death of Cos. Agatha Chapman, a remarkable instance of unshaken faith & earnest piety. It exhibits the peculiar style of religious affection which evangelical ladies feel towards their clergymen (if of the same sentiments). There seems to be something in evangelical doctrine which especially takes with women. I conclude it is because it appeals to the feelings rather than the understanding.

NOVEMBER

2. Assisted at Lovell Squire's lecture on the Useful Application of Science, with some striking illustrations. Davy's lamp & the Bude light, both of which, as well as the invention of gas light by burning carburetted hydrogen, which was invented by Murdock,[1] were of Cornish origin. So that we may claim the merit of illuminating land & sea & the bowels of the earth. Various other examples of the utilitarian view of science were exhibited, ending with the application of the Bude light to the magic lantern. It was a good & useful lecture, well delivered, without pretension or fear.

7. S. Called on Sterling & talked about the Bible, the limits of Inspiration & the Neologians of Germany. Their distinctive peculiarity seems to be that of submitting the Biblical history to the same laws of investigation & criticism as they would apply to any other work.

13. Went off to the Quarantine pool to visit an Egyptian corvette, the *Ashereen*, of about 500 tons, with a cargo of wheat. She is leaky & will probably have to discharge here. The crew were exhibited to me as Consul, a wretched looking set of Egyptians, Arabs & Abyssinians, shivering with the cold. The pilot declares they are fit for nothing. Visited another vessel in Quarantine, on board of which is my old acquaintance Harriet Livermore, on her return from Jerusalem. She looks madder & more nondescript than ever. She insisted in the most peremptory manner to be released from quarantine.

20. Busy trying my hand at a lecture on Public Speaking. There is something in the preposterousness of the idea which pleases my fancy. I may theorise away on the matter as wildly as I please, & I doubt not, embody some useful hints to those as little versed in the art as myself.

22. Cos. Fras. & Rachel Fox with their 2 children arrived in the evening to spend a few days with us. He is a fine, frank, open-faced fellow, with a good deal of practical intelligence & good sense. His wife is a conscientious, nervous little thing. We held a levee of our Egyptian subjects at the Consulate this morning; a precious gang they are. The Captain, Mohammed Said, was taken out of the command of a cutter & put on board the corvette the day before her sailing, & it is said received a basting from his royal master on starting, to make him a good boy on the voyage. He continually straps his men down on the deck, strips them & performs castigation himself. We shall begin discharging the vessel tomorrow. Called on H. Livermore who leaves tomorrow (luckily) for Plymouth. On her mad points, viz, the conversion of the Jews, the approach of the millennium, &c., she is worth listening to, having a fund of imagination & religious enthusiasm. But on matters

1. Wm. Murdock made the first experiments in lighting with coal gas in 1792 and used it in his house and office at Redruth.

of business, the cloven hoof shows itself. She has, in spite of her sanctity, a true Yankee love of money & attention. She has made a vow of celibacy (prudent virgin!) for fear of marrying Antichrist by mistake.

23. A good, practical, clear, perspicuous & important lecture from Dr. Barham[1] this evening on the condition of the Cornish miners, being the cream of his investigation on the subject made by order of the Government. He shows that under the present system mining shortens the average duration of a man's life 10 years. The ameliorations hitherto adopted with good success, are a warm bath & soup on the emergence of the miners, with dry clothes ready to put on & the staves of the ladders 10 inches instead of a foot apart.

26. Harriet Tremayne they say is engaged to John Trelawny, an event I foretold & desired. It would be the greatest pity to throw away so noble a creature on a fool or a bigot. Had a long conference with the Egyptians whom Gowers directs to proceed with the *Ashereen* to Liverpool & which they positively decline.

28. Sunday. This morning looking out of my window, which commands that of the servants' hall, I saw a picture which would have equally suited Wordsworth or Wilkie, Caroline teaching a poor girl to read, who was poor indeed, being blind & deaf & almost dumb. The window formed the frame of the picture & the light fell on their faces, showing the strong contrast of earnest intelligence in the one and the puzzled vacant expression of the other, which artists & poets so delight in. They were poring over a tablet, on which C. had worked in large stitches the Lord's Prayer and was guiding her hand over the letters & words which the other spelt & pronounced in her half-articulate way, now getting thoroughly aground & turning up her sightless eyes with a distressed look, & then returning to her task & now highly pleased, when C.'s approving pat on the hand told her she was right. I thought that if the poor girl learnt nothing else, yet if she learnt that one fellow being in the world took a warm interest in her welfare, forlorn & isolated & unattractive as she seemed, that alone was worth the trouble, & was enough to keep from utterly drying up those invaluable fountains of love & sympathy & gratitude without which the heart is a barren & unblessed thing. Paid a long & interesting call on Sterling.

29. The deluge of 1841. The rain poured down in streams instead of drops, the low lands are inundated, walls & hedges are washed away. The water in some of the houses at Penryn is 4 or 5 feet deep & the inhabitants with their pigs are taking refuge in the top storey according to my father's report, who went to Carclew this morning. The road about Stewart's bone mill is converted into a rapid river 3 or 4 feet deep in some places. The like has not been known in this county within the memory of man. It is a happy thing for the

1. Chas. Barham, M.D., Physician to the Royal Cornwall Infirmary.

old ladies that they can read of the covenant made with our forefathers that the world should never be drowned again, for certainly this looks somewhat suspicious. With Sterling for about an hour in the evening, to my usual edification.

DECEMBER

1. Met a peculiarly pleasant party at Carclew: Tremaynes (father, mother, & daughters) with Harriet's cabaliero Jn. Trelawny, the Dykes & C. Taylor. As easy & social a party as I ever met. Harriet T. & I had a long talk on mesmerism in which she is a believer & operator. Sir W. Molesworth settles down in his mesmeric creed within this limitation, that there does exist a power in man of producing somnambulism in another. Mary was much cast down at the prospect of losing her sister. Sir R. Vyvyan has lately published 'An Electrical Theory of the Universe', in which he proves that all created beings are formed by the light of the moon, except the parasitical plants, which according to him, owe their origin to the reflected light of the creatures! If this be not lunacy – what is?

2. Another wild wintry day. Elizth. Bell to dinner, who fought the cause of mesmerism most gallantly, having practised it with great success. Her first patient was their cook whom she threw into a lethargy & could not get her out of it till Elliotson came to her assistance the next day.

5. Dr. Calvert in so depressed a state as to be talking of suicide and questioning whether it is not lawful for him. Dismal weather.

15. Capt. Said of the *Ashereen* came to me to complain of an assault he received last night in the street of Falmouth from 3 sailors. With some search through the town I discovered their names. All being Packets men I requested Capt. Ellis to order them on board the *Astraea* which he did, and in the evening I took off the Captn. & an actor (who was present & defended him after the attack), in order to identify them. The worst of the 3 had decamped when the officer was sent for him & another was not then brought, but the 3rd, who was on board in irons, confirmed the guilt of Benson who was not to be found, but protested his own innocence. Got a warrant for Benson, who will not shew himself in Falmouth with impunity for some time to come. It is an infamous shame, that a foreigner cannot quietly pass through the street, without a wanton & brutal attack as this appears to have been.

16. Got hold of Benson today, the principal offender 'in re Said' & had him up with four of his comrades before the town magistrates. Capt. Said wrote his oath in Turkish & refused to take any other. The actor's evidence convicted Benson, who pleaded intoxication; he was fined £1 & costs, or in

default 2 months' imprisonment. The other 4 got off for want of evidence, none of our witnesses being able to convict them. We formed a singular procession through the town on our march to the court, Lawyer Tilly & self taking the lead, then the actor, the constable, & C. Clift, then the 2 Egyptians, then 2 Maltese, & lastly a Jewess, Mrs. Moses, & Miss Sharp, followed by a promiscuous multitude. Louisa Power & her cousin, young de Costa, to tea; they landed from the *Maunay*, which put in here damaged on the night of the 11th, on her voyage to Lisbon. The lady was remarkably gay & sparkling & amused us not a little by her descriptions of their drunken Captain's marked & not very delicate attentions to herself during the passage, her interesting position at the time, a subsequent small mutiny & the consequent putting back of the vessel to Falmouth, in all which herself was the most conspicuous figure, & the complete heroine in every exigency.

18. The world is robed in white; yesterday it was all slush & probably will be tomorrow. Dined at the Bank. Walked round the castle with H. Molesworth. There is a great charm to me in the earnest simplicity of his mind, well stored as it is, without a grain of pedantry. He delights in talking about German & is revelling in the grand field of literature which is gradually opening before him. The Madagascar frigate left Falmouth today for Sierra Leone. The sufferings of the Niger expedition from malaria are melancholy to hear. If it continues as the steamers ascend further it will be a death blow to the scheme.

19. S. Called at Sterling's. Talked of Lessing, Carlyle & civilisation. He talks of continuing his Legend of Madrid into an epic embracing the rise of Cromwell & the death of Charles I. Gowers writes that my virtuous conduct towards Capt. Said will be reported to the Pasha, so if he will only have the grace to make me a Bey in return & send the necessary costume, I shall be able to cut a considerable shine at next Yearly. Called with the girls on Miss Power who overflows with gratitude.

21. At Penjerrick. I was grieved to find Betsey much worse, having had a sort of paralytic stroke which had crippled her right arm. Attended Hunt's lecture on the chemical action of light. I took the Egyptian captain there, who excited much attention among the ladies. I went on board his ship in the morning & distributed worsted stockings among the crew. They were drawn up in a line to receive me, all dressed in their uniform, which is a chocolate coloured jacket & Turkish trousers with scarlet cap & sash. Extreme respect was shown to their consul. Capt. Said gave me a young eagle which had perched on his ship in the Mediterranean. I engaged him & his Secretary to dinner for the day after tomorrow.

23. Large Polytechnic Committee. Accepted the offer of the Tresavean Adventurers to adopt Loam's[1] principle for raising & lowering miners. We

1. Michael Loam (1798–1871), of Gwennap, engineer and inventor.

are to pay them £500 when they have succeeded in making it work to our satisfaction at the depth of 200 fathoms. We had the 2 Egyptians, Capt. Mohammed Said & the Hadjah, Sala Effendi, with the Maltese interpreter, to dinner. Nothing could exceed their delight at all they saw & ate. The Hadjah declared he wished for nothing better in heaven & shook his stomach to show how well he had fared. After dinner he favoured us with 3 songs which consisted of the most hideous sounds the human voice is capable of. We took likenesses of them in the evening, which deeply interested them, & showed them the magic lantern & set off a couple of volcanoes.[1] They could not sufficiently express their gratitude & pleasure & departed in a fervid glow of enthusiasm.

24. Christmas eve festivities. We were amongst a select few invited by Sterling's little people to witness the unfolding of a mighty mystery which has occupied their small brains for the last week. The folding doors of the drawing room being thrown open, the inner room appeared like a blaze of light & luxury. In the centre stood a fir tree reaching nearly to the ceiling, covered in all directions with lighted tapers & various gay & glittering symbols, while pendant from the lower branches were numerous presents for children and guests. Papa's ingenious irony had placed a foolscap on the top, immediately overshadowing the man in the moon & the Pope of Rome; crowns & helmets, paper flags & necklaces sparkled amongst the foliage & we all, old children and young, gave ourselves up to the enthusiasm of the moment. My present was a beautiful ivory pen tipped with silver & wreathed with laurel, a most elegant compliment. A.M. & C. were given some very fine engravings. The excitement having somewhat subsided I put off a volcano in the garden. The abandon of the children to their supreme delight was beautiful.

25. Whether this really was the day of Christ's birth is very doubtful yet I would not give up the annual festival for something. As my custom is I joined the Evanses at a good English roast-beef & plum pudding dinner at my cottage. Betsey was able to join us. Tom & I wound up the year's accounts & were mutually pleased at the profitable result. Henceforth he is to share the profits, in addition to his wages, as the just meed of his zeal & industry. Tom's wages are advanced to 10/-, ½ his time to be mine & the other half spent in the higher & lower gardens.

30. According to previous engagement I took Capt. Said & the Hadjah & Pilot to Tregedna to tea, where we found a large & brilliant party already assembled to see the Turks. Two of the Clergy, Kinsman & Ellingworth, the Grove Hill party, Griffins, Uncle A. & boys, & C. were there. The Hadjah recognised Elizth. Bell & Katey Chapman with a scream of joy & then shook hands with every one in the room. He had made enquiries before

1. i.e. fireworks.

as to how far he might go and was rather disappointed when I told him that he must not crack the ladies' fingers nor span their waists, which he declared to be the custom of polite society in Constantinople. After tea he favoured the company with several songs to the very great trial of their risibles. He listened to the girls' singing as tho' it were the music of Paradise & so it certainly was compared with his. At supper seeing nothing but sweet cakes & confiture on the table, he begged for some cheese which he toasted on the tongs over the fire & set to work upon it with right good will. Emma Griffin handed him the mustard which he imagining to be some delicate conserve Inglese, dipped the spoon into & swallowed a mouthful. Painfully finding his mistake he raised the most hideous yell, & twisted his extraordinary face into the strangest possible gesticulations. However he continued to carry on the war with spirit, although I told by illustrative signs that it would make him awfully sick tomorrow. As the best way of ending the scene I ordered the car & told him it was time to go home. He was very obedient & took his leave, declaring that he brought his senses with him from Alexandria, but he was sure that he should not take them back again.

1842

BARCLAY'S HOPES of visiting Italy are dashed by business responsibilities. Indeed it is Uncle Charles who decides to visit Italy and who persuades Barclay to take over the management of the Perran Foundry in his absence. The affairs of the Foundry have been in a muddled state since the previous manager and partner, Benjamin Sampson, died in 1840. To these burdens are added the complexities of Sir Robert Peel's famous budget of 1842, which reduces the duties levied on imported ores and abolishes the rebate given to mine-owners on the duties on imported timber. Nevertheless, Barclay is determined not to allow business to absorb all his time and energies, and is encouraged in this resolve by John Sterling. While on a visit to London he meets J. S. Mill, Wordsworth, and the Carlyles. The central event of the year, as far as Barclay is concerned, is his courtship of Richenda Buxton, the daughter of Sir Thomas Fowell Buxton. He makes two visits to Northrepps Hall, near Norwich, the home of the Buxtons, but in spite of a cordial welcome from Sir Thomas and Lady Buxton, his proposal of marriage is rejected by Richenda.

JANUARY

1. The year opened with fog & mist. It is like living in an atmosphere of wool. Colds prevail & scarlet fever, & stomach disorders, & no wonder. I have agreed to *open* the approaching course of lectures. If one has impudence enough to speak for the first time on the art of speaking, he may as well go further, taking special care to pretend to no remnant of modesty.
2. S. Sterling favoured us with a New Year's address to our family collectively & individually. He concludes by wishing me a 'She, supreme as Harriet'.[1]
7. In confinement with a cold, which gives me the opportunity of progressing with my lecture which is in a forward state, as it needs be, the 18th being fixed for its delivery.
8. An acceptable visit from Sterling, whose tragedy 'Strafford' I finished today. It certainly is a very grand production, though not suited for the stage, there not being incident enough to make it popular. Alex. Bromhead dined here with his sister & Katey. He is a remarkable specimen of simplicity

1. i.e. Harriet Tremayne, for whom Barclay had a great admiration, but who was now engaged to Sir John Trelawny.

& the absence of pretension: an amiable weak desultory youth, fresh from Cambridge, where he asserts that he spends 2 whole hours per day in study.

9. S. Dr. Calvert's weary spirit departed to its long desired rest this morning. A blessed release to him, & a relief to his sister who has long given him up completely. Poor fellow, although invisible for months it feels like a family loss. A kindlier heart than his never beat. A pleasanter companion I never knew. His original & clear-sighted mind with all its varied store of beauty & truth, his tolerance, his gentle & generous nature, were a combination that rarely falls to the lot of one man.

15. Going thro' the town my eye was greeted by innumerable 'R. Barclay Foxes' staring at me from the walls & shop windows, each announcing to the population in fat black letters that he meant to favour them with a lecture on public speaking on Tuesday the 18th inst. Never felt such a public character before.

17. Sterling's epitaph on Calvert has given some offence to the religious world at Falmouth by the use of the term 'Reason thy lamp',[1] which is considered to have something of an infidel tendency, which is perhaps the case. We have no right to wound the conscience of others if it can be avoided, but he couples it with 'Faith' as the star of his existence, & though this perhaps is not a correct image for Faith, which is a *state* & not a *guide* or *goal*, yet the union of Faith & Reason was the remarkable feature of Calvert's spirit, & of course the right use of both will always lead to the same Truth.

18. Made my début (as the young ladies say) before a large & respectable audience, who sat listening for an hour & a half with truly Christian patience. Their silence & attention made it much easier to me & I got through without any difficulty whatever. Sir C. Lemon, who was in the Chair, bestowed abundantly more praise than it deserved. I was obliged to hide behind the reading desk. However the people were generally well satisfied & it is a great relief that it has gone off as well as it has.

19. Dined at Sterling's. Discussed oratory, capital punishment, Oliver Cromwell, &c. My father & the girls joined us at tea, & some scepticism being expressed as to the increase of power which 4 ladies gain by breathing together, so as to lift a heavy man into the air on 2 fingers, the experiment was tried on my father, by which Sterling was convinced.

24. Started with Cos. Joe in his one horse fly on a coasting & trading trip. We called at Burncoose, thence to Tresavean to see the operation of the new machine for raising miners. It was put to work to show us. The plan was very simple, but the power, a small water-wheel is hardly sufficient. I

1. The last two lines of Sterling's epitaph,

> Reason thy lamp and Faith thy star while here;
> Now both one brightness in the light of God

were praised by Wordsworth for their poetic quality.

descended, & reappeared 'at grass' with perfect ease. It consists simply of 2 reciprocating vertical rods furnished with stages for the men to stand on. Proceeded to Wheal Uny on a fine sample of Cornish roads. We had to bundle out of the vehicle twice to escape a capsize. Wheal Uny looks like an automaton school of industry, the whole hillside *busy* with the water-wheels & stamps. Joined the miners in some hot soup which is served out to them daily on ascending from below, a noble plan.

25. Breakfasted at Portreath,[1] inspecting Sim's Foundry in our way. Induced old S. Knight with some difficulty to join us at breakfast. He gives a dull account of Portreath trade on account of the sudden withdrawal of 3 important customers, who send their ore via Hayle to Cwm Avon to be smelted, instead of selling at the ticketings[2] & importing coals the same way. It is highly probable that in process of time the miners will turn smelters & throw the middlemen overboard. A thorough wild ride to St. Anne's. It's well worth visiting. The pier juts out from the cliff in an open savage place & the coals are landed on the cliff, 90 feet high, so that we stood on the landing place & looked down on the caps of the mastheads of a collier below us. 11,000 tons coal were landed here last year. Took some subsist & rattled home to attend Uncle C.'s lecture on American birds.

FEBRUARY

8. My father gave his lecture entitled The Elements of the Planetary system; a recondite & highly instructive lecture tending to elevate & extend the ideas of creation in no small degree in those to whom astronomy is all a terra incognita. There was a very numerous attendance. I rode to Penjerrick & conducted the Coopes over the place. In returning I was spilt, pony & all, in leaping a trench which she did not clear, but no damage was done.

1. Portreath, a harbour on the north coast of Cornwall was an important port for the trade between Cornwall and South Wales. In 1806 it was linked by a 'railway' or tram-road to Dolcoath and this made it much easier to transport the copper ore from the mines around Camborne to the Welsh smelters. In 1837 the first railroad in Cornwall was opened between Hayle (also on the north coast of Cornwall) and Tresavean, and Hayle became a serious rival to Portreath.

2. This system of selling copper ore worked to the advantage of the smelters. The ores were brought to a convenient place where the agents of the smelters took samples. A fortnight later the agents met the representatives of the miners again and produced tickets, or slips of paper, on which were written the prices the agents were prepared to pay for each separate lot of ore. The miners were then expected to sell to the highest bidder. The system was unfair to the miners since collusion often took place between the smelters' agents. See John Rowe, *Cornwall in the Age of the Industrial Revolution*, 1953.

9. A sad letter from Wm. Forster relating Jane's final decision in the negative. He endeavours to bear it manfully.

12. Evening with Sterling. What an evening we had! We discussed first the new corn tariff proposed by Sir R. Peel,[1] a better measure than I expected. Sterling thinks it will not satisfy the anti-corn law associations, which is the grand point after all. We discussed the principles of Chartism on which we differed. He considers the equal division of property to be one of their fundamental principles. My idea was that their requirings do not go beyond the terms of the charter, one of which certainly is Universal Suffrage, which would give the the popular party almost unlimited power, but that they would use it to *equalise* all property I can hardly believe. There is no doubt that one of their principles is a denial of the right of property to confer franchise & possibly they are right, though I am not yet prepared to admit it.

17. At ½ past 8 this morning an earthquake was sensibly felt at Penryn, Constantine, & Helston, accompanied by a low rumbling sound which lasted several seconds. Several houses in Penryn were violently shaken & a man on the quay was *said* to be thrown off his legs. A book in Pollard's house at Constantine was thrown off a shelf & the motion was very de-cidedly felt & remarked by Dr. Wise who was staying in a house the other side of Helston. Some men in Tresavean mine felt the tremulous motion 200 fathoms deep. It was believed all day in this neighbourhood to be caused by the bursting of Tresavean boiler & the number of killed & wounded was confidently stated. Its line of principal action seems to have been NE & SW on the granite range, probably some great heave or slide; no external displacement has taken place that I have heard of.

21. Drove Uncle A. over to Perran to inspect the state of affairs, which we found worse than we had expected. This makes it perfectly clear to me that it is not prudent to go abroad till matters are better arranged, which cannot be done without exertion & close attention. It is somewhat to feel satisfied that the course one has decided on is obviously the right one, though I should have been better pleased, I confess, with a less pungently convincing proof of the fact. My father was not a little alarmed at hearing the true state of things & Uncle A. again wrote Uncle C. on the necessity of returning home.

26. Drove my father to Perran to meet Uncle C. who returned last night. Uncle A. rode out also & we held a serious consultation on the state of affairs in the upper office, which I think will lead to a good result. There is some-thing remarkably disagreeable to my feelings in holding a false position in

1. The Whigs, while in office, were bent upon a fixed but moderate duty on foreign corn, while the Anti-Corn-Law League desired complete repeal. The Conservatives, headed by Sir Robert Peel, pressed for a sliding scale and brought this into effect in 1842 and in the same year introduced a bill for the levying of an 'income tax' of 7d in the pound.

any sphere whether of morals, intellect, or property. With regard to the latter the evil has not gone so far but I think we shall be able to put all right by certain sales & other arrangements, without much difficulty or any great sacrifice. On our way out my father proposed giving up his share in G. C. Fox & Co. to me, I paying him out of it £200 per annum, provided the average profits of 3 years amount to a certain sum. It is a very handsome offer which I of course acceded to. Uncle C. rode home & lodged with us. He & I had a long & interesting walk after dinner. He adheres to his intention of going abroad now & proposed my attending to Perran business during his absence, he allowing me his salary meanwhile. I should have acceded to the first part of the proposition without any reference to the other, but *tant mieux*. He is in a remarkably agreeable humour & although the meeting was somewhat dreaded, nothing of an unpleasant nature passed on either side. How much may be accomplished by a little mutual concession!

28. All are united in the absolute necessity of selling property to square off with the Bankers & of course those who have incurred the bulk of the debt are the right parties to do so. If all debts were paid Foxes & Co. would have a noble balance in hand, the capital (including Portreath) having accumulated to £105,000. Called at Grove Hill in the evening & prepared His Highnesss's mind for tomorrow's éclaircissement & the necessity of disposing of property, which I know will pinch him sore. But desperate diseases require strong remedies.

MARCH

1. Final meeting of the partners of Foxes & Co., held at Grove Hill. Our G.C. not a little shocked to hear the amount of balance against him, but behaved remarkably well. We recommended the sale of one of his estates, but his tenacity for land amounts to an absolute weakness & he prefers parting with half his share of Portreath which pays nearly 10 per cent & is always improving! He suggested laying down his carriage & selling Grove Hill. After dinner at the Bank, Uncle Joshua joined us & was rewarded by a revelation of his circumstances, which he bore well & talked of giving up Tregedna & living by spade & pick axe. Poor fellow! With all his chivalry he is doomed to dependence. He never learnt the art of economy, so must now serve his apprenticeship. No such changes as the parties talked of will be necessary, but it is well they should take the alarm & share the burden. There is property enough & brotherhood enough in the family to prevent any member from going to the wall; once put in order, I hope the old machine will work smoothly & successfully. Rode out with Uncle C. to

Perran to assist in final arrangements. He leaves me in command, both at Foxes & Co. & the Foundry, & wrote the Bankers of both firms to pay due honor to my signature.

2. Uncle C. marched off at 5 for London intending to leave England the beginning of next week. I took my post at the office & fixed on my line of policy during my regency, which is simply to pick up as much & pay as little money as possible. Besides this I mean to make myself acquainted with our mining interest, & don't doubt effecting some good thro' a little extra exertion. Inspected Foundry affairs & returned to Falmouth to dinner.

4. On descending to breakfast had the unexpected pleasure of finding a note from Wm. Forster giving notice of his advent in the evening. Paid the Falmouthians a visit in the middle of the day & returned in time to meet him in the evening. He rolled down from the coach in a monstrous white coat & fur cap & spatterdashes, looking as savage as a buccaneer. Having civilized his appearance thro' stripping & washing & a comfortable tea we set to & talked in good earnest. The refusal he bears like a man. Bradford is uncongenial to him in the extreme & wool is not an article to fatten on (although it may keep the cold out) & in short he'll dissolve the partnership as soon as an opportunity presents. We separated about midnight.

7. Breakfasted with William at the Tregelleses & trudged to Penryn with him to aid his wool business. He is certainly a very fine fellow, honorable, disinterested and intelligent, but impulsive in his actions & perhaps a little too fond of ease.

9. Betsey Evans buried today at Falmouth. I attended the funeral, but left before the service commenced, as the gig was waiting to take William & me to Truro. I feel as if Thomas Evans & I suffered a common loss. We had rain all the way to Truro where we effected each some business in our different lines, he with the wool merchants & I at the smelting house. Returned to Perran, where coffee & a glorious fire awaited us, & we sat together & talked on many topics to mutual edification till 5 tomorrow morning, when he started per *Quicksilver* coach. He certainly is a very fine fellow with a sense of honor almost Quixotic, staunch in his friendship, earnest & sincere, but wants fixedness of purpose, and stability of character. He deeply feels his late disappointment, but now desires most disinterestedly to make Jane over to me as the next best to himself! Thanked him for his kind suggestion.

11. Accompanied my Grandmother & Aunt C. to Perran in the *Regulator*, they proceeding to Frenchay to assist Aunt Mariana in her approaching 'pain & peril', I to Wheal Uny to do my best towards lessening our own. Met Capt. Colmar from Charlestown at the mine & went through all the surface operations with him. Many of his suggestions were very valuable & to be acted on. After dinner laid the question of economy or suspension seriously before Capt. Dunstan who thus fell at once into my views & we decided on

stopping one whim & one range of stamps,[1] which will strike off 30 men from our surface establishment & by an improved system of management, effect the same quantity of work. Reduced the monthly cost according to our calculation £255 per month, but I hope to make it in reality much better than this through increased picking of the ore, which will lessen the expense in every department of dressing. Most of these changes originated in Capt. Tregaskes's brain, who is an invaluable adviser, but prefers keeping behind the scenes in order to prevent jealousy. Rode back to tea & a snug evening at Perran with much satisfaction. After all, if Poverty really stares us in the face, it is the least of evils, far the least. Sickness comes next, then mental disease, & lastly loss of character. So far our family has been preserved from all, for which we cannot be too thankful. But if we have now to retrench & give up some of the luxuries of life through the imprudence of others, what matters it?

12. Morning at Perran Foundry. That concern is in a decidedly unhealthy state.[2] Much is to be done in the way of economising, systematising work & protecting property now exposed to public rapacity. At Wheal Uny to dinner. Found my plans acted on without opposition. Home at eight via Penjerrick. There are wars abroad & distress at home & an almost unprecedented depression of trade throughout the nation. Manufacturing, Agricultural & Mining interests are all apparently at the lowest ebb. What is it all leading to? & how is our increasing debt to be met?

15. Attended Garland's[3] lecture on the Liberty of Opinion, a sound, rational screed on the subject, or as our worthy chairman R. Broad designated it, 'a chaste & recherché dissertation'. Peel's motion to meet our expenditure is one that will make many long faces viz. 7d. in the £ on *income* from property of all sorts but not touching those that are under £150 per annum.[4] I prefer Sterling's idea of a house tax on many accounts. The present is perhaps the

1. A whim was a device for raising ore from the mine and a stamp was used to crush the ore when it had been brought to the surface.

2. The Perran foundry had been started in 1791 by the Foxes and Prices, but the Price connection ended in 1821. At that time Benjamin Sampson, one of the principal shareholders in the Tresavean mine, joined the foundry and became its manager. He died in 1840 and left his interest in the foundry to his nephew of the same name. The Williams family also had an interest; later, in 1848 or 1849, Michael Williams of Trevince became the principal partner and appointed his son, Michael Henry Williams, as manager. The Fox family sold out their interests to the Williams in 1857. At the time when Barclay was writing, the affairs of the foundry were in a confused state because of Sampson's death.

3. Thomas Garland (1804–65), editor of the weekly newspaper *The Cornubian*, published at Falmouth.

4. Sir Robert Peel's Budget of 1842 made considerable reductions in the duties levied on imported goods, but to make good the deficit in revenue he re-introduced a tax on income of all kinds. Such a tax had first been introduced during the Napoleonic wars as a temporary measure only.

most equitable in principle, but is liable to infinite evasions in practice, besides its nature is inquisitional & it bears with equal weight on income from labour & income from property, which does not seem to me right in principle, though I see great difficulty in making any difference between the two.

18. Called on the Williamses & Colan Harvey to consult about the proposed alteration in the timber duties.[1] We are to hold a meeting of the timber merchants on the 22nd. as if they do not allow the drawback on the large stocks now in hand it will be a serious injury to us & a flagrant act of injustice, the timber being imported on the faith of the present drawback. I do not like the principle of either drawbacks or bounties, as they divert the natural course of trade, but if they be anywhere lawful they surely are on the timber used in mines, considering the hazardous nature of the speculation & the vast amount of employment they give. Meanwhile I did my best to dispose at once of our stock on hand by representing to the agents & captains[2] of various mines how much it was in their interest to secure a stock at the present 10/– duty than wait till the 30/– duty comes into operation.

20. S. Sterling sent for me to say he had made up his mind to start for Italy per steamer tomorrow week. I could not but agree in the judiciousness of the move, but should have preferred Madeira as infinitely duller and therefore less likely to be pernicious.

21. Met the Williamses at Copper Office to discuss future proceedings in reference to the alteration in timber duties. After a little chat Uncle A. rode on to a meeting of timber merchants at Redruth & was appointed one of a deputation to our members[3] to endeavour to obtain the drawback at least on stocks in hand, they having been purchased on the faith of that provision. This they may perhaps succeed in, although I am not sanguine, but I have no idea that with all our logic we shall be able to obtain a continuance of the drawback. The principle of the Government is to do away with drawbacks and bounties & I am convinced it is a sound one.

22. An interesting visit to Sterling who, though taking the precaution to remain in bed, does not appear worse. He highly approves Sir R. Peel's principle in the new tariff, viz, admitting the raw material at a duty not exceeding 5 per cent, half wrought materials at not exceeding 12 per cent, & manufactured articles at not exceeding 20 per cent. He only wishes he would carry out his principle to corn, which is also a raw material, & charge

---

1. Peel's 1842 Budget in general terms moved towards free trade but it abolished the 'drawback', or rebate, on duty which had been allowed by previous Acts of Parliament, on timber used in mines. The net result was an increase in duty for the Cornish timber merchants and mineowners. The Williamses of Trevince were mineowners on a large scale, and Colan Harvey a partner in some of their enterprises.
2. The captains were the managers, the link between the adventurers who invested money in the mines and the miners.
3. i.e. Members of Parliament.

5 per cent on it, 12 on flour & 20 on loaves. Walked to Perran & got drenched with rain.

24. Busy morning. Back to Falmouth by the omnibus. Walked out to Penjerrick with my father to join our party over a mutton pie at the cottage. The improvement Uncle G.C. has effected in his place is very striking indeed. On returning I found 4 Norwegian Captains waiting to consult me. One brought a cargo of timber ordered by us, but the other 3 being for market are thrown into a great quandary by the new tariff, & the present uncertainty about the drawback. Gave them the best advice I could, but could give them small encouragement.

27. S. Called on Sterling whose parents were just arrived. The mother seems a remarkably commonplace looking old lady & I cannot conceive how she was capable of producing such a son.

28. Attended a great county meeting convened at Redruth to avert if possible the evils threatened to the mining interest by the proposed alteration in the tariff on ores[1] & timber. A previous meeting of the timber merchants was held at Andrews Hotel which both our county members attended. After much haranguing a committee was formed to communicate with the Board of Trade either thro' a Member of Parliament or a memorial to secure the drawback on all stocks in hand & those now under order. The other meeting was held at the School. J. Tremayne was in the Chair. Treffry held forth with great enthusiasm on the national & provincial importance of the mines & the vast evils to be apprehended from their stoppage. What a sincere advocate a man becomes when his interest is touched. M. Williams gave us some startling facts as to the increased importation of foreign ores. In 1828, 16 tons were imported. The quantity has progressed thro' every succeeding year till in 1841, 8,450 tons of foreign copper ore were imported. Tin was then discussed, the duty of 1/- per cwt proposed on the ore is evidently from ignorance of the vast produce of the foreign ore. We shall probably get 2/6d, but I question whether this is enough. We shall also claim a continuance of drawback on Norway timber tho' I believe with little chance of success. The upshot of it all was that the resolutions of the meeting were transformed

---

1. In 1842 Peel's administration reduced the duties on foreign tin ores to £2. 10s. per ton, but only 10s. was charged on ores coming from British territories overseas. Tin in ingots, bars, etc., was charged duty of £6 per ton foreign and £3 per ton colonial. Imported manufactures of tin were charged a 15% *ad valorem* duty. In 1843 Peel abolished the import duties on foreign tin ores altogether. The competition from Malaya, with its cheap labour force, did not in fact prove disastrous for Cornwall, since it was accompanied by an overall increase in demand for tin. The position regarding copper was rather different. The import duty on foreign ores was progressively reduced until its total abolition in 1848 and this together with a running-out of deposits led to a decline in the Cornish industry generally. See John Rowe, *Cornwall in the Age of the Industrial Revolution*, 1953.

into instructions to a committee of a dozen appointed at the meeting, of whom the first five were named as a deputation to the Board of Trade, to set them right on this important measure. As a Cornishman I wish them success, but as an Englishman I should be sorry to see obstacles thrown in the way of Sir R. Peel's measure, which I cannot but consider a great & bold stride of a sound policy towards the principle of free-trade.

APRIL

1. Took leave of Sterling who starts for Malta tomorrow per *Great Liverpool*. Poor fellow! The haemorrhage has not left him & with his excitable temperament & conversational tendency, I fear there would be a small chance of his overcoming it here. We took an affectionate mutual leave. He has been of no common value to me & indeed to all of us. He talks of meeting us in Town this summer. May it be so. Drove my father to Perran where we spent the morning in inspecting affairs. Called at Carclew & saw 3 superb Nepal rhododendra in bloom. Such dazzling crimson clusters as I never beheld.
5. Capt. Blackwood with 2 of his officers, Evans & Shadwell, & a Capt. Wickham dined with us, all superior, intelligent gentlemanly fellows. They are bound to the S. Seas & then round the world on a voyage of survey and scientific discovery in the *Fly* corvette & *Bramble* schooner. They spent all the morning with my father in the garden studying the instrument,[1] 'the Fox', as I observed they called it. Took them to Uncle G.C.'s lecture on Pompeii which closed the course. It was somewhat elaborate in antiquarian details & more calculated for the few than the many, but a good piece of composition & beautifully illustrated. The Collector, as he always does when possible, made himself particularly ridiculous, passing a drunken vote of admiration & proposing 3 cheers for the lecturer which was responded to by an unrestrained shout of laughter.
14. A few hasty lines from Capt. Tregaskes hurried me to Perran in the middle of the day. An awful event had thrown the whole valley into consternation. Poor Wilson put an end to himself this morning at 7 o'clock. Jas. Carnall, hearing a groan & a fall in the room above, went upstairs & found him on the floor, resting on one arm, down which his life-blood was streaming from a ghastly wound in the throat. The razor was lying on the table. A doctor was sent for immediately. He was laid on his bed & consciousness returned, but it would have been less painful had he never waked again on earth, for he was highly irritable & nothing in the least

1. Robert Were Fox's dipping needle compass.

satisfactory was obtained from him. His only surviving brother arrived just in time to see him alive. He lingered till ½ past 9 & then went to his terrible account. He was about 65 & the third out of 4 brothers who had committed suicide! It appears that he has been labouring under much depression for some time past. The state of the accounts has harassed him a good deal, & it is very likely that suppressed gout was acting on the nervous system. It is to be hoped that this will prove the only assignable motive for such an act. The Coroner arrived at 3. The verdict was 'Temporary Insanity'.

15. To Perran after breakfast. Had an interview with Jas. Wilson in his late brother's parlour & made arrangements for the funeral, &c. He was very deeply affected. Their mutual attachment was great & unvarying.

17. S. Wilson buried this morning. Saw J. M. Williams on his way to Madeira, to see after his brother Charles, of whom the accounts are very unfavourable. Gave him letters of credit on Madeira & Lisbon. Heard a good & cheerful account from Sterling from Gibraltar. His remarks on his fellow passengers highly graphic & characteristic.

21. Very busy all the morning. An unsettled account with B. Sampson, which presented unsurmountable difficulties to poor Wilson, appears to me to have been the immediate cause of his death; certain items having been handed him as a set-off to the balance which he could noways explain from the loose manner in which the books had been kept.

22. Busy morning at Falmouth & Perran. At Trevince to dinner at ½ past 5. Michael Williams & I were alone. He was very communicative & agreeable. He urged me very strongly to undertake the management of the Perran business. He would be satisfied were I there only 3 days a week & would throw all his influence into the scale to make the business flourish. Thanked him for the compliment but took care not to commit myself. Slept at Perran.

23. Busy morning on both sides the river. Young Paddon of Truro called & offered his services as partner & manager of the Foundry, in which case he would invest £6000 in the concern. I believe he's a spooney. The largest piece of wrought iron ever made at the foundry was completed today, an axle of the wheel for the man-machine at Tresavean, weight 46 cwt.[1]

26. Michael Williams met me at 12 this morning by appointment & inspected the trade which he thinks has great capabilities & had a thorough overhaul of the accounts. I kept the ledger out of his way, so he examined the balance sheet only. He will not be satisfied to remain in the House without reform & much wishes me to undertake the management.

28. Had the satisfaction on coming in of seeing the *Ashereen* under weigh.

---

1. The prize offered by the Cornwall Polytechnic Society for a man-engine which would lower and raise men in the mines was won by Michael Loam, and his engine was installed and working at Tresavean by October 1842.

She is the first Egyptian vessel that has visited England. On returning to Penjerrick I found two characteristic samples of female Quakerism, Hester Mills & Elizth. Elliot. The former is all meekness & modesty & unconscious of what an unruly passion can possibly mean. She is quiet, amiable, inanimate, being appropriately clad in the most unpretending drapery of the order. The latter is a strong-minded, abrupt person, gifted with plain sense & sincerity, great conscientiousness as far as she sees, but unable to see good beyond the limits of her own shadow. She is one of the narrow school who virtually think self-denial *in itself* holy & who cannot discern the inward principle except in the outward form in which themselves have been educated.

MAY

2. My poor cow died at 4 this morning in great suffering I fear. This is the first serious loss I have sustained in all my farming operations. Walked into Falmouth to breakfast & after a little necessary business rode on to Perran & thence in the afternoon to Penjerrick, where I found the Grove Hill party at dinner. My father tried the galvanic action of the lodes in Pennance Mine which proved highly satisfactory, showing sufficient strength in the lode to give a constant direction to the galvanometer.

4. Met Benj. Sampson & his factotum Lanyon at the former's house after breakfast, to go into his account. He is evidently a poor soft youth & dare not stir a step without his adviser, who is a tough subject. Got on with him, however, better than I expected, but there are a variety of perplexities in the affair which owing to Wilson's loose accounts & sudden exit we shall find it difficult to unfold.

7. Rode to Perran just in time to be present at the casting of a great cylinder. The sight was magnificent; such an impetuous torrent of white-hot fiery flop rushing from the lips of 2 furnaces through 2 channels to opposite sides of the mould. When this was just full, a rumbling sound like a volcano was heard; the earth shook, a sudden fire spout of huge sparks burst up to the roof & the men fled in every direction. The weight of the column of iron had burst through the core & there it sweltered in a great boiling bed in the centre of it. The casting was of course spoiled.

12. Interesting letter from J. Mill who approves of my lecture, & a glowing letter from Sterling, who is crazed with enjoyment of Naples both as respects nature & art. Grand leave-taking & packing-up as my people pack off tomorrow for London.

13. All ours off by 8, leaving Uncle A. & myself like 2 widowed doves. Slept at Penjerrick. Snug as a hermit with the whole house to myself.

14. Busy day. Spent the afternoon at Perran. Long letter from Uncle C. who wishes me to undertake the superintendence of the Foundry.

19. To Perran to breakfast. M. Williams called before I left & renewed his solicitations on the old subject. I gave him a hint as to comporting himself in case of a meeting of the Partners, which he took well. Took leave of all my old companions in arms. For the Tregaskeses, especially the Captain, I feel a sincere regard & esteem. Rode back to a Library meeting, & *Beresford* meeting in the evening. Taking leave, packing up, &c.

20. A prosperous passage to Plymouth with plenty of passengers, nearly all Irish. One young madcap officer made all manner of fun amongst the ladies & one green young gentleman on whom he played sundry inoffensive tricks, very diverting to the lookers on. The ladies certainly did their parts, entering with much ardour into the pleasures of earth, air & water, forfeits, knight-of-the-whistle &c. There was only one to whom I felt any kind of drawing as she was a lone lady who had never before been so far from Dublin & was now steaming to Town to see her sister. She was reading poetry & had an intelligent forehead which gave me a favourable impression of her, but her conversation did not realise my expectations.

21. Reached Southampton at 7. Glorious terra firma & a noble minded Wm. Hustler who greeted me with undiminished ardour & gave me a solid breakfast which proved highly serviceable. Delightful railway journey to Town, my bodily companion an inoffensive old gentleman & my spiritual one the breathing, soul-searching intellect of Thomas Carlyle as rendered visible in his glorious critiques on Goethe & Burns. Took a bus to 76 Gower Street, our lodgings, & deposited my traps. I joined the girls & Anna Gurney at the *White Hart*, where I met W. E. Forster on the stairs, & off we packed for Upton where all are in a good state of preservation. My father & mother joined us there & we formed a singularly united family.

22. Goodly assemblage at Plaistow meeting, and a party of 35 to dinner at Upton. A beautiful musical sermon from Eliz. Fry on the different offices of different members in the church, comparing them to various parts of one building & the great importance of some parts which are unseen & which give stability to the building. Left Upton at 9 for the Brewery, Brick Lane, as Wm. Forster chooses to consider himself obliged to start tomorrow evening for Bradford. He & I had the house to ourselves & talked a great deal.

23. A visit from Hannah Backhouse at the morning meeting. From her peculiar intonation & spasmodic delivery I lost or rather never gained half of her sermon. What I heard was powerful but sectarian. She termed the ministry of the church 'the bondage of corruption'. Went with William to call on J. Mill, who was warm as ever. Talked on Sterling, Macaulay & Carlyle – difference between 2 latter, the one goes round the outside of a character & points out all the apparent inconsistencies, the other goes to the

inward depth of it & reconciles them. Macaulay meditates a history of England subsequent to the Revolution. Mill hopes he won't write it, because everybody would read it to the exclusion of any more philosophical work on the same subject.

25. Edwin Fox, an intelligent, active youth, breakfasted with us. The morning meeting for worship was interesting & I had to stand a great part of the time. Dined at Bells[1] & Jas. drove me to Wandsworth in the evening in great peril of our necks, owing to the whirling stream of vehicles from Epsom. We called at Carlyle's en route – only the lady at home & she was exceedingly cordial. Went in pursuit of Cavendish; overtook him in the street & accompanied him to his pleasant lodgings in Piccadilly. He was warm as toast, looked well & cheerful, is prosperous in his vocation & I trust will turn out a valuable member of the profession.

28. A most beatific morning. After a peculiarly flat call on Elizth. Bell who is suffering the pangs of 'unregarded love', I proceeded to Carlyle's. Both he & his wife were at home & both very warm & sociable. Engaged us all to tea next week. We got him on Sterling, Emerson, & the Afghan War & a great many things besides. He dislikes Capital punishment, but will not undertake to say that it is not lawful. He thinks Emerson calculated to do much good in England. Laughs at Roebuck's[2] (Bribery Investigation) & similar motions, which are all well as far as they go, but all only skimming the surface. We want a true man to rise up in parliament & speak the great truth of the people of England. In a conversation he had with him, Roebuck said he did not wish to take away the power of bribery because without temptation there could be no virtue. I reminded him, said Carlyle, of one principle at least where there was plenty of temptation, but we did not generally consider it promotive of virtue, – I mean the devil. His laugh is quite refreshing. It comes so palpably from the 'great heart of him'. He was most warm at parting & we proceeded in high spirits to Derwent Coleridge's. Here we saw quite another type of man, the elegant, accomplished scholar, deeply imbued with the ecclesiastical spirit, but very cordial & obliging. He lives in a beautiful place with a large & highly prosperous establishment annexed, for the education of schoolmasters.[3] They are taught many higher branches of education & his plan is to have those that are fit ordained as deacons in the church, to form an intermediate link between the clergy & the people, a most politic plan I think. His wife we did not see, she being laid up with toothache.

1. The Bells were a Quaker family whose eldest son, Jacob, founded the Pharmaceutical Society. Their son, James, and daughter, Elizabeth, were to accompany Barclay Fox to Italy.
2. John Arthur Roebuck (1801-79), Member of Parliament, original member of the Reform Club, and later a supporter of Disraeli.
3. Derwent Coleridge had moved from Helston Grammar School and was now the first principal of St Mark's College, Chelsea, established as a Church of England training college for teachers.

30. The Backhouses to breakfast. Immediately after, I rattled down to the Danish Minister's in Wilton Crescent, to apply for the Consulship. He was very civil & friendly & promised to do anything for us that lay in his power. Joined our party & the Backhouses at the Zoological Gardens at 5 o'clock. Prof. Owen & his wife, & Uncle & Aunt C. & Mildred were also there. The rhinoceros & elephant, the giraffes & orang-outang are the chief interests of the garden. The canter of the giraffe's is most peculiar & graceful. The orang-outang sat on a chair & drank his cup of tea as natural as any old lady. We spent the evening with the Owens at their snug little habitat. His infidelity about animal magnetism is a little shaken, but he has brought up his comparative anatomy to beat down phrenology.

31. Spent a highly interesting hour and half with Owen at the College of Surgeons. He took me through the museum which is decidedly the best in the kingdom. Owen utterly disbelieves the generally supposed fact that mental excitement in the mother produces a corresponding effect in the offspring. When a child is born minus a hand or foot, the mother *remembers* having been shocked at some such sight, but in no instance that he knows of has she mentioned it to anyone at the time. Children are deprived of the extremities previous to birth by twisting the umbilical cord round the wrist or ankle. Went into the city & got thro' a good deal of business satisfactorily. Dined at the Mills with the girls & a magnificent time of it we had. J. Mill was in great force & high spirits. He says he was never yet able to *love* Goethe. He sees so much refined selfishness in him, & can hardly understand how so rugged & concentrative a spirit as Carlyle's can attach itself to one so diverse. His work on logic is to come out in December.

JUNE

1. A busy day in the city. Jordan & Cavendish to breakfast. Accompanied the latter to an anatomical lecture at St. George's Hospital delivered by Dr. Lee.
3. This has been a great & grand day in my calendar. After breakfasting with Gurney & Caroline Hoare, Gurney went off with my father, but then came back & invited us to go over to his mother's to see Wordsworth. The poet had been told that some ladies were very anxious to see him & he accordingly promised to take off his spectacles that they might have a full view. When we arrived he was walking in a shady path with his brother, C. Wordsworth,[1] and his son-in-law, Quillinan.[2] I joined the group & was duly introduced,

1. Christopher Wordsworth (1774–1846), the brother of the poet, was master of Trinity College, Cambridge, 1820–41.
2. Edward Quillinan was the husband of Wordsworth's daughter, Dorothy.

trembling & stammering with excitement, for it seemed like conversing with a spirit. He walked with me into the house & sat him down amongst the ladies, faithfully taking off his spectacles as he did so. He conversed first with my mother, breaking forth into a poetico-religious rapture on the beauty everywhere, on some incidental remark of hers that the beauty of his habitation at Rydall must make other places look tame. This he stoutly denied & contended most truly that the more one lives amongst & *really* sees, i.e. *feelingly* sees, the beauties of Nature, the more competent is he to see & love all other beauty in country & town. 'We see because we feel & we feel because we see.' On my mother's leaving the house, C. & I had the whole of him. We got on Hartley Coleridge whom he does not admit possesses genius, nor in fact, I believe, anyone but himself. He contended that no great genius looked with an atrabilious eye on existing institutions, instancing Chaucer, Shakespeare & Spenser. Hartley is clever but has no genius, he is too metaphysical, too narrow for a poet whose essential quality is diffusiveness. We then got somehow on Faith, which he holds the highest attainment of which man is capable. 'To reconcile the goodness & fore-knowledge of God with the existence of evil is a problem which never will be solved, & used to make me quake in my bed when a child of four years old. Faith only can reconcile the mystery.' It was rather the tone of his conversation than the matter which was striking. When his subject warmed him he talked with the enthusiasm of a poet, sometimes referring to passages in his own works by way of illustration, at other times there was a calm solemnity of manner when he descanted on the infinite revelation of the Deity in his works & the true & high purpose of the poet to interpret this. We left Hampstead for Bury Hill in the afternoon.

4. This was a luxurious day of rest & ease, sauntering to the farm with Uncle Barclay & getting agricultural hints, sitting in the shade & reading & writing. I never saw a place more improved than Bury Hill. The grounds are exceedingly tasteful, beautifully kept & filled with rare & choice plants & trees, the firs especially, which the soil seems to suit. The house is ornamented with various & beautiful works of art, the result of the Italian tour which has had an evident elevating effect on the possessor.

6. Left Bury Hill at half past 10 for Wandsworth. The girls & I proceeded to Carlyle's to tea & a glorious three hours we had with him. He described the careers of Swedenborg & Jacob Bohme, men that saw visions & founded sects with strange wild creeds, but with a real truth at the bottom of them. He gave me some of the former's works. He talked in a dyspeptic strain on the Government & constitution of this country & denies that it is in the power of any man to pay homage to poor little Victoria or to entrust his liberties to Sir Robert Peel. 'I cannot for the life of me worship a velvet chair with gilt nails because it's called a throne, nor the person that fills it, unless it be a

reality & not a sham.' C. made him roar his loudest by telling him that a lady taking it for granted that Herr Teufelsdrock in 'Sartor' was the image of his own existence & career, was curious to know whether he really made his first appearance in the world in a basket. He said he knew of nothing peculiar in his advent into the world except that 11 months after it, he astonished the family by opening his lips in articulate language for the first time on hearing another child squalling in the next room, with the memorable remark, 'I wonder what ails wee Jock'. When my mother came for us with the carriage at ½ past 5, she spoke to him about Elizth. Fry. 'I met her once', he said, '& that was in Newgate. Two other Quakeresses were with her. She was reading the Bible to the prisoners in that clear silver tone of hers & it looked like a little white spot of purity in the centre of a great black, sweltering mass of iniquity.' We reached R. Reynold's at 10, owing to sundry delays & mishaps, a horse falling, losing our way, &c.

8. Went early to town & bus'd to the W. End to attend an African Civilisation Committee as W. Forster's substitute (having offered to relieve him of his black duties during my stay here). Being before time, I strolled down to Westminster Abbey & thought an hour well spent in reading that grand religious poem. On emerging, I could not help comparing this edifice of our fathers with the edifices which we erect in this day. What are they? Railway termini. Religious feeling, call it superstition if you please, has given place to Utilitarianism. Reverence to machinery! From a contemplation of the past & the abstract, I proceeded to the present & practical in the shape of the African Civilisation Committee. The report was read which gave as good an account of the business as could be expected. I think the experiment should not be given up, considering the enormous interest at stake & the value of any sincere effort for an amelioration of that wretched country. After that I spent an hour very profitably at the National Gallery.

16. Took leave of Carlyle or rather his wife (he being out). She was very cordial & affectionate. Returned to the city in one of those arrowy little steamers. The view of St. Paul's from the river where all the details of the dome are distinguishable is extremely grand. Called on Cavendish at the hospital.

17. After a busy morning in the city met the girls at Lombard Street & accompanied them & Sam to the Bank, where we passed through a bewildering succession of offices & passages upstairs into a long room where they manufacture 20 or 30,000 £5 notes daily. Each turn of each press moves a figure in an inner room so that there is no possibility of purloining a note without detection. That is what I call making honest men by machinery. Left the girls & started to the W. End on sundry errands of private & public import & joined them at the Temple Church, where we met Sterling & Edward, the former looking well & sunburnt & full of energy & enthusiasm.

A very rising barrister, W. Smith,[1] known in literature by a first rate work on Law Reform & several tragedies & a novel *Ernesto*, to whom we were introduced by J. Mill, gained us admission, the public being now excluded during the progress of the restoration. It is being restored in all the gorgeous style of the middle ages. The restoration of the interior they say will cost £60,000! J. Mill with his mother & sister joined us by appointment at the Church. I paid him a glorious call in the morning & talked about Afghanistan[2] & Alfred Tennyson, whose poems he reviewed in the *London & Westminster*.

18. Took an affectionate leave of our most kind & hospitable friends of Ham House. We took a luncheon dinner at Uncle David's & my mother & I took a quiet drive to Combe,[3] leaving the girls to follow in a few days. It took us 4½ hours to Bristol! Certainly steam is the one great *Fact* of the present age. To be deprived of it now would feel like going back to Barbarism.

19. At Lawrence Weston[4] meeting, which my mother reached by aid of a donkey & a boy, we met that worthy, simple-minded old saint, Mary Hunt, & to my surprise Jasper Capper & his wife Jane. She is now the mother of 4 children & still looks well with the same sweet mouth & the same oblique line of the upper eyelid which always charms me. Took a walk with them after luncheon & got into J. Harford's[5] woods where we stumbled on some scenery of extraordinary beauty, but how to get out of the place was the puzzle. It was clear we had got into private grounds & all modes of egress we found admirably secured. At length we had to scale 2 successive gates of fearful height & aspect, being furnished with iron spikes & points, which left a memorial of her Sunday walk in Jane's muslin frock. Geo. Hilhouse is an uncommonly odd fellow, far too dogmatic & dictatorial, but really kind in meaning, & a pleasant companion enough when taken in the right humour.

20. A day of little outward incident but a very impressive one to me. My mother & I being closeted a short time before breakfast, we had a little talk about plans. Her womanly penetration gave her an inkling of a certain tendency of mine, though by no means of its force. She warned me faithfully against N—s.[6] I *felt* that it came too late. I feel that an important crisis is

1. Wm. Henry Smith (1808–72), of the Middle Temple, a friend of Mill, Sterling, and F. D. Maurice. He wrote philosophical works and novels, the most famous of which was *Thorndale*, 1857. *Ernesto, a Philosophical Romance* appeared in 1833.

2. The British had evacuated Kabul in January, but of several thousand men only one reached Jallalabad alive.

3. It was now possible to make the journey from London to Bristol by railway since Brunel's Great Western line reached Bristol in 1841.

4. A village near Combe.

5. A Quaker banker of Bristol who lived at Blaise Castle House. The Blaise Castle estate. mentioned in Jane Austen's *Northanger Abbey*, was renowned for its 'romantic' scenery.

6. The following pages make it clear that this is Northrepps Hall, the home of Sir Thomas Fowell Buxton, and that Barclay had thoughts of proposing to Richenda, Sir Thomas's daughter.

approaching. At parting 'she hoped she had not offended me'. Kind loving creature! I walked to Bristol at 1 after taking an affectionate leave of the Combe party & proceeded to Town by the ½ past 2 o'clock train. Lodged at the *Swan with Two Necks* in Ladlane, that being the place whence the Norwich coach starts.

21. I proceeded to the African meeting at Exeter Hall & was forthwith appointed an usher of the white wand to preserve order on the platform. Lord Ashley took the chair at 12. Lord John Russell spoke in a manly, practical & hearty tone on the debt we owed to Africa for three centuries of oppression, the objects & the moral effect on other nations of the late expedition,[1] & the part he had taken in it. He contended that it was not a failure, but much had been effected & the way prepared for much more. Archdeacon Wilberforce seconded the motion. Our principles are those of justice & must ultimately succeed. The natives having united with us to destroy the barracoons[2] is a very important fact. He gave some bitter hints at the ungenerous attacks which have been made on the instigators of the undertaking & the mawkish affectation of pity for our deluded victims. Lord Sandon moved the next resolution about the non-failure of the Expedition & the moral influence of the fact of the British Flag 300 miles up the Niger engaged in the cause of humanity. An Englishman is now distinguished by the natives from all other Europeans & protected. Bishop of Norwich spoke well. It was a strange & pleasant sight to see all creeds & parties united in this great cause. Did it lead to forgetting our own poor? Look around & behold the refutation. This gave him an opportunity of buttering Lord Ashley very thick for his humane exertions on behalf of the miners.[3] Sir T. Acland returned thanks to the chairman with extraordinary animation & zeal & I started to keep an appointment with Cavendish at the Albany. C. & I dined together & renewed the past as we chewed the present. At 8 I started for Norwich per mail.

22. A most glorious moony night, but uninteresting fellow passengers. Reached Norwich at 8. Washed & trudged to Earlham to breakfast. Cos. Eliza Gurney[4] doing the duties of her rank like a queen with perfect ease & dignified simplicity. Cos. J. J. Gurney was suffering from having swallowed some alkaline drops instead of his medicine which burnt the throat & oesophagus considerably, & was only saved from a severe inflammation of the stomach by an immediate dose of castor oil which acted as an emetic.

1. The Niger expedition which had ended in disaster.
2. Barracks in which negroes were penned waiting their transit as slaves.
3. Lord Ashley (seventh Earl of Shaftesbury) was the champion of legislation to regulate the hours and conditions of work in factories and mines, and especially to limit the employment of children.
4. Joseph John Gurney had married his third wife, Eliza, the previous year.

Jane & Hannah Backhouse called after breakfast & Wm. & Anna Forster, the latter far from well, but fond & kind as ever. She likes me for her son's sake & I value her for her own. Dined at the Backhouses at the Grove, a pleasant & edifying opportunity. Ann has an affair pending with John Hodgkin, virtually settled I should think in his favour. Jane looked particularly lovely. A gig conveyed me from Norwich to Northrepps Hall in the evening. Sir Fowell Buxton looked very much broken down,[1] but was exceedingly kind & cordial. Lady B. very unchanged, full of emphasis & feeling & interest, & sitting behind a screen on account of her eyes. Chenda in a light blue afternoon dress, though a little weakened by her late attack, looked as lovely as ever. I never saw eyes with such depth of intellectual expression. The curve of the upper lip & the line of the nose indicate true *nobility*, a *greatness* & a *depth* of feeling combined. She spoke little, but what she said was always to the purpose. Anna Gurney was also there, full of energy & animation. After she was gone Chenda gave us some exquisite touches of music on a very first rate piano, then read a psalm & we retired. Sir T.F.B. was much interested by such scraps of the proceedings at Exeter Hall yesterday as I could remember.

23. Edward Buxton[2] came at 12 to spend a few days. Sir Fowell, he & I rode to Trimmingham, one of the former's estates, where he is planting, farming, rearing pheasants, &c. We drank tea at the Hon. Upcher's at Sheringham, 7 miles off. I drove Chenda in a low pony chair & had some very interesting chat. There is a clearness of vision & soundness of judgment & healthiness of feeling in her remarks which charms me. At Sheringham we met Harry Upcher & his wife who inhabit the Hall, a magnificent place. Mrs. Upcher lives with another son Arthur, the clergyman of the parish, & intended by *his* mother, I hear, & other kind friends, for Chenda's husband. I saw, however, no loverlike attentions pass between them. A pleasant social evening. Mrs. Upcher is evidently a woman of superior cultivation & tastes. After reading this morning Sir Fowell knelt down & lifted up a beautiful prayer for Africa & a strain of thanksgiving for the success of the late meeting.

24. Read some of Tennyson to the ladies which pleased them highly, Chenda especially. Rode with her & Edward to Runton, another estate of Sir Fowell's, about 3 miles off. The wind was high & we rode to some beacon over-looking a fine & very extensive view. Chenda was talking to me of some sea view from the Alban Hill & Lord Byron's lines on it, & as the fresh breeze blew back her curls & gave a deeper rose to her cheek, I thought she never looked so beautiful. It was a very grand sight & one that dwells deep in the memory. Quietly at home all the evening. An opportunity for much

1. The failure of the Niger expedition had been a great blow to him and he died within three years at the age of 59.
2. Sir Thomas's son.

pleasant social intercourse. It is a place where you are made to feel at home. There is an entire absence of style both in the house & grounds. Sir T.F.B. is completely the fine old country gentleman in his manners & appearance, but refined by modern cultivation, natural taste, & deep feeling. Lady B. is thoroughly honest in word & deed, warm-hearted, emphatic & energetic.

25. A day of little outward incident, the principal one being a ride with Sir F.B., Edward, & Chenda to Mr. Johnston's to luncheon & see some plantations. As it came on to rain on leaving the house, Sir F.B. rode home direct & Edward, Chenda & I continued our route & had a drenching, but to me very pleasant ride. Anna Gurney with her satellite, Anna Braithwaite, spent the evening with us. Gave Chenda five pieces of my poetry. She was much pleased.

26. S. Had the double benefit of church with Chenda & Meeting by myself. I was struck by the simple fervent piety of her manner & deportment whilst at church. Everything confirms me in the high estimation I had previously formed of her. There is a certain reserve in her which makes her somewhat chary of the expression of sentiment, but one sees & hears enough to give no ordinary idea of what yet remains to hear & to see.

27. Breakfasted at A. Gurney's with Edward. She is a marvellous creature, full of energy, penetration, talent, cheerfulness in the midst of ailments which which would weigh any common nature to the dust. Rode back in time to join Sir F., Chenda, & Edward in a ride, the last & best. E. & I started after luncheon & Chenda accompanied us to the coach. How it is with her I know not, but I am come to the conclusion there is no recovery for me. I see the variety & greatness of the difficulties which lie between me & my hopes, but love does not calculate. There is no middle course & whether that road leads to madness or matrimony, I must love on. I thought I read something favourable in her parting look but it might have been only fancy. Drank tea with Anna Forster & started per Birmingham Mail at 7, which took me as far as Grantham, whence after breakfast I proceeded via Nottingham, Derby, & Leeds, to Bradford. I found William not returned from a hunt after me, having been to Pontefract & I know not where besides. This gave me time to despatch a letter to my mother telling her the whole history of my long attachment to C.B. & my present confirmation of it, &c. It will be a pang to her & my father who look on memberhood in the Society very differently from what I do, & this alone tries me. For myself I am prepared to endure to the utmost. Wm. arrived about ½ past 11.

29. An uncommonly pleasant & deeply interesting day with Wm. He is improved in appearance by his change of dress which his father has borne without a murmur.[1] Called on the Hustlers & accompanied them to Meeting. Wm. & I dined alone, after which I told him all my story, at which he was

1. He had discarded the traditional Quaker dress.

at first much vexed, having set his heart on my pairing off with another. But finding it was too late, he entered into it like a true friend, gave me some counsel & much valuable information, & we kept it up till ½ past 1 in the morning.

30. A ride with Wm. Hustler in the morning through that murky miserable manufactory which men call Bradford. The Hustlers are a happy family party, very kind, rather flat, & altogether my intercourse with them has been very agreeable. Kept it up with William till the early morning to mutual edification. His friendship for me is a host and I believe will prove so in case of future difficulties.

JULY

1. Took a long ride with William through the valley of the Aire & a beautiful ride it was. At 1 we started in a gig for Wakefield, 15 miles off, & called on Waterton[1] who lives 4 miles from the town. His park is surrounded by a stone wall 3 miles in extent & a fosse outside it full of water. His house stands in the centre of a lake which you cross over by a light & elegant bridge. We found the hero dressed rather à la Uncle Joshua, shabby beaver, jacket & trowsers, a man apparently of 65, very energetic & original. His face was pale & deeply ploughed with toil, & if fame says true, penance & watching. It is reported that in consequence of a vow at his wife's death, he always sleeps on a board with a log for his pillow. He took us over his house & shewed us his various curiosities natural & artificial. He showed us the cayman whose back he rode on, & the boa he had the honour of slaying, a drunken Bacchus by Giordano which he delights in above all his other paintings, & a beautiful St. Catherine by Carlo Maratti. He is well worth knowing, original, uncompromising, & stamped with an energy & vigour of soul, which fits him for any feat, however daring or whimsical. He spoke very highly of Uncle G. who was an old friend of his. W.F. accompanied me to the station & I started for Birmingham a little before 8, feeling the full value of one real friend. Reached my destination at ¼ to 1 but had to wait till 2 before a gentleman turning, left a bed vacant for me. My companion is a little Blenheim spaniel for Aunt C. from Mildred Hustler. There are few in the world I would undertake the charge of such for, all the way to Falmouth, but she is one of them.

1. Chas. Waterton (1782–1865), a naturalist of some repute. He had lived in British Guiana and travelled in Spain, North America and the West Indies. His famous ride on a cayman (a species of alligator) which took place in the course of its capture, occurred during his 1820 expedition to Guiana. He published his *Wanderings* in 1825. The estate at Walton Hall formed a nature reserve and bird sanctuary.

3. S. A very interesting & open time with my mother before breakfast. Wrote my father on *the* subject to break the ice if possible before meeting. I fear he will feel it much. Disownment sounds so like loss of caste. I cannot believe that a religious society has any right to alienate one of its body who concurs with them in faith & practice & commits no breach either of the human, moral or religious law.

4. Left Combe soon after 7 in the morning. I was exceedingly shocked in going thro' Bristol to see placarded round the town a *third* attempt to shoot the Queen. The assassin had escaped & consequently his description is circulated round the country, a hump-backed ill-looking fellow. A pleasant time for social intercourse as we posted from Bristol to Ashburton, where we lodged. Found a note from my father at Exeter, taking the news of my affair in the most sweet & fatherly manner. Heaven bless him for that same.

5. Left Ashburton after an early breakfast & reached Plymouth soon after 10, where I had the pleasure of handing the small dog over to his liege lady. Proceeded to Liskeard. My father met us on the road. He has a troublesome toothache. His greeting was as kind & unconstrained as if nothing had happened.

7. Heavy rain. Reached Perran at $\frac{1}{2}$ past 3. Went home in the omnibus. Everything looking well & homish. Not sorry by any means to be here.

10. S. Uncle & Aunt C. dined with us. Had some conversation with each separately on the plans proposed for the future conduct of the Perran business. Uncle C. feels unequal in health to the sole management. His wish is for me to be united with him in it for a year, after which it should be handed over to me. There is much that is attractive in the idea. I had a little conversation with my mother on *the* subject. It is one of her earnest & daily prayers, but a cloud still rests with her. My father has not yet spoken to me of it. A young man called Rouse drank tea with us. He left the Navy from conscientious scruples to war. He is sincere & intelligent & well-spoken, not without the self-consciousness common to young converts. He refused a lieutenancy which was offered him since his withdrawal. He means to lecture on Peace this week.

15. Michael Williams & his son J.M., Uncles A. & C. & myself met at Perran Counting House & fixed the preliminaries & principles of the new partnership of Foxes & Co., in which the Williamses agree to increase their share from $\frac{1}{4}$ to $\frac{1}{2}$, we taking the other $\frac{1}{2}$. I am to be manager of the new concern, with the clear understanding that I may give a day or two a week to Falmouth business as occasion may require, & leave the management whenever I choose, salary £200 a year & the cottage. The meeting was very harmonious. This will make a great change in my life, but I like the idea of it. My father & I had 2 or 3 hours conversation, first on business, my future situation, & the importance of my not losing my connection with Falmouth. He does not

like my taking the cottage & wished me to put up with the Tregaskeses which I declined. He gives me his share in Perran Foundry with all its liabilities, which I accepted – thankfully. Then he came by degrees to that other subject on which each of us spoke candidly enough. He admits that there is no one out of the Society that he should like so well. He admires her & likes her family, at the same time from his position in the Society I must not expect consent. He very honestly stated the difficulties & inconveniences that presented themselves, & advised deep & calm consideration as a subject of such magnitude requires. The conversation was on the whole a very satisfactory one.

18. I commence my career as manager at Perran, a position that recommends itself to me on many grounds. First it is one of trust & responsibility with a sufficient degree of independence. Secondly it involves Perran Cottage, by far the loveliest nook in the neighbourhood, as a residence. Thirdly I am close to Uncle & Aunt C. Fourthly the salary is £200. Fifthly the clerks & I understand & like one another. Lastly it is a great step gained over the rough ground of prudential consideration on the part of Chenda's parents. I go into court with a stronger case. After a somewhat busy morning, rode home to dinner to meet the Grove Hill party including the Reynoldses & at tea John & Susannah Sterling. J. was in great force & takes a strong interest in my plans & change of abode.

19. Rode to Perran to breakfast. I stay at present in Uncle C.'s house, appropriating only the large room at the cottage, as it seems better not to take entire possession during Grandmamma's absence[1] & during W. Fouracres' presence.

21. Breakfasted at Perran. Took possession of the large room at the cottage & deposited there my letters & MSS not intended for eyes profane. The Grove Hill party to dinner.

24. S. My first bathe for the year. The Gurneys it seems do not come for a fortnight. This is a very great nuisance as I don't see how I can 'go forward' (as the phrase is in such cases) till after their departure. However, I have enough in hand & head likewise, to say nothing of the heart, to keep the time fully occupied meanwhile.

27. Had a great outpouring from T. Evans before breakfast of the state of his affections & its consequences. After hearing all the evidence I could not say a word of discouragement, my own circumstances making me perhaps somewhat more sympathetic. Walked back to Perran via Flushing & had a deeply interesting talk with Aunt C. on *the* subject, of course. Her advice on such subjects is invaluable.

31. S. Mooted to my mother the idea of writing to Sir Fowell before the Gurneys come. It was rather too startling for her at first, as the G.'s write that

1. Barclay was to take over the cottage at Perran which originally had been occupied by his grandmother. Fouracres was the manservant.

they mean to come the evening after tomorrow. I am convinced that under all circumstances it is best to do so. It will prevent the painfulness of fruitless discussion; it will give me a plea to entreat to secrecy in Sir F. & Lady B., so that I may be the first to tell my story, if I mention it to them first after my own family. Besides, my mind being made up, so much precedence is due to them, and I feel that longer delay will injure my cause. (I have already waited 5 weeks.) I today had a grand outpouring of the whole matter to Uncle G.C. who was exceedingly affectionate, telling me with a choking voice that nothing interested him more than my welfare, that he regarded me as his son, & took the announcement of her name infinitely better than I expected. In fact he heartily approved of it & offers to do anything in his power to promote my wishes. Aunt L., whom I saw in the evening, is also deeply interested, & delights in the idea of my marrying the daughter of her dearest friend.

AUGUST

1. This day a few years back the slaves were emancipated in British possessions. This day I was emancipated from a heavy burden of anxieties & fears by dispatching a letter to Sir F. & Lady B. who are staying at Weymouth, declaring my long & deep attachment to Richenda.
2. The arrival of the Gurney party was announced by a suppressed shriek at the Hall door & in burst a torrent of young ladies, Sarah, Bessie, Rachel, & Chenda,[1] followed by their brother Edmund & cousin Harry Birkbeck. They were followed in a more placid frame of mind by the parents, but full of warmth, affection & pleasure. Two of the girls & I quartered at Grove Hill.
3. The elders dined at Uncle A.'s, we young by ourselves, having planned a cruise in the afternoon. Joined a vast family gathering at Uncle Alfred's in the evening. Uncle G.C. went with me into my room & staid till after midnight, talking of *her* & *them*, & what was done, & what remained to do. He is perfectly happy in the idea.
4. Morning at Perran. After an early dinner we took the whole party to Penjerrick & Tregedna. Tea at the latter place was a most abundant & beautiful affair. We were 23 in all. The girls sang, their father romanced, the bloodhounds bayed & all conspired to make the whole scene with its inhabitants somewhat of a novelty & not an unpleasant one to our London guests. As many of the young as *could* stow in the cart were packed in both going & returning, which had a remarkably uniting effect.

1. These were the daughters of Samuel Gurney of Ham House, Upton. The name 'Richenda' belonged to several members of the Gurney family and their circle.

5. Sam Gurney's laugh is as refreshing as a stream in a desert; it comes from the real heart of him. Today was devoted to an excursion to Trebah to dinner where we ate beef & pudding under a marquee & dragged the ladies in a cart to Glendurgan, where Aunt A.'s school children were collected for us to play with, which we did with considerable animation. Wm. Hustler arrived this morning & found himself in his natural element, a complete paradise of girls. He was the life of the party. Uncle J. & daughters joined us on the river & we dragged the ground sean & pursued many other innocent diversions befitting natural young ladies & gentlemen till tea time. Uncle G.'s brake conveyed about a dozen of us home.

7. S. No letter yet. Nothing for it but patience. Better luck tomorrow. Juliet is a great object of attraction to Edm. Gurney. She looks very sweet. The 2 gardeners nabbed 3 boys last night robbing apples in the three-cornered garden. Sent them to prison to be brought before the Magistrate tomorrow. Uncle G.C. deeply interested in talking over my affair.

8. It's come at last! An enclosure with a note from each parent, written in the most liberal, unselfish, noble spirit, leaving the decision entirely to Richenda & giving me full consent to take what steps I think best. Sir F.'s is worthy of himself in every respect, the Mamma's equally full for her but more particular as a Mamma's might be expected to be. She wishes me not to come till after the 17th & to *write* the offer instead of speaking it, at which I kick.

10. Returned to Perran after Meeting via Hayle & the North Coast. A glorious afternoon & the coast scenery looked surpassingly lovely. We met a school of 43 children led out by master & teachers to make the most of a holiday with best array & banners waving. Sam Gurney stopped the carriage & gave them 6d a piece telling them to be good children & mind what their master told them. Met Elizth. Gurney & Bessie & Caroline at Perran, the latter told me of the family gratification at the Buxtons' answers to my proposal & of E. Gurney's[1] excitement & warmth & writing at once to Lady B. a most flowery description both of me & the family. She anticipates, however, some difficulty for me on the part of the lady herself. Well, nous verrons. My mother wrote a very warm & sweet letter to Lady B. & sent it out for me to read before sending it.

11. All the rest of the party excursed to the North Coast in 3 carriages & with 4 or 5 riding horses. I staid to attend to business of which there was plenty. They returned to drink tea with us at the cottage, my first entertainment & a very handsome one it was. My Grandmother, who returned two days ago, falls in with the plan of resigning her tenure to me. She was in fact but a tenant at will of the Co.'s. 20 sat down to tea in the large room. The evening was spent in practical charades.

1. Elizabeth, the wife of Samuel Gurney.

12. Spent the afternoon at Falmouth. My father made a very handsome present, the whole of his share in Foxes & Co., including the mines but not Portreath, worth at least £2,500, & the whole of his share in Perran Foundry Co. say £800. The profits in that House average much better than was supposed, so that in all my income appears to be full £700 & capital (all in business) say £5 to £6000. This, with a house & grounds rent-free, is not a *beggarly* prospect for Chenda or her parents. My father has behaved towards me with the utmost liberality his means admit of. He could not do more if my plans & prospects were quite in accordance with his wishes.

14. S. Spent in sentiment & lounging on the beach. A more than usually impressive Meeting this morning. A note was given me directly after, from Lady Buxton, saying I must not come till I heard again. What an immense bore!

15. The Gurneys left us going away with the brightest possible impression of Falmouth & its inhabitants, & we have exceedingly enjoyed their company. I accompanied them to Perran where I met Uncle C. who put a letter into my hand from Lady B. It cast a cloud over my picture, for it implied that Chenda expressed herself unfavourably towards me when Lady B. spoke in general terms of a *possibility*, in consequence of reports which Lady B. says have reached & vexed her (Chenda). She builds an argument upon it to make me write instead of speak, but I shall do what seems most politic. My plan is to start for London the day after tomorrow & speak to Edward. If he thinks my going will give offence I will write, otherwise I shall appear & whatever be the result strive to bear me like a man. The thing is becoming critical. Chenda's knowing it, or rather having been talked to about it, makes every day important. Cos. Sam Gurney came over to the cottage, where I went to pick some flowers for the girls, & read the letter & advised me not to give up my own plan. He takes the greatest interest in the affair. Nothing could be more affectionate than he & his wife.

16. Rode in to Falmouth to breakfast & communicated my intentions at home of starting for London tomorrow morning & proceeding the next day to Northrepps, should Edward start no sufficient objection to it. They recommend my writing Chenda from Town & paying my personal visit before she could have time to answer me. I think they are right. They started for Penzance & I returned to Perran & succeeded in getting through all that required attention both there & at Falmouth.

17. Started at 6 & enjoyed the companionship of my own thoughts till we were joined at Plymouth by Hicks of Bodmin, & a blustering vulgar fellow called Manning, who pestered me with the most egregious folly such as *proving* that the real revenue of the country is at least double of what it is reported to the public & consequently the surplus forms a private purse for Ministers, government officers & members of parliament to dip into ad

libitum. He has discovered that snuff is an infallible cure for madness & he found out a plan of raising 4 millions a year for the country by a mode which would return to each contributor 10 times the amount of his contribution. He left us at Bristol in order to run down to Birmingham to see the Riots, a pastime which I should think would suit him exactly. Hicks was very amusing. He accompanied me to London where we arrived at 5 in the morning.

18. Called on Edward at the Brewery. He was civil, but cautious in expression. He gave me no encouragement, but hoped the right decision would be come to, &c. He strongly approved my writing to Chenda & not giving her time to answer it, which I accordingly did (my first love letter), warning her that I should probably appear the day after it reached her. A broiling day & not an over pleasant one which I spent principally in a bedroom in St. Paul's Coffee House.

19. Journeyed to Norwich in the *Telegraph*. William was at the Inn waiting to receive me. He says that many bad influences have been at work with Chenda, who is thoroughly distressed & annoyed. A bad beginning. William & Anna Forster were very kind & feeling & cordial. I sat up with Wm. till late discussing the ins & outs of the matter.

20. Started after breakfast for Northrepps by coach with William. A man from the Hall was waiting at the Turnpike & he told us that Priscilla Johnston & Richenda Cunningham were just arrived to stay – a most unconscionable nuisance. Lady B. greeted me kindly at the door & Sir Fowell most heartily. Chenda came down with her sister, looking much excited & flushed. I was self-possessed. While the others were out of the room Lady B. told me that the announcement came on Chenda like a shock & she felt the weight of it & saw nothing but the difficulties. We went into luncheon, after which Sir F. asked which course I should like to pursue & proposed a walk. He said, 'You'll find her reserved, but you may depend she'll give you fair play, only you must be perfectly open with her & conceal nothing, & I most sincerely wish you success.' The walking party was only William, Priscilla, Chenda & I. We got together without any difficulty, & she very soon began with, 'I didn't expect to see you here again so soon, Barclay'. This gave me an opportunity of telling her the whole why & wherefore, in which operation I found no difficulty whatever. I told her that it was necessary for both of us to be perfectly simple & candid with each other, to which she entirely agreed. I said the first step of the consideration of such a matter was to endeavour to discover whether it was opposed to the Divine Will or not, then whether it was impossible or not to return love, then what are the difficulties & are they insurmountable. She contended that it was necessary first to receive every information which could assist her judgment & that judgment was to be submitted to the Divine Will for confirmation

or the contrary. She regretted the thing altogether, as far as she could at present see, that it must end in a refusal, which would be exceedingly painful to her on account of the pain it would give me & others. I begged her not to let that consideration weigh with her in the least. She had simply to consider herself in the matter & it would not do to bias her judgment by feeling for others. She then raised the difficulty I expected, about differences of religious habits. This led to a long disquisition on the nature of true religion, the outward garb of our religion (which I considered *sect* to be) was of very secondary importance. In fact, although rather the exception than the rule, differences on points of doctrine & minor detail *might* be mutually helpful, each in measure supplying what the other lacked. She admitted that it was possible, but thought such an effect was exceedingly improbable. She then wanted to know all about my own family & I took care not to give a very unattractive picture. We got on thoroughly intimate terms & she admitted that she had in great measure got over the horrors of the thing, but still could not give the smallest encouragement. There is a charming simplicity & straightforwardness in her mode of taking the whole thing, & however it ends, I shall be sure that I have received nothing but fair play. After dinner we had another walk & discussed pretty much the same points. I named the various points of similarity between us. I certainly could not profess the same degree of religious advancement as herself, although I believed our standards of excellence might be equally high. 'Oh', she replied quickly, 'if I thought you were no better than myself I would refuse you at once.' This fell upon me like a death-toll & we went into tea. That night was not over pleasant as may be supposed.

21. S. In the depths all day. She looked ill & was evidently much worn. We attended Elizth. Fry's[1] meeting in the morning at her lodgings at Cromer, all the family going too, except Chenda Cunningham & Chenda. It was a remarkably original style of meeting. Sir F. began with a glass of wine & a biscuit, & then put up his legs on the sofa. Lady B. got up to arrange the cushions, & the music of E. Fry's sermon mingled with his snores. Chenda looked wretched at luncheon. I went to Overstrand Church with her afterwards. Precious little attention could I pay to the service, for Wm. told me of a chat he had with her before church, in which she told him that she had endeavoured to seek right guidance & the difficulties had decidedly rather increased than diminished. I sat with her about three quarters of an hour in the upstairs sitting room. She told me that she was still utterly unable to arrive at a clear conclusion, although the tendency of her mind was decidedly against me. We had a walk in the evening in which much passed, but no fresh light was arrived at. She said the difficulty was in understanding one

1. Elizabeth Fry was a sister of Lady Fowell Buxton.

another. Our different habits of mind resulted from our different modes of education; she was a decided church-woman, I was a decided Friend. She could not speak too highly of the generous & considerate manner in which I had treated her throughout, and in spite of herself, her feeling for me & my family made the decision the more difficult to arrive at, besides the many attractive points which presented themselves in the proposal.

22. Whilst walking with Lady B. after breakfast on the lawn, Priscilla ran out to tell her that Arthur Upcher was in the house & wanted an interview. I continued my walk with Priscilla who told me that C.'s difficulties did not seem to give way at all. We had much very interesting talk on the whole subject. After nearly an hour Lady B. joined us & said they had had a somewhat distressing scene with Upcher, but neither she nor Sir F. would consent for a moment for him to interfere whilst I was on the ground. I protested against this. Fair play was all I wanted & I wished him to have the same, & I could not consent to take any advantage from preoccupation. I then went to Chenda's sitting room where she was waiting to see me. I told her the same. She thought her parents had acted quite right & did not wish to be disturbed by any thoughts of Upcher from coming to a clear & full conclusion on the case in point. All her convictions as to the difficulties had become clearer, she said. William saw her afterwards with Lady B. & she told them that she felt so clear, that if she were to give me an answer *now*, she did not believe she would have to repeat it, still she preferred waiting longer. I saw it was all over & determined on leaving the place tomorrow morning. I went with Sir F. & Lady B. in the carriage to Cromer. She & I called on E. Fry whom we found in a deeply sympathetic state. E. Fry & I had a private opportunity & her tenderness unmanned me for a time. I can stand everything but that. She was particularly sweet & consoling, however, & warned me against fleeing to the world for comfort. I then walked on the shore with Lady B. & was gratified to learn from her that C.'s difficulty on the great point of religious unity had decreased, but that at the same time the doctrinal & practical difficulties had *increased*. I told Lady B. what course I had fixed on & could now only beg, & that for C.'s sake as well as my own, that she *would* take time both to come to a right decision & to rest satisfied in that decision & then write me. Lady B. fully agreed that such was the right course to pursue. I accordingly ordered a chaise at Cromer. Lady B. feels really disappointed at the probable issue; Sir F. strongly so, & spoke to Chenda accordingly. I had a short walk with her before dinner & a longer one afterwards, in which nothing but affection & gratitude was felt by each of us. I believed we had both acted with sincerity towards each other. We now knew each other's sentiments on these points of difficulty & therefore further discussion would be useless, & that I had fixed on leaving tomorrow morning. She said she did not wish me to hurry away, but I must act as I thought

best. She believed that she had allowed nothing to prejudice my cause, but that a clearer sense of the difficulties was gradually given her & she could not see that any change would be effected by my staying. I talked to her a little about Upcher, pitied her having to go through a second edition of this sort of thing, with so little respite in case of a final decision against me; trusted that she would take it up with the same simple faith as she had done my proposal & I could not doubt that she would be led to a right result. Whatever that might be, it would be my prayer that it should lead to her happiness. She said she only hoped he would behave half as well as I had & thanked me warmly for the pain I had spared her by my forbearance, &c. It is a great comfort to feel nothing to regret on either side. No one could have received more honourable treatment than I have, & the least I could do in return was to spare her in every way.

23. A calmer night than I could have expected. I feel better than I did yesterday, & more resigned under the increasing conviction that C. has been rightly led. I don't allow my thoughts to wander to myself, for then it seems like a splendid dream vanishing before my eyes. After breakfast Sir F. shook me warmly by the hand & said he would always esteem me as a friend & could have wished to have greeted me in another capacity. Lady B. & I had a loving walk on the lawn for half an hour, when I transferred her to Priscilla & had my last with Chenda. Nothing could be more sweet & cordial & feeling than she was. I gave her a note from E. Fry to me, expressive of her increased regard for me, &c. Chenda said she most truly felt the same. She wished her dear love to be given to the girls. She expressed her belief that the whole affair had been intended for the good of us both. She had felt the last four days like four years. She then went upstairs & I into the drawing room. The chaise drove to the door. Lady B. said that if Chenda could not feel clear in coming to a conclusion without further data, she hoped that I would not take it as an encouragement if she were to write me, in which case I could come back if I preferred that mode. I said of course I should not, I only wished Chenda to be brought to a right decision. I then took a very warm leave of all the party in the drawing-room. I ran up to the sitting-room & found Priscilla standing at the door & Chenda sitting on the sofa. I told her that I was going, she rose & gave me her hand without speaking. 'Give her a kiss', said Priscilla, & Chenda bent forward to receive it. That alone was worth coming for. 'Give her another', said Priscilla. I did so & could not trust myself another moment in the room. We drove off. Neither William nor I felt inclined to talk for the first mile, but before we got to Aylesham I was completely recovered. We dined there & waited for the Coach which brought us to Norwich at 5. W. & A. Forster received us warmly. After tea we went to Earlham where Anna & I had a long & sweet walk. She was overflowing with affection, & had heard from Chenda since we left. Neither

J. J. Gurney nor his wife said anything on the subject to me which was a comfort.

24. As I rose from breakfast to start on my homeward journey, the pony chaise waiting at the door, a letter arrived per carrier from Lady B., requesting me to stop till the evening. Chenda had *no knowledge* of the letter. William wrote back to say I stopped according to her wish & begged her to write per return whether they wanted me back or not, adding, 'Be careful not to allow this act of yours to hurry Chenda's decision'. We spent the morning with Anna in her boudoir very pleasantly & then called on John & Laura, who seem wrapt up in each other & happy as the day is long, then Amelia Opie, who is as young as ever, & then to the post office & to our dismay found no letter from Northrepps for either of us. We dined, William vowing vengeance against the whole family all the time, & immediately after, in spite of thunder, lightning & rain, a most awful storm, he took a gig & started for Northrepps. It was past 7 & as he could not get back till 1 o'clock tomorrow morning I ordered a bed for him at the Hotel.

25. William appeared in my room between 6 & 7 bringing a letter to me from Lady B. & Chenda, expressing deep feeling for me under this fresh trial, &c. Lady B. had written, it appears, both to me & W., & the servant sent them too late for the coach. They do not want me to return. W. says he arrived a little after 9, found the family gone to the Cottage, ran down there, met the carriage returning & jumped up behind. He appeared at the door as they got out of the carriage. Sir F. gave a look of horror, spoke not a syllable but walked straight into his study. The ladies exclaimed, 'What has brought you here?' 'I'm come for an answer to my letter.' Then followed a scene of explanations, declamations, protestations, &c. William asked Chenda to walk out with him for ½ an hour & gave her a very strong flavoured dish of Quakerism. He spoke about her entire submission to what might be revealed to her & told her that she must not hesitate to yield up her opinions which stood in the way, in case that was required of her, become a Friend in fact, &c. She declared she was doing her very best to get at a right conclusion & wished to weigh the matter fully. In the house it was again discussed *en pleine famille*. William pledged himself on my behalf that in case I were recalled from Falmouth for reconsideration, in consequence of any misgivings which might yet arise, I would not think myself ill-treated if even then I met with a final refusal. W. was of course entirely right there. He got back to Norwich at ½ past 1. I never shall forget to the end of life his real practical friendship, displayed so signally during the last 5 days. He returns to Bradford this evening. I reached London at 6 & started per railway at 9 for home.

26. Reached Taunton at 3, Exeter at 7. Then breakfast & off per *Regulator*. A well meaning young clergyman was on the coach with me & a noisy fool,

who I think *must* be a little deranged, called Griffiths. I gave him one or two sets down when he grew unbearable. Reached Falmouth soon after 8. A note from C. informed me at Perran that they were at an anti-slavery meeting in the Town. I called there & walked home with A.M. The rest soon joined us. The past affair seemed to unite us closer than any domestic event that I remember. Chenda's conduct & that of her family excited general admiration, as well it might.

27. Called at the Bank, at Sterling's, the Counting House, &c. There was great delicacy in the conduct of all who knew what I have gone through. A tremendous thunder storm in the middle of the day after which I rode to Perran & had the satisfaction of finding all things going on as I could wish. Rode on to Penjerrick & spent the evening with Uncle G.C. & Aunt L. Both were loving & sympathetic, the former rather savage. Called on T. Evans whom I found with Louisa, his blooming bride, a changed & happy man. Met Uncle Joshua at the assay office, who romanced about my affair in the most extraordinary manner.

28. S. Wrote Chenda today in such a manner as not to lose my character of forbearance & manliness. William sent me a copy of *his* letter to her. It is a great thing to have a friend who will undertake the *pungent* work in these cases; he enforces on her that no consideration must interfere with what is shewn to be her duty, even should it oblige her to become a Friend.

29. After inviting sundry young men to dinner the day after tomorrow & paying an interesting call on Sterling, who looks particularly frail & shattered, I rode out to Perran & got through pretty much work.

30. Aunt C. with me at Perran. Spent a deeply interesting evening with her till long after midnight, she giving me in return for my love-story a long list of hers.

SEPTEMBER

3. On going to the Counting House in the evening I received *the* letter containing my final sentence. The bitterness of death however was past before, and in spite of self I must own it does credit to her head & heart. Religion, poetry, self-respect, sympathising friends, & all that come to my aid. But with all these & a monstrous show of magnanimity, it is a most horrid afflicting intolerable bore and that's the truth of it.

5. At Perran all day. James Magor, an old & trusty servant of the Foundry Co.'s died by the roadside the day before yesterday when carrying a message for the Co. To die in harness in that way has something sickening in the thought of it. I called on his widow today to administer what consolation

lay in my power, but she being old *and* a Bryanite, stood little in need of it. The house was full of the family & the friends, as the funeral was about to take place. I have a design on William Fouracres who will make a capital successor to the departed & would thus be cleared out of the cottage.

10. Had a talk with W. Fouracres. Told him I could not keep him as a servant & offered him Jas. Magor's place at the Foundry which however he by no means jumped at.

11. S. Wet day. Received yesterday a long letter from Priscilla Johnston, very intimate & affectionate, & describing the decided repulse to No. 2 after the second interview. Received also today a letter from William, enclosing two from Chenda describing the late transaction & drawing a contrast sufficiently gratifying to self-love between the two affairs. She is however equally satisfied with her decision in both.

12. Paid Sterling an interesting visit. He lent me Maurice's *Kingdom of Christ*,[1] which is perhaps the best Apology extant of High Church views in opposition to Quakerism on the one hand & Ultra-Protestantism on the other.

15. Two Ministering Friends, Caroline Parkins & Rebecca Sturges, came here to lodge, & held a public meeting at the Methodist chapel, wherein the doctrine of a universal inward light was strongly used. What I dislike in all sermons, or nearly so, of the present day is that the preacher appears rather as an *advocate* for some Christian doctrine than a teacher of Christianity. You know, generally speaking, on hearing his text the line of argument he will take, according to his adherence to this or the other sect, & Truth itself with undue stress on this or the other part of it, ceases to be pure Truth.

17. I returned to Falmouth having much to do & to say at the Office. The Friends dined with us: very quiet & innocuous. Paid a long call on Sterling who lamented the growing power of the Church & the extraordinary fact that no voice was lifted up with power against it. He has interesting letters from Carlyle, who is digesting O. Cromwell & the Puritans. What a grand work it will be when it does come![2]

19. At the office in the morning. With the multitude of vessels that are daily arriving & departing, there is almost a certainty of occasional blunders, which makes close attention necessary. Reform is wanted in some departments. A pilot stupidly ran a vessel on the Black Rock in working out of the harbour yesterday. She is got off, but so damaged as to make the discharge of her cargo probably necessary. This will tell against the port. Perran in the afternoon. A glorious night with Aunt C. till between 1 & 2 in the morning. She favoured me with her confidence which shall not be abused by committing it to paper. It was a valuable lesson & taught me this fact, that

1. F. D. Maurice's *Kingdom of Christ* appeared in 1838. It is hardly correct to call it 'High Church', since it was a plea for religious unity on the basis of a national church.
2. Carlyle's *Oliver Cromwell* was published in 1845.

woman's heart is the most delicate silver-filigree sort of fabric which a harsh word may crush, or a kind word satisfy, & which always must be handled with the utmost caution.

20. News reached us of an accident awful to think of & one that might have proved fatal to my mother & C. Parkins & R. Sturges. They were over-turned in Tregurtha's car last night over a bank 4ft. high in Penryn Street, when on their way to a public Meeting. Fortunately, say rather, providen-tially, none is seriously injured, tho' all more or less bruised. They were able to hold the meeting after it. My father witnessed the accident & heard a cry from the spectators of 'they are all killed'. The meeting was naturally one of peculiar solemnity.

22. Spent an hour at Devoran with Henry Francis, agent to the Railway Co., in convincing him that they had no right to build a dam across the river on our freehold. He accordingly suspended the operation till I should see & talk with R. Taylor, one of the directors. Attended Horticultural Exhibition at Falmouth. Nothing remarkable except a pumpkin from Grove Hill & a mushroom from Enys, which in point of quantity might have dined the whole company present.

23. Rode early to Perran, thence to Copper Office. Rode on to United Mines Association to talk with Taylor & J. Davy about the dam. This was followed by two North Countrymen, who missed me on the road but appeared in the evening smelling mountains high of macintosh.[1] They are J. Hodgson & J. Blain, Engine & Tool Manufacturers who come on a visit to Cornish engines & to suck the brains of Cornishmen. The former is a shrewd clear-headed manufacturer, possessed with a fixed hatred of the Corn laws, at which I do not much wonder, seeing that through them at this day 60,000 cotton-weavers in Lancashire alone earn but 6d a day to support themselves & their families. J. Blain is a youth, with a great deal in him for aught I know, but precious little can be got *out* of him. I had the treat of their undivided attention *all* the evening.

25. S. Mooted to my father the subject of my tour which did not at all take; the oppression of family affairs & a bilious tendency made every difficulty mountainous, till, not the Alps but the Andes seemed to rise betwixt me & Italy.

28. Had the two Lancashire visitors to breakfast. They go away highly gratified with Cornish machinery & Cornish hospitality. An interesting call on Sterling. The three grand objects of Radicalism, according to him, are Free Trade, General Education, & Cheap Law. Aunt C. slept at our house. Sat out the fire & the midnight hour with that bewitching individual.

---

1. Charles MacIntosh (1766–1843) patented his waterproof cloth in 1823.

OCTOBER

2. S. At Falmouth as usual. An interesting walk with Sterling wherein we discussed many topics from the principles of Aesthetics & Art generally to those of the Copper Trade. He contends, & not without plausible reason, that inasmuch as we produce more copper than we consume, the home producer, i.e. the miner, would not be injured by the import of foreign ores, duty free. This is a deduction from the now recognized principle in Political Economy that the price of the surplus produce beyond our consumption regulates the price of the whole.

3. Judging the specimens of Fine Arts all the morning with Sterling, T. Phillpotts, Kinsman, & Cornish at the Polytechnic Hall. The show was decidedly above par. After judging, Sterling drew up a report in his own rapid, vigorous & effective style, not so stringent as last year, but still pointing to a standard which our artists have by no means realised. Capt. Tregaskes's beautiful little instrument for measuring the velocity of the piston at every part of its stroke, was considered by the judges the most ingenious invention in the room & was accordingly rewarded with the first silver medal. A large party of guests at dinner invited from 'the mass', consisting principally of mine-engineers. They are fine intelligent men.

4. Professor Vignoles[1] to breakfast, the celebrated engineer, full of atmospheric Railways. A man of great energy & talent. Adjourned to the Hall at 10. We found, as usual, some grumblers at the award of the judges, as there always must be whilst human nature remains what it is. There was a large party from Carclew. I had the treat of an introduction to Mrs. Strangways, a unique specimen of the female homo, a prodigious rattler, with some brilliance & a brave defiance of conventional ideas; in fact, what ladies designate as 'rather improper'. Sir C. Lemon took the chair at 1 & opened the proceedings by a 'neat' speech, well got up & tolerably delivered. The several reports of the judges were then read. I read Sterling's for he was not equal to it. It was the only report that professed to be composition. The rest were catalogues with remarks. A large party to dinner, Bullers, Treweekes, Carnes, Mary Tremayne, Miss Carew, &c. Everything was conducted quietly & well. I talked philosophy to Isabella, small talk to Georgina, & polemics with Anthony Froude,[2] who is a very intelligent & superior young man. Attended Vignoles's lecture on atmospheric railways in the evening which was highly interesting & practical. The three advantages seem to be cheapness, safety, &

1. Charles Blacker Vignoles (1793–1875), F.R.S., a leading railway engineer and professor of civil engineering at University College, London.
2. James Anthony Froude (1818–74), the historian, brother of Richard Hurrell Froude. He was a Tractarian, but later was to become Carlyle's chief disciple and his literary executor.

a facility for ascending hills. The first comes from the much smaller weight of carriages & rails necessary, the second from the absence of a locomotive engine, & the third from the power being, in every inclination, applied directly & in the direction of the weight. Vignoles is certain that an atmospheric railway might be constructed between here & Exeter at an expense not exceeding £10,000 per mile. The mode of application is by a pipe between the rails, in which there is a horizontal piston, the air being exhausted before it & forced in behind it. The piston is connected with the carriage by a coulter, which opens a slit in the top of the pipe & which is again closed up by a roller, which follows with a preparation of tallow & beeswax. It has been tried in the neighbourhood of London at Wormwood Scrubs for ½ a mile with great success. The Dublin & Kingstown Railway owners are also laying down a few miles of it.

6. Went to the Foundry with the resolve to be industrious but the appearance of Tregellas of Truro dissipated my good resolutions. His Cornish stories of which he gave me a rare specimen are perfect & admirably told. Called at Carclew to see the Trelawnys before they leave. They are a devoted pair. I found a multitude of Bullers, & Mrs. Strangways as extraordinary as ever. Had a glorious evening all to myself.

9. S. A pleasant call on Sterling. Discussed the Copper Trade anomaly of the difference of price at home & abroad. Sterling's explanation is that it is simply the result of the combination of the Copper Companies. Ran out to Penjerrick in the evening to see Uncle G.C. who is invalided. I called on P. Buckett who had something of an epileptic seizure the day before yesterday, the effect, I have no doubt, of long fasts & alcohol. I mean to have a serious talk with him on the subject when he is better able to bear it.

11. Entered my new office, a very snug & genteel looking room. Over Banking accounts all day with the exception of a ride to Stythians to dun one of our debtors. Escorted Aunt C. & Juliet to Ponsanooth to one of C. Parkins's public meetings. A very flat & very noisy opportunity, but a beautiful moonlight walk to & fro made up for it. Heard of Jn. Backhouse's[1] death. He went to bed 2 nights ago as well as usual, but in the night complaining of uneasiness he was lifted out on a chair & expired almost immediately!

13. William arrived at 5 this morning & wisely turned in. He will give me four days, *professedly* spent in wool-gathering. We laid out our time to the best advantage. We rode in to Falmouth, talking over past events & fighting battles over again. Took leave of Uncle A. who starts for town tomorrow, & proceeded with William to Trebah to dinner. We spent a delightful afternoon walking by the riverside with Uncle & Aunt C. admiring the dazzling westward view, over which the sun was setting.

16. Sundry calls at Falmouth. An interesting evening at Perran with William,

1. Jonathan Backhouse, the husband of Hannah Backhouse and father of Jane.

discussing Love, morals & metaphysics. He has certainly 'a kind of thought' in him. He tried hard to impress upon me the duty of falling in love with Jane Backhouse.

19. William left at 5 this morning. He is a rare fellow, staunch, honourable, generous, with a mind of no common order, well read in old books & with a genuine sense of fun. Monthly meeting. The list of overseers proposed by the Committee was read. Aunt L. whose name was down refused to accept office & it was accordingly erased. This caused much female agitation & feeling in the upstairs room.[1] I rejoiced at it as an act of individual consistency versus conformity, for how could she preach scruples to others she does not feel herself.

23. S. Called on P. Buckett & had some serious conversation on his state & its consequences. Whether it be of any use remains to be proved. Called on Sterling who seemed finely. Read Maurice who is decidedly the most, if not the only, philosophical advocate for High Church doctrines. His interpretation & apology for the ordinances are ingenious but do not carry conviction. Today the mail arrived at $\frac{1}{4}$ to 5. $19\frac{3}{4}$ hours from London! It will puzzle the Southampton route to match that.

24. Sterling rode with me to Perran. We discussed Maurice, & rationalism, & Prophecy, & the price of wool. The eagle can fly high or low with equal ease. Read a review of C. Dickens's new work, A Tour in America, which abounds in a fresh genial strain of human-heartedness, unaffected, spirited, & real. It is called 'American notes for general circulation'.

28. Rode on to Falmouth to attend a meeting of long-faces convened to consider how to put an end to Lord Beresford. It was finally resolved to sell her by auction & to call on the shareholders for £12 more per share. Rode back in the evening. I found Aunt C. in great distress about a servant girl called Bant whom she had sent per Auspicious trader, from Portreath to Neath last week, to service at Rebecca Gibbins's, & there is now reason to believe that the vessel has foundered & that all on board are lost.

29. After breakfast rode with Uncle C. to Tresavean to see the first trial of the raising & lowering machine. There was a large attendance & 100 real miners & about $\frac{1}{2}$ a dozen dilettante ones descended to their entire satisfaction & that of the surrounding multitude. Mrs. Strangways' appearance produced many sly grins amongst the miners, who, I'll be bound, never beheld such a high-life oddity before. The machine itself looked a mysterious combination of wheels & rods for the purpose of illustrating to the meanest apprehension the poem we learnt in early life,

> Here we go up, up, up,
> And here we go down, down, down.

1. The women met separately upstairs.

30. S. Had a long talk with Sterling on Neology, &c. The modern school of German thinkers maintain that the Book of Genesis is nothing more than an antique theological theory to account for the existence of evil; & that the prophecies were either descriptions of existing states of things, or the probable future state, which men who reasoned from past experience & cause & effect would be able to predict. Maurice, I observe, hardly touches the subject of Scriptural Inspiration, & yet thereon all forms of Judaic & Christian religion must rest.

NOVEMBER

1. An invasion from Carclew consisting of two Miss Lemons, Sophy Strangways & her daughter Fossey, & Philly Dyke. I took them over the Cottage garden with which they were charmed. S.S. is quite unique, all rattle & 'bustle', but still what's commonly called 'an excellent creature in her way', which to be sure is rather unlike other people's ways. Her daughter is a beautiful child & showed a strong partiality for me. I thought I saw indications of superior sense & taste *before*. C. & I spent a tolerably cozy evening.
2. Occupied the evening to some profit by reading the first hundred pages of Dickens's admirable new work, *American Notes*. There is a freshness, & spirit, & human sympathy in the book which make it most pleasant food. His art, or a considerable part of it, is sketching inanimate objects as if they were living things, humanizing steamboats, & stage coaches, & old houses, & the like, which makes the impression they leave on you vastly more vivid.
4. Sterling joined me at dinner. He is very full of a projected periodical to supply the moral & intellectual wants of the 19th century. He has corresponded with Carlyle & endeavoured to fire my imagination on the subject. In such hands as Carlyle's & Sterling's it might indeed be a formidable engine either for good or for ill. For true it is that the printer's workshop is the real pulpit of the present day. Walked to Penjerrick in the evening & slept at home.
8. Attended Hunt's opening lecture of the course at the Polytechnic Hall, the subject Galvanism, which he treated elementarily. Hunt closed the lecture with a description of perhaps the most extraordinary discovery of this extraordinary age, viz. that polished metal or glass is capable of receiving & retaining the impression of almost any body simply placed near it or on it, & that in perfect darkness. It was first announced by Mosser, a German professor, who considers the agency to be *latent light* absorbed by bodies in the day & given out in the night. Hunt by his researches considers that he has proved this agency to be *heat* & not light. He has succeeded in taking im-

pressions not only from metals, but from engraving on paper, almost as distinctly as Daguerro-type. After contact & a gentle *heat* the plate is exposed to the vapour of mercury which renders the picture permanent. It shows how dangerous it is to be with people promiscuously in the dark where impressions are so easily conveyed.

9. Busy day at Falmouth. News of a large catch of pilchards at Newquay, a glorious Godsend for the poor in the neighbourhood, & a plentiful occupation for us at the shop, circulating the news at home & abroad. Samuel Tuke, the prince regent amongst 'us as a body', came to Falmouth on his way from Penzance where he has deposited two daughters. I was favoured to meet him at the Bank at dinner. He gives a lamentable account of the state of the manufacturing districts. The Society in Yorkshire has raised a subscription of £800 towards a supply for relieving the wants of the most necessitous. He left for Perran in the afternoon.

10. Sterling lent me a tract by Emerson taken from the *Dial* called 'Man the Reformer'. It is a work well calculated to arouse the slumbering manhood of this effeminate & artificial age. It reads like the sound of a trumpet!

17. Was roused from slumber between 6 & 7 & beheld James Carnall as white as a sheet standing by my bedside. He solemnly announced that a terrible accident had happened in the night. I expected to hear that at least half the Foundry men were killed, & was not a little relieved to find it was a breakage of the bob of the Tresavean engine consequent on the snapping off of the gudgeon. Nobody was injured. I breakfasted & rode at once to the mine. The interior of the Engine House presented a strange complexity of ruin. The great springbeam, 16 or 18 inches square, was snapped off like a carrot & the huge end of the bob was resting on the top of the cylinder. On ascending to the top storey I found the breakage on a more magnificent scale, massive plates of excellent iron, $2\frac{3}{4}$ inches in thickness, broken & hanging, & the huge gudgeon 16 inches in diameter, broken clean off close to the shoulder & its box thrown against the wall. No fault could be found with the casting or the quality of the iron which was very satisfactory. For us at the Foundry it was 'like a sick king to a Court Doctor'. We immediately set about casting a new bob & making a wrought-iron gudgeon 12 inches in diameter. The Engineers were with us nearly the whole day.

19. At $\frac{1}{2}$ past 8 one half of the beam was cast. It was a grand sight reminding one of Milton's 'burning Marl', whilst Richard Cloke's vociferations to his grimy Imps added not a little to the Infernal Character of the scene. Two of the Allens tramped out from Falmouth to see it & arrived $\frac{1}{4}$ of an hour after it was over. We breakfasted together at the Clergy's, they not thinking it *quite* prudent to eat & drink alone with a bachelor. Busy at the Cottage, making preparations for settlement, plastering, painting, putteying & mending. I hope to get in there by the middle of next week.

23. The population of Falmouth was thrown into great consternation by the escape of a mad Spanish bull which on being landed on the quay was driven furious by fright or improper slinging. He very soon had the entire control of the quay, then of Quay Hill, & then of Back lane, where he was finally captured with a lasso, having effected general dismay but no injury of importance. Attended the first of Sterling's reading evenings at the Library. About a dozen of us assembled & read Wordsworth's Excursion in turn, Sterling commenting thereon & pausing at the end in solemn silence as if it had been the Bible.

24. Settled in at the Cottage with great comfort & satisfaction as soon as Kitty & Ann Taw were cleared off. I have 3 rooms civilized & habitable & the rest in course of becoming so, a brand new patent kitchen stove which performs all the requisite offices admirably & a temporary servant, a respectable widow, who perform equally well considering their respective advantages. My establishment now consists of the aforesaid Mary, William Fouracres & his daughter Mary Jane. I have specified their respective duties to each & have gone through the alarming catalogue of 'stores' manfully. I read[1] to them in the evening & feel some small shade of increased importance from my new position.

25. All going well in my house, each settling down in his or her respective place & understanding it. The masons & carpenters are still working on my outside. They are the most tenacious class of people in the community.

30. Trudged in to breakfast & packed off a cartload of furniture for Perran. Attended the 2nd of Sterling's Wordsworth's readings in the evening.

DECEMBER

2. Plenty of work. An old woman bitterly complained to me that she had been bewitched by another old woman, Philly Hicks, whom she attacked yesterday for the innocent purpose of drawing blood which it seems would break the spell. She says ever since she set her eye on her she has felt a strange crawling all over her body.

4. Paid Sterling an interesting call. We talked over modern literature, *Signs of the Times*, Puseyism & its antidote Carlylism, the necessity of not prostituting one's being by giving it up to the acquisition of wealth or any other thing 'that is of the earth earthy', but rather to find out the highest work of which we are capable & to do it. I pointed out what seemed to me the weak point in Carlyle's philosophy, viz., directing man to himself for assistance

1. Bible reading and family prayers.

rather than a power above him. He contended that reverence being the very soul of this philosophy it did not refer man to himself, but to that Power within him, called by some the Spirit, by others the Divine Idea, the Divine Reason, &c.

12. Sterling & Hunt suddenly appeared at the Counting House this morning, the latter having received an express from Sir C. Lemon that in consequence of the sudden death of Caroline Tremayne, he should not be able to lecture tomorrow. I was silly enough to consent to supply his place & off I set to Perran & worked at it pretty steadily till 9, when a messenger from Falmouth came with a note from my mother entreating that I would not attempt it; the united disappointment of missing me at the Monthly at Truro & at my Cottage in the evening, being more than she could stand. I accordingly wrote her that I was committed & was well advanced with my work, but I left it to her to find a substitute or make any arrangements she chose.

13. Up at 5 & working till 9, when the parents & sisters appeared at Perran & informed me they had arranged for Patey to lecture this evening, & so took me on to Monthly at Truro instead. Some very pointed things were said to those who were halting between Christ & the world. All our family party honoured me with their company to tea & to lodge. My books being now deposited in their new shelves give the library a very habitable appearance.

25. S. Paid my hebdomadal visit to Sterling who was enjoying the joke of the will of his Uncle which demised £70,000 out of £80,000 to charities in Bordeaux, instead of his mother-in-law Barton & her relations.

26. To Penjerrick to dine with my people as usual on roast beef & plum pudding. Settled accounts which were satisfactory, & had the further gratification of seeing Mary Ann at the Cottage & dining with her new Ma. Got home in time to join the Christmas revels taking place at our house. We had 28 at tea of 6 years old & upwards, from little Minny up to Sterling. The evening went off most brilliantly, & the fund of enjoyment so easily given to so many little hearts, was not the least enjoyable part of it. First the venerable effigies of Father Christmas with scarlet coat & cocked hat, stuck all over with presents for the guests, by his side the old year, a most dismal & haggard old beldame in a night cap & spectacles, then 1843, a promising baby fast asleep in a cradle. Then we had a 'galvanic shock', which was played on Juliet Sterling & myself, blinding us & dressing up our hands & arms into the exact imitation of baby's by the aid of a little paint & flannel, to the no small consternation & surprise of the patient on removing the bandage. Then with the aid of a good mask, nightcap, kneebreeches, pillow, & coat & waistcoat of my father's, I was enabled to make a very passable elderly Friend & bestow some wholesome advice on the children & on Sterling who was vastly entertained. We then had lots of tableaux vivants which were very good,

then supper, then fireworks, then everything else, & we separated in high good humour with ourselves & our company.

28. Dinner at Grove Hill, where Edwin Price nearly blew the house up in manufacturing a volcano, the only death, however, was that of a canary, tho' we were all well smoked. Wordsworth evening at Sterling's. We had some discussion afterwards about Wordsworth's tendency to reverence the past above the present. Sterling compared Wordsworth & Shelley, one the poet of the past, the other of the future. Received an invitation from Jas. Bell to accompany him & his sister Eliza to Rome. Not a little tantalising.

1843

BARCLAY SETS out on a three months' tour to Italy. His journey begins with the overland route through France to Marseilles, where he takes a ship to Leghorn and then Rome. Here he is joined by James and Eliza Bell and together they journey to Naples. After a stay at Naples they return to Rome & then travel northwards to Assisi and Florence. Barclay takes leave of the Bells and visits Venice, and from there he begins his homeward journey through Milan. He crosses the Alps by diligence and makes his way to Zurich and Basle. Here he catches the Rhine steamer on the last stage of his journey home. He arrives in London just in time to join a deputation to the Prime Minister to save Falmouth as a packet port. While in London he also meets Jane Backhouse and we learn that thoughts of a match between Jane and Barclay have been entertained by both Barclay and his family. On settling back into life at Falmouth he finds the leading townspeople exercised with plans for a Cornish railway. A railway line to Falmouth would bring not only greater prosperity but a chance to retain the packet boats there. During the remainder of the year he visits Norwich, where he sees Jane Backhouse again, and London where he meets the Carlyles and John Stuart Mill. While in Italy Barclay has news of the death of Sterling's wife, Susan. Sterling had moved from Falmouth on his wife's death, but Barclay meets him at his new home in the Isle of Wight and in London.

JANUARY

1. S. Rode in to Falmouth & found Sterling alarmingly ill, having had a violent attack of haemoptysis yesterday for which Bullmore bled him. His wife looked haggard & half dead with fatigue & anxiety. He is in bed & not allowed to speak. What a fact in our small world would be the departure of such a Being!
8. S. Called on Sterling, whose rapid recovery has astonished his doctor. He is today up & dressed & reclining in his study.
12. Busy at Falmouth till 12. Trudged out to Perran to dinner. At the Foundry all the afternoon with Uncle C. & the two Harveys,[1] arranging

1. The Harveys owned the foundry at Hayle, which along with the Perran Foundry, was one of the most important foundries in Britain. In 1840 a group of Dutchmen visited Cornwall with a view to ordering an engine for draining Haarlem Lake. They

about the contracts for the Dutch engine & pump-work, amounting with extras to about £12,000. N. Harvey is to start for Holland the beginning of next week & is very anxious that I should accompany him.

13. A most terrific storm last night which continued with more or less violence thro' the day. Some of the finest trees in Perran were blown down. I fear we shall hear of many wrecks after it.

15. S. Rode in to Meeting. Sterling has a sort of relapse, pain in the chest, weakness, &c., but no haemorrhage. Stayed in the house all the afternoon in consequence of a troublesome cold.

18. Monthly Meeting. Benjamin Seebohm present, a German Friend visiting families in this County & Devon. Called on Sterling who is very much pulled down by that vile poison he has been taking (acet. lead) for healing the ruptured vessel. Rode back to Perran to lodge.

19. Busy day. Wrote William to ask about the truth of a rumour about Jane Backhouse's being engaged to Henry Pease. *I* don't believe it. C. joined me in the evening.

23. A memorable day, which if it leaves no profitable effects the fault will be my own. After a bustling morning & a rainy ride I went to the other house to have my 'opportunity' with B. Seebohm, it being too wet to ask him to the Cottage. We sat in the library & he soon began the most striking & impressive address I ever listened to. He told me that the first time he saw me, walking up to the Meeting House a few days since without the slightest knowledge of me, he was filled with a deep interest & gospel solicitude for me beyond the power of all words. He enlarged profoundly & eloquently on the text, Trust in the Lord, &c., & lean not to thine own understanding. He held out to me a prospect of fiery trials beyond anything I do now conceive, but on the other hand, a place of eminent usefulness in case of faithfulness. His earnest & impressive manner reminded me of Goethe's 'And thy *striving*, be it with *loving*'. So affectionate, & fervent, & highly gifted a minister I never had the privilege of meeting before.

27. My father & I busy transplanting shrubs after breakfast. M. Williams called at 1 & we had a pretty close 3 hours of it together over accounts. Uncle C. spoke to him about my going to Italy, in which he fully concurred, but strongly urged that all the *mixed* accounts should be posted under their

---

placed an order for this engine with the Harveys, but the above makes it clear that some of the work was done at Perran. John Rowe, *Cornwall in the Age of the Industrial Revolution*, 1953, describes the engine as follows: 'An immense 144 in. cylinder was cast in July, 1843; the area of the piston was 16,286 square inches; the achievement of the Harveys in melting over 25 tons of iron for this work in less than six months amazed the country at the time. Less than a year later this great engine, then by far the largest in the world, was delivered at Amsterdam, and by October, 1845, part of the lake had been drained.'

proper heads *first*, which is all right & reasonable. The Perran party joined us at tea.

28. My family left me after breakfast. I had a talk with Uncle C. on some of the subjects opened yesterday. I think I can get away early in the week after next. Called at Carclew & saw the remains of last night's ball in the persons of half a dozen tired-out ladies & a sprinkling of young gentlemen playing at billiards. Rode to Falmouth. Called at Sterling's. His state I fear is very precarious indeed. Almost every thing disagrees with his stomach. It is grievously impaired, I should fear, by the lead, & the consequence is that they cannot build him up. Poor fellow! His wife is near her confinement, his governess gone yesterday with a hip complaint, & himself trembling almost on the balance of death and life. What an event to his family & friends would the former be! It is fearful to think of.

29. Sterling has passed another sleepless night. I found his wife tired, anxious & miserable & I could do little to comfort her. I spent the evening at Grove Hill, receiving counsel & information respecting Italy &, what was more to the purpose, sundry guide books & catalogues.

30. Called at Sterling's. The servant described him as having almost 'passed' at 5 o'clock this morning, since which, however, he had revived & ate his gruel with an appetite. Breakfasted with Uncle C. & proceeded in the Bus to a meeting of timber merchants at Truro.

FEBRUARY

1. Sterling, I trust, has turned the corner. He is gaining strength rapidly & eats freely; his tipple is brandy & water. The doctors are in high spirits. The effects of the lead now seem to be passing away, but it had very nearly done for him. It is perilous work to play with mineral medicines. Talked to my father about becoming a partner in the Falmouth House before going abroad, which on many accounts seems desirable. The whole family came out to Perran to stay (not at my house) till the end of the week.

4. Snow on the ground. Last night's storm prostrated one of my largest firs & uprooted another. A busy day, closing worldly affairs. Sold my horse. T.T.L.[1] visit at Uncle A.'s & spent a long evening at Grove Hill to listen to Uncle G.C.'s long lecture on Rome. He has been very kind, giving me 2 sheets of memoranda & 5 letters of introduction to Italian gentry.

5. S. Sterling continues to go on so well that Boase has taken his leave. Paid sundry calls & received much instructive information from Uncle C. whose

1. To take leave.

guide books & catalogues I shall find very useful. What a famous thing it *will* be when I'm fairly off!

6. Accomplished much today in the way of squaring off, amongst other occupations. Ran out to Penjerrick & left final instructions with T. Evans. Took leave of the Tregedna party. All the firm having consented to it, I was today installed partner in the House of G. C. & R. W. Fox & Co. & signed letters accordingly. Took letters of introduction & credit to Genoa, Naples & Venice. Returned to Perran in the evening.

7. After a busy day at Perran attended Wightwick's brilliant & poetical lecture on Shakespeare. It was not a critique but an out-pouring of enthusiastic love. His recitation of the first scene in *Hamlet* was splendidly effective. When he sank his voice to a whisper at the appearance of the Ghost, the audience held their breath & you might have heard a pin drop. Hicks from Bodmin was there & joined us at tea, where I met Sir Ed. Belcher[1] who is here in the *Samarang*, Sloop of War, on his way to China on a surveying voyage. His object in touching at Falmouth is one of my father's instruments, which he is busily learning. Paid a very interesting call on Sterling who wished to see me before I left. He did not look so ill as I expected. He describes what he has passed through as the extreme of physical prostration & misery, but he has not been disturbed, he says, in the least by doubts, or fears, or wavering convictions. Tho' weak & languid at first, he warmed with his subject (Italy) till he forgot his illness & dictated & wrote notes for my guidance there.

8. Went to Perran to breakfast. Finished all business arrangements. Took leave of the Perran party who have been all along the concentrated essence of kindness & returned to Falmouth per bus to finish off T.T.L. calls, &c., as I start tomorrow morning.

9. I started on my long-talked-of, & longer-thought-of, tour at 8 this morning per London mail. My only companion was a pleasing-looking & very intelligent lady, of about 25 I should think, a Miss Broadley, singularly open & artless & with an enthusiastic love of poetry. Consequently we became great allies before we reached Exeter. Wightwick joined us at Perran & was the exciting cause of a continual flow of high spirits & great good humour with ourselves & each other till he left us at Bodmin. Bodmin Moor & the country between that & Exeter was partially snow-clad, the rest was mud. Sufficient time was allowed at Exeter[2] to lay in sufficient food for the rest of the journey & I proceeded to Town without any occurrence worth journalising. The night-air was very sharp & my railway companions were emphatically dull, which was however a relief after incessant chattering all the day.

1. Sir Edmund Belcher (1799–1877), admiral, commander of various survey voyages. In 1852 he commanded the expedition to the Arctic in search of Sir John Franklin.
2. From here the journey was now made by railway.

10. Emerged from the great movement at 5 in the morning, charmed to a due pitch of patriotism with the advantages of steam conveyance. A railway train is a dusky piece of utilitarianism to look at & yet it is not without poetry, particularly when in motion. What a little epitome of the world it contains within its First, Second and Third class carriages, each individual manifesting in his own way the supreme selfishness of human nature. Then look at the magician in front, a grimy potentate in fustian & corduroys called by men the Engineer. He has harnessed to his car a mighty & unseen Strength & drives him on with his ponderous load behind him at the rate of 30 miles an hour. You hear his giant breath as he rushes through the murk. You have no thought of fear, although given up, life & limb, to this terrific guidance, & more helpless than an infant; & dream not of thanking Heaven for your preservation when you return to men after a weird ride of 200 miles through the darkness.

A good wash & hot breakfast at St. Paul's Coffee House proved admirable restoratives & by the time I had paid about 30 calls in & out of the city, got passport, notes, letters of credit &c., I felt as if my day's work was done. I called on E. Sterling who, of course, was exceedingly interested in hearing the last intelligence of his son.

11. Finding a Steamer bound to Boulogne at 7 this morning I thought it would be too good an opportunity to miss & embarked on the *Magnet* accordingly, a name given it perhaps in reference to the *repulsive* property of that instrument, as it has the character of the worst boat on the Station. The accommodations however were not at all to be complained of. The weather was very fine & we ran between the long outstretched piers of Boulogne, which extend like hospitable arms to welcome the voyager, & after a little gentle expostulation with the Custom House officer on the barbarity of condemning me to dirty linen tomorrow morning, I made the best of circumstances & landed with the other passengers, carrying all my effects except the portmanteau, which no entreaty can rescue from official durance before the morning. The examination at the Custom House was a mere matter of form & I very quickly found myself in thoroughly comfortable quarters in the *Hotel Bedford*, dispatched a couple of letters & took a lamplight survey of the town.

12. S. Rescued my portmanteau before breakfast. The porters are all women with baskets strapped over their shoulders into which they toss a trunk & run off with it as if it were only a 'Sensible Species' & not ponderable matter. After breakfast I sallied forth to the Malle Poste office, then to the Diligence Bureau to make sure of one mode or the other. The quay was crowded with most uncomely fishwomen & piles of skates smelling particularly untempting. 3 or 4 little targets were erected in the street at which boys were firing with small cross bows for nuts, surrounded by crowds of Frenchmen who

appeared to take a deep personal interest in the operation. Mine host, an English (gentleman I was going to say) of the name of Lowe is a very hearty pleasant fellow: he joined me for an hour last evening & displayed a true John Bull feeling against the French who, he says, at the present moment can hardly endure the English, yet dare not molest them in any way. Spent the morning quietly alone, dined at 2 & started by the diligence at 4 for Paris. I tried in vain to get a place by the Malle Poste which reaches Paris in 18 hours. These lumbering diligences take 24 &, in the present state of the road, 2 or 3 hours longer. My companions in the interior were a perfectly silent Englishman who looked bilious, another very different, being clever & satirical, a grizzly whiskered Frenchman in a nightcap, a vulgar likeness of Sterling, an old French gentleman, a great wag in his way but with a very indifferent voice which seemed to find its way through chaff or dry hay, and a young French lady from London le Vest End, she told me, from which I conclude she is a governess returning to her parents. The road from Boulogne to Paris is uninteresting. The night was clear & cold, the snow lay upon the face of the earth, & the roads were crisp & vitreous. Each made himself comfortable in his own way as he best could '& thus the night went by'.

13. We did not reach Paris till nearly 8, having been 28 hours on the road with only 2 stoppages for meals. The relays are so quick & the doors of the diligence so tight that by the time one is fairly out to stretch one's legs at the Inn door one must bundle in again. We breakfasted at Beauvais at 11. From thence to Paris the road is better & the country more picturesque. We did not change company in the Interieur. I passed the time in reading *Corinne* which gives a good deal of information about Italy & a good deal of the character of the authoress (Madame de Stael). The French houses strike an English eye from their size & height & thinness of the walls like cardboard houses, built generally either of brick & wood, or lath & plaster, very combustible articles to look at. I was not sorry to avail myself of the comforts of the *Bedford Hotel*, consisting of a good fire & excellent coffee.

14. Well, a month since I did not count on being in this place at this time! What a beautiful city this Paris is! What taste in the arrangement of the shop windows! What grandeur in the places & public buildings. The view from the front of the Tuilleries is truly regal. The majestic avenue is crowded with the fashion & beauty of Paris. The peculiar magnificence of the French has always something theatrical in it. Without the modesty of the Greek or the utilitarianism of the English, French architecture seems to me to be always aiming at *Effect*. The idea which lies beneath it seems to be ever *La grande nation*. In the Louvre I was most grievously disappointed. The principal galleries both of painting & sculpture are closed on account of some alterations which are in progress. Dined at Vevey's, called on Rothschild & arranged about a credit, called at the Post & found a letter from home &

another from James Bell who is now at Arles & wishes me to overtake them there.

15. A little before 7 I started by the Malle Poste for Avignon, nominally a journey of 50 hours. My companions were a young Irishman of birth & fashion on his way to Rome & a quiet but gentlemanly Frenchman who gave me much information on the way. The holding of the land in France begins only from year to year & this accounts for the vast tracts of un-cultivated & half-farmed land over which we passed. The agriculture also is very backward & the implements very clumsy. I saw 4 large horses & 4 oxen drawing a single plough. We had some snow on the way but the night was not particularly cold.

16. The barbarous administration of the Poste-department allows no stop-page of the coach for the sustenance of its passengers till it reaches Moulins, a journey of 25 hours. While the horses were changing, however, I effected a seizure on a partridge, 2 loaves of bread & a bottle of wine which kept me from starvation. At Moulins we dined at 8 in the evening & parted with our French companion. His room was particularly acceptable on the 2nd night. Both he & Atkinson (my other companion) sport beards & moustaches. No man of any pretensions to fashion can do without one or both of these in-dispensables at Paris. Much nicety is shown in the variety of cut which depends on the taste of the cultivator.

17. Reached St. Etienne to breakfast at 11 a.m. where our coach was changed for a light calèche, very snug for two. Eight horses were harnessed thereto & away we went in great style. The whole of the first & half the second stage is up hill, winding along the side of a mountain chain with a deep gorge beneath us & mountains dappled with snow & beautifully clad with forests of dark spruce on our right. By degrees we reached the top of the mountain, the horses walking nearly all the way. Our road led us through the wood which, with the glittering snow between the dark foliage, was highly picturesque. Even my companion's English phlegm was changed into enthusiasm. We passed through Valence in the night, where Pius 6 died after being so unceremoniously transplanted by Napoleon. We crossed the Rhone by a suspension bridge hung on ropes.

18. We reached Avignon at 8, after a ride of 2 days & 3 nights without intermission. I was not at all tired but truly glad of the luxuries of a bath, clean linen & breakfast, after which I sallied forth with the commissionaire to see the famous old palace of the popes, now turned into barracks & capable of holding 4500 troops. In the pope's chapel are some frescoes of Giotto. In the remains of an ancient church I saw the most beautiful carving in ivory I ever beheld. Everybody who goes to Avignon considers it a duty to see it. It is an Image of Christ on the cross, the figure about 3 feet high, the cross of ebony. A nun of the order of the penitents held it, with her eyes cast on the

ground with an expression of reverential love; she reminded me of Mary Magdalene who remained by the cross when all the disciples had left it. A good table d'hote at 5 at which only 7 of us sat down. At 9 bed was really acceptable.

19. S. My only quest in the town today was a pilgrimage to the tombs, first to that of Laura with whose name & that of Petrarch, Avignon must ever be associated. The tomb stands in the garden of an orphan-institution. An Englishman has erected a small monument with a Latin inscription on the site of Laura's tomb & planted cypresses around it. From thence I went to the Cymetry which lies without the walls in search of Robert Fowler's tomb. Twice I made the tour of the cymetry reading every inscription, but without success, & returned tired & disappointed. My landlady at the *Hotel d'Europe* told me much about his illness. She nursed him & was deeply interested about him. Not liking to be foiled I took a car (it being 2 miles off) & the commissionaire who saw him buried, & returned to the cymetry. He could not find it, however, & I should have gone away again unsuccessful but for the Sexton who came to our aid, & knowing the spot, removed a large wooden cross which had fallen down before it. I gave something to the man to remove the weeds & keep it in order & returned to mine Inn. Joined the table d'hote party at 4 o'clock & started by the Marseilles diligence at 6.

20. My companion in the diligence was an uninteresting Frenchman on his way to Algiers. A very slow coach & very heavy rain all night. Daylight opened on another climate. From the sterile champaign about Avignon we were transported into a region of vineyards & olive-yards, orchards of almond & groves of cypress. Limestone mountains crowned with fir, rose on each side of the road, the air was soft as May, notwithstanding the rain continued incessantly. We reached Marseilles at 8 in the morning & there lay the blue Mediterranean in very deed. Deposited myself at the *Hôtel d'Orient*, a sort of palace, the salon about 100 feet long, & everything first-rate. After breakfast I sallied forth to see whatever is worth notice at Marseilles, which is not much. The port itself is the most striking sight. It is an immense dock capable of containing 1500–2000 ships, crowded with a forest of masts from all parts of the world. The town, large as it is, seems destitute of any but commercial interest. Engaged a berth for Genoa in the Italian Steamer *Herculaneum*.

21. The morning was beautiful. I embarked for Italy between 7 & 8 with a beating heart & glorious expectations. At the *Hôtel d'Orient* you must pay for splendour, as indeed everywhere else. They charge 5 francs for a bed! The coast is very mountainous. The clearness of the air of which I heard so much gives a peculiar distinctness (almost telescopic) to distant objects. The rock of Marseilles stretches far into the sea & has 2 quarantine ports in its creeks. We passed Toulon in the middle of the day where part of the French navy

was distinctly visible. There were 35 passengers on board, but the ladies were lost 10 minutes after we got out of port. The others consisted of English, French, Americans & Italians, & all 3 languages might be heard at table at the same time. The breakfast, so called, which was served at ½ past 10, did not descend to the vulgar beverage of tea & coffee but 8 or 10 bottles of wine were placed on the table instead. Read & chatted & lounged till bed-time came, for *bed* is the name which they humourously give to the coffin prepared for you at night, into which you insinuate yourself by a tortuous stratagem, & fancy at first that you can *cover* yourself with the sheet & blanket by bringing them up to the chin & lying particularly straight. But it soon becomes evident that you must submit to partial exposure & it behoves a wise man quickly to resolve which part he values least & sacrifice it to the good of the rest.

22. Woke & found ourselves in the Bay of Genoa & at anchor in the port by the time we came on deck. It rained a flood, but *n'importe*, there it really was with its long grinning fort, its red & yellow towers with bell-shaped roofs. From this quay perhaps where we now land amongst shouting, swearing, hustling raggamuffins, embarked Columbus full of his great idea. Before landing we had to be counted, & after landing, to be inspected by the police, & were then allowed to proceed to our Hotel to breakfast. This being accomplished I took a Valet de Place & sallied forth. I first called on the De la Rue Brothers who were very civil & friendly. They speak of the roads as impassable, 3 mails being due from England! Enquired at the Post Office & found my letter to James Bell still waiting his arrival. It is clear it won't do to wait for him therefore. I saw 4 palaces & the Eglise de St. François before dinner. Table d'Hote at 4 was very good. I am located in the 5th Etage, 111 stairs from the ground, & a falling body from my bedroom window takes 8 seconds to reach the pavement. What strikes an Englishman in Genoa is the enormous disproportion between the classes, the lavish abundance of the aristocracy & the squalid beggary of the poor. They are remnants of the old oligarchical government when both power & wealth were monopolised by the nobles, & since the deposition of the last doge by Buonaparte, time has not permitted the formation of a middle class.

23. I contrived to see the ancient ducal palace now turned into a government-house containing the various city-administrations, the Church of St. Angelo & the Cathedral, a very singular edifice of black & white marble. A letter from home came like a gush of water in the desert. I answered it & wrote Jas. Bell that he would find me at Rome & re-embarked on the *Herculaneum* at 6.

24. Much swell all night. We woke & found ourselves at Leghorn. It was raining streams & the absurd police-formalities delayed our landing till 9 o'clock, & as the steamer was to start at 4 for Civita Vecchia, not much time

was allowed for an excursion to Pisa. A young Frenchman & I determined to attempt it, snapped up a sort of breakfast on board, landed by the first boat, ran to the piazza & agreed with one of the rascally raggamuffin hack coach drivers to take us there in an hour & a half, promising 12 francs if he accomplished the journey both ways within the time & 10 if he exceeded it. We reached Pisa before 11. The road between was fertile but uninteresting, except for the bold outline of the Appenines in the distance. Pisa itself looks like a city of the Dead, the Arno so beautiful in idea is very muddy in reality. The streets appeared to be deserted but shops were not. It has a melancholy grandeur, an appearance of fallen greatness & a stillness which seemed profaned by the rattling of our fiacre over the stones. We drove straight to the Piazza, & what a wondrous sight we beheld therein. We entered first the Duomo, or cathedral, dedicated to Saint Ranieri the patron Saint of Pisa, & my companion prostrated himself before the marble sarcophagus which contains his ashes. I felt, I confess, more reverence for the remains of Pisano & Andrea del Sarto which this church contains in the shape of some of their choicest works. We next entered the Campo Santo & felt as tho' we were treading on hallowed ground. For not only is the soil for 6 feet deep, that of the Holy Land, but this spot exhibits perhaps more than any other the relation between Religion & Art & shews the gradual reawakening of the latter, or rather its *resuscitation* from the darkness & death of the Middle Ages. We spent an hour in this most interesting place which deserves a week of diligent and reverential study. We next ascended the beautiful campanile which was built in 1174. From the top of the campanile is a fine view of Pisa, the Arno, the Appenines with La Chartreuse. We got back to Leghorn about 3, after a well-filled 2-hours' visit to Pisa. Our fellow-passengers, particularly 2 Americans, were much annoyed that we should have accomplished it & not they. At ½ past 4 we left Leghorn with beautiful weather.

25. Woke at Civita Vecchia. The Custom House was not stringent but very troublesome, with no end of paying. Got off at last in an extra diligence with 3 miserable horses – for Rome! Myrtles grew in abundance by the roadside, but on leaving the shores of the Mediterranean the road became abominably bad & the country uninteresting, till the vantage ground of a hill enabled us to see the blue dome of St. Peter's & the far-extended walls catching the western sun. To what fine sentiments the sight would have given birth within me I know not, but they were all quashed by one of my American companions exclaiming to the other, 'Morris, I'll swear it looks like a New England settlement'. We reached the Porta St. Pancrazio at ½ past 7, rattled through the streets by lamplight & came all at once on a mighty Colonnade which proved to be St. Peter's, almost as soon as we entered the city. I had no expectation of such a sight & was almost struck dumb. But away we whisked in another direction, a bridge, then '*This* is the Tiber', 'Yes, &

there's the Castle of Saint Angelo'. My brain was all in a whirl & I couldn't get anything like a definite thought or a distinct feeling till I was favoured with a sense of virtuous indignation at being voided out of the diligence & obliged to submit to a second inspection of my baggage at the Douane, then pay, lock up, get a porter, hurry scurry, go to *Hôtel Îles Britanniques*, no place; *l'Europe*, no room; finally *Grande Bretagne*, one room left, charge 10 pauls a night on account of the Carnival. Well, anything for a quiet life, only before anything else, get me some dinner, for I am almost ravenous.

26. S. Well, I'm in Rome & I know it's raining a stream, & I can do nothing today. However at 11 I managed to get to the English chapel which is nothing more than a large upper room. Heard there an admirable sermon from a Mr. Murray. It was a sermon well calculated to confirm one's good resolutions on coming to this world of fascinations & temptations. Called on Garofalini in the afternoon with Uncle G.C.'s letter of introduction & found him very civil & agreeable. Walked on the Pincian Hill but it was too murky to see anything. I sent to engage Dominico, Uncle G.'s late Valet de Place.

27. I realised the fact of being in Rome at 7 this morning, at which hour I was on the top of the Pincian Hill which rises immediately behind the hotel. The morning was lovely & St. Peter's was bathed in golden light, a light cloud girdled his dome & behind stretched the long outline of the Vatican. On the other side were fertile fields, vineyards, groves, fountains, villas & close beneath me the remains of an old Roman wall. St. Peter's front, the piazza & façade, disappointed me at first sight, but on reaching it I found the illusion arose from the admirable proportions of each part which diminished the apparent greatness of the whole. It is only by standing close to the columns that one is aware of their vastness, & by looking across the piazza, not at the Cathedral, but at the people ascending the steps that one becomes aware of its vast extent. Lifting 2 ponderous curtains I found myself beneath its gilded roof & on its marble floor. My first definite impression was that with all its magnificence it was not a cathedral. You miss the solemnity of the Gothic aisle, you miss its pointed arch which seem like hands that meet in prayer, you find not the mystery of half lights & long shadows. All has too much the effect of a palace. On returning, my way led through the Corso where the Carnival was in full madness. Perfect 'abandon' was the order of the day. In spite of rain in streams the Corso was filled with carriages & these with every variety of costumes. Devils, duchesses & harlequins paraded the street under umbrellas. The windows & balconies were alive with the fashion & the beauty of Rome. At 5 the carriages were turned out of the Corso. The mounted police with naked sabres galloped up & down the street, guards were stationed at all the corners, the centre of the street was entirely cleared & the population of Rome seemed placed under martial law. A drum was heard & half a dozen fiery coursers were led into the 'piazza del popolo',

decked with small flags & ribbons, to which minute spurs were attached, & at the sound of a gun all were let loose; the spurs, the shouts, the fright drove them madly along the Corso. They passed me like a whirlwind. At the other end of the Corso, about a mile distant is a thread painted red & the first horse to break this receives a mark on his chest which distinguishes him as the winner. Called in the morning on Monsignor Medici Spada[1] with Uncle G.'s letter of introduction. He was overflowing in his professions & gave me orders for several sights.

28. My brain aches with the multitude of interest presented to it today. The list is as follows – Trajan's Column & Forum, the Campidoglio, then the colossal statues, then the Tarpeian rock; Aracoeli once the temple of Jupiter Feretrius, then Guiseppe with its miraculous crucifix & its prisons (perhaps the most ancient relic of Rome) containing the post to which St. Peter was chained, the arch of Septimus Severus; the columns of the temple of Jupiter Stator, the temple of Peace, the Forum (20 to 30 feet below the present level of Rome), the temple of Antony & Faustina, the arches of Titus & of Constantine, & the Colosseum; then further off St. John Lateran with its superb Pietà by Bernini[2] in a subterranean chapel. Dominico was my guide, Mesdames Starke[3] & Stael my instructors. The afternoon & evening was devoted to the magnificent fooling of the Carnival. Being the last day it was at its wildest pitch of excitement, amidst all, however, I saw no blackguardism, no drunkenness, no quarrelling. All was abandon & revelry. Garofalini's kindness procured me an excellent place in a balcony on the Corso at the house of Signr. Cecci, a Banker. Sham sugar plums, consisting of grains of corn with a coating of flour baked hard, were flying in showers from the windows on the unlucky carriage loads of English aristocracy & Italian figurantes. Nosegays were thrown to the donnas, who honoured the cavaliers with the same attention. Devils walked the street, arm in arm; harlequins with blown bladders banged passengers between the shoulders indiscriminately. One figure was in scale armour of laurel leaves, another as Hercules in a flesh coloured light suit, apparently quite naked with a club & a garland of flowers, & an Indian chief. All were mingling together in the same spirit of unrestrained hilarity. Then came the moccoletto which consists in carrying lighted wax lights up & down the Corso & putting out everybody else's;

1. Lavinio de Medici Spada (1801–63) was a poet, man of letters and a mineralogist of distinction. The *Enciclopedia Italiana di Scienze, Lettere ed Arti* records that he was 'prelato' without actually taking holy orders (presumably an official of the Church), and that his interest in science was inspired by Humphry Davy who stayed with him at Ravenna. His collection of minerals formed the nucleus of the museum of mineralogy at the University of Rome.
2. Now attributed to Ant. Montanti.
3. Mariana Starke (1762?–1838) was one of the first to produce guide-books for travellers in Europe.

as it became dark the whole Corso was lit in this way the whole breadth of the street, all in motion, & the houses were illuminated from the pavement to the top storey, a most gay & glittering sight. My companions on the balcony entered into the spirit of it & the lady of the house furnished us with tapers in order to be au courant. The imaginative character of the Italians peculiarly fits them for a thing of this sort. I leaned against a column & watched the motley movement, & thought I could have sustained a character better than some bungling Englishmen I saw there. At 11 all was quiet. The Carnival was over.

MARCH

1. Called on E. Wolff[1] with Uncle G.'s letter of introduction & found him in his studio, very civil & highly intelligent. His remarks on art stamped him at once as a man of sense. Took a long interesting & solitary ramble amongst the ruins, ascended the Colosseum & studied the arch of Constantine. Called on Garofalini. His uncle shewed me the most splendid piece of mosaic I ever saw or could conceive. It was a beautiful work of art, made by himself for the crown prince of Russia in the form of a table & representing Rome ancient & modern in 8 compartments. A Russian princess & duchess sat on each side of me & were unbounded in their admiration.

2. Today was given to the Vatican. I spent all the morning in studying Raphael's frescoes. At 2 I gained admission in common with the world to the Statue Gallery, where I walked & wondered till my brain grew bewildered & weary with digesting what the eye could not avoid drinking. No words are rhapsodical that attempt to describe the beauty of Apollo or the grandeur of Laocoön. I am now satisfied that delight in a really fine statue is not dilettantism but is genuine & unavoidable, a fact which I doubted before. I wander'd through gallery after gallery, for miles apparently, till the distance seemed to be infinite. But I found I had more already than I could carry away & trudged home.

4. Hard rain all day with the variation of snow & hail. The only event of importance to me was that of changing my quarters to avoid being entirely devoured by the fleas of which the *Grande Bretagne* is a perfect asylum. This hotel (the *Europa*) is very superior both in accommodation, cleanliness, & charges, & the table d'hote is magnificent. Went in quest of lodgings & found some in the Via Pontifici that look promising & will be vacant early next week. Meanwhile I wait a letter from J. Bell regarding his plans, as if

1. Emil Wolff (1802–79) was a distinguished sculptor and Director of St Luke's Academy in Rome.

they don't 'look towards' Naples. I must post down there before they arrive. Capt. Baynes called (a friend of Uncle G.C.'s of whom he speaks in warm terms). Sensible & polite.

5. S. The service at the Protestant chapel is conducted with an almost Presbyterian simplicity. There is neither music or singing, no clerk to snuffle the responses, no picture, symbol, or decoration of any kind. What a strange contrast to walk out of the Protestant Chapel into the Church of St. Maria Maggiore. No one would believe that the same faith could manifest itself in temples so utterly opposite in the sentiment they express. In St. John Lateran I again descended to the 'Pieta' which filled me with strange unspeakable feelings. Its simplicity, reality, & pathos strike you more the second time than the first.

6. Capt. Baynes called after breakfast & introduced me to Gibson,[1] the first English sculptor now living. His acquaintance is a great acquisition. I found him very intelligent & enthusiastic & he begged me to drop into his studio whenever I liked. Went to Torlonia's[2] for money & letters. The former is easily obtained, but the latter, alas!, appear not. I am thirsting for news from home. Falling in again with Capt. Baynes I accompanied him & a Mr. Thune to the Vatican where we spent the afternoon. A bitterly cold day.

7. At the Post Office I found nothing but a placard saying 'La Corriera d'Inghilterra e di Francia e mancata'. Having thus neither news from home nor any intelligence from James Bell respecting their going to Naples, I thought it best to act independently & accordingly removed into very comfortable lodgings in the Piazza di Spagna No. 31, with an old lady called Belloi. I have two large & well furnished rooms looking out on the Piazza, for which I am to pay her 6 scudi per week (about 28/-).

8. Called on Wolff before breakfast. He was out & his wife asked me to walk in & wait till his return from a walk, but she really seemed so much in deshabille that I felt a little awkward in complying. Such however is the custom of the place, & honi soit qui mal y pense. After calling on Dr. Somerville & Mr. Spada, who were both out, I paid my first visit to the Sistine Chapel. The weather was unfortunate. It requires a bright day & a morning sun to see it to advantage, as in addition to the obscurity of the chapel, a large canopy over the altar, & the smoke of 6 huge candles for 3 centuries, all contribute to make unappreciable except to the eye that patiently & reverently studies it, that chef d'oeuvre of Art, the Last Judgment of Michael Angelo. It is indeed an awful & stupendous conception, calculated by the painful reality of its terrors, 'To rouse the slothful from their sleep of death'.

1. John Gibson (1790–1866), R.A., who lived in Rome. He modelled the statue of Queen Victoria for the Houses of Parliament, 1850–5.
2. Alessandro Torlonia (1800–86) was a member of the banking family who founded the Banca Torlonia in 1814.

9. In the evening I went to one of Torlonia's brilliant soirées, having received an invitation for this & the following Thursdays. The conveyance which took me had to wait in the street a quarter of an hour before it could reach the door of the palazzo. Mounted guards were at all the corners to preserve order. At last I arrived & put on a moderately magnificent air to meet the investigating looks of the lackeys, through whose ranks I marched up a broad staircase, through one or two anterooms into the gorgeous & glittering suite of apartments filled with a more glittering assemblage. 'Snr Frocks', was loudly announced by one footman after another. The Prince de Torlonia came forward, very civil & made some important observation on the state of the weather. Another Torlonia with a red nose was there, but the princess was unquestionably the star of the whole party. She does not look more than 26, has superb flashing eyes, an ever-changing countenance, grace of action & ease of manner. She was dressed in white & wore a magnificent coronet of diamonds which when she sailed amongst her galaxy of guests glistered like the morning-star. I saw some beauty & much fashion, heard a great deal of small-talk, & some very superior music (both vocal & instrumental). Not knowing a soul present, nor even a body except Torlonia's, I had nothing to do but eat ices & make observations. Seeing a young man in a corner with an isolated appearance, I took upon myself to patronise him, for which he was duly grateful, & I found it very difficult to get rid of him, which I was anxious to do as his breath was particularly repulsive & his impediment of speech absolutely distressing. While I was watching the ever varying lights & shadows which played over the face of the Princess Torlonia, Lady Powerscourt was led up the hall & placed beside her. She is also beautiful but of another genus. Italian & English characteristics were well contrasted. Each may be expressed in a word, – Vivacity & Dignity. The party broke up soon after 12.

10. Spent the morning in Wolff's studio copying Prince Albert's leg, not particularly for its own sake but for mine. In order to impress Geography on one's brain the shortest way is to draw maps, so to appreciate anatomical development & beauty of form there is nothing like copying it. Visited the Borghese Palace in the afternoon. The weather was so obscure that nothing could be seen to advantage. Nevertheless some marvels of art were visible, amongst them some most delicate specimens of Francia, Titian's Graces & Sacred & Profane Love, & Raphael's Deposition from the Cross. Here also I recognised a duplicate of that Madonna & Child in the Hall at Tregedna, but the Madonna's hair is auburn instead of golden & I missed the pearly tints of the flesh. This is also called an Andrea del Sarto. Garofalini came in the evening & we commenced our Italian lessons by reading Tasso.

11. Today's post brought me a feast from home, letters from both parents, the girls, & Aunt Charles, good, hearty, cheering news, but also that the

feeble lamp of my Uncle W. Gibbins, so long flickering in its socket, is at length extinguished. He will be missed & lamented. Seeing a crowd near Trajan's Forum I joined it expecting to see some specimen of nationality. It sent a cold thrill through me to see instead a human corpse stretched out in the bare street, cold & livid, apparently a robust middle-aged man. He had fallen down in a fit & died! When sudden deaths or murders occur in Rome, the body has to be left a considerable time unremoved till the *procès verbal* & other legal formalities are gone through.

13. After laughing over a glorious letter from William, & calling on Medici Spada, who was most loving & lavish in his attentions, I trudged to the Vatican & spent nearly the whole time amongst the paintings studying Perugino whom I exceedingly admire.

14. It being a glorious morning I hired a horse & had a gallop of several miles round the walls of Rome, visiting at the Porta di St. Paolo the pyramidal tomb of Caius Cestus which is partly within & partly without the walls. Adjoining it is the protestant cymetry containing the tomb of Keats, which bears the melancholy epitaph he dictated for his tombstone, 'Here lies one whose name was writ in water'. Near him lies the body of William Shelley, aged 4 years. In the other division of the cymetry is buried a son of Goethe, & last named, though the first object of my search, under the shade of 4 fine cypresses, is the simple tomb of Percy Bysshe Shelley. After the name & date of birth & death are those 3 lines from the Song of Ariel,

> 'Nothing of him that doth fade
> But doth suffer a sea-change
> Into something rich & strange.'

The tomb-stone was placed there by Trelawny who has his own grave prepared beside it.[1] How many & strange thoughts does that quiet spot & plain marble slab call forth!

16. Torlonia's party was pretty much the same repeated of this day week. The studied music of Bellini & Rossini has small charms for me. It does not speak to the heart. I picked up an acquaintance with a young English lady whom I had met at the Capitol & she was the innocent cause of what bordered very closely on a catastrophe. After picking up my hat in the anteroom, I was making my way out, & seeing her, was in the act of making a parting bow. I continued my onward progress at the same time, thinking it all plain sailing, since I saw what seemed a passage with many people in it right before me, till I found myself suddenly in violent contact with a large mirror, & immediately after in the butler's arms, who politely but emphatically informed me that that was *not* the way out. The room was of

1. Shelley's friend, Edward Trelawny, did not die until 1881.

course in a titter at my expense & heartily did I congratulate myself that that was all it cost me.

18. At 6 this morning I opened my eyes, & saw a man standing by my bed-side. We gazed at one another in profound silence, but as soon as he opened his lips I recognised to my astonishment & delight, – James Bell. They had pushed on from Sienna on receipt of my letter, travelling 2 successive nights in order to reach this place. We shall now of course proceed to Naples together. At 2 a man from Torlonia's appeared bearing a well filled letter from *both* parents, a delightful letter which made my heart bound to read & put me in extravagant spirits for the remainder of the day. At 3 I escorted the Bells to the Capitol & ascending the Tower of the Senator's House with Eustace's Tour & a map of Rome, we made ourselves throughly acquainted with the relative positions of the ruins &c. The afternoon was glorious & the Bells were excited to a very becoming degree of enthusiasm. Eliza Bell is thoughtful, cultivated, & refined, prone to Germanism & by no means of a common order of mind. Her brother is a capital fellow with much talent, genuine enthusiasm, & a cordial relish of humour. I imagine we shall do well together. I spent the evening with them at the *Europa*. A comet of consider-able extent was visible this & last evening at 7 o'clock. The first I ever saw. The Romans collected in crowds to gaze at it. History & superstitition com-bine to teach them that some disastrous event is betokened by it. Yesterday was the anniversary of Caesar's death, the ides of March.

20. I spent the morning in packing, arranging, getting my passport &c. Spent the afternoon with the Bells at the Sistine Chapel & the Vatican which we saw to very great advantage. James has a great deal of humour & catches the point of a good thing at once, which is a great advantage. His taste is correct & he has much general information which he brings to bear without pedantry. His sister is more reflective & silent.

21. After the multifarious horrors attending passports, packing, paying, and taking leave of Roman friends, we got fairly underweigh in the Naples diligence at 11 in the morning. Each coupé in this conveyance holds 3 which makes it select, but the horses are ponies & the conducteur has a peculiar facility for stopping, which makes the rate, including stoppages, about 4 miles an hour. We made our exit at the Porta St. Giovanni, changed horses at Villetri, & entered on the Pontine Marshes just as night set in. About mid-night while we were in the act of remarking how singularly everything had prospered with us hitherto, there was a fearful lurch, & over went the dili-gence, not quite on its side, but with 2 wheels in a ditch, & the door on its under-side all but resting on the top of a hedge. We all got out cautiously on the higher side & by the light of our lamp saw the whole history of the accident. A cart was in the middle of the road drawn by 4 buffaloes, one of which had fallen down & was still on its side. The sight & smell of these

animals frightened one of our leaders, a young unbroken thing, so as to bolt into the ditch carrying postilion, wheelers, diligence & all after it, & placed it in such a position, as to make it no easy matter to drag it out again. It was a strange & novel scene, & felt very like an adventure. The buffalo still struggling on the ground, the passengers in groups watching the proceedings, the diligence in the ditch at an angle of about 60°, the Pontine Marshes all around us from whence the frogs kept up one long continuous croak, & finally after a very unnecessary quantity of noise from the postilions, 2 buffaloes harnessed in front of our wheelers dragging the clumsy vehicle out, formed altogether a very peculiar picture.

22. Reached Terracina at 1 this morning where we had to turn out & change diligences. While this was proceeding we walked on to a huge old tower or crag (we could not make out which by its dark outline) & there at our feet lay the Mediterranean rippling round the black rocks & spreading a fringe of phosphorescent light round them. The change of diligence being completed we proceeded, but were stopped at Fondi & had all the luggage taken down again to be searched, as we were now in the dominions of his despicable & impotent majesty the King of Naples. The search was merely nominal, the object of the officers being not to discover contraband articles, but to obtain a couple of pauls from each passenger for leniency. The morning light showed us a beautiful country clad with olive trees. We passed one or two aqueducts & other remains of less interest, & a little before 5 that kingly mountain Vesuvius rose before our eyes, dyed ruby colour by the sun, girdled by a cloud & with smoke issuing from one of its craters. After a short detention at the dogana we entered Naples. The bay was pearl colour, the isle of Capri rose before us, on our left was Vesuvius with the white walls of Portici forming bright lines at its base. We drove up the broad street by the arsenal & after the usual horrors of luggage, porters, commissionaires, &c., found ourselves ensconced in 3 handsome apartments in the *Belle Vue Hotel* on the Chiaja, for which they charge 3½ piastres, about 15/- per day!

23. Before breakfast the hills were clad in morning mist & bare-legged fishermen were hauling a ground sean on the beach. After breakfast I called on Turner, to whom I had a letter of credit. He was very civil & recommended our taking advantage of the weather & starting tomorrow for Paestum. On walking back with James along the Chiaja, I saw the shadow of a small hand extended towards my coat pocket, but it was withdrawn before I looked round. I saw & marked the youth, but pretended not to observe him & seeing that he still followed us, we determined to give him an opportunity, keeping a watchful eye on our shadows instead of him, in order to have the pleasure of catching & basting him. We turned up a by-street, he still dodging us. We stared in at shop windows to give him an opportunity of making the attempt, but as we persisted in keeping in the sun he

only followed us. Thinking we had spent time enough in the endeavour to be robbed we turned about. The boy was not to be seen, but as we proceeded we observed a man walking very close behind us & our suspicions being on the alert, I pointed him out to James & kept an oblique glance at our shadows. We commented on his appearance, however, & decided that he looked a grade more respectable than a thief & thought we had wronged him in supposing him capable of such an act. However, we turned down a street where our shadows fell behind us & had not walked above 20 yards when I put my hand in my pocket, & lo! my handkerchief was gone. We turned round. He had also turned & was about a dozen yards before us up the street: we immediately followed him quietly. He stopped at an orange woman's to let us pass, bought 4 oranges & stuffed them in his pockets. He evidently saw we were following him & peeled a little of one & then put the orange half-peeled into his pocket. This nervous action convinced me he was guilty, & we kept very close to him. He went to a cobbler's stall & staid chatting to let us pass, but we persisted in stopping when he stopped. When he left, I walked quietly up to him & begged him to tell me something about a handkerchief I had just lost. He looked the image of convicted guilt, but persisted in denying knowing anything about it. I told him not to waste words but give it quietly back & he should hear no more of it. Still he vehemently denied & exhibited his pockets where it certainly was not, & I came to the conclusion that although not $\frac{1}{2}$ a minute could have elapsed between his taking it & my seeing him, yet that had been enough to pass it into other hands. He said something about a ragazzo, & on pressing him with close questions, he admitted that he had seen a boy walking off with the handkerchief. I told him that I knew he could put his hand on it at once & I would give him a carlino to get it for me, which he agreed to do, begging us to wait for him, to which however we demurred, & said we would go with him. He objected that the boy would make off if he saw us, in which there appeared some sense. We nevertheless resolved not to lose sight of him, followed him up a long street, marked him into a house & walked up the stairs, but just as we thought we were sure of him in the top-storey, we found to our dismay that it communicated with another street, & of course gave up all hopes of ever seeing the face of our friend again. We looked for him up & down the street, but as he had evaporated, we thought it as well to spare ourselves further trouble & returned highly amused with this rare illustration of trying to catch a Tartar. Happily the handkerchief was provided expressly for Neapolitan pickpockets as I paid I think 3/6 for it about 3 years ago. Dr. O'Reilly, the Bells' friend, called on us & said that losing your handkerchief was a matter of course on first coming to Naples, & that the King had lately exported a batch of 800 pickpockets to an island. The trade in handkerchiefs is very great between this & Sicily. The thief lifts the tail of your coat

& lets the handkerchief drop into his hand which he immediately gives to a small boy in his wake. In the afternoon we took a fiacre & drove through the grotto of Posilippo, a lofty tunnel cut through the rock & lit with lamps. We proceeded over rough roads to the Lago d'Argnano, the crater of an extinct volcano filled with water. In the Lake, which has a dismal dead-sea look, is another aperture communicating with the same source & the boiling water bubbling up from thence near the margin of the lake has a singular effect. The guides say that a boat is immediately sucked in & swamped thereby. We made our triumphal entry into Naples in a peasant's conveyance that overtook us, something between a gig & a cart, in which we stowed very close on each other's laps. On entering the town a troop of His Majesty's Cavalry in full uniform & mounted on donkeys excited our risibles to such a degree, that in great wrath, one spurred on his steed to demand an explanation. We had recourse to profound ignorance, & then to considerable surprise at the stoppage, as we had not called him nor were aware that we had ever spoken a word to him. Finding little was to be got by the parley & also that we were somewhat above what he counted on, he left us & we proceeded to our hotel, where we packed up & made all ready for a trip to Pompeii & Paestum tomorrow morning.

24. A railroad & a very fair one, too, conveyed us to Torre del Nunciata where we breakfasted & then hired a fiacre for Pompeii & Salerno. Pompeii is a place of quite unutterable interest. To describe what we saw in the 4 hours we spent there would fill this volume. The effect of it all is that of a complete picture of the every day life & domestic manners of the Romans in the age of the Emperors.

25. A memorable day in my calendar. We left Salerno at $\frac{1}{2}$ past 6 in a barouche & 3 for Paestum. The distance is about 25 miles. The road passes over large plains where herds of buffaloes were feeding. It is bounded by the mountains & the sea, crosses the river Sarno, the transit being made in a large ferry into which the carriage is driven and about 3 or 4 miles beyond it the 3 mighty skeletons of former grandeur rise from the plain. The city wall is clearly distinguishable but all vestiges of the city itself are swept from the earth & from man's memory, or if they exist, the briar & nettle have gained the mastery of them & they are no more visible. A small albergo & one or 2 houses behind it contains all the present population of Paestum. There was a fair when we arrived, held in honour of St. Maria del Nunciata, & before we got out of our carriage we were surrounded by beggars, the most wretched, degraded, clamorous & brutal-looking set I ever saw. They followed us in a troop making the most hideous & savage noises so as to close up all the doors of charity & excite only loathing & disgust. The Calabrian peasantry who had flocked hither from the neighbouring mountains to attend the fair, tho' picturesque in the distance, are, to judge from ap-

pearance, a set of brutes in the shape of men & women, dirty, ragged, abject, bad. I can well believe after having seen them that robberies are of frequent occurrence in the neighbourhood of these ruins. But to return to the ruins themselves, how different is the feeling they excite! After seeing & admiring we spent an hour in sketching & then were glad to get quit of the place for the people were becoming exceedingly troublesome & we looked forward to the pleasure of a robbery on our road home. We stood long on the balcony overlooking the Mediterranean after our return & watched the fireflies like flitting stars dancing in the air beneath us.

27. We embarked on a handsome boat with 4 men for Amalfi & Scorocotajo. The coast is singularly fine. The cliffs about 300 or 400 feet high rise abruptly from the water, their clefts & chasms fringed with aloes & prickly pear which grow here in great abundance. We landed at Amalfi & visited the cathedral. On the assurance of the padrone of our boat who seemed an honest man, that we should save half an hour by going in a smaller boat to Scorocotajo, we consented & found that he had managed better for himself than for us, the boat being a small fishing boat belonging to Scorocotajo with only 3 men, one of whom was 70 years old. However, there was no help for it, and for a time we got on well enough, explored a beautiful blue grotto & admired the stump of St. Antony carved in the rock &c., but by degrees the wind, which is always treacherous in this bay, rose considerably & being right ahead it was all our 3 men could do to weather some of the points where a good deal of sea was running. I tried to persuade the old man to give up his oar to me but he was inexorable, & after 4 hours toiling instead of 2, we arrived at Scorocotajo. From this spot there is a magnificent view of both bays, Salerno & Naples. We made our dinner of fried eggs & part of a sausage, in most primitive style in a very primitive public house which served for shop, inn, & general lounge of the village. Taking a man to carry our bag we wound down the hill to Sorrento & found most comfortable quarters in the beautifully situated *Hotel de Tasso*, the birth-place of the poet himself, tho' now much enlarged & modernised.

28. We are all wild about Sorrento. It realises one's dreams of Italy. I know nothing like it but some of Claude's landscapes. After seeing the antiquities in the town, wandering in a garden & picking oranges, surveying & coveting a little beau ideal of a villa on the top of the cliff with steps winding down to the water's edge, visiting a myrtle tree 430 years old which a man climbed to gather some branches for us, & investing a small amount of capital in 2 very beautiful tables made of the various woods that grow at Sorrento, we descended to the piccola marina & took a boat to the Cave of Ulysses or rather of Polyphemus, no doubt the one from which Virgil took his description. The row under the cliffs is perfectly delicious, the air is so soft, the water so alluring & so exquisitely blue, & the cliffs rise like towers

out of the water crowned with fruit & flowers in luxuriance. After dinner we took a fiacre & drove to Castellamare along a most beautiful mountain path rich in the choicest views of the bay, Vesuvius, Ischia, Capri &c. The train had left Castellamare, so we took a carriage to Naples & changed our quarters there to the *Grande Bretagne*.

APRIL

2. Accompanied the Bells in the evening to call on a family called Maingay from Guernsey, to whom they had a letter. We talked about Italy, of course, & they begged us to stop to tea, & as there was a daughter who collected flowers & wrote poetry, & another with downcast mild eyes & a Madonna face who looked sweet but said nothing, we accepted & got on swimmingly. They had been following in our footsteps to Paestum & Sorrento so there was no lack of topic.

3. Made the most of daylight by breakfasting at 8 & sallying forth seeing sights & making observations till 7. At the Royal Museum we saw in the vast library some of the burnt scrolls of papyrus found at Herculaneum, as well as the ingenious & delicate process of softening & unrolling & deciphering them. But the collection of bronze statues interested us more. A colossal horse's head found in an excavation near the cathedral is superb. They say its body was melted to make bells, the vandals! After dinner we saw the interior of San Carlo, one of the largest theatres in Europe &, what I was peculiarly anxious to see, the Neapolitan letter writers who have each their table & writing materials & 2 chairs, one for themselves & the other for the less literary dictator. Their business is to mould the crude idea into most choice Italian & indite the most appropriate sentiments in an epistolary form whether concerning love or lucre. On the mole we had the privilege of forming part of the crowd who stood listening with profound attention to a young Improvisatore who added the powers of action & gesticulation to his most fluent & animated composition. Catching a glance of us he appropriated a stanza to a hope that his efforts had given us satisfaction & that we would reward them accordingly, with which we of course complied. A little further on an elderly man was reading to another animated group out of a manuscript copy of Tasso which he gave with quite sufficient fuoco & energia. Beyond, another man was exercising his Southern imagination in the capacity of story teller, his tale to judge by the earnest faces round him, was one of thrilling interest. These bits of nationality were delightful. We finished the day with Virgil's tomb, a columbarium in the form of a grotto with brambles all round & a seat on the top of it. We tried in all manner of ways to pump

up a little sentiment or some appropriate classical allusion, but all in vain.
5. James Bell started by diligence at 3 in the morning, there being only one
place to spare. His sister & I follow the day after tomorrow. After breakfast
we drove to Pausilippo to see a newly discovered Etruscan Tomb but the
Custode being at Naples we could see nothing but its mouth. We visited,
however, the Villa of Lucullus in the adjoining garden from whence one
looks down on the ruined walls of the School of Virgil, more than half
submerged, & a little further on, some excavations which have turned up
just relics enough to whet the appetite for more.
7. We were frightened out of our beds at $\frac{1}{4}$ to 3 by the Garçon who had
promised to call us at 2 but had overslept himself. We pitched on our things &
unwashed & unshaven rushed wildly out of the hotel, the diligence-office
being a mile off. The facchino[1] met us at the door, being sent to see for us.
We sent him on to get a carriage & by means of desperate exertion caught
the vehicle on the ground hop & ensconced ourselves in the back of that
great lumbering machine humourously called a *Diligence*. The first remarkable sight was the sun-rise, painting the beautiful Appenines purple, brown,
& blue, whilst here & there rose a broad snowy summit dazzlingly white, the
next was the faces of our fellow passengers. One was a Florentine officer
who talked a 'little Engleese', & had in reading, he informed us, 'De Istrie of
England', 'de Vicaire of Vakfeld' & 'Little Jacq'. On enquiring the author, he
pondered a little, & then replied, 'Milton', which proved a desperate trial of
our good breeding. The other was a canonico-avocato, a most tedious old
drone who bored us with an incessant jabber of common-place. The only
refuge was to read intensely. We partook of a miserable breakfast, after the
miserable fashion of the Italians, in a miserable public house, & on arriving
at San Germano about 3, five of us determined to make an excursion to the
monastery of Monte Cassino & rejoin the diligence at Ceprano. The ascent
was made in donkeys. The vines were magnificent & the road wound about
the mountains 3 miles in length, opening fresh views of the Appenine range.
Monte Cassino is the oldest & one of the largest Convents in Italy. It was
founded by St. Benedict himself since which time it has been 4 or 5 times
destroyed & rebuilt. The interior of the Church is very rich in marbles inlaid
in beautiful patterns. A young monk conducted us over the monastery, which
is remarkable only for its size & a large collection of old manuscripts preserved through the Middle Ages, comprising, besides theology, classics &
philosophy. Only twenty monks reside here now. Those we saw were particularly civil & attentive. Our guides gave us many hints that we were late,
which we did not understand till we were well advanced on the road to
Ceprano, when we learnt that it was a 'lieu suspect'. Certainly if any region
was more favourable than another to assaults from robbers it was this. We

1. The porter.

hardly passed a house in the 20 miles we had to go. Our coachman drove as fast as 4 horses could go, stopping to breathe them only when we reached the sentry boxes of the guards, which are posted at long intervals on this road. We reached Ceprano at 10 & were glad of a good supper & a bed.

8. Started again at 3 in the morning. Exquisite starlight. The road was dusty & comparatively uninteresting, though we did look down into some beautiful valleys & saw some splendid effects of light & shade in the early morning. We entered Rome between 4 & 5 in the afternoon. We saw James in the street & after the usual farce of Custom House examination (which means no more than that every stranger assist in the payment of the officer to the extent of a couple of pauls each) we proceeded to the lodgings which Garofalini had procured for us. A good wash, good meal, & good laugh before going to bed were all very relieving.

9. S. Palm Sunday. The pageant begins at 10 in the morning. Eliza was not able to go. James & I, by means of brass & our insinuating ways, secured a capital place at the head of the nave, very near His Holiness, who was seated on a throne covered with scarlet & gold, a lofty scarlet curtain suspended behind him, his cardinals, bishops, officers, & retinue before & around him. Guards & Swiss lined the nave keeping a wide passage open in the centre. The pope sat like a statue in his robes and mitre. Being seated & cushioned, he was hoisted on to the shoulders of a number of scarlet dignitaries, the palm bearers & olive bearers proceeding & following in a long procession. Six or eight men carried a scarlet canopy over his head, & thus he was borne out of the church & then back again, the choir chanting Hosanna, which I thought bordered very closely on the profane, & the guards & congregation falling on their knees as he approached.

10. Not only misfortunes, but sometimes the contrary come to us in battalions. I received no less than 5 letters today, 2 containing violets & offerings of female affection, & one a power of attorney which I executed before the consul & returned immediately. The letters from home are full of interest. All are well, which is a great blessing. Anna Gurney has accepted J. C. Backhouse which is all right. Called on Medici Spada, from whom I got an order for the Villa Ludovisi, which is capital, being very difficult to obtain.

12. We lionised considerably this morning seeing 19 sights before dinner. The afternoon we spent at the Sistine Chapel where the service of the tenebrae was performed. The Chapel was crammed, all the ladies obliged to be veiled & all the gentlemen in black. The chanting of some of the psalms was exquisite, but the crowd was so excessive that a lady or two 'went off', as they call it, & a little Frenchman fainted away by my side. I wiggled up gradually into a capital place so as to watch the ceremony, which consisted in putting out a candle at the end of each psalm. The ornaments of the chapel were veiled & the chants were all mournful. The last psalm being finished,

the last candle, representing our Saviour, was not put out but carried behind the Altar. There was a short pause and then such a heavenly swell of vocal music as I never before heard, broke forth, rising like a great wave into a note that made the chapel ring, then sinking into a magnificent bass in which the whole choir joined. It was the Miserere of Bai,[1] & that in the Sistine Chapel, with Michael Angelo's Last Judgement before your eyes, was as may be supposed in the highest degree imposing. It really was like nothing earthly. At the conclusion a long peal of mimic thunder seemed to shake the dome. The pope pronounced a few words in a solemn voice, whose import I did not understand, & then the doors opened & we relieved our minds by blowing up a tradesman who had sold us a putrid tongue which we took back to him, exposed him before a shop full of customers & made him refund the money, which we pocketed with a look of severe justice & offended virtue.

13. We drove to St. Peter's & from the steps we saw the ceremony of the pope blessing the multitude who simultaneously fall on their knees, a hollow square of troops in the centre of the piazza doing the same thing. We then crammed into the Southern transept of the Cathedral to see his Holiness wash the feet of 12 fancy Apostles. Dom Miguel[2] was there, a very fine & kingly looking personage. There was *such* a skrimmage among the ladies to get nearest to the ceremony, it was a pleasure to watch the animated expression of the little dears. We then took refuge in the Vatican & spent a very interesting hour in the Gregorian Museum. After satiating ourselves with this we went to the Sistine Chapel & heard yesterday's service repeated. Some parts of the Miserere are exquisitely touching & one of the psalms which is chanted by a single tenor voice sounds angelic, the modulations & changes are *so* beautiful. The senseless, souless, barbarous English ladies were chattering the whole time. After this we saw the ceremony of washing the High altar in St. Peter's which was exceedingly imposing. James was unfortunate. His handkerchief was stolen from his pocket & on returning he amused himself by setting our house in a blaze. I heard him cry 'Fire' & rushed into his room. He was surrounded by it & the light window curtain was blazing to the ceiling. I immediately tore it down & by treading on it & mounting the table & dashing water where we could not reach, we managed to extinguish it. The curtain, table-cloth, & one of James's shirts was all that suffered materially.

14. Spent an effective morning amongst the shops. I bought 3 beautiful little frescoes, either by Annibale Carracci or one of his scholars, & also some

1. Tommaso Bai (1650–1714), Maestro of the Vatican basilica in Rome. His *Miserere* is permanently placed in the services of the Pontifical Chapel, along with those of Allegri and Palestrina.
2. Usurper of the throne of Portugal, who had been defeated by the forces of Queen Maria with the help of the British fleet in 1833.

fine engravings of Massaccio's Life of St. Catherine. We took a carriage &
post horses to convey us to Perugia at the end of next week. In the afternoon
we repaired to St. Peter's. I deposited Eliza in the Sistine Chapel & went into
the cathedral to hear the Miserere there. A double line of guards formed a
wide passage up the nave. At 6 the pope came in procession & knelt at a low
desk in front of the altar which was stripped of all its ornaments. By an
infinite deal of pushing & wiggling I managed to get within 5 or 6 yards of
the railing of the chapel where the sublime Miserere of Allegri was chanted.
The incessant chatter of a group of English ladies behind me & the pushing
of the multitude around me made it impossible to catch the delicate & finely
attenuated notes which seemed to melt into the air.

16. S. High Mass at St. Peter's. The music which was all vocal is perhaps
as striking as the Miserere. Its character, however, instead of being a
lamentation is a triumphal chant, celebrating Christ's triumph over death.
The whole cathedral wears an air of fête. The pope enters in grand procession
& after sitting on his throne for a time & being re-mitred & re-robed by one
of his cardinals walks to the altar, swings the censer before it & reads mass,
the choir chanting the responses. This being over we scamper as many of us
as can, & crowd on the top of the passage leading from the Sistine Chapel to
the façade & look down on the glittering & gay assemblage which fills the
vast piazza. A hollow square of troops is formed in the centre who all fall
simultaneously on their knees when the pope appears at the window of the
vestibule. After reading the benediction he rises & swings his arms like a
windmill, making a cross in the air. Then the band strikes up, the crowd
rise from their knees, & we & other prudent people scramble out of the
press as quickly as possible.

17. In the evening we left our old padrone, the barber, to put away the tea
things & lock up the house, & posted off with Garofalini to the Piazza di
St. Angelo to see the Girandola. It certainly struck me at the time as by far
the most magnificent fire-works I ever saw. On returning we found Garofalini & Eliza, who had arrived two minutes before us, & our old padrone
in a state of mental agony, announcing that the house had been robbed in
our absence. The window was open & a chair stood before it. Eliza's box of
books was carried away bodily & James's & my wardrobes were gone. They
left me a few collars which, without a shirt to fasten them on, are of no great
service. My top drawer contained mosaics, intaglios, silver filligree & a
cameo, all which they took possession of, but had the conscience to leave me
the boxes & the cotton wool to pack others in. We have now nothing to
wear but what we stand in.

18. We spent the morning in agitating the police, the English Consul, &
Medici Spada about our robbery, & wrote a most flowery & pathetic appeal
to the Governor of Rome to exert all his energy to recover our lost property.

Received an interesting letter from my mother in which she informed me of a concern she was about to lay before the meeting to visit some of the meetings in Ireland. How different are the employments of mother & son. Spent the time after dinner in revisiting the Capitoline Museum. Wolff sent us some shirts &c. which are very acceptable. James remarks that we shall be 'sheep in wolves' clothing'.

20. Started at 6 for Tivoli. Foggy morning, but it cleared beautifully about 8. The Campagna looked well, an undulating plain bounded by sunny hills. The gardens of the villa have still the antique olives & cypresses or their children, magnificent trees interspersed with box & laurel & other shrubs. An Italian family went the round with us, & as a bright-eyed laughing donna of 19 was of the party, we soon were excellent friends, doing the attentive to the Mamma & the agreeable to the daughter. The effect of modern Italian gaiety amidst the remains of ancient Roman grandeur had a good effect. The river Anio tumbling head long from its rocky bed, striking on the jagged rocks beneath & sending forth a vast rolling cloud of vapoury foam, illustrated admirably Tennyson's expression in the 'Lotos-Eaters',

> And like a *downward smoke* the slender stream
> To fall & rise, & rise & fall did seem.[1]

Winding down the ravine was a party of 2 ladies & 3 gentlemen, the former beautiful figures & dressed in a sort of Boccaccio fashion with hats & veils. We followed them down the steep ravine by a little winding path cut in the rock. After dinner we made a small circuit on what is called the Circular Terrace. It commands a superb view of the valley of Tivoli watered by the winding river, with the Campagna in the distance, & the dome of St. Peter's rising on the horizon. Both the day & the season were peculiarly favourable & we thought we had never seen any scenery equal to it in our lives. We returned home about ½ past 7.

21. Our day was spent in preparations for quitting; packing up, settling accounts, & taking leave. James & I went before the Tribunal & gave in our depositions of the theft with all the circumstances attending it. Wolff & Garofalini very warm at parting. Both have been of great service to me in their respective lines.

22. Up at 5. Took leave of our old Padrone & set off for Florence in a carriage which I fell in with yesterday & hired for 5 louis. We took leave of the Eternal City with a strange mixture of feelings respecting it: reverence for its ruins & historical magnitude, admiration & love for the various forms of beauty it contains. Its slavish superstition & priestrule disgust us, its fleas devour us & perpetually destroy our peace of mind. Its inhabitants, some have been of

1. The second of the lines quoted should correctly be:
    Along the cliff to fall and pause and fall did seem.

infinite service to us, others have robbed us. However, it has on the whole fully answered my expectations. We posted to Terni without any considerable occurrence. At Nepi an attempt was made to tax us with 3 horses instead of 2, but we stoutly resisted. We sat down obstinately in the post house, the horses were taken out & returned to the stable. Eliza fell asleep in the carriage. At length by means of a douceur to the postmaster we gained our point. At the next stage James gave the postilion a napoleon to change; he took it & rode off. We immediately raised a hue & cry & went in pursuit of him. James bellowed for a horse. I pursued on foot & caught him at the gate & made him refund the money. Whilst he was explaining the meaning of his very equivocal conduct, James hove in sight round the corner, mounted on a raw-boned black charger, a regular Rosinante, very high in action but very indifferent in speed. He came with his great straw hat flapping, blouse fluttering & pegging into his horse's ribs with a large 'bastone',[1] looking bent on desperate revenge. We could not stand the sight & culprit & pursuers (the 2 ostlers & I) rolled with laughing simultaneously. The whole race of Italian postilions that we have had to deal with so far are the most rapacious rascals I ever saw. One's fountain of generosity gets completely frozen by such griping blood-sucking rapacity. It at all events made us resolute & a shower of Italian oaths fall very harmless on us. We reached Terni at 9 & put up at the Poste, apparently a comfortable inn. James was overdone by the heat & exertion & went to bed with a violent headache, to which he is very subject.

23. A tolerably quiet Sunday. The fleas will not allow it to be a day of rest. The cascade for which this place is so celebrated is a most superb sight. The scenery around it is so wildly beautiful, the cliffs so perpendicular & so luxuriantly covered with foliage, that we unanimously voted it superior to Tivoli. James continues far from well. Last night a strange shadow glided into my room. I at first mistook it for a man, then it looked more like a large dog. I told it to get away & it glided out again. I jumped out of bed to shut the door after it & was not a little surprised to find it shut already. I can't account for it now, unless it was some reflection from the yard below.

24. James's symptoms make me rather anxious. He has so much tendency of blood to the head, his eyes show oppression & his pulse fever. I look forward to a laying up somewhere on the road. We started, however, at 6 & pushed on. Let us at all events get somewhere where the comforts of life are to be had. Instead of following the beaten track to Perugia we turned aside to the ancient & interesting town of Assisi. We were dragged up the mountain on which it is built by a pair of oxen. Before we reached the place we were overtaken by a heavy thunder shower which brought after it hail & rain in abundance. We put up at the house of Signr. Carpanelli, an Architect

1. Cudgel.

to whom Dr. Somerville had given me a letter of recommendation. We are treated as guests, payment only excepted, which I understand is very moderate. We have just put James to bed, for he is rather overdone by the journey & Eliza & I have paid a visit to the old church of San Francesco. The subterranean chapel contains the body of the Saint who was born & died at Assisi. Above is a very dark & low church, the walls & ceilings covered with Giottos which it was much too dark to see. Above this church is another called the Modern San Francesco, although it dates from the 14th or 15th century. The walls are covered with frescoes by Giotto, highly interesting & characteristic where they are distinguishable, but the damp has nearly destroyed them. There is an expressive picture of Saint Francis stooping eagerly on his stomach to drink of a stream which is miraculously sent him in the desert. The roof is painted by Cimabue, the father of modern art. His colouring has stood the damp much better than Giotto's. The general effect of what we could distinguish was also more forcible broad & grand than the works of his pupil, but it was too dark to distinguish the details. A little print seller & a thorough-bred Italian volunteered his company in the evening & talked about Art & the Umbrian School while the buxom little Signora sat by knitting stockings.

25. The duomo at Assisi is very quaint & peculiar, thoroughly Byzantine in its character, but altogether it is infinitely surpassed by San Francesco, which we revisited, but on account of its abiding darkness, with little better success. James did not get up till the middle of the day, when we started for Perugia, a post & ½ distant from Assisi. Perugia stands at the top of a very long hill which we ascended with the aid of a pair of bullocks, fine classic mild-eyed, mouse-coloured creatures.

26. All the morning was occupied in nursing. The oppression in James's head continuing, Eliza & I thought it best to apply leeches. Four out of six bit, & one in such good earnest that it was full two hours before we could staunch the blood, & then not without the aid of a surgeon who brought some astringent powder. James nearly fainted with the effort of sitting up in bed. I hope we are not booked for a regular nursing in this out of the way place, but it won't do to run any risks. Another cause of anxiety has been the state of our funds. Herries's[1] notes are not merchantable here & our stock having been much more rapidly diminished than we counted on through incidental charges of Italian posting, we came to the conclusion this morning that we could not stand two or three days detention here & then the journey to Florence. Whilst brooding over our affairs & calculating ways & means I met in the street Mr. & Mrs. Williams who had been introduced to me by Wolff. I thought the opportunity too good to be lost. I laid our case before

1. John Charles Herries (1778–1855), a financier who had been Chancellor of the Exchequer 1827–8, and at this time was Secretary-at-War in the Peel Government.

them & obtained the loan of 5 napoleons as well as a little tin case of arrow-root. This I hope will be enough to provide for all contingencies. Leaving James to his repose I sallied forth to see some of the Peruginos which abound here.

27. James's pulse is reduced to 84. We gave his feet a dose of hot water & vinegar last night which produced copious perspiration. Today I escorted Eliza to see some of the Peruginos & to the Casa Baldeschi where we saw an original early drawing of Raphael's in sepia. At the Church of St. Dominico we saw some fine specimens of Fra Angelico. I spoke to a Dominican monk in Italian and he answered me in rich Irish brogue. His convent adjoins the Church. He was heartily glad of the opportunity of speaking his mother tongue, escorted us round the church & was very attentive. James got up in the evening & by means of chatting & laughing & a good fire we got him a little out of his dumps.

28. We got on to Arezzo today very comfortably. James dreaded the journey, but we rigged up a sort of bed for him & brought a pillow for his head, so that no exertion was required of him but to get in at Perugia & out at Arezzo & counteract the jolts as well as he could. Between Perugia & Cortona we came to the famous lake of Thrasymene where Hannibal showed such consummate generalship & defeated the Consul Flaminius. It looks about twice the size of Windermere. On entering the Tuscan territory we had to submit to a quasi search by the douaniers. A small piece of silver, however, was quite a sufficient evidence to these gentlemen that we were honest people and we proceeded without any detention. We found a marked improvement both in the roads, the posting, & the looks of the women. If anything, also the postmasters were less exacting & the postilions less uncivil. Arezzo appears an interesting town. Petrarch was born here. We arrived before 6 & while coffee was getting ready I visited the 2 cathedrals.

29. Up before 6 & made further researches in the town. I saw the house of Petrarch adorned with a Latin inscription a great deal too long to read, We drove on at a famous pace to Florence, good roads, good horses, smart postilions, no heavy bullocks to drag you at two miles an hour. The face of the country & the faces of the inhabitants show a marked improvement in the Tuscan over the Papal dominions. This is what might be expected (roads & cultivation) seeing that the direction in the one is in the hands of a liberal & enlightened prince, the other in those of a set of ignorant priests. We got the old gentleman through the journey very well & reached Florence in time to see a rich golden sunset streaming down the Arno & glittering beneath the arches of the dark bridges which span it. Our hotel is close to the river. Our suite of rooms are princely. We took a slight sensation of the town while the light permitted. It looks full of interest, activity & cheerfulness. The gloomy grandeur of the Palazzo Vecchio & the other palaces, with their

massive walls & huge iron rings for fastening the family standards, have a very peculiar effect, strangely reviving the old stories of the factions & civil wars with which this city was tormented in the Middle Ages.

30. S. Received a long & deeply interesting letter from home describing R. Barclay's[1] sudden & fatal illness & the overwhelming affliction of the family. There is something startling in the idea of one so full of life & joy & vigour thus suddenly cut down. It may be my turn next. Susan Sterling has realised another girl; her husband was about to start for London probably to the death of his mother. How the two great events of life crowd on each other. I walked today for some time in the Church of Santa Croce & looked at the marble piles which mark the resting places of the mighty dead, for Buonarotti, Galileo, Alfieri & Machiavelli are buried there. Dante's cenotaph is here. The bard himself is buried in Ravenna from whence his offended ghost & the townsmen will not permit his ashes to be removed. After dinner I walked with Eliza to the Cascine about 2 miles & a half up the Arno. It belongs to the Grand Duke who has thrown it open to the public & there the Florentine aristocracy drive in showy equipages & lounge away the afternoon. The days are warm & brilliant but the evenings very sharp & treacherous.

MAY

1. Mayday in Florence brings with it no hideous annunciation of tin horns & birds' eggs as with us, only the hum of life & the clear fresh atmosphere of Northern Italy. The Arno has a delicate sensation of green approaching to pea-soup colour which renders sharply & distinctly the painted houses supported on machicoulies & the piers of the graceful bridges which rise out of its waters. Walked with Eliza to the Uffizi which was shut, then to the Duomo, an imposing pile of black & white marble striated.

2. A day of marvellous sights. We spent the whole morning at the Uffizi & drank a rich draught of beauty. Michael Angelo's Holy Family, almost the only oil painting that is known as his for certain, did not please me. The Madonna's head is thrown back so as to show the under part of her nose. She is coarse nature & her child has no divinity. What a contrast to it is Raphael's Madonna. What angelic purity in the mother & what infantine loveliness in both children. To run thro' this gallery & take a superficial glance of each object that deserves attention is a thorough day's work. I have not half seen it. We spent the evening at Mrs. Brown's, a large & gay party of English, German & Italians. A young lady called Robertson urged my taking part of a

1. Robert Barclay, son of Chas. Barclay of Bury Hill.

vetturino with her & her mother & a French count for Venice. They start on the 6th. It is worth thinking of.

3. Almost every other day at Florence is festa or mezzo festa which means the closing of the galleries & an extra three hours siesta for the custodie. This prevented our seeing the Pitti Palace Gallery today. After dinner Eliza & I took a carriage & drove to Fiesole, a most interesting old town surrounded by an Etruscan wall. We visited Fra Angelico's church & convent, in the former of which is an altar-piece expressive of his pure & holy spirit. On descending, we visited the Villa Palmiere, said to be the scene of the De-cameron. A heavy lowering cloud opposed our inclination to linger in this lovely spot & by hard driving we got back just before it came down in floods.

4. A glorious Italian day. Spent the morning at the Pitti Palace. It is a first-rate gallery but has suffered from over-cleaning & repeated restorations. There are 12 pictures in that gallery which will live for ever in my memory, amongst which are those three Madonnas of Raphael, so widely & so justly celebrated. The Boboli Gardens adjoin the palace & are the finest specimen of an Italian garden I ever saw. The air was loaded with fragrance; the song of birds & bees & the murmur of a fountain were the only sounds. We then drove to the Casa Buonarotti, the domicile of M. Angelo & still inhabited by his family. The custodie was out or asleep, as they always are after 3 o'clock. So instead of viewing the relics of the great, we went & took a warm bath apiece. It was a very luxurious affair. A garçon comes when you ring for him, with hot towels, one of which in the form of a mantle he throws over your shoulders. He then takes your legs on his lap & rubs them with hot towels & moreover gives you a piece of pumice stone to scratch yourself all over to produce friction. James is very much better which is a great relief.

5. Not altogether idle. Visited 5 churches, two academies, the Laurentian Library, the Casa Buonarotti. We also visited the Della Crusca Academy to which we were admitted as a special favour. The Librarian was excessively attentive. After dinner we drove to the Casa Buonarotti, & felt almost on holy ground as we sat in his studio & handled the old man's stick & slippers. The house is inhabited by his family who take great care of all relics of their great ancestor.

6. After breakfast we visited the Palazzo di Justizia to see Giotto's portrait of Dante, lately discovered by the careful removal of the whitewash with which the walls were covered. After coffee I took leave of my fellow pilgrims & started per diligence for Bologna. Their society has greatly increased the pleasure of my journey. We harmonised wonderfully & were much more congenial in taste than travellers thrown together haphazard could possibly expect. I felt quite forlorn & solitary after parting with them. James has almost regained his usual strength, but in case of any return of his indisposi-tion, I shall make a point of rejoining them from Milan.

7. The road from Florence to Bologna deserves all the ill things that are said of it; 60 miles long, 19 hours journey nearly, a little more than 3 miles an hour, up & down hill all the way. How often we had men to drag us up the hill I know not, but four times the men passengers had to turn out & walk. My companions were a Frenchman & his wife, a Milanese, a Bolognese, & a Piedmontese gentleman, all civil & attentive but nothing out of the common. Instead of reaching Bologna at 7 this morning, it was nearly 3 in the afternoon before we arrived. I stayed at the *Hotel de la Suisse*. Thirty-five sat down at the table d'hote which was very fair. Then I went out & called on my future fellow travellers, Mrs. & Miss Robertson.

8. Dismal, wet day. But this matters less at Bologna than any town I know as nearly all the streets have double or single colonnades which give them a very peculiar, sombre & rather grand appearance. I joined the Robertsons & my other companions, a little French Count called Maieux & his son, a thorough little Frenchman of the old regime, very fidgetty, very voluble & liable, I understand, to occasional derangement. His son never opens his lips if he can avoid it.

9. Started at 5 for Ferrara. Breakfasted at Alti & rested the horses. The road was very bad. We reached Ferrara about 4 in the afternoon. Distance 30 miles, time 11 hours! A vetturino to a man pressed for time is the most wearisome thing in the world. The little Count fell down & hurt his leg. Miss Robertson & I kept up a pretty smart fire of conversation. She is lively, good-tempered & wonderfully executive. At Ferrara we posted away to see everything & dragged after us the little Count & his son, much against the grain but they found it worse to be left behind alone. The town has the desolated effect one might expect from its history. Its population is now 30,000, but was at one time 200,000. The library contains some things of much interest: Ariosto's manuscript journal, many of his letters, his armchair & inkstand. We also saw, carefully guarded, a MS copy of Tasso's *Gerusalemme* written by his friend & corrected in numerous places by himself. The hospital of Santa Anna contains the cell where Tasso was imprisoned as a madman for 7½ years. On the walls of the poet's cell Byron has scratched his name, together with Victor Hugo, Lamartine & many others.

10. Wet day & dull road. Crossed the Po & Adige in a pont-volant, a very simple & convenient method. We got through the Custom House on the frontier with a nominal search & a payment of 5 pauls. Reached Montselice about ½ past 6, driving in a mathematically straight line for 7 miles through an avenue of poplars. Before dinner, despite the rain Miss R. & I ran up to the top of the hill above the town from whence is a splendid view of the rich, flat, wooded country round.

11. I am at last in Venice & the Reality is the very Venice of my dreams. To begin at the beginning, we left Montselice before 5, reached Padua at ½ past 7

& saw all that is interesting in that curious old town. After dejeuner à la fourchette we journeyed on for Venice. We embarked at Mestre in a large boat and glided down the lagoons to this Fairy City. The sun set in gorgeous magnificence before we entered its liquid streets & then the moon looked down, clear & round, on the blue waters. What a feeling it was to spring ashore in Venice! I lost little time in running off to St. Mark's. Venetians of both sexes were sipping coffee outside the doors. The moonlight on the canal dotted with gondolas! It was altogether like enchantment. What with gazing, wondering & admiring I could not get to bed till midnight was long past.

12. That gorgeous Duomo loses nothing by daylight. It was the first shrine of my pilgrimage. After breakfast I jumped into a gondola & glided up the Grand Canal. These hearse-like vehicles are the most luxurious things I know. You sink at least $\frac{1}{2}$ a foot when you sit on its down cushion. Two other cushions are placed to support your legs & another your back, the sides have windows & shutters which you can throw completely open if you choose. The gondolier stands behind & with a single oar can send the boat along with wonderful swiftness. I went to the Port, then to Holme's who was very civil. I met there a priest from the Armenian Convent who remembered Byron. Yesterday was the 46th anniversary of the Death of the Republic.[1] The Venetians, although a new generation, lament their loss most bitterly. The Austrians are cordially hated & feared. I met Lord Falmouth in the Hall of the Council of Ten & claimed acquaintance. On returning to the Place St. Mark, I found it filled with Venetians, a military band in the centre, & ladies & gentlemen sitting round & before the cafés. I joined them & scraped a partial acquaintance with a Venetian with 4 fine daughters.

13. Yesterday repeated. Spent an hour in the Ducal Library reading & then visited the prisons. The Venetians in the first enthusiasm of French republicans when they were admitted to these dens of misery, stripped them of their iron doors & set fire to the wood lining of the cells. At the end is the place where the prisoner was 'reconciled' as our guide expressed it & then placed on a stone seat & strangled. Paid another visit to the Academy. Met Lord Falmouth again. I don't think he knows much about painting, whatever may be his skill in politics. The Venetians have no energy to preserve their property after the loss of their liberty & no wonder. Where a palace is falling to ruins, the Austrian Government repairs it & repays itself out of the rents. Lounged in a gondola in the evening with Miss Robertson & the little Count. The French & Italian songs of my companions, the peculiar sound of the gondolier's oar, the rippling waters & the moonlight, had altogether a remarkably Venetian-romantic effect.

14. S. Today being Domenica[2] I did nothing in the way of sight-seeing but

1. By the treaty of Campo Formio in 1797 the Austrians became the masters of Venice.
2. Sunday.

step into a few churches & pay a visit to the ospitale civile, apparently the best regulated-establishment possible. It now contains 970 patients. The wards are lofty, clean, airy & comfortable, the fare capital, the pharmecea wholesale. Holme met me at 2 & we walked together in the Piazza where all the world was promenading, & some of the nobles, a poor & degenerate race. None of Titian's senators are to be seen now. The women want expression & fail generally in the mouth. The standard of morals is subservient to that of fashion, & it is considered discredibtable in a married lady to be without a cavaliere servente. We met a rich old banker with a young wife on his arm, who, on first marrying, tried to take herself off again when she found herself denied this harmless privilege. He told her she was welcome to go if she preferred it, but the money must remain in his coffers. Upon this the lady thought better to remain too. Holme pointed out a celebrated Venetian composer who was walking with a lady to whom he was cicisbeo. So much for Venetian morals! In the evening I wandered down to Napoleon's gardens. What a gay throng, what variety, what endless amusement, here a peepshow, there Punchinello, there an Improvisatore, a comic one, whose gesticulations were quite a study. The group around him were in ecstasies. Then a troop of Albanians, then a drunken English sailor, then what looked like a Persian Emir with a very picture of a beard, white as snow & reaching to his girdle, then black-eyed donnas without bonnets. The evening amusement is to sit outside a café & watch the passers-by.

15. Holme was with me at 9 in the morning & introduced me to a wealthy retail pilchard merchant with whom I arranged to visit the pilchard stores tomorrow morning. He showed me through his cheese warehouses which are kept like a little armoury. I never saw such neatness & order. Met in the Piazza a broad chested John Bull. I asked him his name & county & was answered, 'My name's John Quiller. I keeps the public house to Polperro!' Upon which I of course claimed acquaintance & was charged with remembrances to his wife & family. The Palazzo Mocenigo was inhabited by Byron when at Venice. His rooms are kept as he left them, even to the blots on the table where he wrote. The Palace of the Foscari is a melancholy & interesting sight; a magnificent wreck, the windows of the old salons boarded up with planks. In the top storey I found two poor old women, wretched crones, yet both Countesses, & what is more the last of the Foscari. I chatted with one whose nose & chin met when she spoke to me & shook hands at parting, which I was told afterwards is a great liberty to take with an Italian lady, & is thought a degree worse than kissing. Dined at Holme's. I accompanied the Holmes in their gondola to a Mr. Gale's to tea, an English merchant, & met several gentlemen there. The Gales are thorough old fashioned English people & inveterate whist-players, which seems the quintessence of dullness. Left at 12 & floated about the canal enjoying the exquisite moonlight.

16. Had much to do, packing up, settling, taking leave, passing baggage through Custom House formalities, &c. Venice being a *free* port the Customs Officers give you more trouble than anywhere else. Before breakfast Signor Palazzi, a very large warehouse proprietor & Retail-merchant, took me in his barge to see the mode of preserving pilchards at Venice. Everything of this sort is done with beautiful regularity & neatness. The old pilchard casks are stripped off, the fish cleaned, especially the top row, & placed in new casks with strong brine, & piled in tiers two deep, in which way they will keep 3 years. After breakfast I accompanied the Robertsons & the Frenchman to the Arsenal, the most emphatic remembrance of departed glory. Passing the lions which guard the large bronze door way, we entered the Arsenal, a vast & well ordered place. The Basin was built to contain 21 ships-of-the-line at once & in it now there is one corvette & one ten-gun brig! Below are the barges of the present Royal Family & others. The convicts work here in chains. Poor fellows! I could not help comparing my lot with theirs. Called & took leave of the Holmes & Robertsons & started by the Mail-post boat at 8. The phosphorescence of the water was snow-white & exquisitely beautiful. At Padua, I was joined by a white veil with a pair of black eyes beneath it &, as I soon found, with a fluent tongue beneath them, which could prattle easily in three languages & said its name was Schrank & it was married to a German officer some 12 years, & was going to visit its father at Milan, &c.

17. En route all day & all night. We breakfasted at Vicenza which gave us time to run round to see some of the durable & classic records of his genius which Palladio has left behind him. My little companion was always ready for chat & let me into many of the secrets of Italian domestic life, which in fact by no means deserves the name. We dined at Verona, a fine old town containing about 40,000 inhabitants. A Roman amphitheatre in the Piazza di Bra is what everybody goes to see & certainly is in wonderful preservation. It is very large & is still in use as a theatre; an old gentleman was busy in the arena, not fighting with a lion but painting scenes for the comedy next Sunday. About 10 minutes' walk further on & just outside one of the gates is the garden of a Franciscan convent, & in that garden an outhouse, & beneath that shed a long granite trough used for washing vegetables, &c. It is but an old trough, nevertheless a more interesting sight than any in Verona. This was Juliet's coffin, for Shakespeare's tragedy is one of real-life, only the family name is not Capulet but Scaligeri. Two posts beyond Verona we came to the beautiful Lago di Garda & travelled by the side of its blue water 6 or 8 miles.

18. Reached Milan at 7 this morning. I was glad enough to be on my legs again. The little woman found 2 brothers waiting for her. She grasped my arm, screamed with delight, & then set to & kissed them vociferously. By

means of a warm bath & breakfast I put my inner & outer man to rights & then started for the post office. No letters from home. I had a long hunt for a Chevalier Vassalli to whom I brought a letter of introduction. He was not at home, so I left the letter & he called twice in the afternoon when I was roving. The Cathedral certainly beats every Gothic structure that I have seen in combining elegance & grandeur, decoration & unity. I saw nothing more except the inside of several shops & the outside of La Scala theatre & was not sorry to get to bed somewhat earlier than usual.

19. The Chevalier was with me at breakfast time, an officer-like man of 50 something. Still vigorous & enthusiastic, he was an officer of Buonaparte's whom he accompanied to Moscow when 22. Afterwards he was Equerry to Queen Caroline, always with her & the first witness called on her side.[1] He knows much both of field & Court & is a very entertaining companion. His salary & pension of 300 guineas per annum promised him in the Queen's own writing is still *in nubibus*. He took me first to the Ambrosian Library. The director of the establishment, a cousin's of the Chevalier's, was very attentive & showed me some invaluable MSS: a folio Virgil with notes by Petrarch, & Leonardo's journal or album, a marvellous illustration of his versatility. From thence I went to the Brera. The collection is not large but contains some first rate productions. I then picked up the Chevalier & we trotted off to the old convent of St. Maria delle Grazie to see the great picture of Leonardo's[2] which all the world goes to see, or try to see, for much must be supplied by the imagination. Being painted in oil it is dropping off in flakes, but what remains is the revelation of a mighty & various Master-mind. The Saviour's head is sublime. The soulless monks positively cut away the feet of Christ & his neighbours to heighten a door-way! The afternoon being fine I ran up to the top of the Cathedral & found myself in a forest of snowy pinnacles & an army of statues, everything white marble. The views from this lofty throne 440 feet up are splendid: the snowy ridge of the Alps to the North, Mt. Blanc, the Jungfrau, the Splugen, the Tyrolese Alps, all distinctly visible; the rich & beautiful Brianza nearer; on the other side the far stretching Appenines. The air was so clear that with a telescope I could see the windows of houses sprinkled on the Appenines about 80 miles distant. The appearance of Milan is very flourishing, its streets are wide, shops

1. Queen Caroline, the wife of George IV, was separated from her husband and for a time lived in Italy on Lake Como. When her husband ascended the throne in 1820 she returned to London. The people of England felt sympathy with her because of her husband's conduct, but the Government instituted a Divorce Bill on the grounds of her alleged adultery. Brougham defended her against the charge and the public feeling in her favour caused the withdrawal of the Bill after it had passed the Lords. She assumed the rank of royalty, but was not allowed coronation and was refused admission to Westminster Abbey at her husband's coronation.
2. The Last Supper, on the walls of the refectory of this church.

excellent, palaces abundant. The inhabitants are rich but oppressed by Austrian taxation which amounts to the same as what was wrung from them by Buonaparte during his European war.

20. The Chevalier placed himself at my disposal. His daughter is a pleasing girl of 20, talks English fluently & is much better educated than Italian ladies mostly are. We visited the Cathedral & descended to the subterranean chapel of St. Carlo Borromeo all covered with cloth of gold & silver in bas-relief. The Chevalier having asked me to spend a day at his Chateau in the country which lies in my route, & thinking this too good an opportunity to be lost, I started with him by diligence for the Brianza, a district about 24 miles from Milan, remarkable for its beauty & the rural retreat of the Milanese nobility who go there to rusticate & look after their silkworms. Mulberry trees cover the country the whole way, as in fact they do nearly all the distance between Venice & Milan. On approaching the Brianza the country becomes hilly, wooded, & beautiful, the snowy Alps rising superbly behind it. The Chevalier's house is called Letza & was anciently a convent, but is now a thorough specimen of an Italian chateau, a large old rambling half-furnished house at the foot of a mountain. We had supper & chatted about Italy, England, pictures, men & women, till bed-time. I had a monk's cell for my chamber in which I fared with anything but monastic austerity.

21. S. A delicious Sunday morning & I was waked by the peasantry going to mass beneath my window. Rambled over the estate with the Chevalier who is a very pleasant companion & a thorough good fellow. He has planted extensively & built a large saloon for his silkworms. His plantation consists of mulberries, vines, & olives. In the middle of the day we called on an Englishman called Robinson, a settler of 6 years standing. He is a spirited & intelligent man, but one of those unpatriotic fellows who carries on a very extensive silk thread manufactory, which he showed me after ascertaining that I was not concerned in the silk trade, & also over his grounds which are excessively beautiful. The Brianza is the most beautiful part of Lombardy, perhaps of Italy, & yet English tourists know nothing about it. Wandering beside a beautiful river we visited 2 or 3 very fine cascades amongst the woodlands & some most picturesque points of view, then his mill which is a perfect model of workmanship & machinery. Nothing of the sort in England can surpass it. The motive power is a water wheel 31 feet in diameter. Workmen in the silk mills in England receive 20/- per week. His are paid 3/-. How can we compete with such? He joined us at dinner as did an Italian planter of the neighbourhood & we passed a very social evening together. Robinson is from Norwich & knows the Gurneys. A man of much practical knowledge & energy.

22. The Chevalier called me at 4 & at 5 we bade adieu to his romantic residence, the beauty of which & the frank hospitality of its owner, I shall long

remember. He tried hard to persuade me to spend another day with him, & not succeeding, drove me & my luggage to Como, about 9 or 10 miles through a rich & beautiful district fortified on the North by the snowy rampart of the Alps. At Como we breakfasted & visited the Cathedral. The town is charmingly placed at the southern extremity of the lake. A gentleman about to start by the Milan diligence was suddenly seized with a sort of convulsion in the brain, which manifested itself by a fearful display of the combative principle, till breaking his stick across a man's head, he was made captive & held down by 6 men. His howls were perfectly frightful to hear. Vassalli took a warm & affectionate leave of me & I embarked on board the little Steamer *Falco* which plies daily up & down the lake. The day was faultless & the scenery enchanting, villas & cottages looking at their reflections on the still waters, the hills rising in crags surmounted by sunlit snow & on the other side richly wooded with chestnut & mulberry. The water was the colour of bloodstone & almost without a ripple. We passed many picturesque little towns by the lake-side & finally reached our destination, Colico at the head of the lake, about midday. I landed & in company with a young clergyman called Sockett, whose acquaintance I made on the passage, & whose company was an acquisition, I journied on at once by post chaise to Chiavenna. We travelled under a wall of snow-capped mountains & by the side of lakes & rivers formed by the dissolving snow, & we reached Chiavenna at 3, a little nest overhung by dark beetling mountains which look as if they would swallow it up in a moment. After dinner we explored the environs which are very picturesque, examined the church & scraped acquaintance with a blue-eyed German fraulein who was artless, pleasing, & communicative. My friend is a man of refined tastes & cultivation & we spent an agreeable sociable evening.

23. Today we passed the Splugen. Somebody says the *first sight* of the Alps is an event in a man's life. If so, what must the first passage of them be. From Chiavenna it is one continuous, but not very steep, ascent of two posts to the mountain top. I thought the views in ascending some of the most magnificent I ever saw, Alps above Alps, sternly rising in black array, bristling with pine-groves, & their lofty summits lost in the clouds or glistening with eternal snows. As we ascended higher & higher it became awfully grand. We passed through galleries of considerable length either hewn out of solid rock or built of massive mason-work, through which the snow-water percolating formed icicles as large as a man's body. At length we were above the clouds which veiled the breast of the mountains & lost sight of the earth beneath us with its pleasant green & dashing torrents. We were amongst the region of snow, through which the road has been cut with great difficulty within the last 5 days subsequent to a very heavy fall of snow. The white walls rose on either side us considerably above the roof of the diligence. Nothing was

visible but white snow, exquisitely blue in the crevices, black crags & a sombre sky. We were joined by the Engineer of the road, a robust & intelligent man who gave us his company as far as the Custom House, a little on the Italian side of the summit. Here the diligence was changed for a sledge, the luggage being placed in two others & the conducteur in another. This was the strangest maddest sort of travelling I ever saw. We avoided the road in which a hundred men were at work,* cutting out a passage for future travellers, & floundered through the snow, the horse often buried up to the chest, often sliding on all fours, but ever recovering himself & scrambling forward in the most extraordinary manner. At length we reached the highest point & began to descend on the Swiss side. This was capital fun though sometimes approaching to the terrific. We were wrapt in clouds & snow & rain fell abundantly, the effect of which was to hide the beautiful distance from us altogether. Sometimes we crossed the road, sliding right down into it from a snow bank of 20 feet in height, then rising a similar one with no inconvenience except a few hard thumps on the bottom of the sledge. At length I remarked our driver slipping a bit of chain under the slide of the sledge, which I thought looked ominous. He said he was going to take us a shorter way & down we dashed at a place that looked as steep as the wall of a house. The horse managed admirably. His motion consisted of 2 or 3 jumps & a slide, now almost off his legs but brought up by the snow, & continuing the descent at a most headlong pace. It was far too steep to see his head except when he was thrown on his side. However, our driver gave him the reins entirely & he brought us to the bottom in safety. At the end of our sledge journey which lasted about an hour, we found another diligence waiting us which whirled us down the hill by chasms, torrents, groves of spruce & plains of snow, till we reached the pretty little town of Splugen where we dined. The inn is capital. The people talked German which sounded almost home-ish to my ears. The Swiss bridges, balconies, & wooden houses with their wide eaves, looked highly picturesque. The next post but one brought us to the celebrated Via Mala, a magnificent defile, a mighty chasm in the mountain, the road winding along its side & the pent Rhine dashing over the black rocks far below. In some parts the precipices rise on each side almost perpendicularly upwards of a thousand feet, with here & there rich patches of the mountain spruce. It was the daring work of an Italian Engineer & is certainly the grandest pass I ever beheld. We reached Coire about 10, a queer place. All the travelling gentry in the salon were flirting with the two chambermaids who were nothing backward, & the waiter was playing on the guitar. I was not sorry to get to bed. Here commence the abominable eider-down quilts.

* Those poor fellows are unable to work more than 3 or 4 days together, the dazzling of the snow producing inflammation in the eyes. Many of them wore spectacles or veils.

24. Today's was an easy & delightful excursion amidst highly picturesque Swiss scenery. A diligence which started at 5 in the morning took us to the little village of Walenstadt where a steamer awaited us on the lake of that name. The views on this lake have less of beauty & less of variety but more grandeur than those of Como, for Walenstadt is completely built in with lofty, precipitous & snow-clad mountains with romantic ravines & glens between, rich in firs & pasturage, little emerald intervals amongst the gloomy crags. From Wesen at the other extremity of the lake a gay barge bore us down the canal on a rapid stream into the Lake of Zurich where we embarked on board the steamer *Republikaner* which was crowded with passengers. The shores of the lake are very pleasant to look upon, but the further you proceed the further nature's grandeur is left behind. Two glaciers in the distance were pointed out, but their icy outlines were rounded by the snow which concealed them. The banks seem alive with an industrious & thriving peasantry, whose white cottages & well-cultivated meadows cover the borders of the lake. The steamer performs a zig-zag orbit from side to side of the lake to accommodate the scattered population. We reached Zurich at ½ past 5, a very pretty town with a cathedral & one or 2 churches, some capital hotels & a population of 14,000 inhabitants. After a cup of coffee & an omlette I started by the night-diligence for Basle, bidding adieu to my clerical friend with sincere expressions of regard on both sides. The diligence reaches Basle at ½ past 5 in the morning. The steamer leaves Basle half an hour earlier. In order to catch her, before starting I gave every postilion a gratuity to push on, which they did manfully. I picked up another acquaintance, a Swiss who had spent 4 years in Italy & was glad of an opportunity to practise his Italian. He was simple & intelligent but I lost him at Brock where we stopped to sup & I had 2 fat German bears in his place. They formed a huge bundle of cloak & cap on either side of me & snored terrifically.

25. My efforts & grateful stimulants applied in the right quarter enabled us to reach Basle an hour before our time, but alas all to no purpose. There was no steamer going down the Rhine today. However I made the best of it, cleaned & fed & at the Railway Office, secured a place all the way to Cologne, via Strasburg, & packed myself on the Railroad carriage at 7. The conveyance is good & well regulated, the country flat, well-cultivated & uninteresting. We reached Strasburg before 12. I hailed the Rhine as an old acquaintance & my heart leapt with pleasure when I felt the steamer rushing down the rapid current towards the sea & thought that there was but four days between me & England.

26. The scenery was spoilt by torrents of rain. The passengers were eminently uninteresting & dinner was the great event of the day. However I found one companion in the person of a Prussian Officer who had been in Italy & was fond of paintings. I landed with him at Coblentz & he took me to see a noted

astronomical clock, the work of a poor German monk, & a perfect miracle of art. We reached Cologne at 10, & landed in rain & darkness. The disembarkation was the supreme hour of selfishness. The polite passengers all but came to blows over their respective baggage. One elderly gentleman planted himself firmly in the midst, bestriding a trunk colossus-like, & kept the rest at bay till his belongings were dragged forth from the mass. Took bed at the *Rheinberg Hof*.

27. I rattled across two Kingdoms today & found myself comfortably lodged at the *St. Antoine Hotel* at Antwerp at 10. Other travellers I met in the coffee room stared when I told them I was in Italy 4 days ago. At 5 this morning I visited Cologne Cathedral & found many people at mass, a lesson I thought, for us Protestants. The railroad takes you from Cologne to Liege in 2 hours & a half. Here in concert with 3 other English I took a carriage to Liege[1] which arrived in time to catch the last train to Antwerp. The whole line is to be completed in October which will lessen the distance by 4 hours. The country was generally flat, but rich in corn & hay.

28. S. I have got an inveterate trick of early-rising by being thus continually en route. Feeling it quite strange to be in bed between 5 & 6, I got up, breakfasted, boarded the steamer & secured a good berth, & then made a tour of the churches. The cathedral is a remarkable building. Most unfortunately Rubens's Descent from the Cross was enveloped in a huge cloth to preserve it while whitewashing the church & no persuasions availed to uncover it. At 1 we got under weigh, our steamer, the *Wilberforce*, a large, powerful & comfortable vessel, full of passengers, nearly all English. As we left the city the fretted spire of the cathedral rose beautifully conspicuous. Buonaparte called it, not unaptly, a piece of Mechlin lace-work. I thought myself fortunate in so fair an object as the finish of my tour. What a 3 months it has been! How crowded & crammed with interest. It is not the least enjoyable part of the excursion to be on the way *Home*, to rejoin so many fond & faithful hearts & to enjoy the multiform delights of my singularly favoured allotment. We had a stiff breeze & night ahead.

29. Tempestuous night. On going on deck we found ourselves inside the North Foreland & soon the other Bank of the Thames was visible. The feeling, or at all events the expression, of filial sentiment, however, on the part of the passengers, was damped by the cold heavy rain, varied with intervals of mud colour fog through which we had to pass & wait an hour & a half shivering before a barred door, waiting to hear our names called by the Customs Officer to have our luggage searched. At length in despair at the tardiness of the operation, I jumped into a Railway carriage & rattled up to Town, put up at St Paul's Coffee House & rattled back again to Blackwall. After half an hour longer waiting I got through my examination, washed,

1. The first 'Liege' should probably read 'Aachen'.

dressed, dined & went to Meeting. My entrance though very quiet was soon observed. What a contrast from the churches I have been amongst for the last 3 months. I paid little attention to the business which was some dull discussion about Croydon & Ackworth Schools, for heart & eyes were engaged in hunting out many a friend amongst the wide mass of clean quiet countenances. There was Uncle C., Cousin Sam Gurney, J. T. Price, S. Tuke, & valued worthies without end, & not one amongst them wore a beard! At length it felt more natural & I had time to think of other things, the infinite cause for gratitude on my part & the abominable matter-of-course way in which these favours are received. I greeted old friends & young friends too numerous to mention, & spent the evening with Uncle C. at his lodgings in Christopher St. hearing about home affairs. A letter from my mother shocked me with the news of Susan Sterling's most sudden & unexpected death & the consequent change in J. Sterling's plans. He means to settle in the Isle of Wight for his children to enjoy the advantages of A. Maurice's[1] tuition. What a change for me! What a sorrowful dismemberment. I cannot reconcile myself to the idea at all. Then she tells me how the girls have suffered from their close & active sympathy with the bereaved husband & assiduous care of the children.

30. After breakfast I removed bag, baggage, & self to Uncle C.'s lodgings. I found William there at breakfast, unchanged, & rattled off with him to pay sundry debts & calls. I dined at the Bells, as I promised Eliza they should be the first visited. They had had a good account of James from Venice. I spent a highly interesting evening with Aunt C. who told me much about home-matters. My father has sold the carriage-horses & dismissed William, a sacrifice for the necessities of others, worthy of himself, while I have been indulging self to the full!

31. Attended a meeting for worship at Devonshire House & listened to some unimportant offerings from female 'Instruments' & a powerful address to the young from John Pease. Paid a very interesting visit on Mill at the India House, who was if possible more affectionate than ever, but he looked worn & thin. His work on logic has had an extraordinary sale in the first month after publication. We talked much about Sterling. He thinks his paleness & thinness are to be attributed principally to the lead absorbed into his system. Attended to my boxes at the various London agents & then to part of the evening sitting, which was occupied by considering whether or not to issue a minute of advice respecting the stricter upholding of our external peculiarities. It was unnecessary I thought, for I never saw a plainer Yearly than the present, actually not one specimen of dandyism. Went down to Newington with the Harrises & Aunt C. in the evening. After tea Bella blew out the candles & we told ghost stories. She keeps Pa & Ma pretty

1. Anna (Mrs F. D.) Maurice was the sister of Susan Sterling.

constantly in the fidgets in consequence of a romantic love affair with a youth called Compton who is denied access to the house.

JUNE

1. Paid sundry business calls & dined at the Backhouses. Jane looked like a damask rose. Hannah Backhouse looked & acted her part like a duchess. William & I spent the evening together at St. Paul's Coffee House where we took a sitting room & beds, brought our journals & compared notes, & altogether managed to enjoy ourselves pretty thoroughly. We turned in about 2 in the morning.

2. This was the last day of the Yearly Meeting & was almost entirely occupied by the reading & revision of the various Epistles. William left today for Bradford. I have had far too little of him. I ran down to Tottenham with Cos. F. Fox, & slept at his new house which is thoroughly comfortable. But how I pity his allotment in being tied for life to such a good intentioned but eternal fidget. I believe it would drive me mad.

3. I found by a letter from Uncle A. that I am appointed to join a Deputation coming from Falmouth to make a last effort with the Government about the Packets which they have announced they are about to remove altogether to Southampton. It will be useless I know & will detain me through next week. However the effort *should* be made. Dined with the Backhouses, got through some business-calls in the afternoon & spent the evening at Upton. A large party at Ham House. The Ed. Buxtons & the Johnstons with their respective families were there. I was very glad to renew my acquaintance with Priscilla, & had a long & interesting chat with her. She gives a good account of Chenda, but a poor one of Sir Fowell who is staying at Bath to recruit.

4. S. Brilliant assemblage at Plaistow meeting & a striking sermon from Hannah Backhouse about a surrender of the whole heart & a supplication from Elizabeth Fry which was like the music of a fife. Called on Elizth. Fry who was very affectionate in remembrance of last Autumn. Cos. H. Backhouse gave me a lift to Town in her carriage.

6. Called on the Balls, took leave of Grandmamma & Aunt Charlotte, & then to Town with Uncle C. with whom & his lady I trudged to Guy's Hospital to call on the Maurices.[1] Frederick Maurice gives me the idea of a calm thoughtful & sincere man. His wife is a superior likeness of her sister. They spoke most warmly of the girls & pressed me to come & see them. Drove down to Upton, saw the Gurneys & dined at the Frys. The Backhouses were there. Jane B. looked very beautiful but was particularly silent, like the

1. F. D. Maurice was chaplain of Guy's Hospital, 1836-46.

writing on a mummy-case, very interesting if you could only get at the meaning of it.

7. At length I obtained some news of the Deputation, which Sir Charles tells me are to meet him at the House at 6 tomorrow evening. He believes our case to be hopeless. Hannah Backhouse having entrusted Edmund to my care for the day I took him to the Polytechnic Institution which contains some beautiful models & many things of more than common interest. A lecture on aeronautic navigation was delivered soon after we came in. The principle of the new invented mode of flying does not appear to be unphilosophical but the practical difficulty is the weight of the engine. The inventor[1] asserts, however, that he has overcome that difficulty, having constructed a steam engine of 20 horse-power weighing only 600 lbs. There is no doubt that sails rapidly revolving will raise a weight if not too cumbersome, but how to keep up that rotation & preserve lightness? However time will prove this as it proves everything else. Having sent Edmund Backhouse back to the maternal bosom, I ran down to Carlyle's & found the giant in great force. Both he & his wife were very warm & we spent a long & highly interesting evening together discussing Cromwell, Goethe, Judaism, & the present distresses. Carlyle does not yet know what form his History of Cromwell will take, but the more he studies the man the more is he convinced of his honesty. I got home before midnight.

8. I joined the Deputation, Bond, Broad, & W. Carne, at the Albion & proceeded to the House of Commons. Disappointed by finding 'no House' tonight. We mustered some of our own members, Sir Charles Lemon, Capt. Plumridge, Enys, Vivian, Sir S. Spry, & J. Trelawny, & discussed future proceedings. Spent the evening very pleasantly with the Trelawnys.

9. The Deputation called first on Sanders, the managing Director of the Gt. Western, who is with us heart & hand, & offers to help us in any way we may point out. We then called on Sir Charles, then on Dr. Rashleigh who will also aid us as far as he can, then on Lord Eliot[2] who was very civil & gentlemanly, but held out little prospect of success. He says Goulburn[3] is the man to whom Sir R. Peel will refer us, & he having just lost his son (one of the most promising young men in the Kingdom) we must count on some delay. Dined with my colleagues at the Albion & then trudged down to the House. We met a good many Cornish members & decided on applying for an interview with Sir R. Peel as early as possible. Bond & Broad are meanwhile to get a memorial from Bristol, while W. Carne & myself were

1. Probably W. S. Henson who, in 1842-3, patented a design for an 'Aerial Steam Carriage'.
2. Edward Eliot (Earl of St Germans), M.P. for East Cornwall and Chief Secretary for Ireland.
3. Henry Goulburn, M.P. for Cambridge University, Home Secretary and Chancellor of the Exchequer 1841-6.

dispatched instanter for Liverpool to try to get a similar document from thence. We had little more than 2 hours to go into the City, pack up & be at Euston Square. Found Uncle C. at my lodgings who was vexed at my galloping off just now (as the Backhouses delay their departure till early next week & he wished me much to make the most of the opportunity). I had some open chat with him on the subject.[1] The many external recommendations to such a step keep me back, jealous of the influence of such motives. Found myself in the Railway carriage at ½ past 8 & spent the night in meditating many things.

10. We reached Liverpool at ½ past 5. After the refreshment of a wash & breakfast, W. Carne & I sallied forth on our mission. We called on 20 or 30 of the most influential merchants in the place. We talked to many on 'Change & got, I think, at the general feeling of Liverpool on the subject of the projected alteration of the mails. Those interested in the Gt. Western Railway are strongly opposed to it. Those in the Southampton Railway are as strongly in its favour. In some we succeeded in exciting a useful jealousy of the London merchants being 10 hours in advance of them in the receipt of letters, but the prevailing feeling was indifference. We therefore found it necessary only to seek for a memorial petitioning a delay in the decision of Government till the merits of the case be investigated. We called on Gladstone, the Mayor (brother to the Minister). His leaning was against us, but he gave way a little after hearing our case. Liverpool strikes me as a great Mammon shrine. Not enjoying but getting, seems the universal object of life. You will not hear a hearty laugh from one end of the city to the other. 'Change is peopled by care-worn, pale-faced men who sacrifice the gifts of God to the Demon of lucre. May I be preserved from the like!

11. S. As cold & dismal a Sunday morning as need be. A silent meeting, after which A. Waterhouse took me in his carriage with wife & 3 daughters to his house at Aigburth the most beautiful part of the neighbourhood of Liverpool. He has laid it out with much taste & has had the good sense to retire from business within the last fortnight in order to enjoy life & turn it to more account than a perennial Counting House. His wife is a person of great refinement & would be pretty but for an unfortunate obliquity in one eye. Wrote Uncle C. a full confession concerning Jane. Afternoon meeting also silent. Friends not numerous considering that the population of Liverpool is 300,000.

12. Agitated the city of Liverpool till 4 o'clock. Hard work, desperately uphill having to contend with those obstacles of the worst sort, Prejudice & Indifference. The Memorials we had drawn up for signatures were, however, so modest in their request (simply asking delay till we have an opportunity of

1. It becomes clear that a match between Barclay and Jane Backhouse was now being discussed by the family.

making out our case) that our toil was not wholly fruitless. Took leave of my numerous friends (amongst them W. Rathbone who was vexed at my not dining with him, saying he had invited a large party of his friends to whom he had promised fine sport with a young fox from Cornwall) crossed the river to Woodside & dined with the Frys. They accompanied me 10 miles on the railway to join their little girl who is 'put out' for change of air. I continued my journey to Town.

16. Breakfasted with the Backhouses & agreed either to accompany them or join them at Ewhurst. At ½ past 12 our forces mustered at the Albion, a goodly array of influence & respectability. Having arranged the plan of proceedings we went en masse to the Treasury, mustering about 30. Lords Eliot & Sandon, & Sir H. Douglas being of the number, also Freshfield & Lord Wodehouse, the Bristol members, & of course the Cornish ones. After waiting ½ an hour we were ushered with due form into the presence of His Mightiness[1] who received us with a slight inclination of the head. We took our seats & opened our battery. Sir Charles introduced the subject neatly, Lords Sandon, Berkeley, & Broadwood presented Memorials on the subject from their respective constituencies. Bond then followed with a very good, clear, & pointed speech, showing first Falmouth's advantages over Southampton from its local position at the mouth of the channel, then with respect to the north & west of England, then the fallacy of the argument used against us of the passengers often arriving before the mails, then the continual necessity of the W. India Steamers entering Falmouth for a supply of coals, then the uncertainty of the channel voyage & finally the great injury to local interests which such a change would involve. Lord Sandon fought hard for us but the premier was impenetrable. He spoke in the blandest manner of his pain in injuring local interests, but could hold out to us no prospect of a revision of the Government decision. He recommended us to embody our arguments in a regular memorial to be presented to the Treasury & he promised us it 'should have an answer', no great promise I thought after all. However, I think we have gained a reprieve at least & meanwhile we must not be idle. Ran down to Woking by Railway & thence across the country to Ewhurst, about 18 miles via Guildford, a beautifully wooded spot among the hills, behind which the sun was gloriously setting when I arrived. Found Aunt Mary and the Backhouses at Adeline's Swiss cottage. She was most cordial & affectionate talking over old times. Hopper seemed a gentlemanly sort of country clergyman. They have two children & Adeline looked well & happy. I slept at the Rectory, a very sweet place indeed.

17. After luncheon we set sail. I found a convenient corner in the Backhouses' fly. We turned out once or twice to admire the rich English views which present themselves from various parts of the road. Jane is a great

1. The Prime Minister.

admirer of scenery, but is impenetrably reserved on most topics of interest. Reached Town at 6. Uncle C. & I went down to Upton to sleep.

20. Took leave of the Backhouses, & escorted them to the Paddington Station, Cos. H. Backhouse by a sudden whim having fixed on attending a Quarterly Meeting at Taunton. Jane was silent but less reserved. I fear the repression of all outward show of feeling inculcated under the Jane Gurney[1] dynasty has become an inveterate habit. After all I'm not sure I could find her equal in the Society. Her mother is a grand creature.

21. Fixed on starting by the South Western at 9 but meeting Cos. J. T. Price at breakfast at the *White Hart* I was persuaded to stay with him till 11 examining the Neath Abbey Co.'s finance statement. In these perilous & uncertain times & with the failure of the Harfords[2] staring one in the face it makes one feel careful & Cos. J.T.P.'s report did not diminish the feeling. As it turned out the 11 o'clock train answered exactly. I reached Gosport at ½ past 2, where a steamer was waiting to convey us to Ryde. As we approach home after a long absence I find the nearer we get to it the more anxious are we to be there. The Ryde Steamer was full & had some individualities on board, amongst them an old gentleman of 87 who had outlived nearly all his senses, but retained an almost youthful freshness of mind. In the mid-voyage his hat blew overboard & we decked him out in an old Welsh cap & a lady's boa, making him a regular carnival figure. He entered into the joke & enjoyed being laughed at as few elderly gentlemen would. I landed on the pier, which Sterling well describes as being as long & as wooden as a parliamentary debate. A coach was just starting for Ventnor so I jumped on it & cut across this rich & beautiful island. Sterling was waiting for me at his gate. I jumped off to greet him; he grasped my hand but said little. We walked into his temporary residence & saw the children with their respectable refined & ladylike governess. They gave me a dinner-tea & S. & I trudged off on a walk. We had an interesting time of it & not without profit. Sterling looked ill but seemed to possess more than his usual strength & energy. He made little allusion to his wife, more to his present arrangements & future plans, & the work he is about & has in prospect. We separated at a late hour for him. I slept at the inn close by for he had no room to offer me. He showed me the house he has taken & whither he will remove in 3 months, in which there is no lack either of room or beauty.

22. Breakfasted with Sterling at ½ past 7. Took a warm leave with a promise of a visit from him early next month & at 8 was on my way back to Ryde. This enabled me to reach Southampton via Gosport at ½ past 2, just in time for the *Duke of Cornwall* Dublin Steamer for Falmouth. She was a fine vessel. There was a crowd of passengers & no beds to be had. I met two of the Childs

1. Jane Backhouse's maternal grandmother.
2. The Quaker banking family of Bristol.

of Liskeard, brothers of our worthy little clergyman at Perran, & also a very intelligent young man, a doctor, with whom it was a pleasure to converse. There was such a preponderance of ladies that we had to give up half the saloon to them. A curtain was stretched between & we made ourselves as comfortable as we could on the sofas.

23. Woke at 4 in Plymouth harbour. At 12 I was in Falmouth harbour. As one well known spot after another hove in sight it seemed like the faces of early faithful friends smiling a welcome. My heart beat quicker as the anchor dropped over the bow & I stood straining my eye amongst the boats that shot out from various points, to find some old waterman I knew to take me ashore. Presently whom should I see alongside but A.M. & C. attended by Thomas who acted coxswain. In a very few seconds I was seated between them taking breath after the first salutations, all grinning with pleasure & talking nonsense. We lounged thus for nearly half an hour before descending to thoughts of luggage, which, however, was quickly procured, & in a few minutes I sprang on shore on the old steps, ran up & greeted the old clerks, who hailed me with genuine cordiality. We walked *home*, & while the pie was baking for our dinner at Penjerrick, I took a swim at Gillan Vaise by way of quelling feverish excitement & removing the dust of travel. My father looked, I thought, remarkably well. Conversation flowed as might be expected all the afternoon. In the evening I commenced reading my journal with viva voce annotations. Thomas Evans's grasp of welcome with his strong horny hand was such as almost to 'force the red blood drop from the nail'. It was a delightful reunion for I could trust in all the warm expressions of those who greeted me. It was real in them & I am very sure it was not unreal in me.

26. Devoted to business. Fox & Co. have been progressing satisfactorily in my absence, but the Perran Foundry Co. has been too extravagant. The new manager has effected great changes. The men stand in awe of him & call him Pharoah. He requires a slight check now & then, being apt to hold his head rather too high. Unpacked my boxes from Naples. Nothing injured.

27. I took my seat amongst the Guardians of the Poor, having been elected Tribune for Perran by a majority of 200 to 12. Went through the Penryn Workhouse with my father & looked into the condition of the boys & men therein. The Board proceedings seemed to be conducted in a business-like manner, though perhaps with rather too much of the *Board* & too little of the *Brother* in its feeling. We returned to a late dinner & spent a considerable part of the evening at the Counting House.

JULY

1. Attended a meeting appointed at Falmouth to receive the report of the Deputation concerning their doings in London & Liverpool. Bond held forth & gave a very lucid account of our proceedings for which we were duly & quite sufficiently buttered with praise. My father's proposal to make an offer to the Government to forward the mails ourselves in every instance within 20 hours after their delivery at Falmouth, procured the appointment of a Committee to try & carry the thing into effect. This would take Peel's strongest argument out of his mouth.

2. Called on Mrs. Lake to tell her about her sister at Florence & drank tea with Uncle G.C. to talk about Italy. He made enquiries about Jane Backhouse which I was able to answer clearly. I walked out to the Cottage, but found nobody at home. Walked round the house & found doors & windows carefully bolted; effected an entrance through a bedroom window, got a light & sat down to my writing in the library. Hearing Thomas & Jane come in, I rang the bell, but both were far too frightened to ascend the stairs, thinking it must be a ghost. After a hurried conversation I heard them run out of the house & up the garden steps in order to peer in at the window & try to make out what thing it was that rung the bell. I had drawn the blinds down before & at length Tom with desperate courage rushed upstairs. I quietly asked him if that was what he considered guarding the house in my absence. He could not speak for some time, but at length stammered out a question as to how I had got in. I told him it was very easy & no thanks to him that I happened to be an honest man & not a rogue, as I had full opportunity to carry off the most valuable things in the house. He was thoroughly dumbfoundered. It was a lesson that I think he will remember.

4. Breakfasted at 7 & started for Liskeard en famille. Stopped an hour at Bodmin Asylum to see Hicks & his patients. He gave us a cordial reception. Flamank I hear is recovered. Barham has left. Provis is worse. It is a scene of deep & sad interest & makes one think a little of what use one is making of Reason while one has it. Reached Liskeard at $\frac{1}{2}$ past 4 & after tea, the elders being gone to a Select meeting, we 3 wandered forth. On returning to our Inn we had the surprise of finding Cos. H. Backhouse & Jane arrived about $\frac{1}{2}$ an hour before, most unexpectedly, but Cos. H.B.'s orbit is so eccentric that it is impossible to say today where she may turn up tomorrow. Jane looked well. They go on to Plymouth to attend Aunt Abbott's funeral & will then probably come on to Falmouth.

6. Breakfasted with & took leave of the Backhouses, they are going forward to Plymouth & I am wending my solitary way back again per Plymouth coach. Sterling disappointed me, so after accomplishing some business, I rode in & boarded Sterling in person at Pearce's. He had been overdoing the

thing as usual, travelling 2 nights in succession, but on the whole he was well. Called on Bond afterwards & staid with him till 11, conferring on the packet question & laying down a railway thro' the County.

7. Sterling to breakfast. He was full of chat. We discussed Puseyism which he compared to a return to the old military tactics, shields, armour, &c., when the invention of gunpowder has made them obsolete; Evangelism[1] being those who have adopted fire-arms as the nobler & higher military weapon, but have no modern system of tactics suited to it. Passed a busy day in the city & met Sterling at dinner at Grove Hill where we talked of art & artists. After dinner he accompanied me to Perran where he lodged. After walking round the garden, seeing, admiring, & suggesting, we spent a poetical evening in my library. He read me his 5th Canto of 'Richard Coeur de Lion', a spirited, chivalrous Ariostic work, full of strong thought & manly character, clothed in a light, easy, cantering verse which gives room both for vigorous sketches & flashes of humour.

9. S. Sterling came to breakfast & then accompanied us to Meeting. He confessed afterwards to me that no service had given him as much satisfaction. He felt, however, somewhat tempted to address a few words to the Meeting on the danger of supposing that you possess the principle of Truth on account of an overweening attachment to some of its outward & accidental appendages. After dinner I had much chat with him alone. He is struck by the girls' mental development & progress.

10. Went to Perran per morning coach. We have saved & are carrying hay for which the weather is most favourable. On returning I heard that Sterling has had some return of haemorrhage. Called on him in his bedroom. He looked pale but made very light of it. The Backhouses actually arrived in the evening. The weather was beautiful, the grass just cut, & Jane in a fit of enthusiasm bounded down the lawn, the girls after her. There is a nobility in her face & a depth of womanhood in her eye, worth something if one could get at it. Her mother's face is one of more power, but more narrowness, something of the dogmatism of intense conviction.

11. I offered P. Buckett £20 to join the Total Abstinence Society. Poor fellow! It is the only chance for him. Joined the girls & Jane at Penjerrick. She hurried through the 3 places & then back to a 5 o'clock dinner at Grove Hill. Cos. Hannah ended the visit by a short 'opportunity'. Found Sterling decidedly better. Vigurs is his sworn disciple, a man in whom there dwells a peculiar turn of thought & Coleridgean tendency, to which however he finds it difficult to give utterance.

12. Called on Sterling after breakfast & had much interesting chat. I think he interprets both Cos. H. Backhouse & Jane, but he underrates the former. The latter he calls a 'fresh fountain springing from the side of a dark rock'.

1. i.e. Evangelicalism.

After Meeting, the Rock paid him a religious visit which he did not swallow over meekly. I rode on to Perran to prepare the minds of my domestics for the advent & the digestive powers of Sterling, Jane & the girls. Sterling was brilliant & interested Jane much. He wanted, however, I thought, that serious earnestness which becomes him best. I rode back with them in the afternoon to attend a public meeting held by Cos. H.B., Sterling & Vigurs went with me. Sterling preferred Cos. E. O. Tregelles's sermon, partly from prejudice I think. She is a specimen of a powerful mind, powerfully acted on but cramped by a limited education & association, & tinged with too much dogmatism for a woman, the consequence of being the first in her circle. Sterling paid an interesting visit in the evening & took his leave.

13. The Backhouses departed after an early breakfast. I rode with them as far as Perran, E.O.T. being their squire as far as Bodmin. Jane was very silent, but rather peculiarly beautiful I thought. Her reserve is full of maiden dignity, but not a little provoking. There is no getting thro' the *rind* as a Yankee would say. Her mother is a majestic personage & would have made a splendid Lady Abbess in the Middle Ages.

14. Rode to Falmouth to attend a Packet meeting. Bond, Broad, & I were appointed to draw up the proposal to the Government to put on an extra mail at our own expense. Called with the girls on Easticks from whom I learnt with mortification that Uncle G.C. was today installed as County Magistrate, the very last post for which bounteous Nature intended him.

16. The accounts of the distresses amongst the Foundry workmen in Staffordshire are deeply melancholy. Their rude, earnest, ungrammatical appeal to their fellows to resist the intention of their employers to make a further reduction in their wages is very significant. It cannot be that the enormous inequality which exists & increases between the condition of man & man will be permitted to endure much longer. Meanwhile it behoves each of us to stand prepared for a crisis, & meanwhile perform honestly our individual duties to our fellow men.

17. At Perran. I visited some of the poor of my parish & found them 'poor indeed'. The difference on coming out of their hovels into my library was humiliating to reflect on. If each had his deserts in this world, where should I be? – where many of *them*?

20. Finished Carlyle's *Past & Present*, a regular trumpet blast to a pleasure & money-seeking generation. He shrinks not from telling each class of men the sternest truths. His text is 'Find out thy appointed work & do it'. It is an earnest outpouring from his great sorrowful heart, a book peculiarly suited to the day, & especially addressed to the laissez-faire aristocracy & to the millocracy, whose only Hell is *the dread of not making money*.

25. I am reading Mill's *Logic*, clear, perspicuous & unpedantic.

28. A capital letter from Sterling, who appears to be meditating a crusade

against lies in general. Joined our people at Penjerrick who were in high preservation. Circumnavigated the grounds with my father, planted a deodara pine together with sundry other innocent amusements.

29. Walked in to Falmouth where I found the box from Milan. Bore it to Perran & found the two pictures in very tolerable preservation. They give the library a character it never possessed before. Went to Falmouth to see some mesmeric experiments by Dr Cantor, a German. The patients were boys from our school. Four of the boys were placed in a decided mesmeric sleep which produced different effects on different individuals. The operation consisted in holding the patient's thumbs & looking into his eyes while he looked up into yours, the effect of which was peculiarly absurd. My father contends that the effects are simply physical from the tension of the nerve pressing on the brain. We are to be taught more about it next week.

31. Meeting of the partners at the foundry; on my way out Finch made a bolt at a heap of slates in the street & fell with me on the pavement. It hurt my backbone & sent a strange giddiness into my head so that I couldn't see clearly for some minutes. A crowd collected &, amongst others, Adeline, who greatly sympathising, intimated that it was quite right that 'Pride should have a fall'. I got on again & had on the whole a satisfactory meeting.

AUGUST

1. Harbour Committee at 6 at which letters from Freshfield & Sir Charles Lemon were read showing clearly that we are *jobbed* out of the packets. Sir R. Peel tells Freshfield that the question is referred to Lord Lowther & the Post Office (to whom accordingly Sir C. Lemon without delay presents our offer of putting on an extra mail). Sir G. Clarke on the other hand writes an answer to an enquiry from Sir C. Lemon that the *Treasury* has determined on the removal of the packets & the Post Office has only some minor details to arrange. Here is an obvious discrepancy in the enemy's tactics. Attended an Education Lecture by Dr. Cantor at 8. He spoke of the low grade of school masters in English society, whereas they are the aristocracy of intellect in Germany. Education is there made a study of & has a literature. Compulsory education as practised in Prussia is no hardship. It is a duty parents have to perform to their children; as they are the children of the state, the Government has at least as much right to instruct them as to punish them. There is a range of education in Germany. He spoke of the smallness of the educational grant in England.[1] He referred to the neglect of female-education, which

1. At this time the Government made a grant to voluntary bodies who ran their own schools, and there was no state education as such.

amongst the soi-disant 'higher classes' consists chiefly of 'accomplishments', which means 'modes of accomplishing matrimony'. A female should have a scientific and *household* education, & the more she is instructed in the intellectual parts of it, the less she will despise the culinary. To follow out his rules, we adjourned to the kitchen with Adeline, & learnt accurately how to broil a chop & afterwards to consume it.

7. No lack of work both at Perran & Falmouth. I finished the day by attending a lecture on mesmerism by Dr. Cantor. It was plain & unpretending. He professed no occult property, but contended that the mesmeric power was possessed by all of us. His experiments were triumphant. Four boys on the platform were put into a state of profound & extraordinary sleep apparently by the simplest agency. Hunt, Vigurs, & Cantabrana were operators as well as the Professor. Young Mogg became so thoroughly torpid that it was a long business to waken him. Rickerby exposed himself by a coarse & senseless opposition, which was only excusable on the score of being drunk. In compliance with his demand, the boys were shaken, pinched, hollo'd to, & had pistols fired off close to their heads, without producing the smallest effect, whilst a few movements of the operator's hand before the patients' eyes in most instances awakened them directly. This is perhaps the most unaccountable part of the business, & the greatest poser to sceptical theorists.

11. There was a Railway meeting at Redruth with Pendarves in the chair. It was a spirited & unanimous meeting. I moved that a deputation be sent to Bristol to nail the project with the Directors of the Gt. Western. Bond & W. M. Tweedy are deputed accordingly. Before leaving the room £25,000 were put down, Pendarves giving £5,000. Rode back to the cottage to meet the Tregedna party who spent a very pleasant evening with me. Uncle J. was in raptures with the two paintings. Poor P. Buckett died this morning, another victim of Intemperance! The widow I fear is left almost destitute.

12. Called on P. Buckett's widow but she was ill in bed. Mrs. Dixon saw me & assured me that Mrs. Buckett had done all a wife could do to restrain her husband's evil propensity & to screen his weakness from others. When a woman loves, what will she not do & suffer? Canvassed the town with Bond for the Railway in order to arm him with as strong a list as possible before meeting the Gt. Western people. He is the best beggar I ever saw & will not take a denial.

14. Continued our canvas & by dint of hard driving & impudence collected nearly £4,000 in the course of the morning. In the evening we had a second lecture on mesmerism from Dr. Cantor. He was moderate in his views & reasonable in his deductions. He stupified two boys & two girls very completely, one of the latter seemed rather ashamed of herself on awaking, for having slumbered in public. Dr. Cantor gave some good hints to the audience about trifling with mesmerism lest they should find themselves in the con-

dition of the wizard's apprentice who picked up enough of his master's art to raise a ghost but unfortunately had not the means of laying it.

19. Hard working day. Forgot to mention that last monthly meeting was astonished by the announcement on the part of his Worship G. C. Fox that he relinquished his membership in the Society.

22. Attended a meeting of Vincent's[1] at the Town Hall in the evening & heard an extraordinary display of popular eloquence on the subject of universal suffrage. He completely won the sympathy of his audience & carried them along with him. His mastery of words was wonderful & he made the justice of his cause appear all but self evident, such is the power of appropriate speech. He advocates none but moral force & bases all his arguments on the injunctions of the Gospel; the sophism lying in treating that which may be right in the abstract as right to apply to a corrupt & complicated social system. He was in prison for Chartism & the Welsh insurrection two years ago was for the purpose of releasing him. He is a handsome young man of eight & twenty & wholly self-educated.

23. Breakfasted with Vincent at Cos. Joseph Fox's & discussed universal suffrage till the bus called for him. Had troublesome business all the rest of the day with an American captain & his mutinous crew, & a Jerseyman whose vessel had been wrongfully seized by the customs for having tobacco on board. Joined Bond & Broad in preparing a memorial to the Treasury in consequence of their published determination to remove the packets from Falmouth. Very stormy.

24. A railway meeting of the Provisional Committee was held at Truro to receive Bond's & Tweedy's report of their mission & to arrange future proceedings. A canvass of the county is decided on & a sub-committee appointed to make out the traffic on a South line.[2] A newspaper from Dublin brings the account of the entire success of the experiment of the atmospheric railway. This has important bearings on ours.

26. Busy morning. Perran in the afternoon. Dr. Vigurs spent the evening with me, a thoughtful & intelligent man who once pinned his faith to Hooker but is now a strong Carlylean. An *esprit fort* in his way & a zealous disciple of Sterling's.

29. The Falmouth regatta appeared to be the grand interest of the day, tho' far from grand it proved. No wind, no company, & few yachts, but a diversion of interest was caused by the Queen's expected arrival at Plymouth & a depression of spirits by the decision on the packet question.

1. Henry Vincent (1813–78) the Chartist leader; his conviction at the Monmouth assizes 1839 led to the Newport riots; was imprisoned again 1840–1. Contested parliamentary seats unsuccessfully, 1841–52.
2. The proponents of a southern railway to Cornwall were faced with the problem of bridging the Tamar at Plymouth, but it was to be sixteen years before Brunel managed to do this.

30. Regatta continued. A dull repetition of yesterday. Tom[1] was here in the *Grand Turk*, looking himself with large beard & scarlet cap like a Pasha at least. He is an honest, downright, humorous sort of fellow. After a little chat on business & fun he was off again. Anna Lean came to stay with us, a sort of person who with no single particular one can reasonably object to, is a being wholly devoid of interest. Cries in the ropewalk attracted me on returning late from the Counting House. I found they proceeded from a female who was assaulted by a drunken man. I called him to account, but he protested innocence. On due examination of the case in magisterial form, I decided that neither party was a bit better than they should be, & charged them both to return to their respective homes on pain of being handed over to the constable. The man seemed the more submissive of the two. The Plymouth guns announced the arrival of Her Majesty between 5 & 6 this evening.

31. A widespread rumour with a sort of official authority set the whole town in a ferment under the hourly expectation of the arrival of the Queen & Prince Albert. Rode to Perran nevertheless, & business over, took a Queen-hunting jaunt to Falmouth with the clerks to bless our eyes with Royalty. I found Falmouth on the water in all boats & on all headlands, but after hours of anxious watching never a queen, nor as much as a maid-of-honour, became visible & we turned back again. Finished *Strafford* which Sterling sent me, an exposition of the most critical time in English history & a most vigorous characterisation of the most remarkable man that figured in it.

SEPTEMBER

1. Today we received a call from Albert & Victoria in their steam yacht. The barge was immediately lowered & they rowed round the harbour, which presented the most animated scene since the landing of Donna Maria.[2] Between 400 & 500 boats dotted the glassy surface of the water & thronged around the royal barge, so as materially to impede its progress. When she returned on board, the mayors of Falmouth & Penryn presented addresses from their respective corporations & inhabitants. It was explained to H.M. that the mayor of Falmouth was a Friend & therefore remained covered.[3] The unfortunate H. Lamb, mayor of Truro, in the excitement of the moment, lost his balance & tumbled into the water & as there was not time to hang him up to dry, he lost the chance of an introduction. Uncle G.C. sent off a

1. Tom Fox of Plymouth.
2. See above, p. 47n.
3. Members of the Society of Friends would not remove their hats before any human authority.

basket of fruit & flowers which was graciously acknowledged. She arrived about 1 & left between 3 & 4; so rapid a peep & so full of excitement while it lasted, seemed like the pageantry of a dream. The day was lovely & the little lady could not but express her admiration of the harbour which her ministers have so unjustly despoiled.

3. S. Another glorious day. Dined at Grove Hill. Found Magister low & out of sorts with himself. It is certainly a mistake to disunite oneself from the society in which you were born & educated for a merely *negative* reason.

9. Drove the mare to Perran. She promised to be a very good thing in harness. At 4 o'clock William arrived in high condition & a huge box coat. He will spend a week with me. We had much to hear & tell. I received a packet from Sterling, enclosing some letters sent to F. Maurice by D. MacMillan,[1] a Bookseller in Fleet Street: some of the most interesting things I have seen for a long time. They show the feeling of the young & vigorous minds of the present generation, a deep inward craving for something more real & more believable than the present system of government & religion as outwardly administered, & the inadequacy of the means to the end. The physical & moral debasement of the lower orders make the writer ask, what in Heaven's name are the priests about? The letters are supposed to be written by a young friend of MacMillan's who died at the age of 20 of consumption.

11. William spent the morning at Trebah & joined me at Perran in the evening; chess & chat, and what was better the arrival of my box from Rome. Two of the frescoes are injured, but the books & engravings are all safe. It was a glorious turn out to be sure.

12. A thorough good day's dissipation. The morning was occupied first by Michael Williams, then the girls, who came to take leave of me on their way to Norfolk. I was glad A.M.'s pictures were come just in time. She was highly pleased with them. I rode with William to Truro & attended first a Horticultural Exhibition, then a Bazaar held for the benefit of the Truro Institution. It was rich in animal beauty & a fine field for flirtation. William had on the whole a very fair show of our Cornish aristocracy. A glorious moony night.

13. Business morning at Falmouth. Spent the evening with William at Tregedna, much to his satisfaction, the scene being one to which he is unused at Bradford. The copper smelters have returned to their work, – hunger-driven. How little chance has a poor man in a contest with a rich one! Law is too dear for him, a strike too calamitous, remonstrance *too* ridiculous.

15. William & I enjoyed a luxurious bachelor-evening, tea & a fire in the little dining room, 2 chairs apiece, chat, chess, poetry, &c., a glance at the past & a long look at the future. William drew the points of distinction in

1. Daniel Macmillan, the founder of the publishing house of that name, who was a friend of F. D. Maurice. Maurice at this time was a professor at King's College, London.

our respective characters ingeniously. He gives me credit for the highest practising standard & himself for the highest theoretical one, that in point of evil we are about on a par, but that I reconcile my errors by stretching conscience to allow them, whilst he does the same things, or worse, with a clear perception of their evil or folly. There may be something in this.

16. Rode in to Falmouth to attend a Polytechnic Committee for arranging all preliminaries previous to the next meeting. Dined at Grove Hill at 5, to meet Uncle David & Minny & Bob, who came yesterday for a few days. Uncle D. is a gentlemanly & kind hearted man with good sense, but lacks force of character. Minny, considering her bringing up in the Belgrave Square atmosphere, is remarkably simple & free from airs; there is a little formality of manner which belongs to the surface but wants brushing off. She is tall, genteel, black-eyed & lady-like. Bob is rather a failure, but there is nothing harsh or low about him.

20. Packed William off by the Plymouth coach at $\frac{1}{2}$ past 8 & then accompanied Uncle & Aunt C. to monthly at Redruth. G. Croker Fox was continued a member, having expressed to the Friends who visited him a willingness to waive his resignation, & explaining as his motive a *perplexity* of mind about the sacraments. The whole transaction thus ending in nothing must be a little humiliating I should think. Called on W. Williams, the soldier, who showed me his Jelalabad[1] medal wherewith he means to dazzle the girls' eyes who may have the honour to dance with him.

23. Spent the morning in taking the Barclays to Penryn & Flushing to call on W. P. Williams & the Suttons. While Uncles David & G.C. were at the former's house the rest of us paid a visit to the Archdeacon, whose first question on Minny's being introduced as the daughter of the late member for Penryn, was 'Eh? Eh? How much did he bribe?' I dined at Carclew at 7 to meet Lord & Lady Lansdowne & their brightly beaming daughter, the Lady Louisa Fitzmaurice. Mary Tremayne was there & sat by me at dinner, full of sweetness & intelligence, a fine specimen of English aristocracy. Snr. Bezzi, Silvio Pellico's[2] friend, & the discoverer of Giotto's great fresco at Florence, flanked me on the other side & we had much interesting chat on matters of art.

24. S. Rode in to breakfast since it was the Barclays' last day with us. It was spent chiefly in encouraging the domestic affections. We spent the evening at Grove Hill. Minny & the Tregednas have sworn eternal friendship, which with young ladies of their age means – three weeks!

1. The town in Afghanistan where the British Army had fought an action in the previous year.
2. Silvio Pellico (1789–1854), Italian patriot and writer. He was imprisoned for eight years and gave an account of his sufferings in prison in his *Le mie Prigioni*, a classic of Christian spirituality and faith.

16. A letter from Sterling asking me to dinner in Town to meet Carlyle, Mill & one or two others. Letter from Hannah Backhouse to my mother from which it appears not improbable that I may have the escortship of her & Jane to Norwich. How funny!

19. Started at 9 for Norwich by the *Quicksilver* to fetch the girls, a journey which may be an eventful one, or may not. A cold dull ride to Exeter where coffee & a mutton chop proved highly acceptable. The night was bitter cold. Edmund Turner Esqr. M.P. was my companion from Truro. He made some semi-apologetic remark on his preference for an outside place when I first met him, but on our re-encountering in a second class railway carriage, he sat mute & senatorial, revolving schemes of political economy.

20. After a 6 hours whirl through the frost & the darkness I alighted at Paddington & located myself at the *White Bear*, Piccadilly, which is close to the Norwich coach office. A wash & a breakfast & newspaper occupied the interval agreeably & at 10 I was again en route. Reached Norwich at ½ past 8. Cos. J. J. Gurney looks benignity, a sort of serene, self-conscious Christianity, his wife evidently a woman of strong sense but their mutual attentions are rather too loverlike. The girls arrived from Hingham at ½ past 10. C. looks decidedly better. We sat & gossipped in their room before a good fire to some purpose. They feel flat on the subject of my thoughts & foresee many difficulties.

21. After luncheon we took leave of our hosts & armed with a note of introduction from Catherine Gurney, called on George Borrow,[1] the author of the *Zincali* & the *Bible in Spain*. He is just the sort of man I expected, one who would walk thro' a brick wall if he took it in his head; he is tall & strong-featured & talks like one accustomed to be listened to. We chatted about Spain of which he gives a wretched account & of languages. He says that the language of the Esquimeaux is one of the greatest metaphysical refinement, distinguishing the slighest shade & difference of thought by a distinct word, & yet they are some of the rudest & least-cultured of the Indian races, – a strange anomaly. His old mother was with him. She is almost as great an oddity as himself. We then went to the Grove[2] to commence our visit, although Edmund is our only host. Cos. H. Backhouse gave out that she & Jane were coming in the evening. We accordingly (Edmund & I) rushed out at the advent of every London coach. Cos. J. J. Gurney & lady came to tea & waited anxiously within. Eliza Gurney declared that she felt in her bones

1. George Borrow (1803–81) had been articled to a solicitor in Norwich before his travels abroad. *The Zincali, or an account of the Gypsies in Spain* was published in 1841, *The Bible in Spain* in 1843.
2. Lakenham Grove, the home of Mrs Joseph Gurney, Hannah Backhouse's mother.

that they were near at hand, nevertheless the evening passed over & they came not & we retired disappointed to bed. It is a strange feeling to be here again after a year's absence. Many thoughts come & recollections & comparisons & speculations. The girls think it necessary to leave on 4th or 5th day because Chenda is coming on 4th to see Anna under the impression that we shall be gone, & she has still a horror of encountering me.

23. We dined at the Bishop's palace at ½ past 6, the old gentleman[1] as bright as ever, very unbishoplike in mind, manner & appearance, with no somnolent hierarchical airs but an easy & entertaining companion. He wore his apron & his straight cut coat. His wife is ladylike & his daughters very pleasing. Catherine, the younger, is full of intelligence. C. Wodehouse, the prebend, & his wife Lady Jane & 2 daughters were there. The elder, Isabella, sat opposite me at dinner & looked so like Chenda that I could not take my eyes off her. We returned about 10. Cos. H. Backhouse was gone to bed. Jane looked very lovely & gave us (i.e. my sisters) a warm welcome. She gives a bad account of her mother, who seems to be quite overdone by her exertions.

24. Rode with Jane & A.M. after luncheon. She creeps out of her shell rather more on horseback & acts rather less on the defensive. She is a noble, clearsighted creature, with a depth of feeling which she makes it her study to conceal, & a consideration for others which manifests itself in those small attentions which most people overlook. The beauty of her outward woman any fool can speak to & every fool has fallen in love with already. After dinner sat some time with Cos. H. Backhouse whose symptoms are anxious ones. The swelling of her ankles indicates more than mere exhaustion, but she was bright & animated as usual. Her experiences (many of them at least in her late tour) have been rather humbling than exalting. After tea we had poetry & other reading till bed time. Jane speaks her interest in a subject much more with her eyes than her lips.

25. Called at Earlham with the girls & had a remarkably sweet time with Anna who is overflowing with affectionate feeling. Chenda's affair has had a remarkably uniting influence on Anna & me, in consequence of the confidence & sympathy which it gave rise to. J. J. Gurney took a confidential walk with me round the garden recommending matrimony. Called on Anna Forster & found to my vexation that William is coming tomorrow morning, for our places are already taken for Town. The girls & I had another social sitting with Hannah Backhouse in her dressing-room, & after tea, poetry & a discussion concerning angels. I hardly know what might be the consequence

---

1. Edward Stanley (1779–1849), Bishop of Norwich, 1837–49; a naturalist and geologist; supported Whig measures in the House of Lords.

of a week more of such intercourse, but Chenda's coming & H. Backhouse's state makes our departure unquestionable.

26. Met William at 7 & rode with him to his father's, making the most of our half hour. He vehemently urged me to stop a day or two longer, but in vain. It evidently would not do. We took coach to Harlestone with a strange jumble of inexplicable feelings. Hester Holmes met us there with her carriage & took us to Gardy Hall, a large old manor house inhabited by herself, husband & 2 children, mother & sister. She gave us food & took us to Ticklesburgh, 7 miles off, to meet the London coach. I dropped the girls at Stratford & pushed on to Knightsbridge where Sterling gave me a warm welcome, & we passed an evening of tranquil enjoyment & interesting conversation. Nothing can exceed his kindness. We talked of Ireland for whose grievances one of his remedies is a sort of arbitration court to prevent a tenant being compelled to pay more than a just rent for his land.

27. After breakfast, Sterling & I sallied forth, first to his father's who has lodgings near, & professed to be very ill. We visited Dr. Carlyle,[1] who is his brother *un*-idealised & turned into a strong practical man of the world. We then walked to F. Cunningham's, Sterling's cousin, who has the most splendid private collection of paintings in the kingdom. He has two Sebastians in his grandest style (M. Angelo's hand is evident in them), a Giorgione, a Leonardo, & a superb sea piece by Ruysdael. He has also a very clever wife with perhaps more head than heart. We then called on Linnell,[2] a very clever painter. He showed us Blake's Illustrations of Dante done in the style of the Campo Santo, a sort of mad genius, poor & gifted. Linnell ventured into an argument with Sterling where he was, of course, soon lost. We then called on Carlyle who was in great force. He put on his hat & accompanied us to a steamer, down the Thames to Westminster. Carlyle talked of his visit to Thirlwall[3] with his own peculiar semi-fun, semi-earnest, then got on a discussion whether it was possible that Cubitt[4] the Builder could be a religious man, seeing he runs up houses innumerable simply for sale & not for duration. He spoke of a dandy as a man pretending to be ornamental. Hearing some shipwrights' sledge hammers he called it the most emphatic voice in London. We drink tea with him tomorrow. I joined the

1. John Aitkin Carlyle (1801–79), physician and younger brother of Thomas Carlyle. He had lived abroad as physician to the Duke of Buccleugh, 1838–43, and lodged for a time in Chelsea on his return.
2. John Linnell (1792–1882), portrait and landscape painter. He had been a friend of William Blake.
3. Probably Connop Thirlwall (1797–1875), Bishop of St David's and a contemporary of Sterling's at Cambridge.
4. Thomas Cubitt (1788–1855) carried out a great many building operations in London. He built Finsbury Circus and the east front of Buckingham Palace.

girls at Upton in time for dinner, the party there as warm-hearted & hospitable as ever.

28. Another busy day. I dined at Sterling's & accompanied him to Carlyle's immediately after. It was great fun to hear them fight over the body of Johnson, Carlyle exaggerating his excellencies & Sterling accordingly pulling him to pieces. Carlyle has little or no power of argumentation, altho' he can assert in grand style, consequently he is no match for Sterling. Carlyle has not yet begun his History of Cromwell.

30. Met William just arrived from Norwich & accompanied him to the Old Bailey to hear Zulueta tried for fitting out a slaver. After another round of shopping we joined the girls and Sterling & Harriet Mill at the College of Surgeons. Owen was peculiarly instructive. To see & study those two men together, representing the physique & metaphysique of human science, was not a little interesting. Owen showed us the beautiful organism of the brain, the stomach, the spinal cord &c., while Sterling saw all through a poetic medium & descanted on the connection of spiritual & material laws. William & I paid an interesting call on J. Mill. He was most cordial & delightful as usual. We spent the evening at Ann Hodgkin's,[2] a quiet sincere-hearted creature, conscientous as her mother, without her conflicts. William slept there also.

31. After breakfasting at the unconscionable hour of 7 & a pleasant chat with Ann, we started for Town. William took care of the girls who go today to Eastwick & I got on board a railway carriage to go to Ipswich. A letter from the Ransomes, in reply to an application for a licence from the Perran Foundry, makes it desirable for me to go & have a personal interview. It rained torrents but we reached our destination & after an odd dinner with a large party of Suffolk farmers I waded thro' the streets to the Foundry Offices. Charles May, the principal Manager, was very cordial; he introduced me to his partners & escorted me over the works. I never saw a manufactory in which machinery is introduced to so great extent & apparently with most beneficial effects. Their business increases so that within the last two years they have had to lay out £10,000 in additional buildings. Their implements (agricultural) are admirable & have won for them both fame & fortune. I put up at C. May's who introduced me to his wife, who is the reverse of himself in appearance; he is as broad as she is spare. Robert Ransome joined us at tea after which we retired into C. May's sanctum & talked over the matter between us. They are straight-forward, honest & thorough good men of business. We got on well together & agreed on the principles of an arrangement between us which will be mutually beneficial. After supper C. May & I sat up till ½ past 12 talking over Commerce, Politics & Manufactures. He is a thorough clever fellow.

1. Ann Hodgkin was the daughter of Hannah Backhouse and Jane's sister.

NOVEMBER

1. Directly after breakfast we set to again, drew up a Memo. of Agreement for the approbation of my partners & had some of the machines tried. We went through the works, the pattern warehouse, where everything is arranged in perfect order, & the great warehouse where they have nearly 1,000 varieties of ploughshare all arranged & lettered & all made after their original patent, that of chilling one side.[1] I saw the process. They cast a dozen & a half at each charge & draw 4 charges an hour from a simple cupola (holding about 1½ cwt.) so that a single cupola casts about 60 doz. per diem, which at 12/- per doz. pays not badly. C. May's invention of compressing wood by driving it thro' a conical hole & then steaming it to retain it in its compressed form is very ingenious. They make bolts & wedges for railway chairs in this manner. Old James Ransome, another comfortable old Friend & the senior partner, was introduced to me. He & C. May reminded me of the Cheeryble Brothers. I dined at R. Ransome's & started per 1 o'clock coach for Town. I met William at the *Green Dragon*. He was obliged to start the same evening for Bradford. We had some interesting chat on interesting subjects & then I accompanied him to the Railway Station & put up at the palace-like Euston hotel. Its coffee room is superb.

2. The Dorking coach brought me to Leatherhead at about 11 where Uncle David's groom & gig were in waiting & conveyed me to Eastwick. Hospitable reception. Accompanied Uncle David in an agricultural tour. His farming is excellent. By draining he has almost doubled the value of the land, his stock of sheep is excellent, & what is more remarkable, he makes it *pay*. Eastwick House is wonderfully improved. The great drawing room, 70 feet long, is splendidly furnished & before it a beautiful Italian garden with terrace & statues is now in progress. We had a quiet social evening without any grand intellectual displays, Aunt M. being absorbed in worsted work & Uncle D. in sheep.

5. S. A dull dreary day. Late hours, fire in the bedroom & all the other arts of luxury to shorten human life, don't agree with me at all.

6. Off by the Horsham coach at 8 & got the girls & all their manifold luggage (except one blue bag) safely thro' London, Paddington Station &c., & we emerged at Frenchay about 8 o'clock. Uncle Francis & Aunt Mariana were in waiting with a good tea.

7. Bristol after breakfast with Uncle Francis. I went over Stratton's splendid manufactory of agricultural instruments & bought one or two, Coalbrookdale Co.'s warehouse,[2] remarkable for its beautiful display of small castings, & finally over the *Great Britain* steamer[3] – the greatest experiment since the

1. This patent was the one which made the firm's fortune.
2. The Coalbrookdale Co. was started by Abraham Darby, a Bristol Quaker.
3. The *Great Britain*, completed in 1845, was the invention of Isambard Brunel, and was the first ocean-going screw-steamer. She is now laid up in Bristol and is being restored.

creation. The propellor is not a screw, but a circular fan with 6 arms, radius 8 feet, coming out behind the rudder & working thro' a water tight collar. 5 out of her 6 masts work on joints so that they can be immediately struck; her deck is about 300 feet long. Each pair of engines meet at the top like a letter A where they work a shaft on which is a wheel, which by means of a huge watch chain, works the shaft of the screw. The saloon rather disappointed me. It wants height. The bed places are capital.

8. Aunt Mariana was much afflicted with toothache. Janette (Dr. Francis Fox's wife) joined us at luncheon after which Uncle Francis dispatched us to Combe in his mother's carriage. Met a warm welcome at Combe. Uncle Hilhouse was as mild & pacific as a sucking lamb. Aunt Agatha was full of affection. A pleasant evening.

10. May my worse enemy never know a worse punishment than a steam voyage with wind ahead & a heavy swell. Uncle Hilhouse's carriage conveyed us to Pill[1] where we embarked on the Cornwall steamer. We lay 'the whole of the livelong day' wretched & retching. An unhappy, sallow complexioned gentleman in an adjoining berth made my very heart (as well as stomach) sick by his incessant & ineffectual strivings, travailling in his berth, & bringing forth – nothing but the East wind. It was grievous to see & to hear so much unprofitable labour. The girls were also laid low. At 11 we cast anchor off St. Ives & 'wished for the day'.

11. There is not a negative but a most positive pleasure in the cessation of pain. To step on terra firma, to be cleansed & purified, & to devour a muttonchop breakfast, were so many upward gradations in the scale of bliss. After surveying Harvey's Foundry & the Haarlem engine, we started by railway to Redruth, thence by bus to Falmouth & there into the parental arms. My father has a severe cold but my mother is robust.

17. A.M. & I spent the evening in hanging prints. There is a *cozeyness* in a small room with one congenial companion & a good fire which large houses know not of. I have come to the conclusion that every additional room beyond your real wants (which of course implies some extras for hospitality according to your means) is a positive loss inasmuch as it increases your cares, cost of furniture, servants' labour & claims. A large house is therefore a sacrifice of comfort for conspicuousness & is purchasing Envy at an exorbitant rate. It increases the claims on your purse while it lessens the power of meeting them. It interferes with your liberty of action & enslaves you with the fetters of style.

20. Two great modern improvements bid fair to change entirely the system of railway construction & to diminish to an extraordinary degree the cost of making & working. The atmospheric principle may be said to be established & the process of hardening wood *in vacuo*, by forcing sulphate of iron & lime

1. On the Bristol Avon between Bristol and Avonmouth.

water into the pores, will, if ultimately successful, strike off half the cost of construction at least. Received from Sterling the 6th Canto of his *Coeur de Lion*, a piece of strong chivalrous manhood.

26. S. Blowing a gale. Some talk with Aunt Lucy on our way to Meeting, led to some thoughts on the real meaning of consistency. She leaves the Friends & joins the Church, she continues to attend Friends' meetings as well as Church, is remonstrated with by her clergyman, leaves his & her own Parish Church *in toto*, & frequents one in the country, still continuing part of her allegiance to Friends. In all this she seems to me to have acted consistently throughout. Not feeling easy with the mystic substitute for the ordinance of the Sacrament (the nature of her mind being sensuous rather than transcendental), she submits to baptism in order to entitle her to the benefits of the Communion table. This makes her a member of the Church of England, but the service as conducted in her own church being Puseyite in its character & the Pastor placed over her, one whom she cannot respect, she goes to a neighbouring church to hear what she believes to be a more Gospel ministry & to receive the sacrament from one she can regard as true to his vocation. Meanwhile she attends Meetings for the religious aid afforded by them & because she never in fact objected to them, but only required in addition that which she believed to be an ordinance of Christ. In judging of the conduct of others we must always try to get at *their point of view first*, which will make clear much that seems to us anomalous.

30. Dined at Carclew with Aunt Charles & met the Tremaynes, Enyses, & Lady Dunstanville. The latter is a capital hand for society, such a womanly knack of drawing you out by shewing an interest in what she knows to be your interests. Her dress for an old lady was too low for my taste. Mary Tremayne's singing was more like an angel's than anything I ever heard. Sir Charles Lemon wept when she sang & played the exquisitely touching piece of solemn music called *Ruth*. Aunt Charles was in raptures.

DECEMBER

3. S. Aunt C. dined with us. Read J. J. Gurney's *Papal Hierarchy*, a work of good intention & feeble execution. It is a great misfortune to a man to be the oracle of his circle. This book abounds with specimens of self-satisfied ignorance.[1]

1. J. J. Gurney, the brother of Elizabeth Fry, a minister in the Society of Friends and one of its leading thinkers, had spent a great deal of time and study in trying to define the theological basis of the Society. His critics accused him of leanings towards the evangelical wing of the Church of England, but even so, Barclay's judgement shows an unexpected independence.

10. S. Attended afternoon meeting at Perran. S. Rundell spoke with the power & earnestness of an early Quaker on his invariable theme, the nature & operation of the inward Light. After tea at Uncle C.'s another meeting was got up in which a little close dealing was awarded to Juliet as the 'precious charge' & some weighty counsel on Watchfulness to her parents. On going upstairs Ann Tweedy gave Aunt C. an earnest caution respecting Juliet's affections, as the sagacious old lady thought she detected signs of a sort of liking towards her cousin, which fear was fully conveyed to me immediately on her departure. I had an interesting letter from Sterling yesterday enclosing his last *Hymn of a Hermit*, perhaps the most beautiful thing he ever wrote.

19. Busy morning. Hard work at Board [of Guardians]. Contracts, & one or two ugly cases. A woman had been detected in attempting to produce abortion by drugs, a case for the magistrates.

21. Dined at the other House to meet Sir C. Lemon & Lady Dunstanville, a social, pleasant evening. The *Song of the Shirt*[1] in the last *Punch* is one of the most striking & affecting things bearing reference to present times I have seen anywhere. It describes one of those miserable creatures who make up shirts @ 1¼d. each – 'a woman sat in unwomanly rags'. It will be learnt all over England & deserves to be.

22. Joined Parents at Penjerrick. Too wet to plant. Gave farming directions & talked romance & religion with Uncle Joshua, who is equally *au fait* at both. Returned from Penjerrick in time to attend the Examination at the Lancastrian School. The questions were put by L. Squire, & the boys answered admirably; Geography, Scripture, Mental Arithmetic & Miscellaneous Knowledge, the fellows *would not* be puzzled. The audience which was large was completely astonished.

23. Mud very general. A bright frosty Christmas is a poetical creation. It is very long since we have realised it in these parts. I gave dinners of beef & potatoes to some 40 or 50 in my parish to dress on Christmas day.

24. S. Joshua Pomfrey, a Birmingham manufacturer/brass founder, & an intelligent man, tea'd with us. He can render 12 gross (or 1728) hooks & eyes all silvered & sown on to cards for 1/8d. and make a fair profit. Truly this is the Age of Machinery.

25. Christmas dinner as usual with Thomas Evans at Penjerrick. Roast beef & plum pudding. Everything was satisfactory except the accounts, which shew a heavy loss this year owing principally to the diminished value of produce. Spent the evening at Tregedna pleasantly enough. Groped my way home in darkness & mud, both tolerably dense. The day did not certainly wear the appearance of a happy Christmas.

27. Trudged in to Falmouth & held a family meeting at our house in which

1. Thomas Hood's poem was published anonymously in *Punch*.

a very wholesome resolution was come to – that of letting no individual take money from the House unless he had funds there. Certain sums will be placed at the disposal of certain parties to begin upon, so that they may not be driven into a corner by surprise. Uncle J.'s affairs were also placed on a much more satisfactory footing.

28. Dinner at Trevince at ½ past 6, a party of 20. My companion at the dinner table was a young lady of Truro called Stainton, decidedly above par. She was original, thoughtful, unpretending and animated, plain but expressive. She is an acquaintance of 'Boz', a reader of Carlyle, and an enthusiast in Gothic architecture. Miss Williams who sat on my right was affable but common-place. I left early & got thro' some work after reaching home.

30. Falmouth per bus. Finished 5 Cantos of *Coeur de Lion* sent me by Sterling. It is on the whole the most effective production of his pen, racy, vigorous & in some places highly poetical. We had a large boy-party to dinner, – about 20 I think, – from L. Squire's. We occupied the afternoon & evening with sundry games & gormandizing, a most popular amusement. In playing at 'I Spy' in the garden, one of the boys in attempting an 'artful dodge' amongst the bushes, made a small mistake & tumbled into a pit of abominations, – the receptacle of the main drain from the house. I took him into the servants hall & cleansed him by means of long continued scrubbing.

31. S. Sat up till 12 last night talking over with my father the melancholy ebb tide of some of the family. Consequently I overslept myself & got up with a headache. It is annoying to find one's thoughts continually recurring to such ungenial topics. Life is a joyous thing after all. Its pleasures are continuous, its evils occasional, & poverty is the least. Poor old James Thomas was buried today. Though few seemed to care about him when living, both children & grandchildren wept bitterly on his grave. Of all sad sights on earth I know none sadder than a marriage without a smile or a funeral without a tear. Tea at Grove Hill. The lord & lady were gracious & in good spirits. I sat out the old year & bade him heartily 'farewell', for kind & bountiful has he been to me in pleasures social & solitary, in enjoyment at home & abroad, in affording means of mental progress & formation of character.

1844

MARRIAGE IS the recurrent theme of the year. At the beginning rumours circulate in Falmouth that Sterling has clandestinely married a local girl. Barclay and Aunt Charles try to trace the source of these rumours and discover that they are based on nothing more than gossip. Their concern is perhaps the greater because the entries in the Journal soon reveal that Sterling has proposed marriage to Caroline Fox. The entries are very guarded, but they show Caroline plunged into a conflict of emotions; her great affection for Sterling balanced against a sense of duty to her family, who are concerned at the prospect of her marrying 'out of the Society' to someone suffering from advanced consumption. We see comparatively little of the struggle, partly because of the Journal's reticence, but also because Barclay himself is caught up in his own matrimonial affairs. After a visit to London on railway business, but during which he finds time to see the Carlyles and attend a meeting of the Anti-Corn Law League addressed by Daniel O'Connell, he travels to the North. He breaks his journey at Bradford to stay with W. E. Forster and then goes to Darlington where he successfully proposes marriage to Jane Backhouse. On a second visit to Darlington he hears that Sterling is gravely ill, so hurries back through London to the Isle of Wight. Sterling is so ill that he is not allowed to see him and though Sterling rallies, it is no surprise when news of his death reaches the Foxes in September. At home Barclay is kept busy with the affairs of the Perran Foundry, the fight to keep the packets at Falmonth, plans for the Cornwall railway, and with alterations to his cottage. His hopes of an early marriage are frustrated by the preaching engagements of his future mother-in-law, Hannah Backhouse, who is continually called to different parts of the country by her sense of mission, but eventually in October, Barclay and Jane are safely married.

JANUARY

6. Went to Truro to attend a Railway Committee. I made some investigations respecting an absurd report about Sterling. Walked with Aunt C. who has had some satisfactory chat with her husband today respecting payments, &c. She is Woman all over, with moral feelings & affections to satisfy which she will make any sacrifices.

7. I made some farther investigations respecting the preposterous report of Sterling's second marriage. I called on the Griffins, who profess to have got it from the mother & sister of the bride thro' Mr. Vice's housekeeper.

13. Important Railway Committee at Truro. All my colleagues are converts to the atmospheric principle which is highly satisfactory. Brunel reports favourably & the only question still urged by sceptics is, how will it stand frost? A few weeks will no doubt afford an answer. Pearse of Tavistock came to propose a plan for raising the necessary capital, which he described as a sort of tontine & which he recommended on the grounds that it must succeed because it appealed to the good & evil of our nature. We have fixed on a public meeting for the 26th to form the Company & constitute a provisional Committee since we are only a self-constituted body. Returned to Falmouth to lodge.

19. After breakfasting with Tweedy & his lady I called on Vice. His house-keeper is ill but she solemnly declares that she knows nothing of the report about Sterling beyond hearing it casually at a servants' ball. So instead of being built on an authentic statement of the mother's, it is founded on the fulness of beer & the vulgar gossip of maids. I found that the mother's name was Williams & her residence Ponsanooth. I trudged back to Perran, beat up Aunt Charles's quiet pursuits & off we went to Ponsanooth. We found there that such a report had been spread in the neighbourhood, & a mile or so further on found the old woman herself. She told us she had heard the report of her daughter's marriage to her master & had found that it originated amongst the girls at the Powder Mill. They heard that some Cornish girl had married her master & accordingly fixed on Pamela. Such was the whole origin of the scandal. The mother showed us Pamela's letters which were simple, artless & affectionate. It is no small satisfaction to have the matter thus cleared up.

21. S. [Sterling's letter. C.'s answer.][1] It is a safe rule in inward struggles & perplexities to give sentence in favour of the side which inclination opposes. Today I watched with no common interest such a struggle & victory, & have no doubt that the result will ultimately be self-approval.

22. Wrote Sterling – *rather* an important letter.

26. Letter from Sterling! I trudged to Truro for a Committee appointed for 10. Having met & read the report, fixed on the Working Committee, of which I have the honour to be one, & drawn up the resolutions, we adjourned to the Town Hall which was cram full. Lord Falmouth was in the chair & acted his part like a gentleman. Harvey made a long speech about the line, fancying we were pledged to a Southern, while he was anxious for a Northern line. Treffry made a capital, practical, statistical speech showing from his own experience how cheaply a railway may be constructed in Cornwall. His did not cost £3000 per mile. Bond expatiated on the subject with

1. The words in brackets (which are Barclay's own) are spelled backwards, a device he sometimes uses for items of a confidential nature. This and subsequent entries reveal that Sterling proposed marriage to Caroline, but that after an inward struggle she refused him.

his own enthusiasm. Finally the whole thing was 'carried' as the phrase is, with immense applause. About £70,000 is already subscribed & we must now set to, & work with a will.

28. S. [Poor C.: She bears up nobly but not without praying & struggling.][1] Wrote some lines on the purpose of suffering. Lodged at Perran in order to be early at business tomorrow. Wrote William.

31. Capt. Stanley, son of the Bishop of Norwich, came with his friend Hutchinson of the Indian army, to stay till the end of the week & to test the accuracy of his observations in his late scientific voyage with my father's instrument. Stanley is an entertaining & social little fellow, like his father. Hutchinson was silent but gentlemanly & astonished our weak minds in the evening by his feats of magic & legerdemain. Sterling's final letter to C.

FEBRUARY

1. Scene – Poor C![2] Walked with Hutchinson to the Castle, then to the Patent Slip & left him there, continuing my walk to Perran where I found plenty of work awaiting me. I shall probably start for town on 2nd day to meet Cos. J. T. Price & perhaps someone else.[3]

4. S. Stanley & Hutchinson left us at ½ past 8. I ran out to Tregedna in the afternoon to enquire after Marie, who continues to suffer much from head-ache & sickness. I took the opportunity of using it as an argument with Josephine to convince her of the evils of their present late hours & irregular habits. It is grievous to see those girls wasting their lives at the rate they do. Two Miss Griffins & E. Gilbert were there at tea & I had to escort them home. It was hard work for E.G. was overdone & faint & hysterical & we had to get her home by dint of muscle.

5. I packed up, left orders, & proceeded per bus to Truro to attend the Com-mittee meeting. Treffry was in the Chair. He & Tweedy & Bond & I are deputed to London to raise the capital & confer with the Great Western directors. Cos. J. T. Price is in town & anxious for my aid in reference to our Briton Ferry lease, so I started by the night mail from Truro, escorting Lucy as far as Bristol, where she is going to Miss Graham's finishing school. Fine, clear, moony night. One fat old woman was our fellow passenger.

6. A good wash & breakfast at Exeter were refreshing. At Bristol I deposited Lucy & her maid in a fly for Combe. At Bath the world became white & continued one vast snowfield all the way to London. I helped the journey

1. The brackets are Barclay's.
2. This entry suggests some family quarrel about Sterling's proposal to Caroline.
3. Jane Backhouse.

by reading Dickens's charming Christmas tale,[1] which is healthy reading for all, especially men of business. Reached town at 9 which was one vast *sludge* of snow & black mud. I joined Cos. J. T. Price at that hole he frequents, *The White Hart*, Bishopsgate St., & talked over our Welsh troubles & how to meet them all the evening.

7. Went to Frampton's (our lawyer) after breakfast. He takes entirely the same view as we do of the Briton Ferry question. Spent the evening at Tottenham. Jane Backhouse is gone northward with her brother J.H.[2] Vexing!

8. Early breakfast. Hard frost. Called on Ann Hodgkin who is not yet downstairs, & on Cos. J. Fox who has just lost his wife. He was tolerably well & seemed gratified by the visit. Called on W. Bevan & talked over the Railway business. He engages to procure us £200,000. Joined Sam Gurney Jr. & wife at 4 at Lombard St. & accompanied them in their carriage to Upton. Walked with Sam over his premises & farm & stables. A large party to dinner. The accounts of Cos. Elizth. Fry are neither hopeful nor hopeless, but she suffers much & loses strength.

9. Busy day from breakfast till night. Called on Sir C. Lemon, who was in bed with a violent cold but wished to see me, so I sat by his bedside & chatted over railway & packet business, arranging plans. Called on Capt. Beaufort at the Admiralty with a parcel for Col. Sabine. He was frank & hearty & spoke in high terms of my father. He promised me, as far as his influence extends, that we should have the packets at Falmouth as soon as we had a railway.

11. S. I trudged to Upton bag in hand, no omnibus overtaking me. The party at Ham House was as full of warm life as ever, but clouded by Cos. E. Fry's most lamentable state. She is in continual suffering, sometimes so acute that her screams are heard all over the house. They have a full length likeness of her by Richmond, the most successful of his portraits I have seen. Pleasant sociable evening with the Gurneys. The last account of Cos. E. Fry was rather better. The last 30 hours have seen the most suffering she has ever had.

12. Edmund Gurney drove me to town where I spent the day with the deputation. Bond & I called on Sir C. Lemon who agreed to go with us to the Board of Trade on the Railway question. Ran down to Chelsea & called on Carlyle. Both he & his wife were very cordial. I found him employed in writing a note to the Corporation of London, asking leave of access to the City Records for his great work on Oliver Cromwell. He rails against the booksellers for want of faith. The work is a huge one & requires diving fathoms deep in all manner of old rubbish & many assistants in seeking out the deep hid truths, but none that he has spoken to will supply the means of

1. Dickens's *Christmas Carol* appeared in 1843.
2. Her brother-in-law, J. Hodgkin.

doing it beforehand, tho' when finished they will be ready enough to purchase. He put on his hat & walked with me as far as Hyde Park corner, talking of the Americans, Irish, & early Quakers whom he holds in great veneration, but thinks the peculiar work for which they were sent has now ceased to exist. He gives a poor account of Mill.

13. Joined the deputation at 11. At 2 we had an interview with Lang at the Board of Trade, a thoughtful, low-voiced man. He advises us not to make any application to the Government till we have at least ½ the capital subscribed. At 4 we had an interview with the Directors of the Gt. Western at their office. In the evening I attended a lecture on phreno-mesmerism in Newman St. The lecture was poor, the experiments tried on the audience failed, but 2 boys, one the Deptford youth who alarmed his friends by remaining in mesmeric sleep 3 days, were powerfully acted on. The cataleptic state of one of the boys was very extraordinary. Wit & tune being excited, he sang snatches of some very comic songs, which changed into pious hymns, wit being demesmerised & veneration excited. His imitation developments were capital, taking off fiddlers, dogs, cats, Macbeth, & finally his own Granny. The operators were little more than boys themselves & the Chairman was a goose.

21. I took a cab at ½ past 6 & drove to a great 'Anti-Corn-Law League' meeting held in Covent Garden Theatre. O'Connell's presence was held out as the attraction. About 5,000 persons were present & Wilson[1] was in the chair. After an hour's waiting a distant murmur, as of a far stretching multitude in the street, announced the coming of O'Connell. The assembly was one universal cheer. When the hero of the state prosecution[2] entered the hall & stepped across the platform, the enthusiasm exceeded everything I ever saw. 5,000 men were standing up simultaneously as with the will of one, & cheering, shouting, hollering, to the full extent of their lungs, in a state of enthusiastic distraction for 3 or 4 minutes incessantly. Hats were waved & flung in the air, ladies waved their handkerchiefs from all the boxes & an individual in the gallery, not fortunate enough to possess one, waved a huge brown cotton umbrella. Dan bowed repeatedly in his most emphatic manner, but the cloud of dust & steam which rose from the excited pit prevented his being very distinctly seen. When he did come forward to speak, he evinced a thorough knowledge of the nature of his audience. He said he had no speech to make, but had pleasure in presenting them with a subscription he had just received from a 'Friend of Justice' & threw £100

1. George Wilson (1808–70), chairman of the Anti-Corn Law League from 1841 until the repeal of the corn laws in 1846.
2. Daniel O'Connell was arrested in 1843, on a charge of creating disaffection, and sentenced to a fine of £2000 and a year's imprisonment, but the judgement was reversed on appeal in 1844.

note on the table. He then strove to express the inexpressible exultation, pride & gratification produced by their flattering reception under his peculiar circumstances. 'That shout will be heard across the channel & will echo along the shores of the Shannon & the people of Ireland will thank you for that shout. If there be one virtue in the world more beautiful than another, that virtue is English generosity, & if there be any other quality that may be compared with it, it is Irish gratitude', accompanying the word with a profound bow, his hand on his heart. He confined himself in the main very fairly to the subject matter, denouncing the tax as a legalised robbery of the poor by the rich, & declaiming generally in such style as the stomachs of his audience required. It was impassioned rather than eloquent & when he referred to himself as a conspirator & cleverly threw out the likelihood that a dungeon awaited him, the shouts & excitement of the people knew no bounds. Soon after concluding, he left the theatre, as the Irish Debate is still going on in the House & he has not yet said his say. The rest of the proceedings were comparatively flat.

22. We had at length our long expected interview with Lord Jersey, occupying the time till 12 in calling on merchants in the City. Lord J. listened to the tale of our grievances & to our suggestions in a very gentlemanly manner. We were with him nearly 2 hours & I think impressed him with the idea that his interest & ours were associated, & he promised to give full consideration to our request & see one or both of us again. At 5 I was on the railway & whizzing off for Birmingham which I reached at 10.

23. Spent the morning with Gimblett, Uncle G.C.'s agent. We drove to his estate at King's Heath, about 4 miles off & I went over it with the tenant, examining it as far as the snow would permit. I think we shall succeed in selling & I hope at £60 per acre. I spent the evening at The Farm chatting with Geo. Lloyd, who is a singular & original minded man, with a wry face, a bad asthma, & a set of teeth that point all round the compass.

24. I spent this morning in seeing 2 people who are both rather inclined to purchase the estate at King's Heath & in journeying to the Holt Estate which is from 6 to 7 miles distant. I had great difficulty to get over the steep & narrow lanes on account of the snow, but got back in time to start as directed at 4 by the Leeds railway. From an alteration in the time of starting this month I missed it by 5 minutes & so had to spend 8 hours longer at the Farm.

25. S. Reached Leeds at ½ past 6. A coach took me to Bradford a little before 9 & at 10 I was settled at breakfast with William before a blazing fire in unmingled enjoyment. We did talk a little that's certain – much about the past – more about the future & I fixed to start for Darlington on 3rd day morning. He wrote to Cos. Hannah Backhouse to say I was coming, & so the die is cast. We drove to Meeting in the afternoon & it was worth attending

if only to meet the kindly face & kindlier grasp of Benjamin Seebohm whose earnest & affectionate address to me last year will never be forgotten. 26. A day of intense interest. The morning was spent in plodding through the snow, shopping & calling on the 3 Miss Broadbents, young lady acquaintances of William's. After dinner we went to a Mr. Hall's to meet Spencer Hall,[1] the phreno-mesmerist & 2 or 3 other gentlemen. S. Hall struck me as a highly intelligent & sincere person. I saw no indication of humbug whatever. After tea we had in a remarkable mesmeric patient, a boy of 12 belonging to Bradford, who possessed in the state of 'Coma' the marvellous faculty of clairvoyance. His organ of vision seemed to be the tip of his thumb, with which he was able to see a person who rang the front door bell & could describe his dress & appearance. He was struck by the waistcoat & described it by drawing lines on his hand crossing one another at right angles & saying it was black & white & red; it proved to be a plaid answering the description. But the most remarkable of his gifts, tho' not so easy to test, was that of seeing your interior organization & prescribing the remedy for what he saw amiss. His mode of doing it was to put one thumb in the patient's mouth & one on the pit of his stomach. On looking into our host he became quite sick & would not look at him again. His stomach had been out of order, as he confessed after the examination. On looking into Miller (a young German) he described the lungs as out of order & the quick breathing which caused him a good deal of pain. He prescribed linseed, spanish juice & sugar candy. Miller fully confirmed the boy's account of his affliction, which had been produced by over-exertion. At the lecture 3 young men were brought forward, two of Bradford & one from the neighbourhood. They showed the most marvellous effects on touching various phrenological organs, after being first mesmerised. The greatest fun of all was to see them with their philo-progenitiveness excited, nursing 3 great coats which we gave them with the greatest solemnity. One of them, having had his language & tune previously excited, was singing with deep feeling,

> Hush, my dear, lie still & slumber,
> Holy angels guard thy bed &c.

Another was kissing his babe extravagantly & clasping it to his breast. After these experiments, the youths were completely locked to the floor by a single motion of the operator. No temptations could move them, tho' each of them was offered £5 if he would stir one yard. Similar experiments were made with them separately, & finally the clairvoyant, being once more mesmerised, examined 2 patients & described their diseases. He told one

1. Spencer Hall (1812–85), published *Mesmeric Experience*, 1845; cured Harriet Martineau, 1844; became Governor of Hollis Hospital, Sheffield.

gentleman that one of his lungs was much diseased & all the medicine in the world would not cure him. His doctor told me afterwards that he had frequent fits of haemoptyses.[1] On the whole I never saw anything so closely resembling the preternatural before, & can only suppose that under certain peculiar physical conditions another sense becomes developed which informs the mind thro' some unknown channel. The night was bitter cold. The frozen snow in Bradford streets was like the ruggedness of an iceberg. We did not get home till ½ past 12.

27. William drove me to Leeds in his dog cart in time for the 1 o'clock train to York. At the Darlington Station the coachman's honest face greeted me. He had brought a gig to take me to his mistress's. I was most cordially received. A fire was in my bedroom & dinner was put off till my arrival. Jane blushed no more than might be expected considering the anomalous character in which I came. Edmund was hospitable & gentlemanly. We all got pretty well at ease. I endeavoured to prevent conversation from flagging by recording the wonders of phreno-mesmerism. Cos. Hannah Backhouse went to bed early. Jane stayed half an hour later & did her best to be civil, tho' evidently with an effort.

28. I had a very open conversation with Cos. H.B. immediately after breakfast. No mother could be kinder or more encouraging. I told her my position exactly, which she clearly understood, – that I was very desirous of knowing more of Jane, of whose mind I was at present almost in complete ignorance, that I knew enough to see there were differences between us (the principal one being our different degree of adherence to Quakerism) & how far they might prove a barrier to any closer intimacy I knew not. After luncheon I contrived to get a walk with Jane. We trudged round & round the pond at a fearful pace. Sentiment was quite out of breath, but still the lady walked & I had to do my best to keep up with her & talk as well as I was able. I got on 2 or 3 topics, such as Chenda & W. E. Forster, of a more particular & less general nature, but it was no use. She waxed mute directly & I re-entered the house without having made one inch of way towards closer acquaintance. There is nothing for it but a thorough explanation that's evident. Read Schlegel's lectures on History after tea. I should have said that towards the conclusion of our walk Jane actually proposed a roll in the snow! Of course I seconded it, but this was too great a committal of dignity.

29. A day lost. Breakfast with Joseph Pease,[2] the happy father of 11 children. After Meeting I spoke to Cos. H.B., telling her my resolve to have an explanation with Jane at the very first opportunity. However Jane had arranged a ride & engaged her cousin Jane Pease to accompany us in the capacity of wet blanket, so of course nothing of any interest could be said.

1. Blood-spitting.
2. Joseph Pease of Darlington had married Hannah Backhouse's sister, Emma Gurney.

We rode to Blackwell, John C. & Anna's[1] house, a beautiful snuggery on the bank of the Tees. We walked over the house & grounds & returned to dinner. Jane Pease was with us all the rest of the day.

MARCH

1. I did contrive to get a walk & thoroughly open talk with Jane. I told her of my feeling that we ought to be better acquainted, having hitherto only known each other on the surface, & I had come to Polam in order that we might know each other somewhat deeper. Whether any benefit would arise from it I could not say, for I was conscious of certain differences between us which might bar the way to intimacy. I then told her fully of my *Unfriendliness* which arose from an unsectarian constitution of mind, but confessing my firm adherence to the spiritual principle on which Quakerism is founded. She heard me candidly, but said no more than she could help. She said that I 'set her a pattern of filial obedience at all events'. I was glad to have the opportunity of saying that so far from my present position being a mere piece of filial obedience, neither parents nor sisters *had* the least knowledge of my coming, nor *have*, of my being here. She said agreement of sentiments was not all that was necessary to know. On returning towards the house, I said that if the differences which existed between us were an obstacle to further intimacy, why, I did not come here to persecute her, otherwise I hoped we might soon have another opportunity for open conversation. 'I think', she said, 'we have had quite enough for the day.' On the whole I ought not to complain of my reception. She gave me a fair hearing & I am sure of candour on her part, but she was particularly careful not to commit herself in the least, answering as much in mono-syllables as possible. After dinner we had another walk. We crossed a bridge & scaled a gate & walked in a large meadow. I felt a delicacy at renewing the subject of our morning's conversation in consequence of what she said. She had very little to say & I had to fag very hard to keep up conversation at all. We talked about Uncle & Aunt C., & at last found ourselves again indoors. Cos. H.B. was not well & laid in bed till midday. In the evening she received a note from Henry Whitwell, putting it into her head (or rather enforcing what was there before) that she ought to go to Kendal on account of some recent death in the family. She wrote to Ed. Pease to ask him to accompany her tomorrow, so here's a pretty position for me. My hostess packing off & my lady as sensitive as a nerve; I see nothing for it but to pack too.

2. Ed. Pease declined to accompany our lady mother last evening, & her

1. Anna, the daughter of J. J. Gurney, had married John C. Backhouse of Darlington.

sister, Jane Robson, did the same this morning, so she submits to remaining quiet till next week. I offered to escort her, as no one else would, but she seemed to consider me in my right place. I spent the morning in Jane's room, & made a desperate effort to be on easy terms, telling her it was excessively unfair & disagreeable in her to give me *all* the talking to do. I tried very hard to get at some return in the way of confidence, but in vain. I begged her to let me know what in me she particularly disliked to cause her chilling restraint, but got no light there either. O dear! it *is* uphill work! We took a walk in the meadow beyond the Skyrne & round the pond. In the evening when we were left alone, Jane gave a modest & maidenly explanation of her reserve. It was so *difficult*, she said, to drag forth her opinions & feelings. I asked her whether she had found in the differences between us, anything to prevent further intercourse or intimacy. She acknowledged that she had not. She asked for a truce, tomorrow being a day of rest. She was in a feeling & burdened state, so I did not pursue the conversation but went to bed.

3. S. The truce commanded was observed. In the evening when all had retired to their rooms but Jane & myself, there was a long pause, after which she said, 'So thou'rt going tomorrow.' I said, 'Yes & I hope thou art satisfied with my obedience to thy request.' She said, 'Yes,' – another pause – then her voice trembled not a little as she said, 'However impracticable it may now seem, I believe thou will one day be my protector in life', & then she glided out of the room like a shooting star, leaving me in a state of delirium tremens. It was so far beyond my hopes. I have grievously wronged her in attributing her reserve to coldness & indifference, which spring from her exquisite maidenly modesty. I went to bed but not to sleep.

4. More happened than I can write. Before breakfast there were the fraternal congratulation & the maternal blessing, the latter given with many tears, expressions of deep feeling, enthusiastic love towards Jane, & thankfulness to God that she had at length met with one whom she *could* love & admire. Cos. H.B. spoke most disinterestedly of herself, the precariousness of her health, & her desire that Jane should have a home before she was taken from the world. Nothing could exceed her kindness throughout. After breakfast I had a hurried opportunity with Jane in her boudoir. I could only stammer out my sense of obligation & of blessedness. She tried to make me think that she did not see the thing as practicable, but gave me a letter directed to William, which he was to show me in the evening & contained a key to her mind. We then discussed the time for my next visit. Jane declined giving any opinion, so her mother & I fixed on the day after tomorrow. (They go to Kendal today & I shall join them there if they cannot arrive on 5th day.) 'Nothing like striking while the iron's hot', I say. Bean announced the pony chaise to take me to the station. I took my leave, kissed my mother & I believe something of the same description passed between me & her daughter.

In 20 minutes I was whizzing off to Leeds, with my heart & brain whizzing & thumping & whirling in the strangest manner. At Leeds William met me with his gig & drove me back to Bradford. He was half crazy with delight – noble, disinterested fellow that he is! We could not help drinking Jane's health in a bumper of champagne & then – came the key!! We sat up till past 12 & I went to bed with my love, honour & admiration of Jane vastly increased.

5. I spent the day quietly with William, riding together to Milner Fields, the place he is tempted to take as a residence. I discouraged it. The house is a tempting old hall & enough to set off the imagination, but it will require much repairing & fitting up & it is 5 miles from Bradford & the road is very bad. We dined together at the Hotel & then William started for Bristol. I took possession of his house & spent the evening in writing.

6. Started for Darlington about 12. Edmund was waiting for me at the Darlington Station with the pony chair. I dined with him in good bachelor style at 6 & spent the evening in chess & chat. A note from Jane to him says they intend leaving Kendal tomorrow after Meeting. I shall therefore go & meet them as they must spend a night on the road.

7. I traversed a most wintry scene over a snow covered tract of desolate hills, at the foot of which lay the village of Brough whence 2 roads diverge, one to Penrith, the other to Kendal. As the coach was bound to the former, I descended & took my station at the little inn & endeavoured to kill the time till the hour I calculated for their arrival. However, they came not (Cos. H.B. being on one of her missions of faith) & after exploring the ruins of a mediocre sort of castle, a little reading & a little writing I went to bed.

8. I whiled away the weary hours as I best might, making myself pretty well acquainted with the City of Brough & its environs. However about 1 o'clock they did arrive. Jane looked a little confused & all the more beautiful for it. They were surprised at the rencontre but I think not annoyed. Cos. H.B. was tired & had misgivings about leaving Kendal this week &c. After dinner we returned to Darlington. I gave Jane William's & my notes written on the 5th, which pleased her. We had a few words after the others were gone to bed, one glorious kiss & we parted.

9. Having got clear of the ice, we are sailing on calm seas & in sunny weather. After breakfast we rode to Blackwell, dismounted & wandered thro' the plantations & across the road & through some neighbouring woods & back by the meandering banks of the Tees – with a gale of wind blowing all the time. It was perfectly delightful. It was the first time she took my arm since the commencement of my courtship. She was very charming & (for her) very open. We agreed that our walk was not a little better than those we used to take last week around the frozen pond, which seemed in keeping with the terms we were then on.

11. An interesting chat with Cos. H.B. after breakfast. We were mutually open. I told her my circumstances & prospects. She gave me a general idea of Jane's. I requested that whatever Jane had might be settled on herself. I had enough for my wants. Whatever additional income Jane brought should be applied to rendering her home comfortable. Cos. H.B. told me the sort of establishment which she thought desirable for Jane, a close carriage of some sort, a footman, cook, housemaid & perhaps lady's maid, then as to the house, the number of rooms & offices she thought necessary. Her ideas were quite moderate. She expressed her entire satisfaction in all I told her about myself. Jane & I had a thoroughly pleasant easy social walk in the meadows beyond the Skyrne. She called herself 'a parcel of contradictions'. She rested in her room on the sofa while I read to her. Letters of congratulation & commendation poured in. After supper when the rest had retired, I saw that Jane was rather clouded & uneasy. I catechised her & she confessed that she did not altogether like the idea of her mother's starting tomorrow for Tottenham, as was planned, & my remaining. I protested against the notion of there being any impropriety in it under our present circumstances, nevertheless if she wished it I should make a point of departing tomorrow morning.

12. All the clouds are dispersed & we have glorious sunshine again. Cos. H.B. proposed adjourning her departure till 5th day & taking Jane with her, to which she joyously assented & I, of course, expressed my most entire unity with the plan. Jane & I had a ride & a long walk thro' Blackwell & by the Tees. On returning she laid hold of the letters & there being one to me from William & one to her from Chenda Buxton, she proposed an exchange before opening either, to which I agreed, tho' with some dread as to the free style of speculation that William might indulge in. But as he did not go further than the wedding it did very well. Chenda's was a sweet note, very characteristic of herself, breathing love & good wishes towards us both.

13. We rode together, walked together, gardened together & sat & read together in her boudoir. It was our last day at Polam & a very uniting one. We planned & marked out some new flower beds, our first joint undertaking. In our ride I asked her what she thought of William's bet (that the wedding would be in July). 'Certainly not in July', she said, but I would understand her to say 'not *till* July'. However it seemed to me that she did not wish to delay it much beyond that month. If nothing prevents I am to reappear next month. Jane was perfectly delightful & met my parting embrace as a lover might desire.

14. We gave the finishing touches to our flower beds, took leave of our various relations & immediately after Meeting started for Derby by Railway. Henry Whitwell escorts them on to Town whence he will probably go to France with Cos. J. J. Gurney. We had a choice ride, reading chatting & looking. At Normanton Jane & I had half an hour's walk, when I talked to

her about the cottage. She wishes me to make no alterations except what are essential. I had a capital evening with them at Derby. After Cos. Hannah had retired to bed H. Whitwell considerately went into the Coffee Room & we had a sweet half hour together, not with abundance of words but feelings somewhat deeper. We had an affectionate farewell & at $\frac{1}{4}$ past 11 I continued my route to Birmingham. Reached Birmingham at 1 & retired to bed.

15. After breakfast called on the Lloyds & H. Gimblett about the estate at King's Heath. I have little doubt that I shall sell it now. Proceeded to Gloster at $\frac{1}{2}$ past 12, glorious, glowing weather. A stupidly slow coach from Gloster to Bristol managed to arrive just too late for the 7 o'clock train to Exeter.

16. Reached Beam Bridge at 3 and was there detained more than $\frac{1}{2}$ an hour in packing a pyramid of luggage. Exeter at $\frac{1}{4}$ to 7. William was waiting for me & so was breakfast, but I had only $\frac{1}{4}$ of an hour to eat it, book my place, change my luggage &c. William & I had to exchange condensed sentences between mouthfuls. I had counted on spending the night with him. In the midst of reading a letter from Chenda, the waiter entered to announce that the coach was gone! I bundled up my traps & raced after it. Caught it & reached home at 5. Some sweet notes from loving relatives were showered in at the coach window as I passed thro' the valley. I entered my father's by the back door, made no fuss but quietly went upstairs & regenerated my outward man. I appeared amongst them as they were sitting round the dining-room fire & was greeted with a fullness of affection which made one's heart leap to one's mouth. I sat down & gave them chapter & verse of the whole affair at least so much of it as could be done without betraying confidence. They were all ears. In the evening I had a repetition of the same sort of scene at the Bank. I called at Grove Hill, but hearing Uncle G.C. lecturing to the Perran party *ore rotundo* I did not intrude.

17. S. Received the greetings & congratulations of the whole Falmouth Meeting. The warmest were at Grove Hill. Uncle G.C. walked to the window. The thought of his own childlessness came upon him. I stayed to dinner & he gradually brightened. Aunt C.'s feelings were too much for words & Uncle C. had been telling Uncle G.C. this morning at breakfast that the gift of a Dukedom & £30,000 a year would not have given him half the pleasure. Aunt A. was enthusiastic. Her funny fat brother, the doctor, was with her. Uncle A. arrived from Wales last evening. I wrote Jane my first love letter.

19. I drove my father to the Board at Penryn after sundry plannings for divers alterations; a new entrance to the library & an adjunct of 2 bedrooms above a servants' hall & man's bedroom. I held consultations with mason & carpenter & am half decided. It will cost more than £200 but it is worthwhile.

20. Busy morning. I heard that Sterling is dangerously ill. I wrote to enquire

& to propose a visit if I could be of any use or comfort to him. My party left me after a remarkably snug visit. In the evening came *a* letter, not *the* letter, but a very sweet & sisterly epistle from Ann Hodgkin. Ann says that Jane was well & confessed herself 'refreshed' by my letter!

21. Very busy day. Began operations, clearing away ground for building. After meeting rode to Mylor & had some preliminary chat with Husband about the oyster fishery which I think may lead to something valuable as I see great capabilities. A railway meeting of 4 or 5 'South-liners' at Bond's at 7, after which I rode back to Perran, suspecting a letter. There it was on the drawing room table! A fountain in the wilderness! She says that 'nothing has disturbed the deep & calm repose that dwells in the inmost recesses of her mind'. She speaks of the strangeness of our new relationship & wonders that it does not feel more strange. I wrote an answer by $\frac{1}{4}$ to 1. It is important to prevent any languor in the correspondence. Each letter will be less difficult to her & the more letters we exchange the nearer we shall get. This was quite as affectionately expressed as I could reasonably expect, for the first – & for her.

23. P. Hoskin made a plan of the cottage. By the addition I have planned, I gain a passage, 2 capital bedrooms, & servants' hall & man's bedroom beneath for about £130. The alteration in the staircase making a new access to the library will be a capital improvement. I spent the evening at Perran House & read the *Ancient Mariner* to the girls.

25. Came to Perran to breakfast expecting a letter. One from darling Jane, intensely delightful, showing the exquisite sensitiveness & tenderness of her nature. She is going to Melksham today to join her mother. I wrote, thankfully, of course, & interrogatively as to future plans. There was a beautiful little note of congratulation from Sterling & an improved account of him from the Governess, but the attack must have been a fearful one. Dined at Uncle C.'s.

27. Found on reaching Perran another glorious letter from Jane. Each is an improvement on the one before. There is now a gush of feeling discernible which natural reserve before froze in the expression.

31. S. Last day at Falmouth. Dined at Uncle A.'s. A note came from Jane with an account of their present position & plans, confirming my intention to start the day after tomorrow.

[Interesting chat with my father in the evening about C. Our views agree entirely. He gave me Sterling's letter (self-justificatory) to read, an able production & well answered.][1]

---

1. The brackets are Barclay's.

APRIL

1. Busy morning at Falmouth and afternoon at Perran. I left directions with mason & carpenter about the new access to the library, raising part of the cottage roof, turning bedroom into landing place, &c. Appointed T. Tregaskes 'Inspector of the Works' under my father. Packed up & read & mused on a little note from Jane, informing me that Sarah Gurney, Elizabeth Hoare, *and Chenda*, are all to be at Darlington this week. I feel it a bore on Jane's account not mine. My presence will interfere with her companionship with *her* & *my* friend, but it can't be helped. Uncle C. starts for Bradford in the middle of the month & we must not both be absent at the same time.

2. Glorious morning. Read Macaulay's review of Hallam's *Constitutional History* en route, a beautiful essay, his characterization of Cromwell admirable. Coffee'd at Exeter, Beam Bridge at 11. Bristol at 1. Put up at the *White Lion*.

3. With Cos. H.B. tête-à-tête at the Wheelers' at Clifton before 8 o'clock. She looks well & gave me *another* letter from Jane – beautiful! – containing another to be 'read on the journey'. After breakfast I was closeted for an hour with Cos. H.B. I brought her a nosegay, discussed plans, alterations, establishment &c., &c. I showed her plans of the Cottage with proposed additions which she approved. One point only was not satisfactory. She won't think of any marrying 'before the 9th or 10th month'. I combatted her arguments as far as decency & good taste permitted, but no way can be made at present. I must try Jane. I took an affectionate leave at 10 & proceeded on my travels. Read Jane's enclosure on the coach. I *thought* I loved her *before*, but now! I reached Birmingham at 5 after a hot & dusty ride. After tea I sallied forth in quest of T. Gibbins & discovered his habitat after a long round.

4. Jas. Taylor met me at the Bank & we concluded the sale of Uncle G.C.'s estate, – 4,000 guineas exclusive of timber to be payable at Midsummer. By a letter from William it appears he is in Liverpool, so at $\frac{1}{4}$ past 1 I booked myself for Darlington. I wrote a couple of letters on the Railway & reached port at 10. Thinking it too late to summon up the servants to get tea, &c., at Polam, where the lady would probably be on the eve of departure, I deposited myself for the night at the *King's Head* Inn. To get from Birmingham to Paradise in 9 hours is pretty good travelling, thanks to the Railroads.

5. Appeared in Jane's boudoir at 8, not a little to her astonishment & somewhat I fear to the interruption of her devotions. I was not expected till the evening, but the offence was easily forgiven. She coloured up but rose from her seat with more of smile than frown & the bliss of that moment was somewhat of the transcendent kind. We breakfasted alone, Edmund not having turned out of bed. Our position at the head & foot seemed like a little foretaste of domestic life. We then took a long walk, losing our way of course, & having to make a cut across the country, hedge & ditch, to get

home again. It was a *very pleasant* walk. Jane & I took another walk after dinner, sitting en route in a little old tumbledown wigwam, once called a summer house & gazing on the muddy current of the Skyrne. But it mattered not much what was without. There was better than landscape scenery within. Read *Chartism* in the evening for Edmund's edification and *Christabel* for Jane's.

8. Jane & I dined at Blackwell, having been specially invited by Chenda & Elizth. Hoare, the mistress of the house not being consulted. It was a strange feeling. Those two beings are old & *intimate* friends. Chenda was a *little* frightened at first, as I saw by the way she occasionally looked up under her eyelids, but became gradually easy & social. I sat by her at dinner & we had much talk about common acquaintance. We mustered 10, all young & all 2nd cousins.

11. A particularly nice letter from my father & a particularly sweet day with Jane. We rode to a place called Piercebridge, a beautiful bit of the Tees. We wandered thro' the woods to our hearts' content, reclined on the grass and ate our luncheon. Having no glass, Jane drank the water of the brook in most primitive fashion, out of my hands. Some halcyon moments with Jane when the people were gone to bed.

12. Meeting at 10 whereat Hannah Jenkins officiated, her subject Friendly peculiarities & restrictions, looking hard at Chenda who was seated in the front ranks & might easily be mistaken for a gay Friend. Chenda & I walked together in the garden. She expressed her great pleasure in meeting me here & under such happy circumstances. We made some allusion to the past, but found it more profitable to dwell on the present. She is closely attached to Jane who heartily reciprocates her affection & yet how different are their two minds!

13. We had a walk before breakfast in which more was spoken by silence than by words. The pony chaise drove to the door as reading finished. Jane went up to the school room where I followed her. That parting was beyond description, but can be conceived by the initiated. I wrote some parting stanzas on the railway & sent them from Leeds. I spent a very interesting evening with William. He is becoming sick of Bradford & its society, which gave me no small pleasure to hear. We had much to tell on both sides. He is writing a history of the early Friends.

14. I called at the Post Office before Meeting. A note from A.M., forwarded by Jane, brought me the sad news that Sterling has broken a large blood-vessel & is not expected to rally, though he may linger. His father & the Maurices were gone to him. This changed all my plans. Instead of starting for Bristol tomorrow, William & I drove over to Leeds after dinner, whence he proceeded to Thirsk at $\frac{1}{2}$ past 6, & I to Town at 7 on my melancholy errand. My going can be of little use, perhaps of little satisfaction, but I

cannot do otherwise. I had an ordinary sort of journey & reached London at 5.

15. A South Western train started at 7. This bore me to Gosport at 11 and I was in the Isle of Wight between 12 & 1, – 17½ hours from Leeds. I had to wait at Ryde till 4 for the Ventnor coach. The distance is 13 miles, the time 2¼ hours, for this is the hilliest stage in the kingdom. The blinds of Sterling's house were not drawn, which was something. I deposited my portmanteau at a little cottage-inn hard by, & went there straight. Annie Maurice met me in the hall & took me into an ante-room lest he should hear my voice & there gave me, on the whole, a very encouraging report of him. He has had no return of haemorrhage for nearly a week & his brother has returned to Town. The doctor has discontinued lodging in the house & the only prescription is now perfect quiet & freedom from all excitement. He seems to have expected my visit as he charged A. Maurice to let him know as soon as I came. She asked me to absolve her from her promise & I, of course, would not be a party to interfering with the present system, so obviously the right one. I therefore fixed on starting tomorrow morning. The children were delighted to see me & looked well. I drank tea with old Sterling, who has lodgings close by but is under interdict from all communication with his son, both being far too excitable. He was very entertaining & cordial. I called next on Louisa Gilkes who is here for her health, an affectionate sincere-hearted but *bornée*[1] sort of person. She took me to see Tom Pease, who with his wife & child, father & sister, is also staying here. Poor fellow he did not look a very formidable rival.[2] being pinched by disease. I should fear consumption. Thus 3 hours were pretty fully occupied & after writing a couple of letters I found myself ready for bed.

16. I called at Sterling's & found that he had passed a capital night. I felt well satisfied that I had done nothing to disturb it. I left Ventnor at ½ past 8 and reached Ryde just in time for the Steamer to Portsmouth where the *Brunswick* lay at anchor, bound for Plymouth this afternoon. I engaged a berth on board & occupied the time in going over the *St. Vincent*, the guard ship, a '120' & a magnificent specimen of her species. I dined & strolled about till starting time. There were few fellow passengers & those uninteresting. We stopped nearly an hour at Southampton & proceeded with every prospect of a fine passage. One lady, or quasi-lady, on board, was described as being in a desperate nervous illness at Plymouth, so ill that the doctors had given her up & she had the satisfaction of hearing Dr. Budd say to Dr. Cookworthy, 'Poor dear thing! I should *like to open her*'. About 9 a dense fog enveloped us. We saw a light on our larboard quarter as if a vessel were bearing down on us, & another ahead. We dropped anchor & rang our bell, & presently a

1. Of limited capacities.
2. He had been one of Jane Backhouse's suitors.

blue light was displayed by the thing before us as a warning; whether it was ship or light-house we could not tell, but there we had to remain all night, much to our annoyance.

17. At half-past 10 the fog rolled away & showed us our position, the roadstead of Lymington in Hampshire. Vessels lay all around us & a fine schooner yacht was lying just ahead of us within 5 or 6 times our length. We should have run into her in 2 minutes more. The day proved beautiful, but as night closed the fog came again & prevented our getting into port till $\frac{1}{2}$ past 3 in the morning, when we were all awakened from our sleep by a crash & then the dull grating sound of striking on a rock & dragging over its jagged edges. We all turned out & began to dress in an awful hurry, but it turned out to be only a large government buoy that we had run foul of. So we turned in again, rather ashamed of being frightened.

18. Landed, cleansed, breakfasted & took coach at Devonport for Falmouth at 8. The pleasures of terra firma & 4 good horses after the fogs of the Channel were not small ones. Picked up a trout between Bodmin & St. Austell measuring $19\frac{1}{2}$ inches! & brought it home for my parents. They & the girls were gone to Penjerrick, so I trudged out there. I found them all well & very loving except that C. has a slight cold. Measles & whooping cough environ us. Uncle A. has 7 laid up with the latter complaint. On the chymney piece I found two sweet letters from my Jane, delightful little ebullitions they were & one that my mother gave me, written to her the day I left, more than satisfied the most extravagant desires of a lover. There is a charming simplicity & truthfulness in that creature which wins upon me in a marvellous manner.

MAY

6. I drove my mother & C. to Perran. I found on the table a sadly low letter from Sterling, the first he says he has written (except a few words to his Banker) since his attack, & probably the last. He declines seeing anyone except his constant attendants, as half an hour's conversation might be fatal. He may possibly rally enough, he thinks, to crawl about for a few months at most & that with the certainty of another attack hanging over him. He bids me think of him as of one dead. Poor poor fellow! What a sad winding-up! He calls the attack pulmonary apoplexy. What a star is setting! It was in some measure compensated by a very dear letter from my love. C. stayed with me. We had some interesting conversation on her inward self & interests & duties.

7. I did some shopping with my mother in the furniture department & paid sundry calls. A letter in the evening from Frederick Maurice to A.M. says

that Sterling was seized on the 5th with another severe attack of haemorrhage which was succeeded by another, & whether he is now living is very doubtful. Annie Maurice went to Ventnor at once. How quickly have his prognostications been fulfilled. Now that he is departing from this scene I seem to feel more than ever what he has been to me. May the highest consolation soothe his pillow.

11. An important railway Committee at Truro. Moorsom made his report on the atmospheric principle which he was sent to Dublin to inspect. His opinion is highly favourable. The economy of working, he thinks, will be from 20 to 30 per cent. We resolved on adopting it nem. con. & directed the survey to be immediately proceeded with & to be finished by the end of July, so we seem now to be going ahead.

19. S. Rode in to Meeting. Dined at Grove Hill. I spent the evening at Falmouth where there was a letter from A.M. & C. They have been with Chenda at Bath. She was very affectionate & proposes a visit to me & mine next summer! A letter from Lady Buxton to Aunt Lucy congratulated her on the acquisition of Jane but did not disguise her wish that it had been another!

24. Laid the foundation stone of the new building. Enys called & gave me some valuable hints especially about the verandah & the new road. His eye is wonderfully quick & correct. I started at ½ past 8 per North Mail. Night cold & clear.

25. A hideous old woman was my companion inside. A glorious sunrise. Exeter at ½ past 5. It is a vast convenience having the railroad to that point, nevertheless it was the most tedious railway journey I ever travelled. We lost *nearly an hour* on the road through detentions at the stations & the vast length of the train. I reached my father's lodgings at 7. Nobody at home but a note to say they were all at Tottenham. On arrival at my brother's[1] I found that my parents had gone to their sleeping place, Francis Fox's, being tired of waiting, that my new one was gone to bed, & that my love was upstairs in the study, also a *little* tired of waiting. It was not very long before she was within my arm, her lawful girdle, looking beautiful as ever. Neither of us had much to say, but I felt her heart fluttering & looked into her eyes & was satisfied. Partly out of consideration for me & partly from obedience to maternal injunctions she did not sit long with me after the rest had retired.

28. A walk with my love *before* a 7 o'clock breakfast! I had the satisfaction of finding that my entreaty of yesterday had been followed by a Dr. South in the evening who declared C.'s cough & irritation to be no deeper seated than the tonsils. Called on Cavendish who looked precisely the same as ever. He was most warm & affectionate & most hearty in his congratulations. He

1. John Hodgkin, his future brother-in-law. The 'new one' is his new parent, his mother-in-law.

expects to pass his examination in 2 days. He has had a deal of trouble about his mother's will but is now in quiet possession of a very sufficient property. William arrived in the evening. He came with me to J. J. Gurney's where Cos. Hannah was reclining. Jane came in & met him without awkwardness. I left for Uncle Barclay's where my people were some time assembled. C. was kept at home under medical law.

29. A monstrous meeting for worship at Devonshire House & I had to stand nearly all the time. In the afternoon I called on Carlyle with William, who has been engaged in taking a plan of Marston Moor for his Cromwell. Both he and his lady were remarkably cordial.

30. A very pleasant walk with Jane after an early breakfast. In the summer-house she confessed that she could not meet William under present circumstances, the associated recollections were too trying. She has a true woman's heart & no mistake. Cos. H.B. turned Jane out at Shoreditch into a cab, to speak to me on the subject of the settlement. She referred me to J. Hodgkin to arrange details.

31. William started for Bradford in the evening, making some excuse about wool, but the truth is that frequently coming in contact with Jane was more than he could yet bear. He told me he should keep out of her way till after the marriage.

JUNE

1. Rode to town with J. Hodgkin who is certainly a most intelligent, clear-eyed fellow. I found C. better & starting for Wandsworth. My mother spent the morning with Cos. H.B. & had some satisfactory talk on the subject of *time* (more to the present purpose than eternity). I think she moved her an inch or two, using arguments which women know how to use. I think we shall get in in September unless Cos. Hannah's Western engagements detain her *over* the August Monthly. We slept at Leyton. Jane & I had 2 or 3 delicious turns on the terrace under a full moon before going into the house.

3. Took leave at ½ past 8 of Cos. H.B. who started for Bristol to tourise Somerset & Wiltshire with E. Hunt. I rode to town with Cos. Francis Fox & called on his upholsterer in the city, where I bought a sofa, couch & drawing-room table. I had an interesting shopping excursion with Jane, Aunt C. & Juliet, buying furniture, chintzes, damask, carpets, &c. much to Jane's amusement, who is too straightforward & simple to feel any squeamishness about it. I dined at Belgrave Sq. at Uncle David's. The house is rigged like a palace. I should feel half afraid of myself in such a drawing room.

4. I called on J. Mill for half an hour & talked over common friends & the

success of his great work.[1] I spent a tolerably effective morning amongst the shops, joined our party at Hunter St. & accompanied them to Knotts Green where we found Jane. I gave her a white enamel workbox well fitted up. Other presents made their appearance, a silver teapot from Uncle Pease, a dressing case from Jane Barclay &c. J. Hodgkin arrived in the evening to have some talk with my father & me about the settlement, a matter on which I was profoundly ignorant. His ideas seemed very fair & reasonable.

5. We drove to the Railway Station at $\frac{1}{2}$ past 9 & secured a carriage to our three selves,[2] dressing up a couple of greatcoats into a very respectable & reposeful man & woman friend who occupied the two opposite corners, & effectually kept out all intruders. I had some very pleasant talk with Jane & we read the *Bride of Abydos* together by way of a touch of the profane after so long a spell of the sacred. We reached home at 10. Ann was in bed but Eliza gave us a warm welcome & cold supper.

6. Greeted Ann who received me in a sisterly manner, & her two little step-daughters who already dignify me into Uncle Fox. Many warm greetings at the Meeting House. Jane & I made our dinner at luncheon & rode off across the Tees through fields & shady lanes, stopping in our course to hunt for a peewit's nest, as the 2 parent birds tried vociferously to decoy us from the spot.

8. We had a glorious morning of it. We took a bag of our usual fare with the addition of sandwiches & books & depositing our two selves in the pony chair, drove off to Middleton, a quiet little watering place on the Tees with a very picturesque wood extending about 2 miles along its bank. We discovered a mossy bank by the water's side, well shaded with beech & oak where we ate & read & talked & lounged to our hearts' content. How much time we devoted to that *dolce far niente* I dare not say, but by making a small detour on our way home, crossing the Tees, scrambling thro' some fields, Jane driving & I reading to her, we did not reach Polam till evening.

9. S. This was a day never to be forgotten. The morning was spent sweetly with Jane. It was the first time she walked to Meeting with me. At the morning Meeting Eliza Dale spoke in a strain that has been common in the Meeting for some months, the approach of death, alluding to some present with the expression, 'in a few years, or shall I say months or weeks?'. After Meeting I walked with Jane Bigland to her father's, W. Backhouse, who was looking forward to starting on his Norwegian mission this week. He was cheerful & animated. In the afternoon Meeting after it had lasted about an hour, he rose to speak, put his hand to his forehead & without a word or sign fell down – *a corpse*! Never was such a sermon preached before. The scene in the Meeting was one of bewilderment, terror & amaze. All was done that

1. Mill's *Logic*, published the year before.
2. Barclay, Jane, and Edmund Backhouse.

could be, but it was too late. In the body of the Meeting a great part of the congregation remained standing in groups, whispering with trembling lips, suspecting yet incredulous. Ed. Pease was led from the gallery, faint. I induced Jane to go home & she behaved with calmness & self-possession. I tried to induce others of the female relatives to leave the scene of excitement but in vain. I found on returning to Polam Jane seated with Ann, who asked few questions. Jane walked upstairs with me and it was no small satisfaction that I was able to afford her comfort. W. Backhouse was remarkable for a pure & guileless spirit. If any man was ready for such a call, it was he. He was taken in his Master's service. He fell amongst friends, surrounded by his family. A few days later he would have been on his voyage to a strange land. His family were all settled in life.

14. The mortal part of Wm. Backhouse was laid in the grave today amidst a no common exhibition of public respect & esteem. All the shops were shut & the graveyard was almost filled by the townspeople who were desirous of showing their estimation of unobtrusive excellence. James Backhouse spoke appropriately at the graveside, translating into words the mute eloquence of this strange event. He & Cos. H.B. preached rather striking funeral sermons in the Meeting & Launcelot Marshall a very stupid one, but good or bad, nothing could come up in impressiveness to the fact itself which brought us together. Being the last evening with Jane we made the most of it after the family had retired. A glorious sunset to a rainy day. There is nothing equal to it on this side of heaven.

15. Jane joined me at 7. We walked into the garden but said little, our converse was something beyond words. Mater called me aside before break-fast to talk about the settlement & the time of the wedding, which, however, I contrived to cut short. Sweet flowers & sweeter thoughts were my companions to Leeds where I found William waiting for me with a chaise to take me to Bolton Bridge. We spent our afternoon amongst those exquisite woods on the banks of the Wharfe above the old Abbey, beside the glistening waters which pour thro' the 'Strid'.[1] Our talk was at least as interesting as our walk. We made the most of indoors, comforts & brotherly confidence till midnight. A clean comfortable hotel.

16. A not unprofitable morning in the woods. I believe that William who has laboured so hard for the happiness of others, will have his reward if he do not go wilfully wrong, & few know better the meaning of right. We left Bolton after dinner & attended Meeting at a little roadside place called Rawdon, the site of a Friends' industrial school. I left William at Leeds with profound thanks for a charming excursion & started for Birmingham which I reached at 12½.

1. A rocky gorge; many have fallen into the river with fatal results by attempting to leap it.

18. I breakfasted & started per mail at 5. Slept & read till I reached Perran. I dined, cleaned, attended to business, wrote 2 letters, & inspected progress at the cottage, which is good. C. much better.

19. Monthly Meeting. I duly 'declared my intentions' & handed in the needful certificates. L. Squire & John Stephens are appointed to enquire as to my freedom from other marriage engagements. I gave them due notice after Meeting that if there was anything of that sort in the way it would puzzle them to get it out of me. Walked & talked with Uncle C. & my father. The former starts tomorrow morning to join Aunt C. & Juliet & take them I fancy to some German Bath. Rode with Uncle C. to Perran.

26. Another delicious letter from Jane. She says that the steamer in which W. & Ed. Backhouse were to have taken their passage for Norway has foundered & *all* on board perished! What a sermon for E.! He will consider himself singled out for some special purpose of providence, & if I am not much mistaken will soon commence preaching. I almost think that even I should reform under such a dispensation.

JULY

3. A bad accident today, which might have been much worse. Whilst Tom was driving the gig round from the front door to the back, the grey took fright at a heap of stones & some masons who were building a wall at Miss Cockburn's. He kicked & broke one shaft off, which brought the gig down on his hocks &, of course, terrified him. He capsized the gig, shooting Tom about 20 feet out of it &, starting off again, capsized the gig & himself a second time. From the gardener's manner of informing me, I thought man or at least horse was dead. I went to the stable & found things better than I expected. Tom was shaken & bruised but not injured; the horse was much cut about the hind legs but not deeply. The gig was a wreck. I placed the grey in the hands of a farrier & took Tom in my own, stripped him, bathed his wounds, rubbed in some healing oil & dosed him with rhubarb, instead of going to Meeting. A torrent of rain in the afternoon.

4. Man & horse going on well. My father & mother & A.M. & also, somewhat to my surprise, Cos. J. T. Price, appeared at my dinner table. They report having seen my mother B., the queen B. in fact, at Liskeard. Her ministry had been striking & her society delightful. Cos J.T.P. is come about the Foundry. My Grandmother & Aunt C. arrived in the evening. I went to them at the other house. Both are well & bright.

9. We had a scene at the Board[1] today. A virago threatened one of our

1. The Board of Guardians.

reverend body even in the curule chair,[1] shaking her clenched fist in his face & heaping him bountifully with maledictions. She was removed by a constable. This is an extreme case, but there *is* a dreary want of real sympathy between the working & unworking classes, & the more they are brought into contact in this matter-of-business way, the less is the mutual understanding & confidence.

13. Received a long & interesting letter from Sterling. He says he is decaying gradually & he expects the summer will see him out. He goes into his views on Christianity in answer to a question of mine as to their sufficiency for him in his present state of exile & near prospect of death. He turns off to the larger question of What is Truth? & claims for himself what he allows to others, the right of holding as True that, & no more, than they can individually realise. It must be dreary work poor fellow, for what *can* any of us find in ourselves to rest upon. Conscience has a blotted page to show us, & if God is just & there be no Mediator, what is to become of us?

17. A sweet letter from Jane allayed the aching of a nerve which kept me awake nearly the whole night. The premature decay of teeth is a strong reminder of our imperfect nature. I did not attend Monthly at Redruth as there seemed to be matrimony enough on foot without my presence. Two couples *passed* & I was 'liberated', or whatever the term is, to proceed. I stayed at Falmouth. On going to bed between 10 & 11 I found my old enemy coming on. I ran down to Brougham's & begged him to extract the offending Adam, but he feared doing it by candle light. So there was another night to endure.

18. Another futile visit to Brougham. Sale of the old cottage furniture. Corfield was auctioneer. The library was filled at 2. I did not get clear of them all till ½ past 10. I was tired enough, but it was a good sale & a good job over. The tooth is better.

19. Jane answers my proposition about starting next week, but not very definitely, & inclines more to the other plan of my going early next month & continuing till Monthly, when we pass.[2] However, I see plainly it will *not* do to be absent at the next Foundry meeting early next month. I wrote her so & wrote J. T. Price to fix *his* time for coming here. On their two answers I must shape my plans. Aunt Charlotte called in her way to Truro & offered me a seat beside her, which was too tempting to refuse. We had a most interesting chat. Her clear mind & her unselfish nature & her sense of fun are a charming combination. No-one enters more deeply into my present interest, which like Aaron's rod swallows up all others. Aunt C. dined with me. I cleared off the Corfields & the goods. Received about £80 in all.

1. Literally, the seat of a Roman magistrate.
2. Their marriage had to be approved, or 'passed', by the Meeting of the Friends in Darlington.

20. Rode to Perran after an early breakfast. There was much to attend to & small inclination for work, for I was afflicted with toothache & general all-overishness. Jane's letter, sweet & affectionate as usual, but it did not help to illuminate my plans. I had the rare honour of a visit from W. Tweedy to tea, after a survey of the road together, on which he contemplates some improvement. He is most certainly pleasanter & less restrained out of his house than in it. How I pity from my heart a hen-pecked husband!

21. Rode to Falmouth morning Meeting. Jane's letter of today enabled me to decide on not going at present. After dinner I rode to Penjerrick & spent the afternoon quietly & happily. I was delighted & edified by the sight of the familiar trustful acquaintance between Uncle J. & the robins, which greet him loudly on his approach & alight on his face, hand, &c., taking crumbs from his mouth with perfect fearlessness. It must be pleasant to be on such terms with Nature.

23. Another night of pain & restlessness decided me to suffer extraction. I rode to Truro accordingly & had him out. Such a fearful wrench! My skull felt cloven & my brain swam, but all that I was prepared for. The real trial was when Nathaniel coolly declared to his writhing victim that the tooth was still 'as firm as a rock'. But the knowledge of necessity is often a good substitute for courage & I again resigned myself into his claws, & out sprang my old tormentor across the room, to my no small delight. What absolute pleasure there is in the mere absence of pain, when that has become continuous. Dinner at Penjerrick. Caroline is in fine trim again. Sunny evening. Jane's letter today would have induced me to start this evening, had I not abandoned the plan in consequence of her former letter. She evidently counts on my pursuing the old plan & will now I fear be disappointed & blame herself as the cause. She is so sensitively considerate.

26. The complete success of Capt. Warner's[1] experiment in blowing up a ship at the distance of 300 yds. with some invisible projectile seems to indicate an entire revolution in the art of war. The more certain the destruction, the more war becomes a matter of arithmetic, & the less men will be inclined to engage in it.

AUGUST

3. Attended a Committee railway meeting at Truro. Capt. Moorsom's report of his survey gave satisfaction, & Bond's report on the traffic gave still

1. Samuel Alfred Warner (d. 1853), an inventor who offered the Admiralty 'an invisible shell', but he was later thought to be a monomaniac and his projectile to be useless.

greater. It is clear to me that we can do nothing without the Gt. Western &
it rests with them to float or sink us.

6. A capital railway meeting at Truro. Lord Falmouth was in the chair.
Go-a-head was the general feeling. Rickerby attempted an amendment in
favour of a North line, but found no seconder. Treffry, W. M. Tweedy,
J. Gwatkin & myself were appointed a deputation to meet the Gt. Western
directors in London next week, to find out what assistance we may expect
from them & on what terms.

8. Cos. J. T. Price & his nephew Harry drove up in time for dinner & we
spent the afternoon at the Foundry, whose affairs, present & future, we discussed calmly in the evening, with what effect the result of tomorrow's meeting will show. About 10 p.m., somewhat to my surprise in walked
Cavendish! I did not at all expect him, although having heard that he was
coming from Dublin by the steamer, I sent in a horse & a note of invitation.
He was well & happy & it was a real pleasure to have him beneath my roof.
We talked over old scenes & sympathies, comparing past with present, &
found in spite of diversity of allotment, that the freshness of our boyish
friendship had not worn off. He is the same light-hearted, affectionate,
gentlemanly fellow as ever. He delighted in talking over my prospects &
entering into my happiness. I shared my bed with him, J. T. Price occupying
my only other.

9. Like Hezekiah & the Ambassadors, I displayed to Cavendish my house &
garden & personals, which struck him as a very easy sort of self-denial.
Having much preparatory matter to attend to with J. T. Price, I dispatched
Cavendish at 12 for Penjerrick, where he will stay a couple of days. Uncles
G.C. & A. came to dinner & we fully impressed them with our views,
so that on M. Williams's arrival there was great unity of opinion. We resolved on Bowman's dismissal, in order to effect a renovation & begin again
de novo. His departure will infuse a general delight through the valley. No
act of ours could be more popular. There was just time after it to swallow
some coffee & start per 8 o'clock coach.

10. Exeter station at ½ past 8, Bristol at 1, where I fell in with Moorsom who
had been attending a meeting of the Bristol & Exeter directors & laying a
statement of our railway case before them. They gave him a favourable
reception & wished to have the statement in writing. At the *Albion Hotel*,
London, I found a letter from my Love, and another from William, pressing
me to cut the Polytechnic & divide the time between Jane & him. Did a little
shopping in Oxford St. & turned in.

11. S. Tottenham after an early breakfast. Ann gave me a sisterly greeting &
John Hodgkin is very hospitable. She is much better & he is recovering from
a feverish attack. They could not give me much news of Jane that I did not
know before, but what they know of Cos. Hannah's progress make them

think that her return on the 19th is for good, which *is* good, but I don't count on it. In the afternoon I retraced some of my walks with Jane & found that for me they only had existence through association with her. How differently Nature looks on the man who loves, & on him who loves not! At the evening Meeting J. Hodgkin gave us a powerful, telling sort of sermon on living to the flesh & living to the spirit. A convinced[1] soldier, William Something, & his sister supped with us. He was tried & sentenced to imprisonment by Court Martial for laying down his arms at Deptford, but afterwards procured his discharge & joined the Society.

12. Departed at 8 & got through some shopping in the City. Joined Tweedy, Bond, & Moorsom at the *Albion*. I congratulated Bond[2] on his preferment, which he well deserved, but the loss to us is most serious. Moorsom had drawn up the statement I requested. Tweedy & I took it in hand & spun a new one out of the material, with which we went to Sanders at Paddington & had half an hour's chat with him preliminary to our meeting the directors tomorrow. I spent a busy afternoon buying furniture & called on the Maurices who were out.

13. Our meeting with the Great Western Directors was satisfactory. There were about a dozen of them present. Tweedy, Bond & I palavered & gave them our written statement. They asked some questions, but raised no objections. I believe the only point they have not already resolved on is the *amount* of assistance they will give us & to do this they must confer with their associated companies, whose united answer will be given us next week. Taking leave of my colleagues I cabbed to James Bell's & took luncheon with him & his brother, Jacob, a most strange genius, after which James accompanied me on a furniture hunt. That over I called on Cavendish, who had not returned & on Carlyle who pressed me to stop to tea. His wife went out with old Buller, & Carlyle & I had rather a brilliant hour together, he descanting on the Puritans as a class of beings scarcely possible in our age. Called on Ann Maurice, who is staying at Chelsea, to hear something about Sterling.

14. I started per train for Darlington at 9. It travels almost fast enough for a lover's wishes, doing the distance in 11 hours. I secured a carriage to myself & monopolised it a great part of the way, when I was joined by a silent inoffensive party of ladies & an old gentleman. Edmund was waiting with the pony chair. We whirled home, screaming to the children to get out of the road. Polam!, hall-door, Bean beaming, Robert grinning, jump out, fling them hat & coat & make straight for the drawing room. There she was, dressed in white muslin & looking rather particularly like an angel. The few

1. i.e. a convert to the Society of Friends.
2. William H. Bond, who had been a purser in the Royal Navy and later Mayor of Falmouth, became Secretary of the Reform Club in London, 1845–8, but he remained Secretary of the Cornwall Railway until 1865.

minutes that followed contained as much of heaven as is allowed to weak mortals. After tea Edmund drove off to Blackwell & we had an undisturbed evening for giving and receiving.

18. S. I was in rather a poor temper today owing to Mater's having told Jane that she could not see any time before the Quarterly meeting (Oct. 2.) as fit for our marriage. Jane did her best to bring me back to my better self & to reconcile me to the parental decree.

19. I am in a better mind today owing to Jane's irresistibleness. We read together before breakfast out of doors. This morning a fresh walk in the meadows prepared us for breakfast at which we had the company of the Clarks, who afterwards gave us some good counsel & bright promises in an 'opportunity' at the close of reading. I registered Jane's & my intended marriage at the Registrar's. Jane & I employed the evening in a walk, not to mention a frolic in a hay field, the disputed sovereignty & the united occupancy of a haycock. The stately Jane G. Backhouse is actually come to this!

20. We accomplished the 'passing' satisfactorily. The Monthly Meeting was held at Cotherstone, a picturesque village near the Tees. At the 2nd Meeting Cos. H.B. gave up her certificate with a brief report of her mission. J. Pease entered a minute on the books to record the reason why W. Backhouse's certificate remained in the Clerk's possession.[1] It was beautifully expressed & I observed many eyes wet with tears. Afterwards the men & women, having separated, came on our business. I found Jane disposed for a run, so we galloped down the field while the rest were arranging procedure. All being ready we marched into the Women's Meeting: Edmund and mater, Jane & I, J. C. Backhouse & Aunt Ann, & J. J. Gurney & spouse. It felt uncommonly like the visit of a man-friend under religious concern. I spoke audibily enough for all the ladies to know my business & Jane performed beautifully. I gave the clerk my certificate which was well read by Emma Pease, & J. J. Gurney finished the operation with a prayer for the sanctification of our union. It was 'Ditto repeated' in the Men's Meeting, neither of us blundering out 'wife' for 'husband', or 'husband' for 'wife'. I enjoyed the feeling with which Jane uttered her intentions, her heart & soul consenting. This ended, Jane returned to Meeting with her mother. I wandered beside the Tees, musing on what had befallen me since I wandered there last (7 years ago) with Jane & my sisters, & how different it had all been had I been permitted to follow my own will. During my absence Tabitha Fox's resignation was read & Cos. Hannah, not being satisfied that her work was done, begged for a conference between men & women; the shutters were drawn & a fresh certificate granted her for Glo'ster &c.[2]

1. W. Backhouse, who had dropped dead at a previous Meeting, had been granted a 'certificate' to engage in a mission to Norway.
2. i.e. she was given permission to go on a preaching tour to Gloucester.

21. At breakfast Cos. Hannah propounded her plan of going southward with Jane next week & going to Sunderland today with the Gurneys. We had a little open chat after breakfast about the settlement. We started at ½ past 11. I took Carlyle's *Miscellany* to read to Jane, but J. J. Gurney got hold of it & denounced the man & his works with the awful word 'unsound'. This was perfectly natural. The two men are cast in two moulds & neither can appreciate the other. A large family party assembled in the evening.

24. An hour with Jane in the wilderness. What an hour!, time, place & circumstances favouring us. Our rest was a rustic seat beneath a bower of hazel, close to the rippling Tees. A dove was cooing behind us & something like it within, but the parting came at last, vastly mitigated by the prospect of meeting in a fortnight when Jane expects to be in the S.W. with her mother. The 4 o'clock train whirled me off to York, meditating many things. I had time to run up to that glorious specimen of the embodied faith of the middle ages, York minster, with all its fretted spires & quaint corbels to which the modern houses round look prosaic enough. Reached Leeds at 8. I put up at Scarborough's and ordered a fire in lieu of female society. What a 10 days I have had!

25. William burst into my room between 6 & 7 looking like a windmill. Heartily glad were we to meet & gladder still to be sitting over a comfortable breakfast in his parlour about an hour later. William is like his own self with the additional knowledge of the world which business gives. He is for making a fortune & retire after 5 or 10 years' fag. My ideal is to limit business now to a very *un*engrossing pursuit, be satisfied with little & live accordingly. My ideal is something wherewith money has small concern; his a life of impressive action requiring wealth. The view of Airedale from the hill behind his house is beautiful. My time with William was truly pleasant, discussing present, past & future.

26. I left Bradford at 9 & Leeds ½ past 10. 4 trains in connection whisked me to Bristol by 9, where I found a second rate inn producing third rate coffee & a bench to stretch my limbs on.

27. I left Bristol at ½ past 1 & reached Exeter soon after 4. There I had the comfort of finding a letter from Jane, a draught of rich refreshment. A coach, full inside & out, brought me to Perran by ½ past 2. An ablution & good dinner set me up. That 28 hours should suffice (including 4½ at Bristol for a night's rest) for the journey from Leeds to Perran! Really to good Conservatives like myself it is quite alarming. Things are going on well at the Cottage, but I can't yet get rid of those leeches – the masons & carpenters.

28. I returned to the bosom of my family & plunged from thence into the dissipations of a good, well-attended Polytechnic exhibition. Hicks greeted me in the gallery & his fascinations combined with the crowd prevented my seeing or hearing much of the objects or the orators. There was singularly

little trash. The prominent interests of the exhibition were Coryton Roberts's improved atmospheric Railway (lead vertebrae in a leather case falling into a triangular groove instead of Samuda's[1] valve) & Hearder's[2] contrivance for applying electro-magnetism as a motive-power, the old idea of a wheel turned by breaking & renewing contact of wires. A bazaar was attached where omnium gatherum animate & inanimate were sold, also a sham post office for taking in strangers, charging 6d. for every hoaxing letter, by which several pounds were realised. The fair & gentle Mary Tremayne dined with us & congratulated me warmly. All went off well. C. looks better.

31. Poor Jane has missed my letters & is in a sad way about it, not knowing what has befallen her lover. Would I were by her side! Busy morning. Dined at Carclew at 7. Lord Auckland looks like a Norfolk farmer & is remarkably provident of his sentiments if he have any, but a man who can govern 80,000,000 people must have something in him.[3] His sisters the Miss Edens are dashing, showy conversational creatures. Talbot & Lady Charlotte who came yesterday in their yacht are a superior pair. He is silent, occasionally throwing out a careless, offhand remark, always to the purpose. His lady I sat by at dinner & found her refined, aristocratic & intelligent. Your real aristocracy are easy enough to get on with, it is the millionaire who assumes a stately grandeur which puts you at a distance.

SEPTEMBER

4. On returning to Perran after Meeting I found a letter from Jane urging me to meet them at Bristol the day after tomorrow, spend that day quietly with her & accompany them home. 'Twon't do I believe. The girls can't be ready & I can't leave them in the lurch. Dispatched Tom to Penjerrick to make enquiries & wrote Jane holding out no prospect of acceding.

5. I rode to Penjerrick to breakfast & found things as I expected. The girls were full of generosity & heroism, quite willing to travel alone and urging to follow as love leads. Parents on the other hand rejoiced to find that I had scruples of my own against forsaking the sisterhood, as they did not relish the idea of their travelling alone, so I fixed on waiting for them till the Quarterly Meeting next week. I attended a meeting at Falmouth, convened by Capt. Holland for considering his plan of building large floating docks

1. Joseph Samuda (1813–85), an engineer who experimented with the atmospheric principle 1842–8, but turned to building iron steamships.

2. Jonathan Hearder (1810–76), was electrician to the South Devon Hospital, who patented a sub-oceanic cable. He worked with Sir Wm. Snow Harris on various enterprises.

3. George Eden, first Earl of Auckland (1784–1849), had been Governor-General of India.

between Green Bank & Boyer's Cellars. A very respectable meeting at which a survey & estimate were agreed to be made & a committee appointed for carrying it out. A most acceptable shower in the evening.

7. No letter from Jane who of course counted on my being en route, considering how strongly her will was expressed. I spent a busy morning at Truro & the evening in visiting & haranguing on the bridge the reprobate young men of Perran Well whose conduct of late to peaceful passers-by requires interference. We have sent one youth to Bodmin & have a summons against another.

10. A.M. & C. to dinner, a snug evening together. After dark I walked to the bridge at Perran Well to encounter my Saturday's audience, having heard that some of them threatened to return my next interference by flinging me into the river. The bridge was, however, quite clear. We packed up, gave orders & prepared for starting tomorrow.

11. Beautiful morning. The girls & I underweigh at 6, breakfasting at Probus & reaching St. Austell a little after time (Quarterly Meeting). I found a letter from my love at the Post Office. I dined at the inn with miscellaneous friends. P. Williams warned me that I had a serious undertaking before me. I replied that marriage at the best was that. Others did little but eat their dinners. I took leave of the parents & carried off their daughters to Liskeard where we put up at J. Allen's hospitable well-daughtered house. Talked of railways & other matters.

12. We got no further than Bristol today, leaving our kind hosts at 6. In the passage E. Allen gave me a little address very sweet & suitable, beginning with 'Him that honoureth me, I will honour', referring to my marriage. We reached Plymouth at 10 minutes to 9, but the 9 o'clock coach starting 20 minures earlier by a recent change, we were delayed till the next by which means & the mal-arrangements of railway trains we were forced to stop at Bristol & sleep at the *George*. A very pleasant journey with the girls. C. is evidently in better health & spirits.

13. Started at 6 for Gloucester, reading Dahlmann's[1] *Revolution* en route & Michèlet's[2] translation of Vico. At Worcester we branched off to Malvern on a false scent of the travellers, Jane having spoken of the probability of their being there today & the result of our enquiries at the station confirming it. After a fruitless search at the hotels we went to C. A. Backhouse's who has been for some time here in lodgings with her sisters on account of her health. No news, save of a Friend-corpse & a Monthly Meeting at Worcester which double attraction we doubted not had drawn Cos. H.B. there. We returned to Worcester after an hour's residence at Malvern & hunted the city, but in

1. Friedrich Dahlmann (1785–1860), German historian and politician.
2. Jules Michèlet (1798–1874), French historian, whose monumental work was a History of France in 24 volumes.

vain. We went on to Birmingham & made earnest enquiries at the 3 stations for the promised note, all in vain. We took a fly to the hotel where I learnt that the whole party started yesterday but whither deponent knew not. I tried John Cadbury's next & then to my great satisfaction found the note which had been 3 times to the Station in search of me. It said they were gone home, so there was naught to do but to see my sisters in the Grand Junction train under the protection of a civil guard & to start to Derby as no train proceeded farther tonight. Turned into bed at the *Capital Hotel* at the Derby Station at 8.

14. I rose before ½ past 2, dressed, & being assured by the porter that there was an abundance of time, walked leisurely to the Booking Office. On entering it I found the train had actually started. It was not out of the long shed, however, so out I rushed, leapt into the nearest carriage & the portmanteau was bundled in after me. I reached Polam soon after 9. Bean greeted me at the door & answered my rapid enquiries, 'Any company?', 'Reading finished?', with an unintelligible grin. I marched into the drawing room & found it most desolate. Bean collected his senses & informed me they were not *yet* returned! Edmund appeared & was as much in the dark as to their whereabouts as myself. I went to the bank & waited for letters. One came at length from Jane, from Normanton!, holding out a prospect of their returning *again* to Birmingam to spend Sunday. I returned to Polam & prepared for a start in the afternoon for Birmingham, but while dispatching a note to my parents on the unfortunate issue of my expedition, I heard a well-known voice in the hall & in walked *Mater in lege*, followed by her daughter looking like a guardian angel – an expressive kiss, a little mutual astonishment & mutual explanation. They were brought up at Normanton, by an idea of Mater's that she ought to apply for the Methodist Meeting-house for a public meeting next 1st day, the town hall having been refused her. The proposition was sent to Birmingham Friends who, however, thought better to waive it. So they came on. Jane has picked up a troublesome cold. Alas, she must lie by and nurse.

16. We had it all out this morning after breakfast, chapter & verse, beginning with the daughter's longing for somebody at Bristol, to the mother's perplexities at Normanton about her public meeting. Mater thinks that had I come as intended at first she would have been spared the mess & Jane her cold. It seems that having held a good public meeting yesterday week at Birmingham our lady & her companions started homewards. At Derby 'a stop' came on which induced her & hers to return to Birmingham & apply for leave to hold another Meeting & in the Town Hall. The question took 2 days deliberation, being brought before 2 Town Hall Committees, who at last declined, not liking the precedent. On 5th day accordingly they started again & this time got to Normanton before the 'stop' came. There my

excellent mother did not feel easy without sending an application to a Select Committee of Birmingham Friends for them to ask, if they thought fit, for the loan of the Methodist meeting-house as a substitute for the Hall. The answer from Birmingham was in the negative, Friends preferring to take the burden (or whatever it might be) on themselves & the wanderers returned home accordingly the next morning. Mater went to Select Meeting in the evening & daughter & I held our select meeting together. Mater reported hers harmonious & satisfactory. I think I may *safely* report as much of ours.

17. Monthly Meeting, whereat the certificate[1] was safely returned to the Clerk, & what's more, no fresh one was applied for! A succinct report of proceedings accompanied it. She stated that she should probably have no more business with those parts nor perhaps with any part (I wonder how many believed her). She concluded with a very beautiful prayer. She is a wondrous compound of strength & weakness, or else the result of 2 powerful forces pulling different ways. I did not stay the second Meeting, having a summons from the lawyer about the settlement & preferring to spend the short time that remained in rich luxurious idleness with my incomparable love than listen to the answers to the queries in the men's Meeting. I had the satisfaction of hearing, however, that we are *cleared* & no obstacle now remains. Three flabby female Friends to dinner, 10 minutes after it with my other & purer self in 'great nearness' both of soul & body, when Edmund's dog cart drove to the door, one good wrench like drawing a double tooth & I was on my way to Leeds where William's conveyance was waiting for me. I reached his house about $\frac{1}{2}$ past 9. He appeared at 11 after presiding at a Trade dinner. We spent the evening till 2 perhaps more profitably than appeared at the time.

18. William drove me to Leeds. He will probably attend the wedding. He has given us a magnificent white Morocco bible. He is a noble hearted fellow with one or two weak points. With fixedness of purpose what might he not be.

19. Started at 8 for Bristol. There I went to the Hunts according to agreement with Jane. I found a letter from her with not a bright account of herself. Eliz. Hunt was very cordial. She asked for a private time with me & sent her husband downstairs. She has him in capital subjection. She wanted to know about Mater's and Jane's feelings now & whether they were satisfied or not about the result of the last application for a place to hold a meeting in at Birmingham, &c. I satisfied the lady's curiosity as far as I thought fit. I spent the morning in shopping & at dinner was introduced to her amiable (not lovely) daughters. I was treated by the young ladies with marked respect as Mama's friend's daughter's intended. I started at 7 for Exeter.

20. Up at 4. I found things at the cottage progressing tho' not so fast as if I

1. The certificate that authorised Hannah Backhouse to engage on her mission.

had been at home. After dining, writing & giving orders I rode to Penjerrick & spent a snug gossiping evening with Mater. My father returned late from a Geological meeting at Penzance. Bed early, warm water & gruel in order to stifle in the birth an embryo cold.

22. S. How strangely & wonderfully I am blest! To be loved at all is much, but to be loved by *her* & *thus* is a benison indeed! The post that brought her letter to me brought one of another character to my father. Capt. Sterling[1] in a short note of simple, manly feeling gives the intelligence we had been long expecting. Poor Sterling is at last released from his sufferings. England has lost a Teacher & I have lost a friend. The only particulars of his end are that he was calm & peaceful. May it be as well with him, as I cannot but believe it is! I kept indoors after dinner to nurse a cold.

25. An important railway Committee meeting at Truro. We agreed on the prospectus & arranged its immediate issue; enlarged our Committee & prepared for immediately taking the field. The North line men are very active, holding meetings through the County & holding out golden promises of success. Could they shew me any solid foundation for such hopes I would heartily back them, their line being no doubt best for Falmouth, but, as it is, I fear they will do us mischief, without doing themselves good.

30. At Perran. The cottage full of work, scouring & furnishing. This week I hope will finish it. I issued invitations for the 10th to my wedding dinner at Penjerrick to all the servants in the family, for which the fatted steer is to be slaughtered; all the men to be presented with white gloves & the women with white ribbon.

OCTOBER

1. Tweedy was with me in the morning & proposed my canvassing Leeds, Manchester & Liverpool in conjunction with W. Carne on behalf of the railway, in my way northwards, – a little *too* much to ask. My mother was with me all day, making lists & arranging the store closet.

2. I found people at Falmouth full of the North line scheme. It will be well if we don't fall between 2 stools. Evening at Penjerrick. Uncle J. was more than usually highflown on the subject of the marriage, looking to remote consequences, and equally full of the North line since he is on the committee. I spent an evening with T. Evans arranging the order of the feast.

6. I left my cottage after breakfast never to return to it single & felt no pang in bidding adieu to bachelorhood – not that it is *no* giving up – but the balance is materially against it even in the abstract. In my case, however, the

1. John Sterling's father.

counter-balancing is due to the individual not the abstraction. I spent the day at Falmouth & took leave of old friends.

7. The morning being beautiful we (i.e. parents, Kitty & self) started for Plymouth per *Drake*. The passage was smooth, sunny & rapid. The Exeter coach was cramfull inside & out. A young bride & bridegroom married this morning were amongst us. The former complaining that she was squeezed against the rail, I ascended the luggage on the roof & rode thus enthroned to Exeter. The *petites tendresses* which passed between the happy pair were truly edifying & especially to me. I made a hearty tea supper with parents at Exeter where I left them & reached Bristol soon after 12.

8. Off at 6, and reached Darlington at 7. I found the family at the tea-table enlarged by the addition of brother & sister Hodgkin. Jane is blooming but the *sound* of her cold has not entirely ceased. Perhaps it is only an echo. We had a draught of each other's presence in the evening, being allowed an hour for discourse which was carried on as much without as with words. Our mother is very bright considering, full of her trees which she has been hacking & hewing without mercy.

9. Wedding-eve! My father & mother arrived at 9; the girls, with my Grandmother & Aunt C., in the afternoon. C. has not lost her cough, but both give a clean bill of themselves & bright reports of their northern experiences. The morning was occupied in executing the settlement bond & agreement. We dined at Southend with a large party, including 9 of the bridesmaids. At 7 William appeared seemingly well-strung-up to the occasion. We had much pleasant & interesting chat over the breakfast-room fire till the arrival of Uncle C. & the lawyers put an end to it. He & William in conjunction with J. Hodgkin, & Edmund are our Trustees. This second legal visitation gave me the opportunity of a few last words with Jane who is all herself – free from frights & fancies, considerate of *all*, calm & self-possessed. No perturbation at the thought of tomorrow.

10. The day came at last as all days must come if one waits long enough. The day that ended my old & commenced my new life – a change for the better I have not the smallest shadow of doubt – the day that ends this *daily* journal, having a living tablet to write upon instead, 'The soul's living home' as Coleridge calls it most truly. Jane joined the breakfast party clad in quiet happiness & serenity. William, Edmund and Edward Backhouse were of the party. At ½ past 9 we started, parents & sisters first, then William, Edward Backhouse, & I in Jane's chariot, leaving the Polam coach to follow with its precious burden, after the bridal procession had congregated & formed. We fell short of 2 bridesmaids, Emily B. & Eliz. Richardson, the former from physical the latter from moral indisposition. However, 10 were enough. I presented each with a brooch made of Jane's & my hair. The house was very full & many came from a distance to see a Quaker's wedding. It was a thrill-

ing, throbbing walk up the Meeting House to our place under the gallery. People were extremely silent. Jas. Backhouse preached first, a sermon rather general than particular, but sound, clear & practical. My new mother then knelt & offered a beautiful prayer for us. After, it seemed the right time for us to perform our parts which we did without a blunder, happily, & sat down in our places, man & wife. Brother John then took up the words 'through divine assistance', & made it the text of an excellent sermon, pressing the importance of that other covenant – between the soul & its maker. The signatures to our marriage certificate were very numerous. We left the Meeting as soon as the relations had signed & received the congratulations of new & old kindred in the lady-friends' 'ante-room'. Jane & I rode home alone, ran down to the pond & agreed that we felt very much as we were before, the ceremony only appearing as the public exhibition of an already made contract. Then followed bridesmaids, bridegroom's-men, handshakings, kissings &c., &c. Then we met in our mother's room & she offered up a thanksgiving very full & I thought very noble. There was a dinner party of 80, but neither of us had great appetites. There was no speechifying & no wine, but every delicacy that man could desire in the way of eating. This dispatched, the party split into knots & groups. William & I were much together. I never saw anybody behave better, neither above nor below the mark, self-possessed & a gentleman throughout. He was well pleased that he came. A very large party assembled at tea, upwards of a hundred, to most of whom I had to be introduced & to utter some unmeaning commonplaces. After tea we had a sitting for about ¾ of an hour, & my mother B. spoke with deep feeling & John Hodgkin prayed for us. At 8 the carriage drove to the door. We were heartily tired of the protracted ordeal & after a few more parting words of benediction in my new mother's dressing room & a few hasty kisses to my own kindred, I handed my bride into our carriage & we drove off to Rushyford to lodge.

13. S. Glasgow. Three days of matrimony make a marvellous change to be sure. Few married pairs ever enjoyed life more than we have. Jane mustered courage to introduce 'my husband' to some of her acquaintances at Meeting & it sounded not a little sweet.

20. S. Trossachs. The sweet sabbatism of this day will not be easily forgotten. The morning being wet we were confined to our little inn parlour where we knew something of the fullness of a silence which is beyond words. The afternoon was sunny enough for us to enjoy the heather by the shores of Loch Achray & the sight of the snowy top of Ben Venue. Our walk through the Trossachs & row on Loch Katrine was a beautiful wind-up to a most delightful tour by Loch Lomond, thro' the wild moorlands of Glencoe, around Ben Nevis & down by Blair Atholl, Killiecrankie, Aberfeldy & Loch Tay to this region of enchantment. Tomorrow we wend homewards.

24. Arrived at Polam – warm smiles.

28. Departed – hot tears. My mother said she had never felt any separation so much, not even by death. She was quite overcome. Jane wept freely as the train departed but clung the closer to her new supporter.

29. An interesting visit to Combe. They bear their calamity nobly.[1] Uncle G.H. took me into his room & gave me an exposé of his affairs which are quite satisfactory as regards character. They leave the place probably next month.

30. We reached home at ½ past 7 p.m. As we descended Carnon hill three brilliant lights appeared in the valley & several flashes with a distant booming sound. On reaching Carnon gate our progress was arrested by a dense crowd with torches. A figure came to the carriage window & begged us to alight. On doing so we found the new carriage waiting alongside with a human team (a hundred or so) in harness. After 9 cheers on our getting in, we were drawn through the valley amidst the blaze of tarbarrels, the discharge of cannon & illuminated windows. The reflections of the tarbarrels on the river were beautiful. T. Tregaskes & T. Evans were seated on the box. Old T. Evans was trudging by the carriage door imparting miscellaneous information. Under a triumphal arch of laurel at the Counting House, with an illuminated 'Welcome to the Valley', the carriage stopped, the 'welcome' of the inhabitants was conveyed by T. Tregaskes as their spokesman, then cheers upon cheers – then a short reply – & the carriage proceeded. Over the cottage gateway was another arch with 'Thrice Welcome Here' emblazoned thereon, then more cheering & so at last we reached the cottage where my father, Uncle J., A.M. & C. hotly welcomed us. Jane was taken by surprise but bore all the excitement with her usual equanimity. She stepped out on the balcony with me while I thanked the assembled crowd for their kind exertions. The drawing room was beautifully set up & an elegant supper prepared for us. My father returned to Falmouth & the girls lodged with us. The quiet within our cottage walls was the more deeply enjoyed for the unquiet cordiality without. It looked like peace, & all we felt is not easy to write. If ever heaven seemed to smile on a new married pair it surely seems to now. Gratitude almost fails when I think of all that has been given me.

NOVEMBER

15. A fortnight has accomplished most of the preliminary visiting. Jane feels established. Our young household goes on well on the whole. This evening we gave a supper to the Foundry workmen & our men, about 150, ending

1. George Hilhouse had failed in business.

the repast with a present to each man of a piece of bridecake & a little testament. After supper, speeches of thanksgiving & warm feeling were made by T. Tregaskes & R. Hosking, the men responding with cheers. Uncle C. & I spoke to them in reply. He read them Longfellow's *Village Blacksmith* & did it well. Hunt very kindly gave a brilliant lecture on combustion illustrated by delightful pops & blazes & Tregellas finished the evening with a few rich specimens of Cornish & Yorkshire brogue. The whole thing answered peculiarly well.

DECEMBER

31. Here ends the best & brightest & most blessed year of my life. It is as tho' I had reached the goal of my boy-existence & found it but the starting post of a new one. The mountain tops before me show higher than ever & life is become a more earnest business with a larger sphere & higher pleasures & deeper responsibilities – no longer alone but blest with the companionship of a noble & pure spirit, with the possession of a deeply-loving heart; how abundantly grateful ought mine to be!

Postscript

FROM THE time of his marriage Barclay Fox ceased to make daily entries in his Journal. Instead, the entries now appear, firstly at weekly, then at monthly, and soon at irregular intervals. Their interest lies chiefly in the record they provide of the fortunes of the *dramatis personae* of the Journal proper. Barclay and his wife had ten years of happy married life, with a family that grew to four sons and one daughter. But their happiness was threatened by many troubles. It was a time of commercial depression, accompanied by bad harvests at home and famine in Ireland. Cornish industry was facing strong competition from overseas in a market that had moved towards free-trade. The Cornwall railway was held up by the collapse of the railway boom and by the fears of investors. The Foxes, although they kept their shipping business and their interests at Neath, withdrew from their joint enterprise with the Williamses at Perran Foundry. Barclay himself began to suffer ill-health and moved to Roscrow, which had once been the home of his grandparents, where he exchanged the life of an industrialist for that of a farmer. The anxiety about his health increased with the years; holidays at home and abroad, treatment of one kind or another, all proved ineffective, and the last entry records his departure for Egypt in a last vain bid to recover his strength. Throughout this time of trial he remained considerate of others, playing his part in making society just and compassionate, and showing a loving concern for individuals. Examples of this recorded in the Journal are his visit to Ireland to help organize Quaker relief work, and concern for his bereaved brother-in-law, John Hodgkin.

The following two extracts from letters by Caroline, Barclay's sister, bring the story of the Journal to its close.

[To Elizabeth Carne]
Penjerrick, Nov. 21, 1854.

. . . Robin [Barclay's eldest son] and I have been with Barclay to Southampton, and seen him off for Alexandria in the good ship *Indus*, and then with heavy hearts went to London. Everything on board the *Indus* looked promising; the second officer magnificently gave up his luxurious cabin, and when the bell rang we left our Brother, feeling that we ought to be thankful for the present and trustful for the future. His brother-in-law, John Hodgkin, came down from London that morning to see him off; he was in every way a great comfort and strength, for we had a little time of silence and a solemn prayer before going on board, which, though most touching, was essentially strengthening and helpful. The weather has been so fine since he left that we feel we have had no pretext for anxiety, and all we hear and all we know argues that he is doing the very wisest thing possible, and that there is every probability of its bringing him into a very different state of health from that in which we part from him.

[To E. Lloyd]
Falmouth, April 7, 1855.

It was last Sunday that the tidings reached us that our dearest Barclay had been called hence to be for ever with his Lord. Twenty-four tranquil, peaceful, holy hours succeeded the breaking of a blood-vessel, and then he fell asleep – *literally* fell asleep – and awoke in his Saviour's arms. It was all so painless, so quiet, so holy, that how can we but give thanks, and pray that we may not envy him, but rather bear our little burdens faithfully and meekly for a few short years, and then – !

It was so beautiful that he had asked the Missionary Lieder and his wife to come and visit him at his encampment by the Pyramids, because they were in trouble; so they came, and had some bright, most enjoyable days together; and thus, when the last illness came they nursed him with parental tenderness; and watched beside him in the desert.

Robert Barclay Fox died at Gizeh, Cairo, 10th March, 1855. He was buried at Cairo under a slab of Cornish granite that was sent to mark his grave.

Selected List of Persons

BACKHOUSE, Ann, daughter of Hannah Backhouse; married John Hodgkin; Barclay Fox's sister-in-law.

BACKHOUSE, Edmund, son of Hannah Backhouse; married Juliet Fox; Barclay Fox's brother-in-law; later became M.P.

BACKHOUSE, Hannah Gurney, wife of Jonathan Backhouse of Darlington; cousin of Barclay Fox's mother and to become his mother-in-law; a minister in the Society of Friends.

BACKHOUSE, Jane Gurney, daughter of Hannah Backhouse; Barclay Fox's wife.

BARCLAY, Charles, of Bury Hill, Surrey; brother of Barclay Fox's mother.

BARCLAY, David, of Eastwick Park, Dorking; brother of Barclay Fox's mother.

BARCLAY, Robert, of Leyton; married Elizabeth Lucy Gurney, a cousin of Barclay Fox's mother.

BUXTON, Sir Thomas Fowell, of Northrepps Hall, Norfolk; married Hannah Gurney, a cousin of Barclay Fox's mother; an Evangelical churchman who led the anti-slavery movement after Wilberforce's death; an advocate of prison reform; M.P. for Weymouth 1818–37; a partner in the brewing firm of Truman, Hanbury, and Buxton.

BUXTON, Richenda, daughter of Sir Thomas Fowell Buxton.

CALVERT, Dr John Mitchenson, son of William Calvert, the friend and schoolfellow of Wordsworth; family physician to the second Earl Spencer; friend of John Sterling.

COLERIDGE, Rev. Derwent, son of the poet, S. T. Coleridge; Headmaster of Helston Grammar School and, later, first Principal of St Mark's College, Chelsea.

CROUCH, Lucretia, a minister in the Society of Friends; wife of William Crouch.

ENYS, John Samuel, F.G.S., of Enys; landowner; geologist and engineer who wrote several papers on the design of steam-engines.

EVANS, Thomas, the farm-manager at Penjerrick.

FALMOUTH, Edward, Lord Falmouth, of Tregothnan; created 1st Earl 1821.

FORSTER, William Edward, son of William Forster (a minister in the Society of Friends); entered the woollen trade in Bradford and became Liberal M.P. for the city in 1861; left the Society of Friends on his marriage to Matthew Arnold's sister in 1850; became a minister in Gladstone's administration and was responsible for the Education Act of 1870; appointed Chief Secretary for Ireland in 1880.

Fox, Alfred (Uncle Alfred), of Wodehouse Place and Glendurgan; brother of R. W. Fox; married Sarah, daughter of Samuel Lloyd of Bordesley, Warwickshire.

Fox, Anna Maria, Barclay Fox's sister.

Fox, Caroline, Barclay Fox's sister.

Fox, Charles (Uncle Charles), of Perran and Trebah; brother of R. W. Fox; married Sarah, daughter of William Hustler of Ulverston.

Fox, Charlotte (Aunt Charlotte), sister of R. W. Fox; married Samuel Fox of Tottenham.

Fox, Elizabeth Tregelles, of Roscrow; mother of R. W. Fox and Barclay Fox's grandmother.

Fox, Elizabeth, sister of R. W. Fox; married William Gibbins; Barclay Fox's aunt.

Fox, George Croker (Uncle G.C.), F.G.S., of Grove Hill, Falmouth; cousin of R. W. Fox; married Lucy Barclay, daughter of Robert Barclay of Bury Hill, Surrey.

Fox, George Philip, brother of R. W. Fox; Barclay Fox's uncle; unmarried.

Fox, Joanna, daughter of Joshua Fox; Barclay Fox's cousin.

Fox, Joseph, M.D., son of Richard Fox, M.D.; practised in Falmouth.

Fox, Josephine, daughter of Joshua Fox; Barclay Fox's cousin.

Fox, Joshua (Uncle Joshua) of Tregedna; brother of R. W. Fox; widower.

Fox, Juliet, daughter of Charles Fox; married Edmund Backhouse; Barclay Fox's cousin.

Fox, Lewis, brother of R. W. Fox; Barclay Fox's uncle; unmarried.

Fox, Lucy (Aunt Lucy), daughter of Robert Barclay of Bury Hill, Surrey; wife of G. C. Fox.

Fox, Maria, daughter of Robert Barclay of Bury Hill, Surrey; wife of R. W. Fox and Barclay Fox's mother.

Fox, Mariana, sister of R. W. Fox; married Francis Tuckett of Frenchay, near Bristol; Barclay Fox's aunt.

Fox, Marie Louise, daughter of Joshua Fox; Barclay Fox's cousin.

Fox, Richard, M.D., son of Joseph Fox, surgeon, and father of Joseph Fox (above); practised in Falmouth.

Fox, Robert Were, F.R.S., of Rosehill and Penjerrick; Barclay Fox's father.

Fox, Samuel, of Tottenham; married Charlotte, sister of R. W. Fox.

Fox, Sarah Hustler (Aunt Charles), wife of Charles Fox.

Fox, Sarah Lloyd (Aunt Alfred), wife of Alfred Fox.

Fry, Elizabeth Gurney, daughter of J. Gurney of Earlham; a cousin of Barclay Fox's mother; married Joseph Fry; famous prison reformer and philanthropist.

Gibbins, William, of Falmouth; husband of Elizabeth Fox.

Gilbert, Davies, F.R.S., of Trelissick; President of the Royal Society;

M.P. for Helston and later for Bodmin; patron of Humphry Davy and responsible for choice of Brunel's design for Clifton Suspension Bridge.

GURNEY, Joseph John, of Earlham, Norwich; one of the leading members of the Society of Friends at this time; brother of Elizabeth Fry and a cousin of Barclay Fox's mother.

GURNEY, Samuel, of Ham House, Upton; a brother of J. J. Gurney.

HARRIS, Sir William Snow, F.R.S., of Plymouth; knighted in 1847 for his invention of an improved lightning conductor; Copley medallist; awarded £5,000 by the government for scientific research.

HICKS, Samuel, Clerk and Steward of the Cornwall Asylum at Bodmin.

HILHOUSE, George, of Combe, near Bristol; shipbuilder; married Agatha Barclay, sister of Barclay Fox's mother.

HODGKIN, John, of Tottenham; barrister and friend of J. S. Mill; married Ann Backhouse; Barclay Fox's brother-in-law.

HUNT, Robert, appointed secretary of the Royal Cornwall Polytechnic Society in 1840; published the first treatise on photography in Britain in 1841; in 1843 advanced the theory that there are three distinct properties of the solar ray – light, heat, and photographic power; worked on the Great Exhibition of 1851; elected F.R.S., 1854.

LEMON, Sir Charles, F.R.S., of Carclew; M.P. for Penryn, 1807–12, for W. Cornwall 1832–57.

MOLESWORTH, Rev. Hender, changed his name to St Aubyn by royal licence in 1844; rector of Redruth, 1822–23.

OPIE, Amelia, novelist and poet; widow of the painter, John Opie, R.A.; intimate with the Gurney family and joined Society of Friends in 1825; acquainted with Sydney Smith, Sheridan, Madame de Staël, etc.

PRICE, Joseph Tregelles, a partner in the Perran Foundry but moved to Neath in S. Wales in 1800 to manage the Abbey Iron Works; founder with W. Allen and others of the Peace Society in 1816.

PRICE, Junia, sister of J. T. Price; a minister in the Society of Friends.

REYNOLDS, Jacob Foster, of Carshalton, Surrey; married Anna Barclay, sister of Barclay Fox's mother.

SQUIRE, Lovell, ran a school at Falmouth; meteorologist who started the Falmouth observatory; married Henrietta, daughter of William and Lucretia Crouch.

STERLING, John, educated Trinity College and Trinity Hall, Cambridge; an 'Apostle' and achieved a reputation as a speaker at the Union; tutored by Julius Charles Hare and later served under him as a curate at Hurstmonceaux; studied philosophy in Germany in 1833; a friend of S. T. Coleridge, F. D. Maurice, J. S. Mill, Richard Chenevix Trench, and Carlyle; his *Essays and Tales* edited after his death by J. C. Hare and Carlyle's *Life* gave him posthumous fame.

TREMAYNE, Harriet, daughter of J. H. Tremayne of St Ewe; married Sir John Trelawny, Bt, M.P. for Tavistock.

TUCKETT, Francis, of Frenchay, near Bristol; husband of Mariana Fox.

TWEEDY, William, Head Partner of Tweedy, Williams, and Co., Cornish Bank, at Truro, Falmouth, and Redruth; an elder in Society of Friends.

TWEEDY, Ann, wife of William Tweedy; a minister in Society of Friends.

WILLIAMS, John Michael, elder son of Michael Williams (below).

WILLIAMS, Michael, of Trevince, partner in the Perran foundry; M.P. for W. Cornwall 1853–8; became Chairman of the Cornwall Railway.

Index

413

1839:
work at shipping office, 143–6;
Chartist meeting at Falmouth, 147;
Misericordia Sale, 148–9; shipping
office duties and farming at Penjerrick,
150–8; catches of pilchards at Mevagissey, 159–60; governor of Lancastrian
school, 161; visit from J. C. Backhouse,
162–3; Polytechnic exhibition, 164;
J. Boyne's illness and death, 165–6;
Cornwall railway meeting, 167–8;
Chartist riots at Newport, 169; illness
and death of Uncle Lewis, 170–1;
electors' meeting at Falmouth, 172–3;
1840:
Nadir Bey visits Falmouth, 175–6;
election at Falmouth, 177; Sterling and
Calvert arrive at Falmouth, 178–9;
meets Chartists aboard convict ship,
180–1; meets J. S. Mill, 182–4; visits
Neath and Briton Ferry, 185–91;
London, where he calls on Mill and
Carlyle, and attends an Anti-slavery
convention, 192–202; travels to Woodbridge and Norwich, 202–3; home
at Falmouth, 204–11; Polytechnic
exhibition, 212–13; gales bring
damaged ships to Falmouth, 214–17;
1841:
busy at the office and Penjerrick, 218–
219; Govt. threat to remove packets
from Falmouth, 220; conversations with
Dr Calvert, 220–3; *Fox* v. *Glover* heard
at Bodmin, 224; Sterling settles at Falmouth and becomes a close friend, 225–
234; election at Falmouth, 235; attends
lectures on phrenology, 236–8; attends
meeting of British Association at Plymouth, 238–40; attends Polytechnic
meeting, 241–2; walking tour and
visit to Bodmin asylum, 242–4; office
duties and social visits at Falmouth,
245–55;
1842:
death of Dr Calvert, 256–7; business
troubles, 259–62; 1842 Budget brings
business problems, 263–5; becomes
involved with Perran foundry affairs,
266–8; visits London and meets Mill and
Carlyle, 268–73; visits Northrepps Hall,
274–6; visits W. E. Forster at Bradford,
277–8; takes over management of
Perran foundry, 278–9; visit from
Samuel Gurney and family, 280–2;
visits Northrepps to propose to
Richenda Buxton, 283–8; returns to

duties at the foundry and shipping
office, 289–98;
1843:
Sterling ill, 299–301; tour to Italy, 302–
340; supports attempts to establish a
Cornwall railway, 341–5; visits Sterling
in the Isle of Wight, 346–7; railway and
packets business, 348–52; Chartist meeting in Falmouth, 353; Queen Victoria
visits Falmouth, 354–5; W. E. Forster
in Falmouth, 355–6; visits Norwich,
London, Ipswich, Eastwick, and Bristol,
357–62; returns to Falmouth, 363–5;
1844:
railway business, 366–8; visits London,
Birmingham, Bradford, 369–72; visits
Darlington where he proposes marriage
to Jane Backhouse, 373–7; returns to
Falmouth, 378–9; visits Bristol,
Birmingham, and Darlington, 380–1;
visits Sterling on the Isle of Wight,
382–3; visits London, 384–6; returns to
Darlington, meets W. E. Forster in
Leeds, 387–8; returns to Falmouth,
389–90; visits London on railway
business and then Darlington, 391–4;
returns to Falmouth and escorts his
sisters to Birmingham and goes to
Darlington, 395–8; marriage and return
to Falmouth, 399–403.
Fox, Robert Were (father of R.B.F.), 11,
12, 16, 33, 34, 35, 36, 37, 38, 40, 41, 42,
43, 44, 48, 49, 54, 56, 58, 59, 62, 66, 67,
69, 70, 71, 73, 74, 78, 80, 82, 88, 89, 91,
92, 94, 96, 97, 98, 106, 107, 108, 116,
123, 132, 134, 142, 147, 148, 156, 157,
159, 164, 166, 173, 176, 180, 183, 187,
193, 204, 206, 207, 211, 213, 215, 216,
219, 220, 227, 229, 241, 246, 247, 248,
249, 251, 258, 259, 260, 265, 267, 268,
270, 276, 278, 282, 290, 300, 301, 347,
348, 351, 362, 364, 369, 380, 381, 383,
384, 386, 388, 396, 399, 400, 402
Fox, Robin, 404
Fox, Samuel, 14
Fox, Sarah (Aunt Alfred), 13, 21, 39, 41,
48, 58, 59, 95, 109, 166, 247, 281, 378
Fox, Sarah (Aunt Charles), 14, 21, 35, 36,
42, 44, 48, 53, 54, 55, 57, 58, 59, 60, 72,
76, 77, 78, 90, 93, 104, 105, 108, 118, 122,
128, 132, 134, 135, 144, 145, 151, 163,
165, 171, 172, 192, 194, 197, 210, 211,
223, 225, 226, 261, 270, 278, 279, 288,
289, 290, 292, 293, 341, 342, 356, 363,
364, 366, 367, 374, 378, 385, 388, 400
Fox, Tabitha, 393